MARRIAGE AND MARITAL THERAPY

Psychoanalytic, Behavioral and Systems Theory Perspectives

Marriage and Marital Therapy

Psychoanalytic, Behavioral and Systems
Theory Perspectives

Edited by

THOMAS J. PAOLINO, JR., M.D.

Department of Psychiatry, The Cambridge Hospital/
Harvard Medical School

and

BARBARA S. McCRADY, PH.D.

Butler Hospital/Brown University

BRUNNER/MAZEL, *Publishers* • New York

FIFTH PRINTING

Library of Congress Cataloging in Publication Data

Main entry under title:
Marriage and marital therapy

Includes bibliographies and index
1. Marital psychotherapy—Addresses, essays, lectures. 2. Psychoanalysis—Addresses, essays, lectures. 3. Behaviorism—Addresses, essays, lectures. 4. Social systems—Addresses, essays, lectures. 5. Marriage—Addresses, essays, lectures. I. Paolino, Thomas J., 1940- II. McCrady, Barbara S.

RC488.5.M365   362.8'2   78-17398
ISBN 0-87630-171-5

Published by
BRUNNER/MAZEL, INC.
19 Union Square West
New York, New York 10003

To our parents THOMAS and FLORENCE PAOLINO, MARGARET and JAMES SACHS, and to our children, PIA PAOLINO, TJ PAOLINO and ERIC McCRADY, we dedicate this book with deepest love.

Theory is good; but it doesn't prevent things from existing.

JEAN MARTIN CHARCOT (1835-1893)
Quoted by Sigmund Freud (1893) "Charcot,"
Standard Edition, 3, p. 13,
London: Hogarth Press, 1962.

Preface

The idea for this book has gradually evolved as the Editors have evolved as therapists and researchers. We have continually and progressively been impressed with the two dimensions of human behavior that we have tried to combine in this book: (1) the conceptualization of marriage and marital therapy; (2) the study of human behavior from three scholarly but often opposing perspectives: *psychoanalytic, behavioral* and *systems theory.*

A major reason for our editing this book is that we have been dismayed with the fact that many psychoanalysts, behaviorists and systems theorists manifest a profound sophistication in their respective perspectives but simultaneously display either superficial familiarity with or narrow-minded prejudice towards viewpoints alien to their own. If students and practitioners adhere to one perspective and do not possess substantive knowledge of rival perspectives, then they succeed in reducing truth-seeking about human behavior to a matter of emotional inclination, convention, convenience, or mutual consent among compatible observers. Most, if not all, mental health professionals have observed or experienced various forms of this kind of conceptual chauvinism and intellectual dishonesty. We, for example, have observed an incident where a highly regarded psychoanalyst automatically assumed that the therapist was "acting out his countertransference" because the therapist wondered out loud whether or not his severely alcoholic patient whom he had been treating with psychoanalytically oriented psychotherapy might not benefit more from "behavior modification." There was another occasion when a widely published behaviorist lashed out with eloquent hostility against the teachings of Freud although, when we asked him, he proudly admitted that he had never read any of Freud's writings. There was also an incident when an internationally prominent systems theorist bitterly criticized one of us (TP) for being a patient in psychoanalysis although he never bothered to inquire about the reasons or whether or not the treatment had been helpful. Of course, for each clinician there are some nonscientific and perhaps even irrational reasons behind the choice of models. Nevertheless, we believe that all clinicians should strive for the ideal of selecting models based on academic honesty and scientific judgment.

A fundamental principle underlying the conception and editing of this book is our firm conviction that whether a person is "psychoanalytically," "behaviorally," or "systems theory" oriented, it is far better to approach the conceptualization of marriage and marital therapy from a well thought-out model based on any one or a combination of the three perspectives than it is to approach the subject from no model at all. We agree with Steinglass (Chapter VI) that, by operating from a specific model of psychic functioning and human behavior, the clinician: (1) facilitates the direction of attention to relevant data; (2) clarifies the therapist-patient interaction in a way that indicates when therapeutic interventions are best used; and (3) facilitates making distinctions between the normal and the abnormal.

One of the principal goals of this book is to provide the reader with a choice of models which can be used alone or in combination with the other perspectives so that the student, researcher or clinician can better organize observations. We are convinced that an understanding of all three perspectives will allow the clinician to choose those components of each perspective that can be most effectively applied by the specific therapist-patient combination at a specific point in time. We emphasize, however, that the three perspectives are in many ways unalterably incompatible in such elements as some units of observation, theoretical constructs and theories of change.* Some concepts may appear to be complementary only because one perspective deals with ideas that another perspective might not even address because the concept is theoretically inconsistent with that model. For example, behaviorists don't concern themselves with psychic structures since that metaphor is mutually inconsistent with the social learning model.

---

* We thank Dr. Carlos Sluzki for reminding us of this important fact.

Although there are many, many articles and books focusing on marital therapy, there are relatively few written attempts by clinicians to conceptualize marriage. The separation of chapters in this volume into *"concepts"* and *"treatment"* issues, plus the fact that all chapters focus heavily on operational theories and concepts, should help fill a major gap in the marriage literature. Also, abundant references are provided should the reader wish to go beyond the ideas discussed.

Readership

This book was prepared primarily for advanced clinicians, such as psychiatrists, Ph.D. psychologists, psychiatric social workers, advanced degree psychiatric nurses, and clinical students, such as psychiatric residents, psychology interns, social work students, and advanced degree nursing students, all of whom may be delivering their various forms of psychological and behavior therapy in the mental and community health fields, including social agencies, community clinics and private practice offices. Although the target readership is the clinician, we believe that psychology students will also benefit from the variety of theoretical concepts described that do not require clinical experience to be understood. Also, since one complete chapter and parts of others deal with the empirical outcome research, and all chapters deal with the concepts and techniques that are usually assessed by research, the clinical researcher may benefit from this volume.

By presenting specific perspectives as they apply to marriage, by dividing the subject of marriage into "conceptualizations of marriage" and "marital therapy," and by including a separate review of the research literature and a synthesizing chapter, we have prepared a volume which should be instructive to each reader, regardless of the reader's previous knowledge in specific areas of marriage and marital therapy.

Of course, we are well aware of the fact that clinicians' operational theories of human behavior and clinical interventions often do not fall exactly into a psychoanalytic, behavioral or systems theory model, nor do many aspects of each perspective necessarily oppose many components of the other two. Also, it is virtually impossible to categorically segregate a discussion of "conceptualization of marriage" from a chapter dealing with "marital therapy." Nevertheless, we believe that the format of this volume is a useful expository technique provided that the reader is always aware of the unavoidable overlap.

The Similarities and Differences

Throughout this volume, the reader will note that the three perspectives differ dramatically in some aspects of theory and treatment and are surprisingly similar in other aspects. For example, the concept of transference neurosis is vital to the psychoanalytic approach and of negligible practical value to the behaviorist. Another example: during the assessment period, the systems and behavioral approaches are more oriented towards current events, whereas the psychoanalytic approach relies heavily on historical information. All three perspectives focus on the importance of life cycles, although for the behavioral perspective this is a new concept presented for the first time in the literature by Robert Weiss in Chapter IV of this volume. Each chapter provides the reader with information which can serve to compare and contrast the three viewpoints. Furthermore, the subject is discussed at length by Alan Gurman in his synthesizing Chapter IX, which includes an exhaustive comparison of the three perspectives regarding the focus assigned to the past, unconscious, presenting problems, mediating and ultimate goals of marital therapy, and the role of the therapist.

Overview of Book

The contributors to this volume were selected because of their widely acknowledged leadership in their respective areas. They represent three disciplines: psychiatry, psychology, and psychiatric social work. All contributors are deeply committed to both clinical research and the delivery of clinical services.

Every chapter has been written so that it stands on its own as an exposition but at the same time is an integral part of the complete volume. Each contributor has had the various drafts of the other contributors' chapters during the development of his/her own chapter. Furthermore, a large part of our editorial work involved encouraging or helping the authors to make interstitial remarks. As a result, the volume represents nine integrated contributions.

We should mention at this point that the editors and authors decided that each chapter will *not* critique or review comments made in other chapters despite the fact that, by the very nature of this book, many of the comments made in one chapter are incompatible with some made in others. Of course, the lack of rebutting or critiquing each others' chapters should not imply that the authors or editors are in agreement with all of the various theories and concepts discussed and proposed.

In Chapter I, James and Janice Prochaska provide a historical overview of marital treatment in the twentieth century, and also an overview of current trends in marriage in contemporary American society. The Prochaskas also place in historical perspective the work of the other authors represented in the book.

In Chapter II William Meissner presents a psychoanalytic theory of family dynamics by placing emphasis on the fundamental concepts of object relationships, their internalizations, the introjections and projections derived from the object, and the relationship between the concepts of transference and object relationships.

Chapter III begins with a section by Thomas Paolino which outlines some basic concepts which form the conceptual foundation of all investigative psychoanalytically oriented psychotherapy. After this introductory section, Carol Nadelson discusses the various formats of psychoanalytically oriented marital therapy and then proceeds to examine the different stages of this type of marital therapy. Numerous clinical examples are offered and the technical aspects of the therapy are closely tied into the basic psychoanalytic therapeutic concepts, although some of the techniques discussed by Dr. Nadelson do not conform with what many people consider "classical" psychoanalytic technique.

Chapter IV by Robert Weiss provides a theoretical model for a behavioral conceptualization of marriage, and discusses data relevant to this conceptualization.

In Chapter V, K. Daniel O'Leary and Hillary Turkewitz provide a model for behavioral treatment of marital problems, along with data suggesting the efficacy of their model.

In Chapter VI, Peter Steinglass reviews four major systems theory approaches to marriage, and then provides an integrative, developmental systems model of marriage.

Carlos Sluzki's Chapter VII presents a series of treatment techniques derived from a systems model, and interweaves them into a systems oriented approach to marital therapy.

In Chapter VIII, Neil Jacobson provides a thorough and integrative review of the literature on the empirical outcome of marital therapy.

Finally, Chapter IX by Alan Gurman reviews major concepts associated with each of the three perspectives, compares and contrasts them, and gives an integrative overview of the field.

THOMAS J. PAOLINO, JR., M.D.
BARBARA S. McCRADY, PH.D.

Acknowledgments

We would like to acknowledge our debt and our appreciation to Mr. Frank Delmonico, Director of Administration, Butler Hospital, and Stanley M. Aronson, M.D., Dean of Medicine, Brown University Medical School, who have had major roles in creating the working and scholarly environment at Butler Hospital and Brown University Medical School which provided us with the academic stimulation, time and help which have made this book possible.

This book is a direct outgrowth of the Butler Hospital 1977 Spring Symposium on marriage and marital therapy which we conceived and chaired. We are especially indebted to Jeanne Moore, former Director of Public Relations, to her assistant Linda Mulzer, and to the other members of the administrative staff of Butler Hospital for their services and resources that made the Symposium possible.

We would like to thank David Berkowitz, M.D., Ben W. Feather, M.D., Ph.D., Jonathan Kolb, MD and Paul Rossman, M.D., for reviewing parts of this manuscript and offering their advice. We appreciate the help of our secretaries Shawn McLaughlin and Michele Bokowsky for the vast amount of typing and other tasks demanded for this project. We also thank Erika Schmidt, Librarian, Butler Hospital, for her usual invaluable assistance.

We are especially grateful to the eleven authors and to Bernard Mazel and Susan Barrows of Brunner/Mazel, Inc. The opportunity to get to know our authors and publishers, work with them and learn from them has been unquestionably the highlight of our editing this book.

We consider ourselves lucky to have known, worked with and learned from extremely competent and caring clinicians and researchers who have represented excellence in their theoretical perspectives. By working with them closely and seeing the efficacy of their work, we have learned to recognize the value of multiple orientations, the limitations of each orientation, and the meaningfulness of the therapeutic relationship. In this regard one of us (TP) is especially indebted to Rolf Arvidson, M.D.

We owe a special debt to our spouses, Anne and Denny, who, through loving marriages and the examples of their own careers, have helped us develop balanced, satisfying and joyful personal and professional lives.

The last and most important acknowledgment is to our patients and their families. The joy from our therapeutic successes and the disappointments from our treatment failures have inspired us to edit this book in an attempt to further help and understand those people whom we have had the privilege to know and to serve.

Contents

Preface ix

Acknowledgments xv

Contributors xix

I. TWENTIETH CENTURY TRENDS IN MARRIAGE AND MARITAL
      THERAPY 1
      By James Prochaska, Ph.D. and
      Janice Prochaska, M.S.W., A.C.S.W.

II. THE CONCEPTUALIZATION OF MARRIAGE AND FAMILY DYNAMICS
      FROM A PSYCHOANALYTIC PERSPECTIVE 25
      By William W. Meissner, S.J., M.D.

III. MARITAL THERAPY FROM A PSYCHOANALYTIC PERSPECTIVE 89
      By Carol Cooperman Nadelson, M.D. with an Introduction by
      Thomas J. Paolino, Jr., M.D.

IV. THE CONCEPTUALIZATION OF MARRIAGE FROM A
      BEHAVIORAL PERSPECTIVE 165
      By Robert L. Weiss, Ph.D.

V. MARITAL THERAPY FROM A BEHAVIORAL PERSPECTIVE 240
      By K. Daniel O'Leary, Ph.D. and Hillary Turkewitz, Ph.D.

VI. THE CONCEPTUALIZATION OF MARRIAGE FROM A
      SYSTEMS THEORY PERSPECTIVE 298
      By Peter Steinglass, M.D.

VII. MARITAL THERAPY FROM A SYSTEMS THEORY PERSPECTIVE 366
    By Carlos E. Sluzki, M.D.

VIII. A REVIEW OF THE RESEARCH ON THE EFFECTIVENESS
    OF MARITAL THERAPY 395
    By Neil S. Jacobson, Ph.D.

IX. CONTEMPORARY MARITAL THERAPIES: A CRITIQUE AND
    COMPARATIVE ANALYSIS OF PSYCHOANALYTIC,
    BEHAVIORAL AND SYSTEMS THEORY APPROACHES 445
    By Alan S. Gurman, Ph.D.

Subject Index 567

Name Index 578

Contributors

ALAN S. GURMAN, Ph.D.

Dr. Gurman received his B.A. degree from Boston University in 1967 and his M.A. (1970) and Ph.D. (1971) in clinical psychology from Columbia University. He completed his clinical psychology internship at the Veterans Administration Outpatient Clinic, Brooklyn, New York and a two-year post-doctoral fellowship at the University of Wisconsin Medical School. He is currently Director of the Outpatient Clinic, Co-Director of the Couples-Family Clinic and Associate Professor, Department of Psychiatry, University of Wisconsin Medical School. Dr. Gurman's primary clinical and academic interests are in the practice of marital therapy and in the development of a conceptual model for evaluating the outcomes of marital therapy.

NEIL S. JACOBSON, Ph.D.

Dr. Jacobson received his B.A. degree in 1972 from the University of Wisconsin and his Ph.D. (1977) in clinical psychology from the University of North Carolina, Chapel Hill. He did his clinical psychology internship at the Brown University program at Butler Hospital, Providence, Rhode Island, completing that training in June 1977. Dr. Jacobson is currently Assistant Professor of Psychology, University of Iowa and his primary clinical and academic interests are the analysis and treatment of relationship distress from a social learning perspective and investigations into the causes and treatment of depression.

BARBARA S. McCRADY, PH.D.

Dr. McCrady received her B.S. degree from Purdue University in 1969 and her Ph.D. (1975) in psychology from the University of Rhode Island. She completed her clinical psychology internship at Worcester State Hospital in 1974. She is currently Chief, Problem Drinkers Program, Butler Hospital, Providence, Rhode Island, and Assistant Professor of Psychiatry, Department of Psychiatry and Human Behavior, Brown University, Providence, Rhode Island. Dr. McCrady's primary clinical and academic interests are in the assessment and treatment of alcohol problems, especially from a marital perspective.

WILLIAM W. MEISSNER, S.J., M.D.

Dr. Meissner received his BA degree in 1956, a masters degree (1957) and the degree of Lecturer of Philosophy (1957) all from St. Louis University, St. Louis, Missouri. Dr. Meissner received his M.D. degree from Harvard Medical School in 1967 and completed his medical internship at the Mount Auburn Hospital at Cambridge, Massachusetts in 1968. He completed his psychiatric residency in 1971 in the Harvard Medical School program at the Massachusetts Mental Health Center and also in 1971 he graduated from the Boston Psychoanalytic Institute. Dr. Meissner is currently a practicing psychoanalyst, Chairman of the Faculty, Boston Psychoanalytic Institute and Associate Clinical Professor of Psychiatry, Harvard Medical School. His primary clinical and academic interests are psychoanalysis and psychotherapy.

CAROL COOPERMAN NADELSON, M.D.

Dr. Nadelson received her B.A. degree from Brooklyn College in 1957 and her M.D. degree from the University of Rochester School of Medicine in 1961. In 1962 Dr. Nadelson completed her medical internship at the University of Rochester, Strong Memorial Hospital. She did her psychiatric residency training in the Harvard Medical School program at the Massachusetts Mental Health Center and the Beth Israel Hospital, Boston, Massachusetts and completed that training in 1966. Dr. Nadelson graduated from the Boston Psychoanalytic Institute in 1974 and is currently Director, Medical Student Education, Department of Psychiatry, Beth Israel Hospital, Boston and Associate Professor of Psychiatry, Harvard Medical School. Her primary clinical and academic interests include work with couples and marital problems, the conflicts of women in the context of change, and liaison psychiatry particularly with obstetrics and gynecology and adolescent medicine.

K. DANIEL O'LEARY, PH.D.

Dr. O'Leary received his B.A. degree from Penn State University in 1962, a masters degree (1965) and a Ph.D. (1967) degree in clinical psychology from the University of Illinois. Dr. O'Leary completed his psychology internship in 1967 at the University of Illinois Psychological Clinic and he is currently Chairman and Professor of Psychology; Coordinator, Child and Adolescent Unit, Psychological Center, State University of New York at Stony Brook, Stony Brook, New York. His primary clinical and academic interests are the etiology and treatment of hyperkinesis, conduct disorders and marital discord.

THOMAS J. PAOLINO, JR., M.D.

Dr. Paolino received his B.A. degree from Brown University in 1963 and his M.D. (1967) from George Washington University School of Medicine. In 1968 Dr. Paolino completed his medical internship at the Tufts Medical Service, Boston City Hospital. In 1971 he completed his psychiatric residency in the Harvard Medical School program at the Massachusetts Mental Health Center and Cambridge Hospital Department of Psychiatry. During the production of this book, Dr. Paolino was Chief, Upper East Unit, Butler Hospital, Providence, Rhode Island and Assistant Professor of Psychiatry, Department of Psychiatry and Human Behavior, Brown University, Providence, Rhode Island. Dr. Paolino is currently Clinical Director, Department of Psychiatry, The Cambridge Hospital, Cambridge, Massachusetts and Assistant Professor of Psychiatry, Harvard Medical School, Boston, Massachusetts. Dr. Paolino is also a candidate in training at the Boston Psychoanalytic Institute. Dr. Paolino's primary clinical and academic interests are psychotherapy and the delivery of mental health services in a community setting.

JAMES PROCHASKA, PH.D.

Dr. Prochaska received his B.A. degree in 1964, masters degree in 1967 and Ph.D. in clinical psychology in 1969, all from Wayne State University. Dr. Prochaska did his clinical psychology internship at Lafayette Clinic, Detroit, Michigan, completing his training in 1968. Currently, he is Professor of Psychology at the University of Rhode Island. His primary clinical and academic interests involve the development of a trans-theoretical model of therapy and the application of this model to self-control, marital and sexual disorders.

JANICE PROCHASKA, M.S.W., A.C.S.W.

Mrs. Prochaska received her B.A. degree (1966) and her M.S.W. (1968) from Wayne State University. She completed her field work training at Lafayette Clinic, Detroit, Michigan in 1968. Mrs. Prochaska is currently Director of Professional Services, Child and Family Services of Newport County, Newport, Rhode Island. Her primary clinical and academic interests are aimed at identifying the processes of effective prevention of marital and family disorders through family life education and marital enrichment programs.

CARLOS E. SLUZKI, M.D.

Dr. Sluzki received his M.D. from the University of Buenos Aires School of Medicine in 1960 and the title of Specialist in Psychiatry in 1965 from the Ministry of Public Health, Argentina. In 1967 Dr. Sluzki graduated from the Argentine Psychoanalytic Association Institute of Psychoanalysis. Dr. Sluzki is a F.F.R.P. and Guggenheim fellow, and a M.R.I. Research Associate since 1965. He is currently Director, Behavioral Sciences, Family Practice Residency Program, San Francisco General Hospital and Associate Professor in Residence, Department of Psychiatry, University of California School of Medicine, San Francisco. Dr. Sluzki's primary clinical and academic interests include the study of family systems.

PETER STEINGLASS, M.D.

Dr. Steinglass received his B.A. degree from Union College in 1960 and his M.D. (1965) from Harvard Medical School. Dr. Steinglass did his internship at the University of California Hospitals, San Francisco, and his psychiatric residency at the Bronx Municipal Hospital Center (Albert Einstein College of Medicine), Bronx, New York, completing the residency in 1969. He is currently Associate Director of the Center for Family Research, George Washington University School of Medicine and Associate Professor of Psychiatry, George Washington University School of Medicine, Washington, D.C. His primary clinical and academic interests are the training of family therapists and family interaction research utilizing naturalistic methods.

HILLARY TURKEWITZ, Ph.D.

Dr. Turkewitz received her B.A. in 1971 from the University of Rochester and her Ph.D. in clinical psychology from the State University of New York, Stony Brook, in 1977. She did her clinical psychology internship at the Northport Veterans Administration Hospital outpatient clinic and the State University of New York Psychological Services and Child Development Unit, completing that training in 1974. Dr. Turkewitz is currently Research Associate, Department of Psychology, State University of New York at Stony Brook. Her primary clinical and academic interests are marital therapy outcome research and peer counseling.

ROBERT L. WEISS, Ph.D.

Dr. Weiss received his B.A. degree in 1952 from the State University of New York at Buffalo and his Ph.D. in clinical psychology in 1958 from the same institution. Dr. Weiss is currently Professor of Psychology and Director of the Marital Studies Program at the University of Oregon. His primary clinical and academic interests involve research in assessment and intervention with marital relationships.

MARRIAGE AND MARITAL THERAPY

Psychoanalytic, Behavioral and Systems Theory Perspectives

I

Twentieth Century Trends in Marriage and Marital Therapy

JAMES PROCHASKA, PH.D.
and
JANICE PROCHASKA, M.S.W., A.C.S.W.

Most therapists are about as poorly prepared for marital therapy as most spouses are for marriage. The unavailability or inadequacy of family life education and sex education courses for young people is well known. What is not well known is the unavailability of courses in marital therapy for young therapists being trained in graduate programs in clinical psychology, counseling psychology, social work, and psychiatry. In a survey of 85 percent of the 102 A.P.A. approved Ph.D. programs in clinical psychology, for example, only 7 percent were found to have seminars or practica that give substantial coverage to marital therapy. Of 76 percent of the 21 A.P.A. approved Ph.D. programs in counseling psychology, only 18 percent listed seminars or practica covering marital therapy. Likewise, of 52 percent of the 82 accredited schools of social work examined, only 19 percent had courses concentrating on marriage or marital therapy. While comparable statistics are not currently known on the availability of systematic training in marital therapy within psychiatric residencies, an informal survey of psychiatrists leads to the belief that statistics from psychiatric training programs would be quite similar.

1

Mental health professionals have been and continue to be trained primarily in therapies designed for individuals. According to figures from the National Institute of Mental Health (Parloff, 1976), there are currently 130 therapies available in the therapeutic marketplace (or therapeutic jungle, as it has more aptly been described). Nearly all of the therapies are therapies of and for the individual (Prochaska, in press). As will be seen throughout this book, there are many crucial differences in theory and practice when one is working with couples rather than individuals. Yet most therapists have not been adequately trained to be cognizant of such critical differences.

The inadequate preparation of mental health professionals occurs even though psychologists, social workers and psychiatrists are the three most common providers of therapy to the maritally troubled (Olson, 1970). The unavailability of courses in marital therapy continues even though marital problems are amongst the three most common reasons why people come for therapy. And the poor preparation of mental health professionals for providing marital therapy will probably continue even though, as shown below, the trends in marriage and divorce indicate that the need for marital therapy in American society will continue to increase.

TRENDS IN MARRIAGE AND DIVORCE

When marital therapists proceed to survey marriage in the twentieth century, it is very possible that their perspectives on marriage will be drastically distorted by the fact that so much of their time is spent trying to help couples unravel themselves from disorders of marriage. Nevertheless, we are increasingly impressed with how often the relationship problems we see within our consulting rooms seem to be vivid reflections of what is happening in marriages throughout American society. Increasingly, it can be asked: Are couples in marital therapy the neurotic discontents of our civilization who were miserable before marriage, miserable after marriage, and then blamed their misery on marriage? Are the couples in therapy the failures who were ill-prepared to make a go of an institution that is working well for the majority of people in society? Or has the social institution of marriage itself become the failure? Should we be discussing marital disorders or is marriage the disorder?

Lederer and Jackson (1968) in their well-known work on *The Mirages of Marriage* report that 80 percent of the hundreds of couples they interviewed reported that they had seriously considered divorce at one time or another. Many said that the primary factors that kept them from divorce were economics and concern for their children. Lederer and Jackson conclude that marriage is in a state of calamity.

Scanzoni (1972), on the other hand, takes many of his professional colleagues to task for sensationalizing the statistics of and trends toward divorce. While there has indeed been an increase in the rate of divorce in the United States, Scanzoni presents data that suggest that divorce rates have shown a steady but slow increase over the past 100 years. He found no evidence, however, for the wild speculation that divorce is running rampant and that marriage is a decaying institution. For example, in the three decades from 1910 to 1940, the divorce rate gradually rose from one per 1,000 persons to about two per 1,000 persons. Except for a short-lived but substantial increase in divorce following the Second World War, the trend from 1940 to 1970 was for the divorce rate to follow its long-term gradual increase to a rate of approximately three per 1,000 persons in 1970. Scanzoni argued that the increase in the divorce rate in the past 30 years was one per 1,000 persons, which is the same as the increase that occurred between 1910 and 1940. Where was the dramatic upsurge in divorce that so much of the press and so many professionals seemed to be reporting?

Data more recent than Scanzoni's may provide some support for the conjecture that marriages are indeed beginning to break down at an unprecedented pace. Paul Glick, one of the foremost demographers of marriage and the family, reported in 1975 more recent figures on the rate of divorce. The rate of divorce per 1,000 persons in 1974 had leaped to 4.5. In the four years from 1970 to 1974, the divorce rate had apparently climbed 1.5 per 1,000, compared to an increase of only one per 1,000 in the preceding 30 years.

The rate of 4.5 per 1,000 persons translates into the more common fact that of the 30-year-old women in American society who have married or will marry, 30 percent will go through at least one divorce in their lifetime. The current divorce rate also means that the United States now has the highest rate of divorce in the world. Current trends also indicate that this divorce rate is higher than ever before in history and apparently climbing at an unprecedented pace.

What the data of demographers do not indicate is the pain and the anguish that many people still go through in trying to decide whether to sacrifice for the sake of their marriages or sacrifice their marriages for the sake of themselves. At a personal and practical level, the cliché question had been: *"Can this marriage be saved?"* Gradually the more common question became: *"Should this marriage be saved?"* Then, increasingly, at a larger social and theoretical level similar questions began to be asked: *"Can marriage be saved"* and *"Should marriage be saved?"*

Some of our professional colleagues have made their feelings clear. Dr. Laura Singer, for example, was President of the American Association of Marriage and Family Counselors when she was quoted as affirming: "We know that somehow marriage stinks. We don't know why. We used to make jokes about marriage and stay married and kill each other. Now, for the first time, we feel free enough to say that it stinks and to ask why" (Lear, 1972, p. 12). Singer was cited as an example of the new breed of marriage counselors who are committed to saving the spouses rather than the marriage.

Kaplan (1974), the noted sex therapist and psychoanalyst who uses techniques from behavior therapy, has taken an equally strong stance. She states:

> The destructive effects of the conventional marriage model become clearly apparent when one works with couples. The roots of a person's unhappiness are often not to be found in the individual's pathology but rather in the model, which by its demands constricts, defeats, controls, alienates and then gags and blindfolds its victims so they can have no redress. Thus they are hopelessly trapped and cannot even identify the source of their anguish (p. 520).

David and Vera Mace (1974) are equally critical of the traditional form of marriage. They see it as highly institutionalized, rigid, formal, authoritarian, ritualistic and patriarchal. They believe that the rising divorce rate signals the breakdown of the traditional marriage, thank heavens. Serial monogamy, or divorce as it is so often mistakenly labeled, has risen as one of the major alternatives to what they consider the anachronistic and now destructive institution known as the traditional monogamous marriage.

There are several major cultural changes occurring that are having profound impact on the traditional marriage. Understanding these cultural conflicts is important not only for an adequate theory of contemporary marriage but also because so often the couples in the consulting room are dramatizing on an interpersonal level the conflicts and changes that are occurring at a cultural level. We find in our own practice, for example, that the most common reason for couples coming into marital therapy is that the marriage is being shaken by the wife's struggle for equality. At the same time, at a cultural level it is indeed the historical movement of women working for equality that is having such an impact on the traditional marriage.

As Bernard (1972) documents so effectively, in spite of all the jokes to the contrary, marriage has traditionally been a blessing for many men. Men may leave a particular marriage, but they usually rush right back into marriage as quickly as a new partner becomes available. Marriage as seen through the eyes of the husband is consistently more rewarding than the marriage the wife experiences. The only consistent complaints of husbands have been in regard to the stresses of providing economic support for the family and the sexual exclusivity that marriage traditionally demands. Bernard is definitely bullish on marriage for American males. She believes that the trend toward working wives will lessen one of the husband's chief complaints. She also believes that attitudes toward monogamy are relaxing, though more slowly. A recent survey of 300 students at the University of Rhode Island challenges this latter assumption, however. When students were asked if they would accept premarital sex, not for themselves but for those who chose it, 95 percent said they would. When asked, however, if they would accept extramarital sex, not for themselves or their families but for others who chose it, only three students of 300 said they would.

Traditional marriage has been a blessing for men only at the expense of women. Bernard cites studies suggesting that wives lose ground in personal development and self-esteem during the early and middle years of adulthood, whereas husbands gain ground in these respects during the same years. Wives are found to conform to husbands' expectations much more than husbands do to wives'. Even among women who were in the top one percent of their college freshman class, marriage was found to lead to a marked increase in submissiveness. Bernard concludes that men traditionally enlarge into a husband while women dwindle into a wife.

From a historical perspective, the dominance of the male in the traditional patriarchal marriage found support in an agrarian culture that valued brawn more than skill. With the industrial revolution, however, as skill rather than brawn became most socially valued, the move towards egalitarianism finds cultural support. The twentieth century has witnessed a cultural lag phenomenon in which the traditional marriage continued dominant even though it remained tied to the waning agricultural society. Many modern marriages have been caught in a cultural bind between the emerging egalitarianism of the industrial society and a family socialization process that prepared the spouses for a traditional marriage. As will be seen, the continuing movement toward an egalitarian society has perhaps placed irreversible strains on the traditional patriarchal marriage.

The 1960s witnessed not only a revival in the historical struggle for the liberation of women but an even broader struggle for the liberation of all oppressed people. Freedom became the dominant theme of the '60s: freedom for women, freedom for blacks, freedom from poverty, freedom for students, freedom for gay people, freedom for sexuality among any consenting partners. This radical struggle for freedom in many areas had a clear impact in beginning to liberate many people from the oppressive confines of the traditional marriage. Gay marriages, open marriages, swinging marriages, group marriages, communal marriages, cohabitation and the sexually active single life became popularized if not popular alternatives to the traditional monogamous marriage. The advocates of each of these alternatives worked to have adult relationships become free from the confining restraints of the law and of negative public opinion.

There are those who believe the search for freedom swung too far as trashings and bombings broke out in the inner cities and the universities (Zimmerman, 1972). Those who were high on a dose of freedom were seen as moving away from any restraints, including the inevitable restraints that come with commitment to marriage and to family. *The Death of the Family* was heralded by Cooper (1970) as one of the central steps in the overthrow of oppression. There are others who believe that the quest for freedom did not go far enough. Many people were left with an increased freedom from restraints but found little of value for which to be free. For a while it looked as if a more socially conscious counterculture would emerge as part of the *Greening of America* (Reich, 1970). But soon the invasion of Cambodia, the stagnation of the '70s, and the revelations of Watergate made it apparent that no new America was just over the horizon. For many all that was left was an increase in freedom to "do their own thing," whatever that thing might be.

Tom Wolfe (1976) has characterized the 1970s as the "me decade," in which individuals seem able to care only about themselves. At the turn of the century Nietzsche had predicted that when people realized that God had died, they would need to create a new god in the shape of Superman. Superman is now called the Self. It's not hard to see that in current American society only the Self is really sacred. Unmitigated commitment to self was once frowned upon as selfishness, but now such commitment can be sanctioned in the name of self-actualization. Increasingly, fathers and mothers can withdraw from their families with a sense of virtue.

secure in the knowledge that their quest for self-actualization is the highest good they can know. People are increasingly suspicious that any compromise might involve compromising themselves away. Of course, the idea of sacrifice should be suspect lest it carry its traditional connotation of sacrificing the woman for the sake of the man. But the idea and the action of sacrifice also have an honorable meaning of making sacred, of making some aspect of life one's ultimate concern. Asking spouses to sacrifice in the name of love or in the name of their loved ones sounds too terribly old-fashioned to "turn on" many in the me-generation.

Certainly, some of the increase in the divorce rate in the past decade can be accounted for by socioeconomic changes that are less dramatic than those we have just described. Glick (1975) cites such variable as: (1) an increasing proportion of couples, especially dual career couples, whose income has risen to a level where they can afford a divorce; (2) the increased availability of free legal aid which may provide more impoverished families with the chance to obtain a divorce; (3) the reform of divorce laws, especially the adoption of no-fault divorce; and (4) a greater social acceptance of divorce as a means of resolving marital problems. Glick states that even the Vietnamese War, which threatened to tear apart the nation, helped to tear apart individual families and marriages.

If the worst that marriages had to adjust to in the 1970s were the cultural changes already discussed, the optimism of Bernard (1972), Scanzoni (1972), and the Maces (1974) about the future of marriage might seem more justified. A darker concern, however, is that the 1970s may be witnessing a cultural change that could be truly devastating not only to the traditional marriage but to all forms of trying to find lasting intimate ties. A concern is emerging that we may be witnessing a widespread loss of faith in the future. Witness, for example, the increasing disillusionment with higher education. The blessed B.A. was once believed to be the best means to social mobility. Increasingly, students dread the attainment of the B.A. as a ticket to unemployment or underemployment in unfulfilling work. More students than ever before, nearly 70 percent, now believe that hard work does not pay off in the future (Yankelovich, 1972).

If a people raised on the principle of progress begins to seriously doubt the future, should not increasing dissatisfaction with such social institutions as education, work and marriage be expected? In the past one of the forces that could help troubled marriages through tough times was the faith that, if nothing else, the couple could progress in their standard of living. To start out on a lifetime journey together with the gnawing feeling that the best is already behind could certainly be demoralizing for many marriages.

Ingmar Bergman (1973), in his profound and provocative *Scenes From A Marriage*, captured many of the cultural conflicts discussed here. Marianne's struggle to be her own person, Johan's self-centeredness that passed under the guise of self-actualization, the rigid and ritualistic rules of the traditional marriage are all portrayed in this movie of a modern marriage. When trying to articulate Marianne and Johan's darkest dreads, however, Bergman (p. 209) speaks of this loss of faith in the future. In the middle of the night, in a house somewhere by the sea, Marianne and Johan huddle together in bed.

> *Marianne*: "Do you think we're living in utter confusion?
> *Johan*: "You and I?"
> *Marianne*: "No, the whole lot of us."
> *Johan*: "What do you mean by confusion?"
> *Marianne*: "Fear, uncertainty, folly. I mean confusion. That we realize secretly that we're slipping downhill. And that we don't know what to do."
> *Johan*: "Yes, I think so."
> *Marianne*: Perhaps it's like a poison."
> *Johan*: "Inside us, you mean?"
> *Marianne*: "Just think if everything really is too late."
> *Johan*: "We mustn't say things like that. Only think them."

Of course, there are more optimistic views of the cultural and marital scene. The increasing divorce rate, for example, can be heralded not only as the death of the traditional marriage, but also as the creation of new forms of marriage that are better suited to our times. Certainly divorce and the readiness with which most divorced individuals have remarried have begun to establish serial monogamy as a valid alternative to the traditional marriage. The increasing acceptance of serial monogamy has helped support other alternatives to lifetime monogamy. Open marriages, swinging marriages, group marriages, cohabitation, communes, and a sexually active single life are the better known alternatives that have been popularized since the 1960s. If such alternatives indeed become legitimized, then individuals will find greater freedom to develop adult relationships and marriages that can be much better suited to their values and their life-styles than might the traditional marriage.

The Maces (1974) point out that many professionals make the mistake of assuming that serial monogamy and other alternatives to lifetime monogamy are the only options open to those disenchanted with the traditional marriage. They remind us that during the twentieth century a new form of lifetime monogamy has developed that is more fulfilling for many individuals. Out of the traditional marriage has emerged the companionship marriage.

The companionship marriage is characterized by the development of an individual interpersonal relationship that is based on mutual respect and affection, empathic understanding, and friendship (Burgess and Locke, 1945). The companionship marriage is egalitarian and democratic in spirit and in the style in which rules are established and conflicts resolved. Whereas the traditional marriage has been highly institutional-izel and held together by the external pressures of public opinion, laws and mores, the companionship marriage is seen as being held together by the strengths and significance of the couple's interpersonal relationship (Mace and Mace, 1974).

The problem for most individuals in our society is that they have been socialized and prepared for lifetime living within a traditional marriage. A recent survey found, for example, that the selection of potential dates and mates among college students is still highly restricted by the traditional sexist acceptance of the supremacy of the male (Prochaska, 1977). Two-thirds of the 150 females surveyed reported feeling free to marry only a male who is more intelligent, better paid, and better educated than they are. Seventy percent of the 150 males showed a similar bias, with the exception of an openness to marrying a better paid partner. More striking, however, is that of all the variables surveyed that might seriously restrict freedom to date and mate, the most restrictive was not race, religion or social class. The most restrictive variable was height. Only 3 percent of the males felt free to date a taller female and 3 percent of the females felt free to date a shorter male. Among these students, at least, the tradition still continues of women wanting a man to look up to and men wanting a woman to look down upon.

If dating and mating selection is still restricted by such traditional variables, including such a non-functional variable as height, it can be expected that the transition to a companionship form of marriage in our society will continue to be only a slowly evolving phenomenon. In fact, Bernard (1977) reports that there are little if any data to support the claim that a significant proportion of American marriages have progressed into egalitarian relationships. At this stage in our history, the companionship marriage is more an ideal than a reality.

There is evidence to indicate that attempts to transform traditional marital systems into companionship marriages result in inevitable conflict and strife (Scanzoni, 1972). Part of the problem is that many spouses have not been trained in the behavioral skills that help a companionship marriage function more smoothly. Effective assertion and effective negotiation, for example, are not part of the social learning history of females who are prepared for the wife's role in the traditional marriage. Similarly, deep level communication, especially of feelings, is not a skill that is reinforced in the traditional system of socializing males. No wonder, then, that when couples try to make the transition to a more intimate and egalitarian relationship, their efforts frequently result in a sense of frustration or failure. A more perplexing issue for couples and for marital therapists is whether or not the traditional marriage system is so homeostatic, so resistant to change, that individuals committed to companionship can realistically expect to attain it only by separating and then starting over in a new marital system.

Figure 1 presents a summary of the major trends in marital styles during the twentieth century. Figure 1 is an expanded version of the schemata used by Mace and Mace (1974). On the right is a line representing the traditional marriage which began well before the twentieth century and is shown beginning to die off by the dotted line beginning in the 1970s. In spite of this extreme view held by the Maces, it should be kept in mind that since the traditional marriage has served men well and traditions die slowly, the traditional marriage will, in all probability, remain the dominant form of marriage for decades to come. The popularity of *The Total Woman* (Morgan, 1973), for example, suggests that many women in our society are willing to make considerable self-sacrifices to keep their traditional marriages intact.

The arrows on the right also suggest the emergence of the companionship marriage out of the traditional marriage beginning somewhere around 1930. Again it should be kept in mind that the companionship marriage is more an ideal than a reality and that many marriages are still in transition from the traditional system to a companionship marriage.

On the left is shown the rise of serial monogamy beginning around 1920 and continuing strong into the future. Growing in part out of the legitimization of serial monogamy are the variety of non-monogamous alternatives that became well-known during the 1960s. The alternatives to monogamous marriage include open marriage, group marriage, communal living and a sexually active single life.

There are important questions that arise for couples and therapists alike as marriage continues to change in both structure and function.

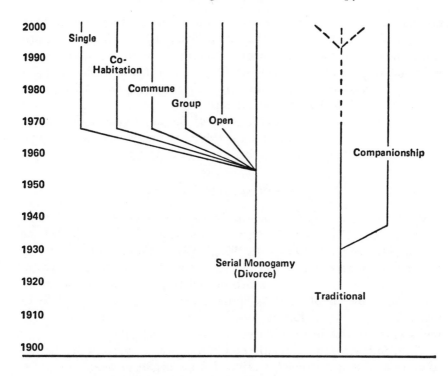

Figure 1. Dominant trends in marital styles during the
twentieth century.

How, for example, does an egalitarian and democratic marital system function effectively in the face of tie votes? With "one person—one vote" being the rule, who will cast the tie-breaking vote when critical differences arise? Perhaps breaking ties is one of the functions of a contemporary marital therapist.

If the second most common form of marriage, serial monogamy, becomes more fully accepted as a valid and valued alternative to traditional marriage rather than being considered a failure of marriage, will marital specialists have to find more appropriate criteria for what constitutes a successful marriage? In the past, successful marriages have generally been judged on the basis of two basic criteria: *stability* and *happiness*. Are we moving into an era in which only one general value will be used to judge the success of marriage and thus the success of marital therapy? Is happiness of the individual partners rather than stability of the marriage becoming the primary criterion for judging successful marital therapy? Is it perhaps anachronistic to expect marriages to be stable when they are being held together primarily by the mutually beneficial qualities of the relationship rather than by external supports and restraints of the larger social system?

The next section will examine some of the developments in marital therapy that have occurred in the twentieth century, in part as a response to the issues created by the changing trends in marriage.

TRENDS IN MARITAL THERAPY

Marital therapy began rather slowly and unassumedly in the United States. In New York in 1929, Abraham and Hannah Stone founded the Marriage Consultation Center. In 1932, Emily Mudd began the Marriage Council of Philadelphia. In 1939, Paul Popenoe established the American Institute of Family Relations which offered help to troubled couples. In 1938, Oberndorf published his classic paper on the psychoanalysis of married couples. In 1942, the American Association of Marriage Counselors was organized by the pioneers in this emerging field.

Then, following the dramatic post-World War II upsurge in the dissolution of young marriages, marital therapy began to progress rapidly. A key year was 1948. Mittleman (1948) published his definitive paper on the concurrent analysis of married couples; Mace (1948) in England published the first book on marriage counseling, which was followed a few months later by the first American book on marriage counseling by John Cuber (1948).

Since psychoanalysis was the predominant approach to therapy in 1948, and since psychoanalysis focused on the pathology within individuals, it was not surprising that the earlier writings generally supported *concurrent marital therapy* in which the therapist saw each spouse separately. The early rationale was that the transference relationship between patient and therapist was central to therapeutic cures and the presence of a spouse during the therapeutic hour would inevitably present reality conflicts that would disrupt the therapeutic transference relationship. By analyzing both partners, however, the therapist was in a better position to discuss which marital interaction problems were reality determined and which were neurotically determined. The therapist could also develop a clearer awareness of the neurotic trends in each patient when information from the spouse was also available (Mittleman, 1948).

In his 1948 paper, Mittleman also presented a psychoanalytic classification of marital problems based on a *complementary needs* view of marriage. The four complementary patterns he described were: (1) one partner dominant and aggressive, the other submissive and masochistic; (2) one partner emotionally detached, the other craving affection; (3) one partner helpless and craving care, the other partner trying to assume a position of omnipotence; and (4) both partners in continuous conflict for aggressive dominance. Concurrent analysis was aimed at each spouse developing insight into the particular neurotic needs that he or she brought into the marriage. With the development of insight in each spouse separately, they could begin to change the way they saw each other and to relate on a more mature rather than infantile level.

Because of the continuing influence of psychoanalysis and psychoanalytic theory, concurrent marital therapy remained the most widely used practice for treating couples throughout the 1950s. Even as late as 1973, Cookerly reported that concurrent therapy was the most common form of marital therapy, though it was fading in popularity. The most significant contribution of marital therapy, however, has been the increasing importance placed on working with the marital relationship per se and not only with the individuals in the relationship (Olson, 1970). If marital therapists are to understand most completely and intervene most directly with the marital relationship, then the couples would need to be seen together in joint therapy sessions. The practice of seeing both spouses together during all therapeutic sessions has come to be known as *conjoint marital therapy* (Brody, 1961; Carrol, Cambor, Lespoll, Miller and Reis, 1963; Haley, 1963; Lehrman, 1963; Satir, 1965; Watson, 1963). Olson (1970) has stated emphatically that marital therapists can be distinguished as a group by their emphasis on the marital relationship and their preference for the practice of conjoint therapy.

Just as the 1960s saw a dramatic increase in the advocacy of new styles of marriage, so too was there a significant increase in the advocacy of new practices in marital therapy. The mixing of conjoint and concurrent sessions became known as *combined marital therapy* (Greene and Solomon, 1963). The use of two therapists, each seeing a spouse separately and then consulting together, became commonly known as *collaborative therapy* (Greene and Solomon, 1963; Martin and Bird, 1963). *Collaborative combined therapy* involved the use of separate therapists for each spouse with all four meeting together at regular intervals for joint sessions (Royce and Hogan, 1960).

As group therapy grew in popularity and respectability, so too did the use of groups for married couples. Spouses in separate groups became known as *concurrent group therapy* while spouses together in the same group participated in *conjoint group therapy* (Cookerly, 1973). The method of bringing couples together in groups led by other couples was created by Ely (1970) and called *conjugal therapy*. Marital groups have also varied in being composed of all couples with one therapist (Boas, 1962; Leichter, 1962; Whitaker, 1958); all couples with co-therapists (Sager, 1966); and couples placed together with unmarried patients (Gottlieb, 1960).

By 1970 all possible combinations and permutations of concurrent, conjoint, collaborative and combined techniques had been practiced either in groups or with individual couples. What did we learn about the effectiveness of each of these methods? Surprisingly little! There have been no adequate experiments which have tested whether working with both spouses, either concurrently or conjointly, is more effective than working with only one troubled spouse in individual therapy. The best data on the subject are from the pilot survey by Cookerly (1973). He surveyed the follow-up records of 773 former marital clients of 21 marriage counselors. He divided the outcomes into six groups: clients who remained married with poor, moderate or good outcome and clients who divorced with poor, moderate or good outcome. He also divided the forms of therapy into six basic practices: (1) Individual therapy with only one spouse; (2) individual group therapy with only one spouse; (3) concurrent therapy; (4) concurrent groups; (5) conjoint therapy; (6) conjoint groups.

The most striking results were as follows. Conjoint therapy was most successful for those couples who remained married but produced the poorest outcomes for those who obtained divorces. Conjoint groups ranked second for couples remaining married and first for those obtaining divorces. Individual interviews were worst for those remaining married, but second best for those who obtained divorces. Concurrent therapy, which was the most common marital therapy at the time, was worst overall, ranking last for those who remained married and second to last for those who turned to divorce.

The problem with these data is that they are as inadequate as they are provocative. The study was not a controlled experiment, but rather a pilot survey. As a result, the many uncontrolled variables confound the data and make meaningful conclusions impossible. For example, the lack of random or controlled sampling could have meant that concurrent therapy was worst because the most troubled spouses were assigned to concurrent therapy.

Thus, the past two decades have witnessed an abundance of innovations in the practice of marital therapy. What has been lacking, however, is the development of adequate theory and data to provide a more systematic rationale and assessment for the practice of marital therapy.

In the midst of the '60s, Manus (1966) aptly characterized marital therapy as a set of practices in search of a theory. In 1967, David Mace concluded that, ". . . marriage counseling is a field in which practice has far outrun theory." By 1970 Olson reported that, "the search for *the* theory of marital therapy is slowly changing to a realization that there needs to be considerably more exploration of various theoretical approaches before a more integrated and comprehensive approach can be developed." The present book is in part a product of the realization that the development of the field of marital therapy can best be carried forward by a systematic exploration into three of the major approaches to the theory of marriage, marital disorders and marital therapy.

An Overview of Three Theories of
Marriage and Marital Therapy

In the earlier drive-dominated days of psychoanalysis, marriage as an institution was seen as continuing the socialization process that had been going on in the primary families of the spouses. Marriage was seen in part as a social means of helping to control the sexual and aggressive drives of the human animal. The control of sex within marriage is obvious. The control of aggression is less obvious, especially given the frequency of arguments and quarrels in marriage (Krupinski, Marshall and Yale, 1970). Nevertheless, marriage is the most successful alternative known for reducing the violence of males, age 16 to 25, the most violent group in our society. Marriage is, in fact, more successful than prison as a means of social control.

The early psychoanalytic view of marriage as a relationship rather than an institution revolved around the concept of complementarity of needs (Oberndorf, 1938; Mittleman, 1944, 1948). A person with strong needs to be submissive and masochistic, for example, will most likely seek a partner with strong needs to be dominant and aggressive. While Mittleman (1944, 1948) used the model of complementary needs as a nosology for marital disorders, Winch, Ktones and Ktones (1954) later generalized the theory of complementary needs to explain the basis of mate selection in normal marriages as well. In the present book (Chapter II), Meissner carries the psychoanalytic theory considerably deeper by accounting for the power of complementary needs on the basis of early identifications and introjections. An individual who has developed a sense of self as victim, for example, has internalized pathogenic introjects that revolve around aggressive conflicts. The aggressor polarity of the pathogenic introject tends to be repressed or split off. The person with a sense of self as victim will have a high propensity to project the repressed or split-off aggressor dimensions of the self onto significant others, such as a spouse. The unconscious and immature need for an aggressor upon which to project the repressed dimensions of the early introjects will lead to the selection of a mate who can provide optimal gratification of these unconscious and narcissistic needs.

The partner then becomes part of the pathogenic process in which a poorly differentiated sense of self results in relationships based primarily on interaction between the more conscious and accepted parts of early introjects and the more repressed and projected dimensions. The divided self is thus transformed into the divided spouses. Conflicts between spouses are at a deeper level a reenactment of the conflicts occurring within each of the separate spouses.

Upon initial reading, Meissner's presentation of a psychoanalytic theory of marriage and the family would appear to be a more sophisticated version of a strictly intrapsychic theory of individuals relating to their own introjections and projections. As Meissner explores deeper into the dynamics of marriage and the family, however, he transforms this radical theory of the intrapsychic individual into a conclusion that the reader may find as challenging as it is surprising.

If spouses are reacting unconsciously to their projections rather than to their partners, to their introjections rather than to their intimates, then therapy must allow for the immature introjections and projections to come into the curative light of consciousness. The classical analytic answer was, of course, to allow a profound transference relationship to develop between an individual patient and the analyst, so that the patient could gradually become aware of how the therapist is being processed through the illusionary lenses of infantile introjections. As Meissner points out, however, marriage itself is, in a very real and profound sense, a fairly stable configuration of transference and countertransference reactions. To bring the spouse into analysis, whether concurrently or conjointly, was traditionally thought to so confound the therapeutic transference relationship that the conscious unraveling of fact and fantasy would be impossible.

Mittleman (1948) argued that the therapeutic transferences could remain uncontaminated if the therapist could remain totally neutral while treating both spouses. Sager (1966) and others have argued that traditional analysts were unduly alarmed over the possibility that the transference developed in individual analytic sessions would be disrupted by concurrent or conjoint sessions. Sager suggests that neurotics and normals both are extremely prone to think and experience relationships in dyadic terms. Thus, the triadic relationship that occurs when the spouse is present will not disrupt the dyadic perception that each patient has of the therapist. The transference relationship and its accompanying dyadic perceptions serve defensive functions that are too important to be readily disrupted.

In the present book (Chapter III), Nadelson suggests how a contemporary psychoanalytic marital therapist can remain sensitive to important transference issues without being unduly restricted in the therapeutic modalities that can be applied. Beginning with an intensive evaluation of the intrapsychic and interpersonal factors involved in a specific marital case, a psychoanalytic marital therapist may recommend concurrent, collaborative, conjoint, or couples group therapy. Or the therapist may indeed decide that individual analysis for just one of the spouses is the treatment of choice.

Nadelson seems to prefer the practice of letting the couples' particular problems and needs dictate the form that therapy will take rather than having theory unduly restrict the format of therapy. What theory does provide for a psychoanalytic marital therapist is an awareness of how the traditional issues of resistance, transference, and countertransference can be the critical concerns in each of the models of marital therapy. Psychoanalytic theory also suggests that the treatment of resistance and transference in couples, as in individuals, involves building a therapeutic alliance followed by an effective use of psychoanalytic interpretations.

At first glance there could probably not be a better counterpoint to a psychoanalytic approach to marriage than to follow with a behavioral view. Introjections, projections, transferences, and changes in consciousness would be expected to collide with the consequences, contingencies and contracts of the traditional behavioral approach to marriage problems. The history of behavioral approaches to marriage would suggest that all that could be expected from comparing psychoanalysis and behaviorism is an increased awareness of two incompatible approaches to humanity.

When behavioral techniques were first applied to marital disorders in the mid-1960s, there were two major thrusts within the behavioral camp. Wolpe (1958) helped to establish *counter-conditioning* techniques such as desensitization and assertiveness training which were based on a classical, respondent or Pavlovian conditioning model of behavior. At about the same time, Lindsley (1956) had begun demonstrating with schizophrenics the potential power of *contingency management* techniques that were based upon the operant, instrumental or Skinnerian principles of behavior. When behaviorists gradually began to work with marital disorders, they turned primarily to an operant explanation of marital interactions and contingency contracting techniques for altering such transactions. Stuart (1969a), for example, was one of the first to apply operant principles to couples who showed the common complaint of the husband wanting more sex and the wife wanting more talking. Though the four couples were already in divorce court, they each negotiated a contract in which the husband could earn a poker chip for every 15 minutes of dialog in which he participated. When the husband earned eight poker chips, he could exchange them for sexual intercourse. Needless to say, the rate of talking went up significantly, as did the rate of sexual relating, and the couples no longer reported a desire to divorce.

Stuart (1969b) extended the operant approach to marriage by incorporating Thibault and Kelly's (1959) social exchange model of relationships. Social exchange theory holds that the amount of social interaction in a dyad is related to the number of mutual reinforcements exchanged. A successful marriage is maintained when there is a high level of reinforcements at a low level of cost for each spouse. Other behaviorists added that successful couples rely on the use of positive reinforcements to modify each other's behavior rather than using punishment or coercion.

Unsuccessful marriages were conceptualized as including: (1) an unfair exchange of reinforcements; (2) excessive cost for the reinforcements gained; (3) a strategy of minimizing personal costs in the face of little expectation of mutual reward; (4) withdrawal or minimal interaction in the face of a lack of mutual reinforcements; and/or (5) the use of aversive or coercive controls to modify each other's behavior.

In Chapter IV of this volume, Weiss builds upon these earlier behavioral conceptualizations of marriage and marital discord, but goes well beyond the traditional operant model. In part he draws upon some of the concepts of the third and most recent thrust in behavior therapy, the cognitive orientation. The cognitive movement within contemporary behavior therapy provides the possibility of some rapprochement with the heavily cognitive orientation of psychoanalysis, especially more contemporary ego analysis. More strikingly, Weiss has also begun to integrate concepts from systems theory into his behavioral approach. Even though the present book was designed to highlight three separate alternatives to conceptualizing and treating marriages, we can see the healthy signs of an emerging integration across the different schools of therapy.

In Chapter V of this volume, O'Leary and Turkewitz reflect how far behavioral marital therapists have come in less than a decade since the classic, though simplistic, contracting studies of Stuart. They advocate a more complex approach to marital therapy that integrates procedures from each of the three major behavioral orientations: (1) counter-conditioning techniques, when there are anxiety-related problems such as sexual dysfunctions; (2) contingency management procedures, such as training in negotiation and compromise; and (3) cognitive processes, such as relabeling and reinterpreting particular behaviors of a spouse. Recognizing, however, that none of the behavioral approaches will be particularly effective if couples lack adequate communication skills, they include a behavioral approach to communication training as an integral part of their marital work.

Following the most important assumption of behaviorists, that therapy be seen as an empirical endeavor that must be tested and validated by the same rigorous, experimental procedures used in investigating any scientific question, O'Leary and Turkewitz proceed to report their recent research on the effectiveness of two forms of behavioral marital therapy. Specifically, they compared communication training plus behavior change contracts to determine which approach was most effective in helping troubled marriages.

Psychoanalysis and behavior therapy were originally developed in the treatment of troubled individuals and then later began to enrich our understanding of relationships as they were applied to marriages and families. Systems therapy, on the other hand, is unique in that it originated directly out of the efforts of researchers and therapists working with troubled families and marriages (Bateson, Jackson, Haley and Weakland, 1956; Haley, 1963; Jackson, 1959; Watzlawick, Beavin and Jackson, 1967). Olson (1970) indicates that systems theory and therapy are, in fact, the most challenging contribution that marital and family therapy have made to the mental health disciplines.

In Chapter VI of this volume, Steinglass makes it clear that there is no single systems approach to understanding marriage and marital therapy. He contrasts the systems approaches of Murray Bowen, Sal Minuchin, the Palo Alto group, and social scientists such as Talcott Parsons and Reuben Hill, in part to demonstrate the diversity of therapists that have emerged from a systems perspective. More importantly, Steinglass wants to demonstrate how each of these separate systems approaches to marriage and the family can be conceptualized as more limited theoretical models that have cut a piece of the pie out of a more general systems perspective. From a more general systems theory, marriage would first and foremost be seen as organized. The relationship between the spouses becomes structured into consistent patterns. Once the spouses are combined in consistent patterns, then the *wholeness* of the marriage becomes greater than the sum of the characteristics of each of the spouses. A marriage can be characterized as a *dynamic steady state* in which there are built-in control mechanisms, homeostatic mechanisms, that allow change to occur in an orderly and controlled manner. Change in marriage follows a *circular causality* so that responses in one spouse serve as stimuli for responses in the other spouse rather than there being a linear causality in which the isolated actions of only one spouse are assumed to be the cause of change in a marriage. The concepts of wholeness, homeostasis and circular causality lead to dynamic interactions in which a change in one spouse will cause a change in the other spouse and, conversely, a change in one spouse cannot occur without a change in the marital system.

In Chapter VII Sluzki illustrates one of the ways in which the basic concepts of a systems perspective can be applied in helping to change disordered marital systems. Originally a part of the Palo Alto group that included Bateson, Jackson, Haley and Watzlawick, Sluzki is especially sensitive to the importance of feedback or communication in controlling a system. Many of his therapeutic prescriptions involve the conscious use of verbal and nonverbal communications to effect change in a couple. Sluzki is also sensitive to how consistent patterns of interactions eventually become rules that govern a marriage or a family. Consequently, his interventions are frequently aimed at trying to change patterns in order to change the rules of a system or, conversely, trying to change a rule in order to allow a change in destructive patterns of interaction. Sluzki presents a series of very practical and parsimonious prescriptions first, and then discusses the theoretical concepts underlying his therapeutic prescriptions. For example, he concretizes the concept of circular causality that governs both marital and therapeutic relationships by suggesting that, "If you (the therapist) don't like what you are getting in marital therapy, change *your* behavior."

In Chapter VIII Jacobson provides a comprehensive review of the controlled outcome research on marital therapy. Adequately controlled research on marital therapy is of very recent vintage, with the bulk of such studies appearing since 1970. In spite of the recent increase in controlled research, data are not available to compare the relative effectiveness of the three major approaches under study in this volume.

Of the three perspectives, only the behavioral approach has a body of literature that permits even tentative conclusions regarding the effectiveness of marital interventions compared to no treatment or to placebo treatments. Behavioral approaches continue to find empirical support as effective methods for helping distressed couples. Ironically, Jacobson's own speculation from the literature is that the communication training component is probably the critical element of a behavioral approach, while at the same time the communication component is the element least unique to behavioral theory. It would not be surprising if working on communication does, as Jacobson suggests, turn out to be the *sine qua non* of marital therapy, since a lack of communication is the most common complaint of couples coming to clinics (Greene, 1974).

The most immediate benefit of the rapid rise in controlled marital therapy research will not be to provide therapists with data on which therapy approaches work best with which types of marital problems. Such data are probably a long way off. Hopefully, the most immediate impact of this research will be to help establish marital therapy as a scientifically respectable discipline that is worthy of much greater attention in the research and service training of young therapists. If marital therapy attains greater respectability in departments of psychology, psychiatry, and counseling and in schools of social work, future therapists may no longer be inadequately prepared for doing effective marital therapy.

In the final Chapter, Gurman begins the difficult task of providing a more systematic comparative analysis of the psychoanalytic, behavioral and systems perspectives. In a critical evaluation of the strengths and weaknesses of each approach, Gurman seems to suggest that in theory, as in life, all too often our most valued strengths are our biggest problems. Thus, a psychoanalytic perspective can contribute a profound appreciation of how experiences from past relationships can be transferred into present marriages in very disruptive and deceptive ways. This theoretical strength can at the same time hinder psychoanalytic marital therapists from appreciating just how much current rather than past transactions can be at the center of many marital disorders. Systems theoretists and behaviorists, on the other hand, are better prepared for analyzing present functioning, but can overlook the many ways in which perceptual distortions due to transference phenomena can disrupt current interactions. In a similar fashion, a systems perspective can be most powerful in conceptualizing the overall patterns and rules of a marital system, but it can at the same time lose sight of the fact that spouses can also be autonomous individuals, with separate wants and desires independent of the marriage, and not just cogs caught in the controls of a larger marital system.

The point is that marriages and marital disorders are probably too complex and too varied to be adequately contained within the conceptual confines of just one theoretical perspective. A comparative analysis of the three major perspectives of this book can perhaps generate the beginnings of a more comprehensive approach to marriage and marital therapy.

REFERENCES

Bateson, G., Jackson, D., Haley, J. and Weakland, J. Toward a theory of schizophrenia. *Behavioral Science*, 1956, 1, 251-264.

Bergman, I. *Scenes from a Marriage*. New York: Bantam Books, 1973.

Bernard, J. *The Future of Marriage*. New York: Bantam Books, 1972.

Boas, C. Intensive group psychotherapy with married couples. *International Journal of Group Therapy*, 1962, 12, 142-153.

Brody, S. Simultaneous psychotherapy of married couples. In: J. Masserman (Ed.), *Current Psychiatric Therapies*. New York: Grune and Stratton, 1961.

Burgess, E. and Locke, H. *The Family: From Institution to Companionship*. New York: American Book Co., 1945.

Carroll, E., Cambor, C., Lespoll, J., Miller, M., and Reis, W. Psychotherapy of marital couples. *Family Process*, 1963, 2, 25-33.

Cookerly, J. R. The outcome of the six major forms of marriage counseling compared: A pilot study. *Journal of Marriage and the Family*, 1973, 36, 608-611.

Cooper, D. *The Death of the Family*. New York: Random House, 1970.

Cuber, J. *Marriage Counseling Practice*. New York: Appleton-Century-Crofts, 1948.

Ely, A. Efficacy of training in conjugal therapy. Unpublished doctoral dissertation. Rutgers University, 1970.

Glick, P. A demographer looks at American families. *Journal of Marriage and the Family*, 1975, 37, 15-26.

Gottlieb, S. Response of married couples included in a group of single patients. *International Journal of Group Psychotherapy*, 1960, 10, 143-159.

Greene, B. The most common complaints of spouses entering marital therapy. Cited in M. Lear: Save the spouses rather than the marriage. *New York Times Magazine*, Aug. 13, 1972, pp. 12-28.

Greene, B. and Solomon, A. Marital disharmony: Concurrent psychoanalytic therapy of husband and wife by the same psychiatrist. *American Journal of Psychiatry*, 1963, 17, 443-450.

Haley, J. Marriage therapy. *Archives of General Psychiatry*, 1963, 8, 213-234.

Jackson, D. Family interaction, family homeostasis and some implications for conjoint family psychotherapy. In: J. Masserman (Ed.), *Individual and Family Dynamics*. New York: Grune and Stratton, 1959.

Jackson, D. The study of the family. *Family Process*, 1965, 4, 1-20.

Kaplan, H. S. *The New Sex Therapy*. New York: Brunner/Mazel, 1974.

Krupinski, J., Marshall, E., and Yale, E. Patterns of marital problems in marriage guidance clients. *Journal of Marriage and the Family*, 1970, 32, 138-145.

Lear, M. Save the spouses, rather than the marriage. *New York Times Magazine*, August 13, 1972, pp. 12-28.

Lederer, W. and Jackson, D. *The Mirages of Marriage*. New York: Norton, 1968.

Lehrman, N. The joint interview: An aid to psychotherapy and family stability. *American Journal of Psychotherapy*, 1963, 17, 83-93.

Leichter, G. Group psychotherapy of married couples groups: Some characteristic treatment dynamics. *International Journal of Group Psychotherapy*, 1962, 12, 154-163.

Lindsley, O. R. Operant conditioning methods applied to research in chronic schizophrenia. *Psychiatric Research Reports*, 1956, 5, 118-139.

Mace, D. *Marriage Counseling*. London: J. A. Churchill, 1948.

Mace, D. Introduction. In: H. L. Silverman (Ed.), *Marital Counseling*. Springfield, Illinois: Charles C. Thomas, 1967.

Mace, D. and Mace, V. *We Can Have Better Marriages*. Nashville: Abingdon, 1974.

Manus, G. Marriage counseling: A technique in search of a theory. *Journal of Marriage and the Family*, 1966, 28, 449-453.

Martin, P. and Bird, W. An approach to the psychotherapy of marriage partners: The stereoscopic technique. *Psychiatry*, 1963, 16, 123-127.

Mittleman, B. Complementary neurotic reactions in intimate relationships. *Psychoanalytic Quarterly*, 1944, 13, 479-491.

Mittleman, B. The concurrent analysis of marital couples. *Psychoanalytic Quarterly*, 1948, 17, 182-197.

Morgan, M. *The Total Woman*. Old Tappan, New Jersey: Fleming Revell Co., 1973.

Oberndorf, C. Psychoanalysis of married couples. *Psychoanalytic Review*, 1938, 25, 453-475.

Olson, D. Marital and family therapy: Integrative review and critique. *Journal of Marriage and the Family*, 1970, 32, 501-538.

Parloff, M. Shopping for the right therapy. *Saturday Review*, Feb. 21, 1976, 3, 14-16.

Prochaska, J. O. Restriction of range on date and mate selection in college students. Unpublished manuscript, University of Rhode Island, 1977.

Prochaska, J. O. *Systems of Psychotherapy: A Transtheoretical Analysis*. Homewood, Illinois: Dorsey Press, in press.

Reich, C. A. *The Greening of America*. New York: Random House, 1970.

Royce, J. and Hogan, P. Co-therapy in a special situation. Paper delivered at the American Group Psychotherapy Association, 1960.

Sager, C. The development of marriage therapy: An historical review. *American Journal of Orthopsychiatry*, 1966, 36, 458-467.

Satir, V. Conjoint marital therapy. In B. C. Greene (Ed.), *The Psychotherapy of Marital Disharmony*. New York: The Free Press, 1965.

Scanzoni, J. *Sexual Bargaining: Power Politics in the American Marriage*. New York: Prentice-Hall, 1972.

Stuart, R. Token reinforcement in marital treatment. In: R. D. Robin and C. M. Franks (Eds.), *Advances in Behavior Therapy*. New York: Academic Press, 1969 (a).

Stuart, R. Operant interpersonal treatment for marital discord. *Journal of Consulting and Clinical Psychology*, 1969 (b), 33, 675-687.

Thibault, J. and Kelly, H. *The Social Psychology of Groups.* New York: Wiley, 1959.

Watson, A. The conjoint psychotherapy of marriage partners. *American Journal of Orthopsychiatry,* 1963, 33, 912-922.

Watzlawick, P., Beavin, J., and Jackson, D. C. *Pragmatics of Human Communication.* New York: Norton, 1967.

Whitaker, C. Psychotherapy with couples. *American Journal of Psychotherapy,* 1958, 12, 18-23.

Winch, R., Ktones, T., and Ktones, V. The theory of complementary needs in mate selection. *American Sociological Review,* 1954, 19, 241-249.

Wolfe, T. *Mauve Gloves and Madmen, Clutter and Vine, and Other Stories, Sketches and Essays.* New York: Farrar, Straus & Giroux, 1976.

Wolpe, J. *Psychotherapy by Reciprocal Inhibition.* Stanford, California: Stanford University Press, 1958.

Yankelovich, D. *The Changing Values on Campus.* New York: Washington Square Press, 1972.

Zimmerman, C. The future of the family in America. *Journal of Marriage and the Family,* 1972, 34, 323-333.

II

The Conceptualization of Marriage and Family Dynamics from a Psychoanalytic Perspective

WILLIAM W. MEISSNER, S.J., M.D.

ORGANIZATION AND COMPOSITION OF CHAPTER

This chapter is an attempt to present certain selective data and to provide them with a theoretical underpinning, which will provide the material out of which a coherent theory of family dynamics based on psychoanalytic principles can emerge. It consists of seven sections: the first section, entitled "General Considerations," introduces the reader to some basic psychoanalytic concepts such as "object relations" and explains why a psychoanalytic approach to marriage must also include a discussion of parent-child normal and abnormal relationships. The second section, entitled "The Evolution of Psychoanalytic Thinking About the Family," gives the reader a brief historical overview of the psychoanalytic theories about marriage and the family as they began with Freud and as they have been modified by Freud's followers. The remaining sections are the author's attempt to utilize psychoanalytic concepts as building blocks for the construction of a psychoanalytic theory of marriage and family dynamics. The third section, entitled "The Individual Personality," discusses the organization of the individual personality, focusing on those interpersonal dynamics in more elaborated and complex social units such as marriage and the family. The fourth section, entitled "The Marital Couple," is a discussion of the interaction of personalities in dyadic relationships, particularly the marital relationship which inaugurates the history of the family. The fifth section, entitled "The Family Unit," is an attempt to enlarge the analysis to embrace the more complex social organization of the family, itself composed of father, mother and one or more children, and the complex interactions which take place, not only between them as individuals, but also more particularly within the family unit as a complex psychosocial integration. The sixth section on "The Transference Model" discusses the transference and how it relates to marriage and family dynamics. The seventh section is a brief summary and conclusion of the chapter.

GENERAL CONSIDERATIONS

When two individuals meet, fall in love and decide to marry, they enter into a process of establishing and defining an interpersonal dyadic relationships which will have certain specificable and enduring characteristics. In entering into this process, each of the individuals brings the psychological heritage that has characterized his/her unique psychological development so that each contributes to the composition of the marital dyad, in respective and proportional ways, elements of his/her own inner psychic constitution. The chemistry of composition will involve a substantially different quality of dyadic interaction depending on the composite elements that are brought to it. The interaction that takes place between two relatively defined and securely differentiated and individuated selves has a quite different quality and quite different implication from that which is composed of relatively undifferentiated selves.

This chapter is an attempt to define the quality of the marital interaction and the correlative nature of the resulting marital dyad as conceptualized from a psychoanalytic perspective. Psychoanalytic theory conceptualizes all family and non-family interactions in terms of "object" relations, their related internalizations, and introjections and projections derived from the object and the relationship. For any given husband and wife, the marital dyadic relationship is so inextricably bound to the parent-child relationship in their families of origin, as well as in their family of procreation, that no comprehensive psychoanalytic discussion of marital interaction can avoid the subject of parent-child interaction. The capacity to successfully function as a spouse is largely a consequence of the spouse's childhood relationships to his own parents. Furthermore, if the family system is conceptualized from the psychoanalytic perspective of object relations, then a logical assumption is that the same strengths and weaknesses are involved in both marital and parent-child relationships. And so, although this book is on marriage, this chapter will not only discuss the marital dyad, but also the father-child and mother-child dyadic relationships, as well as the two parents-child triadic configuration as they occur in normal and abnormal families.

A major thesis of this chapter is that the relative success that the marital partners experience and the manner in which these developmental tasks are approached and accomplished are determined to a large extent by the residues of internalized objects and the organization of introjects which form the core of the sense of self and contribute in significant ways to the integration of their respective identities. The extent to which spouses are unsuccessful in merging these individual identities into a constructive and productive shared marital experience depends in important ways on the extent to which that experience is contaminated by pathogenic introjects they each may bring to it, rather than being organized in terms of a successful differentiated and individuated sense of self and identity.

A key concept in this chapter is that of transference. It has often been said that psychoanalysis is a "one-body psychology," but the charge obviously has only limited validity. The phenomenon of transference has been at the heart of the psychoanalytic enterprise from the very beginning. The transference, in fact, forms a two-body system of complex social interaction, but it is more than that. The study of the transference provides the psychoanalyst with a privileged access to the study of the unconscious, motivational, and transpersonal dimensions of the most basic social unit of organization, the interpersonal dyad. Consequently, even within the limited classical psychoanalytic perspective, psychoanalysis has at the minimum a headstart on the understanding of more complex social interactions.

THE EVOLUTION OF PSYCHOANALYTIC THINKING ABOUT THE FAMILY

The psychoanalytic approach to the understanding of human behavior has its own character in its methodology and theoretical conceptualization. Progress in analytic thinking tends to take the form of refinement, differentiation and deepening of the understanding of its basic concepts and their implications, rather than a surrendering of old concepts in order to replace them with new editions. Thus, psychoanalysis can be said to be essentially a conservative discipline, or perhaps evolutionary in its thinking as opposed to the more revolutionary style often found in other scientific paradigms.

Since this is the case, it is entirely appropriate that the debt to Freud be acknowledged. Certainly, a psychoanalytic understanding of the family and its dynamics must trace its origins back to Freud's contributions and cannot take shape exclusive of them. But the debt to Freud is even more considerable, since it can be safely said that his major contribution was to begin to trace the intricate relationships between the structuring of personality and its developmental vicissitudes within the context of the experience of family life. The oedipal theory, for example, is equivalently a theory about important developmental experience which takes place within the family matrix.

As one reads the classic case histories, for example the case of Dora (1905) or that of the Wolf-Man (1918), it can be seen that Freud was acutely aware of the familial influences on the development and shaping of the patient's personality and the evolution of his psychopathology. In fact, one can go a long way in reconstructing some of the family dynamics from Freud's rather vivid clinical accounts. The emphasis, however, fell elsewhere. As Ackerman (1958, p. 27) has noted:

> The salient emphasis is on the projection of irrational, anxiety-ridden fantasy; the interpersonal reality of the contemporary group environment is largely bypassed.

Yet, from the perspective of a more contemporary understanding of family dynamics, even though Freud brought to awareness the importance of family interactions, there remained an ambiguity. Ackerman (1958, p. 26) has observed:

> . . . hidden in these reflections lies the profound riddle of the inter-relations of individual development and family "belongingness" as they evolve in time. The riddle is persistently echoed in a measure of indecision about how far personality is individual, how far it is familial or social, how far it unfolds autonomously from within, how far it is influenced from without, and how far it moves inward and backward rather than outward and forward. It is the riddle of the relations between the inner and outer face of personality, the secrets of which are not yet fully revealed. They are still somewhat obscured in the reciprocal processes of integration and individuation in family life.

This chapter attempts to determine the degree to which subsequent analytic thinking has succeeded in resolving that ambiguity and solving that riddle.

Subsequent to Freud's early studies, analytic efforts continued to be directed toward the study of the influence of the family on individual personality development, but there was little direct study of the dynamics of the family itself. The high water marks usually indicated are the early work by Flügel, *The Psychoanalytic Study of the Family* (1921), and the 9th International Congress of Psychoanalysis held in 1936, the main topic of which was "Family Neurosis and the Neurotic Family" (Spitz, 1937). Flügel's discussion, despite the somewhat misleading title, focused much more intensely on anthropological data, following Freud's lead in *Totem and Taboo* (1913), and thus provided a discussion of the psychology of individuals who are born, raised and live in families rather than contributing any understanding of the family group process as such. Thus, analysts had not yet taken the bold step of putting themselves in touch with patients' families as a whole. Even the 1936 Congress offers only some preliminary explorations and ideas that arise out of a context of the simultaneous analytic treatment of more than one family member. The treatment of the family group remained a future phenomenon.

Subsequently, the major advances in the direction of family treatment were made by child analysts. Burlingham (1951, 1955) opened the possibility of simultaneous analysis of both mother and child as a way of dealing with the complicated difficulties of this relationship. It was not long after that Adelaide Johnson and her coworkers (Johnson and Szurek, 1952; Giffin, Johnson and Litin, 1954; Litin, Giffin and Johnson, 1956) discussed the transmission of superego defects in children as the result of unconscious parental influences. To this must be added the growing interest in the concurrent analysis of married couples which contributed a much more extensive understanding of the dynamics and vicissitudes of the relationship between husband and wife (Oberndorf, 1934, 1938; Mittelmann, 1944, 1948; Martin and Bird, 1953).

Along with this there were contemporaneous developments in psychoanalytic theory which opened the way toward a more meaningful exploration of the family as a social unit. As Lidz (1962) points out so clearly, we are indebted to Hartmann for making legitimate the psychoanalytic study of the interplay between personality structure and social environment. Hartmann (1944) introduced the problem in the following terms (pp. 26-27):

We know that in hysteria the choice of the affected organ is partly determined by the particular physical characteristics of the organ. Freud described this as *somatic compliance*. There is an analogous relationship between the individual's mental structure and his social environment. This gives us the right to speak of *social compliance*, by which we understand the fact that social factors must also be described psychologically in such a way as to demonstrate their selective effects; they operate in the direction of the selection and the effectuation of certain tendencies and their expression, and of certain developmental trends, among those which, at any given moment, are potentially demonstrable in the structure of the individual. These selective processes are present at every stage of human development.

However, it was left to Erik Erikson (1946, 1950, 1959) to effectively elaborate this sociological dimension of an evolving ego psychology.

In the course of this evolution of analytic thinking, there has been not only a gradual shift from an intrapyschic to a more interpersonal and socialized perspective (Lidz, 1962), but also a parallel shift from dealing with the family as a collection of complexly interacting intrapsychic entities to a consideration of the family as a social unit in itself, having its own inherent and characteristic dynamic properties. The tension in this development is obvious, and it is the inevitable tension which arises between a point of view which takes its orientation from the unconscious and highly individualized psychodynamics of the classic psychoanalytic perspective and an orientation which shifts its focus to the complex patternings of behavior and emotion within the family as a social unit.

The shift to a social perspective has carried with it the risk of losing touch with and ignoring specific unconscious and fantasy-related material. Certainly, as this book demonstrates, there have been theorists who have essentially abandoned a psychoanalytic perspective and turned to a behavioral or systems theory or other theoretical orientation in order to deal with the complex realities of the family process. But such an abandoning of analytic principles is not at all necessary. Ackerman (1958, p. 30) was quick to point out:

> . . . child-parent relations are the core of the psychoanalytic view of human development. It is these very relationships that, as transference phenomena, occupy the center of the stage in psychoanalytic therapy. Yet in pyschoanalysis direct observations of family interaction have not been carried out until very recently, and only now is their importance beginning to be recognized. The attitude of classical Freudians has been, in effect, that the patient's fantasies and dreams are the royal road to the unconscious, that it is relatively

unessential to know the realities of the social environment. . . . on the contrary, I believe that an accurate understanding of the unconscious is possible only when one interprets unconscious dynamics in the context of the conscious organization of experience, the total integrative patterns of personality, and the prevailing interpersonal realities.

In short, the problem for an evolving psychoanalytic theory of family dynamics is not merely a question of integrating data from disparate realms of observation—the intrapsychic and the social—but an involvement with the more difficult and complex problem of developing a theoretical framework within which concepts relating to both the intrapsychic level of functioning and the more complex interindividual and social level of interaction and responsiveness can be adequately comprehended. Too often the conceptualizations of group phenomena, including those of the family group, have been cast in terms which essentially part company with the realm of psychoanalytic discourse which is rooted in the intrapsychic realm. The achievement of a consistent and integrated theoretical framework remains the primary task of psychoanalytic theory in its attempts to understand and conceptualize family dynamics.

This chapter is an attempt to assess the relevant data and to evolve a conceptual framework out of a particular psychoanalytically based understanding of human personality. We will attempt to understand the mechanisms by which such personalities interact to form not merely complex social units, but units which have quite striking and specific affective and motivational components. *It is essential in the course of this construction that the conceptual framework for the understanding of the psychoanalytic dynamics of dyadic marital relations or more complex and multidimensional family relationships should not leave behind or lose its essential contact with the understanding of psychoanalytic dynamic and motivational factors as they operate on an intrapsychic level.* Moreover, an essential quality of the theory developed in this chapter is that it maintain a conceptual continuity in terms of mechanisms and processes as they operate both in the individual component personality unit of themselves and their complex organizations into social systems.

Toward a Theory of Family Dynamics

Individual Personality

From a psychoanalytic perspective, the development of the human personality is a complex process which takes place through a sequence of phases. The process and its vicissitudes have been described in considerable detail in the work of Margaret Mahler (Mahler, Pine and Bergman, 1975). The infant begins life in a state of symbiotic unity with the significant mothering figure, and through a progression of developmental steps gradually is able to separate from this symbiotic dependency and gradually establish an independent and relatively autonomous separate psychic existence. The successful negotiation of this process of separation and individuation leads in the direction of a progressively more differentiated and internally integrated organization of the sense of self and the gradual establishment of an identity which reflects the unique psychological organization of that growing individual and which provides the bulwark for the working-through and successful resolution of developmental crises and the inevitable complexities and conflicts of human life.

The successful accomplishment of this developmental sequence has been focused and articulated by psychoanalytic thinkers in a variety of terms. The successful outcome depends on the establishment of libidinal object constancy which implies not merely the capacity for relationship but, more specifically, the maintenance of attachment to and regard for the object through all the vicissitudes of affective change—in the face of gratifications, frustrations, libidinal wishes, aggressive assaults, disappointments, and disillusionments. It also implies the capacity to delay gratification, to tolerate frustration, and to enjoy the capacity for ego functioning.

In more contemporary terms, the successful outcome of the separation-individuation process leads in the direction of the etstablishing of a coherent and cohesive sense of self, which provides the essential basis for a sense of continuity and sameness within one's own experience of one's own inner psychic processes. By the same token, self-cohesion provides the basis by which one not only achieves initially, but is able to firmly establish and maintain a sense of difference between self and others and a sense of separation between self and others. One of the marks of a mature personality is the capacity to tolerate separateness and differentness of important emotionally involved objects. We have come to recognize all of these elements as contributing to and sustaining a mature sense of personal identity and personality integration. From experience we know that the successful negotiation of this complex developmental sequence is fraught with peril. Very few are able to negotiate it successfully, and most people settle for a more or less successful or unsuccessful developmental career. Some, indeed, fail in this process quite miserably.

One can ask at this juncture what the implications of the relatively successful or unsuccessful achievement of a sense of identity may be for the functioning of the individual personality, as well as for his/her involvement in the family within which he/she grows up. The failure to achieve a differentiated sense of identity means that the developing individuals remain intensely emotionally attached to their families. All their energy and emotional concern are focused on the welfare and well-being of their parents and family rather than on their own well-being. In this dependence on and attachment to the family, they do not have an individuated sense of self that is separate and independent from them. To the extent that this differentiation fails, they imply that they cannot exist without their parents since their own existence and well-being are so intimately tied up with theirs.

This attachment and the conflicts related to it reach a crisis in adolescence when children are caught up in the dilemma of opposing developmental pressures and infantile attachments. They cannot differentiate or separate their own sense of self from that of their parents. They are unable to direct in any meaningful way their energies toward the development of their own lives and interests and to meeting the demands of the environment. Caught in this wrenching and tormenting conflict, they either keep themselves in a position of more or less infantile dependence or resolve the dilemma by denying their dependency and rebelliously adopting a façade of exaggerated adequacy and independence. Even when such children violently rebel or run away from home, they have not successfully resolved the issues of differentiation and detachment from their families, but carry the inner dependency and the related conflicts with them.

Such individuals who have an impoverished or deficient identity never really develop values or beliefs that are clearly their own. They either adopt the values derived from their immediate family or adapt themselves to the strengths they find in other people and thus come to operate with a borrowed identity. The phenomenon was described as a form of character disorder by Helene Deutsch some years ago in her description of the "as-if personality" (1942). Similar phenomena can be recognized in a variety of character pathologies, as reflecting the relative failure of effective internalizations (Meissner, in press). Not infrequently, such individuals become excessively involved and often fanatical in adherence to causes, beliefs, leaders, ideologies—anything which provides them a sense of stability and direction for their faltering and fragile identity.

The most severe cases of lack of differentiation are, of course, psychotic.

In such patients we find little or no motivation toward establishing their own individuality or identity or of moving ahead with a life that is their own, independent of their parents or their families. The schizophrenic child is one who has failed in the process of growing away from and separating from his parents in order to establish his own individuality. The individual with a poor sense of identity tends to blindly accept the views of others, or work at attributing views to them which he then feels he must submit to.

The stance of rebellious opposition reflects the defectiveness of identity just as much as a stance of compliance. The rebel can define his faulty identity only in terms of opposition to the other, and he can take that stand only after the other has made his position known. In fact, however, the rebel has no greater autonomy or independence than his complaint and submissive colleague, but rather presents a façade of adequacy and independence. Such individuals may appear on the surface to have clear values, strong beliefs and a well-defined sense of identity, but their beliefs are often rigid, biased, and dogmatic. They cannot change their position easily, nor can they allow themselves to listen to alternate or different points of view. They are so caught up in defending their own views that they cannot hear what anyone else is saying; their sense of identity is so fragile and embattled that they cannot afford to open themselves to the views of others.

An individual with a relatively mature and secure sense of identity is capable of not only tolerating differences between himself and others, but of accepting and valuing this separateness and difference. Rather than being caught on the horns of the dilemma of rigidly blocking out or submissively swallowing the viewpoints of the important figures around him, he is free to listen, to sample and taste, to learn what is to be learned and to make use of what is helpful and constructive in the pursuance of his own interests and objectives. He has no need to force agreement from others since he can tolerate the fact that they may not agree with or endorse his own point of view. Clinically, one is constantly confronted with patients who struggle with these difficulties. For example, one of the author's patients was a young woman whose marriage foundered on her inability to gain constant approval and endorsement from her husband of everything she did in the family context. The failure to gain his approval left her filled with self-doubt and self-recrimination and continually tripped her up and plunged her into a recurrent depression. She was unable to accept or endorse the validity of her own feelings, attitudes, beliefs, and convictions.

Such individuals are constantly in need of praise and have a poor tolerance for criticism. They are constantly looking to others to build up their fragile sense of self-esteem and they take any criticism as rejection or hostile assault. The person with a mature sense of identity can take it or leave it, can accept praise with circumspection and perspective, and can tolerate criticism and even benefit from it. He is not dependent on either praise or blame for the maintenance of his own inner self-regard. The person with a poor self, however, is hurt, demoralized, and depleted by any rejection or criticism. The major goal of his life seems to be being liked and accepted by others. The more intensely he seeks to please others and gain acceptance from them, the more any rejection is regarded as a catastrophe. Such individuals, who orient their motivation around being the way others in their lives want them to be or toward pleasing those others, are precisely the ones who plunge into feelings of angry and resentful hurt in the face of the failure to gain such approval and turn to the willful hurting of others in retaliation. The more maturely individuated personality who maintains a secure sense of self is not concerned about such rejection or whether or not one is loved and approved. Others are important and valued in one's life experience, but one's life course and attitudes towards oneself are not determined by the attitudes of those others.

One of the most important features of the functioning of the mature and individuated personality is the fact that his emotional functioning tends to be contained within the boundaries of his own self. He is able not only to maintain his own emotional functioning with his own boundaries, but also to buffer himself in relation to the hurts, pain and suffering of others around him. One of the most striking features of families composed of such poorly differentiated individuals is the extent to which emotional stirring in one family member plays upon the emotional functioning of other family members. If there is emotional upheaval, there tends to be a communication of emotion which influences the functioning and autonomy of every involved family member. The individual who achieves a more consolidated sense of identity can live within the field of overflowing emotions yet maintain his own sense of individuality, separateness, and identity. This particular feature of the integrated personality and the relative inability of less differentiated personalities to contain the flow and communication of feeling are of the utmost importance for the understanding of the psychoanalytic dynamics of family systems. This importance concept is returned to later in this chapter

We will now focus on these aspects of personality functioning in terms of a particular set of concepts related to what the author has described at length elsewhere in terms of the "paranoid process" (Meissner, 1978). The particular concepts in question are those which have to do with the organization of the inner psychic world and the integration of the self. The theoretical context for this discussion derives from the work of object relations theorists and developmentalists within psychoanalysis, and takes its point of origin from Freud's early consideration about the role of internalizations. The development of these concepts has been traced in a series of the author's theoretical papers (Meissner, 1970, 1971, 1972); the integration of this theoretical orientation and the connection with the development of identity has been outlined in the early paper by Kernberg (1966) in which he sets forth the theoretical underpinnings of his theory of internalized object relations.

The central concept at this point of the discussion is that of introjection. The notion of introjection is a core concept of the paranoid process and provides the central notion and basis upon which other aspects of the process, which we will be progressively considering, take their derivation. The earliest introjections through which the child's inner world and sense of emerging self begin to be shaped are promoted by the process of separation from the symbiotic union with the mother. To the extent that the process of separation can be successfully and securely negotiated, the child can begin to establish himself as an independent being outside of the orbit of maternal influence. In such cases the introjective process can be positive and constructive in that the child can take from the mother and adopt as part of his own view of himself a selection of elements which he can weave into his own individual pattern or organization. Ideally, such selection and patterning are relatively conflict-free, take place in a relatively autonomous realm which is independent of drive pressures and defensive needs, and set the stage for the declaration of the child's emerging autonomy and sense of differentness and uniqueness as a separate and beginning-to-be integral human being.

From the mother's side, there must be a capacity in her to tolerate this separation and withdrawal on the part of the child as well as to acknowledge, accept, and respond to the child's emerging individuality in meaningful and supportive ways. Where this process fails, whether it be on account of the difficulties on the part of the child—excessive infantile dependence or clinging, fear of separation with its inherent loss and risk, excessive anxiety in pulling away from the protective symbiotic orbit— or from the side of the mother in her excessive anxiety or vulnerability in the loss of symbiotic closeness, her overprotectiveness or her excessive rejecting and thrusting away of the child's dependence, an imbalance is introduced into the process by which the child separates and gradually individuates himself.

The process of introjection is then caught up in the vicissitudes of drives and defensive needs, so that, in situations such as maternal over-protectiveness or rejection, in order to preserve a sense of security in facing the risks of separation the child must carry with him more than he needs of the residues of symbiotic attachment. What he takes in, then, from the mother is excessively colored by infantile dependence or defenses against it, excessively colored with infantile narcissistic needs and its attendant vicissitudes, whether of narcissistic grandiosity or devaluation or narcissistic rage. It becomes contaminated by the intense ambivalence of the tension between the need for increasing autonomy and independence and the impediments of continuing dependence and the obstacles to the freeing-up of a sense of differentiated self.

A result of these developmental vicissitudes is that there is a failure to mobilize positive, constructive and relatively autonomous and differentiating forms of identification which allow the child to establish a sense of inner cohesiveness and of adequate differentiation from the important objects of his dependence. Rather, the child's emerging sense of self becomes organized around these pathogenic introjects with their embedded residues of narcissistic need, defensive conflict, infantile dependence and its associated conflicts, which are spelled out in terms of: (1) a sense of inadequacy or a reactive hyperadequacy; (2) the related ambivalence-embedded conflicts which reflect themselves in the polarities of victimization and aggression; and (3) failures of differentiation of self and of the stabilization of inner structures and their related functions (both of ego and superego) which ultimately compromise adult functioning and place impediments in the establishing and maintaining of a secure sense of identity.

We can speak here of components or configurations of introjective organization; thus, we can describe these various configurations in terms of a victim-introject and an aggressor-introject. These reflect the highly ambivalent and defensive internalizations of the weakness and vulnerability on the one hand and the hyperadequate reactivity and aggression on the other hand of the significant objects of dependence. These introjective forms reflect the vicissitudes of aggression. We can also speak of the internalization of narcissistic residues in terms of the grandiose self on the one hand and of the inferior or inadequate self on the other.

The organization of the grandiose self has been described by Kohut (1971), but in terms of this chapter on the psychoanalytic perspective of marriage the grandiose self is equivalently an introjective configuration in which the residues of primary narcissism are embedded. The introjective configuration is accompanied by its correlative and reactive narcissistic form which expresses itself in terms of inadequacy or inferiority—as a sense of basic shame about the self which occupies the opposite pole to the sense of specialness and uniqueness attributed to the grandiose self.

Special notice should be taken of the polar organization of these introjective components—aggressor versus victim, grandiose versus inferior self. To the extent that the organization and structuring of the self is built around these pathogenic introjects, these introjective components can be found as operative parts of the subject's inner world. One does not find the operation of a grandiose self, for example, without also finding in some form or other, whether repressed or split, the parallel operation of the inadequate self. Similarly, one does not find the operation of the aggressor-introject without finding the parallel constituent of the victim-introject.

The extent to which these introjective configurations are discretely operative or are available to conscious awareness may vary considerably from patient to patient. Frequently, the sense of victimization, for example, may be in the forefront of consciousness and may govern the organization of the patient's pathology, while the hostile, destructive, and aggressive components that reflect the aggressor-introject remain repressed and out of consciousness. Correspondingly, the grandiose self may be more readily available to awareness in some patients, while the inadequate self remains relatively repressed. In more primitive forms of psychology, these components may be split in the terms described by Kernberg (1966, 1967) and may be available to consciousness in a contradictory and alternating way in more primitive forms of character pathology or psychosis.

A central issue in the understanding of the organization of pathogenic introjects of this kind is that the sense of self which forms around them or which is built on them remains fragile, incomplete, and more readily susceptible to regressive pulls and fragmentation. Stabilization and the achievement of some degree of inner stability and cohesion may be achieved through objects or external sources of support, while other resources of the environment may be called into play in the service of complementing the inner deficiency and need. This phenomenon of the inadequately differentiated self has been generally observed and variously described. Erikson (1959), for example, has described the ways in which individuals afflicted with identity diffusion will cling to beliefs, ideologies and causes, or otherwise overidentify with religious, political or other social groupings as a way of stabilizing their fragile and impoverished sense of identity. Kohut (1971) has described the ways in which narcissistic character disorders seek involvement and attachment to important self-objects as a way of completing the inner narcissistic defects and stabilizing the fragile narcissistic disequilibrium which characterizes the organization of the sense of self. Modell (1968) describes the form of transitional object relationship by which he characterizes borderline and psychotic object involvement.

In all of these cases there is involvement with and dependent attachment to an object, but the relationship to the object is not predicated on the basis of one independent, differentiated and relatively autonomous self relating to another independent, differentiated and autonomous self. Rather, the lack of differentiation leaves an element of unintegrated and relatively primitive and unstructured emotional energy which permeates the organization of the self, yet is not contained within, and not differentiated and integrated with the structure of the self. It diffuses beyond it, in a sense, to permeate and contaminate the attachment in an uncontrolled, undisciplined, unorganized, and relatively primary process manner. Thus, the object relationships of such individuals tend to be perfused in varying degrees with this kind of primitive psychic energy which is communicated in subtle and predominantly unconscious ways within the object relationship and comes to affect the functioning and responsiveness of the object, as well as the operations of the subject.

A second important point must be made in regard to the functioning of such poorly differentiated selves. To the extent that the pathogenic introjects form the core of the self, there is a high propensity for projection, particularly into significant object relationships. In terms of the organization of the paranoid process (Meissner, 1978), the projections represent externalized displacements as aspects of the pathogenic organization of the self, usually deriving from the repressed or split-off dimensions of the introjective configuration. These are then attributed to external objects and result in the coloring, distorting, modifying, and influencing of the character and quality of object relationships.

The classic paradigm of this pathogenic process is in the paranoid disorders in which the victim-introject tends to dominate the internal psychic organization, while the repressed or split-off aggressor-introject is externalized and projected to the outside to provide the persecuting forces which attack the victim-introject. Hence the rubric "paranoid process." It is through such projection, arising out of and derived from the respective introjective configurations, that the emotional quality and experience of correlative object relations are organized. It is through these mechanisms, then, that the relatively undifferentiated and primitive flux of instinctually derived emotions not only play into and suffuse the organization of the individual's own subjective sense of self, but come to suffuse and contaminate the organization of object experience and the relationships with objects. It is this phenomenon which provides the basis for transference reactions and interactions, as well as the structure of emotional involvement in the dyad composed of the marital couple and, ultimately, the structure of the family itself.

The Marital Couple

The process out of which the marital dyad emerges is a form of developmental phenomenon and can be regarded as a variety of developmental crises in Eriksonian terms. If this process is divided into sequential steps, one can consider first the phenomenon of falling in love, then the engagement, the marriage and the never ending adjustments after marriage.

1. *Falling in love*

The subject of falling in love is one that was of considerable interest to Freud. Freud saw the fascination with a love object in terms of the libidinal cathexis involved in erotic, sensual, sexual love, but he also maintained that there was a degree of love and affection that somehow transcended these merely libidinal aims. In discussing the adolescent attachment to a love object, he observed (1921, p. 112):

> More often, however, the adolescent succeeds in bringing about a certain degree of synthesis between the unsensual, heavenly love and the sensual, earthly love and his relation to his sexual object is characterized by the interaction of uninhibited instincts and of instincts inhibited in their aim. The depth to which anyone is in love, as contrasted with his purely sensual desire, may be measured by the size of the share taken by the aim-inhibited instincts of affection.

Freud seems to have been reaching here for a distinction between simple libidinal sexual object attraction and what is referred to in more contemporary terms as a mature and mutual object relationship.

What impressed Freud in this phenomenon of falling in love was the overvaluation of the loved object. As he describes it, ". . . the fact that the loved object enjoys a certain amount of freedom from criticism, and that all its characteristics are valued more highly than those of people who are not loved, or than its own were at a time when it itself was not loved" (1921, p. 112). This overvaluation takes the form of a false judgment about the object, a form of idealization. This signals the fact that the loving attachment to the object reflects the overflow of narcissistic libido onto the object so that the object becomes a substitute for some unattained ego ideal of the subject. In other words, what is loved is the object for which one has striven but in some degree has failed to attain, so that the attachment to the object provides a roundabout way of satisfying this narcissistic need.

Freud (1921, p. 113) goes on to describe this situation in greater detail:

> If the sexual overvaluation and the being in love increase even further, then the interpretation of the picture becomes still more unmistakable. The impulsions whose trend is toward directly sexual satisfaction may now be pushed into the background entirely, as regularly happens, for instance, with a young man's sentimental passion; the ego becomes more and more unassuming and modest, and the object more and more sublime and precious, until at last it gets possession of the entire self-love of the ego, whose self-sacrifice thus follows as a natural consequence. The object has, so to speak, consumed the ego. Traits of humility, of the limitation of narcissism, and of self-injury occur in every case of being in love; in the extreme case they are merely intensified, and as a result of the withdrawal of the sensual claims they remain in solitary supremacy.

Consequently this "fascination" or "bondage" of love involves an impoverishment of the ego in which it surrenders itself to the object and places the object as a substitute for the most important inner constituent that serves for the maintenance of self-esteem, namely the ego ideal. Freud contrasts this with the more mature form of love relationship which can result in significant identifications whereby the ego, in fact, enriches itself with properties of the object by a form of introjection of what is positive and valued in the object. As discussed later in this chapter, mutual introjections constitute an important mechanism of the marital dyad.

More recently, Kernberg (1974) has observed that the quality of this experience of falling in love reflects the developmental vicissitudes of what he calls internalized object relations, or, in terms of our present discussion, of introjections and identifications. He also describes a continuum of levels of capacity for establishing mature, mutually satisfying and affectionate, and, in Freud's terms, aim-inhibited object relations. Kernberg writes (1974, p. 487):

> The first configuration along this continuum, represented by an almost total incapacity for establishing genital and tender relations with any other human being, is characteristic of the most severe types of narcissistic personality structure (for example, schizophrenia). The second configuration, characterized by sexual promiscuity (usually heterosexual, but at times polymorphous perverse) is typical of moderately ill narcissistic personalities. The third configuration is characterized by primitive idealization of the loved object, with clinging infantile dependency upon it, and some capacity for genital gratification (the characteristics of this constellation are typical of borderline personality organization). The fourth configuration, characterized by the capacity for establishing stable and deep object relations without the capacity for full sexual gratification, is typical of relatively less severe types of character pathology and neuroses. The fifth and final configuration along this continuum is represented by the normal integration of genitality with the capacity for tenderness and a stable, deep object relation.

The levels of this descriptive continuum can be taken to reflect the degrees to which the personality and the structure of the self have been organized around pathogenic introjects as previously described and the correlative extent to which there has been a failure of the process of differentiation and individuation of the self.

The conclusion of this argument is that the phenomenon of falling in love is a multidetermined result of a number of dynamic factors, but involves in some significant degree the operation of intense narcissistic needs. The intermeshing of and the responsiveness to such needs play an important part in the choice of marital partner. Each of the partners, then, seeks—with varying degrees of conscious or unconscious intention —for a mate who promises to provide optimal gratification of such usually unconscious and predominantly narcissistic needs. To the extent to which such needs are shaped by and reflect the underlying introjective configuration, the need patterns of the marital partners will tend to be complementary, that is they will take the form of dominance-submission, sadism-masochism, superiority-inferiority, etc.—reflecting the pattern of repression and/or splitting of introjective polarities and their respective internalization and projection (Meissner, 1978). Similar patterns of need complementarity have been found in supposedly normal

(Winch, Ktones and Ktones, 1954) and neurotic (Oberndorf, 1938) marital couples.

A second hypothesis has been generated regarding the intermeshing of such complementary and neurotic needs, namely that there is a tendency for partners of relatively equivalent degrees of immaturity and self-differentiation to be attracted to each other. This phenomenon has not been well documented or studied, but retains a certain clinical validity. The tendency for marital partners to be operating at equivalent levels of immaturity or to manifest similar degrees of lack of self-differentiation is sufficiently general to put us on guard, when we find signs of such pathology in one marital partner, for indications of a similar level of personality organization in the other partner.

In reporting on the results of early studies of family dynamics, Bowen (1960, 1961) remarks that clinical experience seems to suggest that individuals tend to choose marital partners who have achieved an equivalent level of immaturity, but who have adopted opposite patterns of defensive organization. In the schizophrenic families he studied, both marital partners appeared to be equally immature, but their relationships tended to fall into patterns of reciprocal overadequacy and inadequacy. Consequently, the hypothesis of complementarity of needs in marital partners seems to concern not only the type of need, but also the level of intensity and developmental immaturity of the need. The perception of prospective marital partners of each other prior to marriage seems to reflect the operation of these needs so that the respective perceptions are governed by projections reflecting the operation of these needs in the introjective economy. When asked about conscious reasons for choice of mate, the partners replied that they admired and were attracted to qualities in the other which reflected their respective façades of overadequacy (Bowen, 1960). It is these qualities that are idealized and seem to fit the narcissistic needs that they respond to in each other. The idealization reflects an idealizing projection by which elements of the ego-ideal become translated into object qualities.

2. *The engagement, marriage, and adjustments after marriage*

Falling in love is followed by a period of engagement, which is terminated by the marital rite of passage. Rapoport (1970) divides the tasks of the engagement period into those which are intrapersonal and those which are interpersonal. The individual pace of working on such tasks may differ considerably—some only beginning to address these tasks in the engagement period, while others may have already resolved them by that time. Intrapsychically, the engagement period is a time of personal preparation for entering into the state of marriage and its accompanying shift in life roles. The individual must prepare to enter into the role of husband or wife, must disengage from old entanglements or attachments that may compete with or interfere with the commitment to the marital relationship, and must modify the patterns of premarital gratification to suit the emerging patterns of the newly-formed marital relationship.

Marriage has been described as one of the most significant of human developmental experiences (Blanck and Blanck, 1968). The level of maturity achieved by the marital partners is of crucial significance for the success of the marriage. Those marriages have the best success in which the respective partners have reached a level of maturity which allows them to enter this significant phase of the life cycle with sufficient resources to allow them to cope with the developmental tasks involved. Others, however, may be burdened by unresolved or only partially resolved developmental conflicts which inevitably are carried over into the marital relationship and create tensions and difficulties. In some of these cases, the developmental impetus and the mobilization of resources within the marriage may allow for further developmental work to be done; in others, however, in whom the organization of pathogenic introjects has blocked the accomplishment of essential developmental tasks, further growth may be impeded or the operation of intrapsychic needs may lead such individuals to try to find gratification in marriage for which marriage is an inappropriate vehicle. The inevitable frustration of inappropriate needs and the inability to cope with the consequent disappointment and disillusionment create an environment of continual antagonism and hostility which results in excessive marital conflict—one of the most frequent symptoms of disturbed marriages.

One of the primary tasks of the marital relation is the establishing and patterning of sexual relations within the context of an enduring object relationship. This requires the final working-through of the prohibitions and inhibitions of childhood sexuality. *If the involvement with and attachment to the parents have not been excessively binding, and the relationship to the parent of the opposite sex not excessively burdened either with incestuous pulls or separation anxieties, the incest taboo can be successfully overcome and a meaningful sexual relation established with a nonincestuous love object.* The attenuation of these fears and anxieties, however, takes place within the framework of a relationship which involves qualities and dimensions that reach beyond the realm of sex alone.

Related to the issue of sexual relations, there is the significant developmental task of confirming and reaffirming gender identity. The image of oneself as male or female enters a new phase of developmental significance with the passage into the marital state. The gender role must undergo a transition to the more specific configuration of husband and wife, emerging in the direction of the more concrete and specific roles of father and mother. The male is able to achieve a more secure sense of masculine identity in the context of a loving relationship with a woman with whom he becomes the progenitor of the next generation. Similarly, a woman finds the fulfillment and maturation of her own sense of feminine identity in the loving and mutually supporting relationship with a man through whom she becomes a mother.

Moreover, the quality of gender identity for both sexes is enhanced and embellished through mutual identifications. Thus, the capacities in the male for tender affection and nurturance can be significantly enhanced by his identifications with his wife, insofar as they become meaningfully integrated with the securely established and supportive pattern of his own masculine identity. Correspondingly, the woman can become more secure and confident of her own capacities for meaningful endeavor and self-assertion in a variety of intellectual and work pursuits by identification with her husband. Such identifications can be constructive forces in the process of marital growth and in the emergence and consolidation of mature and functional identities in both parties, when they take place without the threat of loss of the underlying core of each subject's individual identity and the secure maintenance of a differentiated sense of self which this implies.

Among the significant developmental tasks of marriage is that of the establishing and maintaining a new level of object relationship. If the initial engagement in the love relationship is significantly determined by the underlying needs and the seeking of complementarity in the love object, the progression in the development of the marital relationship must lead beyond the level of need gratification to a point where the relationship is based less on the satisfaction of such needs than on a reciprocal and mutually gratifying basis of object love. Rapoport (1970) regards the degree to which there is a shift from self-orientation to mutuality as a measure of the extent to which the essential tasks of the engagement period, both for men and women, have been accomplished. The normal postadolescent young adult has generally reached a point in the development of his object relations in which he has grown out of the infantile level of need satisfaction to the point where he is able to recognize, acknowledge, and respond to the needs of others. The marriage contract, however, makes him more responsible for maintaining the relative independence of his own needs and for responding to the needs of the marriage partner than he has ever been in any other time of his life or in any other relationship.

The need for the marital partners to disengage themselves from old attachments and relationships that may interfere with the marital commitment introduces a new cycle of psychological separation, particularly from parental attachments. The developmental course itself, from the earliest stages of separation-individuation, involves repeated and progressive separations—perhaps the most critical and most significant, in terms of their impact on personality organization, being those that take place in the resolution of oedipal attachments and at adolescence. Entering into the marital relationship calls for a new phase in the process of the ultimate separation from parental figures, even though in some basic sense that separation is never complete or total.

But this new phase of separation is an inevitable consequence of the need to establish a new, permanent relationship with a nonincestuous object, a relationship which carries with it its own distinctive qualities of intimacy and dependence. The ultimate question for the resolution of this crisis is whether or not this separation can be achieved and an intimate involvement in the new relationship established without sacrifice of hard-won individuation. The success of previous phases of separation and individuation sets the stage and determines the quality of the resolution of this new separation. To the extent that a relatively autonomous and individuated sense of self has already been established, the capacity is inherently available for entering the new relationship and maintaining that individuation intact. Where separation has been less than successful so that the individuation and differentiation of self remain fragile and susceptible to regressive pulls, the entrance into a new relationship will carry with it the residues of old attachments and will introduce into the new relationship the unresolved residues which are carried over from old relationships. This means that the separation vicissitudes are not resolved and the level of individuation attained in the new relationship will correspond to and reflect the level of individuation which was characteristic of those older involvements.

As a result of these patterns of interaction, the new relationship can be contaminated by the effects of the pathogenic introjects inherent in the personality organization of each partner and their intermeshing. As already mentioned, if the personalities which enter the marital relationship are relatively individuated and differentiated, the potentiality exists for positive and constructive identifications that enhance and enrich the personality structure of each partner. Where the personalities are dominated by pathogenic configurations, however, the intermeshing internalizations in such a couple will take place in terms of the organization of such pathological introjects.

What, then, is the quality of interpersonal experience when it is based on such pathogenic introjects or the correlatively poorly differentiated sense of self? The poorly defined self establishes a relationship of dependence upon the other which tends to have a life and death quality. It is as though life and existence depend on the attachment to the important other. Often this attachment has a quality of hostile dependence to it, the "can't live with you, can't live without you" syndrome which is so familiar to clinicians. The most intense form of such a relationship is found in the symbiotic relationship of mother and child, but it is often seen in its most pathological form in the symbiotic relatedness of a schizophrenic child to a symbiotically involved parent, usually the mother. But the same phenomenon can be observed in relatively less intense and mitigated forms wherever there is a defect in the integration or differentiation of the self.

As the person with a well differentiated and individuated identity enters into a relationship as close and intimately interdependent as the marital relationship, he/she is able to enter into, share, and participate freely in the emotional life that takes place between and around the marital partners. The less the degree of individuation or of differentiation of self, however, the more emotion tends to spill over and be communicated to the other member of the dyad in a way which influences the functioning of that other member. Within this complex of implicit and relatively unconscious emotional influences, a pattern tends to establish itself in which one of the partners begins to function with a façade of exaggerated strength and assertion, while the other partner shifts to a position of compliance, submissiveness, and giving-in to the influence and domination of the more adequate partner. Within this emotional matrix there is a phenomenological shift in which one partner seems to attain a degree of hyperadequacy and the confirming of a pseudoidentity, while the other partner seems to lose identity and become a relative nonentity. One seems to gain "self" at the expense of the other.

This pattern can be quite severely pathogenic. Lidz and his co-workers

(1965), for example, have described the effects of this psychoanalytic dynamic in skewed marital relationships. However, there are also a significant group of marriages in which neither partner will "give in" to the pressure of this dynamic process and the result is a constantly conflictual and divisive marital relationship—the schismatic marriage. Where this kind of inexplicit and unconscious emotional communication takes place, the ready spilling over of feelings between the partners and the susceptibility they feel to the level of expressed or unexpressed feelings in each other prevent the communication and sharing of true feelings. The greater the lack of differentiation in the partners, the greater is the tendency of each to react to feelings of the other with feelings of "hurt" and despair; true communication is further inhibited and the partners feel an even greater degree of isolation from each other. In such a communicative and emotionally embedded context, the interchange of feelings is dominated by processes of projection and by the pervasive confusion of fact and feelings.

Where identities are more stable and defined, strong emotion can be experienced without a sense of flooding of the self or of endangering the maintenance of a sense of identity. Situations of intense emotional involvement are inherently difficult for individuals with poor individuation. They tend to avoid such emotional situations by forms of distancing or schizoid withdrawal, or by a relative diffusion of a sense of identity which may result in phenomena of depersonalization or overwhelming anxiety. Individuals with well-differentiated identity, on the other hand, can operate relatively comfortably in situations of intense emotional involvement, with the confidence that such involvement does not impair their ability to remain in contact with reality and to objectively discern that reality from the fantasies and feelings that may be stirred up by the emotional involvement.

Such individuals can allow themselves, therefore, to be in contact with human misery and suffering without being emotionally overwhelmed by it or overidentifying with the suffering of the other. Consequently, they can freely and spontaneously respond in supportive and helpful ways to such suffering of the other. The poorly differentiated individual is easily subject to feelings of pity, remorse, guilt, and shame in the face of emotional turmoil or distress in a significant other. Impulses to help the suffering one come out of feelings of pity or guilt, so that the individual's capacity to address his helping efforts to the reality of actual needs is correspondingly compromised.

On the other hand, individuals with poorly defined self remain extremely vulnerable to such sympathetic and pitying feelings coming from others in their environment. In the face of such pity and guilt-engendered sympathy, their needs to be taken care of and to resort to modalities of infantile dependence actually become more intense so that they tend to move to a position of increasing inferiority and inadequacy as a way of eliciting greater help and caretaking from others and as a way of intensifying the feelings of pity and guilt. The demands for care and help can increase to the point of exasperation and exhaustion of the resources of the helper to continue to be helpful. The helper inevitably becomes motivated by anger and the wish to hurt and destroy the one who is helpless; inevitably, the helper becomes punitive, rejecting, and hurtful. It should be pointed out that the intricacies of these dynamic interactions are quite familiar to experienced clinicians, in the contexts both of psychoanalytic practice and of intensive psychoanalytically oriented psychotherapy, in terms of transference distortions, transference needs, and the corresponding countertransference reactions.

In the kinds of infantile and mutually dependent relationships within which these patterns of emotional reaction take place, it is relatively impossible for the poorly differentiated individual to take responsibility for his own functioning and feelings without blaming the other for his unhappiness and suffering. It is a fairly common experience that one member of the marital couple will blame the other for his own failure or suffering—even as he may have at some other point in the history of the relationship credited that other as being a source of his own happiness and success. There is an implicit demand that the partner become different, somehow, in order to respond to and alleviate this suffering. Any attempt on the part of the partner to establish a clear and well-differentiated identity becomes a threat to this underlying need and is interpreted as an attack, a rejection, a betrayal, and a severely disillusioning disappointment.

In such a situation, each member of the pair ends up making impossible demands on the other, at the same time being caught up in the impossible process of trying to meet the demands of the other. Such interacting demands, counterdemands, compliance, and responsiveness may achieve a sort of functional equilibrium as long as each partner can maintain the position of trying to be for the other what the other seems to demand. But such a system of interaction is perilously fragile and subject to the regressive pulls and vicissitudes of the neurotic needs which drive and determine it. If either partner takes it into his head to assert his own needs in the face of the demands of the other, to establish and differentiate his own self in the face of these regressive pulls and neurotic needs, he can expect the partner to pull out all the stops and use every resource of manipulation, exploitation, pressure, rejection, and force to keep him in the position of compliant dependence and emotional involvement.

Ackerman (1958) has called attention to the fact that the marital relationship represents more than the sum of the personalities which make it up. *One can regard the mechanisms of interaction described in this chapter as the foundation on which the emergent new qualities of the complex marital interaction are based.* Thus, the interactive patterns, the configurations of hyperadequacy-inadequacy, skew or schism, may all be found characteristically in the relatively disturbed marital dyad and are unique characteristics of the relationship, even though the underlying components which contribute to and to some extent determine the emergence and configuration of these patterns can be traced to underlying personality dynamics, specifically to the introjective components of each of the participating personalities. It is important to remember, however, that the interaction of these components, derived ultimately from the lack of self-differentiation and the corresponding organization of pathogenic introjects, creates a newly operative emotional matrix within which the pathogenic influences operate in new and different ways within the dyadic relationship.

To focus these phenomena in terms of the paranoid process, we can say that the emotional matrix that emerges within the marital dyad is contributed to and shaped by the interacting patterns of projection and introjection between the marital partners. To the extent that the partners bring to the marital interaction a relatively undifferentiated self based on pathogenic introjects, there is a residue of unintegrated, relatively unconscious emotion which suffuses the organization of the respective selves and consequently contaminates and pervades the projective and introjective processes as they play themselves out in the interaction. It is important to remember in this context that the individual mechanisms of projection and introjection are being played out on both sides of the marital interaction and are exercising a powerful reciprocal influence on how the interaction is experienced and its configuration.

To the extent that the partners are deeply involved in this emotional interaction—that is to say, to the extent that each of them enters the interaction in terms of a relatively undifferentiated self, the emotional currents at play have a definite interpersonal effect. Such currents of emotion may, for example, be conveyed through the projection of one partner onto the other. To the extent that the second partner is enmeshed in the underlying emotional matrix, the projective elements tend to be internalized and introjected by the second partner. Correspondingly, the projective elements of the second partner will tend to be internalized and introjected by the first. Thus, through the reciprocal interaction of interlocking projections and introjections, internal conflicts of each of the marital partners become translated into concrete modes of perceiving and behaving within the marital relationship.* Mannino and Greenspan (1976) describe the process in the following terms (pp. 139-140):

> . . . One of the partners (the subject) projects certain aspects of himself onto the other (the object), and thus views the other as an embodiment of this characteristic or set of conflicts. Through that process one or both partners misperceive important aspects of the other's character. The object of the misperception is expected to conform to the image projected by the subject through his or her behavior and covertly to gratify certain denied needs of the subject. . . . Whether or not the second partner so acknowledges the other's perception (or misperception) and behaves in a certain manner is not crucial, since the subject will deny or not attend to aspects of reality which do not fit his or her perceptual distortion . . . because the misperceptions serve to meet certain denied needs of the subject, he or she is very strongly motivated to sustain them regardless of the object's behavior or verbalizations. Some amount of collusion also may keep the process operative. When the process functions in both partners, each misperceives the other and each acts reciprocally to the other. As a result, both partners become locked into a discordant relationship pattern which is perpetuated by a defensive pseudo-realistic quality.

---

* This complex interaction is often described in terms of "projective identification" (Greenspan and Mannino, 1974; Mannino and Greenspan, 1976; Zinner and Shapiro, 1972). It is preferable not to use the term "projective identification" and to keep the description of this complex phenomenon in terms of introjections and projections for the following reasons: 1) The term "projective identification" refers to a complex of mechanisms which does not include anything that is not already specified more accurately by the combination of projective and introjective mechanisms; 2) the term is derivative from a Kleinian frame of reference and implies certain theoretical suppositions which may not be generally acceptable; 3) it involves a confusing use of the term "identification" which does not adequately distinguish it from introjections as such. Careful examination of the significance of these terms reveals that a clear distinction must be maintained between introjection and identification and that, in fact, they are referring to and articulating quite distinct and different processes—even though these may often be related in complex ways (Meissner, 1970, 1971, 1972). In any case, what is important is not the particular terminology that is used to describe the phenomena, but the recognition of such an emotionally embedded interactive process as a real phenomenon in marital interaction.

It is important to note that the model of this interaction is based on the understanding of transference phenomena. In the analytic setting, when the emotional involvement of the analytic relationship reaches a certain level of intensity, an emotional matrix is created within which projective mechanisms are mobilized. The transference itself is based on the patient's projections, derived from the pathogenic configuration of introjects which underlie his neurosis or character disorder, and imposed on the therapist. The projections are, as we have noted, based on the underlying introjects, but these introjects themselves derive from the patient's developmental experience and reflect the internalization in relatively pathological terms of earlier object relationships, particularly those with the patient's parents. The therapist or analyst, on his part, maintains the therapeutic context by his capacity to recognize such projective distortions and to avoid a reciprocal countertransference involvement with the patient. As long as the therapeutic quality of the relationship can be maintained in this manner, the potential exists for externally influencing and modifying the projections, along with their underlying introjective basis.

Since the content of the projections ultimately derives from earlier object relations, both in the context of therapy and in the marital relationship, these older object relationships are equivalently reactivated and become available either for pathological expression or for possible reworking in ways that may allow for therapeutic change or psychological growth. To the extent that one approaches the marital relationship with a poorly developed and relatively undifferentiated self, one recreates a pattern of relationships obtained between one's self and one's parents in different stages of the developmental experience. Consequently, a man can look for a substitute mother in his prospective wife and recreate with her the same pattern of conflicts and tensions which were inherent in the maternal relationships. What becomes injected into the marital relationship as a result of this projective process may not simply relate to the opposite sex parent, but may reflect crucial introjections of a pathological sort that derive from both parents in one of the almost infinite vareity of patterns of combination which such internalizations may enjoy. They are different for every individual and reflect the almost infinite variety of each individual's developmental vicissitudes.

As second important point is that a significant component for understanding the transference experience has been contributed by the thinking of Winnicott about transitional objects and relationships based on the transitional mode of experiencing and relating to objects. In describing transitional phenomena, Winnicott (1971) discusses an intermediate area of illusion that takes shape between the realm of the subjective and the objective. In terms of the present discussion, the area of illusion to which Winnicott refers is compounded out of projective and introjective elements of the paranoid process (Meissner, 1978). Thus, the area of transitional illusion, compounded out of components of both self and object and constructed out of interlocking projections and introjections, provides the model for the interactive emotional matrix which emerges from the marital interaction. To the extent that this transitional emotional matrix emerges and dominates the marital interaction, it reflects infantile derivatives that may carry back to the earliest levels of transitional relating between the child and the maternal object, and may thus carry with it relatively primitive emotional currents which interfere with the capacity of the marital partners to relate to each other in realistic and relatively objective terms.

It is obvious that the developmental tasks involved in the establishing of a marital relationship are not accomplished by the marriage ceremony. The developmental tasks involved take time, often a great deal of time. Many couples will have completed a goodly portion of the work involved during the period of courtship and engagement, so that by the time they reach the altar there has already evolved a solid basis and an integrated relationship upon which a firm marital bond can be erected. Other couples at the point of the pronouncement of the marriage vows have scarcely begun the work. For these the work must be done during the early period of marital experience, or it may never be done at all. There are, indeed, a significant number of couples in whom the personal impediments to the work of forming the marriage bond are sufficiently great that no significant work is ever accomplished.

The Family Unit

When the discussion shifts from the marital couple to the family unit, there is a moving to a new level of sociological and interpersonal organization. The emotional matrix compounded out of the interacting personalities of husband and wife becomes the basis out of which an entirely new and considerably more complex form of emotional interaction is elaborated as new members are added to the family unit. This section is an attempt to delineate some of the dimensions and parameters of this complex family interaction.

It is important from the very beginning to have clearly in mind that this section discusses the family as a functional unit. It is the transition from the view of the family in terms of complex interactions between individual members to the focusing of the family process as derived from and functioning in terms of a single organic unit that particularly characterizes and marks as distinctive more contemporary approaches to the understanding of the family (Bowen, 1960, 1961). The implications of this view are multiple. From this perspective the breakdown or illness of one member of the family reflects the operation of emotional processes within the entire family itself. The member who is first referred for psychiatric assistance may be the family scapegoat or may be a substitute for other disturbed family members or for the disturbance of the family itself. Pathogenic conflicts and their associated defenses may be passed contagiously from generation to generation. In severely disturbed families, and often in even not so severely disturbed families, more than one member is emotionally disabled (Ackerman, 1962).

It should be noted here that the concept of role does not play a significant part in the present construction. The organization of the family can certainly be described in terms of roles and their related concepts, but these remain essentially sociological and non-psychoanalytic. While the concept of role provides a bridge between the level of individual personality and the functioning of the group, it does not specifically base itself on nor reflect dynamic issues related to the psychoanalytic structure and integration of personality. This does not mean that there is not an important area for theoretical integration here, but it is not one that we can usefully undertake in the present chapter.

Nonetheless, the family is a primary group which spans the interval between the individual and larger social structures. The study in conceptualization of the family as a unit fills an important conceptual gap between the level of individual functioning and the understanding of the psychological aspects of social processes.

One important aspect of the unitary organization of the family system is the flow of emotion that takes place within it and the intimate exchange of emotional influences which form a sort of emotional contagion (Ackerman, 1958). There are countless examples of the ways in which one family member will manage to be preserved from pathogenic effects of emotional involvements, but at the expense of one or more members of the family. Or the outbreak of symptoms in one member may serve as a protective device which allows other members of the family to maintain an adequate level of functioning. There are family systems in which, when stress impinges on the family system from certain directions, there is an outbreak or exacerbation of pathology in one or another of the members, or in the whole family itself, embracing all of its members. Each family system manifests different patterns of vulnerability and expresses the infinite variety of ways in which, when the family system is put under severe regressive strain, the individual members react—some by developing psychological symptoms, others by developing physical symptoms or illnesses, and still others by various forms of self-destructive or self-defeating behavior. Moreover, such currents of emotional upheaval can be translated across generational boundaries. The author has seen any number of cases in which the death of a significant figure in the grandparental generation will set up shock waves that reverberate throughout the whole of the family system and precipitate pathological reactivity and deviant expressions in multiple members of the family system.

1. *Father*

To focus first on the role of the father, one could ask how father's participation in the emotional matrix of the family affects his behavior and functioning. Fathers of disturbed children are frequently found to be domineering, authoritarian, hypercritical—or else passive, ineffectual, unable to cope with family responsibility, and often engaged in a passive-aggressive undercutting of the mother's authority. In the families of school phobics, the father is often found to be weak, ineffectual, and passive; similarly, in the families of drug addicts, the father is often little more than a shadowy background figure in contrast to the domineering and influential position of the mother. This constellation has also been observed in families of manic-depressives. The effective absence and emotional unavailability of the father have been noted in a variety of contexts (Meissner, 1964; Waring and Ricks, 1965). In these cases Bowen (Bowen, Dysinger and Basamania, 1959) has indicated that the pattern of withdrawal of the father is a function of his exclusion from the intense mother-child relationship. His attempts to intervene and strengthen his own relationship with the child require that he set himself in opposition to the mother by a more or less cruel and dominating approach.

The role of the father in often severe psychopathology was underlined in the studies of the Lidz group of schizophrenic families (Lidz, Fleck and Cornelison, 1965). They noted the importance of the father's impact on the child's development since he is usually the first intruder into the symbiotic mutuality between the child and the mother. The child needs to to develop a sense of mutuality with both mother and father as a unit rather than simply with the mother. Moreover, the mother's own ability to be maternal and secure in her mothering activity depends in large measure on the support she feels coming from the father and his ability to share her with the child. The child's estimation of the mother as a love object similarly is influenced by the degree of father's esteem or enmity toward her. This aspect of the relationship between the parents plays a critical role in the developing identifications for both male and female children. As Lidz and Fleck (1959, p. 335) comment:

> This development will be difficult if the father despises the mother or is so inconsistent that no behavioral pattern appears to satisfy him. The fathers studied were very often insecure in their masculinity, needing constant admiration and attention to bolster their self-esteem. Even the domineering and more tyrannical whom neither wife nor children could satisfy could be recognized as being basically weak and ineffectual by the members of the family.

We can recognize in these configurations the familiar landmarks of overadequacy and inadequacy which seem to characterize the involvement in the family emotional matrix. *But the evolution of such patterns does not exclusively reflect the operation of intrapsychic or intrafamilial dynamics.* The family is, in fact, a channel through which the impact of cultural influences comes to bear on the family members, and particularly on the development of children. As Ackerman (1958) had suggested, cultural patterns operate in such a way as to create a sense of isolation and alienation in men and women, but particularly seem to move in the direction of undermining the sense of masculine identity. One can include in this both the increasing demands of women for a power status along with increasing levels of assertion of aggressiveness and mastery. One can also include the social forces which continually threaten the average man and leave him with a feeling of inadequacy and insecurity in the face of the increasingly ruthless, competitive struggle which characterizes the fabric of our society. In such an arena, the contemporary male is continually threatened with defeat and failure so that the only viable criterion of achieving manhood and masculine identity is a kind of superman achievement or competence. The aspirations become such that they can never be achieved.

It is only recently that attention has been paid to the specific impact of the father on the child's developmental experience. Abelin (1975) has attempted to delineate the role of the father (from a psychoanalytic perspective) in facilitating the phases of separation and individuation. In the practicing subphase, the father plays an important part in facilitating the development of the child's exploratory and early phallic attitudes, and in the subsequent rapprochement subphase he may play a crucial role in supporting the disengagement of the child's ego from the regressive pulls toward symbiosis with the mother. The intrusion of the father into the mother-child symbiosis sets in play a process which leads gradually toward a "triangulation" which requires that the toddler both apprehend and internalize not only aspects of his relationship to his father and his mother separately, but also the relationship between these two intensely cathected objects. Using the parental objects as points of reference, the child gradually evolves an image of himself. The child's image of himself as participating in the mother-father-child triad contributes to the establishing of his own emerging sense of identity and contributes particularly to the shaping of the child's emerging gender identity.

While the experience of fatherhood fulfills a natural biological aspiration and provides a medium for psychological development, this experience is not necessarily free from conflict. As Benedek (1970) has pointed out, there is a tendency for *both* men and women to identify with the child of the same sex. The relationship with that child tends to reactivate conflictual aspects of the relationship of the parent to his own same sex parent. Thus, the introjection of aspects of the conflicted and hostile relationship with the grandparent can serve as the basis of projections of hostility toward the child that can interfere with the exercise of parental love. Benedek even suggests that the desire for children of the opposite sex can be motivated by an intuitive realization that conflicts derived from developmental interactions with one's own same sex parent may serve as the basis for re-experiencing these conflicts with the child.

Thus, the emotional relationship between father and child derives from both the father's identification with the child and his identification with his own father. Normally these two levels of internalization are complementary and are integrated into the fathering experience. The identification with the child serves as a basis for paternal empathy, while the identification with one's own father shapes the internalized norms both culturally and personally of what it means to be a father. As Benedek notes, where cultural changes are slow paced and family structures relatively stable, fathers were less vulnerable to the fears of competitiveness from their sons and the sons found less necessity to struggle against their fathers to establish their own identities. Benedek notes (p. 174):

Just as it is normal for parents to enjoy the manifestations of the constructive aspects of their personalities in their children, it is also normal, in the sense of the psychodynamics of parent-child interaction, that fathers watch with anxious anticipation for signs which indicate that the child might have conflicts and develop problems similar to those they had to struggle against. In either case, the constructive as well as the pathognomic [sic] results of the parents' identification with the child are more direct and effective with the child of their own sex.

What is particularly noteworthy in these patterns is the transmission and interplay from generation to generation of the patterns of projection and introjection, both constructive and destructive as well. Fathers may find themselves with considerable surprise and even a sense of shame and remorse acting toward their sons with the same angry and punitive attitudes that they had experienced from their own fathers. These imitative patterns of behavior pass from generation to generation and reflect the underlying configuration of the introjects which link father and son in the emotional matrix of the family.

Such patterns of intergenerational conflict may lay the basis for paternal rejection of the child. As Ackerman (1958) has observed, paternal rejection may stem from psychologically specific or relatively nonspecific causes. Interference with his role as a father and his capacity to relate to his child may stem from physical illness, emotional illness, alcoholism, demands of work, etc. Some fathers are largely absent due to the nature of their work, but others may be so engrossed in the demands of work that they find little time to spend with their children, or else what little time they do spend with them is filled with distractions which prevent them from real involvement or meaningful communication with their children. If father brings his work home with him or spends his time with the family worried and preoccupied by his workday concerns, he becomes a relatively inaccessible parent.

Often enough the father's own needs to be taken care of, mothered, and supported put him in the position of competition with the child to get these needs satisfied by the mother. Or, if the sexual and emotional relationship with the wife is unsatisfactory, such a father may displace his feelings of resentment onto the child and reject both wife and child together. Such men frequently escape to harbors of male security, the clubs, taverns and other meeting places, or they may seek sexual gratification in extramarital affairs.

In other cases the rejection of the child may be highly specific and can be based on projections by which the child is identified with some critical figure or figures in the father's own experience with whom he had highly conflicted and emotionally intense relationships. Thus, the child may be identified with the father's own father or a brother with whom he might have had an intense rivalry. The child may even become the projective bearer of the aggressive and competitive urges of the father himself, thus intensifying and reviving the father's own sense of masculine inadequacy and deficiency. The connection of such projective phenomena with the father's own introjective economy can often be particularly striking. The father's inner sense of inadequacy and deficiency may be transferred to the son, who then becomes an object of disgust and rejection. It is as though the father's own self-hate is translated into hatred of the child. The son will carry the guilt for the father's evil. The son will grow up seeing himself and feeling himself to be the unloved, unwanted, and rejected son who is unloved because he is inferior and unworthy. Similarly, a father who rejects or keeps a guarded distance from a daughter leaves her with a sense of feminine inferiority and lack of worth in the father's eyes. These affects play a considerable role in the shaping of introjects in such children and provide a basis for a pathological sense of self which they carry into their adult lives. Such fathers may often project onto their children aspects of themselves that have been repressed or have never been accepted or integrated as a functional part of their own selves. The father who was never able to break out of his dependence on his own parents may thus see his own children as rebellious and flaunting parental and societal demands—so that the child's living out of these patterns of behavior provides the parents with a hidden source of gratification and relish.

Similarly, where the emotional relationship with the mother has broken down, the father may seek to gain from the children what he has failed to get from his wife. This may result in exaggerated demonstrations of affection and the demand for love from the children which have not been forthcoming from the wife. Such fathers may become actively seductive so that the child becomes subjected to the father's need and the price of acceptance and love from the father is precisely such submission. The child's own self-esteem and independent needs to be acknowledged and valued in his own right are thus violated. These complex interactions may frequently intensify and bring to a pathological pitch the oedipal involvement. As Ackerman (1958) notes (p. 185):

The child is then neither respected nor valued as a separate being but becomes the object of the father's unsatisfied love needs. Such situations often involve triangular relationships in which tremendous tension is aroused because of the patterns of jealousy and competitiveness. In all this the issue is whether the child fortifies and enhances the father's self-esteem, whether the child adds to the father's feeling of being loved or detracts from it, and whether the father's alliance with the child arouses the mother's jealousy or the mother's alliance with the child mobilizes the father's rivalry and rage.

The father who brings to the family interaction such a poorly defined and insecurely established sense of self provides a defective model for identification for children of either sex. He is a poor model of masculine identity for his sons and provides an inadequate love object for his daughters. It should not be forgotten that important components of the little girl's personality also are derived by way of critical internalizations from the father. In both sexes, the patterning of internalizations through the developmental sequence takes place in relationship to both parents so that elements from both parents are ultimately blended into the child's emerging personality. The most flagrant examples of inadequate fathering and of the turning of rejection and hostility against the child are found in the families of schizophrenic children (Lidz et al., 1965). In these families the disturbed patterns discussed in this chapter seemed to emerge with starting clarity, but, from the point of view of the present consideration, it must be remembered that they reflect the dynamics which are operative within the family system and which characterize a particular emotional matrix of these severely disturbed families.

2. Mother

The role of the mother in the affected family system which produces pathology in its children has been under close scrutiny for many years. It was long felt that the pathologic influence of disturbed mothers in such family systems was even greater than that of the fathers, although that perception has been increasingly balanced by the patterns of paternal influence described above. A good deal of attention has been focused on attempts to define the personality characteristics of mothers whose children have various forms of pathology. The mothers of school phobic children, for example, are described as anxious, ambivalent, hostile, immature, insecure in their mothering function, and demanding (Agras, 1959; Eisenberg, 1958). Children with adjustment problems are described as having mothers who are ineffective, irresponsible, weak, self-critical, competitive for authority, rejecting and hostile (Rexford and Van Amerongen, 1957). Children with ulcerative colitis are said to have mothers who are insecure, inadequate in their maternal role, and ambivalent (Mohr, Josselyn, Spurlock and Barron, 1958). Young addicts tend to have mothers who are controlling, overpowering, guilt-ridden, narcissistic, hostile, inconsistent and seductive (Mason, 1958). Manic-depressives are described as having mothers who are dominant and ambivalent (Gibson, Cohen and Cohen, 1959). And the classic profile of the "schizophrenogenic" mother describes her as dominant, rigidly perfectionistic, lacking in confidence, distrusting, cold, masochistic, low in self-esteem, inconsistent, rejecting, and dependent (Meissner, 1964). The lack of a consistent pattern in the mothers of schizophrenic children has been noted (Fleck et al., 1963; Bowen et al., 1959).

The mother's influence on the children and the general characteristic of the mother-child relation have been intensively studied. Pathology in the children has generally been found associated with maternal conflict and a tendency for mothers to keep the children in a relatively dependent position. The overprotective attitude of mothers of school phobic children is typical: These mothers establish a close emotional relationship with the child which reinforces the child's dependence on the mother and concurrently seems to provide the mother with emotional gratification. A similar pattern is often found in delinquent children, with the added element that these mothers seem incapable of establishing a middle ground in dealing with these children—giving is equivalent to limitless surrender and indulgence, discipline comes to mean total deprivation and hostile, repressive control. Mothers of addicts were similarly found to be overprotective and unable to grant independence to their children. The powerful need to infantilize in such mothers has a profound impact on the children that is reflected in the intense and binding pattern of identification characteristic of this relationship; this may relate to the frequency of homosexual conflicts in addicts. Similar patterns of symbiotic infantilization can be found in psychosomatic disorders and may even reflect a more seriously disturbed mother-child relationship than that found in schizophrenia. In ulcerative colitis, for example, the conflict between the mother's need to keep the child dependent and her own unconscious destructive impulses may be central (Meissner, 1964).

A critical issue in such pathological relationships is the extent to which the child is drawn into the service of neurotic maternal needs. There is a common tendency for neurotic mothers to present themselves as the self-sacrificial victims who bear the loving burden of having and raising their children. The willingness to sacrifice and suffer pain and sorrow thus becomes the hallmark of the mother's love. However, this puts a terrible burden of guilt on the child who is the object of such loving sacrifice. Ackerman (1958, p. 76) has commented in this regard:

> Neurotic mothers are notorious for their martyred agonies, their self-pitying dramatic displays, their exploitation of the theme of sacrifice. In actuality, however, martyred mothers make no sacrifice. If anything, they do precisely the opposite. They exploit their children. They exact an emotional sacrifice. They press upon their children with their imagined wounds, with constant reminders of all they have done for them. Neurotic children take this maternal display seriously; they are mowed down by guilt and seek penance in propitiatory behavior. They attempt in a futile way to make up to their mothers for the presumed sacrifice. Such patterns of neurotic interaction bind the child to mother, deform the quality of togetherness, and sharply restrict the range of development toward a mature autonomy.

A number of patterns of maternal overprotection have been described (Levy, 1970). Most frequently, in clinical terms maternal overprotection masks or compensates a strong rejection of the child. Such motives may be initiated by severe illness, accident or deformity in the child so that such mothers tend to favor these weaker, sicklier and generally more dependent children. Such maternal overprotection is manifested in excessive mother-child contact, infantilization, and the prevention of independent behavior in the child. There may also be a lack or an excess of control over the child's behavior—the former suggesting a deficiency in the mother's capacity to modify the child's behavior so that the child's demands continue to control the relationship, and the latter reflecting a pattern of maternal domination. In the one case, the child's power is exercised in having his own way and in dominating every situation so that he becomes the central figure. Thus, the infantile power tends to expand into a monstrous hold which tends to subjugate the parents. In the latter case, the child's dependency on the mother is fostered so that there is a failure of development and a constriction in the growth of aggressive tendencies. The mothers of dominating children are indulgent, while the mothers of submissive children are dominating.

The pattern of maternal overprotectiveness can be matched by the pattern of maternal rejection. Anna Freud (1970, p. 378) has commented on this subject as follows:

There is, of course, no lack of evidence for the occurrence of rejection of infants. Many infants, instead of being kept as near to the mother as possible, spend many hours of the day in isolation; many are subjected to traumatic separations from their mothers; many, at the end of infancy, have good reason to feel deserted when another child is born; many are, indeed, unwanted. Nevertheless, there is behind these happenings a variety of determinants which decide their outcome. There is not one type of rejecting mother, there are many. There are those who are responsible for their rejecting attitude, who can be exhorted, advised, and helped toward a better adjustment to their children; there are also those for whom rejecting is beyond their control.

Thus the determinants of maternal rejection may be quite diverse and relatively specific or nonspecific. The child may be rejected because of certain characteristics which remind the mother of others in her experience toward whom she has had hateful or ambivalent relations. Or the mother may associate threat or pain with the child such that the rejection of the child reflects experiences or associations that threaten the mother's idealized self-image or her own personal goals or values.

Frequently, the child may become the inheritor of displaced hostilities from other relationships. Thus, the mother may displace the conflicted hostility from her own relationship with her mother to her daughter; or, as in a striking instance in the author's own clinical experience, the mother of an adolescent pre-schizophrenic boy, with whom she maintained a highly ambivalent, conflictual, and mutually rejecting attitude, recalled that when he was born and first placed in her arms she was struck with how angry he looked. She has always regarded him as an angry and unmanageably explosive child. So he has become. This reflected her own hostile, conflicted, and intensely ambivalent relationship with her father who was a violent, alcoholic, and frequently paranoid man, subject to outbursts of temper and violent and destructive behavior. To keep the lines of connection clear, it was not simply that this infant became the object of a displaced perception on the part of the mother, but that, more accurately, he was the object of the projection of her own aggressive and violent impulses which had been internalized, that is to say introjected, from her violent and abusive father.

Maternal rejection, however, may also be influenced by accidental factors. The pregnancy itself may have been accidental and the child unwanted. Or the pregnancy may have come at an unfortunate time in terms of the family finances, or in relationship to the death of significant figures in the family structure, or at a time when the mother is left particularly vulnerable in the exercise of her mothering capacities, as, for example, when the father would be drafted into the army or might have suffered a serious accident or a severe illness.

Basic to the issues of overprotection and rejection is the question of the extent to which the mother herself has achieved a stable and adequate self-image and the degree to which she has been successful in establishing a cohesive differentiated self and a stable identity. To the degree that she has achieved this, she will be capable of accepting the independence and growth potential of her child and fulfill her mothering function without excessive rejection on the one hand or excessively drawing the child into the service of neurotic needs on the other. To be a good mother requires a fundamental acceptance of her own anatomy and physiology and a valuing of its biological potentialities and implications. She must be able to accept herself as fundamentally feminine and as fulfilling the role of wife, before she can comfortably accept the functions and responsibilities of motherhood. Too often, women become mothers who fundamentally deny and devalue their femininity, who are caught in the unfortunate torment of penis envy, who do not value their mothering and nurturing functions, and who tend to relate to their children either as narcissistically compensating or as intolerably burdensome reinforcers of their own sense of self-hate and worthlessness. It will be of great interest to see what changes in the patterning of such maternal responsiveness are wrought by the currently changing status of women in society.

The marital relationship places an important stamp on the developing personalities of the children. The mother's capacity to fulfill her role as wife and to enter into a mutually satisfying and constructive relationship with her husband provides important elements in the family system. Where husband and wife have not developed such mutually supportive roles and a reciprocally reinforcing relationship, they deprive the child of those critical models of adult behavior and functioning, particularly in the context of the relationship between the sexes, which are so essential for the child's development. If a mother is continually expressing her dissatisfaction with her husband and devaluing him, she undercuts his value as an object for the son's identification or his value to a daughter as a model of masculinity and an object for suitable love and esteem. If her own inadequacies or her inability to meet her husband's unreasonable expectations make her an object of her husband's devaluation and criticism, her own worth as an object for identification for both of her children, but particularly for her daughter, is undercut.

If a mother turns from her husband to her son as her major source of emotional support and reinforcement, this will only confuse and intensify the oedipal involvement of the child and make his successful resolution of oedipal conflicts more questionable. The mother who assumes the dominant or domineering position in the family and begins to take on masculine functions and roles within the family only succeeds in offering a disturbed apprehension in the child of masculinity and femininity and jeopardizes his own achievement of a secure sexual identity. Thus, the mother exerts a profound influence on the child's development by the extent to which she can meaningfully and effectively fulfill her functions in the family as wife and mother. But beyond this, as the Lidz group (1965) has pointed out, in most families the mother is the primary teacher and model by which the child acquires a number of the basic skills of socialization and the capacity to relate to other human beings.

MOTHER-SCHIZOPHRENIC CHILD DYAD

That these patterns of overprotectiveness and rejection can have severe pathogenic effects is borne out by studies of the mothers of schizophrenic children. Also, these studies of schizophrenic children and their mothers represent one of the most extensive attempts to observe pathological object relationships. Thus, since this chapter on marriage and family dynamics deals with many of the same concepts as these schizophrenia studies, a brief discussion of a few such studies will be included in this and the subsequent section of this chapter. They suggest that the severity of the mother's disturbance, rather than the type of maternal disturbance, was more predictive of schizophrenia in the child than any other factor.

The studies of Lidz and his group (1965) have concluded that there are two types of "schizophrenogenic" mothers. The first type is more commonly the mother of a schizophrenic son. She seems to be unable to set boundaries and treats the child as though he were an extension of herself. These mothers felt inadequate as women, insecure and anxious about themselves, but even more anxious about the child, particularly when they are not able to fully control his behavior. In such a mother's fantasy it is the child who gives completion and meaning to her life. Her close binding relationship with the child strengthens his primary identification with her and makes the shift to a position of object love as a part of his emerging sexual identity as a male all the more difficult. The mother prevents his exploration of the outside world and makes his decisions for him. The child is prevented from becoming a person in his own right and is held in a symbiotic tie to the mother. She continues to be an omniscient figure who directs her son's thinking and feeling and seems to impose her way of seeing and thinking about the world on the child. He has little opportunity to gain any confidence in his own ability to become an independent and autonomous entity.

The second type of "schizophrenogenic" mother is more frequently the mother of a schizophrenic daughter. She is relatively unable to strongly invest the mother-child relationship, tends to be rather apathetic and indifferent toward her infant, and remains emotionally withdrawn as the child grows older. Even when she is controlling and intrusive, there is an aloof and hostile quality to her overprotectiveness. She is able to give little of herself to the child and provides little foundation for security in the relationship. These mothers provide an inadequate basis to allow the child the exercise of any initiative or for a feeling of increasing security in independent exercise of it. These mothers are profoundly deficient in self-esteem as women and are usually devalued and derogated by their husbands. They gain no gratification from a female child, whom they see as castrated and devalued as themselves. The daughter, in turn, gains no sense of worth of herself as a woman through identification with such a mother. The children of both sexes are deprived of the basis for developing capacities for intimacy and loving affection. With such aloof and hostile mothers to guide them, they do not gain a sense of trust in others or any capacity for trusting closeness with others. Thus, a satisfying marriage for the children of such mothers is highly unlikely.

Bowen (1960) has emphasized the intensity of the mother-child relationship in such schizophrenic families, a point of view that has been reinforced by Cheek's (1970) interaction profiles. Check's findings have lent some support to the profile of aloofness, coldness, and withdrawal in mothers of both male and female schizophrenics, with a higher degree of projected and overt hostility in the relationship with male children. The intensity of the relationship reflects the high degree of ambivalence embedded in it. The mother tends to make two primary demands on the patient. The first, subtle and usually unconscious, is that the patient remain helpless; the other, more overt and verbalized, is that the patient become gifted and mature. Prominent in the mother-patient relationship is the mother's continual worrying, doubting, and concerned preoccupation about the patient.

Bowen (1960) notes that this is a continuation of the mother's over-investment that usually began before the child was born. He has commented on the role of projection in this interaction between mother and child (pp. 360-361):

To summarize this point, the subjects of the mother's overconcerns about the patient and the focus of their "picking on the patients" are the same as their own feelings of inadequacy about themselves. This point is so accurate on a clinical level that almost any point in the mother's list of complaints about the patient can be regarded as an externalization of the mother's own inadequacies. . . . We have used the term "projection" to refer to the most all-pervasive mechanism in the mother-child relationship. It has been used constantly by every mother in every aspect of her relationship with the patient. Accordingly to our thinking, the mother can function more adequately by ascribing certain aspects of herself to the child, and the child accepts. This is of crucial importance in the area of the mother's immaturity. The mother denies her own feelings of helplessness and her wish to be babied. She projects the denied feelings to the child. Then she perceives the child to be helpless and to wish to be mothered. The child, and even the entire family, accepts the mother's perception as a reality in the child. The mother then "mothers" the helplessness in the child (her own projected feelings) with her adequate self. Thus, a situation that begins as *a feeling in the mother, becomes a reality in the child.*

It must be remembered, in addition to this projective aspect of the mother's relationship to the child, that there is a reciprocal activity on the part of the schizophrenic child as well. The child is involved in a similar process to that of the mother, except that whereas the mother initiates her emotional and verbal demands, the child is more responsive to the mother's demands than he is initiating his own. Such a schizophrenic child is involved in a process of trying as well as he can to remain the mother's baby and at the same time to become a mature adult. Ofter the compliance of the patient to the mother's emotional demand is automatic. As soon as the overly anxious mother comes into contact with the patient, she becomes less anxious and the patient becomes more psychotic and regressed. Then the more adequate mother can baby the less adequate patient. With regard to the child's position, Bowen notes (p. 363):

The child makes his emotional and verbal demands on the mother by exploiting the helpless, pitiful position. Patients are adept at arousing sympathy and overhelpfulness in others. All the research families had eventually found their homes geared to the demands of the patient. The parents are as helpless in taking a stand against the patient as the patient in taking a stand against parents.

Other aspects of parent-child relationships

The reader should be reminded at this point that these family interactions take place in connection with an emotional matrix or shared emotional process which seems to characterize the family system. This aspect of family dynamics was noted some years ago by Bowen (1960), who described it in the following terms (p. 368):

> I have used the terms "emotional demand" and "emotional process" to describe the emotional responsiveness by which one family member responds automatically to the emotional state of another, without either being consciously aware of the process . . . it runs silently underneath the surface between people who have very close relationships. It operates during periods of conflict and periods of calm harmony. In most of our families there is much conflict and open disagreement and many stories of injustices and misdeeds between family members.

A similar concept has been elaborated more recently by Slipp (1973). He describes a pattern of interaction which was identifiable in families of various forms of pathology, but to the most extreme degree in families with a schizophrenic member. He describes this "symbiotic survival pattern" as follows (pp. 377-378):

> The essential characteristics of this pattern were that each person's self-esteem and ego identity were felt to be dependent upon the other's behavior. Thus, each member felt controlled by his overwhelming sense of *responsibility* and guilt for the self-esteem and ego identity of the others, and at the same time each needed to *control* the other's behavior.

This pattern derives from the need of the parents to act out their own intrapsychic conflicts in the interpersonal sphere of interaction. This pathological pattern exercises enormous control over the personality and functioning of the child so that he does not learn to integrate sexual and aggressive impulses nor to experience a sense of himself as a differentiated and independent self apart from his involvement with the family. As a result, as the child grows to maturity he fails to establish a stable and autonomous sense of himself and continues to be excessively involved and influenced by the ongoing current of emotion in the family system. The identified patient in such a family is unable to be spontaneous and assertive, but remains constantly reactive to emotional pressures deriving from others in the family system and from the family as a whole. Conversely, the patient is strongly motivated to perpetuate this mutually controlling and symbiotic involvement, since the alternative is the fear of abandonment or, in the most severely disturbed cases, annihilation.

Insofar as the survival pattern and its related emotional closeness is required to maintain whatever level of personality integration has been achieved by its participants, including particularly the parents, the patient's participation and continuing involvement in this emotional process are partly motivated by the need to sustain his own and his parents' personality integration. The psychotic reaction is most often found to be precipitated by a threat to the patient's participation in this family system. Slipp (1973) describes this reaction in schizophrenic families as follows (pp. 378-379):

> Disruption of the symbiotic relationship was experienced as a loss of the self, of not being capable of surviving intact alone, as well as an act of destruction of one or both of the parents. Thus, his *self-definition* continued to remain *reactive* and *relational,* i.e. he continued to remain excessively dependent upon his family relationships for his self-esteem and ego identity. In summary, the symbiotic survival pattern appeared to prevent the differentiation in the child of mental images of self and others, of mental images from external objects, of what is inside and outside (ego boundaries), and hampered the general transition from primary to secondary process cognition in certain areas.

This pattern of emotional interaction within the family establishes a kind of emotional sink or swim which draws the patient into it and impedes his capacities for development and growth to maturity, leaving him consequently with a variety of developmental impediments. Slipp describes this as follows (pp. 394-395):

> The symbiotic survival pattern in the family is characterized as follows: Each person's self-esteem and psychological survival (ego identity) is felt to be dependent on the other's behavior. Each member, therefore, needs to control the other's behavior and feels controlled by his overwhelming sense of responsibility for the self-esteem and survival of the other. Because this system of interaction itself uses magical, infantile, omnipotent techniques to achieve control over past and present object relations, it reinforces magical, primary-process thinking that the child brings to the system innately. The child, thus, continues to use preoperational, primary-process thinking to an abnormal degree in certain areas of personal relationships because: (a) the child's development is fixated at the symbiotic level of infantile functioning; (b) the fixation makes him pathologically dependent upon the family relations for his ego identity and susceptible to continuing influence by this system (this gives the

appearance that the pathology resides solely in the system); and (c) it is reinforced by the ongoing, pathological family pattern of interaction.

While the existence of such an emotional matrix or symbiotic survival pattern can be found in its most dramatic and pathological form in families with a schizophrenic member, the same pattern operating at lesser degrees of intensity and of pathological impact can be found in families with less marked degree of pathology. Moreover, as already suggested in this chapter, the degree of involvement and pathogenic influence exercised by this system is related to the degree of lack of differentiation of self brought to the system by the respective parents, since it is through their emotional interaction that the system is constituted.

The interlocking of personalities and their functioning in this sort of emotional process have been described in transactional terms as well (Boszormenyi-Nagy, 1965). In this view, the family system is compounded of the introjective aspects of individual personalities in transaction with object relational aspects. Thus, more than one individual can be involved in the operation of an action system in which they either complement each other or create a detrimental emotional feedback system. The precocious child can complement a narcissistically demanding parent; or, more negatively, control of impulses in one member of the system may be achieved through the acting-out of the same impulses by others. Consequently, the other member of the system may be regarded as a constitutive agent of the action rather than merely a participant in an indifferent social reality.

Similarly, the fragile autonomy of one family member may be reinforced at the expense of the autonomy of another member. Clinically, improvement in one family member may be accompanied by the movement of another member into the sick role. This has been described in terms of family homeostasis. The interchange of adequate and inadequate roles can take place not only in terms of psychological functioning, but also between the psychological and physical realms. The achievement of greater functional autonomy in one family member who had been previously impaired may be followed by an outbreak of psychological or physical impairment in some other family member or members. In this sense, it is as though certain families can tolerate an autonomous role in one family member only if it is balanced by a relatively nonautonomous functioning in other parts of the family system.

In such family systems where the achievement of autonomy is jeopardized, the system tends to be characterized by a sort of symbiotic involvement which exempts the involved members from the necessity of becoming separate individuals. The members are attached to one another in an engulfing manner which gives the impression of sharing each other's feelings and motivations rather than gaining any mutual recognition and acceptance of differences and divergences. Such intersubjective fusion cannot tolerate autonomous change on the part of its involved members. The unity of the system requires predictability in the action patterns of all its members. As long as all the members are intensely involved and responsive to the demands of the system, the sense of satisfaction and security of its members is guaranteed.

In the extreme examples of such systems, there is no room for individual choice or spontaneous individuality. In less extreme systems, some freedom can be permitted to the members but at certain critical points the demands of the system must predominate and the call for the characteristic and expectable involvement in the system must be responded to by all its participants or else the system is severely threatened. Particularly threatening to the maintenance of the equilibrium of the system is the movement toward autonomy and independence on the part of any of its members. Where the participating selves enjoy a greater degree of differentiation and individuation, the possibility exists of a dialogue in which differences can be clarified and acknowledged. In pathological families, however, relatedness is maintained in a fragile and inauthentic form by the avoidance of differences or by desperate attempts to convince the other of one's point of view or to justify oneself in the other's eyes. This pattern of interaction has been described as "pseudomutuality" (Wynne, Ryckoff, Day and Hirsch, 1958). Real mutuality, however, must be based on the clear differentiation of self and the acceptance of differences rather than merely on the avoidance of conflict. Frequently enough, any movement in the direction of individuation or of the acknowledgement of differences, or any attempt at confrontation and authentic conflict may be labeled as betrayal of the inherent values of the family system—a radical form of treason whose proper punishment can only be isolation and abandonment.

The family emotional system which functions in this way is organized around and functions in terms of the interlocking patterns of introjections and projections which take place between and among the family members. On the part of the parents, such interactions are manifested in their relative insensitivity and inability to respond appropriately to the needs of their children as independent and autonomous persons. The child is seen and reacted to in terms of the parents' own intrapsychic needs rather than in terms of the child's needs. The child is drawn into the emotional interaction in such a way as to sustain the precarious psychic equilibrium of the parents and subordinate his own personality needs and growth potential to this process.

Where the family interaction is based on such an introjective-projective basis, each member of the family tends to represent parts of the other individual's unacceptable self-images, so that any mobilization in the direction of separation and individuation becomes a threat to the inner psychic economy of other members of the system. Where the participants have not achieved self and object constancy, there is a tendency to split off unacceptable aspects of the self and project them onto others, thus setting up the interlocking and emotionally entrapping system. Slipp (1973) describes this very well in the following terms (pp. 384-385):

> Without a stable, integrated, and internalized system of introjects, the parents remained stimulus-bound and needed external objects upon whom to project certain split introjects. In turn, other family members were required to introject, incorporate, and act out these split introjects. However, in order to stabilize the *internal* system of the parents, the entire family became locked into a rigid, mutually controlling *external* system of interaction in which each one's self-esteem and survival was dependent upon the other member's participation.

The implicit demand, therefore, is that other members of the system think and act and feel according to a projected image, rather than as separately motivated individuals. Differentiation of the respective selves is impeded and, when needs are not reciprocally met, the subjects feel rejected, worthless, furious, enraged, and they see the nonresponding other as depriving, controlling or generally evil. As Slipp notes, projective elements may include relatively good and benign aspects, as for example to compensate for the lack of a stable, nonambivalent and good object; this may serve to compensate for feelings of past or present deprivation, or to counter destructive and enraged feelings and thus re-establish a sense of internal balance. Or the projective elements may involve displacement of destructive feelings onto another member of the family system who then serves as a scapegoat. Although scapegoating is only one example of the displacement of destructive feelings to other members, this is a fairly typical pattern. However, other members may also be seen as powerful, intrusive, controlling, domineering, punitive, and with a variety of other hostilely destructive attitudes.

In this fashion the interaction between the parents and the affected child or the designated patient comes to fulfill in the external realm of the family interaction important psychological needs in the participants. The pressures in the system induce the affected member to introject the projective elements which are put on him either separately or collusively by the parents. The patient's participation in this triadic interaction has important functions in maintaining the psychic equilibrium of the parents. The power of these needs and the forces which are brought to bear to control the patient and to keep him in this position vis-à-vis the family are considerable. Slipp (1973) has noted in this regard (p. 395):

> Since intrapsychic conflicts are acted out in the interpersonal sphere, the parents continuously need the patient to stabilize their own personality. Thus, the identified patient cannot achieve his own separate identity with adequate ego control. He requires a symbiotic relation to sustain his *relational* ego identity and acts to perpetuate the system. To break from the symbiotic survival pattern is fraught with the fear of being destroyed, of not surviving intact alone, as well as the fear of loss of control and destruction of the parents. When the individual's adaptational needs are disjunctive with the family system, as a result of developmental growth or outside stress, he may be precipitated into an overt psychosis.

It is within this context, then, that the important patterns of internalization which determine and shape the child's development take place. Where the projective elements are particularly destructive or negative, as they often are in pathological family situations, one or the other of the parental figures is forced into an inadequate or inferior role and is treated in a belittling or contemptuous or undercutting manner by the other parent or other family members. As Lidz and his coworkers have noted repeatedly (1965), the function of the parents is to provide adequate models of identification for children of both sexes. Such internalizations can be harmoniously integrated only when the models are not conflicting and mutually exclusive. The maintaining of an adequate model depends not only on the inherent qualities of that particular parent, but also on the esteem and value placed upon that parent as a love object by the spouse. When the parents are in fact mutually supportive and valued, the potentiality exists for relatively nonconflictual internalizations and constructive identifications.

As mentioned above, one reason for discussing parent-child relationships in a book on marriage is that the psychoanalytic perspective conceptualizes the spouse-spouse and parent-child relationships as closely related. One of the most typical and pathological patterns which evolves in deficient family systems derives from the fact that the parents come to the experience of marriage with unresolved oedipal conflicts and needs and they seek fulfillment of these in the marital relationship. These needs, in fact, usually dictate the choice of marital partner. But when the needs and wishes are frustrated and unfulfilled, there is a regressive retreat, a heightened vulnerability, and an intensification of narcissistic needs which are only aggravated and reinforced by the advent of children. These children are drawn into the service of these consuming and unsatisfied needs which remain largely unconscious on the part of the parent. The child is then drawn into the projective and introjective interaction with the result that his own personality development proceeds on the basis of pathological introjects, particularly of the undeveloped narcissistic residues in the parents, rather than on the basis of differentiated and integrated parental models. Often the neurotic needs of the parents are collusively coordinated, but frequently they are cast in conflictual opposition; in such cases the child is caught in a conflict between the parents so that his response to the needs of one parent means a disloyalty and betrayal of the other. Consequently, his response to the needs of one parent means antagonism and rejection from the other.

These patterns of interaction and particularly the defective qualities of the parental internalization models have been detailed in the studies of the Lidz group (1965). In these studies, the mothers of schizophrenic daughters provided pathetic objects for internalization, not only in terms of their own inner sense of inadequacy and impoverished self-esteem, but also in terms of the contemptuous, derogatory and devaluing attitudes and treatment directed toward them by their husbands. The husbands in their turn tended to be domineering, often grandiose and paranoid, and frequently embittered because the wife would not feed their narcissism by constant admiration and adulation. Similarly, in male schizophrenics, the deficiencies of the father in furnishing an adequate masculine role model are quite striking. Such men tended to be inadequate, passive, seemingly weak and ineffectual—relatively passive and castrated figures constantly belittled by aggressive, domineering, controlling intrusive women who constantly made clear to the patients the degree to which they were dissatisfied with their relationships with them as husbands, belittled and devalued them, particularly in relationship to their sexual function.

Usually, the withdrawal from the father on the part of these women was related to an increasingly solicitous and overprotective involvement with their male children. The relationship of these mothers to their schizophrenic sons tended to be symbiotic, engulfing, and at times highly seductive. It should be noted that, in the context of such pathologically organized family systems, common developmental experiences take on a special coloring and impact on the child's psychic development. Where a hostile projective interaction dominates the family emotional interaction, primal scene experiences or fantasies can be expected to play out in exaggerated ways the derivatives of aggressor- and victim-introjects. As Edelheit (1974) has noted, primal scene representations tend to involve characteristic double identifications which may be either simultaneous or alternating. As noted elsewhere (Meissner, 1978), such primal scene schema contribute to the activation and internalization of victim and aggressor introjective configurations in the child. But it must be remembered that in such pathologically distorted family interactions the normally defensively activated components of such developmental experience are considerably magnified and consequently even more seriously subject to pathological distortion than might be the case in relatively nonpathological family systems.

While the operation of such projective and introjective mechanisms is most blatant and easily observed in families of schizophrenic children, it has also been observed as a predominant mode of perceptual and behavioral interaction in families of disturbed adolescents. The normal adolescent pull in the direction of increasing autonomy and individuation is jeopardized by implicit demands placed on the child to collude with the unconscious emotional assumptions of the family system. From birth these children are introduced into the emotional interaction and come to play a specific role in relation to parental fantasies. From birth onward, these parentally derived pressures play upon the child's own instinctual needs to embed him in the family system as a collusive participant in the process of responding to and fulfilling unconscious parental needs. Zinner and Shapiro (1972) have delineated the common threads of this interaction as follows (p. 525):

> The common threads are: (1) that the subject perceives the object *as if* the object contained elements of the subject's personality, (2) that the subject can evoke behaviors or feelings in the objects that conform with the subject's perceptions, (3) that the subject can experience vicariously the activity and feelings of the object, (4) that participants in close relationship are often in collusion with one another to sustain mutual projections, i.e. to support one another's

defensive operations and to provide experiences through which the other can participate vicariously.

It can be presumed that such projective-introjective interactions are to be found in all family systems, but that the outcome in terms of degrees of pathological impact is determined by a variety of factors, including the intensity and the level of primitive organization of parental defenses, the degree of differentiation and individuation of parental selves, and the corresponding content and level of pathological need embedded in parental projections.

PARENTS-CHILD TRIAD

The arrival of the first child is an event of singular importance in the history of any marriage and marks a decisive turning point in its psychological development. The equilibrium between husband and wife is shifted from a dyadic balance to a triadic configuration. This shift cannot take place without some degree of psychological tension and upheaval (Blanck and Blanck, 1968). The balance of love and hate within this triad is largely determined by the attitudes of the parents, although from the very beginning the interaction is reciprocal. The parents may carry into this new psychological situation residues deriving from experience in their own families of origin. Consequently, they may reproduce patterns of interaction previously experienced in that context, or may shift to a polar opposite set of attitudes as a rebellion against and rejection of those childhood experiences.

Ackerman (1958) speaks in this context of the emergence of a family identity. He writes (pp. 21-22):

> It is the interaction, merging, and redifferentiation of the individualities of the partners of this marital pair that mold the identity of the new family. Just as a child's personality internalizes something of each parent and also evolves something new, so too the identity of a new family incorporates something of the self-image of each marital partner and the image of their respective families-of-origin and also develops something unique and new. From the joined identity of the marital pair each partner seeks further development as an individual, as well as the fulfillment of family goals. If the identity of the marital relationship is impaired, the process of further differentiation of each individual partner will likewise be impaired. The psychological identity of the marital pair shapes the child, but the child also shapes the parental pair to his needs. It is the interaction of family members in reciprocal role relation that provides the

stimulus to appropriate receptivity to new experience and the cultivation of individual initiative. The psychological identity of the marital pair, as well as the evolving identity of each individual partner becomes the core of the expanding identity of the new family.

This chapter has been referring to the progression into the marital bond and beyond into the shaping of the new family group as inherently developmental. As Benedek (1970) has pointed out, with the birth of each child, and with each child in a different way, both parents unconsciously relive portions of their own developmental experience and conflicts. When the circumstances are right, that is, when the child does not stir up deep-rooted conflicts in either of his parents, the child is able to gratify the parents' significant aspirations and enlarge the scope of their own personalities and their marriage. The interaction with the child can thus deepen the meaning of family life for all of its participants and contribute to the further elaboration and consolidation of their respective identities.

The balance in this configuration is disturbed and modified with the addition of each additional child. In this sense it is appropriate to think of the grouping of mother and father with each individual child as forming a triangular configuration which is distinct from the triangular involvement of the parents with each other child. The overlapping and interaction of these respective triads within the family system form a dynamic matrix within which the family emotional processes play themselves out. Bowen (1960) has emphasized that the basic configuration in terms of which family dynamics operate is specifically the mother-father-child triad.

Within the family triad there is a precarious balance between the erotic attachments, which are necessary for the cohesiveness of the family group and normal development of the children, and the incestuous impulses which become disorganizing for the family system and its participants. The desexualization of the parent-child attachment is one of the primary functions of the family as a social and socializing unit. The child's development requires affectionate love from the parents, along with the frustration and attenuation of the erotic quality of this attachment through resolution of the oedipal crisis and the transition to latency. The success of the process depends not only on maturational factors, but also on the child's ability to find a reasonably autonomous and conflict-free position in the family, with adequately consolidated relationships with both parents, and a secure sense of the child's own sexual and personal identity (Lidz et al., 1965).

When one of the parents has an excessive need to gain affective or erotic satisfaction from the child rather than from the spouse and turns to the child for the satisfaction of these needs, this inevitably distorts the oedipal configuration and frustrates the potentiality for satisfactory resolution of oedipal relationships. The stage may be set for the intensification of incestuous tendencies and undermines the normal boundaries between generations which hold the incestuous trends in check. This happens particularly when one parent becomes like another child rivaling the child for the affection of the other spouse, or when a child is used as an emotional substitute for the other spouse. As Bowen (1960) observed in his study of schizophrenic families, when the parents were emotionally more invested in each other than either of them was in the patient, the patient's condition improved. However, when either parent became more emotionally invested in the patient than in the other parent, the patient immediately began to regress.

Moreover, Lidz et al. (1965) noted that in every case the parental relationship and mutuality were not simply deficient, but had degenerated into overt disregard, contempt or hatred in which one parent would continually undermine the worth and authority of the other. There was no sense of mutual support or gratification in the marital relationship. Such parents tend to turn to their relationships with the child for such fulfillment. When the child is so used to gratify the parents' needs, a symbiotic relationship can develop which responds to essentially narcissistic needs in both. In consequence, the child feels undifferentiated from the parent and sexual strivings become increasingly incestuous. Child and parent become bound to each other, since they become essential to the maintenance of psychic integrity of each other.

The objection has often been raised that if the pathological influence on the child's development derives from the amalgamated pathologies of the parents, then it follows that the pathological influence would be brought to bear in the same way on all of the children in the family. This is not the case, since, even in deeply disturbed family systems where there may be one or more schizophrenic children, one or other of the siblings seems to escape the pernicious influence of the family pathology and develops in a relatively normal way (Lidz et al., 1965). The answer is that the family pathology is not uniformly and evenly distributed in the family system, but rather tends to focus itself on particular family members, and in this regard tends to involve one or other of the children more than the rest. There is a focusing of the pathological interaction between the parents so as to involve one or other child in such a way that the parental pathology comes particularly intensely to bear on that child.

This chapter has already described the tendency for these relationships to become organized on a triadic basis. The major pathology of the family may thus be concentrated in a primary triad to which other triadic formations in the family take a back seat. This does not mean that pathological aspects are completely focused in one triadic configuration and not in the others; rather they may all participate, in one degree or other or in one fashion or other, in the pathological influences that are being generated within the family system. There is good reason in this regard to raise a question regarding the so-called "well sibling."

Bowen (1960) has suggested that the selection of a particular child for this form of intense involvement may be determined by the mother's unconscious functioning in the prevailing reality system at the time of the pregnancy and birth. Mutiple influences, however, may come to bear on this involvement which may express itself in varying patterns. Often enough, the first child becomes the leading candidate for this environment, but not necessarily so. Bowen cites the case of a mother whose relationships with her first two children were relatively normal but who then developed an intense symbiotic attachment to a third who was born shortly after the death of her own mother.

The problem of selective involvement in the family pathology has been discussed elsewhere (Meissner, 1964). Particularly in the most severely disturbed family systems, those of schizophrenic families, there is a difference between the way in which the parents relate to the schizophrenic child and the way they relate to the nonschizophrenic child. (Of course, it is unknown to what degree this is a consequence of living with a schizophrenic child.) The parents are able to reach critical decisions about nonschizophrenic siblings quite easily, but decisions related to the schizophrenic child are made only with difficulty and considerable conflict, if at all. The mother's behavior toward the children also may differ considerably: She may be more inclined to leave the nonschizophrenic child alone for longer periods of time, but she is able to leave the schizophrenic child only with considerable anxiety and worry. The schizophrenic child thus becomes typically compliant and responsive to the demands and expectations of its parents, particularly the implicit and unconscious ones, while the nonschizophrenic sibling tends to be more independent and can afford to ignore these parental demands.

The selection of a particular child or children for this involvement is obviously overdetermined and is influenced by a variety of factors which not only have to do with particular characteristics of the child but also reflect the dynamics behind the parental involvement and the operation of other extrinsic factors, particularly those deriving from the extended family. Thus, the prevailing psychological situation in the family at the time of the child's birth has a considerable amount to do with determining the child's role within the family constellation and the character of his involvement with the parents. The affected child was often sickly or in some manner unusual so that it required greater care on the part of the mother. Or, for other reasons, the mother may have been under particular strain at the time of the child's birth.

The selection of a particular child may thus be determined in part by the mother's unconscious functioning in the prevailing reality situation, so that the involved child becomes a particular target for maternal projections. Bowen (1960) gives an example of the close attachment to a deformed child as potentially offering greater fulfillment of a mother's needs than the relationship to a normal child. A case in the author's experience is that of a mother who had six healthy and reasonably well adjusted children, but then delivered a seventh child who suffered from brain damage. The defective functioning of this child seemed to activate her feelings of guilt and self-doubt in such a way that at the birth of her eighth and last child she was highly resolved that there would be no defect or lack in her mothering. This last child now shows every sign of emotional retardation and behavioral difficulties.

THE TRANSFERENCE MODEL

It is beyond the scope of the present consideration to detail all the contexts and patterns of interaction through which the family emotional system expresses itself. We have tried to demonstrate the validity of the description and the concept of such a system and its pathological consequences. The rest of this chapter will describe the aspects of this family emotional system in terms of the psychoanalytic concept of transference.

Transference is the operative model for understanding the family emotional system. The primary meaning of transference refers to that phenomenon occurring within the analytic situation, whereby the residues of prior experiences, and specifically of significant object relationships in the patient's developmental history, are projected onto the analyst so that there is created within the analysis, in part or often to a quite significant degree, a recapitulation of some aspects of those previous object relationships. The transference phenomenon can be variously interpreted, but one way of understanding it is that residues of previous object relationships are projected onto the figure of the analyst so that he becomes in some degree a substitute figure in relation to whom important dynamic issues from the patient's past are recapitulated and can then be reworked and resolved. In terms of the theoretical framework discussed in this chapter, those projective elements derive from the patient's own inner introjective configuration. That introjective alignment itself is the product of the integration of sequential introjects which reflect the vicissitudes of the patient's developmental history.

These dynamics lead in the direction of the establishing of the transference neurosis, in which the infantile conflicts are remobilized and expressed within the transference in relation to the transference object. It must be remembered, however, that the transference phenomenon is not something that is simply evolved within the head of the patient, but rather implies a two-person system which involves both patient and analyst. The analyst in his turn also enters into the transference relationship and becomes a part of it. Countertransference is the name given to the interpersonal phenomenon characterized by the therapist either introjecting aspects of the patient's projection, or contributing his own set of projections to the ongoing interaction and relationship.

The analyst's ability to detect and identify his own countertransference responses and to appropriately modulate and utilize them is a major contribution on his part to the effectiveness of the analytic work. The suggestion made here, however, is that the model of transference functioning which derives from the consideration of transference and countertransference and their dependence on the patient's and analyst's mutually interacting and interlocking projections and introjections provides the working model for the constitution and functioning of the family emotional system. It is as if the family members evolve a more or less stable transference-countertransference configuration among themselves.

This sort of emotional involvement and reactivity is particularly characteristic where the family members are unable to maintain a separate and individuated sense of self and an autonomously functioning identity. Within the analytic setting, it is the capacity of the analyst to maintain himself in a relatively conflict-free, autonomous and differentiated position vis-à-vis the patient's material and his ongoing interaction with the patient, making the therapeutic effectiveness of the analytic setting possible. To the extent that the analyst is drawn into an emotional reactivity with the patient of which he remains unaware and which he is unable to utilize constructively, the psychoanalytic situation would re-create the kind of emotional involvement found in pathological family systems and would do the patient little good. In pathological family systems such as have been described, it can be said that what is in evidence is the operation of a complex transference system in which all of the family members are involved in one or another degree and to which none of the family members is able to bring a differentiated and relatively autonomous sense of self.

In the ongoing family system, therefore, there occurs a set of interlocking transferences around which the family interaction is articulated. Normally, in the analytic situation the transference is brought into the analytic interaction from the family matrix in which the patient experienced the original object relationships. *In the family situation, however, the transferences operate within their native habitat.* The ongoing transference involvement has a somewhat different quality to it since what is being transferred is not something out of the family matrix, but rather reflects earlier vicissitudes of the complex history of object relationships within the family itself. The family emotional process is a natural outgrowth of the earliest dynamic interactions within the family which has its own inherent continuity and history. These interactions, in one important dimension, involve displacement of transference residues that come from earlier levels of experience within the nuclear family itself, i.e., the contemporary pattern of interlocking projections and introjections derives from and reflects internalizations and derivatives of the quality of object relations that were obtained between parents and child when the child was much younger. From another important dimension, however, the transference residues are derived from earlier levels of experience within the extended family; the contemporary transference pattern derives from and reflects internalizations and derivatives of critical object relations in previous generations, between the parents and their respective parents (the grandparents) and even beyond. The family transference system must, therefore, be seen as transgenerational.

Within this transference system in the family it is worth noting the essential triadic construction as has been suggested above. In terms of the dictates of the analytic orientation, the primary attachment and emotional investment on the part of the child is in the parents, so that the triadic involvement of mother, father, and child provides the basic interactive frame of reference within which the important and most central dynamics come to express themselves. This central emotional configuration may be complemented in varying degrees by other significant relationships, but analytic experience dictates an almost universal conclusion that the triadic involvement of the child with its primary objects becomes the radical core of the formation of the child's sense of self and provides the primary introjects which lie at the root of the patient's pathology.

It is precisely these introjects which are inevitably most critically and significantly remobilized in the transference neurosis. These elements are central in the expression of the patient's transference, even though they may vary considerably in intensity and in the sequencing and patterning of their expression within the analysis. It is as though the patient recreates the original emotional triad in his dyadic relationship with the analyst so that the analyst comes to represent, at different times and to different degrees within the patient's analytic experience, the patient's mother, the patient's father, and in differing ways both the patient's mother and father simultaneously.

It is the analyst's capacity to experience the various expressions of transference involvement, to read them accurately in terms of the patient's developmental history, and to respond purposively and constructively in such a way as to allow the patient to rework these developmental experiences so as to modify the configuration of pathogenic introjects at the heart of the patient's pathology. The analyst's therapeutic function, therefore, is to enable the patient to reexperience and rework those basic infantile conflicts which impeded the patient's development and left him with an impaired or distorted sense of self and self-worth. Within the limits of the potentialities of the analytic reconstruction and the modifiability of the patient's personality through corrective experiences of various kinds, the analytic process aims at a reworking of the critical introjects around which the patient's sense of self is articulated.

That reworking takes place through the operation of transference phenomena—through the projecting and reintrojecting, the reprojecting and further reintrojecting in a complex series of interlocking operations. This ultimately offers the possibility of modifying the organization of those introjects in such a way as to make possible the more positive and constructively individuating identifications with the analyst which mobilize the patient's growth potential in healthier and more positive and constructive directions. It is in this derivative sense, then, that psychoanalysis not only is capable of lending some understanding to the phenomenon of family dynamics and to the therapeutic modification of family processes, but is itself inherently, if implicitly, a form of family therapy For the task that analysis sets itself is no less than the reorganizing, reshaping, redirecting and reconstituting of the patient's relationship between his own sense of self, based on critical introjections drawn from the primary family relationships, and the parental images which represent in their turn these critical object relationships.

In summary, *the theory of psychoanalysis is the theory of family dynamics.* The difference lies only in the starting point and perspective from which one chooses to approach the phenomena of human development and human relationships.*

SUMMARY AND CONCLUSION

The present chapter has attempted to present a formulation based in psychoanalytic concepts and theory that can be integrated with the complex understanding of family dynamics. One of the problems for psychoanalytic theory in approaching the whole area of complex social interactions, and particularly in attempting to conceptualize family processes, has been the lack of an adequate conceptual basis which would allow for meaningful and relevant bridging between the level of intrapsychic dynamics, so well understood and explored by the psychoanalytic method, and the intrafamilial dynamics that have been the object of intense study in the last score of years by marital and family therapists.

The key concept in this attempt at an integrated approach is that of the family emotional system. The model through which the family emotional system can be meaningfully related to psychoanalytic dynamics is that of transference. Here transference is viewed as a complex emotional interaction system which is contributed to and compounded out of the emotional responsivities of both analyst and his patient-analysand. Further, the family emotion system and the transference are analyzed in terms of components of the organization of the individual personality which derive particularly from an object relations frame of reference. In these terms, the complex interaction between the individual and his objects can be conceptualized as based on a continual commerce carried on through complex interactions of introjection and projection between the individual and the object world which surrounds him. Through the use of the related concepts of introjection and projection, the reader can gain a theoretical continuity which extends from the intrapsychic level through the interpersonal to the level of social and familial analysis.

Whether the proposed theory can stand the test of time remains to be

---

* The very important psychoanalytic concept of transference is also discussed in the Introduction to Chapter III and in Chapters III and IX.

seen. Nonetheless, it is extremely important to realize and to keep constantly before the mind's eye that the implementation of these principles at each level of analysis is qualitatively different, even though the operation of the same mechanisms can be described. Consequently, the intrapsychic organization of the patient's sense of self through the configuration of introjects is one level of analysis that is characterized by its own inherent properties and principles. As soon as one moves to the level of interpersonal interaction, with the interplay of projections and their derivation from the intrapsychic introjects as well as from the patterns of response and interaction set up within the interpersonal context, one has entered a different realm of understanding and analysis in which one may expect different properties and principles to manifest themselves. It is extremely important for psychological theorists of human behavior, and particularly those who approach these phenomena from the analytic perspective which places such intense emphasis on the intrapsychic perspectives, to keep in mind these qualitative differentiations among these levels of analysis.

In a similar way, it can be said that the shift from a level of interpersonal analysis to the level of more complex and multi-dimensional familial analysis carries with it an additional and quite different and distinctive patterning of variables, qualities of complex and multiply determined interpersonal interactions, and a qualitatively different interaction of projective elements and their correlative introjective consequences. Therefore, the concept of the family emotional system is quite distinctive and different from the conceptual analysis provided at any other level, even though some of the dimensions of the family system have been in part foreshadowed and delineated in the analysis of interpersonal interactions, particularly those of the transference.

While the analytic transference provides the initial model for the understanding of the family emotional system, it is only that. The translation from the understanding of transference dynamics to the level of family analysis must respect the complexity of the new phenomena, and cannot presume that properties discerned and understood within the transference context can have automatic translation or application. Consequently, the appeal to a transference model provides only the first step in understanding and at best opens the way to a richer and more fully congruent understanding of family dynamics and the application of analytic principles to that understanding. Conversely, one can sincerely hope that the increasing understanding of patterns of family emotional involvement and responsiveness will contribute significantly to the view of human behavior and functioning as it is understood in psychoanalytic terms, particularly in reference to the genetic, dynamic and adaptive aspects of human behavior.

REFERENCES

Abelin, E. L. Some further observations and comments on the earliest role of the father. *International Journal of Psychoanalysis*, 1975, 56, 293-302.

Ackerman, N. W. *The Psychodynamics of Family Life*. New York: Basic Books, 1958.

Ackerman, N. W. (1962). Family psychotherapy and psychoanalysis: The implications of difference. In: N. W. Ackerman (Ed.), *Family Process*. New York: Basic Books, 1970.

Agras, S. The relationship of school phobia to childhood depression. *American Journal of Psychiatry*, 1959, 116, 533-536.

Benedek, T. Fatherhood and providing. In: E. J. Anthony and T. Benedek (Eds.), *Parenthood: Its Psychology and Psychopathology*. Boston: Little Brown, 1970.

Blanck, R. and Blanck, G. *Marriage and Personal Development*. New York: Columbia University Press, 1968.

Boszormenyi-Nagy, I. A theory of relationships: Experience and transaction. In: I. Boszormenyi-Nagy and J. L. Framo (Eds.), *Intensive Family Therapy: Theoretical and Practical Aspects*. New York: Harper and Row, 1965.

Bowen, M. A family concept of schizophrenia. In: D. D. Jackson (Ed.), *The Etiology of Schizophrenia*. New York: Basic Books, 1960.

Bowen, M. The family as the unit of study and treatment. I. Family psychotherapy. *American Journal of Orthopsychiatry*, 1961, 31, 40-60.

Bowen, M., Dysinger, R. H. and Basamania, B. The role of the father in families with a schizophrenic patient. *American Journal of Psychiatry*, 1959, 115, 1017-1020.

Burlingham, D. T. Present trends in handling the mother-child relationship during the therapeutic process. In: *Psychoanalytic Study of the Child*. New York: International Universities Press, 1951.

Burlingham, D. T., Goldberger, A. and Lussier, A. Simultaneous analysis of mother and child. In: *The Psychoanalytic Study of the Child*. New York: International Universities Press, 1955.

Cheek, F. E. The "schizophrenogenic mother" in word and deed. In: N. W. Ackerman (Ed.), *Family Process*. New York: Basic Books, 1970.

Deutsch, H. (1942). Some forms of emotional disturbance and their relationship to schizophrenia. In: *Neuroses and Character Types*. New York: International Universities Press, 1965.

Edelheit, H. Crucifixion fantasies and their relation to the primal scene. *International Journal of Psychoanalysis*, 1974, 55, 193-199.

Eisenberg, L. School phobia: A study in the communication of anxiety. *American Journal of Psychiatry*, 1958, 114, 712-718.

Erikson, E. H. Ego development and historical change. In: *The Psychoanalytic Study of the Child*. New York: International Universities Press, 1946.

Erikson, E. H. *Childhood and Society*. New York: Norton, 1950.

Erikson, E. H. Identity and the life cycle. In: *Psychological Issues*, Monograph 1. New York: International Universities Press, 1959.

Fleck, S., Lidz, T. and Cornelison, A. Comparison of parent-child relationships of male and female schizophrenic patients. *Archives of General Psychiatry*, 1963, 8, 1-7.

Flügel, J. D. *The Psychoanalytic Study of the Family*. London: Hogarth Press, 1921.

Freud, A. The concept of the rejecting mother. In: E. J. Anthony and T. Benedek

(Eds.), *Parenthood: Its Psychology and Psychopathology*. Boston: Little Brown, 1970.

Freud, S. (1905). Fragment of an analysis of a case of hysteria. *Standard Edition, 7,* 1-122. London: Hogarth Press, 1953.

Freud, S. (1913). Totem and taboo. *Standard Edition,* 13, vii-162. London: Hogarth Press, 1955.

Freud, S. (1918). From the history of an infantile neurosis. *Standard Edition,* 17, 1-122. London: Hogarth Press, 1955.

Freud, S. (1921). Group psychology and the analysis of the ego. *Standard Edition,* 18, 65-143. London: Hogarth Press, 1955.

Gibson, R. W., Cohen, M. B. and Cohen, R. A. On the dynamics of the manic-depressive personality. *American Journal of Psychiatry,* 1959, 115, 1101-1107.

Giffin, M. E., Johnson, A. M. and Litin, E. M. Specific factors determining antisocial acting out. *American Journal of Orthopsychiatry,* 1954, 24, 668-684.

Greenspan, S. I. and Mannino, F. V. A model for brief intervention with couples based on projective identification. *American Journal of Psychiatry,* 1974, 131, 1103-1106.

Hartmann, H. (1944). Psychoanalysis and sociology. In: *Essays on Ego Psychology.* New York: International Universities Press, 1964.

Johnson, A. M. and Szurek, S. A. The genesis of antisocial acting out in children and adults. *Psychoanalytic Quarterly,* 1952, 21, 323-343.

Kernberg, O. Structural derivatives of object relationships. *International Journal of Psychoanalysis,* 1966, 47, 236-253.

Kernberg, O. Borderline personality organization. *Journal of the American Psychoanalytic Association,* 1967, 15, 641-685.

Kernberg, O. Barriers to falling and remaining in love. *Journal of the American Psychoanalytic Association,* 1974, 22, 486-511.

Kohut, H. *The Analysis of the Self.* New York: International Universities Press, 1971.

Levy, D. M. The concept of maternal overprotection. In: E. J. Anthony and T. Benedek (Eds.), *Parenthood: Its Psychology and Psychopathology*. Boston: Little Brown, 1970.

Lidz, T. The relevance of family studies to psychoanalytic theory. *Journal of Nervous and Mental Disease,* 1962, 135, 105-111.

Lidz, T. and Fleck, S. Schizophrenia, human integration, and the role of the family. In: D. Jackson (Ed.), *The Etiology of Schizophrenia.* New York: Basic Books, 1959.

Lidz, T., Fleck, S. and Cornelison, A. R. *Schizophrenia and the Family.* New York: International Universities Press, 1965.

Litin, E. M., Giffin, M. E. and Johnson, A. M. Parental influence in unusual sexual behavior in children. *Psychoanalytic Quarterly,* 1956, 25, 37-55.

Mahler, M. S., Pine, F. and Bergman, A. *The Psychological Birth of the Human Infant.* New York: Basic Books, 1975.

Mannino, F. V. and Greenspan, S. I. Projection and misperception in couples treatment. *Journal of Marriage and Family Counseling,* 1976, 2, 139-143.

Martin, P. A. and Bird, H. W. An approach to the psychotherapy of marriage partners. *Psychiatry,* 1953, 16, 123-127.

Mason, P. The matter of the addict. *Psychiatric Quarterly Supplement,* 1958, 32, 189-199.

Meissner, W. W. (1964). Thinking about the family—psychiatric aspects. In: N. W. Ackerman (Ed.), *Family Process.* New York: Basic Books, 1970.

Meissner, W. W. Notes on identification. I. Origins in Freud. *Psychoanalytic Quarterly,* 1970, 39, 563-589.

Meissner, W. W. Notes on identification. II. Clarification of related concepts. *Psychoanalytic Quarterly*, 1971, 40, 277-302.

Meissner, W. W. Notes on identification. III. The concept of identification. *Psychoanalytic Quarterly*, 1972, 41, 224-260.

Meissner, W. W. *The Paranoid Process*. New York: Jason Aronson, 1978.

Meissner, W. W. Notes on the differential diagnosis of borderline conditions. In press.

Mittelmann, B. Complementary neurotic reactions in intimate relationships. *Psychoanalytic Quarterly*, 1944, 13, 479-491.

Mittelmann, B. The concurrent analysis of married couples. *Psychoanalytic Quarterly*, 1948, 17, 182-197.

Modell, A. H. *Object Love and Reality*. New York: International Universities Press, 1968.

Mohr, G. J., Jesselyn, I. M., Spurlock, J. and Barron, S. H. Studies in ulcerative colitis. *American Journal of Psychiatry*, 1958, 114, 1067-1076.

Oberndorf, C. P. "Folie-à-deux." *International Journal of Psychoanalysis*, 1934, 15, 14-24.

Oberndorf, C. P. Psychoanalysis of married couples. *Psychoanalytic Review*, 1938, 25, 453-475.

Rapoport, R. Normal crises, family structure, and mental health. In: N. W. Ackerman (Ed.), *Family Process*. New York: Basic Books, 1970.

Rexford, E. N. and Van Amerongen, S. T. The influence of unsolved maternal oral conflicts upon impulsive acting-out in young children. *American Journal of Orthopsychiatry*, 1957, 27, 75-87.

Slipp, S. The symbiotic survival pattern: A relational theory of schizophrenia. *Family Process*, 1973, 12, 377-398.

Spitz, R. Familienneurose und neurotische Familie. Bericht über den IX Kongress der Psychoanalytiker französicher Sprache. 1936. *Internationale Zeitschrift für Psychoanalyse*, 1937, 23, 548-559.

Waring, M. and Ricks, D. Family patterns of children who become adult schizophrenics. *Journal of Nervous and Mental Disease*, 1965, 140, 351-364.

Winch, R. F., Ktones, T. and Ktones, V. The theory of complementary needs in mate-selection. *American Sociological Review*, 1954, 19, 241-249.

Winnicott, D. W. Transitional objects and transitional phenomena. In: *Playing and Reality*. New York: Basic Books, 1971.

Wynne, L. C., Ryckoff, I. M., Day, J. and Hirsch, S. I. Pseudomutuality in the family relations of schizophrenics. *Psychiatry*, 1958, 21, 205-220.

Zinner, J. and Shapiro, R. Projective identification as a mode of perception and behavior in families of adolescents. *International Journal of Psychoanalysis*, 1972, 53, 523-530.

III

Marital Therapy
from a Psychoanalytic
Perspective

CAROL COOPERMAN NADELSON, M.D.
with an Introduction by
THOMAS J. PAOLINO, JR., M.D.

INTRODUCTION: SOME BASIC CONCEPTS OF
PSYCHOANALYTIC PSYCHOTHERAPY

by THOMAS J. PAOLINO, JR., M.D.

All psychotherapy can be broadly defined as a relationship between a person suffering from a psychical problem and another person who has the training, skills, and motivation to alleviate that suffering through some interaction with the patient. Every responsible therapist has the same ultimate goal, namely, "the *practical* recovery of the patient, the restoration of his ability to lead an active life and of his capacity for enjoyment" (italics in the original) (Freud, 1904, p. 253). Since psychotherapists request that their patients engage in the *painful* task of abandoning their maladaptive satisfactions, it is sometimes overlooked that the goal of psychotherapy is a more permanently meaningful and pleasurable existence.

Although the ultimate goal is the same, therapists differ in their operational models of the mind and human behavior. As a result, the approach which they take to therapy differs in accordance with the specific operational model. These different approaches lead to different categorizations or types of therapy. Therapies called "psychoanalytic," "behavioral," "systems oriented," and others less easy to label all have, to some degree, different rules, procedures and formats, although, as noted by Frank (1971), Karasu (1977) and others, all forms of psychotherapy have certain common elements, such as a therapeutic ideology provisionally accepted by both patient and therapist; the preparation for a new knowledge which is transmitted by an increased self-awareness, by example or from directives; persuasive powers of the therapist which lead to increased hopefulness, and facilitation of abreaction.

The psychoanalytic therapist conceptualizes the mind of the patient as operating by Freudian principles. (The term Freudian is being used to refer not only to the ideas of Freud himself, but to those post-Freud followers who have expanded his basic ideas.) In psychoanalytic therapy, both the therapist and the patient are devoted to discovering the psychic truth about the patient and they engage in an interaction that is characterized by a combination of intimacy and deprivation unlike any other form of human relationship.

Following this section on basic concepts of psychoanalytic psychotherapy, Nadelson describes the implementation of one form of psychoanalytic therapy, namely, psychoanalytic marital therapy. In order for the reader to fully grasp the therapeutic concepts from which psychoanalytic marital therapy has evolved, it is necessary to understand some basic concepts which can be grouped into the following six categories: (1) the meanings of the terms "psychodynamic" (sometimes called "dynamic") and "psychoanalytic"; (2) the relationship between mental symptoms and unconscious intrapsychic conflicts; (3) the desirability of making the unconscious conscious; (4) the presupposed connection of serial associations; (5) the therapeutic effect of thoughts and feelings as opposed to action; (6) the occurrence of a duplication of the neurosis within the therapy (including transference). Because of space limitations the following discussion on these concepts might appear simplistic when in fact they reflect phenomena and ideas that are as complicated as human functioning itself. Nevertheless, the complexities of the mind from a psychoanalytic perspective should not discourage us from attempting to isolate some of the basic principles which identify psychoanalytic psychotherapy.

The Meaning of the Terms "Psychodynamic" ("Dynamic") and "Psychoanalytic"

The term "psychodynamic" is confusing and is used in a variety of ways throughout the psychological literature. In fact, at a conference held by the American Psychiatric Association in 1952 and attended by 86 psychiatrists, including 24 psychoanalysts, agreement on this subject could not be reached (Fromm-Reichmann, 1954). Despite the complexities of the problem, however, the issues of how "psychodynamic" and "psychoanalytic" are used must be clarified, especially since those terms are used throughout this volume.

The term "psychodynamic" is frequently used in the literature synonymously with the term "psychoanalytic" (for example, see the otherwise excellent review by Karasu, 1977). This interchangeable use of these terms is often confusing and erroneous. It is not at all uncommon to find two authors differing on some subject of psychodynamic theory or technique but, on closer inspection, the difference is semantic rather than theoretical since each of the authors is discussing different phenomena based on two different operational definitions of "psychodynamic." If these terms refer to certain theories of pathogenesis, psychosocial development, or treatment techniques, then they might be correctly used as synonyms, depending, of course, on the specific concepts being discussed. At other times, however, they refer to totally different and even opposite positions—for example, many psychodynamic therapeutic techniques are in direct opposition to the techniques of classical psychoanalysis.

All three perspectives discussed in this book (psychoanalytic, behavioral and systems theory) agree with the fundamental hypothesis that a person's thoughts, feelings and behavior, both normal and abnormal, are based on complex interactions between the mind, body and external environment. The "external environment" consists of the physical world external to the body of the person in question, the past and present interpersonal interactions, and the past and present surrounding social and cultural settings. Keeping this fundamental hypothesis in mind, the term "psychodynamic" can be broadly defined as referring to theories that expand on the fundamental hypothesis by applying various specific *mentalistic* concepts that include dynamically interacting components of the mind. A "psychodynamicist" clearly describes isolated components and experiences of the mind as possessing various differentiating attributes and functions so that the mind consists of a coherent arrangement of separate, hierarchically ordered psychic processes and functions that operate in specific ways and directions. The psychodynamic functional anatomy of the mind always includes specific identifiable factors that are often in conflict and are psychological, powerful, usually unconscious, motivating forces of human behavior.

If the above definition of "psychodynamic" is accepted, then "psychoanalytic" can be considered a term referring to one specific variety of "psychodynamic." It can be defined as a term used in reference to one of three meanings:

(1) *In reference to Freudian principles of psychic functioning and human behavior.* These principles can, as a body of knowledge, be categorized into theories of resistance; the unconscious; repression; narcissism; the developmental importance of the libido, anxiety and aggression, and their intrapsychic conflicts; the significance of infancy; the phenomenon of transference being derived from a sexual content; the metapsychological concepts of the id, ego and superego; and the strict adherence to the concept of psychic determinism.

(2) *In reference to the psychoanalytic instrument of investigation by which one can learn more about the workings of the mind.* Sometimes the most effective psychoanalytic method of *investigating* the mind is not the most effective psychoanalytic approach to *treating* a disturbed mind.

(3) *In referring to "psychoanalytic technique" as a method of treatment.* This usage also involves reference to the techniques that distinguish the psychoanalytic treatment modality from non-psychoanalytic therapy such as the behaviorist, systems theorist, or non-psychoanalytically oriented psychodynamicist.

It should be noted that the term "psychodynamic" refers both to theories of psychic functioning and to therapeutic techniques based on such theories. It should also be emphasized that not all psychoanalytic techniques and theories are in opposition to approaches that are psychodynamic but not psychoanalytic. For example, the psychodynamic Sullivanians agree with the Freudians that transference and resistance to making the unconscious conscious constitute an integral part of the therapy, although, of course, they differ in their conception of those unconscious psychic elements that are transferred or resisted against (Fromm-Reichmann, 1954). The reader should also be aware that many, if not most, psychoanalysts agree with Freud, who often expressed doubt that the value of the clinical results achieved by psychoanalytic therapy could ever match the value or potential value possessed by psychoanalytic theory as a body of knowledge or as a research tool.

According to the above definitions, psychoanalytic theories and techniques are psychodynamic, but not all psychodynamic theories and techniques are psychoanalytic, since there are various theories of the structural mind and techniques that attempt to change the psychic apparatus but are not founded on Freudian principles. Of course, neither the behaviorist nor the systems theorist perspective is "psychodynamic" since neither focuses on specific structural concepts of the mind, nor does either attempt to alter specific components of a postulated psychic apparatus. "Sullivanians," "Kleinians," and "Jungians" can be considered "psychodynamic" but not "psychoanalytic" since their theories and treatments, although strongly mentalistic, are nevertheless not largely operating on Freudian principles. (For an exhaustive review of the various psychodynamic perspectives, the reader is referred to the comprehensive works of Ellenberger (1970) and Munroe (1955).)

Of course, this condensed description is a simplification of a very complicated issue. Nevertheless, to try to resolve the issue of how and when these terms are accurately used, interchangeably or separately, would take the reader into areas not relevant to the intent of this volume. Thus, for purposes of clarity and uniformity, the terms "psychodynamic" and "psychoanalytic" will be used throughout this book as defined above and not as synonyms, although the term "psychodynamic" will occasionally be used in a way that encompasses the term "psychoanalytic."

THE RELATIONSHIP BETWEEN MENTAL SYMPTOMS AND UNCONSCIOUS INTRAPSYCHIC CONFLICTS

This therapy [psychoanalytic therapy] *then is based on the recognition that unconscious ideas—or better, the unconsciousness of certain mental processes—are the direct cause of the morbid symptoms* (Freud, On Psychotherapy, 1905, p. 266).

An unhappy marriage is often the final common pathway that results from a collection of psychic "symptoms" belonging to one or both partners. According to psychoanalytic theory, all psychic symptoms must be understood from five "metapsychological" perspectives: dynamic, economic, structural, genetic, and adaptive (Rapaport and Gill, 1959). All five aspects of psychoanalytic metapsychology presuppose that mental symptoms result from the mind's attempt to adjust to unconscious intrapsychic conflicts and to the signal anxiety that is generated from such conflicts (Freud, 1926). A symptom serves three functions: (1) It economizes the mental effort to resolve an intrapsychic conflict; (2) it alleviates the anxiety; and (3) it avoids the danger signaled by the anxiety. The ineffectiveness of this solution is what identifies the thought, feeling or behavior as a symptom. An alleviation of symptoms can result from a conscious cognitive and emotional awareness of these mental processes.

In essence, the symptom is a secondary adaptive phenomenon that represents a reaction to the primary psychological cause of the mental problem. The primary component of the symptom is the reaction of the ego to the instinctual demands of the id and the moralistic demands of the superego (Nunberg, 1933). A corollary to this idea is that, although symptoms bring emotional pain and suffering, they also serve a practical purpose in that they in some way prevent the emergence of thoughts or feelings which are consciously or unconsciously considered by the patient as even less acceptable than the symptoms. Thus, a mental disease does not consist only of symptoms, and the cure of the disease involves more than a removal of symptoms. If symptoms are removed without dealing with the basic intrapsychic conflicts leading to those symptoms, then there remains the likelihood that new symptoms will form. This concept of "symptom substitution" is in direct opposition to the principles of therapy underlying "behavior modification."

An intrapsychic conflict is a phenomenon whereby different psychic parts of the same person oppose each other. Starting with Freud and continuing with all subsequent adherents of the psychoanalytic perspective, it is a psychoanalytic theme that mental symptoms and neurotic anxiety result from some force drawing the mind away from a specific object, whereas some other influences are attracting the person toward the same object. This theme is basic to psychoanalytic theory. It makes no difference whether Freud was discussing dreams (*Interpretation of Dreams*, 1900), the history of civilization (*Totem and Taboo*, 1912-13), the neurological mind (*Project for a Scientific Psychology*, 1950), religion and mythology (*Moses and Monotheism*, 1939), psychological theories of the mind (*Interpretation of Dreams*, 1900, Chapter 7; *The Ego and the Id*, 1923b), or the pathogenesis of neurosis (General Theory of the Neuroses, Lectures 16-28 of *Introductory Lectures*, 1917), there was always the basic concept that there were simultaneously existing opposing forces toward and away from a specific object.

Critics frequently complain that the psychoanalytic therapists avoid or minimize current stress and the developmental intrapsychic tasks that occur at all stages of life. It is true that the developmental aspects of psychoanalytic theory focus on the psychosexual stages up to six years of age, but it is inaccurate to say that psychoanalytic therapists avoid the importance of current situations. The complete psychoanalytic therapist, following the pioneering work of Erikson (1950), accepts that life continues after the age of six and that every human life cycle from birth to death creates new psychological tasks and new inner crises. Not only does investigative psychoanalytic therapy accept the importance of current crises and developmental psychic tasks, but a fundamental presupposition is that the key to the understanding and treatment of unconscious pathogenic conflicts lies in the interaction between the various external and internal (real) stressful experiences and the multitude of preexisting ideas, feelings, attitudes, and conflicts. The preexisting psychic elements are not static and, in fact, gain new meaning as they interact with various aspects of the current situation. Therefore, in order to understand the genesis of the specific clinical material under study, the therapist and patient must be as familiar with the central problem with which the patient is currently dealing ("context," Langs, 1973, p. 316) as with the developmental and intrapsychic variables. The therapist must keep in mind, however, that an awareness of context itself might be defended against, in which case the primary therapeutic task is to discover the specific context which in turn will lead to the underlying pathogenic psychic elements.

THE DESIRABILITY OF MAKING THE UNCONSCIOUS CONSCIOUS

The psychoanalytic therapist focuses interactions with the patient on interventions that make the patient conscious of the pathogenic intrapsychic conflicts and help the patient make the inner changes that lead to a resolution of these conflicts.

Early Freudian Theory

The fundamental theories of contemporary psychoanalytic psychotherapy are in some ways quite different than those of the early Freud and his associates during the beginnings of the psychoanalytic movement. One of Freud's earliest therapeutic principles was that cure resulted from making the unconscious conscious (for example, see the case histories discussed in *Studies on Hysteria* [Breuer and Freud, 1895]). By "the unconscious" Freud was referring not only to forgotten memories but to current psychic processes within the patient of which the patient is unaware. The therapeutic goal of making the unconscious conscious was based on the presupposition that a major cause of psychopathology is the separation of anxiety-arousing thoughts and feelings from conscious awareness. According to this principle, all that was necessary for the therapist to do was to observe the various abnormal and normal preconscious and conscious derivatives of the unconscious, formulate the contents of the unconscious and its relationship to preconsciousness and consciousness, and then communicate this knowledge to the patient. A cure was anticipated contingent upon the patient's ability to cognitively understand the therapist's communication.

Later Freudian Theory

Freud soon learned that the basic therapeutic doctrine of an automatic cure by making the unconscious conscious was oversimplified and perhaps even potentially clinically dangerous. Repeatedly, Freud closely observed his patient, discovered the patient's unconscious motivation, and then communicated this knowledge to the patient. Sometimes the patient agreed with the formulation and would even change his (the patient's) intellectual and cognitive outlook on his symptoms. However, the emotional nature of the condition usually remained the same and sometimes deteriorated following the therapist's explanation of the unconscious dynamics. Freud learned early in his psychoanalytic career what many psychoanalytic therapists never learn: the fact that merely remembering a forgotten past experience or merely achieving intellectual insight does not have much capacity to change the motive forces responsible for intrapsychic conflict. Repression involves far more than making and/or keeping a psychical event unconscious.

And so, current psychoanalytic therapy is based on therapeutic principles different from those of the early Freudians, and Freud himself was instrumental in this change. The major difference from those earlier times is the added presupposition that some kind of emotional experience must be associated with the intellectual self-awareness in order that any clinical change result. The patient must not only know the forgotten wish or idea, but must feel the emotions associated with it. If this feeling-idea complex is kept from again slipping into unconsciousness, then the patient might learn to readjust to the situation in a more beneficial way than he did to the original situation.

In essence, then, later Freudian theory led to an expression of the principle that symptomatic relief results from more than just making the unconscious conscious. Most, if not all, contemporary psychoanalytically oriented psychotherapists agree that no matter how painful self-awareness might be, an increased awareness of the unconscious combined with the appropriate emotional experience will ultimately result in more peaceful, effective and mature resolutions or adaptations of the problems of intrapsychic and external life.

Supportive Psychoanalytically Oriented Psychotherapy

The basic concepts outlined in this section apply mostly to the "investigative" as opposed to the "supportive" forms of psychoanalytic therapy. However, psychoanalytically oriented therapists do sometimes deliver supportive therapy which is not aimed at an emotionally meaningful uncovering of unconscious pathogenic elements. Supportive psychoanalytically oriented psychotherapy, although still grounded on Freudian principles and still requiring extensive training in theory and technique, is based on the underlying assumption that derivative intrapsychic conflicts and symptoms can be significantly resolved without resolution or even awareness of primary and more basic unconscious intrapsychic conflicts and of the resistance and transference associated with those conflicts. The procedures by which symptomatic relief is achieved through supportive psychoanalytically oriented psychotherapy are rarely discussed in the literature, although Alexander (1954a) categorizes them into five groups: (1) the indulgence of dependency needs which in turn reduce anxiety; (2) abreaction; (3) advice (suggestion), which of course is often facilitated by the dependent relationship that the patient in supportive therapy often has with the therapist; (4) support of psychic defenses; defense mechanisms can be supported through verbally encouraging adaptive defenses and confronting maladaptive defenses (Gill, 1951); and (5) manipulation of the external environment.

THE PRESUPPOSED CONNECTION OF SERIAL ASSOCIATIONS

It is a rule of psycho-analytic technique that an internal [intrapsychic] connection which is still undisclosed will announce its presence by means of a contiguity—a temporal proximity—of associations; just as in writing, if "a" and "b" are put side by side, it means that the syllable "ab" is to be formed out of them" (Freud, 1905, Fragment of an Analysis of a Case of Hysteria, p. 39).

Another basic concept of psychoanalytic psychotherapy is that in listening to the patient's verbalizations, it is presupposed that associations that follow one another have some conscious or unconscious connection to each other. In fact, although the therapist certainly does not always learn the meaning of all communications, it is assumed that *every* expression of the patient during the session has one or more unconscious meanings. A corollary of this basic concept is that any and all of the patient's uninhibited, uncensored and freely expressed communication could and probably will eventually lead to the primary intrapsychic conflicts causing the symptoms for which the patient is in treatment. For example:

> Mrs. O is a 25-year-old woman with a long history of fear of sex to the point that she experienced severe pain during all attempts at intercourse. In discussing one of her recent unsuccessful attempts, she associated to her husband inadvertently hurting her during intercourse, a childhood incident in which one of the other children hit her on the head with a hammer, another childhood incident when she was struck on the head with a stone, and her father spanking her. All of these associations to sex have one thing in common, namely violence. Thus, she associates violence with sex, thereby giving some clue as to the reason for her fear of sex. The therapist has suspected that such was the case well over a year before this series of associations. However, it wasn't until the patient associated herself in this way that she became meaningfully consciously aware of the relationship between sex and violence in her mind and she essentially made the interpretation herself.

In carrying this basic concept of serial associations even further, it is assumed that each psychotherapy session is in some way related to a previous session or sessions. Of course, not all of the various associations, communications or meanings are of equal importance and one of the primary tasks of the therapist is to determine which material is of most clinical significance.

The Therapeutic Effects of Thoughts and Feelings as Opposed to Action

The removal of the symptoms of the illness is not specifically aimed at, but is achieved, as it were, as a by-product if the analysis [investigative psychoanalytic psychotherapy] *is properly carried through* (Freud, 1923a, p. 251).

A fundamental assumption of psychoanalytic psychotherapy is that there is a certain kind of influence possessed by the verbal and emotional expression of thoughts and feelings that is superior to the therapeutic influence of deeds. This principle is, at first glance, in direct opposition to the "behavior modification" approach, although there certainly are areas of convergence between learning theory and psychoanalytic theory that have useful clinical applications (Ainslie, in press; Feather and Rhoads, 1972). A basic concept of psychoanalytic psychotherapy is that it is usually more effective to verbalize and "feel" thoughts and feelings than to act out those thoughts and feelings. In fact, psychoanalytically oriented therapists often go so far as to say that it is frequently destructive to the patient's well-being for him to employ behavioral solutions to intrapsychic conflicts and anxiety. Emotional insight must come first, then behavioral changes will follow.

Of course, most psychoanalytic therapists would agree that in certain cases behavioral treatment might be quite appropriate and, in fact, achieve immediate symptomatic relief. Most psychoanalytically oriented therapists would, however, question whether any permanent solution is possible without some modification of the underlying intrapsychic conflict itself. Furthermore, the psychoanalytic psychotherapist is always concerned that the patient might employ behavioral attempts at cure as a way to avoid the psychic pain of dealing with the intrapsychic conflict. Such "acting out" frequently occurs with destructive denial and repression to a maladaptive degree (Langs, 1973, p. 164). If the "acting out" is minimized, then the verbal and emotional expressions will serve as stimulants for additional thoughts, feelings and insight, which are all considered to be superior to direct action.

A natural corollary to this basic concept is that the patient has nothing to fear from any thought or feeling, no matter how irrational that thought or feeling might seem. According to the psychoanalytic perspective, if behavior is encouraged as a substitute for thoughts and feelings, then the patient who lives in dread of his feelings and hidden thoughts will perceive the behavioral approach as confirming the fear. These perceptions will in turn reinforce maladaptive suppression and repression.

THE OCCURRENCE OF A DUPLICATION OF THE NEUROSIS WITHIN THE THERAPY

For a patient never forgets again what he has experienced in the form of transference; it carries a greater force of conviction than anything he can acquire in other ways Freud, 1940 [1938], p. 177).

Another basic doctrine of intensive psychoanalytic psychotherapy is that the various past and present psychic variables that are involved in pathogenesis of the mental disorder interact with each other during the course of the psychotherapy so that the neurosis is duplicated within the therapy itself.

The transference neurosis is the prototype by which the neurosis is expressed within the therapy. The first case history in which transference was fully discussed was Freud's report of Dora (Freud, 1905), an 18-year-old woman whom Freud treated in 1900. Most students of Freud consider the discovery of transference to be Freud's most significant contribution, since transference has proven to be the most effective process by which the patient can overcome the natural resistances to an aware-ness of those pathogenic painful thoughts and feelings that have been repressed into the unconscious.

Transference is a regressive phenomenon by which unconscious intrapsychic infantile and childhood conflicts are gradually and progressively mobilized, reexperienced and resolved in the current treatment setting (Freud, 1912). The revitalization of the conflict manifests itself in the interactional processes occurring between the therapist and patient and thus a psychical reality and an affective impression are achieved for the patient. Of course, the totality of one's life cannot be resurrected in the transference. Clinical experience has shown, however, that the most significant pathogenic intrapsychic conflicts that were once reflected in a child-family relationship will invariably be reflected in the relationship between the adult patient and therapist if the therapist has the knowledge and technical skill to facilitate the process (Alexander, 1954b).

As Freud (1914) emphasized, transference is formed with all people at all places and at all times. However, psychoanalysis (Bird, 1972; Orr, 1954; Szasz, 1963) and the intensive investigative type of psychoanalytically oriented psychotherapy differ from all other situations in which transference occurs in that these treatment modalities first of all purposively attempt to facilitate the formation of keenly sensitive transferences and, secondly, attempt to observe and learn from the transference phenomena without acting them out.

The therapeutic goal of "investigative" or "uncovering" psychoanalytic therapy is for the patient to master the transference neurosis. (The resolution of the transference neurosis will not occur if the therapist employs the techniques of "supportive" therapy mentioned above.) In investigative psychoanalytic psychotherapy, the patient experiences the intrapsychic conflicts within the contemporary transference neurosis as if the conflicts were the original pathogenic problem. The primary conflict, however, usually is resurrected in a less intense form than in its original (usually childhood) situation. By utilizing the therapeutic alliance and by reexperiencing the conflicts within the contemporary transference situation, the patient is able to apply his more adult secondary process modes of thinking and reality testing to the old problem. Since the patient is now an adult and has undergone ego development and maturation, he is less helpless and less impotent to find resolutions to the conflicts that he experienced as a child. Furthermore, since the transference is a somewhat reduced duplication of the original intrapsychic conflict, the patient not only has more ego with which to work, but also is confronted with a weaker conflict. Another favorable element in the treatment setting is the therapist's reaction to the patient's transference behavior. The therapist's behavior should be less intimidating and less punitive than that of the parents of childhood and so once again the transference situation facilitates resolution of the intrapsychic conflict (Alexander, 1954b). A resolution of the conflicts on this second time around not only alleviates symptoms, but often frees the patient from previous maturational retardation that might have occurred as a result of the conflict.

The concept of transference is also discussed by Meissner, Nadelson and Gurman (Chapters II, III, and IX of this volume).

MARITAL THERAPY

by Carol Cooperman Nadelson, M.D.

Organization and Format

The rest of this chapter consists of five main sections and two appendices. The first section, entitled "General Considerations" consists of a general discussion of the psychoanalytic perspective of the marital relationship as it involves choice of mate, intrapsychic processes and marital conflict.

The second section, entitled "Formats of Marital Therapy," discusses some of the theories, advantages and disadvantages of individual therapy with collaborating and non-collaborating individual therapists, conjoint therapy, co-therapists, and couples group therapy. There is also a discussion of combined, individual and conjoint sessions with a co-therapist. The author favors this combined format.

The third section, entitled "Psychoanalytic Considerations of the Therapy Process" deals with four psychoanalytic concepts that are fundamental to psychoanalytically oriented marital therapy: transference, countertransference, resistance, and the therapeutic alliance.

The fourth section is entitled "The Evaluative Process" and is a discussion of the various principles and procedures by which the author evaluates a couple in the initial few sessions. The evaluation process focuses on: (1) psychic processes of each spouse, including the ego strengths and weaknesses; (2) motivation for treatment; (3) goals of therapy; and (4) establishing a therapeutic alliance. These concepts are exemplified and amplified by 19 examples from the author's clinical experience. The clinical examples throughout this chapter not only serve to clarify the various concepts discussed but also give the reader some idea as to how the psychoanalytically oriented marital therapist conceptualizes his clinical cases and the terms he uses in describing these patients. The concepts and terms used in these clinical examples can be contrasted to the concepts and terms used in the chapters of this book written by the behaviorists and systems theorists. It is assumed that both marital partners should be evaluated even if individual therapy for only one of them is the eventual disposition. An underlying theme of this section is that an inaccurate or incomplete evaluative process in the initial sessions will significantly reduce, if not outrightly negate, the chances of a constructive therapeutic alliance and a successful clinical course of marital therapy.

The fifth section is entitled "Stages of Couples Treatment" and entails a discussion of the initial, middle and terminal stages of marital therapy, acknowledging, of course, that the "stages" exist only for purposes of clarity of presentation, since in reality much overlap occurs. As in the other sections, this discussion entails the application of psychoanalytic concepts and techniques (for example, transference, resistance and interpretation) to marital therapy. There is, however, material that is not usually considered part of any "psychoanalytic" treatment, such as a brief discussion of the use of videotapes in psychoanalytically oriented marital therapy. Again, as in the previous section, clinical examples are offered.

The sixth and seventh sections are Appendix A and B which are reproductions of questionnaires given to all couples being evaluated for marital therapy at the Department of Psychiatry, Beth Israel Hospital, in Boston.

GENERAL CONSIDERATIONS

Success in marriage has been defined on the basis of endurance, absence of marital counseling, and reported or judged happiness. While these assessments are operational, they neglect the observation that many marriages are far from ideal, yet never reach the stage of divorce, separation, or marital therapy for reasons having little to do with marital adjustment and more to do with cultural and intrapsychic factors.

The marital relationship requires that individual partners bring together preexisting psychological and cultural histories which may be quite disparate. In addition, expectations are often romanticized fantasies, rather than reality based. The idea that "love conquers all" does not account for the complexities involved in the development of a working partnership. Couples often expect that they must share goals, understand and accept each other totally, and be satisfied and happy simultaneously. Furthermore, romantic expectations often preclude consideration of the realities of daily life or of the developmental changes which occur as individuals proceed through life.

Values in marriage have undergone a radical change in the past century. They have shifted from an emphasis on survival and economic security to a focus on companionship, love and communication. This shift has involved changes in societal expectations as well as in individual development and goals. Self-fulfillment is a value that has superseded more traditional concerns about family loyalties and responsibilities. Thus, rather than attempt to resolve conflict, the couple often sees divorce as a solution to frustration and disappointment. Weiss (1975) comments that the rising divorce rate appears to be related to the "intensity of our impatience with barriers to self-realization" (p. 8).

Another societal change of considerable importance has been the emergence of the women's movement and the implications of changing roles and expectations for women. This has brought new demands, fulfillments and conflicts for the individual and for the family. While the conceptualization of marriage as an adult partnership between equals, with specific sex roles and characteristics, is not a new one (Erikson, 1950), this concept has evolved in a way that questions assumptions about gender-determined roles and expectations. The partnership concept has taken on new dimensions. The style of marriage has shifted from that of two closely intertwined persons with clearly designated gender-determined roles to that of two independent people with individual goals, style and personalities.

Recent work in adult development (Levinson. Darrow, Klein, Levinson and McKee, 1974; Gould, 1972; Butler, 1968; Lidz, 1968; Neugarten and Datan, 1974) has indicated that important developmental shifts occur throughout life, thus expanding previous work on the life cycle and normative stages of development.

The concept of a marital life cycle has also evolved (Blanck and Blanck, 1968; Berman and Leif, 1975). Critical stages in the individual life cycle are related to critical stages in marriage. Thus, issues that appear to be either individually determined or dyadic often result from the interaction between marital and individual crisis points (Berman and Leif, 1975). During the course of marriage, there is a shift of tasks, expectations and demands. Children are born, careers wax and wane, relationships with relatives and friends change, and the physical environment varies. Complementary shifts may not occur in a partner, thus disturbing the homeostatic balance of the relationship and potentially producing conflict.

According to the psychoanalytic perspective, intrapsychic factors, conscious and especially unconscious, exert a significant influence on marital object choices and affect the quality of the relationship, the nature of interactions with spouse and children, and the kinds of conflicts and resolutions which are possible.

The purpose of this chapter is to focus on the psychoanalytic view of intrapsychic influences on the marital system, the implications these have for therapy, and the approach that this perspective provides. In any consideration of the psychoanalytic approach to the understanding and treatment of marital conflict, it is important to differentiate the theoretical framework and the language used to conceptualize the individual and couple dynamics from the treatment process. The understanding obtained from this perspective provides a framework for therapy; however, the technique as applied may or may not differ from the technical procedures and interventions used by those approaching marital problems from a different theoretical model. The difference is, of course, that the technique discussed in this chapter is applied with a psychoanalytic operational theory of psychic functioning and human behavior.

Choice of a Mate

The choice of a marital partner is one of life's most difficult decisions. Most often the ambivalence which is experienced is based on the uncertainty of predicting future events and behaviors, as well as anxiety about the possibility that feelings will change and that, despite attempts at working out the complexities of a relationship, it will fail for unknown or uncontrollable reasons. As we will see, psychoanalytically oriented marital therapy focuses on some of the unconscious determinants of marital choice.

Freud (1914) formulated an individually based theory in which object choices were seen as anaclitically or narcissistically based. The person who makes an anaclitic choice is oriented primarily toward nurturance and protection, and is focused primarily on the gratification of dependency needs. A narcissistic choice is made by a person who sees himself or herself as the object. The person who is chosen represents the ideal self or a projected ego ideal; or is chosen in an attempt to recapture a past self, a projected past object, or a person who was once part of the self. The chosen partner may represent a part of the self, i.e., "my wife is my phallus" (Stein, 1956, p. 66). This is often expressed in discussions of the spouse as "my better half."

Part of the process of selection of a mate is based on unconscious signals by which the partners recognize in each other the possibility that they can jointly work through unresolved conflicts which exist intrapsychically in each of them. Mate selection can allow for the identification with the loving aspects of parents and parental introjects and relieve rivalries and repressed sexual feelings.

The choice of a mate can also fulfill frustrated longings and allow new opportunities for self-realization. At the same time, partners sense that mutual defenses and collusive "joint resistance" will prevent working through and integration (Dicks, 1963). Thus, marriage can become a repository for old conflicts (Main, 1966). The projection of archaic objects onto the spouse may back a couple into a sadomasochistic type of interaction, with the partner bearing the hated aspects of the self. The partner then ceases to exist as a separate object.

The ultimate goal of a relationship is the fusion of the ideal self with the projected ideal spouse. However, since the fantasy about the chosen object must face the reality of who that person is, each individual can only approach this fantasy goal. There is a degree of profound unconscious ambivalence in the choice of object. As discussed in more detail by Meissner in the previous chapter, the level of psychological readiness to make the commitment to an intense object relationship is an important factor in the success of a marriage. While some individuals have attained a level of differentiation and individuation which prepares them to cope with the tasks of marriage, others are burdened by unresolved early conflicts, unrealistic expectations (conscious or unconscious), or severe psychological deficits which make the resolution of marital tasks more difficult. Those individuals who enter a marriage in less differentiated developmental stages can grow toward maturity within the marriage; however, those who either cannot cope or cannot resolve infantile desires are vulnerable to disturbance if their goals for the marriage differ from their spouse's goals.

Marriage can foster development in a number of important ways (Blanck and Blanck, 1968). While these have been discussed by Meissner in Chapter II of this book, they will be summarized since they have an important bearing on therapy. The establishment of a close and sexual relationship offers the opportunity for partners to work through the prohibitions and inhibitions of childhood in the context of the establishment of a new level of object relations. This involves the ability to relate with another person on a reciprocal basis. It implies that individual development has proceeded beyond the stage of need gratification and that separation from early objects has occurred. The self must be perceived as autonomous.

Marriage does, however, present a paradox, especially for people who marry before they have resolved the critical tasks of adolescence—separation and identity consolidation. The marital agreement, symbolized in the marriage ceremony, requests that the two become one. Or in the words of the Bible, Genesis I:24: "For this cause shall a man leave father and mother and shall cleave to his wife and the twain shall be one flesh." Yet, the task of developing and maintaining a separate identity is an important developmental issue. For those whose conflicts around separation-individuation actually precipitated the desire to marry, the need for dependency gratification may be projected onto the partner, who then becomes the parent in fantasy, and the developmental tasks of adolescence are not mastered. If, however, the individual can integrate these opposing forces, a new level of ego control is possible and new opportunities for identifications are possible. When this process occurs in the more autonomous environment of adulthood, rather than in adolescence, infantile pressures are less intense and the danger of object loss or identity diffusion is less fearsome. Thus, less anxiety is experienced and greater choice is possible.

The Marital Relationship and Intrapsychic Process

The marital relationship has been seen as consisting of two fully differentiated individuals, both with clear sex roles, who work together to satisfy each other, themselves and their responsibilities to society (Erikson, 1968). This is further specified by Fairbairn's (1954) conception of mature dependence which "is characterized by a capacity on the part of a differentiated individual for cooperative relationships with differentiated objects . . . it is a relationship involving evenly matched giving and taking between two differentiated individuals who are mutually dependent, and between whom there is no disparity of dependence" (p. 145). This statement describes an idealized state which is never actually realized, because no individual reaches the point in development where a state of non-libidinally demanding object relatedness can be obtained. In the ideal two-person relationship each partner is seen by the other as a separate individual with his or her own desires and needs. Within this ideal dyad, there is an attempt by each partner to fulfill both his or her own needs and those of the partner, without resorting to pregenital or infantile modes of interpersonal interaction. However, while the idealized state exists in theory, it is not likely that the kind of interaction proposed is attained consistently and predictably, even in those individuals who attain a level of development where mutuality is possible. Some of the reasons for this relate to complex intrapsychic and interactional phenomena.

In the previous chapter, Meissner has considered in detail the individual psychological structure as it evolves and begins to establish a marital dyad. He has discussed concepts of interaction and need complementarity and has emphasized the clinical observation that individuals of equivalent degree of maturity and self-differentiation are attracted to each other. In order to help elucidate some of these aspects of psychological development and to extend the propositions and hypotheses presented as they relate to treatment, this chapter will review attachment and its ramifications in object relations theory.

The early attachment between mother and child has been shown to be a critical experience (Bowlby, 1968). If there is not "good enough mothering" to provide an attachment experience, subsequent personality development is impaired (Winnicott, 1965). The first object relationship, that between mother and child, is therefore of primary importance, and it affects the pattern of subsequent relationships, including marriage. The nature of the original object ties is precarious and unpredictable, as a consequence of the realities of the process and requirements of mothering. Thus there are many instances where suspicion and even rejection of object relationships later in life, deriving from early difficulties, are inevitable. All individuals have some degree of mistrust and reluctance to be giving and loving because past attempts have not always or consistently been reciprocated (Fairbairn, 1954). When the individual reaches adolescence and powerful new libidinal drives emerge and create conflict between the wish to regress to earlier objects and the desire to move toward new ones, he or she not only defends against the intensity of the pressure to form new object ties, but may also feel incapable of loving and drive the love object away in anticipation of disappointment. Thus, in addition to the importance of early life experiences which were in reality unsatisfactory, anticipation of object loss or disappointment by the object may play an important role in the development of adult object ties.

Ambivalence, then, is a part of early object relations, and ego development occurs by passage through a succession of positions of ambivalence toward objects. This begins with the "good" and "bad" objects of early infancy and evolves toward an integration of ambivalence which can be tolerated in the self and in others without the necessity of splitting the antithetical components from each other (Dicks, 1963). This provides a basis for an internalized object constancy, where anger, aggression and absence can be tolerated and mastered.

Since marriage is the nearest adult equivalent to the original parent-child relationship, an important condition for a marriage is to allow freedom for bringing out the deepest infantile and regressive issues without loss of dignity or security, knowing that the partner accepts, because he or she can projectively identify or tolerate, as a good parent, the neediness of the other. For some people, then, the search for a mate may be for a person who can be unconditionally loving, permissive and strong, so that all part objects can be fused. For them the ideal mate is a good parent and they may repeatedly fail, or find a partner who complements them in this need (Dicks, 1963). This ability to regress, to return to a state of helplessness and lack of control without feeling threatened with annihilation, is crucial for adult sexuality, as well as for adult interaction at other levels. It implies a capacity to trust and to conceptualize oneself as separate from the object.

Marital Conflict

Marital conflict occurs because of differences in beliefs, interests, desires, values, or expectations as well as from competition between the partners, or differences in life stage or intrapsychic organization. Conflict, however, is not necessarily destructive (Deutsche, 1969). Productive conflict may be characterized by mutual recognition of different interests, open and honest communication, and the presence of trust. If this occurs, both parties can find creative solutions to their differences. Destructive conflicts are characterized by tendencies to rely on strategies of power, tactics of threat, coercion and deception. This leads to mutual suspicion, lack of communication, and disappointment.

Historically, psychoanalytically oriented therapists have concentrated primarily on individual psychodynamics and psychic conflict in people who sought consultation for marital conflict. They have tended to place less emphasis on the significance of the object tie and the contributions of the partner in the system. The opposite view, that it is possible for a marriage to be non-functional without the partners demonstrating significant individual pathology, has been proposed by the systems theorists. From this systems oriented perspective, the marital therapist would focus on how the partners view themselves and the people in their lives; how the partners perceive their problems, the gratification sought, and the original expectations of the marriage, the changes occurring in the marriage, and the precipitants of the current therapeutic contact. Individual histories and individual dynamic formulations would not necessarily be relevant. The best integrative view of the etiology of marital psychopathology is that masked, or double bind, communications arising from a "collusive" process which are built on mutual "projective identifications" bind the partners together in a relationship around which a "joint ego boundary" develops (Dicks, 1967). The double bind communication is used by each partner to protect himself or herself, the partner and the dyad from his or her own *unconscious* objects, which are perceived as potentially destructive and thus must be disguised, denied or projected. The marriage, then, serves a defensive purpose. Instead of growth promotion, e.g., strengthening of object relationships and final resolution of oedipal ties, it is used to defend against a fear of symbolic merger, loss of identity, depression, or object loss or to prove a stage of object relatedness or gender identity, e.g., heterosexual competence. Communication and closeness then might threaten the ego because they would make available material that has been kept from consciousness since infancy, when the primary objects were split off because they were threatening. The psychoanalytic concept of projective identification has been discussed by Meissner in Chapter II of this book. Here we will focus on this mechanism as it affects marital disturbances and treatment.

When the individual has had an unsatisfactory parental figure who has not satisfied early needs, the relationship becomes frustrating, and arouses hate and anger. That relationship (the libidinal cathexis to that object) is split off from the ego and repressed. It lies dormant until reactivated by a new situation of intimacy, i.e., marriage recalls it. At this time the ego must renew its defensive processes to keep the infantile affects from awareness because the demands also recreate the fears and frustrations of the childhood experience.

Since inevitably each individual will have repressed elements which will be reactivated, degrees of regression will occur. In a healthy relationship, the partners will accept and tolerate these without causing a loss of dignity or self-esteem. If the relationship does not allow for this process, then both partners must employ defensive maneuvers to deny the dependent needy parts of themselves (Dicks, 1963). Problems are intensified when children are born because their neediness and demands more actively seek fulfillment and reactivate infantile disappointment, acutely and unrelentingly. The parent may defend by identification with the lost part of himself or herself in the child, or may even reject the child. With each developmental stage of the child, new challenges emerge which must be reconciled with the individual developmental issues of the parents and with the developmental process of the marriage.

The mature individual accepts the partner as a whole object, including the dependent and regressive part, whereas the pathological relationship maintains the collusive dyadic system which cannot tolerate communication without threatening disruption of a fragile balance. If the defenses and collusive resistances are too rigid, then they can cause individual distress and symptom formation, and even threaten each partner's sense of identity. Thus, the infantile situation is repeated, but not resolved, making further maturation difficult or impossible (Ackerman, 1958). For both marital partners defensive processes maintain the repression of the split-off parts of the ego, and thus preserve the shaky self-image of the individual. However, for the marriage to maintain its balance, each partner must remain as the other wishes him or her to be, and must also remain as she or he wishes to be. Any change in the system reactivates defensive rather than adaptive mechanisms.

In addition to the collusive mechanism, idealization can also be used defensively. Idealization is a process by which an object is aggrandized without any alteration in its nature (Freud, 1914). The partner can deny ambivalent hate or anger and project these onto the partner, who then becomes the hated object. The partner, however, may also project the good onto the other and retain the negative components himself or herself, thus becoming bad. The partner, then, is no longer a real object, and mutuality cannot be established or developed. The development of symptomatology and regressive behavior occurs if there is pressure to bring previously repressed ambivalent feelings to consciousness. The collusive sharing of idealizations is protective. Thus, a couple can live in what appears to the observer to be an unsatisfactory balance, but it is perceived unconsciously by those involved as less dangerous than the repressed affects.

The attempt to complete the self entirely or in part through a union is an element of this collusive process. This type of interaction can result in one partner being seen as sadistic or persecutory toward the other, in the same way as the original lost object was toward that individual. Mutual accusations occur: *"You made me,"* rather than internalization of responsibility for an act or feeling: *"I get upset when. . . ."* This projective identification toward the spouse closely resembles the transference of the analytic situation (which will be discussed in more detail later) and provides a conceptual bridge between an understanding of individual and interpersonal psychodynamics.

The frustration of infantile needs by the partner may result in the manifestation of the other side of the ambivalence toward that partner. The collusive partner may likewise become more manifestly ambivalent, and regression in both occurs. Each partner blames the other and thus does not experience himself or herself as playing any part in the interactional conflict. On the other hand, if the need for idealization is sufficient, one partner may accept all of the guilt and blame to maintain the goodness of the other partner. It is clear that many embattled marriages are sustained by this collusive process.

The existence of joint ego boundaries is exemplified by the appearance of signs of psychopathology in a non-patient spouse when the patient begins to improve (Oberndorf, 1934; Kohl, 1962). Fixed or overdrawn complementary patterns may represent a discrepancy between the demands of the marital role and unconscious conflict around activity-passivity, dominance-submission, or other polarized ambivalent needs. The partners may assume one part and be unable to relinquish that role despite circumstances which call for more flexible coping or adaptive capacities. Thus, a partner may be seen as the aggressor in order to justify the other partner's hostile and aggressive feelings toward the object and to dissipate guilt about these feelings. The examples of stereotyped, macho or compliant masochistic behavior are often responses to conflict about the opposite affect or impulse. Each partner reflects anxiety about the emergence of repressed part objects. In each there is also provocation and permission provided by the response. Each party may retreat to martyrdom or pseudo-cooperation in order to avoid open conflict (Dicks, 1953). These roles may be exerted as a means of repressing, suppressing or denying the opposite. Passivity may be a defense against aggression, and aggression defends against passive longings. These roles require a compliant or complementary spouse to be successful; they cannot exist without a reciprocal.

A classification of marital relationships based on complementary interaction of mates has been developed (Mittleman, 1948). The patterns of interaction described are: one partner emotionally detached, the other craving affection; rivalry between the partners for aggressive dominance; one partner helpless, the other ostensibly strong, but in reality seeking the dependent role; and one of the mates alternating between periods of dependency and self assertion while the other alternates between periods of helplessness and unsatisfied need for affection. In these relationships both partners may find security, satisfaction and enhancement of their self-esteem through mutual support. The dependent partner feels safer with a strong mate, while the "stronger" supporting partner allays his or her unconscious fear of helplessness and abandonment by helping. The danger is the potential for the helper to identify with the helpless, or for the partner not to live up to expectations or follow the assigned role consistently, making the deficiencies of the other partner more apparent.

Marital patterns which are frequently seen clinically because of the conflict which arises include: the relationship between the "hysterical" wife and "obsessional" husband where intimacy is limited; the "hysterical" husband and "obsessional" wife where dependency issues are most prominent; the relationship between two people with similar rather than complementary dynamics where each expects the other to be the responsible need gratifier; and the paranoid relationship where mistrust and jealousy are often overwhelming (Martin, 1976). Other types of partnership combination classifications have been focused on the profile of each partner and the complementary mate, thus clarifying the interactional dimensions. Partner profiles include equal, romantic, parental, childlike, rational, companionate and parallel (Sager, 1976). Each of these combines in a pattern of interaction at conscious and unconscious levels.

While these are described in terms of behavioral variables or intrapsychic conflict, some consideration must be given to sociocultural determinants and expectations, as well as to developmental stages and issues. All of these patterns involve the conflict between fantasy and reality, explicit and implicit, conscious and unconscious understanding of expectations, obligations and roles. These vary at different times during the life cycle of the marriage and of the individuals. The concept of marital contracts, written and unwritten, is an ancient one. It has been discussed in the contemporary literature as a way of understanding each individual's expressed and unexpressed, conscious and unconscious concepts of the obligations, expectations and roles of both partners. These contracts range from being externally detailed written contracts to verbal communications which may be reinforced and renegotiated periodically (Sager, 1976; Martin, 1976).

While the terms of the marriage contract are determined by unconscious expectations of each partner, the individual is usually not aware that attempts to fulfill the partner's needs are based on the fantasy that his or her own wishes would thereby be fulfilled; the individual is also unaware of the expectations of his or her mate. As a result, when aspects of the contract are not fulfilled, the disappointed partner may respond as if an actual contract had been broken. A schematic model of the contract includes: a level of conscious, verbalized expectations where each partner tells the other about his or her expectations; a conscious but not verbalized level where expectations, plans, beliefs and fantasies are not verbalized; and the unconscious level (Sager et al., 1971). An understanding and clarification of these contracts may become an explicit part of marital therapy (Sager, 1976).

FORMATS OF MARITAL THERAPY

While a variety of procedures and techniques have been proposed to deal with marital problems and the indications and contraindications of each have been discussed, it is important to emphasize that each therapist brings another viewpoint and style and that there is no infallible technique or answer to the multiple and complex problems of this work. The reader must bear in mind Marmor's (1966) admonition that no one therapy has been proven better than others, but that favorable results may depend more upon the therapist's personal characteristics, empathic capacity and clinical maturity rather than on his or her theoretical inclinations.

Methods of diagnosis and classification, as well as treatment rationales, are based on the utilization of psychoanalytic, role, systems and learning theories. Since these theoretical positions are increasingly more often combined and tailored to the needs of each couple, the therapist should have an understanding of the principles of each orientation and its therapeutic application. Frequently, semantic systems and interactional models are deceptive. Therapeutic principles and procedures may not differ as much as their theoretical underpinnings would lead us to believe.

While this chapter will focus on the therapeutic interventions which derive from psychoanalytic theory, it is important to emphasize that a theoretical perspective deriving from psychoanalytic theory does not necessarily commit the therapist to psychoanalysis or to psychoanalytically oriented psychotherapy. Recent work in the area of sexual dysfunctions has amply demonstrated the usefulness of understanding psychoanalytic principles, while using an approach to therapy which relies heavily on learning and systems approaches (Kaplan, 1974). When a patient presents with sexual symptoms, the therapist can prescribe a sensate focus exercise to help him or her experience sexual feelings, while an interpretation of underlying conflict can be made from the patient's verbal productions.

Marital therapy has been proposed as a treatment of choice when (1) techniques of individual psychotherapy have failed or cannot be used; (2) a patient has a sudden onset of symptoms related to marital conflicts; (3) it is requested by a couple directly because of conflict and stress which they are unable to resolve; (4) it appears that improvement in a patient involved in individual psychotherapy will result in a change in the equilibrium of the marriage and cause increased conflict (Haley, 1963).

The field of marital therapy, from whatever perspective it derives, is no longer oriented at only one level. It can be understood descriptively, genetically and functionally (Ackerman, 1958). At a descriptive level, one can delineate groups of symptoms such as sexual failure, economic or social failure, etc.; at a genetic level, one can focus on the dynamic evolution of a relationship and trace the impact of life phases, including courtship, early marriage, the arrival of the first child, and the expansion of the family with more children; and at a functional level, marital disharmony may be seen as related to perceptual distortion (transference), disturbances of communication, frustrated dependency needs, threats to adaptive defenses, fears of the unfamiliar, and unresolved conflicts with parents. It is possible, however, to focus on one aspect of the marital problem and develop treatment plans accordingly. For example, in terms of conflicting levels of communication, one can focus on the reciprocal interaction of the couple rather than on the domination or dependency of one partner (Haley, 1963), and work with a couple on communication.

The major methods of treating couples from a psychoanalytic perspective are based on an initial decision about whether to use a more supportive or counseling orientation, stressing sociocultural factors and focusing on the implications of the current life situation, or an exploratory approach which proceeds in greater depth, is less directive, uses psychoanalytic principles to understand and treat the couple, and concerns itself with unconscious motivation and conflict. It may also include the use of interpretation, and the resolution of the transference situation.

A therapeutic approach may be focused on ordering the environment, resolving crises, or understanding the reciprocal interaction between the two partners. This may be done by working with the two partners separately or together. The following section discusses the various formats of psychoanalytically oriented marital therapy. There are three general categories: one therapist, co-therapists, and group therapy. Of course, there is some overlap in these categorizations. For example, co-therapists could see the spouses individually, conjointly, or collaboratively with other co-therapists. Also, despite the fact that this chapter is about the application of psychoanalytic principles to marital therapy, there is nothing about these formats that is unique to the psychoanalytic approach; the same formats could be applied to the behavioral and systems theory perspective.

Individual Therapy

No spouse inclusion or therapist collaboration

Explorative marital therapy has been performed in a number of different ways. The classical psychoanalytic approach to the treatment of marital partners is for each to be seen individually by a therapist or analyst who does not see the spouse or collaborate with the other's therapist. In a couple where one or the other partner has intrapsychic issues contributing in a major way to the problems of the couple, and/or where the other partner has the ability to change as the partner in treatment changes, significant improvement can result from an individual approach. "Successful resolution of the marriage problems by this method necessitates a patient with basic ego strengths which allow for structural changes and continuing problem solving without dependency upon initiating change in the marriage partner" (Martin, 1976, p. 110). Among the advantages of this technique are: (1) It requires that individuals assume responsibility for personal growth and change. (2) It presupposes that unresolved individual conflicts seriously interfere with the ability to effectively negotiate the marital relationship. (3) It allows for independent work especially where one partner has decided upon divorce

(Cookerly, 1973). (4) It protects the confidentiality of partners where there are secrets (for example, extramarital affairs, homosexuality, past history of illness or prison term). While the issue of maintaining secrets can and has been debated, it is likely that "secrets" are usually known by the partner. The individual must assume the ultimate responsibility for disclosure.

Other advantages of this approach are its success with individuals who are threatened by the inclusion of their partner, who are narcissistic, paranoid or who have major problems with sibling rivalry. In addition, when mates have different goals and expectations, it is sometimes advantageous for them to explore these and search for independent solutions.

This approach has been criticized because it has been reported, in about 7 percent of cases, to result in serious psychological disturbances in the mate (Sager, Gundlach, Kremer, Lenz, and Royce, 1968), it may have no effect at all on the marital disturbance, and it has also been cited as a cause of marital dissolution. In addition, it is long, expensive and may involve the individuals in issues they are unwilling or unable to pursue. In this approach, the therapist is unaware of the nature of the interaction or of distortions, denial, omissions or projections which may occur. Likewise, the therapist may be unable to recognize serious problems in the partner or to facilitate communication and problem solving.

CLINICAL EXAMPLE #1: INDIVIDUAL THERAPY—SPOUSE NOT INCLUDED

Mrs. A, a 28-year-old teacher, married for three years, requested therapy because she felt increasingly less interested in her husband and sexually attracted to other men. She expressed ambivalence about ending the marriage because she objectively felt that her husband was a "good person" with whom she had much to share, and she was uncertain about the reasons for the change in her response to him. She requested individual therapy and did not want her husband included because she felt that he would be hurt and angered if he knew of a recent affair with a mutual friend. She was seen in intensive psychoanalytically oriented psychotherapy twice a week for six months. During this time the role of her unresolved oedipal conflicts in her search for another more sexually attractive man became increasingly apparent. She began psychoanalysis at this time, focusing on her intense desire to please her father and her competitiveness with her mother. She became aware that she viewed her husband as very different from her father and that this factor had played a significant part in her choice of him. The affair she'd had was with a man who more closely resembled her father in his manner and way of relating to her. The realization of these factors and her ability to work through the oedipal issues resulted in her decision to remain with Mr. A and to make a commitment to the marriage.

Consecutive therapy with same therapist

Consecutive psychotherapy is more of historical interest since it was proposed early as a form of marital therapy (Oberndorf, 1934). This technique in which the same therapist treats one spouse, terminates when clinically indicated, and then treats the other spouse was seen as adding clarity to the marital conflict areas because the therapist or analyst could recognize in the second partner some of the unresolved issues in the first and the partner could benefit from the fact that the analyst or therapist had clarified his or her understanding. In addition, the complementarity of neurotic problems would be clearer. Among the disadvantages of this technique are the length of time before the second partner is involved, the competition generated, the negative responses of the first partner to giving up the therapist or analyst, the conflict in allegiances and other sibling-related issues, and the potential countertransference problems in the therapist or analyst. In addition, differing goals in the therapy or analysis may not be adequately addressed if marital goals are defined as primary.

Concurrent therapy with same therapist

In this format, both spouses are simultaneously but individually treated by the same therapist. This format was proposed because the therapist or analyst can obtain a more comprehensive picture of the realities of the interaction (Mittleman, 1948). Since the relative advantages and risks are understood, the opportunity for changing the emphasis of interpretation is possible. In addition, information can be obtained which might not be otherwise recognized and might be highly significant, especially if it can be worked with to affect the interaction with the spouse. Most of the criticisms of this approach involve the problem of resolution of the transference neurosis, since the essence of the transference projection is the patient's self-representation (Giovacchini, 1965). When the analyst has a relationship with both spouses, there may be competition and confusion in the transference, and in the countertransference. In addition, confidentiality is more apt to be a problem because each partner may be fearful that it will be violated; in fact, the therapist or analyst may be more vulnerable to violation because of the increased difficulty of keeping the partners clear and separate. In addition, problems of competitiveness may arise and block therapeutic work if they are severe.

Concurrent therapy with different but collaborating therapists

Collaborative therapy where the marital partners are treated by different therapists who communicate with each other has also been called stereotypic therapy (Bird and Martin, 1956). With this approach, the understanding of reality distortions may lead to the rapid recognition of defense mechanisms and the impulses behind them. The presence of two collaborating therapists provides a broader perspective and may diminish some of the potential pitfalls of the consecutive or current techniques with regard to competition, revelation of secrets, or countertransference problems.

The major problem with this technique is that each therapist tends to defend his or her own patient, often related to the countertransference. The therapists must work out this problem. If the therapists meet regularly, it is possible that the resistance to the recognition of this phenomenon can be dealt with early in the process. This approach also intrudes on the cofidentiality of the therapist-patient relationship. It may become problematic if therapists have different status and ability, or even different vacation plans, office furnishings or patterns of work.

Conjoint Therapy

Conjoint therapy is where both partners are seen together in the same session by the same therapist. It is currently the most widely used modality. Recommendations for conjoint couple therapy are made in family relationships where distortions are gross and reality-disruptive, and where speed in halting family disintegration is critical. Conjoint couple therapy is also recommended for couples where the problems involve acting out and are of a characterological nature. It can also be useful where the partners are "poorly motivated" and "not ready" for individual treatment (Watson, 1963). In addition, it may be important to include both partners in a program when one is severely disturbed, since a relationship in which equilibrium is based on one partner's mental illness is unstable. As has often been noted, when the "sick" partner improves, the "healthy" one may develop difficulties. Conjoint therapy may also be combined with individual sessions and has extended to include other family members. Conjoint sessions may be indicated at different times in the individual treatment process, since among other advantages it can help to "concretize" gains made in other forms of therapy (Brody, 1961). The therapist may use a psychoanalytic approach or be oriented toward a system focus or behavior therapy. In each case the technique varies. Conjoint therapy is seen as effective and economical. It may focus at varying degrees of depth. It involves an intense level of interaction between the partners, and also actively includes the therapist. The interaction evolves rapidly and has the potential for clarifying the homeostatic balance of the system early. Mutually shared communications reinforce that balance and if change occurs both partners participate.

In the conjoint format, the underlying interpersonal dynamics are more rapidly apparent, as well as the conscious and unconscious aspects of the marital contract. It is possible to reinforce mutual strivings and interdependent needs while ameliorating mistrust and hostility. Spouses also have the opportunity to understand each other in greater depth and thus to develop empathy as well as the ability to perceive the spouse as separable and real. The therapist has the advantage of being able to directly observe and evaluate behavior, thus limiting distortion, and he or she may have an opportunity to focus on the positive aspects of the relationship and to reinforce mutual goals and desires. The therapist may also be better able to limit destructive behavior and to facilitate the development of the observing ego of each partner so as to enable them to reality test more effectively (Martin, 1976).

This form has been recommended when marital problems are acute and ego alien (Grunebaum, Christ and Neiberg, 1969). If a marriage is imminently about to dissolve, it is not likely that conjoint therapy will be effective since in that circumstance the spouses are rarely willing or able to work with each other in a positive direction, or to reach an agreement about the goals of therapy. Thus, it is not the severity or type of pathology that determines the recommendation for conjoint therapy, but the motivation to work together, the commitment to the marriage, the acuteness of symptomatology, and the discomfort of the partners.

Among the disadvantages of this modality are the possibility that the partners may unite with each other and project onto the therapist their negative feelings about authoritarian or omnipotent parents, and thus potentially defeat the therapist's efforts to effect change. Another problem is that the partners may have differing goals and expectations, and the confrontation with this may be destructive, especially if the therapist is unable to effectively intervene, or an intensely pathological conflict of one or both partners emerges. Suggested contraindications to conjoint therapy include inadequate tolerance of anxiety, inability to control hostility within a therapy session, one partner who is actively psychotic, fragility of defenses of one partner, severe character disorders, patients with paranoid reactions, patients with excessive sibling rivalry or attitudes that preclude the sharing of a therapist, patients in whom severe psychoneurotic reaction might develop if the homeostatic balance of neurotic marriage transactions is disturbed, patients who persistently use a therapeutic situation to manipulate their spouses, and situations where the individual's diagnostic interviews communicate information about acting-out behavior, such as infidelity or homosexuality, of which the other partner is unaware.

Arguments and counterarguments can be made for each of these proposed contraindications and there is no clear evidence that these are valid. In fact, probably the most important contraindication is the therapist's inability to prevent a spouse from utilizing the conjoint session for destructive purposes against his or her mate (Sager, 1966).

A Combined Format

A *combined therapeutic* approach using elements of individual and conjoint therapies has the advantage of responding to changing needs, and promotes adaptation to variable marital patterns (Greene and Solomon, 1963). Within this format one can combine psychoanalytic principles and techniques with techniques based on communication and interaction. It is often used when an impasse is reached with other formats or when there is acting out in one partner. In addition, the rigidity of one partner or the potential threat to a partner may make individual or joint sessions more productive.

However, if the plan of therapy is not made explicit and the rules are changed, confusion may occur (Hollender, 1971). Other disadvantages do not differ from those described above for conjoint or concurrent approaches.

The Use of a Co-therapist

An aspect of these therapeutic approaches which has been widely discussed is the use of a co-therapist. Among the reasons for recommending a co-therapist are that the co-therapist makes possible more flexibility in scheduling individual sessions and a dyadic relationship with one therapist can be developed, when this is necessary. In addition, co-therapists provide an additional perspective and way of approaching a problem. The co-therapist can support a partner who feels attacked or can react with a more mollifying or tactful approach if the other therapist has produced excessive anxiety. The co-therapist can also be a model for identification and support to the same sexed partner, or can help defuse an intensely sexualized transference. Countertransference responses can be minimized and new parental models are available. From the therapists' perspective, mutual support and reinforcement, as well as constructive criticism, may facilitate therapeutic work.

Among the disadvantages of introducing a co-therapist are the expense and time problems. More important, the potential for conflict between co-therapists who have not worked out their own competitive or status-oriented conflicts is very great. Co-therapists may be more confusing to some couples, and they may revive negative parental transference images and thus interfere with therapeutic progress.

One area where the use of co-therapists has been especially recommended is the treatment of patients with sexual problems.

CLINICAL EXAMPLE #2: COMBINED FORMAT WITH CO-THERAPIST

Mr. and Mrs. B were being seen in conjoint therapy by a co-therapy team. The initial presenting problem was Mr. B's impotence. In the early sessions, it gradually became apparent that Mr. B viewed his wife as overly aggressive and forward and he became anxious when she approached him sexually. Mrs. B was confused by his response, felt rejected and inadequate, and withdrew from him. Although they were able to talk about these issues openly, they found it difficult to explore more deeply or to change their behavior. The co-therapists decided to see each partner individually with the same sexed therapist, to attempt to break the impasse. In his first session, Mr. B talked about how in some ways his wife's active approaches reminded him of his mother's controlling behavior toward him. While this had always been a problem, it was intensified when his parents divorced when he was 12. He felt deserted by his father and helpless because of the fear that if he did not comply with his mother's wishes he would be abandoned. He also felt guilty, seeing himself as responsible for the marital rift. As a result, he felt compelled to be a companion to his mother. In the second session he related these feelings to his anger at his wife. He said that it was helpful to talk to the therapist because he had always found it easy to talk to his father and had missed him.

Mrs. B in her sessions revealed a chronic problem with self-esteem. She had always maintained an outward appearance of competence and self-assurance, but never felt that it was a reflection of her internal feelings. Both of her parents were insecure people who could not support her. She found it easier to explore some of these issues with one therapist alone, initially because she was fearful that her husband would feel that her need for reassurance was a demand and he would reject her.

Following two individual sessions, Mr. and Mrs. B were again seen together by the co-therapists. The couple was able to explore some' of the issues that had emerged in their individual sessions, to share their own feelings and each other's responses, and to feel less vulnerable. Gradually, over the next two months, the sexual problem abated and they reported feeling closer, more empathetic, and more able to see each other as trusted friends rather than adversaries.

Couples Groups

Another important modality of couples therapy has been the couples group. This format applies an understanding of group interaction in terms of unconscious group tensions and psychodynamics (Ezriel, 1950). Through the correction of perceptual communicative disparities, the recognition and alleviation of reciprocal enmities, and the understanding that a couple's problems are not unique to them, it is often possible to facilitate sharing and the development of problem-solving techniques. It is also possible to reality test with regard to expectations and goals. Group therapy has been recommended for marital problems that are chronic and ego syntonic, that is, if the problem appears to be a way of life (Grunebaum, Christ and Neiberg, 1969). In the couples setting, the interaction not only is described but can be enacted with another partner with immediate feedback. A group composed of individuals with similar developmental issues and capacities for object relatedness facilitates the process (Neiberg, 1976).

Among the disadvantages of this format is the mutual communication of hopelessness, or the potential for group members who are excessively destructive or disturbed to be disruptive and prevent group cohesion. When there are family secrets or the fear of self-revelation by one partner, this modality is contraindicated. It may also be seen as threatening to an individual who is more restrained or insecure in groups.

PSYCHOANALYTIC CONSIDERATIONS OF THE THERAPY PROCESS

While, as already noted, perspectives on therapeutic approach are based on different theoretical and practical considerations, these views do not necessarily contradict one another. In fact, they may be complementary and reinforcing. This chapter focuses on the psychoanalytic framework of understanding and then approaches therapeutic techniques from this orientation. The synthesis of methodologies will be evident in the procedures.

Transference and Countertransference

Since marital conflict may be viewed as a result of the mutual projection, by each partner, of early internalized objects (see Meissner's discussion in this volume), and thus may become the battleground for past conflict, the therapist must be aware of each spouse's transference projection onto the partner as well as onto the therapist. In order to understand these complex interactions, a more comprehensive definition of transference will be used (Rioch, 1943, p. 151):

> The transference is the experiencing of the entire pattern of the original reference frames, which included at every moment the relation of the patient to himself, to the important persons and to others, as he experiences them at that time in the light of his interrelationships with the important people. . . .

When a couple presents for treatment, there is already an intense ongoing transference interaction between each partner. The therapist must deal with at least five transference manifestations: (1) man to woman; (2) woman to man; (3) woman to therapist; (4) man to therapist; (5) couple to therapist. Just as there are multiple transference reactions, there are multiple countertransference responses.

The dyadic transference which occurs in individual therapy does not essentially change with participation in conjoint therapy, despite the therapist's involvement with the spouse. Since the transference neurosis is not based on current reality, it will not be significantly influenced by current reality factors. However, transference reactions to the therapist in the triadic session may differ from those which occur in individual sessions, just as family members react differently depending on which others are present at a particular time.

While the therapist is present in a conjoint setting, the dyadic transference continues to be important. A couple who present with marital conflict because the wife feels that the husband is not supportive enough, and the husband feels that the wife is too demanding may be responding to each of their past histories. The husband may have had a demanding mother and the wife an unresponsive father, or there may have been other family situations which produce anxiety in the new situation. Both

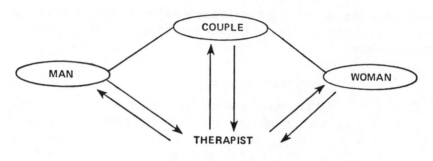

Figure 1

transference and countertransference responses may be significant. The therapist must choose the level of clarification or interpretation depending on the situation. The goal at the particular time is most important to consider.

While some feel that the marriage rather than the individual should be the end point (Main, 1966), others disagree (Sager, 1967). The resolution of both dyadic and triadic transference is required for the working through of neurotic difficulties (Sager, 1967). One or the other may be a primary problem with a particular patient. It is important to emphasize that the transference-countertransference complexities are multiplied in the conjoint setting and that they influence the triad, which now includes the therpist, just as they were factors in the marital dyad.

At times, direct and early interpretation of this transference is important, especially in the conjoint setting (Main, 1966). When negative images are projected onto the spouse, he or she will respond to these projections. The unconscious collusive process which occurs perpetuates the problem. An interpretation of the unconscious etiology can result in change in the partners. Thus, if one partner becomes overly controlling, the other might respond as if the partner were a primary object and behave as he or she did in the past, i.e., withdraw; this might cause the controlling partner to become even more controlling, also a pattern developed during childhood.

Five foci of transference transaction have been elucidated by Greene and Solomon (1963) from their work in concurrent therapy. They describe first the relationship to the therapist as a real person and as a new object. Second is the experiencing of the therapist as a symbolic figure with fantasied qualities. The third focus is the dyadic transference neurosis which is manifested in regression. The three foci are basic to all transference relationships. When, however, the transference reactions of both spouses are directed toward the same therapist, as well as toward each other (as in concurrent or conjoint therapy), two additional foci called the triangular transference transactions are introduced. The first of these is the triangular transference neurosis which reproduces, for example, the oedipal constellation. In the second, the triangular transference transactions involve the production of adaptive feedback toward the analyst, and toward the other spouse, and vice versa. As an example, Greene and Solomon (1963) cite the displacement of positive sexual transference from the analyst to the other mate, who in turn reacts to these positive feelings, setting in motion a "constructive, cyclical transactional process."

An aspect of transference which emerges in conjoint treatment includes the stereotyped, changing and regressive responses the partners have to each other. These are well established before the couple present themselves for treatment and may be manifested in therapy sessions very early. Similar manifestations of dyadic transference evolve more slowly in individual therapy or in psychoanalysis.

Early symptomatic improvement may derive from interpretation of transference behavior between marital partners since the interpretation provides a rationale for what was seen as irrational behavior and may relieve guilt, confusion or frustration that had resulted from self-blame for the spouse's responses (Sager, 1967). With the development of triangular transferences later in treatment, the interpretations and focus include the therapist, thus broadening the transferential base. The manifestations of transference will be described in more detail in the discussions on the therapeutic process later on in this chapter.

Resistance

Resistance is an aspect of couples therapy which evolves from the working through of transference reactions. Often, when change begins to take place which might mean giving up previous mechanisms of adaptation, resistance may arise as a defense. This is particularly apparent in conjoint therapy, and may result from the failure of one spouse's transference to arouse familiar and expected countertransference responses in the other spouse. When this occurs, the response may be to intensify efforts or, failing that, to attack the therapist or the process. At times the spouse who has made some changes will unite with the other to placate him or her, out of anxiety about potential loss of the relationship (Sager, 1967). Another resistance to change is the unwillingness of one spouse to discuss a particular issue, often citing the potential for disturbance to the other as a reason. The tendency to talk to the therapist rather than the partner, to attempt to ally the therapist on one or the other side in a particular disagreement and the threat to leave therapy or change therapists are other manifestations of resistance, as is the perpetual creation of one crisis after another to generate affect via displacement from the real issues—for example, discussions of money when the major concerns are in other areas. In this situation the focus on crisis resolution may prevent therapeutic work in more depth.

Resistance patterns tend to be repetitive and occasionally become autonomous; they appear in interactions even when there is no conflict at the time. Resistance patterns have been described as having a preconscious quality, so that they can be available to consciousness if attention is specifically directed to them. They are similar to the preconscious defenses which interfere with free association and communication in psychoanalytically oriented psychotherapy or psychoanalysis (Titchener, 1966).

Resistance seems defensively to exclude the therapist from participation since he or she may not be aware of the meaning of particular references or symbols, especially at the beginning of therapy. Resistive patterns of interaction also block awareness of affect or participation in treatment and thus they block the process.

Therapeutic Alliance

Another important concept in therapy is that of the therapeutic alliance. It is defined as the working relationship between patient and therapist (Greenson, 1965; Zetzel, 1970). In the course of psychoanalytically oriented therapy or analysis, this alliance evolves by an ego splitting mechanism, whereby the observing part of the patient's ego identifies with the therapist in order to modify the pathological defenses which were being used to ward off internal danger. A trusting relationship between therapist and patient is necessary for this to occur; the capacity for object relationships in either cannot be at a primitive symbiotic or need gratifying level. This definition can be extended to the marital therapy situation where the capacity of the ego of each partner to relate to objects is of primary importance. While psychoanalytically oriented marital therapy is not identical to psychoanalysis, some aspects of the mechanisms of the development of a therapeutic alliance apply.

Thus, the task of allying with the observing ego in order to understand conflicts, as well as the identification with the therapist to form a working partnership, occurs in marital therapy. Even when the transference neurosis causes distortions in the perception of the reality of the therapist's identity, patients can ally with the rational and caring parts of the therapist. This requires a sense of the self and therapist as separate. In the marital situation, the problem is more complex since *each* partner must be willing and able to ally with the therapist in order for the therapeutic process to succeed.

The development of a therapeutic alliance thus requires not only the ability to form mature object relationships, but the motivation to work with the therapist. It is evident, then, that the assessment of the goals of the therapy and motivation for change are critical elements. Indeed, in the author's own work (Nadelson, Bassuk, Hopps and Boutelle, 1977), it has been found that the motivation of both partners to achieve the goals they set is the most important determinant of success. This implies that the therapist has some understanding of both conscious and unconscious motivations. These may derive from pressure from the partner, fear of loss, guilt, anxiety, competitiveness, or the genuine desire to improve the relationship.

In order for a therapeutic alliance to develop, the couple must be able to agree on goals and expectations, and they must be willing to look at the determinants of resistances as they arise. Assumptions that are not shared make therapy impossible, i.e., the couple may state that they want their marriage to work when one partner has invested in another relationship and really wants to end the marriage.

The recognition and understanding of resistance can facilitate the giving up of neurotic or maladaptive behavior. "The blocking of the therapeutic alliance through inappropriate or incompatible motives should be seen as a resistance. Its recognition and eventual understanding by the couple are just as essential to the work of marital therapy as is any building of insights about their interaction" (Smith and Grunebaum, 1976, p. 370).

THE EVALUATIVE PROCESS

The decision about the approach to marital therapy derives largely from the orientation of the therapist. As noted, if it appears that the difficulties lie in the marital relationship, then it is appropriate to consider marital rather than individual therapy. There are no absolute criteria. Instead, there is a spectrum of treatability determined largely by motivation to work together. For this reason, the evaluative procedure is particularly important. In addition to providing information, it forms the basis for treatment.

The procedure to be described will focus on the method which has evolved over the past 10 years and has in the author's clinical experience resulted in successful resolution of conflict for those couples who were motivated to work together in this process. A presenting complaint of marital difficulties requires that both partners participate in the evaluation procedure in order for a recommendation to be made. This derives from careful study and understanding of the interpersonal relationship as well as of the individuals. Since the person making the initial contact is often defined as the "sick" partner and is accepting of that role, the first line of resistance may be manifested by statements like, "My husband won't come in," "My wife won't have anything to do with it because it's my problem." At this point the evaluator may reassure the patient by making a statement such as, "It sounds as if you are committed to solving the problem, so that it really isn't as important to point a finger at who is responsible, but more to work together to solve it. In order to do that, it is really important that both of you participate in understanding the problem, so that we can find the best way to solve it." At times the evaluator may offer to call the spouse himself or herself if the partner feels that he or she cannot do so. This approach attempts to establish an opened communication and to break through early *resistances.*

The procedure followed by the author is to first of all evaluate each spouse individually and then to see the couple together. The therapist must agree to respect the confidentiality of each partner in the individual meeting. This agreement presents some problems, particularly if secrets exist, since the therapist can be seen as being in collusion with one partner. An insistence on total revelation, however, may result in either holding back relevant material or leaving therapy if the individual is too threatened. Since the evolution of *therapeutic alliance* begins at this point, too much pressure on one partner may seriously impair the possibility of developing a good alliance. In addition, the individual may respond to the authority of the therapist and the response may be related to the actual act of the therapist rather than deriving from early life experiences and fantasies.

Each partner is seen individually in order to assess his or her psychic processes, ego functioning, and goals for therapy, and to establish a relationship. The individual has the opportunity to confide any "secrets," thereby exploring ambivalence and motivation for therapy in a setting where the other partner cannot be intimidating or coercive. While partners are encouraged to share secrets with each other, when secrets are not shared with the therapist they often appear in the therapy as resistances, or they may block therapy entirely and the therapist may be unaware of the reason. For example, the spouse who is having an affair may insist on continuing it; he or she may be coming to therapy without motivation for change and only to appease the partner.

In a situation where individual contact is not made, these and other aspects of the history may be entirely unknown and the therapist may continue to work with a couple unproductively. Another important factor for choosing to see each partner individually is to facilitate a decision about the treatment plan, since a request may be made for couple treatment as a resistance to recognizing an intrapsychic problem that may be more apparent in individual therapy. While the opposite possibility also exists, it has been the author's experience that the request for individual treatment to avoid facing marital problems is rarer and is more readily recognized by therapists oriented toward couples therapy.

Since, as noted above, there is already an intense ongoing transference interaction between each partner when the couple presents for treatment, the individual evaluation also sets into motion the development of the transference of each partner to the therapist. This aspect may be important to the future therapy since it can prevent the development of resistances of the type which ally the couple together against the therapist and prevent the establishment of the therapeutic alliance. Clearly, the opposite case can be made, that the importance of reinforcing the integrity of the couple should be stressed. In the final analysis, it is probably most important to begin at a place where the therapist feels that he or she can function most effectively.

A conjoint session at the end of the evaluation is important because individual goals, wishes, and complaints may differ significantly and this session can provide an opportunity to explore these differences and clarify mutual problems and goals. Frequently, unconscious or preconscious issues emerge which can be elucidated and discussed with the partner. The conjoint session may intensify motivation by clarifying difficulties in the context of a positive relationship with the evaluator. The individuals often feel more supported and motivated toward exploration and solution of their problems when they have each had a chance to tell their own story.

In order to expedite the evaluation process, to obtain more specific and detailed history, and to involve the couple more actively and directly, the author and her colleagues at Beth Israel Hospital in Boston have developed a questionnaire which is filled out by the couple during the course of the evaluation (Appendix A of this Chapter). Each partner is asked to complete a separate form and to return it without sharing its contents with the other partner until after it is returned. When the presenting problem is a sexual one an additional form is requested (Appendix B). The experience with the use of this material has been positive. Most couples feel that they are more involved in the process, that it increases their motivation, and that they are able to focus more clearly on pertinent problems, and on areas of communication difficulty. In the conjoint meeting following receipt of the questionnaire, the evaluator is able to elicit, while discussing the effects of writing the questionnaire, the motivation and goals for therapy. This often facilitates the couple's engagement in an alliance toward therapy. The model used in the procedure is not very different in its conceptualization from the marriage contract (Sager, 1976). It is, however, less complex and less penetrating. It begins as a part of the evaluation process, not as an initial part of the therapeutic procedure. It helps the couple and the therapist to further define and clarify goals and expectations. In addition, transference manifestations and resistances begin to emerge. This enables the evaluator and the couple to formulate a more realistic therapeutic plan.

The assessment of motivation for treatment is critical to its ultimate success. Ambivalence, differences in motivation, or other conscious or unconscious needs and desires may interfere with the development of a therapeutic alliance (Smith and Grunebaum, 1976). Couples frequently present with an acute crisis which they cannot solve themselves. Underlying the request for help in problem solving may be a basic uncertainty about the integrity or value of the marriage.

Clinical Examples on Evaluation

Following are some clinical examples which will help the reader understand the above comments on the evaluative process.

CLINICAL EXAMPLE #3

Mrs. C was a 33-year-old administrator, married for five years to Mr. C, a 38-year-old college professor. At the time they came for help, Mr. C was interested in a job in another city and he wanted his wife to leave her job to come with him. Mrs. C was fearful that she would not be able to obtain as good a job elsewhere. She also did not want to leave her friends and family. She expressed ambivalence about the plan. Further exploration revealed that Mrs. C believed that Mr. C did not care enough about her to consider her needs and that he saw her career as unimportant. A task of the evaluation was to clarify the reality, since it was not clear if Mr. C indeed felt the way Mrs. C perceived him to feel, or if she was projecting her ambivalence onto him.

CLINICAL EXAMPLE #4

Mrs. D, a married mother of three children, presented with an acute depression. She was seriously decompensating and hospitalization was recommended. The evaluation revealed that a determinant of her symptomatology was the interaction between her and her husband. She tended to use hysterical defenses in contrast to her husband's more obsessive style. The more emotional, demanding and infantile she became, the more withdrawn and intellectualized he became. Their battleground involved finances, housekeeping, and Mr. D's athletic activities. She would interpret his interest in athletics as a rejection of her and would become angry and demanding. She felt helpless and worthless, unable to change her situation. Clinically, she appeared increasingly more depressed. While Mrs. D was the most blatantly symptomatic, Mr. D's defensive style masked his symptoms. While the problems of each individual were significant, interactional components clearly contributed to the presenting problem.

Couples sometimes present for treatment when a decision to end the marriage has been made and the partner who made it feels guilty about abandoning the other or not trying hard enough to effect another solution. Marital therapy is doomed if the therapist is not aware of this decision, and the partner then feels entitled to the *"I did all I could"* position. His or her guilt is relieved. A therapeutic alliance may never take place if these motives are not confronted.

At times one partner may take the position that the marital difficulties would be solved if the other partner would change, or solve his or her individual problems. Often, when this is presented in an individual session, it is a way of expressing some conscious or unconscious understanding of one's own part in the etiology of the presenting problems. It can then be dealt with as a defense. The partner may be too anxious to look at his or her part and may need the permission and support of the therapist to alleviate that anxiety and face himself or herself. A marital therapist who is not aware of the individual issues may miss the subtle dynamics and may increase unconscious resistance if the anxious and defensive partner does not have a face-saving way of approaching the problem. At times, this may be an individual session or a chance to be be seen as a part of a process rather than as the culpable party.

CLINICAL EXAMPLE #5

Mr. and Mrs. E were negotiating about conjoint co-therapy because of sexual difficulties manifested by Mrs. E's increasing lack of of interest in sexual activity. She initiated the request for therapy because she feared losing her husband. The couple had been married for 15 years and had known each other for five years before marrying. When seen together, they described a satisfying sexual life and apparent harmony in other areas until two years before. Mrs. E blamed her lack of sexual interest on "menopause" (she was 38) and Mr. E agreed. He encouraged her to seek therapy, however, to see if anything could be done. In his individual evaluative session, Mr. E described a "normal" childhood and family. He sounded like a successful husband and father and reported no unusual stress. Mrs. E came from a close, and sexually inhibited family. She revealed considerable sexual anxiety throughout her life. She accepted herself as the "sick" partner. After the first conjoint evaluative session where there was a discussion of commitment to working on the sexual problem together, Mr. E called to request an individual session with the male co-therapist. He insisted that it was important for him to see the therapist alone. He seemed anxious and distraught. The therapist suggested that at the next session the four discuss it together. Mr. E refused and stated he could not tell his wife. At the individual meeting, Mr. E told the therapist that he was actively involved in a sexual affair with another woman. He was willing to give this up, but did not want to tell his wife about it. He stated that it was not his wife who had lost interest in sexuality with him, but it was he who had lost interest in her sexually. Her compliance and desire to please him had led her to take the blame. He was anxious about his sexual adequacy and recognized after the initial session that he could not blame her and avoid confronting his own problems.

Mr. and Mrs. E serve as an excellent example of how sometimes the latent agenda of the individual or couple is to seek an ally in the therapist. The therapist may be seen as the omnipotent parent who provides strength and reassurance for the weak, helpless child (patient). It is important to understand the unconscious motivation for seeking help. Is it to gain strength to remain in the relationship? Is it an attempt to stand up to the partner? Is it to leave the relationship? Is it to remain a victim? Depending on the nature of the interaction, the choice to remain or leave may be seen as an ego strength and the therapist's task is to ally with the evolving strength of that partner rather than to necessarily see the salvation of the relationship as a solution.

CLINICAL EXAMPLE #6

Mrs. F, a 28-year-old housewife, presented initially because of violent arguments with her husband and physical abuse by him for the entire 12 years of their marriage. She and Mr. F, a 29-year-old carpenter, had married when they were teenagers because Mrs. F was pregnant. From the beginning there was marital conflict. When Mr. F would become abusive, Mrs. F would take the children with her and go to her mother's home. Recently, she had become more involved in her children's school activities and had volunteered to be a teacher's assistant. She felt that she had started to feel like a "real person." This angered Mr. F who saw his wife moving away from him and felt rejected. He responded with increased attempts to control her, and with rage when she didn't capitulate. Mrs. F wanted the therapist to ally with her against the husband. In this situation, the therapist felt that Mrs. F had shown evidence of developmental progress in a more autonomous direction while Mr. F demanded that she remain where they were at the beginning of the marriage. The therapist was able to ally with Mrs. F in the direction of ego growth rather than regression. However, he did not allow himself to get into a position of siding with the "right" or "wrong" partner, but rather supported maturational goals. By not taking sides in the manner requested, he enabled Mr. F to be less threatened and begin to look at his fears of abandonment and isolation. Mr. F was also able to grow.

At times patients present their helplessness or "sickness" as a reason for their inability to take responsibility or to change, and they ask that the therapist ally with them on that issue. The therapist would then be in a position to encourage the partner to capitulate and to be more understanding and less demanding. As in the case of Mrs. F, the therapist could have been destructive by permitting regression rather than fostering growth. In addition, this position would have failed to take account of the interaction, and the unconscious needs of the partners to take sick or well positions as part of their contract with each other. Therapeutic progress is not likely to occur if the therapist becomes part of the collusive system. In this situation, it is not necessary that the marital partners themselves be designated as the patient or the "sick one," since other family members frequently act out or highlight problems.

Another aspect of the problem of seeking an alliance is the search on the part of one partner for a therapist who will "really understand" because the therapist is of the same sex, race, religion, etc. The patient may actually seek such a therapist and, if the therapist is not aware that the patient may be using the request defensively, the therapist may not offer what is most necessary. It is important to interject here that such a request is not always defensive. Many patients have had negative past experiences. In addition, the availability in a therapeutic role of a person of similar values, race, sex, etc., as the patient can facilitate the development of a positive alliance and the patient can approach issues more quickly because there are areas of identification and similarity. However, differences can be focused on and used as resistance to the establishment of an alliance.

CLINICAL EXAMPLE #7

Mr. G requested therapy because he felt that he could no longer tolerate his wife's argumentativeness and anger. During the first visit, Mrs. G attacked the male therapist, using a feminist argument to state that he couldn't possibly understand her. The therapist found it difficult to be objective since he had always viewed himself as sympathetic to women's issues, and was quite surprised by her reaction to him. Mrs. G requested a female therapist and Mr. G agreed. With the new therapist it became clear that Mrs. G's anxiety about the possible loss of her husband had been displaced onto the therapist, and expressed in her attack upon him. The ideological issue was not primary. The fact that she had regained control and had a therapist of her choice, however, facilitated the development of an alliance and enabled her to sort out the issues with fewer resistances and greater objectivity.

CLINICAL EXAMPLE #8

Mrs. H had been in individual therapy in the past, and had adored her "fatherly" therapist. When her 15-year-old daughter, P, began to act out sexually, her former therapist suggested that Mrs. H seek help from a therapist who had more experience with adolescents and family work. In her meeting with the new therapist, P revealed that her parents had not slept in the same room for three years and that there was enormous friction between them. When Mr. and Mrs. H were seen, Mrs. H presented as the disorganized, explosive partner for whose care Mr. H was responsible.

While it was clear that Mrs. H had a borderline personality organization and Mr. H was a severe obsessive compulsive, it was not clear that these diagnoses were sufficient to understand the situation. Mr. H used the fact that Mrs. H was in therapy to reinforce her role as the sick one. Mrs. H saw her husband as ungiving and unloving. Unconsciously, each saw the other as the "bad" parent. P became the recipient of that "bad" parenting and behaved as a "bad" child. The sexual acting out symbolized the sexual rift between her parents and it abated rapidly when her parents began couples therapy.

Couples also frequently present for therapy when one delivers an ultimatum and threatens to leave or to change the system in some way unless the partner changes or the marital system is restructured. The partner desirous of the change may define a specific problem—sexual or financial, for example—or may present with vague dissatisfaction or accusations such as *"He is sick."* The other partner may feel helpless, impotent, attacked or enraged. It is obvious that an alliance is not possible when one partner or both want vindication rather than therapy, or when other problems may be masked by the demand or symptom. This must be clarified before any therapeutic contract is possible.

CLINICAL EXAMPLE #9

Mr. and Mrs. I came for therapy because Mr. I was uninterested in sex and Mrs. I felt that she could no longer tolerate his rejection of her. In his individual session, Mr. I revealed that he was suffering from a serious bipolar depression for which he was being treated. It had a recurrent history predating the marriage. He was terrified that his wife would leave him and recognized that the sexual problems were manifestations of his depression. He felt trapped by Mrs. I's ultimatum. In her individual session, Mrs. I focused on the sexual problems because she was frightened about the future and angry that she had been deceived by Mr. I, who had not told her about his problems prior to the marriage. She felt overwhelmed by Mr. I's demands and his "selfishness." In the conjoint evaluative session, these issues were aired. Mr. I's understanding of the reasons for the ultimatum made it possible for him to include her in his otherwise narcissistic preoccupation and to agree that they needed to work together. Mrs. I gave up her insistence on sexual satisfaction "or else" and was able to commit herself to working on some of the issues she had raised during the evaluation.

An optimal situation for seeking therapy is when the couple recognize a mutual need and request help. Most often, such couples have sought previous consultation or have been in therapy in the past. A recognition of the need often has evolved in the course of exploration of individual problems. At times, however, the appearance of mutuality may be a way of avoiding significant conflict and ambivalence.

Thus, in assessing a couple for marital therapy there are several areas to consider, each of which offers important information contributing to the assessment of motivation for treatment, as well as to the understanding of the interactional components of the relationship. The evaluator can consider how the referral was made, who made the recommendation, and who made the initial contact. While the partner making the contact often presents himself or herself as the "sick one" and assumes responsibility for the marital stress, this may be a simplistic view of a complex interactional problem.

In the process of evaluating each partner, a good developmental history and an assessment of ego functions are necessary. An understanding of each partner's coping ability, adaptational patterns, self-image, and ego defenses can lead to a better understanding of how these interact in the relationship. In addition, one should learn how each partner manages affect, frustration and disappointment. Another ego function which should be assessed is the capacity for empathy, as it is manifested both within and outside of the relationship. A knowledge of personal values and goals, as well as of those of the family of origin, can contribute significantly to understanding the problems of the couple. It is important to know how the marital problem is seen by each partner. This includes the factors leading to the request for therapy, the threat to the integrity of the marriage, and each partner's motivation for marital therapy. There are times when the secondary gain of symptoms may be so great that the individual is unwilling to give them up, or when a partner expressly wants to leave the other but cannot confront the partner and hopes that the therapist will help with the painful task.

In assessing a couple, it is important to understand why they came for therapy at the particular time they chose. Initially, symptoms and complaints may be presented which feel "safer" to the partners but which mask more deep-seated difficulties or which may avoid confrontation with issues which are more damaging to self-esteem.

CLINICAL EXAMPLE #10

Mr. J, a 45-year-old businessman, urgently requested couples treatment because he felt that he had lost interest in his wife sexually. A change in the marital relationship had occurred after Mr. J had had a business failure. Mr. J had withdrawn because he was ashamed of his inadequacy and felt that he was unlovable. Individual treatment was recommended to help Mr. J with his depression. Intermittent couples meetings were also part of the therapy plan in order to support Mrs. J and to help both reestablish an equilibrium in the marriage.

Currently, since it is acceptable to admit to sexual difficulties, these may be the presenting symptoms even though other problems may be more seriously interfering with the relationship. The presentation of sexual symptoms may represent an attempt to find a rapid, magical solution to a painful problem. It is critical that the evaluator have a good understanding of the dynamics of the interaction before embarking on an attempt at symptom relief which may produce even greater anxiety. While a number of sexual problems are amenable to behavioral approaches, it is not infrequent that major problems in communication or more extensive pathology is masked by this focus.

CLINICAL EXAMPLE #11

> Mr. and Mrs. K had been married for three years when they sought therapy for sexual problems. The initial complaint was that Mr. K was impotent. During the evaluation, Mrs. K revealed that she was not orgasmic. They insisted on a behaviorally oriented approach to treatment. They both felt that the symptoms had started with the birth of their son one year before. Mrs. K was very involved with the child. She spent little time with her husband and complained of fatigue when he made sexual advances. Mr. K responded by spending more time at work. Mrs. K then felt uncared for and unloved.
>
> Mr. K was openly jealous of his son, recreating an early experience in his life. Mrs. K revealed that her mother had died early in her life and when her mourning father withdrew from her she felt rejected. Both Mr. and Mrs. K were terrified of the intensity and depth of the early feelings stirred up by the birth of their son. Their anger and disappointment about past experiences were critical issues, since they were manifested in their interaction.
>
> After beginning a behaviorally oriented sexual therapy, they found themselves unable to proceed. They requested a change in therapy perspective and began to explore in psychoanalytically oriented marital therapy the problems between them and to understand the underlying determinants of their conflict, as well as their resistances to the previous therapeutic approach.

Communication problems are pervasive in couples seeking therapy. In addition to sexual communication, other areas are frequently problematic. Couples may be unable to communicate affectively, they may be unsupportive or lack empathy or the ability to express affection. They may be unable to problem solve in the daily tasks of living, or they may be rivalrous or competitive. The balance of power and the use of power and physical force may prevent communication in any meaningful way.

A couple may have assessed each other incorrectly when they married and they may be deeply dissatisfied. They may be unable to share or to develop the flexibility necessary to negotiate compromise.

CLINICAL EXAMPLE #12

> Mrs. L, a 32-year-old librarian, requested couples therapy after four years of what she termed an "unsatisfactory" marriage. The precipitating problem for her request was an episode of physical abuse by her husband. During their marriage, Mr. and Mrs. L rarely saw each other. He worked a night shift and she worked during the days, including weekends. They came from different economic and intellectual backgrounds, and in whatever free time they had they pursued different interests. Mr. L was invariably late for appointments, when he remembered them, and he procrastinated consistently in paying bills. Finally, Mr. L abruptly deserted Mrs. L without discussion, leaving her with enormous debts. He broke off all contacts with the couple therapist and instituted divorce proceedings. Mrs. L elected to continue in individual psychotherapy to understand why she had so misjudged him. She felt that in the couples therapy she had understood her husband for the first time, and revealed a sense of relief about his desertion of her.

An understanding of marital identity is also important before embarking on a therapy program. Although individual expectations, goals, values and conflicts may differ, this can be resolved if the couple can find an area of common interest and aspire to some common goal. The partners' styles of adaptation and areas of conflict may be such that they cannot find mutual areas of satisfaction or they cannot compromise. As discussed in Chapter II, the issue of trust and ability to share are among the most critical components of marital identity. Often partners view each other as the enemy, or they may recreate an early sibling competition or an oedipal situation. They may feel themselves to be deprived and ungratified. They may find that they cannot tolerate regression or dependency in the other or that they are invested in the strength or weakness of the partner and cannot tolerate any shift. They may be unable to acknowledge their own or their partner's strengths or weaknesses, so that a rigid or even stereotyped interaction is all that is possible.

CLINICAL EXAMPLE #13

> Mrs. M, a 30-year-old teacher, came for treatment because she felt there was "nothing left of our marriage." She related that her husband had been extremely critical of her in their five years of marriage and that he had never really wanted to be married. She

had always felt inferior to him and felt he only tolerated her. The myth of this marriage had always been that he was the strong, independent partner and she was the weak, dependent one. The equilibrium of the relationship had been upset when Mr. M left the company where he had been a respected employee to develop "his own business," and was not immediately successful. When Mrs. M left Mr. M after a period of abuse and criticism of almost every facet of her existence, Mr. M began to decompensate and was unable to work. This revelation to Mrs. M that her husband actually needed her prompted a reconciliation.

STAGES OF COUPLES TREATMENT

For the purpose of clarity the stages of treatment are being carefully delineated as distinct structural entities, though in reality they overlap considerably. A discussion about which therapeutic format is optimal is based on many factors. These include the realities of time, motivation, finances and other pragmatic considerations as well as ego resources and coping ability of the partner. As Gill (1954) has stated, "The choice of treatment may be divided between the minimum necessary to restore the ego function and that which strives for maximum change. The gross major decision is based on defenses of the ego which parallel the strength of the ego" (p. 77).

Contract Negotiation

When the decision to recommend conjoint therapy is made, it is discussed with the couple and a therapeutic contract is negotiated. This includes a reaffirmation of the couple's motivation and goals. Since goals differ for each marital pair, there is a continuous reevaluation of the goals of therapy by the partners and the therapist during the process of assessment, as well as while they are working in therapy. For example, an agreed-upon divorce may be the new goal of the couple.

The first step in therapy involves the administrative aspects. These include negotiating fees, vacations, and appointment times of each weekly session. Problems with these aspects are reflections of communication issues between the partners and may be an indication of future resistances. Couples may discontinue therapy after the first few sessions for a variety of reasons, including the realization that the therapist will not magically cure them, that they may be confronted with painful feelings, that fantasies may become more explicit, or that they will, by virtue of the commitment to work with their spouse, be required to look at their own contributions to problems and their resistance to change. Often

couples or individual partners cannot express their feelings and dissatisfactions explicitly and will communicate via acting-out behavior, missed
appointments, failure to pay bills, failure of both partners to come for
appointments together or requests by one partner to be seen alone when
they have made a contract for conjoint meetings. For those therapists
who are psychoanalytically trained, it is often tempting to see a partner
alone or to focus on the needs and conflicts of that individual. While
this approach may be useful at times, it may also involve the therapist
in a collusive interaction with one partner and potentially sabotages the
couples therapy. In this situation it represents a countertransference
problem. Some of the reasons for seeing a partner alone, particularly in
the contract negotiation phase, include an acute crisis, a serious depression, an inability to live up to the terms of the contract, or information
which one partner wants to impart which he or she does not want to
discuss in conjoint session because of fears of retaliation. The "secret"
may be that the partner is physically abusive, has committed a crime, or
is having an affair.

The decision to work in a co-therapy setting should be made at this
point. While there are many possible indications and contraindications
for co-therapists, it is perhaps a most important consideration when
there is concern about the possibility of countertransference responses.
This includes the situation where the therapist does have values or ideas
which differ from those of the patient(s); for example, the wife may
want to pursue her career and both her husband and the therapist believe that women with children should remain at home to care for
them. This kind of belief is more likely to evoke countertransference
responses in less experienced therapists, or in those who are less flexible
or are defensive about a particular goal or value. At times, one partner
makes an explicit request for co-therapists or for a therapist of a particular sex which, as noted above, may occur because that partner feels that a
therapist of the opposite sex will not understand and will side with the
spouse. Or else, that particular partner may not be comfortable talking
intimately with a person of the opposite sex, because of early background
or past experiences. While this can be seen as a resistance, and it may
be, the facilitation of the development of the therapeutic or working
alliance is most important. The therapeutic alliance cannot evolve productively if there are feelings of mistrust or suspicion of collusion, or if
the therapy becomes focused on a struggle for power or control between
the therapist and the insistent spouse, rather than on the commitment
to work together with both partners.

Initial Phase of Treatment

The initial stage of treatment involves the clarification of communication patterns and the development of tools for effective problem solving, as well as the establishment of a therapeutic alliance. To understand their problems, the couple must become aware of the nature of their interaction as two separate individuals, with different past experiences, needs and perceptions, who have entered a partnership. When the individual contributions to the difficulties of the marriage can be appreciated, they can begin to learn new patterns of verbal and nonverbal communication. The therapist can help to elucidate interactional problems by using techniques of clarification, suggestion, manipulation, abreaction, confrontation, and interpretation. During this early phase, however, interpretation is generally employed less frequently than it is later in the therapy when the alliance has consolidated and transference issues developed. Initially, the presenting symptoms are explored and the couple is encouraged to negotiate. Concrete and specific concerns are most frequent at this time—for example, budget, housework, division of labor, disciplining of children, relationships with other family members, or planning vacations.

Early in treatment, a significant issue is the inability of each partner to predict the inevitable result of certain behaviors or interactions despite their repetitive nature. The development of the ability to predict the outcome of a behavior is an important goal of this phase of treatment. Another issue at this early phase of treatment, noted earlier, is the attempt of one partner to engage the therapist so that he or she takes sides. This is often seen around the issue of role-based expectations. The therapist must be aware that this polarization is occurring and be able to define what is expected of him or her. This behavior is an early manifestation of transference and may evoke countertransference feelings on the part of the therapist.

Countertransference is not necessarily to be considered as a negative factor. It can be viewed as an active constructive element in the therapeutic situation (Benedek, 1953; Alexander, 1959). Countertransference feelings play a particularly important role in the management of triangular transactions (Solomon and Greene, 1963), especially if the therapist can clearly identify the etiology of his or her responses. These include the increased risk of unconsciously identifying with one partner, of responding to threats of divorce or acting out, or of feeling guilty for causing further disruption in the relationship by upsetting one partner. The primary focus of the initial phase of treatment is on the symptoms.

While underlying intrapsychic issues and transference feelings are identified, interpretations are more often focused on the couple interaction and those psychic elements that relate to it. Emphasis is on communication and role patterns. Many couples therapists consider treatment complete once the couple has developed workable problem-solving techniques. This may also be seen as the initial stage of therapy. Treatment can stop at this point if the couple agreed that they have reached their goals and do not wish to proceed. If the working through of unconscious conflicts is indicated, more extensive transference work can be done. The decision about the continuation of treatment depends on the couple's ability, motivation and need to work with transference issues in an insight-oriented approach, and their ability to develop a therapeutic alliance.

If a decision is made to proceed, then the question of a co-therapist can be reconsidered. The co-therapist can balance the triadic competition if this is seen as a particularly troublesome possibility. In addition, individual sessions may occur which will evoke more intense and deeper transference responses and facilitate work in the next phase of therapy.

Long-term and often intermittent supportive rather than insight-oriented couples therapy is indicated for couples with more tenuous functioning. This may be especially beneficial to the couple when one partner appears to be more disorganized or "sicker" than the other. The encouragement of the better integrated partner to support the other is facilitated by the observation and reinforcement of seeing the therapist in that role over a period of time. Some degree of modeling and identification may facilitate the therapy and strengthen the relationship.

CLINICAL EXAMPLE #14

Mr. and Mrs. N presented at the time of Mr. N's impending retirement. He had worked 40 years as a laborer. He was rarely at home during the rearing of the children. As he became more available after his retirement, Mrs. N pushed him to participate more in family activities. She found, however, that she was unable to get along with him. He was impulsive, erratic, and drank heavily. He was quite frightened of the impending push toward a closer relationship with his family. Mrs. N was a masochistic, obsessional woman who maintained control of all of the activities at home. During the intermittent therapy, Mrs. N was able to learn to appreciate her husband's anxiety and to tolerate his need for distance. She benefited from observing the therapist and was able to relinquish some control. Mr. N became less anxious when he had more distance. No attempt at basic personality reorganization was made. However, significant improvements occurred in both partners.

Middle Stage of Therapy

Many therapists prefer an individual approach when deeper intra-psychic conflict is apparent. It is often possible, however, to facilitate and intensify the therapeutic process as well as to foster the consolidation and interaction of the couple by working with them conjointly. The therapist can help them to strengthen their alliance with each other by permitting them to share past experiences and traumata. This enables them to be more empathetic and supportive with each other. The therapist's skill in promoting the strengths of their relationship and the positive value of their understanding of each other can lead to a renewal of their earlier commitment to each other.

CLINICAL EXAMPLE #15

Mr. and Mrs. O, a professional couple in their twenties, had been married for two years. Mr. O was a graduate student who had a very competitive relationship with his older brother. His mother had been a very controlling woman and his father had been passive and subservient to her. Mrs. O, a law student, was an only child whose distant father and mother continually castigated and depre-cated her. Both partners were insecure and felt sexually inadequate. Mr. O saw his wife as competitive and controlling while Mrs. O constantly sought her husband's approval and attention. When Mr. O spoke of his concerns about his masculinity, Mrs. O reinforced his anxiety by complaining that he could not bring her to orgasm. When these patterns and their earlier derivatives became apparent to the therapist, he suggested that more intensive couples work might be beneficial. They gradually became comfortable enough with each other to raise painful issues and to discuss feelings which had been hidden because each feared that the other would be critical and rejecting. They could begin to really test their fears and get feedback which was not as damaging as expected. They shared an understanding of each other which enabled them to be more supportive while working through conflictual issues. When Mrs. O dreamed that she had had a baby, both partners could understand it from their own perspective. Mrs. O spoke of her wish for a baby as a wish for unambivalent love, while Mr. O saw himself as the baby. He was conflicted about the helplessness he felt in the face of her constant demands. He recognized that he projected his conflict about being a baby, about being controlled yet nurtured by his mother, onto his wife. Mrs. O also spoke of her view of her husband as the sibling she never had, whom she competed with yet yearned for.

The understanding of transference and dream material can be useful in the middle stage of the therapeutic process and become an integral part of the therapy, as in the above example. Interpretative work, including dream work, can begin in the middle stage, with the inclusion of the therapist as a participant in the interaction. The therapeutic alliance representing the real object relationship between therapist and patient, the identification with the therapist, and the positive transference (Daniels, 1969) are consolidated when the "therapist is allied with a relatively conflict-free part of the ego of one of the marital pair and uses it to make observations toward pathological defensive portions of the ego to the other. The form and content of the alliance is constantly changing" (Titchener, 1966, p. 331). The therapist can use it to interpret and clarify pathological defensive maneuvers of the pair, but he or she must be constantly aware of the triadic nature of the transference and be able to use it as effectively as the dyadic transference.

CLINICAL EXAMPLE #16

Dr. and Mrs. P initially presented because of frequent arguments and increasing distance between them. Both partners had been working until the birth of their son two years before. At that time, Mrs. P left work to stay at home. Dr. P increased his work commitments in order to make up for the decreased income, and Mrs. P was left alone with the child for greater lengths of time than she had anticipated. She began to feel that Dr. P did not care about her, she suspected that he was interested in other women, and she felt "stupid and dull." Dr. P denied her accusations, but he did acknowledge that she was not as spontaneous and interesting as she had been when she was working. He complained that all she did when he arrived home was to berate him for his inattention and order him around. He stated that he felt he "just lived" in the house and was like another child (burden) to her.

When they decided on marital therapy, Dr. P complied with Mrs. P's wish to have a woman therapist because she thought that a man would merely side with her husband and see her as responsible for the difficulty because she could not understand the demands of her husband's work.

In the initial phase of therapy, the couple began to look at the evolution of their inability to communicate. After several weeks, they were able to talk with each other without becoming so angry that one or the other would feel impelled to leave the room. However, as the therapy became more intense, Dr. P became seductive with the therapist and developed a full-blown transference neurosis, based on his unresolved oedipal conflicts. Mrs. P became enraged at the therapist whom she accused of having "everything" because the therapist was a professional woman with a family. She felt demeaned by the therapist and accused her of being "as bad as a man." Mrs. P had grown up mistrustful of men. She stated that they never gave anything. On the other hand, she feared her powerful mother who had controlled and managed her father and the rest of the family, but who never gave her enough. She projected her anger at her mother onto the therapist.

Because Mrs. P had developed enough of an observing ego early in the treatment, had substantial ego strengths, and had a positive alliance with the therapist, she was able to tolerate the intensity of her anger and recognize its origins in her childhood experiences. She became aware that the therapist and her husband had become parental figures and that she related to them as she had in the past. Dr. P's oedipal conflicts were more difficult to work through. He repeatedly attempted to involve the therapist as a colleague, in order to avoid the intensity of his oedipal anxiety. The therapist and Mrs. P both became maternal objects, and it was essential to help him understand the split he had made. An important insight came to him in one session when he clearly confused the therapist with his mother in a question he asked.

There are several levels of transference of one spouse to the other and to the therapist (Sager, 1967). These must be dealt with in the middle phase of therapy. These include transference manifestations that are characterological (Dr. P's view of all women as sexual objects), symbolic (Dr. P's verbal confusion of the therapist with his mother), and regressive (Dr. P's behavior toward the therapist as if she were his mother). In the middle phase of therapy, then, motivation is not enough for successful therapeutic work. The individuals must have the ability to develop a true therapeutic alliance, to tolerate delay and anxiety, and to develop an observing ego which enables them to look and integrate in order to produce change. Thus, if one partner does not have this capacity and the other does, it is likely that they will either stop at this phase of earlier conflict resolution (initial phase of treatment). Or if the symptoms are too ego alien for one partner, that partner may desire to end the marriage.

Another issue which emerges in this stage of therapy is the capacity of the therapist to work with the regression that occurs in the partners once the working alliance is established. This regression is another manifestation of transference and does not necessarily indicate that the therapy is faltering. Issues which appeared to have been resolved in the initial stage of treatment arise again within the context of the transference. The partners can work toward an understanding of the unresolved conflicts which each brought to the marriage. Individual transference issues are dealt with primarily when they are manifested symptomatically. "So long as the patient's communication and ideas run on without any obstruction, the theme of transference should be left untouched. One must wait until the transference, which is the most delicate of all procedures, has become a resistance" (Freud, 1913, p. 139).

This position is applicable to psychoanalytically oriented couples therapy as well as to individual therapy. When a couple present for treatment, psychoanalytically oriented aspects of the transference have already become a resistance, as evidenced by the marital symptoms. The therapist elucidates the pathological transaction patterns and interprets the defensive patterns of each partner, as well as the complementary defenses evoked in the spouse. The therapeutic alliance shifts as each partner's defensive maneuvers are modified within this dynamically operating system.

Psychoanalytically oriented couples therapy, like other psychoanalytically oriented psychotherapies, is not necessarily directed toward the complete resolution of the transference neurosis. It is also designed to accomplish a multitude of other therapeutic results. For example, it may prove a point, teach, or set an example. Some defenses are supported; other defenses are analyzed. The transference is only interpreted insofar as it affects the couple's interaction in a pathological fashion, i.e., serves as a resistance. The timing and mode of presentation of interpretations are of critical importance, as in individual therapy. In order to maintain neutrality, especially early in the process, interpretations should be made that relate to the communication distortion and that are relevant to both spouses. As material is brought up by one partner and interpretations are made, the observing partner can maintain some distance and thus improve his or her ego's capacity to perceive. This can progressively diminish the narcissistic identifications between the partners and augment the capacity to be rational and to communicate (Watson, 1963).

The ultimate aim of interpretation and working through in psychoanalytically oriented marital therapy is the neutralization and integration of aggressive and libidinal needs so that behavior is motivated more in the service of the ego and less by impulse and intrapsychic conflict. Neutralization occurs by a process of acquiring more adaptive mental mechanisms for drive control. Interpretation of resistances and defenses repeatedly over time can facilitate the acquisition of these more adaptive mechanisms. Maturity in marriage consists of a relative neutralization of instinctual drives so that each partner reciprocates with the other. Interpretive work does not extinguish or encourage aggressive expressions; rather it attempts to explore the sources of these feelings and understand their appropriateness and meaning in the relationship. Since the instinctual drives derive from early relationships, they may result in defensive mechanisms which are inappropriate and confusing in the marital relationship (Titchener, 1966).

CLINICAL EXAMPLE #17

Mr. and Mrs. Q were both in their late twenties when they married. They sought therapy initially because of conflicts about Mrs. Q's relationship to Mr. Q's two children by his previous marriage. Mrs. Q felt that the children demanded a great deal of her and that their presence compromised the relationship between the couple. She had previously had a brief marriage which ended in divorce when she was 19. Mr. Q had been married for six tumultuous years and decided on divorce after the birth of his second child when he felt that his wife was no longer interested in him. Neither partner had ever shared the affective components of their earlier experiences with the other. In the evaluation, Mrs. Q revealed that she had come from a rather distant, unemotional family whose ethic was to bear pain silently. Mr. Q had come from a divorced family and spent his childhood being shipped to various relatives and schools, never feeling cared about.

In the early conjoint sessions, both partners were able to talk about their losses and their failures, to mourn, and to comfort each other. Mrs. Q cried about her earlier marriage and about a miscarriage that she had never talked about with her husband. Mr. Q shared his feelings about his parents' divorce when he was 10, and his guilt about causing his children to be in the same situation as he had been in as a child. As therapy progressed, Mrs. Q was able to discuss her desire for a child, while Mr. Q talked about his fear of failing as a father, just as his father had failed him. He also explored his early feeling that he had contributed to his parents' divorce. He felt that he had repeated his own problems with his children and that he was incapable of sustained and giving relationships with them. The therapist interpreted Mr. Q's over-solicitousness with his children in the light of his past history of deprivation and guilt. Mrs. Q could respond empathically and feel less threatened and competitive when she understood the source of his behavior. They discussed their feelings about having children of their own. Mrs. Q was able to recognize that Mr. Q was not as enthusiastic about children and, because she now understood his past, she could appreciate his fear of the potential destructive effect of children on the marriage. Her ability to reach out to him enabled him to recognize that she was not part of his past and that she had wishes and desires which were part of her separateness from him. She was able to tolerate her own affect, to see it as non-destructive, and to allow him to move closer to her.

In this therapy situation the therapist was not only a model for the exploration and expression of emotion but permitted and encouraged it in a way that countered the past and provided an alternative. This could occur only in the context of a positive therapeutic alliance.

Use of videotape

In the middle, as well as in the initial stage of psychoanalytically oriented marital therapy, videotape playback has been a useful adjunct to treatment. The playback to couples and the supervisory potential facilitate dealing more effectively with transference and countertransference phenomena, as well as with communications issues. The response to videotape playback has been characterized as including an "image impact," the patients' first response to seeing themselves on the playback screen, a response during the process of playback, and a residual response (Alger and Hogan, 1967; Hogan and Alger, 1969). A strong positive or negative image impact leads to more involvement in the therapy and greater and faster change. Therefore, this response may be used prognostically.

Among the effects of using video playback is the ability to see the interaction with some degree of distance. The partners can develop an "observing ego" and may be able to see the "blame pattern" of charges and countercharges between themselves, and become aware of the multiple conflicting messages given by each of them. Videotape is not in itself a therapeutic modality; like free association for the psychoanalyst, it is a tool which can assist a skilled therapist in understanding a complex multilevel interaction.

CLINICAL EXAMPLE #18

Mr. and Mrs. R were both teachers in their late thirties who came for couples therapy when Mrs. R threatened to leave Mr. R because she felt that he did not understand her and was constantly critical and patronizing toward her. Their interaction in the couples sessions revealed that Mr. R paid no attention to her statements, spoke in a paternalistic manner, and treated her like a child. He was unaware of how he was responding. Mrs. R, on the other hand, was unable to see that she was provocative and self-effacing. She responded to him by bursting into tears, exclaiming to the therapist, *"See what I mean?"*

After careful preparation about the purpose and nature of the videotape, the therapist played back selected segments over a period of several weeks. The couple was asked to view their interaction on the tape and consider the potential effects on each other of what they did or said. At times, the therapist asked them to role play possible alternative responses. This technique proved to be very successful as both partners gradually came to see that their actions produced predictable responses and that the patterns could be altered. The use of videotape was continued throughout the treatment and included dealing with transference issues as they evolved.

Another use for videotape is to facilitate refocusing on issues that had been taken up previously and dropped. This technique is more difficult in couples therapy than in individual therapy because of the increased complexity of transference and countertransference patterns and the necessity for observing both interpersonal dynamics and nonverbal communications while simultaneously attending to the frequent intervening crises, which distract the participants and the therapist. In addition, material like a partner's dream which is important to understand, and may not have been adequately understood or explored when it emerged can be retrieved. The videotape can thus be a stimulus as well as a way of obtaining additional associations.

For some patients the loss of control inherent in the situation of being a patient in therapy may be difficult. The ability to maintain control through the use of intellectual defenses may facilitate an alliance and help resolve early resistances. Videotape playback has been useful for patients who use intellectual defenses or denial, since it offers the patient an opportunity to maintain some distance, utilizing familiar defensive styles, and to feel less attacked or threatened.

The use of videotape for supervision or self-monitoring can reduce the conscious and unconscious retrospective distortion which occurs and record nonverbal behavior more accurately. Events can be put in perspective and self-instruction is possible (Benschoter, Eaton and Smith, 1961). Countertransference can be monitored and more careful process analysis can occur (Nadelson et al., 1977).

Because of the increased transference and countertransference complexity inherent in the situation when co-therapists work together, videotape playback may be helpful. It enables them to work out their own relationship by providing an opportunity for close study of their verbal and nonverbal interactions with each other and with the couple.

Termination Phase

Termination of psychoanalytically oriented couples treatment is similar to the termination phase of individual psychoanalytically oriented psychotherapy. Once a termination date is set, many conflicts and defenses re-emerge. The therapist's task is to help the couple identify and work through the anxiety about the impending loss and review and clarify therapeutic gains. Individual and couple dynamics dealing with separations are clarified and interpreted. The goal during the process of termination is to decrease each partner's ambivalence about separation, to reinforce gains that have been made, and to foster techniques for continued psychic growth. The end point of therapy is usually the acceptance and understanding of the integrity of each partner by the other and the development of mechanisms of conflict resolution which evolve from this mutual respect and commitment. The couple must give up fantasies about what they could have gotten from the therapist and what could have been accomplished in therapy. They must accept the limitations, compromises and successes involved in separating, in much the same way as occurs in individual therapy or analysis, as well as in life. Generally, in psychoanalytic couples therapy, because of the nature of the contract and the specificity of the goals, as well as the multiplicity of transference reactions, there is less profound dependency and less difficulty with separation than occurs in individual therapy. Because of the triadic nature of the therapeutic format, the partners are not as likely to feel angry or rejected.

At times, separation or divorce, rather than consolidation within the marriage, is the result of treatment. This can be a positive growth-promoting situation and is not necessarily a treatment failure. Despite the fact that it is a loss, the loss is not equated with failure or defeat. When marital dissolution is agreed upon, one or both partners may desire individual psychotherapy or psychoanalysis. Often this was not considered previously because the marital relationship was so tenuous that they dared not risk any additional strain. Or else they projected all of their difficulties onto the partner, thus defending against the recognition of individual responsibility for or contribution to the problem. The couples therapy may have facilitated the recognition of individual intrapsychic issues by allowing them to reach consciousness. Individual therapy may also be sought to consolidate gains and avoid repetition of the same "error" in future object choice or relationships.

CLINICAL EXAMPLE #19

   Mr. and Mrs. S had been married for two years when they sought therapy. The reason given for seeking therapy was that Mrs. S, age 29, was interested in having children and a more stable home life, while Mr. S, age 38, was unwilling to make that commitment. When they had initially married, each had assumed that the other shared the same values and goals about a future family. In the initial phase of the treatment, they each discussed these goals and communicated more explicitly about their expectations than they had ever done before. While Mr. S had been clear about his desires, Mrs. S had previously been unable to tell Mr. S what she wanted because she feared his anger and his disapproval of her for her "middle class values." In her own background, Mrs. S had idolized her father and performed to meet his standards, a goal she never felt she had attained. Her behavior with her husband was very similar. She felt that to have a differing opinion or belief was "bad." Mr. S, the only boy in his family, was adored and pampered by his mother and sisters. His father expected perfection, yet was threatened by his own son's competitiveness, so that their relationship was highly ambivalent. Mr. S not only expected compliance from his wife but also wanted her to share his views and agree to the correctness of his positions.

As the therapy proceeded, Mrs. S began to understand the transference aspects of her relationship with her husband. She developed more autonomy and her self-esteem grew. She became increasingly more invested in her work and more confident about her desire to have children. The therapist provided support, a model for identification, and a means of helping her to see herself as autonomous and acceptable. On the other hand, Mr. S feared parenthood because of the nature of the conflicts and identifications with his father. While he became more tolerant of his wife and supported her development because he could see her as separate from his mother and sisters, he was convinced that what he wanted was to express his creativity in his career. He did not want children. For him, the therapist was the non-condemning or demanding part of his father, as well as the self confident part of his mother. The couple decided to separate and were able to do so painfully but amicably.

A one-year follow-up revealed that both were doing well, and that they remained on good terms. Mrs. S had entered individual therapy, had obtained a new job, and was in a satisfying relationship with a man. Mr. S was in psychoanalysis and progressing in his professional development. He had no interest in a commitment to a permanent relationship.

When the issue of termination emerges, some couples attempt to prolong therapy because they have grown attached to the therapist, have developed a pattern of interaction and a habit of working together with the therapist, or are uncertain about their ability to sustain the level of interaction and communication that developed in treatment. Generally, these issues must be worked through in the treatment process; however, there are some couples for whom follow-up visits over a period of time are helpful and can be viewed as a part of the therapeutic process. These visits may occur if symptoms recur or they may be set up to review and reinforce gains. This is facilitated because the therapeutic alliance continues to exist. The meetings can be spaced depending upon the specific needs of the couple. There is, in fact, a distinct advantage in couples therapy, as in individual therapy, to setting up follow-up visits. These provide an updating of the patients' status, they are a way for the therapist to assess his or her work, and they provide a reevaluation mechanism for the patient and a way of consolidating treatment results.

If one of the partners desires individual therapy, it can be discussed at termination or in a follow-up visit. The advantage of utilizing the follow-up visit for this purpose is that the individual has had time for thoughtful consideration and has hopefully integrated the therapy in such a way that the request is not solely a response to loss and a search for a replacement. An assessment of the goals for therapy can occur in this context. It is generally preferable to refer the individual to a therapist other than the couples therapist because of the nature of the transference-countertransference tie and the potential for re-evoking a rivalrous situation in the couple. Furthermore, since periodic return visits, especially at crisis times, may occur, the potential for optimal use of these visits may be diminished if a new and different set of transferences are evolving simultaneously and the nature of the alliance is significantly changed.

CONCLUSION

The evaluation of the effectiveness of couples therapy is complex and difficult, especially since there is considerable disagreement about criteria for marital success, the goals of therapy, the indications and contraindications for therapy, and the techniques to be used. (The research literature on outcome is reviewed in Chapter VIII of this book.) What is perhaps most critical is that the criteria for success differ for each couple. Both the therapist and the couple must arrive at some consensus about goals and expectations. These may need to be modified as resistances emerge in the therapy and as the motivation and limits of the partners become clearer. The presence or absence of a particular symptom or complaint does not alone determine the end goal or result.

Neither togetherness nor divorce, neither continued open conflict nor its absence can give a picture of the efficacy of the modality employed. However, it is clear that most experienced and competent therapists do not differ as much in their techniques as they do in their theory, their use of language, or their focus. Therapists with opposing perspectives are merely, as in the tale of the blind men and the elephant, describing different aspects of a problem and reporting results from different vantage points. The shape and form do not have a unity until those groping for the answer can agree to common considerations and assessments. However, in the final analysis there is value in maintaining differing perspectives if the ultimate goal is to continue to re-examine and clarify the problems and improve treatment techniques.

APPENDIX A

COUPLES' EVALUATION QUESTIONNAIRE
BETH ISRAEL HOSPITAL—DEPARTMENT OF PSYCHIATRY

THIS RECORD IS CONFIDENTIAL: Please try to answer all questions. If you need more space, please use a separate sheet of paper.

COUPLES EVALUATION

Date: ....

Name: ....

Address: ....

Telephone No.: Home .... Work: ....

Sex: .... Race: .... Citizenship: .... National Origin: ....

Religion: ....

    Were you brought up with a formal religion?
    Do you practice that religion or any other?

Place and Date of Birth: ....

    Were you adopted?
    (If yes, at what age?)

Marital Status: ....

List previous marriages—state if they ended by divorce or death: ....

....

....

Level of Schooling (include any academic degrees): ....

....

....

List Jobs Held: ....

....

....

MEDICAL HISTORY

Illnesses: ....

....

... .   -   ....

Operations: ....

....

Accidents: ....

....

Were you ever hospitalized? ....

   At what age?

   For how long?

Last complete physical: ....

Name of family physician: ....

Have you ever been hospitalized for psychiatric reasons? ....

   When: ....

   Why: ....

Have you ever consulted a psychiatrist? ....

MENSTRUAL HISTORY

How old were you when your period first started? ....

Are your periods—regular .... irregular .... other ....?

During your periods, do you have: severe cramps, heavy flow, feel depressed, feel

   nervous? ....

Any other symptoms associated with period: Painful breasts, ankle swelling, spotting

   between periods, fatigue? ....

CONTRACEPTION HISTORY

Please indicate which you use—and how you chose that method: ....

   Rhythm; condom; diaphragm; pill; "withdrawal"—coitus interruptus (pulling
   out); IUD; douche; foam

Are you satisfied with current method? ....

Have you changed recently? ....

PREGNANCY HISTORY (BOTH PARTNERS)

1. How many pregnancies have you had? ....

   Or been involved with (male)?

2. Miscarriages? .... When? ....

3. Still births? .... When? ....

4. Abortions?   .... When? ....

5. How did your spouse react when you were pregnant? (i.e., sympathetic, helpful, jealous, distant, etc.) ....

6. How did you feel about having sexual relations during pregnancy? ....
....

7. How did you feel about having sexual relations after the baby was born? ....
....

CHILDREN

Please list all children living with you:

Name	Age	Sex of Child	By This Marriage, Previous, Adopted	Living at Home

Who else lives with you? ....

1. How many living children? ....

2. Were they planned? ....

3. Have you adopted any children? ....

4. Have any children died? .... Cause: ....

5. How did having children affect your relationship with your spouse? ....
....

6. a. How did you see yourself as a parent? ....

    b. How do you see your spouse as a parent? ....

7. What problems have you had being a parent? ....

PARENTS

	Mother	Father
Name:		
Age:		
Religion:		
Race:		
Occupation:		

State of Health: ....

If deceased—cause of death: ....

date of death: ....

Was this a first marriage: ....

Please list other marriages: ....

....

Educational level: ....

Did parent work during your childhood: ....

Does parent work now: ....

What kind of work: ....

Was your home disrupted by: ....

    Separation

    Divorce

    Death

If yes—how old were you? ....

With whom did you subsequently live: ....

To whom were you closest in the family? (include siblings, or other relatives) ....

....

What kind of contact do you maintain with your family? (visit, phone calls, letters,

    etc.) ....

BROTHERS AND SISTERS

First Name	Age	Marital Status	Number of Children	Occupation
....	....	....	....	....
....	....	....	....	....
....	....	....	....	....
....	....	....	....	....
....	....	....	....	....

SELF-IMAGE

1. As you see yourself, what are your attributes? ....

    faults? ....

2. How do your friends and your family view you? ....

3. Has your view of yourself changed recently? ....

COUPLE RELATIONSHIP

1. What attracted you most to your spouse? ....
   Is that still present as you see him/her today? ....

2. Did you experience any "second thoughts" after marriage? Explain: ....
   ....
   ....
   ....

3. Do you spend spare time together or separately? ....

4. Do you confide in one another? ....

5. What do you enjoy doing as a couple or family? (e.g., TV, movies, theater, concerts, socializing, sports, etc.) ....
   ....

6. Who decides on the activity? How do you decide on activities, vacations, etc. ....
   ....
   ....

CURRENT PROBLEMS

1. What's the problem you come with? (Try to describe details: length of time, any specifics you consider important, why you came now) ....
   ....

2. What other marital problems have you had? ....
   ....

3. Do you have some idea how they developed? ....

4. Do you feel that your sexual relationship is a problem? Explain: ....
   ....

5. Have you shared any of these concerns about your relationship with your partner? If not, why? ....

6. What have you done about your problems (any professional help?)? ....
   ....

7. How do you think therapy could be helpful? ....
   ....

8. Do you think partner would answer these questions differently? ....

APPENDIX B

SEXUAL FUNCTION

(Supplement to Couples Evaluation Questionnaire)

THIS RECORD IS STRICTLY CONFIDENTIAL.

CURRENT SEXUAL HISTORY

1. How would you describe your current sexual relationship? What problems do you have? ....

....

2. How often per week do you usually have intercourse now? ....
Has there been any change? ....

3. What has the most influence on when or how often you have intercourse (i.e., partner's desire, work, tension, vacation, etc.)? ....

4. Who usually initiates sexual activity? ....

5. Does lovemaking always lead to intercourse? ....

6. Do you have a preference for a particular time of the day and situation for lovemaking? (Describe) ....

7. Can you let your partner know what you find pleasurable sexually? (Explain)......

....

8. Is your partner able to let you know what he/she finds pleasurable sexually? (Explain) ....

9. Do you experience orgasm ("come")? How? ....
In the past? ....

10. Do you ever have orgasms in your sleep, masturbation, intercourse or other means? ....

11. Has there ever been any trouble with erection ("hard on")? Please explain: ....

....

12. Has there ever been trouble ejaculating ("coming")? Please explain: ....

....

13. Do you feel free to express your sexual desire at any time and expect a warm reception? . ...

14. Are you able to say "No" to your partner's advances if you don't feel like it? ....

....

15. How do you feel if your partner says "No"? ....

16. Have you ever used means other than sexual intercourse to bring sexual pleasure to you or your partner? (Please describe): ....

Was it successful? ....

Was it accepted by partner? ....

Would you like to do it more frequently? ....

17. What are the other methods of sexual practice your partner has used with you for sexual pleasure? ....

Were you both satisfied with such measures? ....

Were you bothered, frustrated, angry, or guilty? ....

18. How do children affect sexual relations? ....

   a. Not at all

   b. Troubled by the possibility of their interruption

   c. Have they "caught you in the act"?

   What did you say?

19. How do you ensure privacy while having sex? (Lock on door, etc.) ....

20. How much (if any) sexual activity has occurred on your part outside of the relationship? ....

21. Does your partner know about this? ....

22. How would you feel about your partner having other sexual relationships? ....

....

23. Do you feel comfortable about the way your body looks? Please elaborate: ....

....

   MEN: Are you circumcised? .... How do you feel about it? ....

   Are both testes in scrotum? ....

   Have you wondered about the size of your penis? ....

PRESENT SEXUAL HISTORY

1. How did you learn about sex? ....

2. What family attitudes were you aware of? ....

3. Did you masturbate? If yes, describe any fantasies, concerns: ....

....

4. Did you have sexual relations before you were married? Yes: .... No: ....

   If yes, please describe: ....

   If no, would you make a different decision now? ....

5. If there was a prior marriage, describe sexual relationship: ....

6. Describe first sexual encounter (with whom, thoughts, feelings): ....

7. Have you had any homosexual experiences or fantasies? ....

Do you think your partner would answer these questions differently? (Please explain):

....

Is there anything else you feel we should know? ....

....

REFERENCES

Ackerman, N. W. *The Psychodynamics of Family Life.* New York: Basic Books, 1958.

Ainslie, G. A behavioral understanding of the defense mechanisms. *Archives of General Psychiatry,* in press.

Alexander, F. Psychoanalysis and psychotherapy. *Journal of the American Psychoanalytic Association,* 1954 (a), 2, 722-733.

Alexander, F. Some quantitative aspects of psychoanalytic technique. *Journal of the American Psychoanalytic Association,* 1954 (b), 2, 685-701.

Alexander, F. Current problems in dynamic psychotherapy and its relationship to psychoanalysis. *American Journal of Psychiatry,* 1959, 116, 324.

Alger, I. and Hogan, P. The use of videotape recording in conjoint marital therapy. *American Journal of Psychiatry,* 1967, 123, 1425-1430.

Benedek, T. Dynamics of countertransference. *Bulletin of the Menninger Clinic,* 1953, 17, 201.

Benschoter, R. A., Eaton, M. T. and Smith, P. The use of videotape to provide individual instruction in techniques of psychotherapy. *Journal of Medical Education,* 1961, 40, 1159-1161.

Berman, E. and Lief, H. Marital therapy from a psychiatric perspective: An overview. *American Journal of Psychiatry,* 1975, 132, 583-592.

Bird, B. Notes on transference: Universal phenomenon and hardest part of analysis. *Journal of the American Psychoanalytic Association,* 1972, 20, 267-301.

Bird, H. W. and Martin, P. A. Countertransference in the psychotherapy of marriage partners. *Psychiatry,* 1956, 19, 353-360.

Blanck, R. and Blanck, G. *Marriage and Personal Development.* New York: Columbia University Press, 1968.

Bowlby, J. *Attachment and Loss: Attachment,* Volume I. London: Tavistock, 1968.

Breuer, J. and Freud, S. (1895). Studies on hysteria. *Standard Edition,* 2, 1-307. London: Hogarth Press, 1955.

Brody, S. Simultaneous psychotherapy of married couples. In: J. Masserman (Ed.), *Current Psychiatric Therapy,* I. New York: Grune and Stratton, 1961.

Butler, R. N. Toward a psychiatry of the life cycle. *Psychiatric Research Reports of the American Psychiatric Association,* 1968, 23:233-248.

Cookerly, J. R. The outcome of the six major forms of marriage counseling compared: A pilot study. *Journal of Marriage and the Family,* 1973, 35, 608-611.

162   *Marriage and Marital Therapy*

Daniels, R. Some early manifestations of transference. *Journal of the American Psychoanalytic Association*, 1969, 17, 995-1014.

Deutsche, M. Conflict: Productive and destructive. *Journal of Social Issues*, 1969, 25, 7-41.

Dicks, H. V. *Marital Tensions*. New York: Basic Books, 1967.

Dicks, H. V. Experiences with marital tensions in the psychological clinic. *British Journal of Medical Psychology*. 1953, 26, 181.

Dicks, H. V. Object relations theory and marital studies. *British Journal of Medical Psychology*, 1963, 36, 125.

Ellenberger, H. *The Discovery of the Unconscious: The History and Evolution of Dynamic Psychiatry*. New York: Basic Books, 1970.

Erikson, E. *Childhood and Society*. New York: Norton, 1950.

Erikson, E. *Identity, Youth and Crisis*. New York: Norton, 1968.

Ezriel, H. A psychoanalytic approach to group treatment. *British Journal of Medical Psychology*, 1950, 23, 59-74.

Fairbairn, W. R. D. *An Object Relations Theory of Personality*. New York: Basic Books, 1954.

Feather, B. W. and Rhoads, J. M. Psychodynamic behavior therapy. I and II. *Archives of General Psychiatry*, 1972, 26, 496-511.

Frank, J. D. Therapeutic factors in psychotherapy. *American Journal of Psychiatry*, 1971, 25, 350-361.

Freud, S. (1900). The interpretation of dreams. *Standard Edition*, 4 and 5, 1-626. London: Hogarth Press, 1953.

Freud, S. (1904). Psychoanalytic procedure. *Standard Edition*, 7, 247-255. London: Hogarth Press, 1953.

Freud, S. (1905 [1901]). Fragment of an analysis of a case of hysteria. *Standard Edition*, 7, 1-123. London: Hogarth Press, 1953.

Freud, S. (1905 [1904]). On psychotherapy. *Standard Edition*, 7, 255-269. London: Hogarth Press, 1953.

Freud, S. (1912). The dynamics of transference. *Standard Edition*, 12, 97-109. London: Hogarth Press, 1958.

Freud, S. (1912-1913). Totem and taboo. *Standard Edition*, 13, 1-162. London: Hogarth Press, 1955.

Freud, S. (1914). Observations on transference love (Further recommendations on the technique of psychoanalysis III). *Standard Edition*, 12, 157-172. London: Hogarth Press, 1958.

Freud, S. (1917 [1916-1917]). General theory of the neuroses, Lectures 16-28 of Introductory Lectures on Psychoanalysis. *Standard Edition*, 16, 241-478. London: Hogarth Press, 1963.

Freud, S. (1923a). Two encyclopedia articles. *Standard Edition*, 18, 233-259. London: Hogarth Press, 1955.

Freud, S. (1923b). The ego and the id. *Standard Edition*, 19, 1-60. London: Hogarth Press, 1961.

Freud, S. (1926). Inhibitions, symptoms and anxiety. *Standard Edition*, 20, 77-179. London: Hogarth Press, 1959.

Freud, S. On beginning the treatment, 1913. *Standard Edition*, 12, 121-144. London: Hogarth Press, 1961.

Freud, S. (1939 [1934-1938]). Moses and monotheism: Three essays. *Standard Edition*, 23, 1-139. London: Hogarth Press, 1964.

Freud, S. (1940 [1938]). An outline of psychoanalysis. *Standard Edition*, 23, 139-301. London: Hogarth Press, 1964.

Freud, S. (1950 [1895]). Project for a scientific psychology. *Standard Edition*, 1, 281-360. London: Hogarth Press, 1966.

Fromm-Reichmann, F. Psychoanalytic and general dynamic conceptions of theory and of therapy. Differences and similarities. *Journal of the American Psychoanalytic Association,* 1954, 2, 711-721.

Gill, M. M. Ego psychology and psychotherapy. *Psychoanalytic Quarterly,* 1951, 20, 62-71.

Gill, M. Ego psychology and psychotherapy. In: R. Knight (Ed.), *Psychoanalytic Psychiatry and Psychology.* New York: International Universities Press, 1954, p. 77.

Giovacchini, P. L. Treatment of marital disharmonies: The classical approach. In: B. Greene (Ed.), *The Psychotherapies of Marital Disharmony.* New York: Free Press, 1965.

Gould, R. L. The phases of adult life: A study in developmental psychology. *American Journal of Psychiatry,* 1972, 129, 521-531.

Greene, B. (Ed.). *The Psychotherapies of Marital Disharmony.* New York: Free Press, 1965.

Greene, B. and Lustig, N. Treatment of marital disharmony: The use of individual, concurrent and conjoint sessions as a "combined approach." In: B. Greene (Ed.), *Psychotherapies of Marital Disharmony.* New York: Free Press, 1965.

Greene, B. L. and Solomon, A. P. Marital disharmony: Concurrent psychoanalytic therapy of husband and wife by the same psychiatrist—the triangular transference transactions. *American Journal of Psychotherapy,* 1963, 17, 443-456.

Greenson, R. The working alliance and the transference neurosis. *Psychoanalysis Quarterly,* 1965, 34, 155.

Grunebaum, H., Christ, J. and Neiberg, N. Diagnosis and treatment planning for couples. *International Journal of Group Psychotherapy,* 1969, 19, 185-202.

Haley, J. *Strategies of Psychotherapy.* New York: Grune and Stratton, 1963.

Haley, J. Marriage therapy. *Archives of General Psychiatry,* 1963, 8, 213-234.

Hogan, P. and Alger, I. Impact of videotape recording on insight in group psychotherapy. *International Journal of Group Psychotherapy,* 1969, 19, 158-164.

Hollender, M. H. Selection of therapy for marital problems. In: J. H. Masserman (Ed.), *Current Psychotherapies.* New York: Grune and Stratton, 1971.

Kaplan, H. S. *The New Sex Therapy.* New York: Brunner/Mazel, 1974.

Karasu, T. B. Psychotherapies: An overview. *American Journal of Psychiatry,* 1977, 134 (8), 851-863.

Kohl, R. N. Pathologic reactions of marital partners to improvement of patients. *American Journal of Psychiatry,* 1962, 118, 1036.

Langs, R. *The Technique of Psychoanalytic Psychotherapy.* New York: Jason Aronson, Inc., 1973.

Levinson, D. J., Darrow, C. M., Klein, E. B., Levinson, M. and McKee, B. The psychosocial development of men in early adulthood and the mid-life transition. In: D. F. Ricks, A. Thomas and M. Roff (Eds.), *Life History Research in Psychopathology,* Vol. 3. Minneapolis: University of Minnesota Press, 1974, pp. 243-258.

Lidz, T. *The Person.* New York: Basic Books, 1968.

Main, T. F. Mutual projection in a marriage. *Comprehensive Psychiatry,* 1966, 7, 432-439.

Marmor, J. The nature of the psychotherapeutic process. In: G. Usdin (Ed.), *Psychoneurosis and Schizophrenia.* Philadelphia: J. B. Lippincott Co., 1966.

Martin, P. *A Marital Therapy Manual.* New York: Brunner/Mazel, 1976.

Mittelmann, B. Concurrent analysis of marital couples. *Psychoanalytic Quarterly,* 1948, 17, 182-197.

Munroe, R. L. *Schools of Psychoanalytic Thought.* New York: Dryden, 1955.

Nadelson, C., Bassuk, E., Hopps, C. and Boutelle, W. Conjoint marital psychotherapy: Treatment techniques. *Diseases of the Nervous System* (in press).

Nadelson, C., Bassuk, E., Hopps, C. and Boutelle, W. The use of videotape in couples therapy. *International Journal of Group Psychotherapy,* 1977, 27 (2), 241.

Neiberg, N. The group psychotherapy of married couples. In: H. Grunebaum and J. Christ (Eds.), *Contemporary Marriage: Structure Dynamics and Therapy.* Boston: Little, Brown, 1976.

Neugarten, B. L. and Datan, N. The middle years. In: S. Arieti (Ed.), *American Handbook of Psychiatry,* 2nd ed., Vol. 1. New York: Basic Books, 1974, pp. 592-608.

Nunberg, H. The theoretical basis of psychoanalytic therapy. In: S. Lorand (Ed.), *Psychoanalysis Today: Its Scope and Function.* New York: Covici Friede, 1933.

Oberndorf, C. P. Folie à deux. *International Journal of Psychoanalysis,* 1934, 15, 14.

Orr, D. W. Transference and countertransference: A historical survey. *Journal of the American Psychoanalytic Association,* 1954, 2, 621-670.

Rangell, L. Psychoanalytic and dynamic psychotherapy: Similarities and differences. *Journal of the American Psychoanalytic Association,* October, 1954, 2, 734-744.

Rapaport, D. and Gill, M. M. The points of view and assumptions of metapsychology. *The International Journal of Psychoanalysis,* 1959, 40, 153-162.

Rioch, J. The transference phenomenon in psychoanalytic therapy. *Psychiatry,* 1943, 6, 147-156.

Sager, C. The treatment of married couples. *American Handbook of Psychiatry,* III. New York: Basic Books, 1966, pp. 213-225.

Sager, C. Marital psychotherapy. *Current Psychiatric Therapies,* 1967, 7, 92-102.

Sager, C. The conjoint session in marriage therapy. *American Journal of Psychoanalysis,* 1967, 27, 139-146.

Sager, C. Transference in conjoint treatment of married couples. *Archives of General Psychiatry,* 1967, 16, 185-193.

Sager, C. *Marriage Contracts and Couple Therapy.* New York: Brunner/Mazel, 1976.

Sager, C. J., Gundlach, R., Kremer, M., Lenz, R., and Royce, J. R. The married in treatment. *Archives of General Psychiatry,* 1968, 19, 205-217.

Sager, C., Kaplan, H., Gundlach, R., Kremer, M., Lenz, R. and Royce, J. The marriage contract. *Family Process,* 1971, 10 (3), 311-326.

Smith, J. W. and Grunebaum, H. The therapeutic alliance in marital therapy. In: H. Grunebaum and J. Christ (Eds.), *Contemporary Marriage Structure Dynamics and Therapy.* Boston: Little, Brown, 1976.

Solomon, A. and Greene, B. Marital disharmony: Concurrent therapy of husband and wife by the same psychiatrist. *Diseases of the Nervous System,* 1963, 24, 21-28.

Solomon, A. and Greene, B. Concurrent psychoanalytic therapy in marital disharmony. In: B. Greene (Ed.), *The Psychotherapies of Marital Disharmony.* New York: The Free Press, 1965.

Stein, M. The unconscious meaning of the marital bond. In: V. Eisenstein (Ed.), *Neurotic Interaction in Marriage.* New York: Basic Books, 1956.

Szasz, T. S. The concept of transference. *International Journal of Psychoanalysis,* 1963, 44, 432-443.

Titchener, J. The problem of interpretation in marital therapy. *Comprehensive Psychiatry,* 1966, 7, 321-327.

Watson, A. S. The conjoint psychotherapy of marriage partners. *American Journal of Orthopsychiatry,* 1963, 33, 912-922.

Weiss, R. S. *Marital Separtion.* New York: Basic Books, 1975.

Winnicott, D. W. *The Maturational Processes and the Facilitating Environment.* New York: International Universities Press, 1965.

Zetzel, E. *The Capacity for Emotional Growth.* New York: International Universities Press, 1970.

IV

The Conceptualization of Marriage from a Behavioral Perspective

ROBERT L. WEISS, PH.D.

INTRODUCTION

At first glance the union of *marriage* and *behaviorism* appears to be that of two most unlikely bed partners. The legitimacy of marriage within the field of psychology has not been enthusiastically accepted. In fact, the study of marriage, for the most part, has been the domain of colleagues in sociology and, to a lesser extent, social psychology (for example, Levinger, 1965). On a popular level, the juxtaposition of marriage and behaviorism—the latter viewed as a mindless form of experimental psychology—conjures up images of "Clockwork Orange." The emphasis on behavior control, the reflexive chants of "ends justifying means," and other currently held, unpopular views of behavior modification make abhorrent to many the application of a technology of control to idealizations of marital intimacy.

On an academic level it can be argued that marriage is not a psychological variable; it may be a state of mind or, more appropriately, a contractual arangement, with rights and privileges regulated by statute. At best, the argument might continue, perhaps one could study components of marriage, such as satisfaction, but, alas, the problem is not unlike the scientific study of beauty. The study of aesthetics may not lend itself to experimental control. How, then, comes the question from both quarters, can mindless behaviorism be used to illuminate the nuances, the subtlety, the symbolic fulfillment, characterized by adult intimacy and commitment? The purpose of this chapter is to provide a systematic analysis of what behavioral psychology offers to our understanding of marriage relationships and marital therapy. As will be shown, the offering has had a considerable impact on the field.

As the chapters in this volume demonstrate, there may be many construals of one of the most popular, interesting, albeit elusive forms of interpersonal behavior, marriage. To invite different points of view also suggests that there may be no persuasive evidence to recommend one over many other approaches; one's point of view is still very much a matter of personal taste, value, or simply stubbornness. Aside from their aesthetic value, theories are interesting insofar as they lead to alternative outcomes. If after considering each of the construals of marriage relationships, together with the corresponding treatments, little substantive difference among the treatment techniques is found, the utility of proposing three different theories would be questionable. The editors, anticipating that theories should lead to discernably different applications, have included companion chapters on therapeutic interventions which reflect a conceptual heritage of the theoretical chapter in each case. The degree of overlap between the two companion chapters need not be extensive, as in the present case, where the model has given rise to specific assessment and intervention procedures somewhat different from those described by O'Leary and Turkewitz in Chapter V of this volume and presented elsewhere (cf., Weiss, Hops, and Patterson, 1973; Weiss and Birchler, 1978).

Although the behavioral point of view has had considerable impact on the field, the acceptance of this point of view by others trained in very different traditions has been somewhat less enthusiastic. The reasons for this are worth considering here as a means of helping focus on what is peculiar to the behavioral models and what they may actually share with others.

A popular misconception is that there is one doctrinaire behaviorism, while in fact there are different behavioral points of view. As noted before, a model of marriage and marital distress, and a technology for marriage therapy may be quite dissimilar, yet both would be recognizable as behavioral in orientation. Behavioral approaches to marriage all share a commitment to some learning-based network of concepts, a commitment to objectifying conditions responsible for producing behavior change, and a particular point of view about the functional causes of behavior. Within the framework of these general tenets, one is free to wander about introducing this or that innovation. Similar differences within systems theory approaches are documented by Steinglass in Chapter VI of this volume.

Another commonly-held but erroneous view of behavioral models is that they are basically mechanistic, best describable as "mindless behaviorisms" that totally ignore the role of "thoughts," "feelings," and other forms of distinctly human activity. The caricature of the behavioral psychologist includes one who uses reinforcers, tokens, M & Ms, verbal praise such as "That's good, Johnny!" and so on, as well as the more alarming use of electric shock and other nefarious forms of behavioral control.

Behavioral approaches are certainly concerned with how certain consequences, made contingent upon behavior, lawfully regulate future behavior. In the past, the emphasis was on external arrangements, which contingently controlled behavior, whereas current emphasis in behavioral psychology incorporates many forms of cognitive processes. Today, a rapprochement between what might have been both a mindless behaviorism and the excesses of cognitivism (cf., Mischel, 1973) is emerging. Indeed, there is marked enthusiasm for the various approaches to behavioral psychology which involve notions of "cognitive learning" (cf., Mahoney, 1977; O'Leary and Turkewitz, Chapter V, this volume). In large part, this "humanizing" of behavioral psychology reflects a technological advance as well. It is now possible to systematically introduce techniques which allow a degree of control over cognitions and to observe the effectiveness of these operations. It is no longer possible to represent behaviorism in its mindless state of yesteryear and still maintain fidelity to the state of the art. Nor does this change mean that behavioral approaches are indistinguishable from the avowedly more psychodynamic models. There are still many differences in basics, but an outmoded reflexology applied to adult intimacy is not presented here. Nor do the recent successes of behaviorally based sexual therapy (cf., Marks, 1976) contradict this point, given their heavy emphasis on behavioral technology. These approaches reflect carefully thought-out applications of behavioral principles, which, in these instances, bring about changes in sexual functioning without elaborate excursions into the symbolic meanings of the behavior. Thus, behavioral approaches introduce cognitive components as these appear to be needed in dealing with the problem at hand; if behavior change can be effected at a skill training level, further cognitive elaboration may be unnecessary.

Persons attracted to behavioral psychology found the emphasis on controlling behavior compatible with their point of view. The maximum understanding one may have of an event is to be able to reproduce the conditions which "cause" that event and then to observe the occurrence of that event. In a sense, being able to predict events, like eclipses or effects of unobserved planets, means that one has functional control over the necessary and sufficient antecedent conditions, thereby making prediction successful. Although natural forces cannot always be moved around at will, the conditions which must exist before an outcome will be observed can be specified. It is this emphasis on control *as understanding* which often distresses nonbehaviorists and reinforces the idea of an authoritarian, control-oriented technocracy.

This chapter has been organized into five main sections: *Conceptions of Marriage: An Overview,* which briefly sets the stage for this inquiry; *Behavioral Analysis,* which is both an introduction to behavioral learning concepts and a review of the various social learning approaches to marriage therapy; *Behavioral Systems Approach to Marriage,* a presentation of the author's model within a behavioral framework, followed by *Evaluation of Behavioral Position.* The last section *Summary and Perspective* is a look forward. The chapter moves from more basic considerations in early sections to more research oriented considerations in later sections. The focus throughout is on conceptual issues rather than the techniques of marital therapy, and a somewhat selective review of research which identifies the robustness or, at times, the anemia of behavioral concepts applied to marriages.

CONCEPTIONS OF MARRIAGE: AN OVERVIEW

As part of a systematic review of behavioral conceptions of marriage, it will be helpful to identify some of the broader issues addressed by various conceptions of marriage. What is the relationship between marriage and quality of life adjustment? Does what takes place within marriage have relevance for basic health and adjustment, or do conceptions of marriage steer clear of the private, at times nonrational, occurrences between two consenting adults? One practical last question: Should marriage therapy be covered by health insurance policies?

Asking these broader quality-of-adjustment or health-related questions focuses on some of the important differences between and among models of marriage and marriage therapy. Many forms of psychological distress *are* viewed as being health-related, enough to be included in insurance payment plans. Do persons with existing forms of psychopathology come together, thereby producing a marital illness (the assortative theory of mating), or do persons produce psychopathology as a result of their lives together (the interaction theory)? Admittedly, such cause-effect determinations are beyond current knowledge, but the correlational data are worth noting.

A problem as professionally annoying as alcoholism has many familial tendrils. Paolino and McCrady (1977) have drawn together the various conceptual and treatment approaches involving alcoholic marriages. Interest in the association between marriage and depression is demonstrated in studies by Overall, Henry and Woodward (1974), Coleman and Miller (1975), and Weiss and Aved (1978). In a retrospective statistical study of 1,624 psychiatric outpatients, Overall et al. (1974) found marital complaints to be a part of a broader depressive spectrum disorder, but further stated, ". . . it must be concluded that a highly significant relation between complaints of marital problems and history of parental discord exists separate and apart from the depressive spectrum in the psychiatric patient population" (p. 450). In an earlier study, Overall (1971) showed that for some 2,000 university hospital patients, rated psychopathology (on inpatient rating scales) was inversely related to *number of marriages*: multiply-married persons showed less severe forms of psychopathology than either the never marrieds or the married-once groups. These results may show that, at least for this population, ability to get into and out of close heterosexual relationships is not so much a sign of personality instability as of social skillfulness.

Coleman and Miller (1975) and Weiss and Aved (1978) have both shown significant correlations between various measures of marital satisfaction and depression, and a general index of physical health status. As Crago (1972) has observed, although the incidence of mental disorders is lower in married couples than in any other marital status group, there still is no direct evidence for causality.

The effects of marital discord on children are now being actively studied, as well as the expression of intrafamilial violence. Estimates still indicate that intrafamilial homicide accounts for a significant proportion of reported deaths. Although marriage may simply provide an arena for problems to be acted out, it may also represent an ideal target for intervention into a wide number of socially significant problems.

The various theoretical models presented in this book probably differ most greatly along three dimensions: (1) conception of the determinants of behavior; (2) interface between cognitions and behavior; and (3) appropriate unit of analysis for effecting relationship change. Each of these will be considered in turn.

Determinants of Behavior

If the determinants of behavior are viewed as being largely within the individual, models of marriage will reflect concepts which include various personality trait variables, or various enduring dispositional constructs (cf., Mischel, 1968). These are usually need-based theories, which define various motivational structures, which are presumed to have relevance for the ways individuals select mates. These individualizing models also view marriages from the perspective of the individual's thoughts, feelings, and awareness of personality dynamics. Interactions are explained in terms of individual needs, and particularly in terms of projecting early familial introjects (see Meissner, Chapter II, above).

Alternatively, if the determinants of behavior are viewed as largely outside the individual, our model of marriage will stress situational determinants, one popular variant of which has been role-theory (Crago and Tharp, 1968). An extreme situationalist view would hold that knowledge of the situation predicts likely behaviors of individuals. Role-theory is a somewhat milder form of this argument, since concepts of role expectation and role enactment suggest first that the learning of role appropriate behavior must take place and that failures of role enactments (given expectations) produce distress. The credulity of role-theory, as applied to marriages, has been weakened by the current feminist position (cf., Laws, 1971). Laws has written an incisive critique of the marital literature, noting repeatedly how various role conceptions of marriage have operated to disadvantage females in our society, largely because researchers have taken traditional acceptance of role prescriptions without basing their theory on interactional data.

The various "systems theory" approaches seem to take a midway position between the individualizing and situationalist views. Situations and the organization of behavioral transactions over time suggest an interest in patterning (higher orders of traits?), but one clearly focused on interactional regularities.

Behavioral theories are inclined to make a functional analysis of the situation-behavior-consequence network, albeit a smaller network than that dealt with by systems approaches. Here the interest is in behaviors determined not by developmental constructions (such as traits) but by situational and reinforcing control of outcomes. These behavioral concepts will be elaborated on at length in subsequent sections.

Interface Between Cognitions and Behavior

Speaking of the interface between cognitions and behavior raises an epistemological question: How do persons utilize the events of daily life to form cognitive products (thoughts, attitudes, beliefs) about themselves, and, more importantly, about their relationship with another? When we recall that so much of our popular culture emphasizes that love is inaccessible to rational analysis (for example, one is struck dumb with love, one falls in love, marriage is a ball and chain, etc.), it should not be surprising to discover that as individuals most persons are terribly unskilled in tracking cause-effect relationships in their daily environs. Such commonplace expressions as "You never want to spend time with me" may be a conclusion drawn from only a few instances, or from a defective assessing program—how many invitations actually have been proffered in the past! Is it a psychologically meaningful question to ask couples, as in such standard assessment devices as the Locke-Wallace Marital Adjustment Scale (Locke and Wallace, 1959), to indicate ". . . the degree of happiness, everything considered, of your present marriage"? Certainly, the empirical issue is whether response to that question predicts anything significant about relationship behavior (which it seems to do); but as important is whether it is possible to index "happiness" in this global sense, without tapping various habits regarding good impression management. Many of the individualizing approaches to persons foster use of cognitive labels rather than observation of events (cf., Weiss and Margolin, 1977; Weiss and Isaac, 1976). If, indeed, cognitions about marriage are independent of the empirical (daily) events of the marital interaction, all that would be required is a technology for changing attitudes independent of behavioral events. Thus, whether or not one actually is treated considerately (appointments and other agreements kept), it would still be possible to increase the cognition, "I am well treated." Clearly, the more that thought and action diverge, the greater the likelihood for social concern!

Global, retrospective self-reporting has characterized much of the work that has provided the empirical basis of marriage and marital interaction (cf., Hicks and Platt, 1970; Laws, 1971; Weiss and Margolin, 1977 for methodological appraisals), but this approach has generally failed to illuminate the relationship between cognitions held about relationships and the behavioral support for these beliefs. Neither has there been much information on the circular relationship between cognitions and behavior, that is, how each provides corrective feedback to the other. As behaviors change, we would expect that cognitions catch up with these changes, as well as the more traditional view that behaviors change after cognitions change.

Different models of marriage therapy emphasize the role of cognitions over behavior intervention techniques. The understanding ("insight") so familiar in psychodynamic therapies is such a case in point. The communication oriented therapies, favoring a systems point of view, stress the flexibility in how events may be construed, which defocuses the individual in favor of the situation itself. Behavioral models, as noted above, are moving more toward incorporating the role of cognitions in behavior change, but the emphasis continues to be on behavioral outcomes, the effects of actions taken or not taken.

Units of Analysis

Finally, models will differ in what is proposed as the unit of analysis for effecting behavior change. From a "systems theory" point of view, the minimal unit most often is the triad, husband, wife, child, whereas from the individualizing points of view the person is the unit appropriate for intervention. (Still larger units can be described as either collectives or communities; see Chapter VI.) For some theorists intervention into a dyadic relationship when the natural setting includes other members is ill advised; rather, family therapy is the intervention of choice (Whitaker, 1975).

Systems approaches and behavioral approaches share, if not always the appropriate unit for intervention, a highly functional orientation to outcomes. The former is concerned with system dynamics having relevance for distribution of commodities: how attention is garnered, how decisions are made, and so forth. A similar concern with outcomes, effectiveness of actions, and problem-solving attainments characterizes the behavioral point of view. The emphasis in either case is on transactions rather than the internal processes of individuals. O'Leary has offered preliminary correlational data to suggest that treatment gains in parent-child behavioral therapy are unrelated to pre-treatment marital satisfaction. If these results are replicated over samples of more typically distressed clinical couples, it would have to be questioned whether the systems view is necessary in all cases of family and marital intervention (Oltmanns, Broderick, and O'Leary, 1977).

Where Angels Fear to Tread

One last consideration about models of marriage and marital distress before moving more directly into a consideration of the behavioral point of view: There are probably more authoritative myths about marriage than about any other area of human study. Not only has our knowledge of marriage been based upon retrospective survey data, but it has depended largely upon theoretical prescriptions often reflective of traditional value orientations. As Laws (1971) and others have noted, researchers have started with little more than a popular conception about male and female roles and then set out to demonstrate how reality fits these construals. Significant longitudinal observation of marital interaction is simply not available. The level of theoretical sophistication of these models has done little to endear the topic of marriage to scientific study.

The arrival of behavior modification onto the marriage scene is therefore both a delusion and a snare. It is a delusion in the sense that once again a theory of human interaction has been developed which is derived from what is essentially a collection of technologies, in this instance guided by some assumptions about empiricism. Behavior modification is not a theory of human interactions; it is better described as a technology derived from learning principles, which are quite frankly mute on the issue of a theory of adult intimacy in long-term committed relationships! It is a snare in that the more the tool is used the more uses are found for it. While many of the techniques may be found effective for bringing about relationship behavior changes, the techniques will never answer value questions of what behavior should be changed (cf., Weiss and Margolin, 1977).

The alternatives at this point appear to be laid out clearly: (a) return to the easy chair and conjure up "ideal marriages," positing this or that degree of openness, traditionalism or egalitarianism; or (b) accept the metaphors of others, using engineering, systems, or computer analogies to marriage models, including models of individual cognitive processes; or (c) close shop and await some quality data on what transpires daily in marital interactions, then build theory upon the observational data. The approach taken here is to boldly take hold of the data produced by those working within a learning theory model, and to weave back and forth between what the technology illuminates and the data seem to support.

BEHAVIORAL ANALYSIS

This section will briefly review basic learning concepts which form the basis of behavior modification or social learning approaches to human problems. Since the emphasis of this chapter is on interactional behaviors and the conditions under which persons learn social behaviors, this discussion will not focus on the more symptom oriented behavioral approaches in which symptoms predominate, such as anxiety, compulsive eating, bedwetting, and so on. Rather, discussion will be with how persons learn, change, and influence the behavior of others. Examples will be drawn more from naturalistic settings rather than from the laboratory, since most interesting interpersonal behavior occurs in small groups of intimates, marriages and families.

Situations × Persons × Behaviors

The world is populated with Situations, Persons, and Behaviors, which is to say the earth is not round, it is a cube. Any of these domains (faces) can be sampled, but Persons is most often sampled. To study the range of human potential, though, it would be necessary to specify a broad representation of Situations in order to discern just what it is persons may accomplish. The output or response face, Behaviors, can be judged only in terms of the demands of the Situations. A behavioral analysis requires a set of concepts for each of these three faces of a cube, and a set of rules for relating each face to the others. The cube may be illustrated as in Figure 1.

One immediate conclusion suggested by the cube is that discussions of person similarity may mean (a) persons in the same situation, (b) persons with similar behavior capability, or (c) persons with similar organism characteristics. The cube also suggests that adaptability may be defined as being capable of diverse behaviors across situations; the more a person is capable of making differing responses in differing situations, the greater his or her adaptability. Thus, a person who emits the same behaviors in differing situations may be inflexible; much of assertiveness training seems directed at increasing response variability across situations.

Situations

Situations can be specified as *stimuli*, noting that there are four different stimulus functions that behavioral theorists describe: *eliciting* stimuli, *discriminative* stimuli, *neutral* stimuli, and *reinforcing* stimuli.

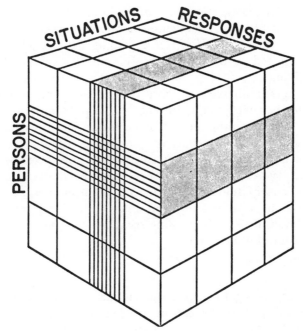

FIG. 1. Person by situation by response cube.

When some aspect of a situation reliably produces behavior (response), it is said to be an *eliciting stimulus*. A hot stove is an eliciting stimulus for rapid hand withdrawal; stimuli which reliably elicit such responses are part of a stimulus-response-reflex. But it is also possible through learning to have responding reliably associated with particular stimuli, so that sights, sounds, or smells of objects can become associated with particular responses. Most of these kinds of stimulus-response units seem to fall within the domain of *classical* or *respondent* conditioning and are typically not associated with verbal control. However, thoughts ("What will I say if she says no!") can elicit physical responses such as sweating or dryness of the mouth.

From a social learning framework *discriminative stimuli*, or S^D's are of particular interest. A stimulus is said to function as a discriminative stimulus when it signals the occasion that some response will be followed by a consequence. S^D's have a cueing function, making some response more probable. Discriminative stimuli have a controlling function over behavior; stop signs, insignias, a question, or a note pinned to the refrigerator door. These stimuli have been associated with consequences but are not themselves consequences of responding.

Neutral stimuli have no function regarding behavior, but conditions could be arranged so that a previously neutral stimulus is associated with responding.

Reinforcing stimuli refer to those situational events which are consequences for behavior and which change the probability of occurrence of the responses preceding them. Note, according to this definition, that not all pleasurable consequences are reinforcing stimuli. A consequence may be a reward, a desirable outcome such as unexpected money, but unless some class of responses is strengthened by the response → consequence relationship, reinforcement has not occurred. Observers may rate some consequences as pleasing but unless behavior rates change the pleasing stimuli are merely pleasing stimuli having no significant function in the control of behavior.

Persons*

Persons vary along biological dimensions, such as physiological response capability, neurological integration, genetic, and biochemical functions. Behavior is biologically based and controlled by the physiological limits of organisms.

Interpersonal behavior is more often related to cognitions, the symbolic ways in which persons represent experience to themselves and others, through language, thought, images, and so on. Thoughts and feelings interact in a stimulus → response sequence, and self-statements are often effective controlling stimuli for other behaviors. While thoughts are private unless spoken, the variables which influence behavior also influence thought processes.

Behaviors

The stimulus counterpart of situations is in the same relationship as *responses* are to behavior. Typically, a response does not mean an isolated twitch; this term is used to denote behavioral events rather than undefined behaving. Responses may be covert or overt, but in either

---

* As drawn, Persons and Responses are not independent in the same sense that both are independent of Situations. It is not possible for Responses to be independent of Persons. The point of the illustrative cube is to show how each face may contribute relative to the others. Thus, it is possible to focus on Responses per se, ignoring individual (Persons) differences. The author appreciates Dr. Carlos Sluzki calling this asymmetry to his attention.

case defining the stimulus conditions which control responses is of most interest.

Responses are usually defined as *respondents* or *operants*. The former are under the control of eliciting stimuli, and therefore occur on "call"—that is, the frequency of the stimulus equals the frequency of the response (until physiological adaptation takes place). The consequences of respondents typically do not alter the frequency of their occurrence.

Operants refer to behaviors which have a statistical frequency of occurrence over time when an eliciting stimulus is either unknown or not present. A person may cry frequently, usually followed by attention from others. This behavior-consequence relationship (contingency) is quite likely to produce a higher rate of crying when people are present. Children move about in ways which annoy adults; adults often seek explanations of this "hyperactivity." But the behavior has a countable frequency over time which probably is stable for specific situations. Consequences for such behavior include yelling at the child to sit still, threatening glances, offering books, toys, and so on; if the behavior rate increases contingent upon such consequences, the behavior is said to be reinforced by the consequences. Operant behaviors—behaviors which have any rate greater than zero—can be reinforced quite independently of the intention of others.

This first section defined terms relating to the three sides of the cube, stimuli, person-variables, and responses. The next section considers some rules which describe operations relating to these three domains.

Reinforcement Control

Consequences of behavior are reinforcing to the extent that they affect the rates of behaving. The rate of a behavior (such as talking) can be accelerated or decelerated. Consequences which accelerate the rate of a behavior are *reinforcers;* consequences which decelerate behaviors are *punishers*. Reinforcers may function in two ways: a *positive consequence* may follow upon a response or an *aversive consequence* may terminate after a response is made. Both outcomes will change rates of behavior. The positive case is termed positive reinforcement, while the termination of aversiveness is termed negative reinforcement. If one smells natural gas upon entering the house, one seeks for a turnoff valve; those responses which terminate the aversive gas smell are strengthened (reinforced) and, given the S^D (discriminative stimulus) of gas, the turn-off response is made promptly. If one is threatened with attack, submission may reduce the overt threat, thereby reinforcing submission as a response to threat.

Punishment involves either the presentation of aversive stimulation (hitting, yelling) or withdrawal of positive stimulation (loss of benefits). In either case the rate of ongoing behavior is suppressed. Punishment and negative reinforcement are often confused although it can be seen that they involve very different contingencies. A response which removes an aversive stimulus is thus negatively reinforced, whereas the presentation of aversiveness (or loss of benefits) suppresses or punishes ongoing responding. Unscheduled opportunities for punishing behavior are plentiful: A call to say that one will be late is often met with a criticism, which may have the effect of suppressing phone calls announcing lateness. A distinction is required between being informed and the content of the information: The content may be abhorrent but the availability of the information should be reinforced positively.

Reinforcers and punishments may be either primary or secondary, referring to their status as natural events or learned outcomes. Pain, food, natural holocausts are all examples of primary reinforcers or punishments requiring no learning. Most social behavior is controlled by secondary or generalized reinforcers or punishments: Stimuli which are regularly associated with positive or negative outcomes take on reinforcing properties of those primary outcomes. In most situations, various forms of attention, such as eye contact, are secondarily reinforcing. Approval of others is another example of a learned reinforcement. Because of the effectiveness of generalized reinforcement (for example, money), it is possible to reinforce a wide range of behaviors without clearly intending to do so. Paying attention to a person when that person is engaging in some undesirable behavior may strengthen that behavior. Money can be used to reinforce a diverse set of behaviors because it is associated with so many other reinforcements.

The withholding of reinforcement contingent upon responding defines *extinction*. Inattention to a response which had previously been reinforced with attention is a case of extinction; behaviorally, a decrease in the rate of the original response results, the response eventually reaching its operant level. The interesting observation that much human behavior continues in the face of no apparent reinforcement (such as slot machine responses) suggests that withholding reinforcement does not produce an immediate cessation of responding.

Discussing the relationship between a response and its consequences defines the *contingencies* governing that response. The amount and frequency of reinforcement can be made to vary contingently upon responding. *Reinforcement schedules* refer to the relationship (either temporal or determined by response frequency) between responding and occurrence of consequences. A slot machine is programmed to pay off variably after so many lever pulls, but not after every lever pull. Much behavior is reinforced only aperiodically, and oftentimes noncontingently! Praise may come when a person feels least effective; an effortful production may be followed by disinterest.

Scheduling of reinforcements is important in social behavior because response rates are strengthened according to their reinforcement histories. When reinforcement occurs aperiodically (other than on a one-reinforcement-to-one-response basis), extinction and reinforced trials become blurred. It typically takes much longer to give up (reach baseline levels) after an aperiodic reinforcement history.

Stimulus Control

As noted earlier, stimuli can function as discriminative occasions for responding; that means that reinforcing consequences are more likely when given the stimulus. The examples of interpersonal cueing are legion; for example, couples often use physical objects, such as a particular light, to signal the desire for sexual intercourse. Combining discriminative stimuli (S^D) with stimuli which reliably signal that reinforcement will not occur, stimulus delta (S^Δ), provides the conditions for concept learning. Learning to make a response when S^D is present and to withhold that response when S^Δ is present is to learn a discrimination. Behavior may be appropriate under some conditions but not others, which is another way of referring to concept formation.

Much behavior is sequentially organized and not a matter of discrete isolated responses here and there. Typing, skiing, driving, talking are a few examples of complex behavior chains. Behavior is chained when each response functions as the S^D for the next response. A popular example of response chains which are confused with intelligence is that of the white rat who has been trained to push a lever to release a ball which is then put into a chute, and so on, until a final response (riding a cart on a track) is made to produce a food pellet. The rat obviously appears to be intelligent since so many different responses unnatural to rats are required. But in training the animal each response was trained contingent upon the preceding response(s), thereby creating a sequentially organized chain. By omitting a critical response somewhere in the chain, the rat would be very confused or prematurely make responses normally occurring later in the chain. The same thing happens with typing. The letters at the end of a word come forward in time. Thus, each response can set the stage for the next response in a sequence.

Finally, learning can occur by *successive approximations* or *shaping*. No animal trainer would expect a horse to jump over a 10-foot rail until it had mastered five-foot jumps. Yet one spouse may berate another for having completed only part of a desired task, rather than reinforcing the effort! A youngster bringing home a B is admonished for not getting an A, and so on. Shaping refers to the process of reinforcing smaller approximations to the target behavior; it is an integral aspect of chaining.

However, the fact that shaping is also involved in negative behaviors is less obvious. In many aversive situations, persons wait until the intensity level is very high before responding. The classical (albeit pedestrian) example of this type of shaping is the child with harried parent shopping in the supermarket at 5:30 p.m. Bored child begins making mouth noises, asks for an ice cream cone, wiggles dangerously in the pushcart, yelps, reaches a tomato display and sends it resounding to the floor. At *this* point the parent turns to the child and admonishes the child's behavior! What the child has now learned is that attention is equated with high rate, high amplitude behavior; never mind this penny nickel stuff!

Learning and Performance

The concepts and principles described above are useful in understanding how responses (behaviors) are maintained under conditions which are either counterintuitive or more often stupid. However, much of the learning that takes place according to these rules pertains to overt responding. Adult learning probably occurs very quickly because of the considerable human facility in symbolic representation. Language fosters learning, as does simple observation of others. Some make a distinction between acquisition and performance (Bandura, 1969), suggesting that reinforcement principles govern performance (responding) but that learning is basically a one-trial affair, probably mediated by observation, as in modeling. This brief review of learning concepts has omitted the role of cognitions, self-verbalizations, feelings, and so forth, other than a passing note that such inner events can function as stimuli controlling overt behaviors. A considerable amount of adult relationship behavior is overt, in that each partner provides a very rich stimulus network to the other. Reinforcing exchanges should result in chained relationship behaviors, wherein one person is the stimulus for the other person's next response, and so on.

The next section considers some of the concepts about relationships that may be derived from three perspectives: individual, behavioral, and systems views.

Concepts from Individual, Behavioral, and Systems Theories

This section will briefly draw out threads common to three influential approaches to persons and persons in small groups—namely, individualizing, behavioral and systems points of view. The subsequent section will summarize the current views on relationships as developed within a modified behavioral or social exchange theory. This section provides a transition between stimulus-response behavior theory and the more eclectic social learning conceptions of marriage conflict and accord.

Individualizing theories of persons have been prominent in both our professional and artistic awareness (as in literature and drama); these theories have come to explain life as we know it. One unmistakable contribution of all personality theories has been the emphasis on individual consistency: *Theories of personality are theories of person consistency.* The specific structures which give rise to these consistencies differ from theory to theory—that is, drives, needs, motives, perceptual-cognitive consistencies, to name a few. The result is that attention is directed to inner forces, dynamics, or organizations which are largely responsible for directing the individual to this or that end. The psychoanalytic approaches represented by Meissner (Chapter II) and Nadelson (Chapter III) are excellent illustrations of models of person consistency. In fact, mate selection itself is largely determined by intrapsychic factors.

Some of the newer individualizing approaches, emphasizing cognitive more than drive-like consistencies, have stressed human ability to cognize experience, to impose order on experience, and to ignore contradictory input. In the earlier writing of George Kelly (1955) and now again in recent work (Mischel, 1973), the point is made that scientists may have erroneously reserved for themselves the right to form constructs of experience, often disregarding that nonscientists function daily in the same manner. All persons evolve construals of experience, and some of these construals are highly valued as part of the definition of self.

Individualizing approaches thus direct attention to the fact that persons (scientists and others) actively construe their own experiences, and that theory and value are ways of imposing a conceptual template onto experience. The issue here is not whether a particular construal is better than another but rather that construing is given.

The current interest in attribution theory (Kelley, 1973; Jones, Kanouse, Kelley, Nisbett, Valins and Weiner, 1972) reflects a professional interest in how persons attribute causality to the events around them. An illustration of how attributions about causality affect behavior: In a series of six studies showing essentially the same functions of person attributions, Langer (1975) offered office workers an opportunity to purchase lottery tickets; each prospective buyer was either (a) allowed to choose the ticket desired from the set, or (b) given a ticket chosen by the vendor. A lottery, of course, is a chance event and selection of ticket would not affect outcome. At a later time, under the ruse of someone else wanting to enter the lottery, and having sold all the tickets, the vendor offered to buy back the original ticket for whatever amount the person would sell it. The vendor went to great lengths to assure the person that he personally did not care whether the person sold the ticket back; it was strictly a matter of the other person's wanting a ticket.

Those persons who initially chose their own ticket demanded a significantly higher amount of money than those whose ticket had been selected by the vendor. Since both groups had been asked to sell their tickets and since originally all tickets cost the same, there was no issue of one holding a "winner." Rather it seems that an *illusion of control* was involved in determining the behavior of subjects. Rather than labeling the behavior as irrational—assuming a fair lottery, it seems more profitable to speak of attributions about causality directing behavior. Again, the emphasis here is not with the validity of attributions held, but rather that persons may be quite active in attributing causes to outcomes.

Behavioral approaches, as should be painfully obvious from the previous summary, focus primarily on situation-behavior relationships, seeking lawful relationships between stimulus conditions and responding. Unlike most other approaches, the learning model postulates as little as possible about unobservables, such as illusion of control. Behavior has statistical structure in that consequences (contingencies of reinforcement) change operant rates of responding; the scheduling of reinforcing consequences is particularly well suited to the study of interpersonal situations simply because of the density of stimulus → response → consequence sequences that persons in ongoing relationships provide one another. The potential for exchange between partners is considerable, as is the potential for reinforcing or extinguishing behaviors.

As noted above, the behavioral approaches are totally neutral as to what constitutes a reinforcer. Whereas individualizing approaches often lead us to rely on what persons say (as reflections of cognitive structures), the behavioral approach focuses only on outcomes: What is the effect of behavior A or B? What a person says and what a person does may differ widely because each system is under different stimulus or reinforcing control. Two illustrations may help make this point clearer. In his own research and that of his students into parent attitudes and child deviant behaviors, Stephen Johnson has found that children referred to parent-child clinics do not differ greatly, relative to "normal" families, in their behaviors coded in home settings, but rather parent attitude (or mood states) predicts parental response to the child more than the child's behavior itself. This was especially true in one study in which automatic audio recording "bugs" were placed in homes (thereby removing the reactive effects of a home observer) (Lobitz, 1974; Johnson, S. M., personal communication, April, 1977). Studies of preschool children have also indicated that parents and nursery teachers differentially reinforce stereotypical sex role appropriate behaviors, guided by their cognitions rather than by child behavioral activities (e.g., Margolin and Patterson, 1975).

A second case of the use of ongoing situational feedback can be illustrated with the following fictional example. Designate outcomes as positive (+) or negative (—): We note the car is dripping oil (—), someone narrowly misses hitting us in making their unsignaled left turn (—), we find a convenient parking space (+), and so on throughout the day. What kind of day has it been? If events are tracked (+'s and —'s) in their probabilistic structure, the proportion of "favorable" to "unfavorable" would answer the question empirically. Tracking most recent outcome ignoring density or *trend* leads to very different conclusions. From a social learning point of view, tracking the sequence of outcomes would be necessary in answering the question, regardless of what verbal statement one makes about the quality of the day.

Systems theory approaches, especially those proposed by developers of family therapy (Laszlo, Levine, and Milsum, 1974; Satir, 1964; Sluzki, Chapter VII; Steinglass, Chapter VI; Watzlawick, Beavin and Jackson, 1967) have had a considerable impact on thinking about marriages. The emphasis on communication and rules in communicating systems has been discussed extensively. Beyond the assertion that behaviors in one part of a system influence behaviors throughout that system, the systems approach is philosophically compatible with the functionalism of the behavioral models. Behavior is under the control of systems principles to the extent that the latter define the range of potential moves. *Systems theory also considers the situational control of behavior.* Rules, as metacommunications about permissible behaviors, are discriminative stimuli, such that rules are like system rather than individual attributions. Being in a particular relationship (system) also provides "meanings" to the behaviors of the participants. Rules of relationships constrain what may and may not take place, and rules define power relationships among the participants (cf., Haley, 1963; 1973). A helpful distinction may be that between having the opportunity to speak at a meeting versus having the capability of setting the agenda for the meeting; those who set the agenda have strategic control of the meeting. Stuart (1975) refers to respecting the *core symbols* of a relationship, those that define the security of the partners and which may not be compromised or negotiated without destroying the system.

Assuming that relationship behaviors are controlled by rules or system principles, how these develop is of interest. In other forms of partnerships, persons may contractually spell out rights and obligations. In intimate relationships it is more likely a matter of trial and error, together with available tribal wisdom. Current society provides an interesting opportunity for observing how couples will accomplish the blend of rule definition and daily behaviors in their quest for establishing egalitarian marriages. Egalitarianism, as a guiding principle, still requires that partners work out the daily behaviors within that type of relationship. Thus, behavior in such a relationship is controlled by its consequences. However much thought is given to explicit rule definition, the daily behavioral exemplars are like skills that must be developed. Particular environments may not support the goals as defined—for example, inadequate architecture or temporal imbalances such as working swing shifts.

It would seem that from a systems point of view behaviors are under situational control, that often one can construe more or less explicit rules by which participants interact. Such rules may be functionally important regardless of their conscious elaboration.

This selective review of individualizing, behavioral, and systems points of view leads to the conclusion that, in addition to response control, there are cognitive or representational modes of behavior control. The review has shown how individual attributions about causality affect behaviors, how in specific instances cognitions may be controlled by variables different from those controlling overt behaviors (observers and subjects need not agree), and how systems models emphasize rule governance of behaviors, which is a higher order of stimulus control (situations govern interactions). Decisions are always necessary whether one or another level of analysis is appropriate to the behavior under study, that is, whether to focus on individual responses, cognitions, or system rules. Rather than arguing for the application of one model it may serve better to differentiate among the complexes of the behavior and select a model accordingly.

The next section presents a brief review of the currently promising behavioral models that have directed much of the clinicial work with couples, showing how learning principles and some of the cognitive points of view have been brought together in these current models.

Integrative Behavioral Approaches

This section briefly traces the development of current models for applying behavioral principles to marriage relationships, focusing largely on current social learning approaches. This literature has been comprehensively reviewed by others (Jacobson and Martin, 1976; Patterson, Weiss, and Hops, 1976; Weiss and Margolin, 1977) and will not be covered in detail here. Since the approach to marriage relationships being proposed by this writer draws heavily upon this literature, this section is a transition to the next where a particular model will be offered.

Behavioral approaches to marital conflict were characteristically atheoretical in earlier reports. The focus of relationship therapy was often no more complex than attempts to change the behavior of one person. Thus Goldstein and Francis (1969) trained five wives to selectively extinguish undesirable husband behavior while reinforcing desired behaviors. Goldiamond (1965) reported two case illustrations of treating couples which focused on either self-control procedures or interdependent reinforcement contingencies; individuals were taught to bring their behavior (a) under stimulus control by rearranging their interaction settings or (b) under reinforcing control by making a desired outcome contingent upon accomplishing a targeted behavior (for example, keeping an appointment with each other). Lazarus (1968) employed desensitization and assertiveness training (cf., also Fensterheim, 1972). These reports have been of single case applications where the focus was largely on some specifically targeted behavior, not necessarily relationship behavior.

The major attempts to go beyond changing some targeted behaviors of individuals, who happened to be in relationships, are based on very similar theoretical elaborations by different authors; much of this development was concurrent and the confluence of points of view made individual contributions difficult to credit. Stuart (1969) published an important integrative model which he labeled an "operant interpersonal treatment" for marital discord, drawing heavily upon social psychology (notably exchange theory) and the earlier work of the communications people within systems theory (such as Lederer and Jackson, 1968; Watzlawick et al., 1967). During this same period, Patterson and Weiss were developing a social learning approach to child-parent conflict (for example, Patterson and Reid, 1970; Patterson and Cobb, 1973). Azrin (Azrin, Naster and Jones, 1973) also presented a carefully reasoned model for marital interaction based exclusively upon operant principles which further elaborated on Stuart's model.

Thibaut and Kelley's (1959) theory of social exchange has provided the basis for subsequent elaboration of reciprocity. Exchange models are a form of behavioral economics, appropriating concepts such as benefits and costs; the former are defined as satisfactions, the latter as dissatisfactions. As applied to intimate, ongoing relationships, exchange theory emphasizes an interdependence of reinforcing control, in terms of individuals striving to maximize benefits (affectional and material gains) and minimizing costs (aversiveness of the other's behavior). The joint payoff matrix, for couples, contains an inherent confusion. As Gottman, Notarius, Markman, Bank, Yoppi, and Rubin (1977) note, based upon Gergen's (1969) analysis of exchange models, benefits and costs derive from two different types of events, one in which the person emits (exhibits) a behavior, and the other in which a person receives behavior from another. Thus, not only can behaviors be viewed in terms of their intrinsic reward value (benefits), but they must also be viewed in terms of the extrinsic benefits *and* costs. Although teasing may be intrinsically beneficial (intrinsically high reward-low cost of teasing), the response of the person being teased provides an extrinsic reward-cost dimension as in threatened withdrawal of affection if teasing continues. In a satisfying marriage, not only should the intrinsically beneficial behaviors be low cost to the other, but each person must receive highly beneficial behaviors from the other; it follows that one person's received beneficial behaviors also should be low cost (therefore, easier to give) behaviors for the other. (If benefits are provided begrudgingly, at high cost of emitting, very negative sentiments may result.) The interdependency of this exchange requires that each person have potentially high reward value for the other; the positive reinforcingness of each for the other must be high. Thibaut and Kelley suggest that behavioral exchanges follow a norm of reciprocity over time so that parity or equilibrium is established for the exchange. When rewards and costs become imbalanced, attempts are instituted to bring the relationship back into equilibrium. From the earlier operant model proposed by Homans (1950), frequency of social interaction is said to be a direct function of number of mutual rewards exchanged in the relationship. Further, positively reinforced encounters also increase positive sentiment toward the relationship itself.

Stuart has elaborated the social exchange concept by assuming that the marriage relationship at a given time represents the best of available rewarding alternatives for the couple, that is, it represents the best balance each can achieve between individual and mutual rewards and costs (Thibaut and Kelley, 1959, p. 12). Over time, the expectation of reciprocity is developed and maintained, a *quid pro quo* arrangement (Lederer and Jackson, 1968). In a successful marriage, both partners work to maximize mutual rewards while minimizing individual costs. (The nature of the payoff matrix concerns mutual reward.)

"In an unsuccessful marriage" the exchange process shifts since "both partners appear to work to minimize individual costs with little apparent expectations of mutual reward" (Stuart, 1969, p. 675). Each person can trim costs by giving less value (withdrawal) or by shifting to a process involving negative reinforcement and punishment, the *coercion process* defined by Patterson and Reid (1970). In coercive interactions one member seeks to gain positive reinforcement in exchange for negative reinforcement.

As Patterson et al. (1976, p. 244) state it:

> An aversive stimulus is presented in either of two ways. It can be delivered contingently following a certain response which is to be suppressed, or it can be presented prior to the behavior which is to be manipulated and then withdrawn only when the other person complies. "Punishment" and "negative reinforcement" described the processes involved in coercion.

Stuart (1969, p. 176) cites an example of how this occurs:

> . . . a husband might wish his wife to express greater affection; following the failure of his amorous advances, he might become abusive, accusing his wife of anything from indifference to frigidity, abating his criticism when he received the desired affection.

This approach is self- as well as relationship-defeating, since, as Stuart points out, by making himself abusive the husband lowers the chances of his receiving reinforcement from wife, his abusiveness denigrates the reward value of wife's affection; if she complied under these coercive circumstances, it must appear as appeasement rather than "genuine affection," a credibility problem of no mean proportion.

Reciprocity has also been stressed by Azrin et al. (1973) and is operationally defined as providing reinforcement for reinforcing behavior. If each partner pleases the other (reinforces the other), it is necessary for each to reinforce the occurrence of pleasing behavior. Therefore, frequency and variation of reinforcers are critical to Azrin's approach; the greater and more varied the reinforcement exchanged over a wide range of behaviors, the greater the reciprocity and the marital happiness.

To be sure, each of these formulations has been subjected to much critical debate, and the supporting empirical literature has been thoroughly picked over (cf., Gottman et al., 1977; Gurman and Kniskern, 1978; Jacobson and Martin, 1976). Gottman et al. (1977) have suggested that the behavior exchange theory described above is unclear regarding the nature of reward-costs payoff, and more importantly, researchers have essentially failed to test the reciprocity notion. As noted, because Gottman et al. detected ambiguity in how rewards and costs are presumed to operate in marriages, they asserted that there has been no adequate test of perceived value of rewards exchanged, only tests provided by outsiders (e.g., trained coders) who label behaviors as (potential) rewards. Thus, when Birchler, Weiss, and Vincent (1975) report that dysfunctional couples, relative to nondistressed couples, emit significantly less positive and significantly more negative coded behaviors, this does not support exchange theory since no attempt was made to determine how the recipients themselves rated the reward value of the behaviors exchanged. Gottman et al. argue further that reciprocity can be demonstrated within social learning formulations only as reinforcing control, a point for point reciprocity; a positive husband response, for example, begets an immediate positive wife response. (The conditional probability of wife positive given husband positive must exceed the non-conditional or base rate probability of wife positive.) The implication of Gottman's argument is that the *intentionality* of communications must be accounted for what each person *intended* to send as well as *impact* of the message on the receiver. If there is a misalignment between intended and received messages, Gottman argues, the case for a *communication deficit* model of marital distress would be strengthened. The deficit exists only when intention and impact do not agree, not when they are both negative. A wife intending to send negative and husband receiving negative have a problem with negatives, not with communication!

Thus, while communication has been widely implicated as a source of marital distress (by couples and therapists), there is remarkably little direct evidence reported in support of any particular theory. Gottman's approach is exciting since his research follows directly from this analysis of exchange theory failures.

To summarize and draw whatever conclusions possible at this point: Current social learning models of marital accord and distress are based upon social exchange concepts which, in turn, stress quasi-behavioral economics; partners enter marriage with the expectation that the ratio of rewards to costs of relatedness will outrun the rewards to costs of singleness. In well-functioning relationships, partners should be exchanging benefits, which are bolstered by the fact that each person has reinforcement value for the other. Since relationships such as marriage involve behavior exchanges over a wide spectrum of possibilities, there are numerous opportunities for rewarding exchanges likely to maintain the relationship.

The failure of relationships is thought to be explained by deficient reward exchanges. In fact, it is said that the reward system shifts from a positive to a coercive control system in which each person attempts to coerce positive reinforcement in exchange for negative reinforcements. Forced rewards, like solicited compliments, lose their value.

In addition to contingency control, marriages may become distressed because of communication deficits, and within the social learning framework there is at least one spokesperson for the communication deficit position.

These elaborations of behavioral principles increasingly mention cognitive variables—if not always attributions about causes, at least the role of expectations and the building of sentiments. These points of view also reflect the significance of stimulus control and, to a somewhat lesser extent, the kinds of system control noted in systems theory approaches. The main contribution from systems points of view seems to be in dealing therapeutically with communication in marriages.

BEHAVIORAL SYSTEMS APPROACHES TO MARRIAGE

This section brings together the assorted wisdom of the various approaches to marriage relationships discussed in previous sections and, taking a broad based social learning view, proposes a behavioral systems approach to marriage. This approach will, of course, draw heavily on applications of social exchange, reciprocity, and communication points of view.

Specifying Criteria for Relatedness

Marriage relationships involve commitment, mutual independence, and change. Marriages can be assigned to either of two gross categories, *obligatory* or *beneficial* types of relationship. Obligatory relationships are defined as tradition-controlled, role-structured forms of commitment wherein success and satisfaction accrue by living up to externally imposed standards of excellence; doing what is correct is more important than individual expressions of personality or selfhood. There are also many economic and political ramifications of such orderings of intimacy not considered here.

Beneficial relationships are more often based upon an egalitarian, co-partner type of relatedness ideology emphasizing success through personal accomplishment, personal growth, and humanistic concerns. Although beneficial relationships also may be rule-governed, the ideological basis is likely to be quite different: The individual partners are seen as having far greater control over which rules shall operate. The contributions of the partners are emergent and define the "success" of such marriages.

Of the customary distinctions between types of marriage relationships drawn by sociologists, the concern here will be with beneficial (socioemotional) rather than with instrumental (traditional) forms of relatedness. Traditional relationships, when in need of help, are served by tradition-oriented providers, and since one-half of all married women between 25-54 are regularly employed, marriages are headed toward arrangements of financially contributing partners more than ever before. This author's value judgment, which should be made explicit, is that the concern of professionals in this area should be with prevention and not curing—prevention of the destructiveness that spouses can wreak upon one another, not of marriage. An effective theory of intimate relationships should point the way to providing individuals with relationship skills prior to the time that they have acquired skillfulness in aversive control. *Thus, it would seem that behavioral approaches to marriage are best suited to relationships which already subscribe to more egalitarian than traditional ideological components.*

It is interesting to note that the rising divorce rate signals greater ease in withdrawing from nonbeneficial relatedness, but the relatively stable remarriage rate also suggests that the dissatisfaction is not so much with marriage but with specific relationships (Carter and Glick, 1970). The political and economic effects of the feminist movement are also consistent with increased attractiveness of beneficial relationships. Finally, the behavioral model seems particularly appropriate to second marrieds, where relationship concerns are often about resource allocation and maintaining individuality within the dyad. But as the Prochaskas (Chapter I) observe, the transition from traditional to companionship marriages is far from complete; companionship marriages may be more the ideal than a reality.

Marriage relationships differ in many important ways from any other two-person ongoing relationship, such as roommating, business partnerships, and so forth. In a marriage, behaviors are exchanged in a relatively closed system* where producer and consumer are mutually dependent upon one another for repeat business. With the exception of the telephone company, most business can be taken elsewhere if dissatisfied. While it may be good business sense to aim for the short-term gain —make a killing and leave—marriages, like the corner store, cannot afford this zero sum game tactic. If there is to be an exchange of commodities of value, the closed system limits the extent to which one can maximize individual gains.

Another feature of marriages is the pervasiveness of exchanges: Both parties operate a general store which makes available love, sex, status, and life support systems! Taking a gain in one area of the commodities market is certain to produce retaliation in some other areas of the market. The specialization of function in other relationships—visiting a friend for conversation, a physician for health needs, an auto mechanic, lawyer, and so on—is not possible within marriage relationships. The same person with whom one struggles over finances, plans with for vacations, helps with one's infirm parents, keeps the child from becoming a neighborhood menace, is also the source of sexual gratification and understanding comfort! From a learning point of view, the number of discriminations required by this arrangement are legion and likely to break down without well programmed control. Quality of sex may have more to do with getting the roof repaired than time since the last sexual encounter!

Marriage relationships contribute one additional element not running through most other transactions. Not only are commodities exchanged over a wide range of possibilities, but all marital transactions potentially have relevance to self values. These behaviors may have objective market value, but more often they relate to the self-esteem or personal worth of

---

* The use of the phrase "closed system" is not contradictory to Steinglass's descriptions of living systems as open (Chapter IV). The intention here is to focus on the consistency or regularity of the behavioral changes. (Cf. Steinglass's definition of system emphasizing elements organized by consistent interrelatedness.)

the partners. Failure to accomplish a better savings in a commercial transaction may lead to feeling foolish, but it is unlikely to profoundly affect one's sense of personal worth. Couples often use their behavior with one another as a means for providing information about the other's *intent*. The attribution of causality is a well developed skill. For example, failing to get gas for the car or calling to announce one's lateness are not just simple omissions which require remediation; they are commissions having to do with love, consideration, or caring: "It is because you don't care enough about me. . . ." A 2 × 2 matrix may be constructed with high and low objective value and good or bad intent as the rows and columns. An object may have considerable value (a diamond ring) but the wrong intent (it belonged to a previous wife!). The subjective rating of intent may effectively contradict the objective value.

To summarize to this point: Marriage relationships are governed by *ideologies, stage of their own development,* and *allocation of resources.* The less a relationship is governed by clearly stated rules (traditional versus egalitarian relationships), the greater the potential for idiosyncratic solutions, that is, far greater trial and error approximations. Relationships based upon beneficial ideologies require considerable accommodation without benefit of seasoned rules to dictate outcomes. Relationships are also committed to change; the partners grow older together and requirements change with life situation. Finally, a closed system must deal with the allocation of resources—one person's gain or loss has implications for the gain or loss of the other. In this sense the relationship is said to be mutually interdependent; as one example, by increasing relationship benefits unilaterally, one necessarily reduces the total amount of benefit available within the system. If a person chooses to drink heavily, for example, for whatever real or imagined gains this produces, the behavior diminishes relationship resources in terms of both finances available for other goods and the quality of consciousness of one member of the group.

This quasi-economic view of beneficialy based relatedness suggests evaluative criteria in terms of *satisfaction with skill competence.* By definition, such relationships exist to provide benefits to the members. *Satisfaction is an accomplishment within such a relationship.* Accomplishments may be either chance events or the result of behaviors directed toward ends. *Accomplishment is related to skillfulness as well as effort.* Couples may exert effort but lack skills, which would result in fatigue but not satisfaction.

A behaviorist would empirically define those behaviors necessary to accomplish the objectives of a satisfactory relationship, perhaps by noting what successfully married couples do. This would yield a long and probably confusing list of accomplishments. The task could be simplified somewhat by systematically sampling the various stages of the family life cycle (cf. Rollins and Cannon, 1974; Spanier, Lewis and Cole, 1975) or stages of personal development (cf., Erikson, 1950; Haley, 1973; Sheehy, 1976) and describe the demands of each life stage. Psychoanalytic and systems models, as represented in Chapters II and VI, currently incorporate some concepts of life stages which are applicable to marital adjustment. Such taxonomies can become prescriptive rather than descriptive. Not every couple *must* have children to meet anyone's definition of marriage or the good life (cf., Laws, 1971); role theorists have in the past relied too heavily on survey data rather than interactional data, and have often reflected traditional value systems rather than human adaptability. But such developmental taxonomies are useful if used in a conditional probabilistic way: *Given* that a couple has a child, what accomplishments are necessary? Persons remaining in marriage beyond 20 years are a very select sample since by that time many dissatisfied others have had an opportunity to leave the sample. Situational demands met by those remaining couples may be similar, but their coping may reflect resignation more than creativity. Fortunately or otherwise, little present interactional information is based upon older couples.

Clearly this theorizing runs far ahead of the data; descriptive information about couples and their coping with relationship accomplishments is not available. In the absence of normative data, available data, based on dysfunctional couples are drawn upon. A theory of relationships based on data from dysfunctional interactions is as hazardous as in the field of psychopathology. Given these cautions, the next section presents a tentative model, bolstered with data in the final section of this paper.

Stimulus and Reinforcement Control in Marriage

Specifying contingencies of adult reinforcement is difficult. Most persons are not well practiced in contingency control management and lack adequate tracking skills. Scheduling is very complex with adult reinforcement: Persons may be reinforced after variable intervals, thus making an entire *sequence* of behaviors more probable than a single response. Reinforcing stimuli are often noncontingently available. A couple may have a fight which is followed by a "making up" period, so that the expected aversiveness of fighting does not operate. The sequence is fighting leads to pleasurable interactions, which shapes masochistic behavior. Similarly, for adults verbal mediators, thoughts, cognitions intervene between responses and consequences. Specifying reinforcing control on a point-for-point basis is likely to remain difficult. Similarly, because of the availability of many otherwise positive behaviors (tasty meals, pleasuring, listening, instrumental accomplishments), persons may become satiated with noncontingent consequences, or at least take them for granted. In order for these events to gain reinforcing status, they would require intensity shaping. Reinforcing behaviors can be put on a schedule which reduces their effectiveness; they may actually lose their discriminative properties.

An alternative focus could be on stimulus control, the cue functions of stimuli. Language facilitates cueing through thoughts, talking to oneself, attitudes, and so forth. Persons also bring their own behavior under stimulus control by making lists for themselves.

Rules are the highest embodiment of stimulus control: Behavior guided by rule expectation is analogous to control of a super list. Traditional relationships provide ready-made rules which are condensed into a single stimulus—"mother," "wife," "provider."

Finally, situations themselves provide occasions of stimulus control of behavior. If one studies at the same table that provides dinner, hunger seems to attack frequently. Social gatherings may effectively control rates of drinking or smoking. Reid (in press) has shown how drinking in bars can be brought under the stimulus control of the drinking behavior of a model, who drinks heavily or minimally.

Because intimate relationships provide benefits in a metavalue system— self worth value of behaviors—partners in such relationships seek the guidance of symbolic meaning of behavior. These meanings become codified in trait descriptive labels, such as, "He's a very considerate person." It is easier to deal with a person if we have the person's rules, for example, considerateness. The other is reinforced for his/her *considerateness* rather than for the behavior itself. The flowers may be lovely, but the thought behind the flowers is what counts. Considerateness is born from such transactions and may become disembodied from behavior, floating about as merely a label (the flowers may have long since died).

Communications theorists are most helpful, if not downright brilliant, with these kinds of stimulus control operations. The works of Watzlawick et al. (1967), Haley (1963), Lederer and Jackson (1968) are a few examples of how sophisticated communications rules and their meanings may become. These higher orders of patterning which determine interactional behaviors can be addressed empirically (cf., Phillips and Metzger,

1976; Rogers and Farace, 1975) by communications analysis. *It is important to note that stimulus control, as the term is used here, does not imply ability to verbalize the rules.* A dyad may function reciprocally without ever being able to state the rules governing their behavior. Interruptions and contingent attending may characterize an interaction between spouses when discussing a child's misbehavior, but not when discussing a weekend recreational plan.

The aim of a behavioral systems approach, then, is to identify classes of events which control behavior in complex, multichoice relationships. Person A, for example, seeks satisfaction on a cognitive level: "Show me you care"; person B delivers responses much like behavioral commodities. The likelihood of satisfaction is predictably low in this arrangement. The value of adult regard is conditioned by meanings. As therapists it behooves us to utilize these meanings in selecting behavioral enactments which are designed to provide contingencies of reinforcement. A therapist may urge one partner to be more affectionate to another—such as in providing a "love day" for that person—while ignoring an interfering attribution held about the giver: "He is only interested in himself!" Affection in such cases is not affection regardless of the response topography.

The intensity of reinforcers is difficult for outsiders to control. In principle, a class of stimuli could be identified which would make probable a response that acknowledges the true affection of the giver: "He *does* care about me!" However, routinely making one behavior contingent upon another, often done in contingency contracting, risks heaping more disfavor on one or the other partner. In other instances, such contingencies work effectively and predictably.

Reciprocity and exchange theories of marriage encounter difficulty with these kinds of considerations. One hypothesis is that for couples who successfully provide relationship satisfaction (who accomplish in varied areas of relatedness), functioning is rule-controlled. Rule-based exchange achieves parity over time, not on a moment-to-moment basis of reciprocity; point-for-point exchange reciprocity suggests that a relationship has shifted to reinforcing control rather than stimulus control. When satisfactions are low, one carefully tracks payoffs. The partners force a payoff matrix that is response contingent: "Where the hell is my affection?"

We also suspect, as a methodological aside, that the topography of positive and aversive behaviors is very different. In discussion settings, where most marital observations are made, the range of potential negative behaviors far outruns that for positive behaviors. There are numerous put-downs, both of a verbal and nonverbal nature, which can be emitted in an interview room, while there are relatively few equal magnitude but sign-reversed behaviors possible in that same setting. One could hardly produce flowers, a gourmet dinner, or a trip to Hawaii in that setting, whereas one could be insulting, rejecting, abrasive, to use the common trait designators. We quickly satiate to a person's rapid fire headnodded "ummhmms"; positive value decays quickly if given too frequently or without sufficient variation. Thus, within the limits of a discussion in a room, it appears to be relatively easier to generate negatives than positives.

The concept of reciprocity has been used in two contexts: Short-term reciprocity may characterize dysfunctional relationships and long-term reciprocity (or exchange) would characterize nondistressed relationships. There are some tentative findings to support these notions, especially in findings of negatives being reciprocated on a day-to-day basis where positives are reciprocated over longer periods (two weeks). A couple may have a rate of positive exchanges which identifies them like a signature. Over time, one observes their particular exchange rate of positives.

Behavioral Exchange—Change Model

The purpose of beneficial relationships is to provide gains not available from (a) other relationships, or (b) remaining single. With Stuart, it is assumed here that at any given stage of a relationship the partners have the best behavioral exchange of rewards and costs they can effect. One aspect of the ideology of egalitarian relationships, not usually fully elaborated, is *fate control*. When two persons form a beneficial relationship, they are in a sense giving over to one another a degree of fate control.* Each is now expected to have the capacity of changing the feelings states of the other, if not actual self evaluations. The relationship is thus mutually interdependent on fate control.

Typically, this assumption of fate control is workable since the partners assume an obligation for the well being of the other. *The failure of fate control in a closed system is not a lessening of magnitude, but rather*

---

* The controlling aspects of marriage have been conceptualized differently by psychodynamic, systems, and behavioral models. For psychodynamic theory, Meissner details the almost inevitability of persons coming together because of historical (developmental) need residues. Steinglass's analysis of the "communication" model within systems theory emphasizes the "command" function of communications which continually inform about the status of the relationship regarding who controls what. Views that one person exercises limiting control over another are likely to be bothersome to proponents of a free-spirit ideology.

a change in direction of control capability. If a person drinks to escape a nagging spouse, seeks an affair, or engages in other relationship-threatening behaviors, that person, nonetheless, is acting within the system defined by the original two partners. Total separation is the only effective way to extinguish fate control; even here there is a considerable period around separation when one obsesses about the past relationship.

The range of points of contact between two people in a committed intimate relationship is, as pointed out above, considerable. Persons provide confidences to one another, pleasures and displeasures of all sorts, financial dealings, resource allotment, personal services, and the like. Living together does indeed encourage interdependencies. Both behaviorally and ideologically, each person has fate control over the other.

Behavioral Exchange can be depicted as a Give-Get equilibrium. Although the range of commodities that can be exchanged is vast, "market value" is defined largely within the relationship. Since there is no common medium of exchange, such as money or gold, the partners are free to define value. As noted above, value interacts with intent, which further removes the exchange from public view and control. Relationship exchanges, therefore, are not subjected to consensual validation since no one else would understand!

How couples bring the Give-Get function into equilibrium should it move out of balance is central in this model. A third operation, behavior change, is necessary. The relationship is represented as in Figure 2.

The valve that regulates the balance between Giving and Getting is Behavior Change—the method by which couples go about instituting changes in the relationship to accomplish beneficial parity. If asked how

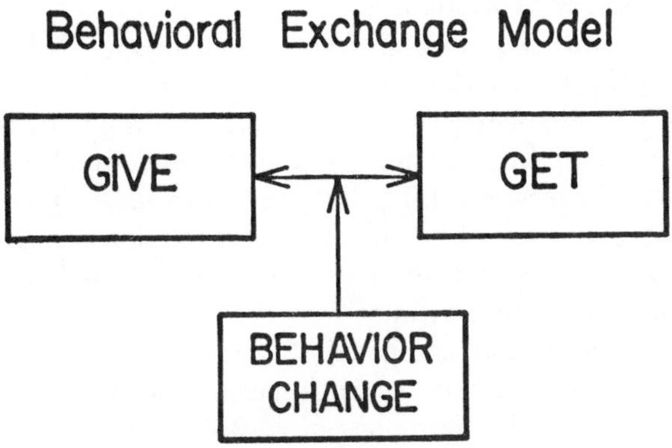

Behavioral Exchange Model

FIG. 2. Give—Get behavior change model.

they realign imbalances, spouses usually list such behaviors as "nagging, crying, withdrawing, threatening, feeling sorry for myself," and so on. Rarely do they suggest alternatives like "shaping desired behaviors, reinforcing X or Y, making assertive statements of my desires," and so on. The readiness with which aversive control procedures are mentioned reflects how a society relies on the use of aversive control to socialize young and control adults. ("Thank you for not smoking" signs are a pleasant exception.)

One reason that aversive control procedures are readily called upon is that punishment effectively stops ongoing behavior. The reinforcement (effectiveness) of punishing stimuli is immediately apparent to all; the troublesome behavior *does* stop! The application of aversive stimulation also produces audience responses; for example, crying elicits many kinds of concerned responses. Responses which are effective in accomplishing ends are themselves learned. If crying gains attention (a generalized reinforcer), which is then followed by a desired outcome (affection, increased resources), then crying as a tactic is strengthened.

As long as response-contingent reinforcement occurs, the system will move to a different equilibrium, for example, one person may effectively dominate another through sickness and health. However, if reinforcement—effectiveness in controlling outcomes—is noncontingent and, in the extreme case, if efforts at producing effects are futile (a noncontingent arrangement), conditions thought necessary for producing "learned helplessness" (Seligman, 1975) are present. In both animals and humans it has been possible to demonstrate that responses which are only randomly effective in terminating aversiveness produce a generalized nonadaptiveness, or learned helplessness, which in humans has been offered as an explanation of depression.

Thus, there are two possibilities for detrimental behavior change operations in the Give—Get relationship balance: one based upon an active reciprocity involving coercive control (trading negative reinforcement for positive reinforcement), and one based upon noncontingent reinforcement of effective coping, leading to learned helplessness.

Finally, there appears to be an interesting relationship between marital satisfaction and the occurrence or nonoccurrence of specific behaviors in individual areas of marital interaction.

The Oregon group has construed 12 areas of marital interaction in which spouses can demonstrate skillfulness; these particular categories have been derived from a number of sources, but are most similar to those defined by Azrin et al. (1973) in their Marital Happiness Scale.

TABLE 1

Twelve Categories of Marital Interaction

Appetitive	*Instrumental*	*By-products*
I. Companionship	VII. Child Care	XI. Personal Habits
II. Affection	VIII. Household	Appearance
III. Consideration	Management	XII. Self & Spouse
IV. Sex	IX. Financial &	Independence
V. Communication	Decision Making	
Process	X. Employment-	
VI. Coupling Activities	Education	

Items I through VI have in common the appetitive or sought after goals of interaction—those that reflect the gains one would expect to get from relatedness. The instrumental items label the work of a relationship: They may provide joy, but are not typically the affective basis for relatedness. Finally, the sequelae of marital production are labeled by-products of the interaction, results of, and certainly not reasons for seeking, relatedness. The popular cognitive labels for these subcategories have purposely been retained to communicate better with couples.

Couples seen for counseling or therapy state their complaints in decelerate terms: "I want her to stop . . .," or, "If only he wouldn't. . . ." Problems are behaviors which occur at too high a frequency. Couples focus on reduction of aversiveness, but have difficulty expressing accelerates: "I want him to do more of . . .," or, "If only she would give me more of. . . ." Plotting these categories against an idealized satisfaction scale generates a sigmoidal function called the Pleasure Sine Wave.

In idealized form, Figure 3 illustrates that the reduction in rate of aversive behaviors, those toward the right hand part of the wave, merely reduces dissatisfaction but does not in itself add to satisfaction. If all annoyances fell to zero rate/hour, one would be quiescent but not necessarily satisfied; soporiphic drugs might accomplish the same end. On the other hand, the occurrence of behaviors in categories I through VI, those on the left hand side of the sine wave increment satisfaction. *Their nonoccurrence would be expected to decrement satisfaction in a fairly nonspecific way.* It is most difficult to track the absence of behavior, the rate at which something did not happen. Therefore, decreased rates of

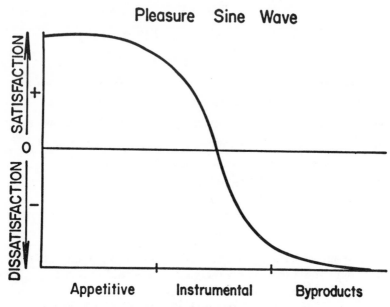

FIG. 3. Pleasure sine wave.

appetitive behaviors decrement satisfaction while increased rates of aversive behaviors increment dissatisfaction, the nonoccurrence of annoyances does not increment satisfaction.

Four Areas of Relationship Accomplishment

To return to the original question, the specification of relationship criteria: The foregoing concepts lead to a fairly straightforward taxonomy of relationship accomplishments. To set the stage for these:

(1) Relationships based upon beneficial ideologies must accomplish *the exchange of beneficial behaviors.* Persons do not live by reason alone; there must be a hedonic component to relatedness.

(2) *Relationship behavior is under the control of stimulus and reinforcing conditions;* stimulus control refers to discriminative stimuli (S^D's), the controlling function of rules and situations. Persons tend to focus their attention on inner causes of behavior, when often the control imposed by settings is far more important to understanding behavior outcomes. Reinforcing control refers to response-consequence contingencies.

(3) Relationships require *methods for communicating* about the host

of interaction possibilities, both hedonic and instrumental. In intimate communication, it is often possible to lose effective stimulus control of symbols, relying instead on private meanings of behaviors.

These are three relationships processes. However, it is possible to specify how these processes are manifested in the four areas of relationship accomplishment: *Objectification, Support/Understanding, Problem-Solving,* and *Behavior Change.* Under each, the role of hedonic, situational, and communicative functions will be indicated.

Objectification

Objectification refers to the *denotative* or pointing aspect of relatedness. Spouses need to make reliable discriminations in their behavioral environments among (a) the benefits received, (b) the situations which control behavior, and (c) discriminations among communication options.

Behavioral environments contain numerous stimulus-response sequences to which persons attach value; objectification refers to making these discriminations. Tracking events, determining the statistical structure of outcomes, noting what consequences follow which behaviors, these are all instances of discriminating behavioral environments. Typically, there is a lack of labels for such events in other than global terms (traits, motives, and so on). Thus, a partner is not lazy, in this sense, but the rate of some particular behaviors is too low; the reinforcing contingencies controlling such behaviors are possibly ineffective because of (a) noncontingencies (there are *no* consequences to emitting the responses) or (b) consequences are temporally too distant from the accomplishment itself (recalling two weeks afterwards that someone did a fine job).

The Marital Studies Program at the University of Oregon has developed a number of assessment and training techniques to help couples make discriminations in benefits received, the situational control of their relationship, and, of course, in communication skills—for example, learning pinpointing, opening statements, and so on, which are described elsewhere (for example, Weiss and Margolin, 1977).

Support/Understanding

Accomplishments in this area refer to skills which provide *companionship, comforting,* and *"understanding"* behaviors. Knowing how to discriminate between and among behavioral events (objectification) is not the same as having skills for accomplishing supportive-understanding objectives. Couples can be expected to provide these benefits to one another in affectional, companionship, and indeed, all the headings listed under appetitive in Table 1. Similarly, couples can provide supportive-understanding skills in their control of situations which support these behaviors. For example, "love days" are utilized with couples to help teach what happens in their relationship if they designate a single day during which one spouse provides a substantial increase in the Give part of the Give—Get relationship. These behaviors are tracked on special tracking forms and indicate which pleasures are being increased. Support/understanding in communication refers to those listening skills which communicate understanding (not necessarily agreement) with what is being said. Whereas Objectification refers to denotative meaning—"Did you say X?"—Support/Understanding here refers to *connotative meaning*, the feeling or implication of the message. Reflecting skills, use of paraphrases, identifying and using idiosyncratic helping aides (such as those suggested by Gottman et al., 1976; Margolin and Weiss, 1977) all qualify under this heading.

Spouses often attempt to trade management functions (cooking, providing a house, baby sitting, and so forth) as instances of support and understanding, whereas these are more properly labeled instrumental and personal services. One can be supportive and understanding *about* such functions, but that is different from personalized support and understanding. A couple may have an attractive house and properly socialized, neatly dressed children, yet fail miserably on support/understanding skills in appetitive areas of exchange.

Problem Solving

The accomplishment in this area is defined by the *producing of products* and *meeting objectives*. Problem Solving is the application of reason, intelligence, or experience to the production of some outcome, such as planning a recreational event, decision making about children, resources, sex, and so on. The processes involved in Problem Solving are different from those identified in the two preceding areas of accomplishment; skillfulness in these prior areas precedes success in problem solving. *Problem solving cannot occur if objectification has failed, or if one person is seeking support while the other is problem solving.* Problem-solving skills can be applied to benefits, situations, and the communication process itself. For example, agenda making is a way of ordering alternatives and can be applied to benefits or to situations which themselves control problem-solving behavior, for example, by limiting meeting times, scheduling administrative sessions, and so forth. Problem solving may be applied to communication by tracking on-target responses, using modality checking, stating positions rather than feelings, and so on.

Behavior Change

The last of the accomplishments to be defined deals with the control valve itself between Give and Get balances, namely Behavior Change. Relationships must be understood in terms of their stage of evolution, which of course implies that they change in some orderly fashion. Change may result from a crisis mentality, new relationship elements emerge out of each crisis, or change can be negotiated and planned. Relationships usually do not need further training in the use of crisis mentality approaches to change. *Couples often use individual responses to bring about changes when actually the change should be under rule control.* For example, fighting is generally under response control, each response serving as an S^D in a chain for the next response. While there are many who support a "fair fighting" approach to relationship change failures, the approach described here deals with fighting strategically by removing the situational antecedents which lead to fighting. Thus, in this system the focus is not on the rules for fighting but on the rules for providing successful outcomes. Similarly, problems with personal habits are often dealt with on a response level when they too might be more successfully handled as a problem of rules and resource allocation.

The explicit behavior change that is taught to couples usually involves accomplishments at each of the three preceding levels, and then introduces negotiating and contracting skills. It is important to note that within this model not all behaviors are candidates for contracting change operations. There are many case examples in the literature which would lead one to conclude that the standard treatment for sexual complaints is to make sex and conversation contingent upon one another: If conversation, then sex. Other, more sophisticated arrangements have been reported in which tokens are earned for some noncontroversial behavior, which are then exchanged for controversial behaviors, for example, tokens exchanged for sex or tokens exchanged for conversation.

Much can be accomplished with the first three areas so that relatively few problems require the full treatment of contracting and negotiation training. These procedures are best reserved for couples whose skill levels are very low and whose natural reinforcing effectiveness is simply too low to be trusted for adequate behavior change. However, in any event, couples must accomplish behavior change through positive and not aversive means.

Accomplishments × *Areas of Interaction* ×
Stage of Life Cycle

The model has stressed marital accomplishments as well as 12 categories of marital interaction; the latter were shown to contribute differentially to marital satisfaction-dissatisfaction (the Pleasure Sine Wave). One method for illustrating the interaction between these major classes is depicted in Figure 4.

Focusing first on the two-dimensional surface (Areas × Accomplishments), the model directs us to assess satisfaction among 48 cells (12 × 4 = 48). Each major accomplishment (Objectification and so on) can be viewed in terms of a "content" category, given by the 12 areas of interaction. In a sense, the model proposes a profile of marital satisfaction by determining how well a couple functions in each cell.*

The third dimension of the model, Stage of Life Cycle, is provided to emphasize differences in the requirements for interaction as a function of where a relationship is in time. The accomplishments for newlyweds are vastly different in quality from those of persons in post childrearing years. Yet, each life stage requires the accomplishments listed across the bottom of the figure. While the categories of Support/Understanding would be expected to change with stage of life, the requirement for Support/Understanding functions would not.

Of the three positions represented in this volume, only the psychodynamic model has attempted to specify developmental stages in detail, although these are pre-relationship stages. The ahistorical systems approaches and the behavioral approach described here allow for relationship changes because of the ". . . external psychosocial context within which the marital system is structured and functions" (Steinglass, Chapter VI). Certain similarities between the behavioral and systems models should now be apparent. Steinglass makes an important distinction between steady state and transition functions of systems; the former he sees as involving homeostatic mechanisms while negentropy is involved in the latter. Thus, he emphasizes, as does the present model, the necessity for conceptualizing maintenance versus transitional requirements of a relationship (system). The emphasis here on Behavior Change as the regulatory valve for the Give—Get balance is very similar to this

---

* Functioning in each of the cells is equated with satisfaction although it is an empirical matter whether individual cells will contribute more directly to reported marital satisfaction than do others. Only under the condition described by "love is blind" would no relationship between accomplishments and satisfactions be observed.

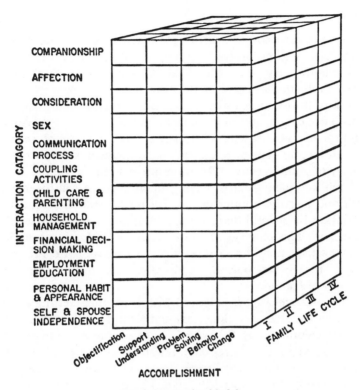

FIG. 4. Integrative Model.

suggestion. Of particular interest in this regard is the distinction between stimulus control (rule governance) and reinforcing control (point for point reciprocity) as two processes which may distinguish between distressed and non-distressed states of a relationship. As Steinglass notes, "adaptational mechanisms are critical during transition periods."

The model illustrated in Figure 4 takes a contemporaneous view of relationships, suggesting that there are accomplishments (genus) in specific areas of interaction (species), and that specifics within this interactive system change over time, that is, stages of life dimension. The model differs most from Meissner's exemplary account within a psychoanalytic framework in its nonadherence to the historical inevitability of current functioning. Like Steinglass's system, the focus is on relationship behaviors now, relative to the environmental context.

Summary

The behavioral exchange model presented here is quite dynamic in the sense of being responsive to system changes. Four areas of relationship accomplishment were identified: Objectification, Support/Understanding, Problem Solving, and Behavior Change. It was proposed that relationships shift between stimulus control and reinforcing control of relationship exchanges. Stimulus control functions refer to behaviors under the control of cues, either situational or in the form of relationship rules. Reinforcing control refers to behavior under the control of contingencies of reinforcement. Relationship distress is viewed as a shift toward reinforcement control relying upon aversive contingencies, punishment and negative reinforcement. Distressed couples frequently state complaints as behavioral decelerates, asking that some behavior decrease in frequency. The removal of aversiveness is reinforcing but does not increment satisfaction in a relationship. A pain avoidance strategy is not beneficial since it can only bring dissatisfaction to zero, but does not increment satisfaction.

A behavioral exchange is proposed with holds that Getting and Giving are in some balance over time, that imbalances in the relationship exchange are modulated by Behavior Change operations: Spouses institute actions to realign the Give—Get relationship. Choices for Behavior Change are many, but typically couples resort to use of aversive control, through nagging, threats, and the like. The goal of behavioral marriage counseling is to provide couples with behavior change operations based upon positive control procedures.

In terms of relationship accomplishments, it was proposed that stimulus and reinforcing control functions can be represented as accomplishments having to do with benefits, situations, and communication. Thus, objectifying benefits, situations, and aspects of communication process are all instances of teaching stimulus control of behavior. When these same three processes are viewed under the accomplishment of Support/Understanding, the focus shifts to reinforcing control. Teaching couples how to utilize supportive benefits, or how to put themselves in situations which are conducive to supportive outcomes, is the goal for this acomplishment.

The accomplishments are seen as sequentially ordered, such that Objectification is a prerequisite to the other three. It is also proposed that many relationship ills can be remedied by lower-level accomplishments, thereby making unnecessary the use of more complicated outcomes, such as Behavior Change in the form of negotiation and contracting. However,

Problem Solving and Behavior Change operations can be taught systematically to couples for use when the Give—Get balance is misaligned.

Finally, a three-dimension model was presented which integrates the areas of accomplishment with the specific areas of marital interaction. These two faces were then extended in time, in order to denote the importance of accomplishments as a function of stage of life of the relationship. Similarities and differences to the other models in this volume were noted.

The focus in the final section is on the empirical research which provides tests of these propositions, especially within each of the four major areas of accomplishment.

EVALUATION OF BEHAVIORAL POSITION

This section will summarize the nature and extent of empirical support for the behavioral concepts developed in previous sections. Following the plan of the previous section, this section will review the evidence under four headings of relationship accomplishment: Objectification, Support/Understanding, Problem Solving, and Behavior Change.

Objectification

The major issue for Objectification is whether the subjectivity of marital satisfaction can be partitioned into events capable of outside evaluation. Should the reporting of relationship satisfaction be unrelated to the actual happenings of daily life, primary focus would have to be on attitude or belief system rather than a causal behavioral system. Objectification, as a relationship accomplishment, therefore stresses ability: (1) to denote cause-effect relationships; (2) to make discriminations in one's behavioral environment, including knowledge of situational control of behavior; and (3) to be able to pinpoint desires. Not all categories are covered in the available literature, but the evidence germane to each category will be reviewed.

Sociological studies

Consider first the broader issue of marital satisfaction. Global, retrospective, survey type assessments of satisfaction, while most prevalent in the literature, are of limited value for current purposes (cf., Weiss and Margolin, 1977). Most important is evidence that *events* of a relationship add to or subtract from satisfaction. Behavioral marriage therapy seeks to increase behaviors which are productive of satisfaction; it is important to determine whether satisfaction and marital events are lawfully related.

In an extensive sociological interview survey of some 5,878 persons, Bradburn studied the structure of psychological well-being and provided interesting data for marital satisfaction (Bradburn and Noll, 1969). Bradburn focused largely on behaviors and feelings in the recent past rather than upon global recollections, and found marital happiness to be highly related to general happiness—somewhat more so for females. Marital happiness was inversely related to negative affect measures: a smaller relationship was found between positive affect measures and marital happiness! Negative affect scales included being bored, depressed, and so forth. Consistent with their findings about psychological well-being, positive and negative aspects of satisfaction were unrelated to one another, yet both related to overall satisfaction. Thus, it was found that scales labeled Sociability, Companionship, and Tensions were each related to marital satisfaction, but that the positive scales (Sociability and Companionship) were unrelated to the negative (Tensions) scale. The absence of tension items did not predict to presence of positive items; it simply means recording fewer tension items (for example, disagreements about specifics of the relationship, money, in-laws, and so on). There were also indications that tensions influenced satisfaction more than did positive items. Bradburn also showed that both novel experiences and social participation were associated with general satisfaction, but were not associated with dissatisfaction.

The sociological picture that emerges is that companionable and togetherness (intimacy) events positively affect marital happiness, and that tensions (disagreements about functions) adversely affect satisfaction, but that these two classes of events are independent. A similar conclusion holds for overall satisfaction, that both classes contribute to satisfaction, but are not in a complementary relationship.

The family life cycle literature, also within a sociological perspective, may illustrate situational regularities in marital satisfaction. The literature is somewhat confusing, suggesting (a) marriage satisfaction declines, or (b) does not decline, with longevity of the relationship (cf., Hicks and Platt, 1970). Others have shown a U-shaped function suggesting recovery after a period of decline (Rollins and Cannon, 1974). Miller (1976), using survey interview data, sought to establish through multiple regression path analysis evidence for the theoretical relationship between antecedent life variables and satisfaction. A finding of major importance was that ease of most recent family *role transition* and frequency of *com-*

panionate activities directly affected marital satisfaction: (a) how well respondents "dealt with" most recent family role demand (such as birth of first child, child entering school, and so on) and (b) companionship events (for example, visited friends, took a drive) were both predictive of satisfaction. Since Miller's study sampled persons at the various stages in the family life cycle, it was possible to simulate relationships between life stages, satisfaction and companionship. The very lowest level of satisfaction was found for "First Child in School" and for persons married from six to 10 years. Companionship was at relatively lowest levels early in the span, starting at six years of marriage, and increased only in very late years. Companionship described a U-curve for "most recent role transition" and for "years married." Satisfaction and companionship tended to increase in tandem after the first-child stage until retirement. When plotted against years married, both factors fell sharply until the 6-10 year interval, with satisfaction showing a sharp increase thereafter and companionship a U-shaped recovery. While theoretically interesting, Miller's simulated longitudinal data points were based on very small frequencies.

From these sociological studies it would appear that marital relatedness can be partitioned into statistically meaningful components indicating discriminative properties. Companionship, sociability, and tension are three likely candidates, with the first two positively and the latter inversely related to satisfaction. These positive and negative clusters are independent of one another. Self-reported success in making the transition to the next (demanding) family role and amount of companionate activity are effective antecedents of reported marital satisfaction; the years of maximum child rearing involvement are also associated with a decline in companionship, which in turn is associated with the decline in marital satisfaction. Whatever the popularly acclaimed benefits of child rearing, they were not discernible in the family life cycle studies.

A social-psychological effort has been reported by Rosenblatt and his co-workers (Rosenblatt and Budd, 1975; Rosenblatt and Cunningham, 1976; Rosenblatt, Titus, and Cunningham, 1977), focusing not on companionship but the other side of this issue: separateness. Rosenblatt was concerned with person and setting variables which lead to couples maintaining separateness within ongoing intimate relationships. In the study by Rosenblatt, Titus, and Cunningham (1977) the apartness issue was addressed by defining person variables of abrasiveness and perfectionism and determining how persons classified in these categories dealt with major annoyances, such as big fights, minutes annoyed or angry. Two sets of findings from the data (obtained from interviews of events in the past 24 hours) are of particular interest, although the present inter- pretation is somewhat at variance from the interpretation the original authors have given their data: (a) Agreement between spouses (r's) for specific events in the past 24 hours ranged from a low of $r = .23$ to a high of $r = .71$ for measures of togetherness-apartness (median $r = .47$, $N = 68$) and from a low of $r = .23$ to $r = .56$ (median $r = .25$, $N = 71$) for measures of tensions or fights. *Spouses may not show remarkable agreement on events presumed to affect them both,* such as fights. (b) Couples who are unlikely to express negative behaviors (below median on abrasiveness) tend to distance if they fight; to a somewhat lesser degree couples who do not express negative affect openly and who have clear separation of household roles do not report having much fighting. (c) Couples who described themselves as perfectionistic and who have high role separation tend not to report fighting and tend to remain angry or annoyed with spouse.

The first set of correlations is interesting in establishing the amount of agreement (or lack thereof) between intimates on behavioral events. (Clinically, this discrepancy is also seen for mutual activities like inter- course!) From a behavioral point of view, therefore, couples cannot be expected to report with great accuracy events which might otherwise be assumed to be reported with great fidelity. But from Rosenblatt's model the findings regarding apartness are interesting. They call attention to the need to define differences among couples in skill at distancing, since it appears to be possible to preselect couples on this skill dimension. Couples who have clearly segregated instrumental roles (only one person works on checkbook, only one cooks evening meals, and so on) report less fighting (annoyances) if they are alo high in perfectionism. If only companionship is emphasized, ability to distance may be overlooked, even though distancing might be beneficial to the relationship.

Psychological studies

A number of studies have been done using variations of spouse obser- vations and observations of trained observers (cf. Weiss and Margolin, 1977). The prototype study along these lines was reported by Wills, Weiss and Patterson (1974) and attempted to capture the distinction between affectional (or socioemotional) and instrumental pleasures/displeasures as correlates of marital satisfaction. Using multiple regression analysis, the task was to predict variance in daily marital satisfaction ratings from knowledge of daily frequencies of spouse-received pleasing and displeasing behaviors; these were further categorized into affectional (kisses, hugs) and instrumental (washing car, feeding dog) behaviors. Quality of nonmarital outside experiences was included as the fifth predictor variable. For a small number of nonclinic couples, a highly significant multiple correlation (R) was obtained which accounted for 25 percent of the variation in satisfaction by the appropriate combination of the five predictors. Of the variance accounted for, 65 percent was accounted for by affectional and instrumental *displeasures;* exchange of displeasures within the relationships of these people decremented satisfaction more than occurrence of pleasures incremented satisfaction. Similar to the sociological literature, pleasures and displeasures were independent of one another. Given the difficulties of spouses' perceptual accuracy already cited, 25 percent of the satisfaction variance is not trivial.

Weiss and Isaac (1976) were also concerned with components of marital satisfaction. They focused on the interface between cognitions about satisfaction and specific behavioral events as these two figure in spouses' estimates of marital satisfaction. These authors first had judges sort some 400 specific pleasure-displeasure items into categories labeled to capture popular marriage-related concepts*—Companionship, Consideration, Affection, Parenting, Household Management, and so on. Each category was formed by a priori agreement of at least 70 percent of the judges. A sample of 92 married persons rated the pleasingness (displeasingness) of each of 84 items which may have occurred in the past 24 hours. (There were 12 popular categories and seven items representing each category; items were randomly printed on the response sheets to avoid suggesting the category.) Subjects also rated their satisfaction with the category name for the same past 24-hour period, such as, satisfaction with Affection. Finally, respondents were asked to provide an overall rating of marital satisfaction for the 24-hour period. The overall rating corresponded to the "daily rating" in the Wills et al. procedure. The sum of the values of the weighted items (those actually rated per person) corresponded to an item-derived measure of satisfaction; the satisfaction for that 24-hour period thus was the total value of the weighted items. The correlation between the two measures of satisfaction, overall (cognitive) rating and weighted item sum was .576 ($p < .01$), indicating that again 28 percent of the variance in satisfaction rating was shared by the weighted item sum. Of particular interest to this survey was the relationship between categories of behavioral items and overall rating of satisfaction: Affec-

---

* These are the same categories listed in Table 1.

tion, Communication, and Child Care category item scores were used as predictors to overall satisfaction and the $R = .999$, indicating that 98 percent of the satisfaction rating variance was accounted for by these three specific categories of behavioral items.

These two studies establish the groundwork for the conclusion that satisfaction can be partitioned, that quality of events in the past 24 hours related to satisfaction with spouse, and that affectional, companionate, and instrumental behaviors (helping with child care) are important components of rated satisfaction.

The application of this strategy for assessing marital satisfaction of distressed or dysfunctional couples has also been reported. In a behavioral analysis of the reported *quality of time together*, Williams (1976) made a careful determination of time spent together for distressed and nondistressed couples; distressed couples were in marital therapy. The distressed couples spent a mean of 5.2 hours together daily, whereas the nondistressed couples' daily mean was 6.6 hours. The ratio of *positive* to *negative time* was 15.3:1 and 6.3:1 for nondistressed and distressed respectively. For the distressed couples, not only was less time spent together but the saturation of negative time was significantly greater than for nondistressed couples—18.2 minutes vs. 26.6 minutes of negative time for nondistressed and distressed respectively. Whereas the couples in either grouping were comparable in their recording of actual time segments, there was a significant difference between groups for within-couple agreement about *quality of time spent together*, whether it was positive or negative. The rating of daily marital happiness was significantly different for the groups; distressed husbands and wives both scored the day as less satisfying.

The pleasure-displeasure spouse observation procedure was also employed by Birchler et al. (1975) with 12 distressed and 12 nondistressed couples, where it was found that, on average, P:D ratio for nondistressed couples was 19:1, but for distressed couples the ratio was 3:1. (The difference between the averages based upon individual ratios was highly significant in favor of the nondistressed group.) Williams' data agree with the earlier Birchler et al. findings, using different methods.

In a study designed to provide systematic information about how couples observations of themselves are congruent with those made by trained observers, Robinson and Price (1976) have provided still other important data on the behavioral correlates of satisfactions measures. Couples were selected on the basis of their marital adjustment (Locke-Wallace) scores; four couples scoring below 90 were matched with four couples scoring above 110. Couples first responded to a variant of the SOC (which in this study included rating affectional behaviors) by scaling the pleasantness value of items for the past seven days. Couples were observed for one-hour periods in their homes during a one-week baseline period, and were rated on nine positive interaction behaviors, such as attending, agreement, approval, positive physical interaction, and so on. After baseline, couples were trained to make observations on these nine interaction behaviors during periods which overlapped with the home observers being present. This "intervention phase" was designed to determine whether controlled practice in observing the exchange of positive behaviors would systematically increase marital happiness ratings. Also, during the intervention phase the couples continued to take daily pleasure data, as well as filling out the Marital Happiness Scale daily.

Results indicated that estimates of frequency and weighted frequency of pleasure-displeasure behaviors (SOC) were systematically related to the succeeding daily measures of marital happiness. The combined weighted frequency for instrumental and affectional pleasures and instrumental displeasures correlated .51 and —.59, respectively, with Marital Happiness ratings. These findings are most similar to the Weiss and Isaac (1976) findings for a 24-hour period, where, it will be remembered, the correlation between weighted items and overall satisfaction was .576. From 33 percent to 37 percent of the satisfaction variance seems to be accounted for by behavioral events.

Consistent with the Wills et al. finding, it was shown that daily estimates of pleasurable events received from spouse and rated marital happiness correlated .60 ($p < .001$); these relationship pleasures accounted for 36 percent of the Happiness variance. (This figure is somewhat inflated since Robinson and Price also found amount of time spent together and marital happiness to be correlated, $r = .57$; variations in time together could also influence the pleasures.)

The relationship between trained other and self observation was higher for frequency of positive behaviors emitted ($r = .57$, $p < .001$) than for frequency of pleasurable behaviors received ($r = .41$, $p < .001$); recalling the Rosenblatt et al. finding for within-couple agreement, these findings indicate that under relatively controlled conditions (hourly in-home observation sessions) agreement is only moderate. Robinson and Price report that the correlations for specific couple-observed items (agreement and concern) were highly related to daily ratings of Marital Happiness (r's .58 and .62).

Although the trained observers did not record significant differences between High and Low marital adjustment groups' mean rates of positive behaviors, the couples themselves in these groups reported mean differences for both emitted and received pleasurable behaviors. (Note, these results pertain to the overlapping hourly observation sessions.) The High group reported greater frequencies of pleasure. Taking a much broader data base, the daily report of pleasures over the weeks of study, the differences between the High and Low groups were also significant; the couples classified as maritally more adjusted, on average, reported in excess of three times the frequency of pleasures reported by the low adjusted group. These data are consistent with the earlier Birchler et al. data based on a one-week sample of P's and D's.

No effects of observation practice, as an intervention, were found in the study; actual rates of emitted pleasurable behaviors did not increase over baseline observations, although for the high-adjusted group there was a significant increase in Marital Happiness, indicating that the four weeks of tracking positives heightened their subjective happiness.

While certainly making a contribution to observational technology, these results are somewhat limited. The range of possible interactions during the hourly home visit was, of course, curtailed, and to use these periods to predict to broader classes of behavior over larger time segments is troublesome. Robinson and Price have shown that couples' observations may be colored by subjective factors, but not entirely since there was agreement between trained observers and couples on behavioral occurrences. Subjectively coded behaviors, however, predicted better to satisfaction ratings than did the observer ratings. (These results may be expected on the basis of similarity of methods.)

Effects of home observation on couple interaction were also reported by Follingstad, Sullivan, Ierace, Ferrara, and Haynes (1976) for data gathered during an extended baseline period. Couples were classified as functional (volunteers) or dysfunctional (having sought marital therapy). Interobserver agreement was high between coders (.95); behavior codes included eye contact, agreement, criticism, interrupt, and disagreement, among others. While expected significant differences in behavioral rates between the two groups were found, especially on a negative triad of Criticism, Interrupt, and Disagreement, both eye contact and agreement were significantly higher for the dysfunctional couples. These same five response codes were all negatively correlated with a measure of Marital Happiness (r's ranged from —.43 to —.58, $p < .05$). None of the "positive" codes were related to the self-report measures. No data were taken on how couples observed themselves, but these results do suggest that in-home behaviors can be identified which discriminate functional and dysfunctional couples, and that intracouple consistencies (across three observational sessions) can be found.

In an earlier analysis of couples in treatment, Patterson, Hops, and Weiss (1975) reported rank order correlations between Facilitating coded behaviors (on the MICS) and baseline reporting of pleasures-displeasures; for wives rho $= .85$, for husbands rho $= .61$ (p's .01 and .05, respectively). The out-of-session (baseline) exchange of pleasures was associated with in-laboratory observation of interactional behaviors; negative behaviors did not generalize across the two settings.

Using the Birchler-Vincent data on 24 couples, Weiss et al. (1973) reported that a rating of interview behaviors was related to (a) P/D scores, $r = .56$, (b) reported conflicts recorded in a weekly diary, $r = .43$, and (c) percentage of activities engaged in with spouse, $r = .53$ (all p's $<$ .05). The greater the rated couple distress, the greater the Displeasure relative to Pleasure, the greater the number of conflicts self reported, and the more time spent in activities with persons other than spouse.

In summary, a review of the literature pertaining to whether satisfaction can be partitioned into behavior-related events within a relatively restricted time frame—days or weeks, rather than months or years— indicated that marital satisfaction (ignoring the theoretical issue of whether that also means adjustment) is seen to covary with significant identifiable relationship events. Satisfactions and tensions are not inversely related; rather they seem to be independent. This has been demonstrated on both a survey and interactional level of analysis. The reported satisfaction with a relationship is lawfully related to stage in the life cycle. Child rearing, especially in the early years and because of its cost to companionship, is associated with lowest levels of satisfaction. Competence in taking on new roles within the family is also related to satisfaction; the greater the ease of making necessary changes, the more satisfaction. Data continue to indicate that husbands and wives vary greatly in their agreement on whether specific relationship events have occurred in the past 24 hours. Helping couples problem solve when agreement about the events themselves is at issue may be putting the cart before the horse!

We know relatively little about distancing as a couple skill in containing conflict (dissatisfaction). Initial survey data suggest that couples may differ meaningfully in likelihood of distancing and that those who distance report having fewer fights or the usual sequelae of fighting.

A large number of psychological studies have been reported which focus on the interactional aspects of pleasurable-displeasurable exchanges within a relationship. These two categories of events were seen to be unrelated to one another, yet both relate to satisfaction. Employing a variety of data collecting procedures, the amount of variance in satisfaction measures accounted for by behavioral events is around 28 to 30 percent on the average, but may go as high as 98 percent. Distressed couples across studies consistently differ from nondistressed couples in their pattern of providing fewer pleasures relative to displeasures. Not only do distressed couples understandably report lower satisfaction, but in tracking their daily behavior they also confirm that they are receiving less pleasure.

Subjective evaluations of behavior compared to those made by trained observers do not always agree. Behaviors likely to be classified as positive (such as agreement) may be observed more frequently in *distressed* couples relative to nondistressed couples. The observational setting probably requires far greater thought than is currently the case, and many of these "discrepancies" will no doubt be related to representativeness of settings. Home to laboratory relationships between important relationship behaviors have been reported, suggesting that pleasures and displeasures have validity for relationships beyond the specific setting of a laboratory.

Truly experimental studies in which components of satisfactions are systematically varied and observed are lacking. Most of the data are correlational, and no specific data are available on other aspects of objectification training. The focus has been on marital satisfaction and behavior; the evidence supports the attempts to help couples change their behavior, since these changes could be expected to produce the desired effects. From the data considered here, objectification can gain control over events which are likely to enhance their affective well being.

Support/Understanding

The research pertaining to support-understanding accomplishments in marriage relationships is both plentiful and scarce. Certainly the influence of nondirective therapy, especially applications to couples (Harrell and Guerney, 1976; Rappaport, 1976), has provided numerous instances in the literature on self-report measures that training in paraphrasing and reflection significantly increases marital satisfaction ratings. While attempts are often made to separate out various aspects of satisfaction with communication, halo effects (generally feeling better about one's relationship) probably account for the N different ways of expressing satisfaction on self ratings. This literature is summarized brilliantly by Gurman and Kniskern (in press). Clear evidence is lacking that training on support/understanding skills also produces incremental satisfaction as well as change in how couples function supportively over time.

The lack of direct evidence is attributable in part to the understandable tendency of clinician-researchers to be concerned with offering clients effective treatment alternatives. Therefore, packages not dissimilar from that developed by the Oregon Marital Studies Program have been the order of the day. These are often truly multivitamin blitz approaches which cover all the outcome objectives mentioned here, with special reference to communication and negotiation training (Azrin et al., 1973; Rappaport and Harrell, 1972; Stuart, 1976; Weiss et al., 1973). There is now a considerable literature consisting of comparative treatment studies, single treatment studies, case and anecdotal reports, most of which have been reviewed by Jacobson and Martin (1976) and Patterson et al. (1976).

The focus here will be on the literature pertaining to the processes of support-understanding as defined in terms of potential accomplishments in relationships. While it may be necessary to look at selected therapy studies, this is not the main objective.

Support-Understanding? Who says?

The issue of subjective versus objective (or public versus private) events looms large in this consideration of supportive-understanding functions. Gottman, Notarius et al. (1977) have joined the issue by noting potential differences between what the couple and what outside observers label as supportive behaviors. This has led Gottman et al. to a search for the relationship between *intent* and *impact,* and their preliminary analyses have indicated that distressed and nondistressed couples did not differ significantly in the reported intent of messages sent; each intended to send messages of the same mean value of positiveness; however, the rated impact of messages indicated that distressed husbands coded 36 percent of wife behavior as positive while nondistressed husbands coded 57 percent of wife behavior positive; similar results were found for wives. (Gottman et al. report situational variations in that wives assigned higher positive codes to low conflict discussions than high conflict discussions, but these details need not detract from the general review.) These findings led the authors to consider that marital distress is a matter of a communication deficit; sent and received message-affect are out of synchrony. Clearly Gottman et al. have made a first step toward documenting the attribution of intent, data that are much needed.

The alternative approach that has been popular in behavioral laboratories is to define assessment (coding) procedures which allow outside trained observers to make observations of behaviors *a priori* labeled as being supportive, for example, Facilitating versus Disruptive codes (Patterson et al., 1975). (These measures have been reviewed elsewhere, cf., Weiss and Margolin, 1977.) In the first attempt along these lines, Birchler et al. (1975) were concerned with whether spouses from either distressed or nondistressed marriages were either locked into exchanges of increased negatives (or decreased positives) or whether skill in emitting such responses was truly trait-like and therefore could be observed with spouses and strangers alike. The question was whether facilitative or disruptive behaviors (defined as positive and negative responses) were under stimulus control provided by the spouses and therefore not likely to appear under similar conditions with non-spouses, or whether they reflect a person deficit observable in any situation. The findings clearly indicated that distressed and nondistressed spouses emitted significantly different rates of negatives *and* of positives, and that although positive responses were in the repertoire of distressed spouses, their occurrence was controlled by own spouse interactions; stranger spouse dyads emitted positives. These data were derived from observations of trained coders using the MICS system for coding dyadic interactions.

It must be asked, what can coders know about *real* support and understanding? Two studies pertain to this issue. Royce and Weiss (1975) employed university student judges to discriminate between samples of distressed and nondistressed interactions between actual spouses which Birchler et al. had previously videotaped. Judges' "hit" rate, while significantly different from chance, was unimpressive, 63.3 percent correct identification of distress status. Further, the cues that they indicated they had used to make their discriminations between distress and nondistress seemed more heavily to weight aversive behaviors than positive behaviors; means of judges' ratings of stimulus couples correlated with couples' (coded) aversiveness scores —.41 ($p < .01$), but not with (coded) positive scores ($r = .05$, $p = $ ns). The weighting of identified behavioral cues also differed from the weighting that statistically best discriminated the couples, and a Problem Solving → Agreement sequence was a highly reliable differentiator not used by the untrained observers! Since the Birchler et al. tapes originally produced differences in couples positive and negative interchanges, the original coding was not suspect—only the new sample of untrained observers.

Is this also true for therapists? Would therapists be able to identify "supportive or helpful" behaviors in videotapes of distressed and non-distressed couple interactions? Engel and Weiss (1976) sought an answer to that question. Prior to participating in a marital training workshop for therapists, the number of "helpfulness" responses identified discriminated between the two types of interactions; this difference in identified "helpfulness" became more obvious after the workshop training (which did *not* involve training in the MICS coding system). Most important, after the workshop the therapists were in greater agreement with MICS definitions of helpful behaviors than prior to the workshop. A control group of counselors in training without benefit of the workshop did not show the pre-post changes, although they too significantly discriminated between distressed and nondistressed types.

These investigations indicate that what couples do on camera can be read by outsiders, and that at least one coding system detects important interaction behaviors.

Gottman, Markman, and Notarius (1977) provide initial information on supportive-understanding skills (in the laboratory communication settings) by a detailed verbatim analysis of couple interaction using a coding system (trained coders) which exceeds the current capabilities of the MICS. In addition to defining communication-specific faults (such as Mind reading attributions, Summarizing Self, Disagreement) they included nonverbal behaviors indicative of the quality of message affect, whether positive, negative or neutral. With this degree of detail it is possible to code *content* of message and *how it was delivered,* for example, mindreading-positive and mindreading-negative reflect the difference between a sympathetic probe of the other's feelings versus attributing motives to the other in a hostile manner. The Gottman et al. analyses also were concerned with issues of reciprocity versus behavior exchange, as already indicated in earlier sections of this paper.

Both the husbands and the wives of distressed and nondistressed couples differed significantly in their percentage of Agreement (Ag divided by Ag + DisAg); husbands differed by one and a half times, while wives differed by a factor of two; the percentage Agreements scores always were in favor of persons from nondistressed relationships.

For distressed couples, when agreement was made with neutral affect it was more likely to lead to the spouse's next message being delivered with negative affect. Neutral agreements can serve as discriminative stimuli for escalating conflict in distressed couples. Distressed couples also, on the average, delivered more of their messages in the "summarizing-self" rather than "summarizing-other" category, suggesting that little paraphrasing or reflection was going on. Distressed couples, significantly more than nondistressed couples, accompanied Problem Feeling, Mind-reading, Agreement, and Disagreement responses *with negative affect.* Disagreement can be communicated verbally, on a content level, but the addition of negative affect means the message is being acted out, a form of behavior more typical of the distressed couples.

Particularly noteworthy, from the point of view of the shaping that can take place in relationships, was the observed difference in listening behaviors of spouses as a function of the speaking spouse's affect quality. Husbands listened with *positive* or *neutral* affect when distressed relationship wives spoke with *negative affect.* The reverse was true for wives listening to their speaking husbands: Wives from nondistressed relationships listened with *positive* or *neutral* affect when their husbands spoke with *negative affect.* To oversimplify, the negative affect communicated by distressed wives was reinforced by attentive positive listening of their husbands, while negative affect of nondistressed husbands is reinforced by positive listening wives. The role reversal in these two groups is most interesting; these couples were married on the average only three years and may reflect a pattern in young marriages.

While adding interesting findings by the very expensive use of affect-codes, Gottman et al. have also replicated the Birchler et al. findings for content categories: Distressed couples did emit fewer "positive" behaviors than nondistressed couples.

In her dissertation research, Margolin (1976) sought to determine whether a deliberate attempt to manipulate a mutuality relationship attribution would significantly enhance the effectiveness of behaviorally defined communication training. Three groups of distressed couples were seen for either (a) behavioral, (b) behavioral-attribution, or (c) non-specific communication training. (Couples were selected on multiple criteria of distress, which included Locke-Wallace, $\bar{x} = 71$, interview rating of marital distress ranging from 1 to 8, $\bar{x} = 2.0$, and Areas of Change Questionnaire, $\bar{x} = 24.1$, all of which score sufficiently below "average" norms to warrant calling status distressed.) Therapy consisted of structured communication training sessions and specifically designed homework exercises. The two behavioral groups learned to identify helpful communication behaviors by a signalling device which enabled identification of (a) sending helpfulness responses, (b) receiving helpfulness from the other, and (c) agreement that helpfulness was sent and received; the latter were referred to as agreement intercepts and were intended to provide a behavioral measure of mutuality. In addition, all groups tracked daily pleasures and displeasures, with the two behavioral groups receiving additional training on identifying particularly important pleasures. The emphasis in the behavioral-attribution group was on *couple* accomplishment scores, rather than individual scores; the couple functioned as a unit to increase relationship pleasures and communication supportiveness. The nonspecific communication group focused on identifying feelings in the context of nondirective training.

A multilevel set of criterion measures was employed, including self, spouse, and trained other observation. The communication training device is described further in a case illustration by Margolin and Weiss (1977). The entire training program, including pre and post assessment sessions, lasted for four weeks, a total of eight hours.

The behavior-attribution group showed a highly significant increase in MICS coded supportive behaviors ($p < .025$) pre to post training, an effect which exceeded that for the other two groups. All groups increased in their identification of helpfulness received from partner (a "goodwill" effect), but only the two behavioral groups identified significantly more helpfulness sent (to partner). On helpfulness agreements (agreement intercepts), the behavioral group (*without* the attribution) improved pre to post ($p < .01$) as did the nonspecific control group ($p < .05$); the behavioral attribution group did not change significantly. (The mutuality requirements imposed an unintended hardship on this group, making the task exceedingly difficult, cf., Margolin, 1976). However, on the MICS measures of helpful or supportive responses coded by trained coders, it was the behavioral-attribution group which exceeded the other two, both in significant within group pre-post increase and a significantly greater increment than the other groups.

Margolin reported results which indicated that, consistent with much of the marital therapy literature reviewed by Gurman and Kniskern (1977), a reduction in negative category behaviors is achieved fairly readily. In fact, Margolin's nonspecific communication group—which was designed to mimic most other communications oriented marital therapies—showed the greatest within group reduction of MICS coded negative behaviors ($p < .005$). A post treatment "Counseling Readiness Questionnaire" was administered to all couples to determine whether they had acquired social learning knowledge by the end of treatment. The mean scores for the two behavioral groups were significantly higher ($p < .01$) than the nonspecific group; the latter group mean was almost twice as low as the behavioral groups. In an unpublished report, Follingstad, Haynes, and Sullivan (1976) employed a volunteer group of seven couples (mean Locke-Wallace scores 82) and demonstrated that an educational phase consisting of two conjoint sessions of training in behavioral principles relating to relationships (discussion of aversive chains of behavior and how to break such chains) was also effective in significantly decreasing "negative behaviors" coded from home observations; the decrease was from .275 to .131 behaviors per hour ($p = .05$).

The Margolin results demonstrated a generalization effect from one type of task to another and indicated that spouse-defined helpfulness responses can be identified and trained to the couple's advantage. Her results also lend support to the importance of the mutuality attribution, that couples work toward relationship rather than individual gain. The ease with which negative behaviors can be reduced (e.g., Margolin; Follingstad et al.) suggests that perhaps active contact with concerned outsiders may be beneficial in controlling the display of these behaviors; whether long-term effects might be expected to persist is another issue.

Gottman's findings are particularly important in showing how affective communication controls subsequent responding—how for relatively young marriages, distress-nondistress status predicts very different listening patterns between husband and wives in terms of what affective content is attended to by listeners. Unquestionably, Gottman's fine-grain analysis (multiple coding from verbatim transcripts of interactions) is a technical achievement depicting how the affective component of communication either facilitates or disrupts communication.

Spouse versus outside observer definition of supportive behavior was also considered in the Robinson and Price (1976) report reviewed in the preceding section on satisfaction. Although observers and spouses showed moderate agreement in their coding of positive behaviors (during home observation periods), only the spouses' ratings of such behaviors correlated with daily measures of Marital Happiness, especially agreement and concern (r's .62 and .58, respectively). The subjective definition seemed to account for variance in happiness that observation by others did not. These authors also report that while both high and low adjusted groups were not very accurate (based upon ratio of agreements to agreements plus disagreements with observers in their homes) in recording specific behaviors, the high adjusted was significantly more accurate in estimating the overall rate of pleasurable behaviors ($p < .05$), which agrees with Gottman's communication deficit notion. An alternative interpretation would implicate the role of attributions; the overt instrumental behavior may be topographically acceptable but not read as "genuine" by the spouse.

Robinson and Price (1976) and Follingstad et al. (1976) provide data to indicate that merely recording positives (and negatives) does not provide an effective intervention in that couples did not increase the rate of reported positives in their marital happiness as measured by the Locke-Wallace. An earlier paper by Welch and Goldstein (1974) using nondistressed couples showed Locke-Wallace marital satisfaction increases as a result of charting and focusing on the exchange of positives. Robinson and Price did find, however, that their well-adjusted couples (high Locke-Wallace) reported significantly greater Marital Happiness (Azrin measure) as a result of the four weeks of tracking—pre-post happiness $t(5) = 2.11$, $p < .05$.

Communication training

Wieman (1976) has reported a controlled study which is germane to the support/understanding accomplishment and deserves attention here. The comparison was between Conjugal Relationship Modification (a Guerney type program; cf. also., Rappaport, 1976) and Reciprocal Reinforcement therapy patterned after Stuart's approach. Groups of couples met for eight weekly sessions; a waiting list control group was employed. The treatments stressed either (a) speaker listener roles, empathically reflecting feelings of other, or (b) pairing desired behaviors from each spouse for contingent control, that is, making desired behaviors reciprocal. Spouses in each group provided weekly measures of "ownership" and "reflection" of feeling counts or frequency counts of number of "reinforcements" delivered by each spouse.

Both treatments were effective through the 10-week follow-up, and did not differ significantly from one another, although both were superior to the control group which showed no changes. The communications training was utilized during the first but not the second half of treatment in extra-therapeutic conversations; the reciprocity trained couples increased their proportion of positive statements made about mates during the *second* half of treatment and accelerated their rates of reciprocity reinforcing behaviors throughout treatment. Of all process measures, only the change in delivery rate of reinforcing behaviors (pre to post treatment) correlated significantly with change in "marital adjustment" ($r = .43$), ". . . supporting the contention that, with an increase in the frequency of positive reinforcement exchanged by spouses, a concomitant enhancement of marital functioning may be expected" (Wieman, 1976, p. 2).

An enrichment communications training approach has been reported in specific detail by Rappaport (1976), which indicated once again that communication listening-reflecting skills produced significant self-reported marital satisfaction increases in 20 couples; ratings of tapes also indicated that couples significantly mastered the content. At this point the results indicate that a didactic approach can be used to accomplish these objectives, and as Rappaport suggests, such training may serve as an effective precursor to negotiation training.

Problem Solving

As indicated earlier, Problem Solving is *outcome oriented,* requiring some form of product. Studies tend to confuse problem solving with other elements of marital therapy, most notably communication skills of all sorts. As a relationship accomplishment, problem solving refers to bringing resources to bear on specific achievements. Problem solving as accomplishment answers the question, "How do we get from here to there?"

We may consider two aspects of Problem Solving (PS): (a) Factors which impede PS, and (b) Skills peculiar to PS.

Factors impeding PS

Conceptually, any behavior which sidetracks a discussion from reaching its goals is disruptive to PS. Patterson et al. (1975) defined Facilitating and Disruptive behaviors, as coded with the MICS, as two empirically derived criteria for discriminating therapy outcome. Clear evidence demonstrating that specific factors impede PS is still lacking, but we will consider the available findings.

The reciprocity and coercion hypotheses are germane to isolating behaviors which impede PS. Nontask behaviors which escalate reciprocally—behavior of one elicits behavior of other, and so on—are certain to produce a reduction in PS.

The most stringent statistical test of reciprocity between dyads has been presented by Gottman and his students (Gottman et al., 1976), and, as noted previously, the evidence for negative reciprocity was not strong. It is important to note, however, that Gottman's tasks were not always representative of couple interactions. Couples either talked in controlled speech units (turn taking imposed by the Talk Table) or discussed fairly trivial problem-solving issues. For older couples, it was found that tasks which elicited more conflict better discriminated distressed from non-distressed couples. But the evidence did not support a reciprocity of aversiveness, that is, an escalation effect.

Although specific point-for-point escalation of aversiveness has not been shown empirically, there are other "base rate" data to suggest that distressed and nondistressed couples differ significantly in their output of PS behaviors. Vincent, Weiss, and Birchler (1975) demonstrated such a difference, using the MICS codes for 12 couples classified as either distressed or nondistressed. These effects have been replicated by subsequent studies conducted by Birchler (1977) and Vincent (1976). Similarly, the Royce and Weiss (1975) judgment study indicated that a PS $\rightarrow$ AG sequence was a major predictor in differentiating distressed from non-distressed tapes; higher rates of PS $\rightarrow$ AG characterized the nondistressed group. Finally Mead (personal communication, 1976) has found similar MICS coded differences between couple distress status.

The Vincent et al. (1975) study indicated that PS behaviors were emitted by spouses in distressed relationships to stranger spouses, suggesting that the former are not bereft of PS skills. Observations of fewer (base rate) PS responses among distressed couples reflects not so much a response deficit as a performance deficit: Something about the two-person interaction prevents performance of these otherwise useful responses. In a later study, Vincent (1976) asked whether distressed and nondistressed couples could change their performance if asked to do so; specifically, if asked to "fake good" or "fake bad," would it be possible for couples from both distress classifications to change their performance appropriately, consistent with instructions? If, when told to "fake good," distressed couples produce higher levels of PS related behaviors than under baseline conditions, the evidence would favor a stimulus-control theory of observed lowered rates of PS among distressed couples.

Vincent's (1976) results essentially supported the stimulus control position, and, like the earlier study, concluded that distressed couples could increase their performance rates of facilitative PS behaviors when told to "fake good." Interestingly, nondistressed couples also increased their performance rates under these instructions, but the distress distinction was still evident thereunder; distressed couples did not change in the positive direction to an extent which made them look like their non-distressed counterparts. Vincent was particularly interested in the effects of instructions on nonverbal behaviors (also measured by the MICS) and found that couples were far less able to change their nonverbal performance given the differing sets. He concluded that verbal behaviors were susceptible to manipulation by instruction, but that nonverbal behaviors were not under voluntary control.

These data do not meet Gottman's conditional probability criteria for reciprocity, but they continue to support the view that couples differing in distress status function differently in ways detectable by trained coders, and that performance deficits are attributable to the disruptive stimulus effect each spouse has on the other rather than reflecting some absolute lack of appropriate PS behaviors. If the data continue to implicate the role of nonverbal behaviors (a) as being less susceptible to manipulation and (b) major contributors to impact variance, our retraining efforts will have to focus in on such communication channels very early in treatment.

Skills relevant to PS

The best single source of data on the PS issue has been provided by Jacobson (1977), who conducted a treatment control comparison using (unfortunately for present purposes!) *both* problem solving training *and* negotiation/contracting training. While this mini-package was highly effective relative to the no treatment controls, the relative effectiveness of the components was not examined. (Jacobson's study is somewhat better than other package studies for present purposes in that he employed only two identifiable active agents, whereas others (Azrin et al., 1973; Stuart, 1976; Weiss et al., 1973) have utilized numerous techniques.)

There have been many reports in the literature describing behaviorally conceptualized training techniques for problem solving skills; Blechman has modified the MICS to code parent-child interactions in her Family Contract Game (Blechman and Olson, 1976). The game is a particularly clear demonstration of how stimulus control can be utilized to keep players on task and help them reach solutions.

Harrell and Guerney (1976) utilized as part of their educationally based training package a series of steps which provide increasing stimulus control over potential conflict responses. However, their training did not affect marital satisfaction, although other coded differences between trained and control couples were found.

Patterson and Frederiksen (1976) have been developing problem solving steps as part of negotiation training with psychiatrically distressed couples. While their data are essentially case illustrations, their technology looks promising. Similarly, some very innovative work has been reported by Carter and Thomas and their associates (for example,

Carter and Thomas, 1973; Thomas, Walter and O'Flaherty, 1974) which contains numerous suggestions for discriminating specific problematic communication behaviors.

Thus, Problem Solving is a major component of behavioral approaches but ironically has received little direct controlled observation. One approach that further researchers might consider is to actually assess couples who have been treated by various therapy points of view to determine whether they now demonstrate *a priori* defined PS skills. The prediction would be that couples showing evidence of these skills will maintain their benefits for a longer time than those not demonstrating such skills.

Behavior Change

If the current conception of the four areas of accomplishment is essentially correct, there should exist little evidence for Behavior Change as an isolated accomplishment because, (1) Behavior Change techniques are more likely to be successful after accomplishments at earlier stages have been strengthened, and (2) it would be relatively impossible to track the differential effects of Behavior Change per se without invoking these other skills. Most of the behavioral intervention package approaches include some form of behavior change training, but determining its effectiveness *in vitro* is well nigh impossible. In the Azrin et al. (1973) package, individual elements were successively introduced for reciprocity training (approximating a multiple baseline design), but only a single self-reporting Marital Happiness scale was used throughout. Stuart (1976) has recently reported a high degree of success with his package which includes contracting for changes toward the end of the program; some 174 couples out of an initial 200 remained married on five-year follow-up. Given that a higher percentage of the 200 came initially to decide whether to stay together, this outcome is noteworthy.

Contracting

Negotiation training which eventuates in quasi-formal contracts is a major vehicle for training couples in behavior change wisdom. It is useful to distinguish between *negotiation training* and *contracting*, since the former is really a form of guided problem solving. Assertiveness training, learning to state desires in a positive pinpointed manner, keeping affect either neutral or positive when making requests for change, are some techniques allowing the couple to order their positions on issues without confusing the process with emotionality. Contracting, on the other hand, provides a method for objectifying stimulus and reinforcing control of the agreed-upon behaviors. The contract may impose rewards and penalties for performance; these may be contingently arranged in the various quid pro quo arrangements or the good faith model suggested by Weiss, Birchler and Vincent (1974). Reciprocity contracts require that desired behavior "GET" be made contingent upon desired behavior "GIVE," behaviors each spouse desires from the other.

Once again Jacobson (in press) provides the only direct evidence on contracting per se. As part of his dissertation research, Jacobson compared the two major forms of contracting *qua* behavior change technology, quid pro quo, and good faith (cf., Weiss et al., 1974), and included a nonspecific treatment group (NS) and a wait-list control. Among his major findings: (a) both quid pro quo (QPQ) and good faith contracting (GFC) were equally effective in producing pre-post treatment changes on four criterion measures (Marital Happiness, Positive and Negative behaviors coded from the MICS, and Locke-Wallace MAS), but did not differ from one another in technique effectiveness; (b) QPQ and GFC combined exceeded the wait-list control on all four measures; and (c) the combined QPQ and GFC exceeded the nonspecific group on three of the four measures (the Marital Happiness Scale was similar for both groups). All the above differences were at least $p < .01$. The NS group increased significantly in self-reported Marital Happiness. While the NS couples were obviously satisfied with their treatment, the effects thereof were not discernible on either behavioral measures or the Locke-Wallace MAS.

Jacobson's results would argue for no difference in the two major forms of contracts since both were equally effective. Since the quid pro quo arrangement is simpler to effect, he obviously recommends that procedure.

Follingstad et al. (1976), whose study of seven couples has been mentioned from time to time in these sections, addressed themselves to the question of the sequence of modules—for example, whether "communication" followed by "contracting" is more effective than the reverse clinically unorthodox order. (This study, it may be recalled, found a significant reduction in negative behaviors from the educational module early on in intervention.) While significant repeated-measures analyses of variance were found, not all effects were in expected directions, nor was there any evidence that the order effect was important to outcome. These results are difficult to interpret in view of the marked differences these investigators seem to find relative to others. For example, agreement decreased, whereas most indications are that agreement or agreement percent is higher for nondistressed couples. Most measures were home observations of small behaviors like eye contact, smile, agreement, and so forth. Of the nine significant home observation outcomes, only three were in expected direction, Negative Behavior, Criticism, and Interrupt. No reference is made to the outcome of contractual items, although the Locke-Wallace MAS increased significantly for all couples over time. Harrell and Guerney (1976) also found an unexpected decrease in "agree" and "approve" statements, which further analyses showed was probably due to the increased frequency of a more complex (program trained) response. Spouses were taught to summarize their messages to each other, which apparently substituted for specific agree responses. Clearly, the topography of the response class is important, and simply recording smiles or eye contact, or agree responses (which might also include nonverbal "mm-hmm"), is likely to miss other facilitative behaviors occurring at rates higher than during baseline.

In an earlier report, Rappaport and Harrell (1972) present a rationale and case illustration of behavioral exchange contracting which is a lucid presentation of this point of view, but no data were provided on its comparative effectiveness.

That part of the Harrell and Guerney report (1976) that dealt with behavior exchange contracting indicated that "contracting" skills did not generalize sufficiently to be reflected in measured marital satisfaction (Locke-Wallace) and on a number of self-report and audio-tape coded measures designed by the authors. The authors cite insufficient time in the testing situation as a major reason for not detecting differences.

Wieman's dissertation report (1976), as noted in an earlier section, did find that "reciprocal reinforcement" therapy was effective, and that only the rates of these contracted behaviors during the last half of therapy correlated significantly with pre to post difference in marital adjustment. Again, providing sufficient time for skills to consolidate and for having a precise specification of the response topography seems necessary in the evaluation of contracting effectiveness.

Summary

This section has briefly reviewed some of the empirical literature which pertains to the behavioral model of marital accomplishments. Recognizing that studies have not been specifically designed to test this elaboration of relationship accomplishments into Objectification, Support/Understanding, Problem Solving, and Behavior Change, studies have nonetheless been found relevant to the model.

Objectification pertains to the denoting functions between intimates: being able to specify relationship elements in terms of costs and benefits, or pleasures and displeasures. The studies reviewed indicated that pleasures and displeasures, defined in various ways, are independent of one another, yet both are related to measurable relationship satisfaction. The amount of variance accounted for by behavioral events labeled "pleases" or "displeases" varies from a low of 25 percent to a high of 98 percent depending upon the study methods. Asking couples to develop skills in denoting pleasures and displeasures is reasonable since these events do contribute to reported marital satisfaction. A number of methodological issues about agreement between couple and observer definition of contributary behaviors were also discussed.

Support/Understanding is frequently emphasized in non-directive approaches to marital therapy, but has been represented in the behavioral literature as well. The major issue is whether observer-labeled supportive behavior agrees with subjective ratings made by spouses. Identification of specific reinforcing behaviors may prove difficult, but the studies generally show that facilitative behaviors can be labeled and that both parties (observer and spouses) are more in agreement than disagreement. Specific behavioral techniques are available for training relationship-defined supportive behaviors, and in at least one study generalization was found to other observations made of couples' interaction. More recent work has emphasized the relationship between message intent and impact, weighing the subjective factors of supportive/understanding communications. Distressed marriages seem to be characterized by significantly fewer positive behaviors and more negatives (in terms of base rates), greater tendency for spouses in the former to receive spouse behaviors as more negative than sender intended, and for distressed relationship couples to record observed positive behaviors by a factor of one half less than nondistressed couples. Distressed relationships clearly are deficient in supportive/understanding accomplishments. Some studies were reviewed which suggest that training in these behaviors makes a difference to the couples' functioning.

Problem Solving as an accomplishment has been isolated to a lesser degree than the preceding accomplishments. Typically, measurement of PS has been imbedded in other aspects of training. When a strictly behavioral focus on Problem Solving has been reported, it has produced significant changes in relationship behaviors. Data are not available to either totally support or refute the hypothesized occurrences of escalation of nonfacilitative PS behaviors. The only direct test for reciprocity in marital interactions failed to demonstrate a point-for-point reciprocity of negatives, but evidence for spouses controlling one another's outputs was presented. In a controlled study of problem solving effectiveness, it has been shown that PS training was superior to a control comparison in producing increases in relationship satisfaction.

Finally, Behavior Change is most often equated with some form of contracting and negotiation training. *In vitro* effects of contracting are not likely to be demonstrated since most workers agree that prior skills training is necessary before this form of Behavior Change can be taught. However, various reciprocal arrangements have shown therapeutic effects of contingency contracts, and most recently, a direct comparison has been reported between the two major types of contracting, suggesting little practical difference in their effectiveness, while both forms are superior to other active controls.

SUMMARY AND PERSPECTIVE

The odyssey has been long and touched many shorelines. The main arguments may be summarized briefly here as section summaries were provided throughout.

(1) Behavioral approaches to marriage and marriage therapy are certainly based upon learning principles, a strong commitment to empirical demonstration of propositions, and a view of relationships in terms of mutual behavior shaping. Unlike the mindless forms of behaviorism that have remained in the public's image, current approaches actively incorporate "cognitive" variables. However, the phenomenal representation of experience need not directly depict those conditions which are responsible for maintaining or changing behaviors. Self descriptions (or even explanations) of important relationship events may be colored less by the statistical structure of behavioral rates and more by attitudinal factors.

Differences among various approaches probably relate to issues of what class of variables determines behavior, how cognitions and overt behavior interface, and the units deemed appropriate to the analysis of marital relationships. Among the common threads discerned for individualizing, behavioral, and systems approaches was the emphasis on person consistencies in the form of attributions about causality, and the func-

tional emphasis of the behavioral and systems approaches, both emphasizing the consequences of ongoing behaviors.

(2) A capsule view of learning theory was provided which emphasized
the basic shape of the world as a cube: Persons × Situations × Responses
seemed to describe the three faces of events germane to relationships.
The operant reinforcement model seemed most fitting, and this has been
elaborated further in what is commonly labeled the social learning
approach. How persons learn to influence one another's social behavior
is of most interest.

Learning is governed by the consequences of behavior. The contingencies of reinforcement were discussed, noting those consequences associated with increased or decreased rates of responding. Both positive and
negative consequences were seen to affect behaviors differently; one
tending to increase rates of responding, the other to decrease rates of
responding. The heavy reliance on use of aversive control techniques
reflected a fact of nature: punishment and negative reinforcement are
effective; they produce immediate results in changing behavior. The use
of positive control techniques, while these are available, is less likely in
intimate relationships.

Probably of most interest to the social learning formulation of marital
interaction are the variants of social exchange theory which hold that
partners function in a quasi-economy involving the exchanges of costs
and benefits. Intimate relationships cover a wide range of potential behavioral exchanges, making adequate stimulus control most difficult.
Distinctions carefully guarded in other relationships readily break down
when one lives with the same person who is lover, financial expert, cook,
child rearing partner, mechanic, and even oracle. The coercing of positive outcomes (affection, sex) from the other simply leads to a downward
spiral of benefits.

(3) A model of relationships derived from behavioral concepts was
presented which emphasized four areas of accomplishment, Objectification, Support/Understanding, Problem Solving, and Behavior Change.
These accomplishments are thought to be hierarchically ordered, each
depending upon the previous one. Relationships involve a Give → Get
dynamic balance, which reflects the exchange of costs and benefits. It is
hypothesized that when this balance is tipped in either direction for the
partners, attempts at restitution are made which are labeled Behavior
Change. Spouses engage in Behavior Change operations designed to increase gains or reduce costs. Unfortunately, these tend to reflect reliance

on aversive control procedures, which are reinforced and used more persistently.

Couples therapy focuses on each of the four areas of accomplishment by further discriminating some 12 areas of marital interaction, involving such commonplace activities as companionship, affection, parenting, household management, and so on. Couples may have specific deficiencies in accomplishment across these areas of interaction. Behavioral marital therapy is thus highly situation oriented, seeking to provide skills to deal with areas of interaction as appropriate to the major accomplishments. Typically, such approaches end with specific skill training in behavior change techniques, as with negotiation and contracting.

(4) A selective review was made of the empirical literature which offered tests of these conceptual propositions. While specific studies were not designed with this model in mind, sufficient work has been reported to at least lay out some important directions.

The interface between cognitions about spouse (relationship satisfaction per day) and events transpiring between spouses (per day) can be lawfully stated. Satisfaction with the relationship can be accounted for in part by specific interactional events; from 25 percent to 98 percent of the variance of satisfaction can be related to events.

Although couples focus on negatives, often seeking the reduction of negatives as a therapeutic goal, the model and the data support the notion that positive and negative relationship events are independent of one another, and that reduction of negatives can only decrease aversiveness but not increase positiveness. Couples often lack skills in tracking positive events, and distressed couples compared with nondistressed couples underestimate by half the actual occurrence of positive events. However, it may be argued that distressed couples do not subjectively rate behaviors as pleasing, although the intent of the sender is positive. Other studies have shown how partners reinforce "deviant" communications by attending to complaints differentially. Outside observers can code the same classes of positive behaviors as couples code, but generally the subjective definition of pleasant relates to reported relationship satisfaction better than observer's estimates of positive behaviors exchanged. Numerous accounts have established that distressed and nondistressed couples differ in total amount of positive and negative behaviors exchanged, and that problem solving statements also differ with distress status.

While treatment effectiveness was not the focus of this chapter, some studies included for review demonstrated that, compared to various control groups, behavioral therapy modules are effective in producing changes in marital satisfaction and in targeted behaviors important to the interaction. What is often, yet understandably, lacking in such studies is whether a specific module dealing with one of the four accomplishments is the effective agent of change or whether the "package" is necessary in its entirety. For example, it has now been established that the two major forms of contracting (and negotiation training) necessary for Behavior Change are quite similar in their relative effectiveness with couples demonstrating a moderate amount of distress. Both procedures surpassed the effects of placebo control groups.

What then lies ahead? A few brief words about next steps within a behavioral framework.

The behavioral approach is criterion oriented; satisfaction with relationship accomplishments also requires an outside evaluation of skillfulness. Couples may express considerable contentment with their "problem solving" but, based upon objective assessment of these skills, still appear to be deficient in problem solving. "Feeling good" about the other person is not the same as being competent in each of the areas of accomplishment. We need far greater accomplishments in our ability to accurately record skills in these difficult-to-observe areas of marital interaction.

It was suggested in the current model that a shift in control from stimulus to reinforcing control might be indicative of marital distress. Stimulus control, it was suggested, more closely approximated the rule governance of relationships often described by systems theorists. Reinforcing control refers to the maintenance of some behaviors by the quality of consequences. Often, distressed couples tend toward problem solving based on reinforcing control, using specific responses of the partner rather than rules to predict to their own next response. For example, a couple may attempt to decide the larger issue of division of resources (in a second marriage) on the basis of some tit-for-tat discussion of who got what item last Saturday, rather than on the basis of how much income is joint and how much separate. The next large-scale move for behavioral therapists will be in determining the conditions under which couples operate best with stimulus control or reinforcing control. Behavioral approaches are not embraced by couples with equal enthusiasm, as most clinicians have learned. What accounts for these differences, since we are generally confident that the medicine is well formulated? Where have we misunderstood the cognition-behavior interface with regard to gaining greater compliance with our helping technology?

The functionalism of behavioral approaches holds great promise for far better descriptions of dyadic environments than has been accomplished. Most clinicians working with couples are struck with the situational similarity between couples and their complaints. It can of course be argued that people only present what is easy to talk about and that real differences lie buried deep within. But a simpler hypothesis is that marriage and intimacy in general set up fairly common requirements which have to be met by the participants. Whether the family life cycle is too gross a level of analysis remains to be seen, but something akin to a taxonomy of situations is needed. Armed with this, marital therapy may then be approached still more rationally than is being done now.

The relationship between one's marital adjustment (a quality of relationship measure) and other areas of social functioning, including physical health status, is one that empirical investigators should attempt to describe. If, as many current reviews would indicate, marital therapy must be done with both partners conjointly in order to be effective, it can also be asked whether both partners effectively control these broader aspects of social adjustment. Sociological surveys are useful up to a point, but considerably more is needed in terms of interactional studies and effects on better defined measures of adjustment. Such a move would be entirely consistent with the current ecological emphasis in our culture.

REFERENCES

Azrin, N., Naster, B. and Jones, R. Reciprocity counseling: A rapid learning-based procedure for marital counseling. *Behavior Research and Therapy*, 1973, 11, 365-382.

Bandura, A. *Principles of Behavior Modification*. New York: Holt, Rinehart & Winston, 1969.

Beck, D. F. Research findings on the outcomes of marital counseling. In: D. H. L. Olson (Ed.), *Treating Relationships*. Lake Hills, Iowa: Graphic Publishing Company, 1976, pp. 431-474.

Birchler, G. R. A multimethod analysis of distressed and nondistressed marital interactions: A social learning approach. Paper presented at the Western Psychological Association Meetings, Seattle, April 1977.

Birchler, G. R., Weiss, R. L. and Vincent, J. P. A multimethod analysis of social reinforcement exchange between maritally distressed and nondistressed spouse and stranger dyads. *Journal of Personality and Social Psychology*, 1975, 31, 349-360.

Blechman, E. A. and Olson, D. H. L. Family contract game: Description and effectiveness. In D. H. L. Olson (Ed.), *Treating Relationships*. Lake Mills, Iowa: Graphic Publishing Company, 1976, pp. 133-150.

Bradburn, N. M. and Noll, C. E. *The Structure of Psychological Well-Being*. Chicago: Aldine Publishing Company, 1969.

Carter, H. and Glick, P. C. *Marriage and Divorce: A Social and Economic Study*. Cambridge, Massachusetts: Harvard University Press, 1970.

Carter, R. D. and Thomas, E. J. A case application of a signaling system (SAM) to the assessment and modification of selected problems of marital communication. *Behavior Therapy*, 1973, 4, 629-645.

Coleman, R. E. and Miller, A. G. The relationship between depression and marital maladjustment in a clinic population: A multitrait-multimethod study. *Journal of Consulting and Clinical Psychology*, 1975, 43, 647-651.

Crago, M. Psychopathology in married couples. *Psychological Bulletin*, 1972, 77, 114-128.

Crago, M. and Tharp, R. G. Psychopathology and marital role disturbance: A test of the Tharp-Otis descriptive hypothesis. *Journal of Consulting and Clinical Psychology*, 1968, 32, 338-341.

Engel, K. and Weiss, R. L. Behavioral cues used by marital therapists in discriminating distress. Paper presented at the Western Psychological Association Meeting, Los Angeles, April 1976.

Erikson, E. H. *Childhood and Society*. New York: Norton, 1950.

Fensterheim, H. Assertive methods and marital problems. In R. D. Rubin, H. Fensterheim, J. Henderson and L. P. Ullman (Eds.), *Advances in Behavior Therapy*. New York: Academic Press, 1972.

Follingstad, D. R., Sullivan, J., Ierace, C., Ferrara, J. and Haynes, S. Behavioral assessment of marital interaction. Paper presented at the Association for the Advancement of Behavior Therapy Meetings, New York, December 1976.

Follingstad, D. R., Haynes, S. and Sullivan, J. Assessment of the components of a behavioral marital intervention program. Unpublished manuscript, 1976.

Gergen, K. *The Psychology of Behavior Exchange*. Reading, Mass.: Addison-Wesley Publishing Co., 1969.

Goldiamond, I. Self-control procedures in personal behavior problems. *Psychological Reports*, 1965, 17, 851-868.

Goldstein, M. K. and Francis, B. Behavior modification of husbands by wives. Paper presented at the National Council on Family Relations Annual Meeting, Washington, October 1969.

Gottman, J., Notarius, C., Gonso, J. and Markman, H. *A Couple's Guide to Communication*. Champaign, Illinois: Research Press, 1976.

Gottman, J., Notarius, C., Markman, H., Bank, S. and Yoppi, B. Behavior exchange theory and marital decision making. *Journal of Personality and Social Psychology*, in press.

Gottman, J., Markman, H. and Notarius, C. The topography of marital conflict: A study of verbal and nonverbal behavior. Unpublished manuscript, 1977.

Gurman, A. S. and Kniskern, D. P. Research on marital and family therapy: Progress, perspective, and prospect. In S. L. Garfield and A. E. Bergin (Eds.), *Handbook of Psychotherapy and Behavior Change: An Empirical Analysis* (2nd ed.). New York: Wiley, 1978.

Haley, J. *Strategies of Psychotherapy*. New York: Grune and Stratton, 1963.

Haley, J. *Uncommon Therapy*. New York: Ballantine Books, 1973.

Harrell, J. and Guerney, Jr., B. G. Training married couples in conflict negotiation skills. In D. H. L. Olson (Ed.), *Treating Relationships*. Lake Mills, Iowa: Graphic Publishing Company, 1976, pp. 151-166.

Hicks, M. W. and Platt, M. Marital happiness and stability: A review of the research in the sixties. *Journal of Marriage and the Family*, 1970, 32, 553-574.

Homans, G. C. *The Human Group*. New York: Harcourt Brace, 1950.

Jacobson, N. S. Problem solving and contingency contracting in the treatment of marital discord. *Journal of Consulting and Clinical Psychology*, 1977, 45, 92-100.

Jacobson, N. S. Specific and nonspecific factors in the effectiveness of a behavioral approach to the treatment of marital discord. *Journal of Consulting and Clinical Psychology*, in press.

Jacobson, N. S. and Martin, B. Behavioral marriage therapy: Current status. *Psychological Bulletin*, 1976, 83, 540-566.

Johnson, S. M. and Lobitz, G. K. The personal and marital adjustment of parents as related to observed child deviance and parenting behaviors. *Journal of Abnormal Child Psychiatry*, 1974, 2, 192-207.

Jones, E. E., Kanouse, D. E., Kelley, H. H., Nisbett, R. E., Valins, S. and Weiner, B. *Attribution: Perceiving the Causes of Behavior*. New York: General Learning Press, 1972.

Kelly, G. A. *The Psychology of Personal Constructs*. New York: Norton, 1955.

Kelley, H. H. The processes of causal attribution. *American Psychologist*, 1973, 28, 107-128.

Langer, E. J. The illusion of control. *Journal of Personality and Social Psychology*, 1975, 32, 311-328.

Laszlo, C. A., Levine, M. D. and Milsum, J. H. A general systems framework for social systems. *Behavioral Science*, 1974, 19, 79-92.

Laws, J. L. A feminist review of marital adjustment literature: The rape of the locke. *Journal of Marriage and the Family*, 1971, 33, 483-515.

Lazarus, A. A. Behavior therapy and marriage counseling. *Journal of the American Society of Psychosomatic Dentistry and Medicine*, 1968, 15, 49-56.

Lederer, W. and Jackson, D. *Mirages of Marriage*. New York: W. W. Norton, 1968.

Levinger, G. Marital cohesiveness and dissolution: An integrative review. *Journal of Marriage and the Family*, 1965, 27, 19-28.

Lobitz, G. K. Referred versus nonreferred children: A multimethod comparison. Unpublished doctoral dissertation, University of Oregon, 1974.

Locke, H. J. and Wallace, K. M. Short marital adjustment and prediction tests: Their reliability and validity. *Marriage and Family Living*, 1959, 21, 251-255.

Mahoney, M. J. Reflections on the cognitive learning trend in psychotherapy. *American Psychologist*, 1977, 32, 5-13.

Margolin, G. A comparative evaluation of therapeutic components associated with behavioral marital treatments. Unpublished doctoral dissertation, University of Oregon, 1976.

Margolin, G. and Patterson, G. R. The differential consequences provided by mothers and fathers for their sons and daughters. *Developmental Psychology*, 1975, 11, 537-538.

Margolin, G. and Weiss, R. L. Communication training and assessment: A case of behavioral marital enrichment. *Behavior Therapy*, in press.

Marks, I. M. Management of sexual disorders. In H. Leitenberg (Ed.), *Handbook of Behavior Modification and Behavior Therapy*. Englewood Cliffs, New Jersey: 1976, pp. 255-300.

Miller, B. C. A multivariate developmental model of marital satisfaction. *Journal of Marriage and the Family*, 1976, 38, 643-657.

Mischel, W. *Personality and Assessment*. New York: John Wiley and Sons, Inc., 1968.

Mischel, W. On the empirical dilemmas of psychodynamic approaches: Issues and alternatives. *Journal of Abnormal Psychology*, 1973, 82, 335-344.

Oltmanns, T. F., Broderick, J. E. and O'Leary, K. D. Parents' marital adjustment and the efficacy of behavior therapy with children. *Journal of Cosnulting and Clinical Psychology*, 1977, 45, 724-729.

Overall, J. E. Associations between marital history and the nature of manifest psychopathology. *Journal of Abnormal Psychology*, 1971, 78, 213-221.

Overall, J. E., Henry, B. W. and Woodward, A. Dependence of marital problems on parental family history. *Journal of Abnormal Psychology*, 1974, 83, 446-450.

Paolino, T. J. and McCrady, B. S. *The Alcoholic Marriage: Alternative Perspectives.* New York: Grune and Stratton, 1977.

Patterson, G. R. and Reid, J. B. Reciprocity and coercion: Two facets of social systems. In C. Neuringer and J. Michael (Eds.), *Behavior Modification in Clinical Psychology.* New York: Appleton-Century-Crofts, 1970, pp. 133-177.

Patterson, G. R. and Cobb, J. A. Stimulus control for classes of noxious behaviors. In J. F. Knutson (Ed.), *The Control of Aggression: Implications from Basic Research.* Chicago: Aldine-Atherton, 1973, 144-199.

Patterson, G. R., Weiss, R. L. and Hops, H. Training of marital skills: Some problems and concepts. In: H. Leitenberg (Ed.), *Handbook of Behavior Modification and Behavior Therapy.* Englewood Cliffs, New Jersey: Prentice-Hall, 1976.

Patterson, G. R., Hops, H. and Weiss, R. L. Interpersonal skills training for couples in early stages of conflict. *Journal of Marriage and the Family,* 1975, 37, 295-302.

Peterson, G. L. and Frederiksen, L. W. Developing behavioral competencies in distressed marital couples. Paper presented at the Association for the Advancement of Behavior Therapy, New York, December 1976.

Phillips, G. M. and Metzger, N. J. *Intimate Communication.* Boston: Allyn and Bacon, Inc., 1976.

Rappaport, A. F. Conjugal relationship enhancement program. In: D. H. L. Olson (Ed.), *Treating Relationships.* Lake Mills, Iowa: Graphic Publishing Company, 1976, pp. 41-66.

Rappaport, A. F. and Harrell, J. A behavioral-exchange model for marital counseling. *The Family Coordinator,* 1972, 21, 203-212.

Reid, J. B. The study of drinking in natural settings. In: G. A. Marlatt and P. E. Nathan (Eds.), *Behavioral Approaches to Assessment and Treatment of Alcoholism.* New Brunswick, New Jersey: Rutgers University Center for Alcohol Studies, in press.

Robinson, E. A. and Price, M. G. Behavioral and self report correlates of marital satisfaction. Paper presented at the Association for the Advancement of Behavior Therapy, New York, December 1976.

Rogers, L. E. and Farace, R. V. Analysis of relational communication in dyads: New measurement procedures. *Human Communication Research,* 1975, 1, 222-239.

Rollins, B. S. and Cannon, K. L. Marital satisfaction over the family cycle: A reevaluation. *Journal of Marriage and the Family,* 1974, 36, 271-282.

Rosenblatt, P. C. and Budd, L. G. Territoriality and privacy in married and unmarried cohabiting couples. *Journal of Social Psychology,* 1975, 97, 67-76.

Rosenblatt. P. C. and Cunningham, M. R. Television watching and family tension. *Journal of Marriage and the Family,* 1976, 38, 105-111.

Rosenblatt, P. C., Titus, S. L. and Cunningham, M. R. Perfection, disrespect, tension, and apartness in marriage. Unpublished manuscript, 1977.

Royce, W. S. and Weiss, R. L. Behavioral cues in the judgment of marital satisfaction: A linear regression analysis. *Journal of Consulting and Clinical Psychology,* 1975, 43, 816-824.

Satir, V. *Conjoint Family Therapy.* Palo Alto: Science and Behavior Books, 1964.

Seligman, M. E. P. *Helplessness: On Depression, Development, and Death.* San Francisco: W. H. Freeman and Company, 1975.

Sheehy, G. *Passages: Predictable Crises of Adult Life.* New York: E. P. Dutton & Company, Inc., 1976.

Spanier, G. B., Lewis, R. A. and Cole, C. L. Marital adjustment over the family life cycle: The issue of curvilinearity. *Journal of Marriage and the Family,* 1975, 37, 263-275.

Stuart, R. B. Operant interpersonal treatment for marital discord. *Journal of Consulting and Clinical Psychology,* 1969, 33, 675-682.

Stuart, R. B. Behavioral remedies for marital ills: A guide to the use of operant-interpersonal techniques. In: A. S. Gurman and D. G. Rice (Eds.), *Couples in Conflict: New Directions in Marital Therapy.* New York: Aronson, 1975, pp. 165-175.

Stuart, R. B. An operant interpersonal program for couples. In: D. H. L. Olson (Ed.), *Treating Relationships.* Lake Mills, Iowa: Graphic Publishing Company, 1976, pp. 119-132.

Thibaut, J. and Kelley, H. H. *The Social Psychology of Groups.* New York: Wiley, 1959.

Thomas, E. J., Walter, C. L. and O'Flaherty, K. A verbal problem checklist for use in assessing family verbal behavior. *Behavior Therapy,* 1974, 5, 235-246.

Vincent, J. P. The susceptibility of marital observation data to faking. Paper presented to Western Psychological Association Meeting, Los Angeles, April 1976.

Vincent, J. P., Weiss, R. L. and Birchler, G. R. Dyadic problem solving behavior as a function of marital distress and spousal vs. stranger interactions. *Behavior Therapy,* 1975, 6, 475-487.

Watzlawick, P., Beavin, J. H. and Jackson, D. D. *Pragmatics of Human Communication: A Study of Interactional Patterns, Pathologies, and Paradoxes.* New York: W. W. Norton, 1967.

Weiss, R. L., Hops, H. and Patterson, G. R. A framework for conceptualizing marital conflict, a technology for altering it, some data for evaluating it. In: F. W. Clark and L. A. Hamerlynck (Eds.), *Critical Issues in Research and Practice: Proceedings of the Fourth Banff International Conference on Behavior Modification.* Champaign, Illinois: Research Press, 1973.

Weiss, R. L., Birchler, G. R. and Vincent, J. P. Contractual models for negotiation training in marital dyads. *Journal of Marriage and the Family,* 1974, 36, 321-330.

Weiss, R. L. and Issac, J. Behavior vs. cognitive measures as predictors of marital satisfaction. Paper presented at the Western Psychological Association Meeting, Los Angeles, April 1976.

Weiss, R. L. and Margolin, G. Marital conflict and accord. In A. R. Ciminero, K. S. Calhoun, and H. E. Adams (Eds.), *Handbook for Behavioral Assessment.* New York: John Wiley & Sons, Inc., 1977, pp. 555-602.

Weiss, R. L. and Birchler, G. R. Adults with marital dysfunction. In: M. Hersen and A. S. Bellak (Eds.), *Behavior Therapy in the Psychiatric Setting.* Baltimore: Williams and Williams, 1978, pp. 331-364.

Weiss, R. L. and Aved, B. M. Correlates of physical health status among nonclinic married couples. Paper presented at the Western Psychological Association Meeting, San Francisco, April, 1978.

Welch, J. J. and Goldstein, M. K. The differential effects of operant-interpersonal intervention. Unpublished manuscript, 1974.

Whitaker, C. A. A family therapist looks at marital therapy. In: A. S. Gurman and D. G. Rice (Eds.), *Couples in Conflict: New Directions in Marital Therapy.* New York: Aronson, 1975, pp. 165-175.

Wieman, R. J. Behavioral and Rogerian group marital therapy: A comparison. Paper presented at the Association for Advancement of Behavior Therapy Meeting, New York, December 1976.

Williams, A. M. Behavioral analysis of the quality and quantity of marital interaction. Unpublished doctoral dissertation. University of Florida, 1976.

Wills, T. A., Weiss, R. L. and Patterson, G. R. A behavioral analysis of the determinants of marital satisfaction. *Journal of Consulting and Clinical Psychology,* 1974, 42, 802-811.

V

Marital Therapy
from a Behavioral Perspective

K. DANIEL O'LEARY, PH.D.
and
HILLARY TURKEWITZ, PH.D.

THE BEHAVIORAL TREATMENT OF PAUL AND SHARON O'SULLIVAN

Mr. and Mrs. O'Sullivan were referred to the Stony Brook marital therapy program by a local mental health clinic which had a lengthy waiting list. They presented themselves as follows in the initial interview.

Sharon: An attractive 32-year-old woman who said that the major marital problems were lack of communication, lack of mutual interests, sexual naivete, and decreasing affection. She felt that she had a low tolerance for frustration and that she was depressed. She was a housewife with three children, aged eight, five, and three. Sharon was very dissatisfied with the marriage, she reported feeling like a prisoner, and she resented her husband's "over-involvement" in Alcoholics Anonymous.

Paul: A neat, reserved 35-year-old salesman who noted only one major marital problem, lack of communication. However, he reported that his wife displayed misdirected anger and had a minimal tolerance for the shortcomings of others. Paul had been a heavy drinker since his college graduation and throughout their 12 years of marriage. Fortunately, he had been abstinent for the past three years during which he was an active member of A.A.

This couple was seen for a total of 10 conjoint sessions and one initial one-hour interview with each spouse. Therapy was deemed successful by the therapist and both clients. The major treatment procedures included:

(1) Teaching communication skills—particular emphasis was placed on listening without interrupting and minimizing punitive statements and questions which sounded like declarations.

(2) Encouraging Sharon to engage in more activities outside the home (for example, a prayer group, a women's group, and Al Anon) to increase the positive feedback she might obtain from people other than her husband.

(3) Encouraging both Sharon and Paul to volunteer to do things which satisfied each other's needs. They were asked to sign a weekly therapy plan sheet to indicate that they understood the nature of their behavior change agreements and that they were committed to making these changes. The necessity of mutual compromise as a vehicle for alleviating distress was emphasized.

(4) Prompting Paul to display some form of affectionate behavior once per day as improvements were made in the relationship.

(5) Helping Sharon learn to ask Paul directly to meet more of her needs—especially her needs for his affection. In brief, she was encouraged to be more expressive of her needs.

(6) Asking Sharon and Paul to entertain the notion that her criticism of A.A. and Paul's involvement in it (for example, "Most of the members are sick," and "You spend too much time there.") resulted from his failure to be affectionate and to tell her at least several hours before going to an A.A. meeting that he needed to go that evening.

(7) Having Sharon contemplate the possibility that when Paul went to bed before she did and politely said "Good night," he was not putting her down and she need not feel jealous.

In summary, the treatment procedures included:

(1) Communication training.

(2) Negotiation and compromise.

(3) Therapist's suggestions that Sharon find social reinforcers outside the marriage.

(4) Therapist's suggestion that Paul be more affectionate.

(5) Insight, that is, reinterpretation or relabeling of certain behaviors.

Before describing these procedures in detail, a brief outline of the general thrust of this chapter follows. The major goals are to describe: (1) the behavioral approach; (2) the development of behavioral marital therapy; (3) the assessment and treatment procedures of the Stony Brook program; (4) treatment outcome data; and (5) future treatment directions.

WHAT IS THE "BEHAVIORAL APPROACH?"

The treatment procedures used with Sharon and Paul were conceptualized within a behavioral framework emphasizing two features, operant and cognitive. However, present behavior therapy in its broadest sense draws from three approaches: operant, respondent, and cognitive, and these three streams of influence on behavioral marital therapy will be discussed before the specific treatment procedures are further elaborated.*

Operant Conditioning

In 1953, B. F. Skinner published *Science and Human Behavior,* which was a major conceptual innovation regarding abnormal behavior. Most importantly, Skinner argued that behavior problems should be regarded as important subject matter in their own right. That is, he stated that we should not be wedded to the notion that a behavioral problem has to be regarded as a symptom of some psychic conflict. In his model he advised accepting a behavior, such as a communication difficulty or a sexual difficulty, as the problem to be addressed and corrected. As he noted, the emphasis on overt problems as mere symptoms in the 1950s encouraged therapists to avoid specifying the behaviors to be corrected. "Above all," he wrote, "it has encouraged the belief that psychotherapy consists of removing inner causes of mental illness, as the surgeon removes an inflamed appendix or cancerous growth or as indigestable food is purged from the body. . . . It is not an inner cause of behavior but the behavior itself which—in the medical analogy of catharsis—must be 'got out of the system' (Skinner, 1953, p. 373).

In his attempt to persuade mental health personnel to focus on observ-

---

* As Weiss (Chapter IV) noted, behavioral approaches to marital therapy have been generally atheoretical and not all behavior therapists would espouse this three-fold model. Instead, many behavior therapists argue strongly for one of the three approaches. Others, like Weiss, employ the social exchange and reciprocity models of social and operant psychology and communications paradigms as the basic theoretical springboards for treatment.

able behavior, Skinner argued vehemently for the eschewal of thoughts and images as primary data for psychology. Instead, he recommended a focus on observable behavior because it could be quantified according to frequency and rate. This reconceptualization by Skinner of abnormal behavior was a major impetus for a drastic change in therapeutic procedures in schools, hospitals, and outpatient facilities. More specifically, it provided the decisive impetus for the establishment of behavior modification and behavior therapy as a treatment-oriented approach. Lindsley, Skinner, and Solomon in 1953 first used the term "behavior therapy" in their description of the modification of a simple, lever-pulling response in psychotic patients. Initially, work utilizing an operant framework was executed primarily with children and psychotic adults, but more recently this approach has been successfully used with delinquents, obsessive compulsives, alcoholics, and distressed spouses (O'Leary and Wilson, 1975).

One of the first applications of operant learning principles to marital therapy was reported by Stuart (1969) who explicated a reciprocal reinforcement paradigm with couples. Spouses learned: (a) to list behavior they desired in one another; (b) to record the frequency with which the spouse displayed the desired behavior; and (c) to specify exchanges for the desired behaviors. More specifically, the couples gave tokens to one another immediately after they displayed the desired behavior; those tokens were redeemable for communication and affectionate or sexual behaviors.* The basic operant model has been modified and extended by Azrin, Naster, and Jones (1973), Weiss, Hops, and Patterson (1973), Stuart (1976), and Turkewitz and O'Leary (1976). Common to these approaches are emphases on increasing reciprocal reinforcement, decreasing aversive control, increasing communication, and teaching negotiation and contracting skills. The treatment procedures used to achieve these goals will be described in detail in a later section of this chapter.

Classical Conditioning.

Wolpe was a major pioneer in the development of behavior therapy procedures for adult patients with fears and neurotic reactions. Anxiety was deemed the causal agent in these patients' problems, and the anxiety was defined as a persistent response of the autonomic nervous system

---

* It should be noted that Stuart and almost all other behavior therapists no longer use tokens in marital treatment, but this study is cited because of its clear historic import.

acquired through classical conditioning. Wolpe's etiological and thera
peutic concepts were presented in a now classic book, *Psychotherapy by
Reciprocal Inhibition* (1958), in which a procedure called systematic
desensitization was described.

Systematic desensitization involves having a patient deeply relax and
imagine anxiety-provoking stimuli of increasing magnitude. Minimal
fear-provoking scenes are usually presented to the patient first. When
the patient can imagine those scenes without anxiety, other, more fear-
arousing situations are described. According to Wolpe, anxiety is extin-
guished by a process called reciprocal inhibition. Basically, Wolpe held
that anxiety is reduced if "a response antagonistic to anxiety could be
made to occur in the presence of the anxiety-evoking stimuli so that it is
accompanied by the complete or partial suppression of the anxiety response" (Wolpe, 1958, p. 71). Responses that are antagonistic to anxiety
include relaxation, eating, and assertion. Wolpe found that 90 percent
of his adult psychotherapy patients were either cured "or markedly improved" by such reciprocal inhibition therapy. This success rate was unprecedented with such patients and, more importantly, the duration of
therapy was only several months, not several years, as had been the case
with many other therapies with similar patients.

The pioneering clinical work of Wolpe and Lazarus in South Africa
was the major impetus for much of what is presently called behavior
therapy with adults. It is now clear that systematic desensitization can
lead to decreases in anxiety in speech phobics, in individuals with dating
and social anxiety, and in patients with fears of heights (acrophobia).
Further, desensitization has proven successful with monosymptomatic
phobias as well as polysymptomatic anxiety (O'Leary and Wilson, 1975).
However, it has not been demonstrated that either the hierarchial presentation of feared stimuli or the relaxation training is critical in the
successful treatment of various anxieties (Kazdin and Wilcoxon, 1976).
In brief, while systematic desensitization seems well accepted as a viable
treatment method, the processes contributing to the effectiveness of desensitization have not been identified.

Classic applications of the respondent conditioning paradigm to marital
problems have largely been in the area of sexual dysfunctions. Wolpe
(1958) pioneered in this area and the following examples illustrate his
contribution. When he ascertained that anxiety responses had been conditioned to sexual activities, he advocated various treatment procedures
depending upon the extent of the anxiety. If great amounts of anxiety
had been conditioned and sexual responsiveness had been almost totally

inhibited, systematic desensitization was advocated. With moderate amounts of anxiety regarding sexual activity, patients were told not to perform sexually unless they had an "unmistakable, positive desire to do so" (p. 130). For example, for a partially impotent male patient, he recommended the following:

"The patient is told to inform his sexual partner (quoting the therapist if necessary) that his sexual difficulties are due to absurd but automatic fears in the sexual situation, and that he will overcome them if she will help him, i.e., if she will participate on a few occasions in situations of great sexual closeness without expecting intercourse or exerting pressure toward it. He is to ask her to be patient and affectionate and not to criticize. Assured of her cooperation, he is to lie in bed with her in the nude in a perfectly easy, relaxed way, and thereafter to do just what he feels like doing *and no more*. He has no duty at any stage to reach any criterion of performance. It is found that from one love session to the next there is a decrease in anxiety and an increase in sexual excitation and therefore in the extent of the caresses to which the patient feels impelled. He has increasingly strong erections, and usually after a few sessions coitus is accomplished and then gradually improves" (1958, p. 131).

About the same time as the publication of Wolpe's book, *Psychotherapy by Reciprocal Inhibition* (1958), Masters established a clinic for the treatment of sexual dysfunction at Washington University School of Medicine. The work of Masters and Johnson was predicated on treating the marital relationship as the patient. The sensate focus procedures described in their classic text, *Human Sexual Inadequacy* (1970), bear strong resemblance to in vivo extinction and reinforcement of alternative responses described by Wolpe (1958). Other than these brief comments, the focus in this chapter will be confined largely to the treatment of couples without specific sexual dysfunctions or where the marital relationship is the primary focus and sexual problems receive secondary import. Thus, the treatment of sexual dysfunction as illustrated by Masters and Johnson (1970), Lobitz and LoPiccolo (1972), and Marks (1976) will not be covered. Nonetheless, sexual and marital problems are frequently inextricably related and thus it is often necessary to treat sexual problems during the course of marital therapy.

Cognitive Therapy

Many behavior therapists have placed increasing importance on the role of perceptions and thoughts in determining one's emotional reactions to external events. Behavior therapists, of course, are not unique in this view, but only recently have they clearly begun to ascribe special status to cognitive meanings,* labels, and structures. One of the earliest comprehensive treatment approaches utilizing cognitive methods was that of Ellis (1962). His interventions, labeled rational emotive therapy, are based on the proposition that most, if not all, psychological disorders arise from irrational thoughts. Basically, Ellis noted that people have faulty assumptions about themselves and the world about them. In turn, these assumptions lead to self-statements or "internal sentences" which are self-deprecating. For example, Ellis stated that a key proposition or belief held by many individuals with psychological problems is as follows: "One should be thoroughly competent, adequate, and achieving in all possible respects if one is to consider oneself worthwhile" (Ellis, 1962, p. 63). The therapist's goal is to help a client alter such beliefs. Like Wolpe, Ellis described his own therapeutic efforts in a summary case study fashion and reported that 63 percent of the clients he treated with psychoanalytic psychotherapy improved, whereas 90 percent of the clients he treated with rational emotive therapy improved. His self-reported success rates are plagued by the usual case study report problems, and particularly by his own change in therapeutic orientation during the time these clients were treated. More specifically, he treated the psychoanalytic group first and the rational emotive therapy group second. However, Ellis' writings have continued to influence researchers who have incorporated many cognitive methods into their therapies (for example, Beck, 1976; Goldfried and Goldfried, 1975; Mahoney, 1974; and Meichenbaum, 1974).

Other cognitive therapeutic methods successfully employed within a behavioral framework include teaching subjects or clients to use self-instructions to guide their behavior (Meichenbaum and Goodman, 1971; O'Leary, 1968; Robin, Armel, and O'Leary, 1975), and problem solving, which involves: (a) problem definition and formulation, (b) generation of alternatives, (c) decision-making, and (d) verification (D'Zurilla and Goldfried, 1971; Robin, Kent, O'Leary, Foster, and Prinz, 1977). Cognitive therapeutic procedures, such as thought stopping (Wolpe, 1958) and covert reinforcement or extinction (Cautela, 1967), are frequently used by behavior therapists, but the therapeutic efficacy

---

* See Weiss (Chapter IV) for a discussion of factors influencing judgments about intent and of rules as "the highest embodiment of stimulus control."

of these procedures has not been documented (Criaghead, Kazdin, and Mahoney, 1976).

Cognitive learning approaches to marital therapy have been almost nonexistent when applied in isolation from operant or respondent approaches. The most relevant cognitive behavior modification work is that of Ellis, who argues that marital disturbances result from neurotic disturbances of either or both spouses. His theory is that most couples enter marriage with two general expectations, the hope for regular sexual satisfaction and the enjoyment of intimate companionship and love. If these two expectations are prejudiced or illogically exaggerated, marriages will be disturbed (Ellis and Harper, 1961). According to Eisenberg and Zingle (1975) who evaluated Ellis' rational emotive therapy (RET) with marital clients, disturbed marital interactions are simply an extension of the disturbed individuals and thus can be dealt with accordingly. In brief, the assumption is that separate theoretical frameworks and procedures are not needed for marital therapy as contrasted to individual therapy. Data supporting this assumption are sparse. For example, Eisenberg and Zingle compared couples seeking marital therapy with randomly selected couples in the same community on a questionnaire designed to assess belief in Ellis' 11 basic irrational ideas. They found that the clinic couples had significantly higher irrational idea scores. While such data provide some support for Ellis' assumption concerning irrationality and marital dissatisfaction, there was no correlation between the irrational idea inventory scores and a general measure of marital adjustment (Locke and Wallace, 1959).

Specific applications of cognitive learning approaches have not been utilized or tested with any sophistication in the marital area. Nonetheless, the present authors would argue that much of what occurs in good marital therapy of *any* variety involves discussions of the assumptions that each spouse has: (1) about what was expected of the marriage, and (2) about what the marriage is providing relevant to those expectations. In this sense, the writings of Sager (1976) regarding the development of informal contracts appear to have critical yet unrecognized import for behavior marital therapists.

In summary, the behavioral or social learning approach to marital therapy includes contributions from the areas of operant, respondent, and cognitive learning (Bandura, 1969). As will be seen in the following description of the development of behavioral marital therapy, the operant paradigm has predominated in the conceptualization and formulation of treatment procedures.

DEVELOPMENT OF BEHAVIORAL MARITAL THERAPY

Marital discord has only recently begun to receive systematic attention from behavior therapists. Behavioral marital treatment programs have been described as being in "embryonic stages" (Greer and D'Zurilla, 1975). The research in this area has similarly been labeled as in the "initial stages" (Jacobson and Martin, 1976) and "prescientific" (Patterson, Weiss, and Hops, 1976). Nevertheless, an increasing number of empirical investigations suggest that the behavioral approach to marital discord is a viable one. The literature in this area will be reviewed with an emphasis on the development of therapeutic strategies, rather than on research methodology or data collection.

One explanation given for the "late arrival" of behavior therapists to the treatment of marital distress is that behavior modification, with its emphasis on the application of principles derived from general experimental psychology, tends to focus on the individual rather than groups or dyads (Greer and D'Zurilla, 1975). This focus is reflected in the early reports of behavioral marital therapy in which the therapists saw the spouses concurrently, in individual sessions (Goldiamond, 1965), or would treat only one of the partners. In two of the three marital case studies that Lazarus reported in 1968, only the wife was involved directly in the therapy. The treatment techniques used were: (a) desensitization, to help a wife accept her husband's past history of drunkenness now that he was no longer drinking, and (b) assertive training, to help a wife argue more effectively with her husband. A second tack taken in treating only the wife in a distressed marriage was to train her in the behavioral principles of reinforcement and extinction so that she could attempt to shape her husband's behavior in desirable directions (Goldstein, 1971; Goldstein and Francis, 1969). These authors reported significant positive change in eight of 10 cases. However, the focus on just the wives, with no reports from the husbands, does not allow one to make any statements regarding the overall marital relationship.

The more recent behavioral marital treatment programs involve conjoint rather than individual therapy. The assumption is that both spouses need to be present to insure that the dyadic structure is altered in a way that is satisfying to both. Conjoint therapy gives the therapist an opportunity to assess the marital interactions in vivo, it provides a context for directed practice of new skills, and it increases the probability that both partners will accept and support the changes that occur in the marriage. In a comprehensive review covering all approaches to marital therapy,

Gurman (1973) found considerably more studies of group and conjoint than individual therapy. Thus, it appears that the behavioral therapists' preference for having both spouses present is shared by marital therapists from a wide variety of treatment orientations. Additionally, in a more recent review, Gurman and Kniskern (in press) conclude that there is little research evidence for the continued practice of individual marital therapy and that conjoint and conjoint group therapy are clearly more effective.

One way in which the behavioral approach was first applied to the conjoint setting was to teach the spouses behavioral principles—either to help them shape positive behaviors in one another (Liberman, 1970) or to have them analyze the consequences of their behavior and learn to interrupt negative interaction chains (Friedman, 1972). These mutual behavior change attempts were structured even further with the introduction of behavioral contracts. The contracts took the form of written agreements, with each spouse agreeing to make changes that the other desired. Rappaport and Harrell (1972) listed several advantages that a written contract has over a verbal agreement:

(1) It serves as a reference so that memory does not play a significant role. This is a very important advantage because in using verbal agreements when one or both spouses are reluctant to change (which is almost always the case), lack of memory of the agreement is the first and most frequently cited reason for not following the assignment. Having a written contract precludes this "excuse" and thus makes it easier for the therapist to discuss the factors prompting the spouse's resistance.

(2) A written contract is easier to renegotiate and modify.

(3) Placed in a visible location, it can serve as a constant reminder to the couple of their commitment. It is also possible that a written, signed, or initialed contract will produce more commitment to follow-through than a verbal agreement.

Although Rappaport and Harrell had couples contract for reductions in undesirable behaviors, the more common procedure is to have spouses specify and contract for increases in positive behaviors (e.g., Weiss, Chapter IV).

There are several reasons for this emphasis on accelerating positive behaviors. One of the therapist's goals is to teach the couples a more positive means of changing one another's behavior. All too often, distressed spouses are quite skilled in punishing each other for the occurrence of undesirable behaviors, and one goal of therapy is to eliminate the use of aversive control strategies.

One direct way to change this pattern is through a focus on positively reinforcing desired changes rather than on punishing undesirable behaviors or reinforcing the absence of these behaviors. Weiss, Birchler, and Vincent (1974) pointed out that it is easier to reinforce the occurrence of something than to reinforce a nonoccurrence. For example, reinforcing nonoccurrences of criticisms can be difficult because a spouse would not know all those occasions when an individual *might* have been critical but chose not to be. Additionally, an individual may not notice the absence of an aversive event as easily as the occurrence of an unexpected positive behavior. These authors also noted the useful strategy of accelerating a desirable behavior that is incompatible with an aversive one—for example, contrast for increasing two-way conversation during dinner hour as opposed to decreasing TV watching during dinner. In this way, the undesirable behavior will decrease without the use of punishment.

One method used to increase the likelihood that desired behavior changes will be executed is to use tokens, which spouses give to one another upon the occurrence of a desirable behavior (Hickok and Komechak, 1974; Stuart, 1969). The advantages cited for the use of tokens are that they serve as immediate reinforcement, they are concrete and unambiguous, and the exchange of tokens can provide the occasion for a positive social interchange. Both case study reports of this technique presented favorable outcomes. However, as there is much evidence indicating that successful contracting can take place without tokens, the present authors think they should not be used for the following reasons:

(1) Tokens are often perceived by clients as highly artificial and mechanistic.

(2) Spouses desire that behavior changes in their partners occur largely voluntarily, and token and back-up reinforcers contribute to the perception that behavior change is externally prompted. This attribution may prompt resistance by the clients and a fear that the externally prompted behavior will not be maintained.

(3) Tokens were originally used to aid individuals in bridging the temporal gap between the occurrence of a behavior and the back-up reinforcers. However, most marital clients do not have serious problems in bridging such gaps, and thus tokens can be viewed as superfluous.

(4) Whenever tokens and back-up reinforcers are introduced in the

reinforcement of behavior, a transition period is necessary in which maintenance of behavior has to be assessed in the absence of token and back-up reinforcers. This transition period and the necessary gradual fading of external rewards are avoided if token and back-up reinforcers are not employed.

There are two major forms of contracts that are used in behavioral marital therapy. The first is the quid pro quo (or tit-for-tat) contract (for example, Azrin et al., 1973; Lederer and Jackson, 1968; Rappaport and Harrell, 1972; Stern and Marks, 1973; and the token programs of Hickok and Komechak, 1974 and Stuart, 1969). In the quid pro quo contract, spouse behavior changes are cross-linked, in that the contract is written so that *if* one spouse engages in the desired behavior, *then* the other spouse will also change in the requested manner. For example, if Tom would like Sue to figure the household budget and Sue would like Tom to play cards with her, a quid pro quo contract might be written as: (a) "If Sue figures the household budget, then Tom will play cards with her for one hour," or (b) "If Tom plays cards with Sue for one hour, then Sue will figure the household budget." It is clear that in the quid pro quo contract the spouses' behavior changes are dependent on one another. If the first part of the contract is not executed, the second spouse is under no obligation to change. Thus, it is possible that the spouses will play a "you go first" game, with neither wanting to make the first move.

The second major contract format is a "good faith" contract introduced by Weiss, Hops and Patterson (1973). This contract is written so that if a spouse engages in the desired behavior, he/she receives a positive reinforcer that is independent of change in his/her partner's behavior. Again consider the example of Tom, who would like Sue to figure the household budget and Sue, who would like Tom to play cards with her. A "good faith" contract between them might read, "If Tom plays cards with Sue for one hour, then he is entitled to choose the TV programming for that evening; if Sue figures the household budget, then she gets private time for an evening while Tom watches the children." In such a contract, there is no benefit in waiting for one's partner to change first. Each spouse can receive his or her own rewards, from either their partner, the external environment, or the therapist (for example, a fee reduction) for changing in the desired direction. Good faith contracts have also been written to include penalties for not engaging in the desired behavior. However, once again, caution must be recommended in using penalties, particularly spouse-controlled aversive consequences.

Weiss, Birchler, and Vincent (1974), in a detailed explication of behavioral contracts, noted that in constructing good faith contracts with spouse-controlled reinforcers, the therapist must be careful in guiding the spouses' choices of these reinforcers. For instance, one would not want a husband's reinforcer to be something that may be highly aversive to his wife. An example of a problematic contract described by Weiss et al. was as follows: having a wife sleep in the nude (if sleeping in the nude is an aversive event for this woman) if her husband engaged in future-planning conversations with her. Weiss et al. stated that if this contract were employed, and the husband did not engage in future-planning discussions, not sleeping in the nude would be sanctioned and the contract would inadvertently be strengthening the wife's avoidance behavior (p. 329). More important, if the wife finds sleeping in the nude highly aversive, she will probably find a way to make it very difficult for her husband to engage in future-planning conversations, and thus promote his failure to carry out the contract. This subversion will occur when the negative aspects of sleeping in the nude outweigh the positive effects of future-planning discussions. The general rule for the therapist is to insure that both spouses agree on the reinforcers chosen. Even if the woman would not subvert the contract, as will be noted later, contracts for sexual behavior are ill-advised.

There are several theoretical and practical considerations a therapist should note in making a choice between quid pro quo and good faith contracts. Quid pro quo contracts may be more powerful since the most significant reinforcers for a spouse would presumably be the changes they are requesting in their partner. In addition, Jacobson and Martin (1976) argued that quid pro quo contracts are more efficient, as it is time consuming to identify separate reinforcers and arrange for the individual reinforcement of each behavior change. However, the problem of waiting for one's spouse to "go first," noted previously in the discussion of quid pro quo contracts, prompted Weiss and his associates to advocate the good faith contract particularly for seriously distressed and extremely hostile couples. Jacobson (in press) compared the effects of the two contracts and found both equally effective. However, it is possible that there may be a difference if couples are extremely disturbed. Knox (1973) combined both of these contracts, using the good faith contract first, until appropriate positive changes had been made, and then switching to the quid pro quo agreements.

In addition to contracting, training in communication skills has become an increasingly important aspect of behavioral marital therapy. Much of the process of constructing a contract involves problem-solving discussions that include: specification of the desired changes, "brainstorming" or generating alternative ways of effecting these changes, and predicting and evaluating the consequences of different agreements. Couples are taught to communicate in ways that are conducive to effective problem solving. These skills are taught through modeling, role playing, structured exercises, instructions and feedback (Jacobson, 1977; Patterson, Hops and Weiss, 1973; Patterson, Weiss and Hops, 1976; Stuart, 1976; Weiss et al., 1973). The spouses are also strongly encouraged to verbally reinforce one another for desired changes that occur. Azrin, Naster and Jones (1973) used what they termed the "Positive Statement Procedure" to increase the socially reinforcing aspect of spouses' interactions. This procedure requires that each spouse include a positive statement with any negative remark they make (for example, "What you said earlier made great sense, but the comment you made just now is illogical").

One additional technique employed is the use of "Love Days" (Weiss et al., 1973) or "Caring Days" (Stuart, 1976). On these days the spouse is requested to make a special effort to please his/her partner by engaging in significantly more of the behaviors that the partner desires. The assumption is that these displays of caring will hasten the flow of positive feelings between the spouses. While the technique has been used successfully, it should also be noted that there are couples who find this task too burdensome or whose attributions do not allow them to perceive their spouse's efforts as reinforcing (Liberman, Levine, Wheeler, Sanders, and Wallace, 1976; Weiss, 1975).

In summary, the central emphasis of the behavioral approach to marital therapy is on helping spouses learn more productive and positive means of effecting desired behavior changes in one another. The techniques used to reach this goal include communications skill training, problem solving, and marital agreements or contingency contracting. Three issues that have not been directly studied in published research on behavioral marital therapy are: (1) whether to use co-therapists; (2) whether conjoint or group therapy is the most effective setting; and (3) whether therapy should be time-limited.

Co-therapy is recommended by some professionals because of the opportunity for modeling in the interaction between the therapists. At times the co-therapists have even discussed the couple's conflict between themselves, each presenting the argument of the same-sex spouse. Thus, the modeling of effective interactions occurs regarding issues of greatest relevance to the couple. It may also be useful to have co-therapists when giving negative feedback, as when the therapists want to identify a counterproductive communication pattern. At times a spouse may attempt to dismiss negative feedback from an opposite-sex therapist by saying (or thinking) such things as: "Of course she'd think that, she's just like my wife," or "All men have trouble understanding the woman's point of view." However, these reactions can be overcome if the therapist is clear in explaining the rationale behind the feedback and if he or she is sure to be "fair" in the dispensing of feedback. Gurman (1973) compared the improvement rates in studies of all approaches to marital therapy and did not find that couples showed greater improvement when they had co-therapists than when they had a single therapist. Since it is important to develop a treatment package that would be appropriate for practicing clinicians in non-university settings, and staff and economic limitations often make co-therapy untenable, the Stony Brook project involves individual therapists.

The cost of conjoint marital therapy prompted Liberman et al. (1976a) to recommend group marital therapy. However, in addition to economic factors, the group setting was recommended for the wide variety of models, the potency of the feedback, and the positive expectations derived through seeing progress in other couples (Liberman, Wheeler and Sanders, 1976). Reports of treatment programs in which the exclusive emphasis was on training communication skills, without the behavioral problem-solving or contracting approach, almost universally have involved group therapy (Ely, Guerney and Stover, 1973; Hickman and Baldwin, 1971; Pierce, 1973). In contrast, there are very few descriptions of behavioral group marital therapy (Liberman et al., 1976a, 1976b; Turner, 1972). Although Liberman et al. reported successful use of groups, the couples involved in these programs attended approximately one to three conjoint interviews before joining the group. Gurman and Kniskern (in press), in reviewing all marital therapy approaches, found no difference in outcome when group and conjoint therapy were directly compared. In the absence of data indicating which setting is preferable for behavioral therapy, the present authors decided to see the couples in conjoint therapy.

Almost all of the recent reports of behavioral treatment programs involve time-limited therapy, that is, the number of sessions is specified in advance. One possible explanation for the prevalence of time limits is that the investigators are conducting research evaluations which require uniform treatment across couples. However, the present authors feel that there can be advantages to time-limited therapy that go beyond research considerations. As Stuart has noted (1975), when couples know the termination date in advance, they may maximize their use of therapy time. For example, they may be more committed to working out their problems from the beginning of therapy, including completing assignments at home between sessions.

However, it is advisable for the therapist to be willing to make exceptions to the time limit. Two examples of situations in which therapy might be extended are when the couple is in the midst of a new crisis (created by an external event such as loss of a job or death of a family member) and when significant information becomes available toward the end of therapy. As with the issues of co-therapists and group therapy, the choice of length of therapy and time-limits in behavioral marital therapy cannot be dictated by available data. Gurman and Kniskern (in press) reported conflicting evidence regarding the use of time limits in that in some cases time-limited therapy was more effective, while other investigators found no differences.

Whether or not one uses a time limit, the present authors believe that it is always advisable to set a specific time at which progress in therapy can be evaluated. During the first session the therapist can state that the couple's progress will be evaluated at the eighth session. If at that time there is some positive change but the couple and therapist think that further gains can be made, therapy will continue. If there is no change by that time, the therapist should discuss referring the clients elsewhere, since another therapist may be more effective in working with that particular couple. In a recent review of the literature, it was found that the average duration of behavioral marital therapy is typically about eight sessions. The present authors' treatment program consists of an intake interview and 10 weekly sessions. As Gurman (1973) reported an average marital therapy length of 17.45 sessions, the behavioral programs are considerably shorter than treatment programs of other orientations. While this difference may be due to the use of an upper limit, Weiss et al. (1973), who did not set time limits, reported treatment durations of $1\frac{1}{2}$ to 13 weeks, which were still shorter than the average.

There are several research evaluations of conjoint behavioral marital therapy. Azrin et al. (1973) evaluated a "Reciprocity Counseling" procedure with 12 couples and reported significant increases on a 1 to 10 rating of various areas of marital satisfaction. These results were replicated with five couples by Wolf and Etzel (1976). Weiss et al. (1973) and Patterson, Hops, and Weiss (1975) evaluated a total of 10 couples on a variety of measures, including questionnaires regarding marital satisfaction, spouses' recordings of pleasing and displeasing behaviors, and the couples' interaction on a problem-solving task. They reported significant improvement on most of their measures. While the above studies did not include control groups for comparison, Jacobson (1977) compared five couples who received behavioral marital therapy with five who were in a waiting list control group and found that the treated couples improved significantly more on a problem-solving task and reported significantly greater increases in overall marital satisfaction. In a second study, Jacobson (in press) compared behavioral therapy to an attention control group and found the behavioral program significantly more effective. For a more detailed description of the outcome research on behavioral marital therapy, the reader is referred to Chapter VIII by Jacobson. A report of the present authors' research evaluation will follow the detailed account of the Stony Brook treatment program. However, prior to this description, an overall view of the process of marital therapy will be presented.

TREATMENT PROCESS

To maximize therapeutic effectiveness, a therapist must be attuned to the nature of his or her relationship with the clients. It is useful to conceptualize the overall treatment process in terms of this therapeutic relationship and the way in which it changes over time. The four stages of the therapeutic relationship can be conceptualized as (1) courtship, (2) engagement, (3) marriage, and (4) disengagement. The parallel between the first three stages and the couple's own relationship process is clear. The fourth stage, disengagement, is a necessary aspect of the therapeutic relationship, but its counterpart, divorce, is typically not a stage that couples seeking marital therapy desire in their own relationship.

During the courtship stage, the therapist establishes rapport with the clients, while they are deciding whether the therapist is a person who can be helpful to them. During this stage, a therapist should show warmth and understanding and may even occasionally self-disclose to increase the likelihood that the clients will place trust in him or her (Johnson and Matross, in press). The clients are also actively engaged in "winning" the therapist to their side. While this activity of trying to gain the therapist's support against one's spouse may and often does continue past the courtship stage, it is particularly salient in these first few sessions.

Although assessment of problems and/or progress clearly takes place throughout therapy, during the courtship stage the therapist completes his or her initial assessment. In the present authors' treatment program, the couples also complete several questionnaires and engage in a problem-solving exercise during this stage. In this assessment process, rapport is enhanced by focusing on specific behaviors that can be changed and by showing a serious concern for the spouses' feelings toward one another.

During the engagement stage, the therapist solidifies a working relationship with the couple. It is at this time that the therapist explains the treatment model and rationale and clarifies his or her expectations regarding the couple's commitment to therapy. Although the present authors do not have the couples sign an explicit therapeutic contract during the engagement stage, several behavioral marital therapists do.

The first two stages of courtship and engagement generally comprise only the first two or three sessions of therapy. Just as the marriage stage is obviously the most involved part of the couple's relationship, it comprises the major part of the treatment program and will be the stage described in greatest detail.

Disengagement involves preparing the couple for termination of therapy. The treatment program involves the teaching of general strategies for resolving conflicts, and the expectation is that these strategies can and should be used after termination. In that sense, the couple is being prepared for termination continually throughout therapy. However, during the disengagement stage the therapist actively begins to withdraw his or her direction and control to insure a greater probability of maintenance of treatment effects.

Each of these stages will now be described in more detail with an emphasis on particular therapeutic strategies and techniques.

Courtship

As noted, the courtship stage is primarily the setting for assessment and the building of rapport. The assessment of marital problems within a behavioral framework will be described in some detail. However, the following discussion will emphasize the assessment procedures found useful in treatment; those measures which would be confined largely to a research context will be discussed only briefly.

Any assessment endeavor is intricately tied to one's conceptualizations both of appropriate treatment and of "good marriages." As Weiss and Margolin (1977) have noted, however, research on the critical factors that constitute good marriages is relatively sparse. Nevertheless, a number of studies indicated that problems regarding sexual relations (Clark, 1961; Gebhard, 1966), child rearing (Oltmanns, Broderick and O'Leary, 1977), communication (Bienvenu, 1970; Gottman, Notarius, Markman, Bank, Yoppi and Rubin, in press; Navran, 1967), and recreational activities (Weiss et al., 1973) are some of the factors which significantly differentiate distressed from nondistressed couples. It is important to note that changing these problematic areas by encouraging the distressed couple to behave more like a nondistressed couple will not necessarily create a happy marriage. However, it is clearly important to assess these dimensions of the relationship. At present, with the exception of particular sexual dysfunctions, marital problems are not highly differentiated or differentially diagnosed, and the Stony Brook program's referrals from local mental health clinics include clients with highly heterogeneous problems. Consequently, the initial assessment procedures are designed to provide the therapist with an extensive rather than intensive survey of the couple's problems. Specifically, assessment areas include general marital satisfaction, change in particular target behaviors and marital problems identified by each spouse, positive feelings toward one another, and communication patterns.

The behavioral assessment of marital discord is an admixture of standard marital assessment devices, ratings of particular behaviors deemed important to change, and the clinical interview. Generally, the standard assessment devices are used to obtain an index of the severity of the couple's problems and a generalized measure of marital happiness. Occasionally, standardized self-report assessment measures may also be used to provide the therapist with an index of individual pathology of either one or both of the spouses. Standardized observations may be used in research contexts to assess the couple's style of communication by having them attempt to resolve differences of opinion about standardized problems or problems of their own (Olson and Ryder, 1970; Turkewitz and O'Leary, 1976; Weiss et al., 1973). On occasion, a clinician may choose to use a structured problem-solving task to obtain a sample of the couple's interaction, but the coding of such data is too costly and time-consuming for general clinical use. Another type of assessment procedure that may be used is to have the couple observe and record pleasing and displeasing behaviors that occur at home (Weiss et al., 1973). This practice is more clinically relevant than using standardized ratings of problem-solving interactions. However, because daily telephone calls are advised to obtain reliable recordings of pleasing and displeasing behaviors (Patterson et al., 1976), this procedure was not used. Nonetheless, it is advisable to ask clients to take mental (and, on occasion, written) note of whether their spouse is engaging in desired behaviors.

Self-report questionnaires

GENERAL MARITAL HAPPINESS

The present authors use the revised Locke-Wallace Marital Adjustment Scale (MAT) (Kimmel and Van der Veen, 1974) because of its brevity, reliability, and validity. The revised Locke-Wallace is a 23-item questionnaire which requires only 10 to 15 minutes for spouses to complete and less than 10 minutes to score for both spouses. The questionnaire is an omnibus one which briefly assesses various aspects of marriage such as communication, sexual compatibility, affection, social activities, and value differences. The construct validity of the Locke-Wallace MAT has been demonstrated in several studies. The reliability coefficient computed by the split-half technique and corrected by the Spearman-Brown formula is .90 (Locke and Wallace, 1959). Further, the factor scores of the revised form are remarkably stable over a two-to-four-year period (range .69-.78) (Kimmel and Van der Veen, 1974). Its predecessor, the Terman Marital Happiness Test, is even predictive of marital happiness in men across a 30-year period (Sears, 1977). The discriminant validity of the Locke-Wallace has been established largely by a contrasted-groups method in which discordant couples seeking marital therapy are compared with couples who are not reported as having marital problems (Eisenberg and Zingle, 1975; Locke-Wallace, 1959).

Like most self-report measures, the Locke-Wallace MAT is subject to the social desirability set, a tendency to perceive and report relationships in a positive manner even when the relationship would not be viewed as such by an independent assessor. However, it is not clear whether this set has any serious negative consequences for the validity of the MAT. While it is true that social desirability and self-reported marital adjustment are correlated, the data of Murstein and Beck (1972) on social desirability and the MAT lead one to question whether the problem of social desirability is as serious as Edmonds (1967) and Edmonds, Withers, and Dibastia (1972) have asserted. The social desirability set is clinically important in areas where denial of problems is a critical symptom such as in assessment of ulcerative patients. However, even if both spouses view their marriage in more positive terms than would most independent judges, it is not clear that the reliability or predictive validity of the MAT would be adversely affected.

SELF-DESCRIPTION OF CRITICAL PROBLEMS

Each spouse is asked to complete a questionnaire on which he/she describes the most important problems that he/she would like to see changed (a) in the marriage, (b) in the spouse, and (c) in him or herself. Such descriptions provide the general foci for treatment, and in many ways these self-descriptions of critical problems are the most important questionnaire data obtained.

The strategy of obtaining self-descriptions and ratings of the most important problems to change is a clinically focused strategy that has been used with marital distress, conduct disorders, and hyperactive problems of children. Although the formal reliability and validity status of these self-descriptions and ratings of critical target behaviors has not been established, such measures have been found to be sensitive to treatment changes and to be of clear face validity to both clients and therapists (Kent and O'Leary, 1976, 1977; O'Leary, Pelham, Rosenbaum, and Price, 1976; Turkewitz and O'Leary, 1976).

SELF-REPORT OF FEELINGS TOWARD SPOUSE

The current authors developed an 18-item questionnaire designed to evaluate the emotional quality of the marital relationship. The purpose of the "Feelings Toward Spouse" questionnaire (Turkewitz and O'Leary, 1975) is to assess feelings that are not *necessarily* communicated, either verbally or nonverbally. Several examples are: "How often do you look forward to being alone with your spouse?" "Do you feel positive about your spouse's personal successes?" "How often do you think about particularly good experiences that you and your spouse have shared?" The spouses are asked to rate the frequency of these feelings, using a 5-point scale. A measure of this kind is useful for several reasons: (1) it is clear that the existence of positive feelings is a necessary component of a successful marriage; (2) the extent of positive feelings may be predictive of success in therapy; and (3) it is important to be able to assess the changes in feelings that accompany or follow behavioral changes. Scores on the "Feelings Toward Spouse" questionnaire correlate significantly with scores on the revised Locke-Wallace, the measure has adequate test-retest reliability (Turkewitz and O'Leary, 1975), and the current authors have obtained some evidence indicating that it can be predictive of outcome in therapy (Turkewitz and O'Leary, 1976).

SELF-REPORT OF COMMUNICATION

The Locke-Sabagh-Thomes Primary Communication Inventory (Navran, 1967) is used to assess communication patterns. This 25-item questionnaire contains a 5-point scale that the spouses use to report the frequency of such communication behaviors as talking about pleasant or unpleasant events of the day, sulking, discussions of sexual matters, and understanding of spouse's tone of voice or facial expressions. This questionnaire has discriminant validity in that couples seeking counseling score significantly lower than nonclinic couples (Navran, 1967). Since improving communication is so often one of the primary goals in marital therapy (Olson, 1970), it is helpful to have an efficient questionnaire that can serve both as a means of identifying particular areas of deficiency before therapy and as a measure of the impact of the treatment program.

Clinical interview

A good clinical interview is the sine qua non of assessment of marital problems. It is the context in which trust is built and the "courtship" actually begins. As is true for all therapies, the substance of the clinical interview is determined by one's theory or model of treatment. A clinical interview that follows a social learning framework would be designed to:

(1) Specify and elaborate the target behaviors noted on the questionnaires.

(2) Develop some understanding regarding the etiology of the problem.

(3) Provide the therapist with an opportunity to learn whether there are critical problems other than those mentioned, that is, to ascertain whether there are hidden agendas.

During the initial interview, the present authors also solicit information regarding the physical health of the spouses. If a physical examination has not occurred in the past year and there is any suspicion of a physical problem (such as impotence, blood pressure, ulcers, vaginismus), an immediate physical is recommended.

In addition, individual problems of spouses should be assessed and attended to. For example, extreme generalized compulsiveness, alcoholism, or depression should be addressed over and above or, in certain instances, instead of the marital problems. Of course, if any of these conditions is relatively limited to the marital interaction, then individual therapy would be contraindicated.

Two primary goals of the initial clinical interviews are to build positive expectations and to establish rapport with the clients. Clients' expectations of a therapist's ability to help them have been shown to influence outcome in many therapeutic endeavors (Goldstein, 1962). Thus, some statement by the therapist regarding expectations of benefit from therapy is certainly desirable in the courtship phase, following assessment. Especially where it is felt that the spouses care a great deal about one another and the general prognosis is good, it can be of great benefit to the clients to learn that the therapist feels that he or she can definitely help them resolve many of their problems.

On the other hand, where it is unclear to the therapist that he or she can help the clients resolve their joint problems, it may be useful to state such. For example, the therapist might discuss with the clients that given a minimal level of caring, a long history of aversive control, and the reluctance of one partner to change, the program's effectiveness may be lessened. (Age, length of marriage, and feelings of caring have been found to be predictive of therapeutic change [Turkewitz and O'Leary, 1976].) Such discussions convey an impression to the clients that they clearly have to work to produce a satisfactory result.

Secondly, reasonable statements from the therapist regarding the likely gains to be made over the course of the 10-week treatment program will produce more trust in the therapist's judgment than would overly optimistic statements implying that he or she has a panacea for marital problems. Finally, it is important to assess the client's expectations regarding therapy to insure that they are not either unrealistically high or low.

Building rapport can be enhanced by creating both the physical setting and interpersonal demand characteristics that will facilitate treatment. The physical setting can be arranged so that the room is comfortable and well designed and the therapist can sit equidistant from each client. Personal mementos, pictures, plants, diplomas, and licenses can also convey an attitude of warmth within a professional setting (Goldman, 1972).

Fortunately, behavior therapists are beginning to discuss interpersonal factors that enhance the therapeutic relationship (Wilson and Evans, 1976), but they have conducted few research investigations concerning the application of learning or social influence principles to this process. Because of this gap, the present authors provide a number of suggestions for enhancing rapport in marital therapy that are drawn from clinical practice and the writings of therapists of diverse theoretical persuasions. The establishment of rapport can be facilitated by very careful listening with minimal interruption during the initial interview. As each spouse has a tremendous investment in having the therapist understand his or her point of view, accurate, nonjudgmental reflections of *both* clients are particularly crucial at this stage. Having a therapist listen in a nonjudgmental fashion has long been felt to lessen a client's anxiety through extinction and counterconditioning. A further way to reduce anxiety in marital therapy is to make occasional comments in the initial sessions about treating other clients with similar problems or to simply state that most couples have similar problems.

Although the selection of therapeutic goals does not take place during the courtship stage, it is worthy to note here that this selection is one clear way in which a client senses in the therapist either an obtuseness or a sensitivity to his or her needs. Occasionally, one may decide to work on modifying a target problem that will not be viewed as crucial by one or both of the clients. If such is the case, it is especially important to explain the rationale for this intervention—that the behavior change in question will facilitate other desired changes. Since women usually make the initial referral call, it is incumbent upon the therapist to also motivate the male in the first session. Of course, the reverse holds true if the husband was the initiator of the therapy appointment. There are several additional relationship issues of import, such as the influence of the therapist's values or life-style, empathy, self-disclosure, and style of communication. These will be discussed in the present courtship stage, although the therapist should clearly be cognizant of these factors throughout therapy.

The choice of working toward resolution of marital problems versus working toward divorce counseling may be influenced by the therapist's marital status. It is advisable for divorced therapists to be alert to the possibility that they may work less intensely toward resolving marital difficulties than married therapists. Similarly, a married therapist needs to be more aware that he or she may strive too hard to continue a marriage when such may not be desired by one or both of the clients.*

While most therapists strive not to have their values unduly influence their clients, it seems clear that that influence occurs by the questions asked, the reputation of the therapist in the community, and the therapeutic targets the clients are helped to establish. At times, a therapist is well advised to declare simply and honestly his or her strong personal biases regarding options clients may be considering (such as adultery or

---

* We are grateful to Drs. Richard Stuart and Ronald Kent for emphasizing these issues with us.

swinging) (O'Leary and Wilson, 1975; Wilson and Evans, 1976). The therapeutic process can then proceed with candor as the clients are free to consider and discuss the therapist's opinion; often a strong bias left unsaid may result in a more subtle or insidious influence process which would be counterproductive.

As in many therapeutic endeavors, empathy is probably facilitative of change in marital therapy. Gurman and Kniskern (in press) found that degree of therapist empathy was related to outcome in family therapy. Since family and marital therapy have clear commonalities, empathy is likely to have considerable impact in marital therapy as well. In fact, the present authors assert that where communication skills are a problem, as is the case with the majority of distressed couples, empathy becomes a particularly important factor in therapy. Although certain behavior therapy procedures apparently can be successfully implemented without a therapist or with therapists who presumably demonstrate only a moderate amount of empathy (for example, enuresis treatment, Lovibond, 1974; self-administered self-desensitization, Paul, 1966; programmed instruction counseling, Gilbert and Ewing, 1971), such is not likely to be the case with marital therapy. While a special technology is needed for treating marital problems (Koch and Koch, 1976), such "nonspecific" factors as empathy and interpersonal skill will continue to be an essential aspect of the therapeutic intervention.

In addition to warmth and empathy as trust facilitators, self-disclosure by the therapist regarding his or her perceptions of the client is associated with self-disclosure by the client (Davis and Skinner, 1974). Self-disclosure of feelings regarding a client is not synonymous with self-disclosure regarding one's personal problems, and the latter is generally advised against. On occasion, it may be helpful to disclose one's problems to a couple when those problems have been successfully overcome or, more importantly, when certain marital practices are found especially rewarding to a therapist (for example, ways of conveying caring, ways of structuring one's day so that regular communication is guaranteed). Nonetheless, as Wilson and Evans (1976) have noted, therapists should avoid the temptation of presenting themselves as idealized individuals to be emulated in all situations. Presumably, an effective therapist model is one who models that he or she is generally coping well, but clearly coping, not simply breezing through life.

Lastly, the language a therapist uses should be as nonmechanistic as possible. It has been demonstrated that behavior modification and behavior therapy are terms that have less endearing qualities to educators

(Woolfolk, Woolfolk and Wilson, 1977) than terms like humanistic education. Nonetheless, when behavior therapists have repeated contacts with clients and teachers, they have been evaluated almost uniformly as understanding, warm, sincere, and interested (O'Leary, Turkewitz, and Taffel, 1973). Azrin, Naster, and Jones (1973) avoided all technical jargon in their behavioral marital therapy program, and were apparently successful in increasing the marital satisfaction of their clients. Although there were no evaluations of the therapists, and the possible contribution of the avoidance of technical language is unknown, their strategy regarding language usage seems highly commendable. Terms like reinforcement, extinction, training, and operants should be reserved for the experimental psychology laboratory, not for treating individuals with marital problems.

In summary, during the courtship stage, while conducting the initial assessment of the marital problems, the therapist begins to develop a warm, trusting relationship with the clients. Through the building of this relationship and the expectation of benefit, the therapist is preparing the clients to make an active commitment to the treatment program or to "become engaged" in the therapeutic process.

Engagement Stage

As previously mentioned, the engagement stage involves the solidification of a therapeutic relationship. More specifically, the therapist conveys a commitment to aid the couple in reaching their goals and outlines his or her expectations of the clients: that they will complete the 10-week treatment program and will invest a considerable degree of time and effort in working out their conflicts, both in sessions and during the week at home. It is not expected that the clients can honestly make this commitment prior to the courtship stage or before they have a good understanding of the treatment approach and the rationales underlying the interventions. It is explained to the couple that they will be working with the therapist primarily to improve their communication and understanding of one another, and to increase their satisfaction in the marriage through mutual behavior changes. The therapist may also discuss working on alleviating sexual dysfunctions or such specific areas as child management problems, if necessary.

With regard to communication enhancement, the rationale given is that marital distress is often caused by faulty communication patterns. The therapist may also note that even if the couple's problem were not the result of communication difficulties, problems in other areas generally produce hostile or defensive communication patterns which then serve to maintain or increase distress. At this point the therapist can give feedback to the couple on both positive and negative aspects of their interactions, explaining how these particular behaviors can affect their feelings about each other and their ability to resolve their conflicts. If this feedback is accurate and the clients perceive it as relevant to their problems, they are much more likely to accept the rationale and make a therapeutic commitment.

The process of working on negotiated agreements to effect changes that each spouse would like to see in the other is briefly described during the engagement stage. The rationale presented is that couples are often unhappy because of a failure of both spouses to be responsive to each other's needs—that is, the spouses may not feel rewarded for their efforts (feel "taken for granted") and may feel that their partner does not care for them. It is generally not difficult for each spouse to agree that he or she would like certain changes in his or her partner. However, there are clients who resist the notion that compromise is necessary to resolve the conflicts. Either these clients feel that they should not have to change ("It's all his/her fault") or they feel that they have made all the efforts to work on the relationship in the past and now it is their partner's turn to change. Some discussion may be necessary at this point regarding the tactics the couple has used to resolve conflicts in the past. That is, the couple may be able to see that their recent attempts to change each other have only resulted in hostility or withdrawal, and that they need to try a totally different approach to break the destructive pattern of demands and noncompliance that they have developed.

Following the discussion of the treatment model, when the clients have at least tentatively accepted the relevance of the goals of communication enhancement and changing desired behaviors, the first "homework assignment" is given. The procedure described here is adopted from Azrin et al.'s (1973) "Reciprocity Awareness Procedure." Each spouse is asked to make a list of the current behaviors in his or her partner that he or she finds satisfying or pleasing. This list is to be completed at home, but to avoid the possibility that the clients will return to the next session claiming they could not think of anything, the therapist uses information obtained from the assessment to help the spouses start their lists during the session. The behaviors that can be listed cover the entire range of marital interactions, including sex or affection, financial support, child care, meal preparation, or social activities. Thus, it is unlikely that there are no current satisfactions. In the cases where a couple is so severely distressed that they are truly living as independent units without providing any support to one another, they are asked to list those things that attracted them to each other initially or the satisfying interactions they remember from the past. However, it is much more common to see spouses who can generate at least three behaviors in their partner that they currently find pleasing.

The spouses read their "satisfaction lists" to each other during the next session. The therapist insures that the lists are understood and points out what the spouses may be learning about their partner's reactions to them and the importance of giving positive feedback to one another.

Most clients respond quite favorably to this intervention. They report that it gives them a good feeling to pay attention to the positive aspects of their relationship; they also enjoy receiving positive feedback from their partner. This intervention falls in the engagement stage of the treatment program since the positive feelings produced facilitate increasing the couple's involvement in the therapy. While the couple may be prepared to make a tentative commitment to the therapy after the discussion of the treatment model and rationale, this positive experience tends to strengthen that commitment. An additional facet of this procedure is that the couple is asked to describe the satisfying behaviors in as specific terms as possible, and the therapist helps them do this during the session. As the treatment program continues, the clients will also have to be very clear and specific in their requests for changes. Thus the construction of their "satisfaction lists" prepares them for writing behavior change agreements and in that way sets the stage for the problem-solving process.

At the conclusion of the engagement stage, the spouses can make an active commitment to the therapeutic program since they understand the rationale, they have at least tentatively accepted the relevance of the treatment approach to the alleviation of their distress, and they have some direct experience with the possible beneficial effects of involvement in the therapy. The treatment program then proceeds to the most intricate and difficult stage, the marriage stage.

The Marriage Stage

The marriage stage of the present treatment program has two primary emphases: (1) improved communication, and (2) written marital agreements that are used to aid the couple to effect desired changes in one another. Communication enhancement involves helping the couple solve problems more effectively and promoting a more open, clear, and warm pattern of interactions. Written commitments to change in desired ways are used to prompt spouses to satisfy more of each other's needs. The extent to which communication enhancement or written behavioral agreement is the focus of therapy depends upon the problems or deficits of each couple. Generally, however, both of these strategies are employed throughout this stage of the program. The marriage stage is analogous to the couple's relationship to the extent that the spouses learn to modify the nature and structure of the relationship which they have developed.

Communication enhancement

Enhancing communication primarily involves four major therapeutic goals: (1) teaching problem-solving skills, (2) helping the couple reduce and clarify misunderstandings that arise in general conversation (outside the context of problem-solving discussions), (3) increasing positive verbal interactions, and (4) increasing the appropriate expression of feelings. There are a variety of techniques the therapists use, including modeling, role-playing and feedback. In addition, the spouses are encouraged to follow explicit rules or guidelines to promote good communication. The specific strategies the therapists adopt to work toward the four goals cited will be discussed in detail.

PROBLEM-SOLVING SKILLS

The aspect of communication patterns that has received the most attention from behavioral marital therapists is the teaching of appropriate problem-solving skills.* The present authors agree heartily with the statement made by Liberman et al. (1976a) that "contingency contracting is worth just about the paper it's printed on without the family members having adequate interpersonal communication skills" (p. 32). It is clear that couples will not be able to negotiate on their own if the spouses cannot communicate clearly regarding their desires. In addition, there are many non-productive communication patterns that interfere tremendously with efficient problem solving, such as overgeneralizations, content shifts, and references to past transgressions. Throughout the discussions that take place during therapy, which may focus on particular crises that arise or on the major problematic issues for that particular

* We are here using the term *problem-solving* to describe a general process, not the specific procedure of D'Zurilla and Goldfried (1971) and Robni et al. (1977) discussed earlier.

couple (such as sex, in-laws, commitment), the therapist attempts to shape appropriate problem-solving skills.

One method of shaping such skills is to clearly state rules for problem-solving discussions and to provide feedback on the application of these rules. Some examples of these rules are: be specific; phrase requests in terms of positive changes, as opposed to attacks on negative behavior; respond directly to a complaint or criticism, rather than responding with a cross-complaint of your own; keep the topic of conversation confined to the present or future; wait for your spouse to complete a thought before giving your reactions or comments; confine your comments to observable behavior, rather than making remarks about motives or character analyses. As can be seen, these rules are phrased in the positive, in terms of what should be done, rather than in terms of what not to do. The rationale for this positive phrasing is the same as for wording the spouses' behavioral agreements in the positive: It is easier to reinforce the occurrence of a behavior than its non-occurrence. The therapist reminds the couple of these rules through both positive and negative feedback. The negative feedback typically takes the form of specifically pointing out a nonproductive behavior and explaining the negative consequences that ensued. For example: "When you told Bill that last year he didn't visit his mother enough, the two of you started arguing about what 'enough' was and exactly how many visits there were instead of continuing on with your future-oriented discussion of how to plan visits this year. You were both sidetracked from solving the problem at hand."

A second technique for teaching productive problem-solving behaviors is behavior rehearsal, or role-playing. The couples practice the new communication skills during the session and the therapist provides feedback. A modified form of behavior rehearsal is "re-playing." The couples present a frustrating discussion or hostile argument they had during the week and are asked to replay the sequence. The therapist interrupts the interaction to help the spouses pinpoint the destructive behaviors that contributed to the negative chain, and the couple is asked to generate alternative responses that would be more productive. This re-playing generally results in a more satisfying interaction so that the reinforcing value of the new communication skills is directly demonstrated.

One additional problem-solving tactic that behavioral marital therapists teach couples is the use of stimulus control strategies, The couple is instructed to bring their problem-solving attempts under the control of particular times and settings, as, for example, "Administrative Time"

(Weiss et al., 1973). More specifically, regular times are scheduled during the week, such as after dinner with coffee, when the spouses can engage in problem-solving discussions.

CLEAR COMMUNICATION

A very common presenting complaint among distressed couples is "lack of understanding." Often, underlying this complaint is the statement, "If he/she really understood me, then he/she would do what I want or need." However, "lack of understanding" is certainly not always tied to a lack of desired behaviors. There are some data indicating that distressed spouses hold more discrepant meanings for concepts significant to marriage (Katz, 1965) and have more difficulty interpreting each other's statements (Gottman et al., in press; Kahn, 1970) than do happily married spouses. That is, distressed spouses actually do have a difficult time understanding each other.

The confusion that results from discrepancies between the message sent and the message received often leads to unnecessary arguments and hostility. As an example, Jane and Larry, a couple in therapy, were calmly and happily discussing their weekend plans. They were having a small party for friends, and although there was much work to be done in preparation, both of them felt good about their plans because they felt that their marital problems had for several years prevented them from having such parties. In the course of the discussion, Jane mentioned in passing that Larry had agreed to help her clean the floor. Larry looked surprised and responded that he had not agreed, that his wife could get her daughters to help her, and that he had enough of his own work to do. Jane felt hurt, saying that Larry had, in fact, agreed to help her and that she didn't like his going back on his word. At this point, the therapist interceded, asking them *which* floor they were discussing. In actuality, Jane was talking about the den floor, but Larry thought that Jane was talking about the kitchen floor. With a clarification of messages, the couple discovered that they were beginning to argue about a nonexistent disagreement.

While the aforementioned example may seem trivial, it is also clear that if the couple had been discussing this at home, the argument might have escalated and involved insults and hurt feelings before the spouses realized the mistake each was making. The misunderstanding would have resulted in yet another aversive experience for both of them. Couples have to learn to ask for clarifications and specific elaborations of each other's messages. These requests serve to interrupt the behavioral chain of escalating arguments. Each spouse must attend to his or her negative reactions, and investigate whether these reactions are warranted. If their partner says something that surprises or puzzles them, instead of supplying their own meaning and assuming the worst, they are urged to stop the ongoing interaction and clarify the situation. The spouses' emotional reactions can serve as a cue, or discriminative stimulus, to ask questions. For example, Larry felt surprised that Jane was requesting that he clean the kitchen floor, since he thought they had made a different agreement. He assumed the worst, that she was being unreasonable and demanding, and proceeded to defend himself. It was pointed out to Larry that a constructive alternative would be for him to use that surprised feeling as a cue that he may have misunderstood, and to ask Jane, "Do you want me to clean the kitchen floor?" By the same token, Jane's assumptions that Larry was "weaseling out" should have been held in abeyance, and she was instructed to use her hurt feelings as a cue to seek clarification.

Training in empathic skills is also used to increase clear communication (Ely et al., 1973; Pierce, 1973). (Weiss' [Chapter IV] notion of support/understanding is similar to the concept of empathy). The spouses are taught to reflect what they hear their partner saying. Initially, this skill is taught in the context of very structured discussions of non-problematic issues. One spouse is designated as the speaker and limits his/her speech to a couple of sentences. The therapist then summarizes what has been said, to provide a model of empathic listening. After the therapist models, the spouses speak to each other, alternating speaker and listener roles, with the listener reflecting both the content and feelings in the message. The speaker is always given the opportunity to comment on the accuracy of the reflection and make corrections when needed. With some couples it may be necessary to start with the speaker saying only one sentence at a time. This is particularly important when the listener leaps to conclusions that are interpretations rather than reflections of what was stated. Another precaution is that some couples need to become more comfortable in establishing and maintaining eye contact, prior to empathy training. However, all couples should first attempt the exercise with a nonthreatening topic. Empathic listening is such a radical departure from the couples' typical conversational style that it is too difficult for them to learn this skill if emotional reactions are provoked by the content under discussion.

Once the spouses have demonstrated that they can provide accurate summaries of short verbal statements, more active empathic listening is introduced. The therapist models how one can interject supportive, reflective comments, and the spouses then interact in this way, still remaining in the speaker and listener roles. The therapist gives feedback to the active listeners throughout the exercise, immediately following the short interactions. Following the first introduction to empathy training, the couple is given a homework assignment to practice this skill in half-hour structured discussion three times during the week. The time in speaker/listener roles is kept to about five minutes, so that the spouses alternate these roles several times in the course of each discussion. They are told to practice with "safe topics" at times when they are not angry with each other. As empathy training continues, the time in speaker and listener roles can be extended, and more emotionally charged issues are introduced as topics for discussion. The homework assignments parallel what has been accomplished in the sessions; the talks become more involved. Once the spouses have mastered the skill in structured discussions, they are prompted to use these reflecting skills at other times, such as when a spouse is hurt or angry.

Therapists should be cautioned that some clients may use empathic reflections to avoid taking responsibility for their behavior or dealing directly with a complaint of their spouse. For example:

> *He*: You said you'd call the insurance agent today.
> *She*: You really think it's important that I call?
> *He*: Yeh, what happened? How come you didn't?
> *She*: You're starting to get angry thinking about how I didn't call.
> *He*: Well, did you not want to call or did you forget?
> *She*: You're not sure what happened.
> *He*: That's right, damn it; why don't you answer me?
> *She*: Now you're really angry.

In this instance, it is apparent that the husband was communicating clearly and that the wife was accurately reflecting his feelings. However, the empathic responses were used to avoid giving information and dealing directly with the issue at hand. It is important for the therapist to give feedback regarding the appropriate and inappropriate use of empathy. Empathic responses are particularly appreciated by a spouse who is venting feelings or requesting support. In addition, empathy training helps to promote cooperative efforts between the spouses and often increases feelings of closeness and caring.

One important aspect of the treatment program that is related to clear communication, but does not involve working directly with verbal interactions, is having the spouses examine and re-evaluate their interpretations of each other's behavior. All behavior communicates something within the context of the dyad: Not doing chores may be interpreted as a lack of caring; keeping long hours at work can be seen as avoiding spending time with one's partner. Distressed spouses, in particular, often interpret their partner's behavior as a negative relationship message, even though the partner had no such intent. For example, a wife's renewed interest in going back to school or work is often perceived as threatening to the relationship. This step toward more independence may be interpreted as boredom with the husband, preparation for divorce, or a desire to become involved in an extramarital relationship. The therapist must help the spouses reinterpret each other's behaviors in a more positive and/or realistic way.

POSITIVE VERBAL INTERACTIONS

To insure the continuation of new behavior patterns, it is essential that spouses verbally reinforce one another for the desired changes. In addition, the present authors emphasize the importance of communicating positive feelings spouses have that may not be directly related to target changes, such as compliments on appearance, cooking, or work in the house and yard. It is clear that distressed couples have fewer positive interchanges than nondistressed couples (Bienvenu, 1970; Birchler, Weiss and Vincent, 1975). However, this dearth of positive comments is not due only to a lack of positive thoughts or feelings. Many spouses report that they have positive reactions but choose not to share them. They explain their reluctance in a variety of ways: "I don't want him to get a swelled head," "I felt good about that but I was still angry about what she did yesterday," "When was the last time he said something nice to me?" Particularly because of comments like the last one, the therapist can choose to select "saying positive comments" as a mutual behavior change and ask the spouses to carry out a written agreement such as: "I will make one positive comment to my spouse each day."

Since the reason for working on positive comments is to increase reinforcers exchanged, it is important to insure that the positive remark is received as such. This is noted particularly because Kahn (1970) found that distressed husbands were more likely to attribute negative connota-tions to their wives' attempts to communicate happiness than were non-distressed husbands. In this study, the spouses were asked to read a neutral statement, such as "We're having chicken again tonight," and to communicate that they were feeling either happy, angry, or neutral about this. Distressed couples could not discriminate what their partners were communicating as well as nondistressed couples did. Thus, the therapist should (a) ask how the positive remarks are heard, and (b) recommend that the remarks be explicit and unambiguous, to lessen the probability that they will be heard as either neutral or negative.

APPROPRIATE EXPRESSION OF FEELINGS

Very often couples in therapy are all too comfortable expressing negative feelings and asserting themselves. However, there are also many spouses who will not share their feelings. Distressed spouses report more fear of expressing their feelings than do nondistressed mates (Bienvenu, 1970), and there are some data indicating that there is decreased self-disclosure in distressed marriages, although the empirical support for this difference is not very strong (Cozby, 1973). Clinically it seems as though husbands, more frequently than wives, are reluctant to express their negative feelings. This observation is consistent with the finding that husbands in distressed marriages are reluctant to self-disclose about issues that are anxiety-laden (Katz, Goldston, Cohen, and Stucker, 1963). These husbands may say: "I would be happy if she were," "Nothing is important enough to get upset about," "Why can't she be as rational and unemotional as I am?" In some cases the client is stating how he honestly feels. However, in others, the client is not expressing negative feelings for fear that he will be punished by his wife for this, or because he has learned that it is not "manly" to express feelings.

The present authors think it is important to increase feeling expression in the above cases for several reasons:

(1) Assuming that there are behaviors in his wife to which the husband does react negatively, these reactions must be expressed so that mutual behavior change agreements can be made. Therapy cannot proceed successfully with unilateral changes.

(2) In these couples the expression of feelings is often a target change the wife desires. The wife reports feeling distant from her husband; his sharing his feelings (positive and negative) would be a powerful reinforcer for her behavior change attempts.

(3) These findings are often expressed non-verbally or indirectly (through sulking, avoiding the spouse) so that the partner is getting a negative message but cannot easily respond to it. For example, Stan maintained he was happy in his marriage and there was nothing his wife could change. When Linda then asked why he was often angry and yelled at her frequently, he responded that he was not angry, but just

spoke in a loud voice. Stan denied any significant variations in the volume of his voice and said Linda was imagining it. This client needed feedback during the therapy session about when he was raising his voice. The couple was then able to discuss what prompted the increase in loudness, and Stan began speaking about what was frustrating to him about his wife's behavior.

In addition to giving feedback on nonverbal behavior or subtle cues that indicate an emotional reaction, the therapist can help the clients use several other strategies to increase "feeling talk" in one another. At times the reluctant spouse can be encouraged to talk about feelings he or she has that are not related to the marital relationship, as this is apparently less threatening. Using this shaping process makes it easier to prompt expressions of relationship-related feelings. Initially, the therapist should use this procedure and model how to encourage the spouse who is reluctant to express feelings; the couple can then learn to use this strategy at home.

Another way the therapist can increase the likelihood that a spouse will admit to and discuss feelings is to start with very low level empathic reflections of statements made by a "nonfeeling" spouse. That is, if the client's nonverbal behavior indicates he or she is very angry, the therapist might reflect that the client seems "annoyed" rather than saying, "You appear very angry about that." Initially, the reticent client is more likely to agree with a reflection that minimizes the emotional component of his or her remark. Gradually, the therapist can increase the level of emotion reflected. Maintenance of increased feeling talk is sometimes difficult since the spouse requesting an increase in expressiveness may readily support a positive feeling statement but may not support an expression of negative feelings. For this reason it is important to insure an empathic response to attempts at feeling expression.

The strategies to increase communication of feelings can be used for both positive and negative feelings. However, the authors certainly do not recommend the expression of any and all feelings. Each partner has the right to private feelings, and there are instances in which the expression of certain feelings could be destructive (as, for example, the relating of extramarital sexual fantasies). As noted previously, promoting the expression of negative feelings or reactions in some couples may be necessary to facilitate problem solving and to allow conflicts to be addressed directly. However, there are certain ground rules established regarding negative comments. Expressing negative feelings regarding something a spouse cannot change (such as height, family members) is not likely to be productive and is not encouraged. Additionally, a clear distinction is made between hostile, hurtful comments and the expression of a negative feeling. Saying "I hate you" is counterproductive; the statements to be encouraged are in the form of "I am very angry because you said or did X." One ground rule is that *feelings* are to be expressed, not insults. "You're a slob" is to be replaced with "I get angry when you leave your clothes around." Spouses may attempt to express feelings in a hurtful way by saying things like "I feel you're a slob." Clearly this "subversion" must be discouraged; negative labels do not constitute a helpful or honest expression of feelings. Thus, while the communication of negative emotions may be encouraged, the spouses must be clear on the distinction between a punishing remark and a statement made in the interest of openness and problem solving.

In summary, the communication training aspect of this behavioral marital therapy program involves: teaching behaviors conducive to constructing successful behavior change agreements, increasing clarity in general communication patterns, increasing the expression of positive feelings, discrimination training between hostile remarks and the productive expression of negative feelings, and, when necessary, promoting the expression of negative feelings. The techniques used to help achieve these goals include modeling, behavior rehearsal, instruction, feedback, shaping, and structured exercises. For additional examples of structured exercises used to enhance communication, the reader is referred to *The Mirages of Marriage* (Lederer and Jackson, 1968) and *A Couple's Guide to Communication* (Gottman, Notarius, Gonso, and Markman, 1976).

Marriage agreements

Behavior change agreements or contracts have been a cornerstone of behavioral marital therapy (Lederer and Jackson, 1968). Although the present authors disagree, Weiss (1975) and others have stated that all work in communication is designed to facilitate negotiation and contracting.[*] A contract in behavioral marital therapy generally has the following elements:

(1) A written agreement by each spouse to engage in certain specified behaviors desired by the other spouse.

---

[*] In fact, Weiss (Chapter IV) has recently changed his opinion regarding the necessity of marriage agreements or behavior contracts. In this chapter he stated that relatively few problems require negotiation and contracting and that "These procedures are best reserved for couples whose skill levels are very low and whose natural reinforcing effectiveness is simply too low to be trusted for adequate behavior change."

(2) A written documentation of the positive and/or negative consequences which should occur if the specified behaviors are or are not displayed. The contracts are employed to (a) help spouses identify desired and undesired behaviors, (b) "establish the public market value of targeted annoying behaviors which occur at either high or low rates," and (c) provide a system of rewards and penalties for compliance or noncompliance with the contract (Weiss, Birchler, and Vincent, 1974, p. 323).

At the Stony Brook marital therapy clinic, the method used to increase behaviors that are desired between the spouses has been to develop informal marital agreements. There are several components in the process of constructing these agreements:

(1) The spouses specify the behaviors they desire to see increased in one another.

(2) The spouses reach an agreement regarding the behavior changes that will take place, and a list of these behaviors is made and signed by each spouse.

(3) The intrinsic positive consequences to the spouses of following the agreement are discussed. These components will now be discussed in some detail.

SPECIFICATION OF DESIRED BEHAVIORS

In his recent book, *Marriage Contracts and Couple Therapy,* Sager (1976) described the expectations that each spouse has as he or she enters a marriage and importantly noted that these expectations rapidly become solidified. These solidified expectations, in turn, become viewed as contracts which, if violated, cause serious marital discord. Although Sager discussed the contracts from a psychoanalytic framework and stressed unconscious defenses, his general notion of a marriage contract is consistent with the behavioral approach.

In attempts to have spouses specify desired behavior changes, a brief history of the desired behaviors (such as affection or communication) is obtained, and changes in expectations during the marriage, if any, regarding these behaviors are discussed. One valuable aspect of having the spouses specify their desires is that their expectations regarding marriage and their partner can be identified and evaluated. Often a distressed spouse will have unrealistic expectations, such as: My spouse will fulfill all of my personal needs; my spouse will agree with my opinions on all major issues; my spouse will "read my mind" and know what I want without my having to ask. These expectations are clearly counterproductive since they cannot be met. It is thus necessary for the therapist to help the spouses modify some of their expectations. At times it can also be helpful to give normative information regarding such areas of marriage as the frequency of sexual intercourse, amount of time individuals generally spend talking per day, and typical behavior problems of children, to help spouses re-evaluate their expectations.

The clients' initial statements regarding changes they want in their marriage are generally quite global, such as more caring, better communication. It is not a simple task to change these statements into specific descriptions of desired behaviors. At times, the spouses may resist, stating that their partner knows what they mean by "caring" or that they cannot describe what they mean. The therapist explains the necessity of clear communication and assists the spouses in finding behavioral referents for the global complaints. That is, the therapist might ask, "What is it that your husband (wife) can do that would demonstrate his (her) caring for you?" Once the desires are specified, the therapist assists the couples in selecting targets for change.

CONSTRUCTION OF MARITAL AGREEMENTS

Initially, spouses are encouraged to request behaviors of each other which they feel realistically could occur the following week, such as spend time watching T.V. with me, have coffee and dessert with me each night, talk for five minutes. If communication skills are extremely poor and there have been highly aversive interchanges for the past few years, encouraging five minutes of communication may even be too high an expectation. The therapist must make an assessment regarding the likelihood that the behavior change requests will be fulfilled and then give the couple feedback if he or she feels the requests are unreasonable for the early stages of therapy. The couple is told that, as the treatment program progresses, more difficult behavior changes are incorporated into the agreements. This shaping procedure is used to increase the probability of a success experience early in therapy. It is explained to the couple that it is best to begin with "small" changes and to work on increasingly complex problems only as they become more skilled in the problem-solving process. One tack taken to facilitate the implementation of the first marital agreement is to have the spouses choose a request from their partner's list that they feel they can fulfill. This procedure works well as long as both spouses feel that the agreement is fair. It should be noted that the perceived equity of the agreements is always important and the therapist should be attuned to the spouses' feelings about this.

The therapist should also be cognizant of the way in which his or her values may affect the selection of targets for change. Additionally, there may be times when a therapist may recommend against certain agreements. For example, while a husband may list staying home more as a behavior he wants from his wife, promoting such an agreement may serve to increase the wife's depressed feelings, minimize her current rewards, and miss the critical issue of the husband's jealousy. It may also lead the wife to feel that the therapist is in an unfair alliance with her husband (particularly if the therapist is male).

With regard to the couple's sexual relationship, it is the authors' opinion that changes in sexual behavior per se should not be incorporated into standard written marital agreements. Sexual relations which are prompted by a contractual agreement in the absence of positive affect are ill-advised since it is likely that such sexual interchanges will be resented. Contracts could also result in establishing a pattern where sex occurs solely because of feelings of obligation. Rather, the therapist can help the spouses identify the factors that would enhance both their enjoyment of and desire for sex. For example, if the husband is requesting that his wife engage in sex more frequently, the therapist would help the wife identify the behavior changes in her husband that would prompt her to *want* to engage in more frequent sex (such as more affection), and would suggest that the husband engage in these behaviors. In brief, changes in sexual behavior are accomplished through identifying the factors inhibiting satisfying sex and helping the spouses overcome these problems. An agreement written to modify sexual behaviors that does not deal with these inhibiting factors is likely to fail; the reluctant spouse will not change.

A written list of the behaviors each spouse agrees to engage in is prepared at the end of the session, and each spouse is asked to sign the list. If possible, the use of prepared marital agreements with carbons for the therapist is preferred. As noted previously, the advantages of the written agreement are that "memory failures" are minimized, the process of clarification is facilitated, and increased commitment is fostered when a spouse is asked to sign an agreement.

The types of behaviors specified in the marital agreements will clearly depend upon the particular couple's needs. The following example is given to demonstrate the form of the agreements.

MARITAL AGREEMENT

Date ....

This week I agree to:

(1) Spend one evening or afternoon engaging in an activity with the whole family (e.g., playing cards, hiking, going on a picnic, bicycle riding, playing board games).

(2) Call my wife on the phone to tell her when I will be coming home if I will be more than 15 minutes late from work.

Signature of Husband ....

This week I agree to:

(1) Greet my husband when he comes home from work and show interest (i.e., ask questions) regarding his day.

(2) Go to a sporting event one night this weekend.

Signature of Wife ....

Signature of Therapist ....

DISCUSSION OF THE POSITIVE CONSEQUENCES
OF AGREEMENT FULFILLMENT

In the absence of data indicating the necessity of explicit rewards or punishers in marital contracts, the use of such has been avoided for several reasons. The long-term efficacy of using strong reinforcers and punishers for behaviors specified in the contract has not been established. The palatability of such contracts with many clients is questionable; the very term contract implies a business-like or legal approach to the marital relationship, which is to be avoided. Finally, it is doubtful whether couples would apply strong aversive consequences if such were specified in a marital agreement.*

Rather than contracts with formal consequences, the Stony Brook program emphasizes a discussion of the natural positive consequences that would result from the desired changes. For example, increased cooperation and an increase in positive feelings would be likely beneficial changes in the relationship. In addition, the spouses may *choose* to do nice things for one another as a result of a desired change, but these "favors" are not written into the marital agreement.

One general method of increasing the likelihood that agreements will

---

* Personal communication with S. Wolf confirms this suspicion, August 10, 1977.

be fulfilled is to write them so that the spouses are actually helping each other change. This approach was noted in regard to sexual behaviors but can also be used in other areas. A good example of this procedure, cited by Jacobson (submitted for publication), involved a wife's request that her husband spend more time with their daughter. The husband felt uncomfortable about this as he did not feel he knew how to entertain the child. A marital agreement regarding this problem could entail having the wife plan activities for the husband and daughter so that he would feel more comfortable and be more likely to carry out his part of the agreement of increased time with the child.

The spouses are *strongly* urged to verbally reinforce one another for following the agreements. The clients are given several reasons for the importance of verbal reinforcement: (1) if you don't mention the change that you see, your partner will think that you didn't notice and could decide that the change is not worth the effort; (2) everyone needs support for making a change, and your partner will not continue to follow through on agreements if you do not provide this support; (3) telling your spouse when something pleases you is actually a very clear and productive way of communicating your desires. Your spouse will be better able to make you happy in the future if you give direct and immediate feedback now; and (4) your spouse will probably not continue to compliment you if you do not also make positive comments. When the spouses report complying with the marital agreement, the therapist often asks, "Did you feel that your husband/wife appreciated what you did?" This frequent question serves as a reminder to give positive feedback in the future and often prompts the spouses to direct a compliment to their partner during the session. Of course, the therapist models verbal reinforcement throughout the treatment program.

In the present treatment program, the process of constructing marital agreements initiates behavior change through clear communication of specific requests, written commitments, and therapist suggestion. The agreements are maintained via positive changes in the relationship and verbal reinforcement between the spouses and from the therapist.

Couples have completed approximately 63 percent of the weekly assignments in the Stony Brook program. There has been no significant discrepancy between assignment completion by men and women. Resistance or noncompliance should signal the therapist to:

(1) Assess whether the spouses actually have the requisite skills required to engage in the requested behaviors.

(2) Ask whether the spouse stopped displaying the desired behavior after one instance in which an expected reward did not occur.

(3) See if the task the spouse agreed to fulfill was deemed unfair or, in fact, detrimental to the individual's welfare.

(4) Ascertain if the person with lesser communication skills feels he or she was criticized and thus punished—whether directly or indirectly—for attempts to communicate.

(5) Assess whether one spouse feels wronged (as in the case of discovering an adulterous relationship) and is thus waiting for the spouse who has "transgressed" to atone for past wrong deeds.

(6) Obtain an estimate of the noncompliant person's feelings toward the other. It may be the case that one spouse has so little feeling or, in fact, such strong negative feelings toward the other that they do not wish to comply with a marital agreement which has the implicit goal of more affection and ultimately sex. In a related vein, couples sometimes are reluctant to comply because they are afraid they will have to face an unresolved sexual problem such as premature ejaculation or orgasmic dysfunction.

One additional problem a couple may present is depicted in a form of skepticism regarding the "real" motivation for therapeutic change. For example, a wife may be skeptical of any change her husband makes and state that, "He only does this because he has an agreement to fulfill—not because he cares about me." The therapist generally responds that it is true that the husband is engaging in certain behaviors partly because of the therapeutic plan and the particular marital agreement. However, if he finds that such behaviors have positive consequences for him, he will be likely to continue to engage in them in the future. It is also predicted that as spouses experience positive changes in their relationship, their feelings will be likely to change; they will care more for one another and then be motivated to maintain behavior changes on the basis of these feelings. It is important for the therapist to be aware of the possible client concerns regarding marital agreements and the more common reasons for noncompliance. However, most couples respond very well to this phase of the treatment program, and difficulties in completing agreements can be minimized though careful assessment and the gradual introduction of more difficult conflict areas into the problem-solving process.

The two major aspects of the authors' treatment program, communication enhancement and marital agreements, have been described in detail. The program has been presented as it applies generally to couples experiencing marital distress. Clearly an assessment of each couple's problems will dictate the exact nature of the intervention. That is, the time spent on either communication or marital agreements will be determined by such factors as the severity and nature of the interactional difficulties and the degree of cooperation between the spouses. If a therapist feels uncomfortable about writing marital agreements or anticipates that clients will react negatively to such written assignments, it seems highly appropriate to execute the marital agreements by simple verbal exchange. Further, there are some motivated couples where simple direct communication about past or present desired behaviors is sufficient to bring about dramatic improvement in the relationship, and written agreements are superfluous.

The present authors employ such procedures as specific sex therapy techniques, assertive training, or training in child management if such are deemed necessary. Finally, as illustrated in the case study noted in the introduction to this chapter, individuals often need to be encouraged to seek reinforcing activities outside the context of the marriage. In many cases one spouse, particularly the wife, if she is a housewife, is too dependent upon the marital relationship for need satisfaction. Encouraging more activity outside the home (social activities with friends, adult education programs, pursuing interests or hobbies) helps decrease this dependency and has a positive effect on the relationship.

Disengagement

The disengagement is technically not a distinct or separate stage but a gradual process of shifting control of the therapy from the therapist to the clients. The point at which disengagement begins will necessarily depend upon the couple's progress in the marriage stage. One way in which disengagement is accomplished is by placing increasing responsibility on the couple for the construction of marital agreements. For example, after the couple has been able to construct several marital agreements while working with the therapist, they are asked to arrive at, but not carry out, a new marital agreement at home, between sessions. This agreement is discussed in the following session to insure that both spouses feel it is fair and are amenable to executing it. If this agreement is then successful, the couple is given the homework assignment to negotiate *and* carry out another new agreement. This fading procedure clearly provides the therapist and the clients with an assessment of whether or not the spouses have the cooperative set and interactional skills necessary to resolve conflicts following termination. If the first independent attempt is not successful, the therapist can help the clients identify what interfered (for example, unrealistic demands, lack of clarity in communication) and work on reducing the hindrance. If the attempt is successful, it provides the clients with more confidence regarding the course of their relationship following termination. This is particularly important since, as noted previously, spouses may initially state that their partner is doing certain things only because the therapist suggested it, and they need to see that constructive change is possible even when the therapist is not directly involved in the problem-solving process.

Another way in which the intervention can be modified over the course of therapy to increase maintenance of gains is to change from written to verbal agreements. Knox (1973) conducted a questionnaire follow-up of 10 couples he had seen and reported that none of them continued to use written agreements following termination, although the beneficial treatment effects appeared to be maintained. The implications seem to be that either further negotiations were unnecessary or the couples were working out effective verbal compromises and problem resolutions. Since it is almost inevitable that couples will be faced with additional problems and areas for compromise following termination, the finding that they do not use written agreements on their own suggests that the therapist should shift to verbal agreements once the couple is successful with their independent written agreements. Successful fading of the control of a written agreement should also serve to increase the spouses' confidence and trust in each other.

Additionally, as therapy progresses, the therapist can give the couple an increasing degree of responsibility for correcting and improving their communication. Whereas initially the therapist may identify specific communication rules that would be helpful to the couple and suggest alternative modes of responding, he or she can prompt the clients to provide more input to this process. For example, instead of interrupting a problematic interchange and modeling or suggesting ways in which the clients could have responded differently, the therapist can have the clients suggest the alternatives. This procedure is best accomplished by having each spouse generate their own alternatives, by answering the question, "How could I have handled this differently?" It is advisable, however, to avoid a situation where the spouses are telling each other what to do. Each one should take equal responsibility for producing the interaction, and thus each should consider ways in which they can change. The clients should also become adept at recognizing when an interaction is going poorly before it is out of control, so that they can analyze and interrupt the negative chain. This self-analysis can be prompted by having spouses jointly discuss both verbal and nonverbal cues that are precipitants of negative affect and by encouraging spouses to discuss these negative feelings when they are at a minimal level. To facilitate this analysis, the therapist should indicate the cues (in addition to obvious hostile verbal remarks) he or she is responding to when interrupting the couple's discussions during therapy; facial expressions, shifts in body posture, reduced eye contact. When the couples can identify the "danger signals" and stop the ongoing interaction, they can change the course of the discussion by making an effort to use empathic listening or clarify the messages.

Through the treatment program it is important for the therapist to be cognizant of the ways in which disengagement can be accomplished so that the couple is gradually prepared for termination.

The Present Authors' Outcome Research

The authors conducted an outcome study involving 30 couples to evaluate the therapeutic approach described herein. Since the current chapter is treatment rather than research oriented, the emphasis of this presentation will be on the clinical implications of the results. However, it is necessary to briefly describe the research design and methodology employed.

The couples were matched in groups of three on the Locke-Wallace Marital Adjustment Test and the number of years married, and then randomly assigned to one of three groups: (1) Communication Therapy, (2) Behavioral Marital Agreements and Communication Therapy, and (3) Wait-list Control Group. The difference between the two treatment programs primarily involved whether or not the couples were writing and executing behavior change agreements.

To be included in the program, a couple had to be married at least five years, living together, and score in the distressed range on the Locke-Wallace. Couples were to be excluded if there was evidence of chronic alcoholism or psychotic disorders, or if the marital problem was primarily due to a sexual dysfunction. (Four couples who requested treatment were excluded and referred elsewhere on the basis of these criteria—three due to alcoholism and one because the male was impotent.) Two-thirds of the couples were referred by local mental health clinics or private practitioners; the remaining third had responded to announcements of the marital therapy program in local newspapers. The couples averaged 12.4

years of marriage, 35.4 years of age, two children, an annual income of $12,000, and a high school education. In brief, the participants were representative of a general clinical population.

At intake, termination, and a four-month follow-up interview, the couples completed the questionnaires described previously (Locke-Wallace, Primary Communication Inventory, Feelings Toward Spouse, Target Marital and Individual Problems, and Spouse Behavior Changes) and engaged in a problem-solving exercise that is a variant of Olson and Ryder's (1970) Inventory of Marital Conflicts. The spouses tried to resolve differences of opinion; discussions were tape-recorded and then coded by undergraduate raters. The couples on the waiting list completed the assessment procedures for a second time after a 10-week wait and were then offered therapy. Five therapists of varying theoretical and educational backgrounds participated in the study—the two authors of this chapter, a social worker, a clinical psychologist, and a doctoral student in clinical psychology. The therapists' training included readings, discussions, and role plays. In addition, the therapists followed detailed therapy manuals and met for weekly group supervision throughout the program.* Each therapist saw two couples in each treatment group.

The questionnaire data obtained at termination of therapy demonstrated that the couples in both treatment groups experienced significantly greater positive change than the control group on: (1) the communication measure, (2) the client-identified marital problems, and (3) the behavior changes desired in the spouse. With regard to client-identified individual problems (those problems not seen as being tied to the marital relationship), the wives in the therapy groups reported significantly greater gains than did the wives in the control group; the husbands did not. Although the treated couples changed significantly on the Locke-Wallace and Feelings Questionnaire while the control group did not, the differential gains between the three groups were not significant. The behavioral data on the problem-solving exercise did not demonstrate differential gains of the treated couples over the control group, but all couples changed in a positive direction on several of the categories. Analyses of the follow-up data indicated that the treated couples across both groups reported significant improvement in their communication patterns and a significant increase in marital satisfaction from pre-treatment to follow-up. There were no differences in effectiveness between the

---

* The therapy manuals and a full research report can be obtained from the authors by sending a check for $3.00 payable to SUNY Stony Brook.

two treatment groups as measured by the changes from pre- to post-treatment and post-treatment to follow-up.

In light of this finding of similar effectiveness, it was essential to document that the therapists were, in fact, behaving differently across the two groups. Therapist behavior was assessed in two ways: self-report of activities engaged in during each session and the coding of therapist behavior by undergraduate raters (unaware of the nature of the treatment groups and experimental hypotheses) who listened to randomly sampled 20-minute segments of half of the therapy sessions in each treatment group.

Analyses of both self-report and behavioral data confirmed that the therapists were helping clients with behavior change agreements significantly more in the marital agreements treatment group than in the communication therapy group. In fact, the raters scored the category of working on marital agreements only once across the 50 rated tapes of the communication therapy group. The ratings also demonstrated that the therapists were verbally reinforcing behavior changes not related to communication significantly more in the marital agreements group. With regard to communication therapy, analyses of the behavioral data indicated that the therapists were conducting structured communication exercises twice as often in this treatment group as they were in the marital agreements group. This difference approached significance.

The self-report data were consistent with the behavioral data in that the therapists reported working on structured exercises and on generalized communication patterns significantly more with couples in communication therapy. An additional indication that the therapists were behaving differently across the two treatment programs is that the husbands in the marital agreements group rated their therapists as significantly more empathic and more competent than did the husbands in the communication therapy group, although, as noted, the same therapists saw couples in both groups. This result is particularly interesting, given that the overall treatment effects were similar for the two approaches. It is possible that the clients perceived their therapists as more directive and "businesslike" in the behavioral agreements program and thus judged them to be more competent. Since the therapists involved had differing educational backgrounds and training and reported feeling equally comfortable using both treatment manuals, these factors probably did not influence the ratings of competence. With regard to greater empathy, one hypothesis is that the therapists' working with the husbands to help them effect desired changes in their wives was seen as a more significant indication of empathy or understanding than was the offering of empathic reflections.

That is, the therapist was "behaving" empathically in helping the husbands change certain behaviors in their wives, rather than just "speaking" empathically and helping the wives to do likewise. It should be noted that the wives' ratings of the therapists were so uniformly high that no differences could be detected.

The clear implication of the finding of no overall treatment differences is that the writing of the behavior change agreements is not a necessary part of the behavioral treatment program; approximately two-thirds of the clients will experience significant clinical gains, whether or not the therapist uses written agreements. However, examining mean changes over 10 couples can mask the possibility that the effectiveness of the procedures may vary, depending upon the characteristics of the couples and the problems they were presenting.As age and years married were demographic variables that were highly correlated with therapeutic outcome in the program, the effectiveness of the two treatment approaches was compared in terms of change on the Locke-Wallace and the communication questionnaire, across the younger and older couples in the sample. The couples were rank ordered according to age, and each treatment group was split into two groups of five couples. Thus, the responses of young (average marriage length of 7 years, average age of 29) and older (average marriage length of 18 years, average age of 41) couples were compared across the three experimental groups—two treatments and the control. The pattern that emerged was that the behavioral marital agreements program was highly effective for every younger couple but was not very helpful to most of the older couples. The younger couples in this treatment group showed significantly more improvement than the waiting list couples. However, the reverse was true with regard to the communication therapy, in that it was the older couples who showed significantly greater gains than the controls. This interaction of age and treatment approach was also evidenced in the follow-up data obtained from the Locke-Wallace.

Several hypotheses can be entertained to explain this finding. Perhaps the older couples, with a longer history of distress, have a more firmly entrenched pattern of hostile and destructive communication and thus need more intensive therapy regarding communication patterns. The younger couples may be in the process of trying to define a satisfactory structure and set of rules for conflict resolution and thus respond well to the structure imposed by the therapist (negotiated change, compromise, and written agreements). Further research is clearly necessary, both to increase our understanding of the variety of factors which influence response to therapy and to replicate this age-related finding. However, one possible implication of this study is that interventions should be client-tailored to maximize effectiveness for a particular couple and that age should be a determinant of the type of intervention used.

SUMMATION AND FUTURE DIRECTIONS

Fortunately, the various behavioral treatment programs discussed have shown that couples show significant improvement on one or more outcome measures. However, most measures of outcome, especially self-report measures, are subject to demand characteristics. Consequently, comparative studies of behavioral and nonbehavioral marital therapy with multiple outcome measures are needed. Judging from outcome data to date, no approach is definitely superior (c.f. Beck, 1976; Turkewitz and O'Leary, 1976). Both communication therapy and negotiation/contracting approaches have shown considerable promise in effecting significant marital changes.

The approach in the Stony Brook program has been twofold: (1) to improve communication and (2) to increase mutual satisfaction by promoting clear communication about desired changes, and, where those changes appear reasonable, prompting their occurrence through therapist suggestion and the encouragement of social reinforcement between the spouses. As noted previously, written marital agreements have proved facilitative of amelioration in marital discord with young couples, whereas older couples appear to respond more favorably to intensive communication than to a focus on marital agreements and negotiation. Given the paucity of treatment research with couples in serious distress and with couples over 30 years old (Gurman and Kniskern, in press; Patterson, Weiss, and Hops, 1976), research with this population is encouraged. In addition, if the efficacy of particular procedures is ever to be determined, certain process research is sorely needed. Consequently, outcome research with correlational data relating treatment procedures and therapy change (for example, Sloane, Staples, Cristol, Yorkston, and Whipple, 1975) *as well as* individual subject design experiments with component analyses are necessary. At present, only communication approaches appear to be the sine qua non of effective marital therapy since communication enhancement is a common denominator of any marital therapy approach.

Behavior therapy has changed significantly during the last decade, and marital therapy, in particular, has moved from a stress on reinforcement to problem solving and communication (Turkewitz and O'Leary, 1976; Weiss, Chapter IV). It is the present authors' guess that communication therapy is best for some problems and reinforcement oriented programs are more effective with others. Unfortunately, there is almost no research documenting the effects of various marital procedures with clients with different diagnoses or problems. Problems such as jealousy and infidelity would appear to be ameliorated by different therapeutic strategies than would differences over child-rearing and role definition. When treating parent-child dyadic relations, evaluation does not focus only on global change in such problems, and one general treatment program is not used for all parent-child difficulties. Instead, specialized treatments exist for hyperactivity, withdrawal, enuresis, autism, and other specific childhood problems. In the same vein, it is necessary to develop problem-specific therapeutic programs for alleviating different couples' marital distress. At this point, even multiple case studies illustrating treatment methods for dealing with particular problems and client evaluations of such are advisable. In addition, sophisticated client evaluations of treatment efforts on a session-by-session basis would be very useful.

That negative interactions are characteristic of distressed couples is a commonly observed and reported phenomenon. It has not been convincingly demonstrated that an exclusive emphasis on increasing positive interactions is best advised, and there are at least two reasons why deceleration of destructive behaviors may be an appropriate therapeutic target. First, as Weiss (Chapter IV) has noted, from both survey and interactional analyses it can be concluded that pleasant and unpleasant occurrences are independent of one another, yet both are related to marital satisfaction. Given the assumption of independence, it would follow that simply focusing on increasing positive interactions would not necessarily result in a decrease in negative interactions. Second, even one highly aversive interaction (such as physical violence) is detrimental to both the self-esteem of the participants and to the relationship, and may be sufficient to undo weeks of effort at increasing positive interactions. The need to decrease certain destructive interchanges is so crucial that in the Stony Brook program the couple is told of the import of such change and the person likely to display the highly aversive behavior is advised to call the therapist at any time he/she feels that he/she is going to engage in the behavior. While the clients almost never make such phone calls, the message regarding the importance of these changes is clear and the destructive interactions do decrease in frequency.

As noted previously, many behavior therapists argue that it is inadvisable to use written marital agreements for decelerating behaviors as these agreements may encourage criticism and aversive control. Rather than use this negative strategy, the major emphasis of written marital agreements is on building positive interactions through social reinforcement. However, as evidenced by the example cited above regarding the instruction to telephone the therapist, other therapeutic techniques should be developed for the particular problem area of highly destructive interchanges.

With the exception of some drop in marital happiness during early child-rearing years, there do not appear to be drastic changes in marital happiness over the life cycle (Spanier, Lewis, and Cole, 1975). However, younger and older clients report differing reinforcers, and it would be helpful for therapists to have demographic or actuarial data on what "happy" couples do and on what they find reinforcing. Such information could be obtained from both longitudinal and cross-sectional approaches.

There is an increasing trend in psychology in general to "go cognitive" (Dember, 1974); in behavior therapy specifically, this trend is very salient (Bandura, 1974). As Wilson (1977) aptly stated, "Behavior therapy is not, nor was it ever, a monolithic structure," and the cognitive trend within certain circles makes the structure of behavior therapy even more ambiguous. However, as Wilson noted, the term behavior therapy "identifies a common core among *all* present behavioral approaches—a commitment to measurement, methodology, concepts and procedures derivable from experimental psychology." The cognitive trend, however, has not made significant inroads in the practice of behavioral marital therapy. That is, *principles* from cognitive learning laboratories have not had much impact on practicing marital therapists or even the university researchers in the area. There are several areas, however, where cognitive learning research would likely be of great benefit to the marital therapist. Assignment of meaning to behavior and specifically attributing the intent of caring to particular behaviors are critical factors in marital happiness, yet we know little about how such meanings are determined. Given that couples in distress interpret messages intended to be positive as neutral or negatively valenced (Kahn, 1970), it would be helpful to know why such results are obtained and how to reverse the attributional process. If communication enhancement is the sine qua non of effective marital therapy, principles of effective communication are sorely needed. That is, in addition to having information on differences between distressed and nondistressed groups, marital therapists must have data on how the implementation of certain communication practices affects marital interactions.

As this chapter concludes, Etzioni's projection in *Science* (April 29, 1977) should be considered:

> At the present accelerating rate of depletion, the United States will run out of families not long after it runs out of oil. The proportion of married households out of total households declined from 72.5 percent in 1965 to 64.9 percent in 1976. . . . Depending upon one's assumptions about how this acceleration will progress, the United States will not have a married household left a generation or so from now. . . . The projection suffices . . . to show that the family is an endangered species.

It could be concluded from the above that marital therapists will be out of business within a generation. Etzioni's projection may be an exaggeration. One would need the yearly figures to accurately project the rates. However, his point is worth contemplation. It may be the case that marriage as an institution is threatened and that more than remedial efforts are necessary if it is to survive. For example, premarital counseling programs could be used to prevent serious marital discord by teaching couples the necessary skills to establish a satisfying marriage. To aid existing marriages, certain public policy changes are definitely needed. For example, it is highly unfortunate that treatment of marital discord is not recognized by government and private insurance companies despite the fact that these agencies have ample data documenting the negative sequelae of family distintegration. This public policy change is particularly important since, in contrast to Etzioni's prediction, it is clear that at present marriage is still a sought-after life style for the majority of the population. There are surveys which indicate that over 90 percent of young people want to carry (Cole, 1976), and that 75 percent of divorced persons remarry within three years (Norton, 1976). Given these statistics and the prevalence of marital distress, it is essential to develop effective therapeutic programs.

As discussed throughout this chapter, there is no one behavioral approach. The Stony Brook behavioral marital therapy program has been outlined in the hope that others may replicate these endeavors and in order to receive feedback from other therapists. Social learning theory as described by Bandura (1969) has been most useful heuristically and pragmatically for conceptualizing the authors' program. However, psychoanalytic and systems theorists have very intriguing and intellectually exciting frameworks for conceptualizing marital problems. The very structure of this text, with three treatment approaches to marital problems represented, illustrates the view of the editors that no conceptual or treatment procedural domain has all of the answers to the amelioration of marital discord. Hopefully, this chapter has presented some partial answers; progress in marital therapy will undoubtedly occur with the integration of various aspects of these approaches.

REFERENCES

Azrin, N. H., Naster, B. J. and Jones, R. Reciprocity counseling: A rapid learning-based procedure for marital counseling. *Behavior Research and Therapy*, 1973, 11, 365-382.

Bandura, A. *Principles of Behavior Modification*. New York: Holt, Rinehart, & Winston, 1969.

Bandura, A. Behavior theory and models of man. *American Psychologist*, 1974, 29, 859-869.

Beck, A. T. *Cognitive Therapy and the Emotional Disorders*. New York: International Universities Press, 1976.

Bienvenu, M. J. Measurement of marital communication. *Family Coordinator*, 1970, 19, 26-31.

Birchler, G. R., Weiss, R. L. and Vincent, J. P. A multi-method analysis of social reinforcement exchange between maritally distressed and non-distressed spouse and stranger dyads. *Journal of Personality and Social Psychology*, 1975, 31, 349-360.

Cautela, J. R. Covert sensitization. *Psychological Reports*, 1967, 20, 459-468.

Clark, L. Sexual adjustment in marriage. In: A. Ellis and A. Abarbanel (Eds.), *The Encyclopedia of Sexual Behavior*. New York: Hawthorn, 1961.

Cole, S. Teenage girls. Unpublished manuscript prepared for *Newsday*. SUNY at Stony Brook, 1976.

Cozby, P. C. Self-disclosure: A literature review. *Psychological Bulletin*, 1973, 79, 73-91.

Craighead, W. E., Kazdin, A. E. and Mahoney, M. J. *Behavior Modification: Principles, Issues, and Applications*. New York: Houghton-Mifflin, 1976.

Davis, J. D. and Skinner, A. E. G. Reciprocity of self-disclosure in interviews: Modeling or social exchange? *Journal of Personality and Social Psychology*, 1974, 29, 779-784.

Dember, W. N. Motivation and the cognitive revolution. *American Psychologist*, 1974, 29, 161-168.

D'Zurilla, T. J. and Goldfried, M. R. Problem solving and behavior modification. *Journal of Abnormal Psychology*, 1971, 78, 107-126.

Edmonds, V. Marital conventionalization: Definition and measurement. *Journal of Marriage and the Family*, 1967, 29, 681-688.

Edmonds, V., Withers, G. and Dibastia, B. Adjustment, conservatism, and marital conventionalization. *Journal of Marriage and the Family*, 1972, 34, 96-103.

Eisenberg, J. M. and Zingle, H. W. Marital adjustment and irrational ideas. *Journal of Marriage and Family Counseling*, 1975, 1, 81-91.

Ellis, A. *Reason and Emotion in Psychotherapy*. New York: Lyle Stuart, 1962.

Ellis, A. and Harper, R. *A Guide to Successful Marriage*. Beverly Hills, Calif.: Leighton Printing Co., 1961.

Ely, A. L., Guerney, B. G. and Stover, L. Efficacy of the training phase of conjugal therapy. *Psychotherapy: Theory, Research and Practice*, 1973, 10, 201-207.

Etzioni, A. Science and the future of the family. *Science,* 1977, 196, 487.

Friedman, P. H. Personalistic family and marital therapy. In: A. A. Lazarus (Ed.), *Clinical Behavior Therapy.* New York: Brunner/Mazel, 1972.

Gebhard, P. H. Factors in marital orgasm. *Journal of Social Issues,* 1966, 22, 88-96.

Gilbert, W. M. and Ewing, T. N. Programmed versus face-to-face counseling. *Journal of Counseling Psychology,* 1971, 18, 413-427.

Goldfried, M. R. and Goldfried, A. P. Cognitive change methods. In F. H. Kanfer and A. P. Goldstein (Eds.), *Helping People Change.* New York: Pergamon, 1975, 89-116.

Goldiamond, I. Self-control procedures in personal behavior problems. *Psychological Reports,* 1965, 17, 851-868.

Goldman, G. The establishment of a private practice. In G. D. Goldman and G. Stricker (Eds.), *Practical Problems of a Private Psychotherapy Practice.* Springfield, Illinois: Charles Thomas, 1972.

Goldstein, A. *Therapist-Patient Relationships in Psychotherapy.* New York: Macmillan, 1962.

Goldstein, M. K. Behavior rate change in marriages. Training wives to modify husbands' behavior. *Dissertation Abstracts International,* 1971, 32 (1-B), 559.

Goldstein, M. K. and Francis, B. Behavior modification of husbands by wives. Paper presented at the National Council on Family Relations, Washington, D. C., 1969.

Gottman, J., Notarius, C., Gonso, J. and Markman, H. *A Couple's Guide to Communication.* Champaign, Illinois: Research Press, 1976.

Gottman, J., Notarius, C., Markman, H., Bank, S., Yoppi, B. and Rubin, M. E. Behavior exchange theory and marital decision making. *Journal of Personality and Social Psychology,* in press.

Greer, S. E. and D'Zurilla, T. J. Behavioral approaches to marital discord and conflict. *Journal of Marriage and Family Counseling,* 1975, 1, 299-315.

Gurman, A. S. The effects and effectiveness of marital therapy: A review of outcome research. *Family Process,* 1973, 12, 145-170.

Gurman, A. S. and Kniskern, D. P. Research on marital and family therapy: Progress, perspective and prospect. In: S. L. Garfield and A. E. Bergin (Eds.), *Handbook of Psychotherapy and Behavior Change: An Empirical Analysis* (2nd ed.). New York: Wiley, in press.

Hickman, M. E. and Baldwin, B. A. Use of programmed instruction to improve communication in marriage. *The Family Coordinator,* 1971, 20, 121-125.

Hickok, J. E. and Komechak, M. G. Behavior modification in marital conflict: A case report. *Family Process,* 1974, 13, 111-119.

Jacobson, N. S. Problem-solving and contingency contracting in the treatment of marital discord. *Journal of Consulting and Clinical Psychology,* 1977, 45, 92-100.

Jacobson, N. S. Specific and nonspecific factors in the effectiveness of a behavioral approach to marital discord. *Journal of Consulting and Clinical Psychology,* in press.

Jacobson, N. S. Training couples to solve their marital problems: A behavioral approach to relationship discord. Manuscript submitted for publication.

Jacobson, N. S. and Martin, B. Behavioral marriage therapy: Current status. *Psychological Bulletin,* 1976, 83, 540-556.

Johnson, D. W. and Matross, R. Interpersonal influence in psychotherapy. In: A. S. Gurman and A. M. Razin (Eds.), *The Therapist's Contribution to Effective Psychotherapy: An Empirical Approach.* New York: Pergamon, in press.

Kahn, M. Non-verbal communication and marital satisfaction. *Family Process,* 1970, 9, 449-456.

Katz, I., Goldston, J., Cohen, M. and Stucker, S. Need satisfaction, perception, and cooperative interactions in married couples. *Marriage and Family Living*, 1963, 25, 209-214.

Katz, M. Agreement of connotative meaning in marriage. *Family Process*, 1965, 4, 64-74.

Kazdin, A. E. and Wilcoxon, L. A. Systematic desensitization and nonspecific treatment effects: A methodological evaluation. *Psychological Bulletin*, 1976, 83, 729-758.

Kent, R. N. and O'Leary, K. D. A controlled evaluation of behavior modification with conduct problem children. *Journal of Consulting and Clinical Psychology*, 1976, 44, 586-596.

Kent, R. N. and O'Leary, K. D. Treatment of conduct problem children: BA and/or Ph.D. therapists. *Behavior Therapy*, 1977, 8, 653-658.

Kimmel, C. and Van der Veen, F. Factors of marital adjustment in Locke's Marital Adjustment Test. *Journal of Marriage and the Family*, 1974, 36, 57-63.

Knox, D. Behavior contracts in marriage counseling. *Journal of Family Counseling*, 1973, 1, 22-28.

Koch, J. and Koch, L. *The Marriage Savers*. New York: Coward, McCann and Geoghegan, 1976.

Lazarus, A. A. Behavior therapy and marriage counseling. *Journal of the American Society of Psychosomatic Dentistry and Medicine*, 1968, 15, 49-56.

Lederer, W. J. and Jackson, D. D. *The Mirages of Marriage*. New York: W. W. Norton & Co., Inc., 1968.

Liberman, R. Behavioral approaches to family and couple therapy. *American Journal of Orthopsychiatry*, 1970, 40, 106-118.

Liberman, R. P., Levine, J., Wheeler, E., Sanders, N. and Wallace, C. J. Marital therapy in groups. A comparative evaluation of behavioral and interactional formats. *Acta Psychiatrica Scandinavica*, Supplementum 266, 1976 (a).

Liberman, R. P., Wheeler, E. and Sanders, N. Behavioral therapy for marital disharmony: An educational approach. *Journal of Marriage and Family Counseling*, 1976, 2, 383-395 (b).

Lindsley, O. R., Skinner, B. F. and Solomon, H. C. *Studies in Behavior Therapy. Status Report 1*. Metropolitan State Hospital, Waltham, Mass., 1953.

Lobitz, W. C. and LoPiccolo, J. New methods in the behavioral treatment of sexual dysfunction. *Journal of Behavior Therapy and Experimental Psychiatry*, 1972, 3, 265-272.

Locke, H. J. and Wallace, M. Short marital adjustment and prediction test: Reliability and validity. *Marriage and Family Living*, 1959, 21, 251-255.

Lovibond, S. H. *Conditioning and Enuresis*. Oxford: Pergamon, 1974.

Mahoney, M. J. *Cognition and Behavior Modification*. Cambridge, Mass.: Ballinger, 1974.

Marks, I. Management of sexual disorders. In: H. Leitenberg (Ed.), *Handbook of Behavior Modification and Behavior Therapy*. New York: Prentice-Hall, 1976, 255-303.

Masters, W. H. and Johnson, V. E. *Human Sexual Inadequacy*. Boston: Little Brown, 1970.

Meichenbaum, D. H. *Cognitive Behavior Modification*. Morristown, N. J.: General Learning Press, 1974.

Meichenbaum, D. H. and Goodman, J. Training impulsive children to talk to themselves: A means of developing self-control. *Journal of Abnormal Psychology*, 1971, 77, 115-126.

Murstein, B. I. and Beck, G. D. Person perception, marriage adjustment, and social desirability. *Journal of Consulting and Clinical Psychology*, 1972, 39, 396-403.

Navran, L. Communication and adjustment in marriage. *Family Process*, 1967, 6, 173-184.

Norton, A. J. U.S. Census Bureau. Personal communication, January 19, 1976.

O'Leary, K. D. The effects of self-instruction on immoral behavior. *Journal of Experimental Child Psychology*, 1968, 6, 297-301.

O'Leary, K. D., Pelham, W. E., Rosenbaum, A. and Price, G. H. Behavioral treatment of hyperkinetic children. *Clinical Pediatrics*, 1976, 15, 510-514.

O'Leary, K. D., Turkewitz, H. and Taffel, S. J. Parent and child evaluation of behavior therapy in a child psychological clinic. *Journal of Consulting and Clinical Psychology*, 1973, 41, 279-283.

O'Leary, K. D. and Wilson, G. T. *Behavior Therapy: Application and Outcome.* Englewood Cliffs, N. J.: Prentice-Hall, 1975.

Olson, D. H. Marital and family therapy: Integrative review and critique. *Journal of Marriage and the Family*, 1970, 32, 501-538.

Olson, D. H. and Ryder, R. G. Inventory of marital conflicts (IMC): An experimental interaction procedure. *Journal of Marriage and the Family*, 1970, 32, 443-448.

Oltmanns, T. F., Broderick, J. E. and O'Leary, K. D. Marital adjustment and the efficacy of behavior therapy with children. *Journal of Consulting and Clinical Psychology*, 1977, 45, 724-729.

Patterson, G. R., Hops, H. and Weiss, R. L. A social learning approach to reducing rates of marital conflict. In: R. Stuart, R. Liberman and S. Wilder (Eds.), *Advances in Behavior Therapy*. New York: Academic Press, 1973.

Patterson, G. R., Hops, H. and Weiss, R. L. Interpersonal skills training for couples in early stages of conflict. *Journal of Marriage and the Family*, 1975, 37, 295-303.

Patterson, G. R., Weiss, R. L. and Hops, H. Training in marital skills: Some problems and concepts. In: H. Leitenberg (Ed.), *Handbook of Behavior Modification and Behavior Therapy*. Englewood Cliffs, N. J.: Prentice-Hall, 1976.

Paul, G. L. *Insight versus Desensitization: An Experiment in Anxiety Reduction.* Stanford, CA.: Stanford University Press, 1966.

Pierce, R. M. Training in interpersonal communication skills with the partners of deteriorated marriages. *The Family Coordinator*, 1973, 22, 223-227.

Rappaport, A. F. and Harrell, J. A behavioral-exchange model for marital counseling. *Family Coordinator*, 1972, 21, 203-212.

Robin, A. L., Armel, S. and O'Leary, K. D. The effects of self-instruction on writing deficiencies. *Behavior Therapy*, 1975, 6, 178-187.

Robin, A. L., Kent, R. N., O'Leary, K. D., Foster, S. and Prinz, R. An approach to teaching parents and adolescents problem-solving communication skills: A preliminary report. *Behavior Therapy*, 1977, 8, 639-643.

Sager, C. J. *Marriage Contracts and Couple Therapy.* New York: Brunner/Mazel, 1976.

Sears, R. R. Sources of life satisfactions of the Terman Gifted Men. *American Psychologist*, 1977, 32, 119-128.

Skinner, B. F. *Science and Human Behavior.* New York: Macmillan, 1953.

Sloane, R. B., Staples, F. R., Cristol, A. H., Yorkston, N. J. and Whipple, K. *Psychotherapy versus Behavior Therapy.* Cambridge, Mass.: Harvard University Press, 1975.

Spanier, G. B., Lewis, R. A. and Cole, C. L. Marital adjustment over the family life cycle: The issue of curvilinearity. *Journal of Marriage and the Family*, 1975, 37, 263-275.

Stern, R. S. and Marks, I. M. Contract therapy in obsessive-compulsive neurosis with marital discord. *British Journal of Psychiatry*, 1973, 123, 681-684.

Stuart, R. B. Operant-interpersonal treatment for marital discord. *Journal of Consulting and Clinical Psychology*, 1969, 33, 675-682.

Stuart, R. B. An operant interpersonal program for couples. In: D. H. L. Olson (Ed.), *Treating Relationships*. Lake Mills, Iowa: Graphic Publishing Co., 1976.

Stuart, R. B. Behavioral remedies for marital ills. In: A. S. Gurman and D. G. Rice (Eds.), *Couples in Conflict*. New York: Jason Aronson, 1975.

Turkewitz, H. and O'Leary, K. D. Positive feelings questionnaire: The relationship between positive feelings towards one's spouse and general marital satisfaction. Unpublished manuscript, SUNY, Stony Brook, N. Y., 1975.

Turkewitz, H. and O'Leary, K. D. Communication and behavioral marital therapy: An outcome study. Paper presented at the Annual Meeting of the Association for the Advancement of Behavior Therapy, New York, December, 1976.

Turner, A. J. Couple and group treatment of marital discord: An experiment. Paper presented at the 6th Annual Meeting of the Association for the Advancement of Behavior Therapy, New York, October, 1972.

Weiss, R. L. Contracts, cognition and change: A behavioral approach to marriage therapy. *The Counseling Psychologist*, 1975, 5, 15-26.

Weiss, R. L., Birchler, G. R. and Vincent, J. P. Contractual models for negotiation training in marital dyads. *Journal of Marriage and the Family*, 1974, 36, 321-330.

Weiss, R. L., Hops, H. and Patterson, G. R. A framework for conceptualizing marital conflict: A technology for altering it, some data for evaluating it. In: L. A. Hamerlynck, L. C. Handy and E. J. Mash (Eds.), *Behavior Change: Methodology, Concepts and Practice.* Champaign, Illinois: Research Press, 1973.

Weiss, R. L. and Margolin, G. Marital conflict and accord. In: A. R. Ciminero, K. S. Calhoun and H. E. Adams (Eds.), *Handbook for Behavioral Assessment.* New York: John Wiley & Sons, Inc., 1977.

Wilson, G. T. Cognitive behavior therapy: Paradigm shift or passing phase. Paper presented to University of Houston, Houston, Texas, April, 1977.

Wilson, G. T. and Evans, I. M. Adult behavior therapy and the therapist-client relationship. In: C. M. Franks and G. T. Wilson (Eds.), *Annual Review of Behavior Therapy: Vol. 4.* New York: Brunner/Mazel, 1976.

Wolf, S. S. and Etzel, B. C. A behavioral analysis of reciprocity marital counseling procedures. Paper presented at the Tenth Annual Meeting of the Association for the Advancement of Behavior Therapy, December, 1976.

Wolpe, J. *Psychotherapy by Reciprocal Inhibition.* Stanford, Calif.: Stanford University Press, 1958.

Woolfolk, A. E., Woolfolk, R. L. and Wilson, G. T. A rose by any other name. . . . Labeling bias and attitudes toward behavior modification. *Journal of Consulting and Clinical Psychology*, 1977, 45, 184-191.

VI

The Conceptualization of Marriage from a Systems Theory Perspective

PETER STEINGLASS, M.D.

Imagine, for the moment, the following fictitious scenario:

Bob and Alice F. are a married couple in their mid-twenties struggling through their fifth year of marriage. For the past six months a series of increasingly contentious fights have erupted with disturbing frequency and they now fear for the integrity of their relationship. Although these fights have covered a wide range of manifest issues, they have centered primarily around a series of conflicts familiar to all marital therapists. Mrs. F. feels her husband is increasingly unavailable to her, keeps long work hours, fails to appreciate either the magnitude or strain created by her mothering and housekeeping duties, and is driven to distraction by what, from her point of view, is her husband's total irresponsibility regarding money and his inability to plan logically and rationally for the future. Mr. F. for his part, finds Mrs. F. increasingly difficult to talk to, critical, negativistic and depressed. He feels that her lack of sexual responsiveness predetermines his tendency to pull away from her, and that she is pressuring him to accept an economically secure but intellectually boring choice of occupation.

Recognizing that their levels of tension and dissatisfaction are becoming associated with overtly symptomatic behavior, and feeling that their marriage is clearly on the rocks, they turn in desperation to a professional for advice and guidance. If they were asked to make the rounds of some of the prominent therapists in the field, what experiences might they have as a result of these referrals? Suppose, just to make it manageable, they are restricted only to those people who have called themselves *family systems therapists*. A representative series of contacts might unfold.

First, they visit Murray Bowen. He starts by addressing a series of questions to Mr. F., then turns his attention to Mrs. F., then to Mr. F., then to Mrs. F., and so forth and so on for one year's worth of visits. If at any point they attempt to talk to each other, he interrupts them, insisting that they talk one at a time and only to him. He asks them how they "see" this and that; he seems very interested in their families of origin; he talks at length with them about triangles and one-on-one relationships; he draws complicated diagrams he calls family genograms; and he gently but firmly urges them to spend much of their waking hours contacting, thinking about, and developing new "differentiated" relationships with members of their extended family group.

Next they go to Salvador Minuchin. Arriving with their newly developed skills from their sessions with Bowen, they talk, as they're sure they are supposed to, one at a time, and only to Minuchin. Much to their surprise he demands instead that they talk to each other, breaking in every time they look or talk toward him with a gentle but firm, "No, no, Mr. F., I want you to talk to her!" He seems totally disinterested in their by now burgeoning knowledge of their extended family and the wonderful anecdotal stories they have uncovered, insisting instead that they talk about what is happening *now*. Every time they settle down to what they think will be a comfortable discussion, he has them change their chairs, and he is continually giving them tasks without explanations. And he seems particularly interested in how they are dealing with their young child, a subject they managed to totally avoid in one year's worth of discussions with Bowen.

Somewhat perplexed, they are sent on their way and come to rest in the office of a therapist trained by the late Don Jackson. And what they find is, of course, a paradox. Communication *is* behavior and suddenly their words (what they are saying and the way they are saying it) become supremely important. And they are given a curative prescription: They are to fight regularly about exactly the same issues and they are to do so for six days a week; they are allowed to talk civilly to each other only on Sundays.

The scenario should, of course, have Mr. and Mrs. F. at this point living happily ever after, having benefited from the skills of three masters. But how are they to organize the experiences they have gone through? The simplest explanation might be that they had been treated by professionals from three of the wide variety of psychotherapeutic schools they know to be blossoming at an ever-increasing rate. Their assumption surely would be that their three therapists come from widely disparate theoretical backgrounds. But of course, as pointed out at the beginning, each therapist, far from being a stranger to the other's point of view, has vigorously staked out his claim as a bona fide member of a systems perspective theoretical school.

Now Mr. and Mrs. F., being novices to the field, cannot be expected to reconcile these seeming discrepancies. For the professional, however, it is another story. This clinical anecdote underscores an important point right from the start: System theory, as it has been applied to marriage and marital disorders, is at the moment more a series of loosely connected concepts than an integrated theory of marriage. In fact, many people would characterize it, perhaps pejoratively, as nothing more than a style or stance of thinking, certainly not a body of theory in the form of a comprehensive model. In order to render a balanced judgment on this issue, it will be necessary to devote considerable space to a careful discussion of general systems theory itself, especially basic concepts of living systems; then we will be prepared to move on to a discussion of marriage and marital disorders.

Another difficulty should also be mentioned before beginning. Although this chapter addresses marriage and marital disorders alone, systems theory emphasizes the relationship between individuals, the marital system, the family system, and the community system. Marriages have frequently been described as subsets of family systems, and therefore examples may frequently address family and marital issues simultaneously. In fact, theoretical statements unique to marriage and marital disorders are sparse. Olson (1975), in his comprehensive review, makes this state of affairs quite clear. He concludes that "it is apparent that the field of marital therapy is in serious need of a theoretical base from which to operate. The past work in this area generally serves as an example of what are not fruitful approaches regarding theory development" (p. 32).

GENERAL SYSTEMS THEORY

In 1928, Ludwig von Bertalanffy introduced the first of a series of concepts that, taken together, were intended to develop an "organismic" approach to biological problems. In 1945 these concepts were collectively given the title General Systems Theory (von Bertalanffy, 1968). Historically, these concepts were developed in response to major dilemmas that had been arising in the biological sciences, dilemmas which von Bertalanffy felt were related primarily to limitations imposed on scientific explanation by existing theoretical approaches to science. The core of the problem as he saw it was the exclusive reliance on what has been called the reductionistic/mechanistic tradition in science.

In essence, the reductionistic/mechanistic approach explains events by developing a linear series of stepwise cause and effect equations, each of which is intended to unearth a fundamental precedent event assumed to be causally explanative of the final behavior under study. In psychology, the stimulus-response model is perhaps the clearest example of this approach: an attempt to explain behavior as a series of two-step events, one being the cause or stimulus, the other being the behavior or response.

Von Bertalanffy attempted to reverse this prevailing trend in science by urging that attention be paid not only to reductionistic principles, but also to those more *general* principles that might be used to explain biological processes that lead to increasing complexity of organization (for the organism). Phenomena of this second type had previously been relegated to the realm of vitalism. The resultant theoretical principles, known collectively as General Systems Theory, have been either heralded as a new revolution in scientific thought—or felt to be by and large commonsensical and perhaps somewhat mystical.

In the field of human behavior, systems theory has had an uneven reception, being embraced to a greater or lesser extent depending upon the primary interests in question. Systems theory has been attractive to theorists whose interests are directed toward relationships among individuals or groups of individuals (sociologists, social psychologists, marital and family therapists), and less attractive to those primarily interested in individual behavior (experimental psychologists, psychoanalysts). In the mental health field, although systems concepts have been applied with some success to an analysis of complex social organizations (such as community mental health centers), and to multivariate analysis of specific health problems (such as a systems analysis of drug abuse), by far the most extensive use of systems theory has been its application to the study of families and family pathology. Interest in the marital system has been subsumed under the wider family umbrella. This chapter therefore discusses a popular and clearly attractive model of marriage and marital disorders.

The Systems Perspective

What, then, is general systems theory all about? In an introductory chapter in their book, *General Systems Theory and Psychiatry*, Gray, Duhl and Rizzo (1969) describe general systems theory as

> ... a logical-mathematical field which deals with the new scientific doctrines of wholeness, dynamic interaction, and organization. It is a new approach to the unity-of-science problem which sees organization rather than reduction as the unifying principle, and which therefore searches for general structural isomorphisms in systems (p. 7).

When von Bertalanffy was first invited to speak at an annual meeting of the American Psychiatric Association in 1967, he chose to describe the aim of the general systems theoretical approach as follows:

> Looking into those organismic features of life, behavior, society; taking them seriously and not bypassing or denying them; finding conceptual tools to handle them; developing models to represent them in conceptual constructs; making these models work in the scientific ways of logical deduction, of construction of material analogues, computer simulation and so forth; and so come to better understanding, explanation, prediction, control of what makes an organism, a psyche, or a society function (von Bertalanffy, in Gray et al., 1969, p. 36).

As these statements make clear, the key notions being introduced are *wholeness, organization* and *relationships*. They are being urged in opposition to reductionism, cause and effect, and Newtonian mechanistic views. Although originally introduced as an alternative scientific model, the general systems model has appeared to many observers to be a fundamentally different approach to knowledge. Bateson (1972) talks of "new" versus "old" epistemologies in discussing systems concepts. A recent review of family therapy theories contrasted the organismic (active organism) versus mechanistic (reactive organism) *world views* (Ritterman, 1977). In the systems-oriented think tank, the phrase "That's linear thinking" would be voiced with a condescending sneer.

Unfortunately, systems terms, such as wholeness, or circular causality, are easier to talk about in the abstract than they are to apply conceptually to specific problems in biomedical and behavioral science. Many researchers merely throw up their hands when faced with multivariate explanations that force reliance on computer analysis, because of their unfamiliarity with such statistical analyses or because of the difficulties encountered in attempting to simultaneously keep track of the significance of the interacting variables.

Since considerable time will be spent discussing marriage from a systems perspective, some rudimentary notions about such a perspective need first to be developed. Perhaps the best means for accomplishing this goal is to begin with traditional biomedical problems and contrast a typical reductionistic approach with a systems approach. Pay attention especially to what happens when the reductionistic approach reaches its natural limits, and whether systems thinking need really to be thought of as so esoteric.

The traditional reductionistic approach, as already mentioned, deals with explanation in science through a funneling process that reduces each complex phenomenon under observation into a series of less complex reactions. The gene model in genetics, for example, stimulated a long series of brilliant experimental investigations, each of which progressively narrowed down the definition of a gene as the biochemical puzzle slowly unraveled. Even if a number of critical questions must be set aside as this process of narrowing down proceeds (such as, why do cells, in the process of embryological growth, undergo differentiation such that some become nervous tissue, while others develop into muscle), the traditional approach assumes that one can always return to the starting point and begin again with a new series of reductionistic experiments addressing the temporarily bypassed issues.

Advocates of the reductionist approach have argued that, although it may not always present the "whole picture," one can trust in the predictive validity of scientific conclusions arrived at via such an approach. However, argue systems advocates, retrospective assessment often leads to the conclusion that efforts to simplify have inadvertently generated simplistic explanations. The complex organisms under study refuse to behave in the straightforward fashion predicted.

This problem is clearly illustrated in the history of investigation into the etiology of infectious disease. The classical approach had four basic steps: (1) reproduce the infectious disease in a laboratory animal by inoculation with samples from the infected human; (2) prepare bacterial cultures from the infected animal; (3) identify and isolate each organism present; (4) reintroduce the organism to a healthy animal, and observe the re-emergence of disease. Utilizing this elegant experimental design, the pneumococcus might have been identified as the etiological agent *causing* one form of pneumonia. However, when leaving the laboratory to return to the site of original concern, the patient, it is discovered that the pneumococcus does not invariably produce pneumonia. Instead, the emergence of pathology appears to be influenced by a highly complex set of factors, some of which are related to the host environment. The *relationships* among these variables are as important as the variables themselves. Thus, when returning to the in vivo situation, a new concept, that of host-agent interaction, helps immensely in understanding the differential expression of the pathological condition of interest.

The example of pneumonia is particularly cogent in that it relates to one of the triumphs of a reductionistic-mechanistic scientific approach. However, even when the limitations of the traditional reductionistic approach are appreciated, it might nevertheless still be concluded that, because of the inherent complexity of biological and behavioral phenomena, systems approaches are unmanageable. Such a conclusion would be unfortunate and unwarranted. It is perhaps true (as will be seen later in the discussion of issues related to marriage and family) that all appropriate variables cannot be considered simultaneously in the analysis of problems. However, if the *essence* of a systems approach is defined as attention to organization, to the relationship between parts, to concentration on patterned rather than on linear relationships, and to a consideration of events in the context in which they are occurring rather than an isolation of events from their environmental context, then the systems approach may be found both masterable and useful.

The following example from the field of pathology illustrates this point. A pathologist examines a slide of an organ tissue biopsy and is required to answer several questions regarding the type and severity of pathology present. As part of his routine examination of the slide, the pathologist utilizes a series of microscopic magnifications which increase magnification 100, 400, and 1000 fold. At 100 fold magnification, tissue structure is clearly seen, but differences between cells are hard to distinguish. At 1000 fold magnification, characteristics of individual cells allow subtle but necessary distinctions to be made, but tissue structure is no longer apparent. One might be hard pressed to even correctly identify the source of the biopsy if forced to use this magnification alone. The beautiful organizational structure of cells, whose particular pattern distinguishes one type of tissue from another, is lost, in effect violated, by examining the tissue structure at the highest level of magnification available. If the questions being asked relate primarily to the tissue structure itself, then this ability to "see better" has suddenly become a hindrance. For example, if the pathologist wishes to distinguish a hepatoma (liver cancer) from a uterine carcinoma, that judgment can best be made at low magnification. If, on the other hand, he/she wants to judge how primitive (anaplastic) a particular tumor is, high magnification examination of cells will be most helpful.

Patterning, organization, structuring, wholeness—these are the concepts of interest. The pathologist employs these principles as a routine part of his/her work. Although he/she might not call him/herself a systems thinker, clearly he/she has incorporated such an approach or perspective in making judgments.

At the risk of oversimplification, it could be argued that the critical distinction is between the reliance on pattern-recognition versus deductive reasoning as the basic format for making sense out of the world. When things are seen as fitting together in a pattern, rather than being related in a linear cause and effect fashion, then the systems perspective is being employed.

It would, perhaps, be easiest at this point to jump into the fray and deal directly with "systems concepts" of marital function and pathology. Instead, the next section will outline and detail the major tenets of general systems theory to help place in context the individual variations in theoretical concepts about marriage and family that have emerged in the ideas of such family thinkers as Bowen, Minuchin, Jackson and Hill. As shall be seen when exploring these different ideas, they often appear to vary widely, but nevertheless all lay claim to the title "systems theory." Perhaps if the basic tenets of "pure" systems theory can first be sketched, those aspects that have been easily utilized to advance understanding of psychopathology can be better appreciated, and why and with what impact other tenets seem to have fallen by the wayside can be evaluated.

The Core Concepts of Living Systems

1. The concept of organization

The concept of organization is the starting point because, in effect, it is virtually synonymous with the concept of the system. If a *system* is defined as a set of units or elements standing in some consistent relationship or interactional stance with each other, then the first concept is the notion that any system is composed of elements that are *organized* by the consistent nature of the relationship between these elements. Consistency is the key; consistent elements are related to each other in a consistently describable or predictable fashion.

a) WHOLENESS

The first major principle regarding organization is that this collection of consistent elements, once combined, produces an entity that is greater than the additive sums of each of the separate parts. This is the concept of *wholeness*. It is a deceptively straightforward concept, perhaps easily acceptable if only because we have heard about it so often. Yet perhaps of all the concepts introduced by General Systems Theory, it is the most revolutionary. It proposes, in effect, that no system can be adequately understood or totally explained once it has been broken down into its component parts. Furthermore, it proposes that any single element or sub-group of elements within a system cannot be thought of as acting independently. Nor can one state that Element A will occur if Element B is also present (covariance). Instead, an organized entity is proposed in which "the state of each unit is constrained by, conditioned by, or dependent on the state of other units" (Miller, 1965, p. 68).

This concept that the universe can be conceptualized as a series of organized systems has, as one of its most immediate consequences, a direct effect on the language that must be used to "explain" events. Causal models have a strong pull. Both inductive and deductive reasoning is directed toward the discovery of preceding causes; such discovery allows the uncovering of a linear series of events and the placing of them in their proper sequence. The holistic systems approach, on the other hand, forces the use primarily of a *descriptive* language in which the critical elements and the relationships between these elements that comprise the *system* are identified. The fit between these elements helps us greatly in understanding what is observed, but explanatory statements that are the usual goal of scientific inquiry are difficult. Marriages are therefore defined as bona fide systems insofar as they are composed of consistent elements (husband and wife) and consistent relationships, but the use of systems concepts should be avoided if the goal is to explain why, for example, factors in Mrs. B's marriage are causing her clinical depression.

b) BOUNDARIES

It is very easy to give lip service to these "organismic" concepts in systems thinking. Organization, wholeness, relationship of parts, and the phenomenal intricacy and beauty of biological organisms are easily appreciated. But the concept of a marriage as a system may be more troublesome than it appears at first glance. One of the difficulties lies in another major concept associated with organization, that of *boundaries*. If systems are consistent elements relating in a consistent fashion, then they are also elements bounded by the nature of the relationship between them. Sometimes, as shall be seen, the bounding takes place in a spatial context, in other instances bounding occurs in a time context, but the clarity of the boundary that emerges is directly proportional to the clarity of pattern determined by relationships.

When the relationship of elements in space is so highly patterned that a physical boundary can be easily identified, then the system identified can be physically perceived (seen, felt). A single cell, or an animal, is such an example. Boundaries are easily identifiable. The cell membrane or the animal's skin clearly separates or delimits the boundaries of the system. The concept of a marital system obviously has no such clear-cut boundaries, but notions of organization demand that they be described. These boundaries can be represented in the form of systems diagrams, and the use of a language derived from cellular biology is easy to apply. The boundary between a marriage or a family and its surrounding environment is therefore frequently described in terms of its *permeability* (the relative ease or difficulty outside persons or elements experience in moving into and outside of the marital system), which implies a physical property analogous to that of the cell membrane (see Figure 1).

It is relatively easy in looking at these diagrams to conjure up images of a husband and wife huddled behind double brick walls, in a house with barred windows and "beware of dog" signs liberally sprinkled across the front lawn. But this is clearly not what is intended. Instead, permeability is an abstract concept useful in envisioning a marital relationship as a separate organized entity.

The concept of boundaries seems particularly critical for understanding living systems, a point Skynner (1976) makes with dramatic clarity. Concentrating upon the concept of boundary as a structure that facilitates or impedes the passage of materials between the organism and its surrounding environment, he illustrates its critical importance:

> Failure of the boundary to restrict exchange across it leads to a loss of difference between the living thing and its surroundings, of its separate identity; instead, there develops an identity of inside and outside, one meaning of death. Too impermeable a boundary, preventing any exchange, brings another form of death, the fixed and stained tissue we see beneath the microscope (p. 5).

FIGURE 1. Boundary Permeability in the Marital System

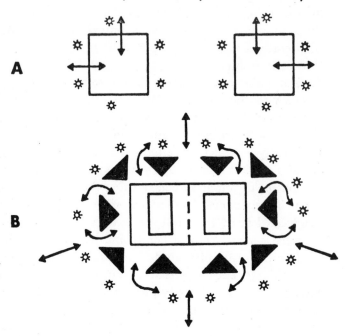

Boundary permeability, the ability to move in and out of the structural exterior of the system, obviously varies greatly from individual to individual. Capacity for intimacy and closeness are terms that are used to describe the relative permeability of individual-level boundaries. However, the marital system also has boundaries, and its permeability characteristics are not a simple distillation of the relative openness of husband and wife as individuals. In the marriage illustrated above, each spouse (level A) is a relatively open individual and interpersonal access is straightforward. Their marital system (level B), however, is surrounded by a more complex boundary structure (triangles). A friend or acquaintance, knowing the husband or wife to be an open person, easy to relate to, might approach the individual anticipating easy access, only to find that if the individual is now a marital spouse, openness has been replaced by relative impermeability. The subjective feeling is that one is now relating to the marriage. Many close individual friendships are stressed to the breaking point following marriage when these new and at first confusing boundaries emerge around the fledgling marital system.

c) HIERARCHIES

The third principle related to organization that will be particularly useful is that of *hierarchical* organization. The notion here is that systems are themselves organized one to another according to a series of hierarchical levels, often analogized to a series of Chinese boxes (see Figure 2). Each system is envisioned as composed of component subsystems of smaller scale, and, in turn, as being a component part of a larger suprasystem. Once again, the emphasis is on a notion of the universe organized along ordered and highly structured lines, with clearly identifiably differential levels of complexity that relate in logical fashion one to another. Marriages would therefore be conceptualized as comprising two individual subsystems, husband and wife, and being, in turn, a subsystem of the family system. Families, in turn, are subsystems of a community system, and so on, as Chinese boxes are placed one inside another.

However, a particular system may be simultaneously affiliated or connected to multiple suprasystems. Therefore, a husband/father is a member of both a marital system and a family system, but at the same time he is a member of a corporate system, a community system, etc. Concentric circles replace Chinese boxes when this point is being made (see Figure 3).

2. *The concept of control*

The second major tenet in systems theory relates to concepts of control, embodied in the characterization of the living system as a *dynamic steady state*. Much has been made of the emphasis in systems theory on balance and stabilization within systems. Often this is mistakenly translated as rigidity—a sort of forced and inflexible patterning of behavior. On the contrary, the concept of control introduced by systems theory allows the development of highly complex, fluid, interactional models that increase options rather than diminish them. It would be unfortunate to misconstrue these concepts and imply that systems behavior is automated behavior, which, in humanistic terms particularly, implies automatic rather than responsive behavior. Instead, control suggests an image of elements in constant dynamic interaction, but able to relate meaningfully to each other because of an intricate and delicate series of available mechanisms that, first, keep them within an acceptable set of limits and, second, permit adaptation to occur. It is this second point particularly which is often overlooked. Controlled adaptation, as shall be seen, is the key to meaningful change. Controlled adaptation also appears critical to the

FIGURE 2. Hierarchical Organization in a Complex System

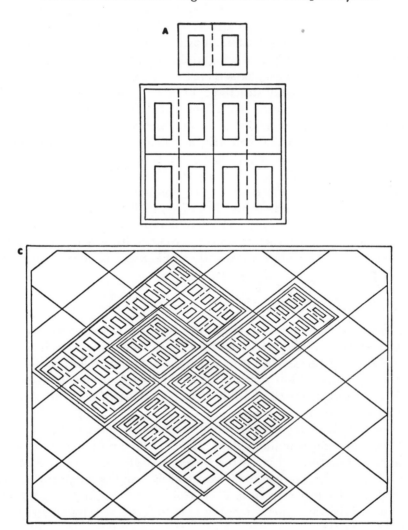

FIGURE 3. Multiple Subsystem membership

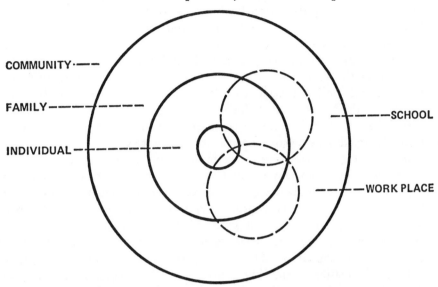

Systems, especially social systems, characteristically have considerable overlap. The same individual is simultaneously a member of multiple systems, including marital, family, work, educational and community-based systems. The individual's personality and behavioral characteristics may differ dramatically from one system to another. For example, assertive behavior at work does not necessarily predict assertive behavior within the marriage.

(Figure from Skynner, A. C. R., *Systems of Family and Marital Psychotherapy.* New York: Brunner/Mazel, 1976, p. 7)

issues of growth and development that are so central to living versus non-living systems. Controlled growth leads to differentiation and development of tissues, organs, and individuals. Uncontrolled growth, cancer, kills the living system.

a) HOMEOSTASIS

What concepts of control have proven most useful? To draw upon the notion of a living system as a steady state, the concept of balance or *homeostasis* must first be considered. The term homeostasis was first introduced by Walter Cannon (1939), the physiologist, to describe a set of mechanisms within the neuroendocrine system whose function appeared to be the maintenance of a constancy of the internal environment of the organism. Hormonal and autonomic nervous system regulation was found to be organized in such a way as to control critical biological functions, such as electrolyte concentration, blood pressure and blood flow, acid-base balance, temperature, water content, and so on, keeping these functions within acceptable biological ranges. Growing sophistication over the years has not only helped to flesh out understanding of how the biological organism regulates its internal environment, but has also led to the discovery that these mechanisms play a significant part in the mediation of the organism's responses to its natural or social environment. Characteristic mechanisms for adaptation to stress, a cornerstone of psychosomatic medicine, are an example of this expanding focus.

The concept of homeostasis and the corollary notions of positive and negative feedback loops have been inventively adapted by Jackson and his colleagues in their theoretical notions of family homeostasis. Jackson (1957, 1965) proposed that a series of mechanisms can be identified whose primary purpose is the maintenance of an acceptable behavioral balance within the family. The notion is that families tend to establish a behavioral balance or stability and to resist any change from that predetermined level of stability. Events causing a state of imbalance may occur related to behavior generated either within or outside of the marriage. In either case, emergence of the state of imbalance activates a set of built-in mechanisms that ultimately act to restore the homeostatic balance of the family. Although anecdotal evidence from clinical situations provides much of the evidence that family homeostasis does, in fact, exist, a growing body of research data also exists that seems supportive of such a concept.

To cite two recent examples, Minuchin and his colleagues (1975) have demonstrated striking patterns of free fatty acid production (a stress-response measure) in family members during conjoint interviews. These coordinated responses, Minuchin thinks, are indicative of a family-level pattern of response to stress, a pattern that is being demonstrated on a biological level.

On a behavioral level, Reiss (1977) and his colleagues, in their studies of multiple family therapy and discussion groups, point to a striking stability of family-level behavioral measures, such as speech interaction rates, as examples of regulatory mechanisms being expressed at a family level. Furthermore, family-level stability is not merely an additive reflection of individual-level stability. Individuals within the family might vary markedly from session to session, but their fluctuations are balanced by the performance rates of other members within the same family.

Lastly, the stability occurs most strikingly in terms of the family's *relative* activity rate as compared with other families in the same group. Speech rates for the group as a whole might vary from session to session, but high interaction families remain high, and low interaction families remain low, seemingly adjusting their activity rates to fit an acceptable range in relation to the social environment in which they are interacting.

Nevertheless, at this point in time, the conviction that homeostasis is a useful concept when applied to behavioral systems rests primarily on a multitude of clinical experiences. For example, a sudden flare-up of adolescent promiscuous behavior is observed following the first session in which two parents have talked openly and directly to each other; or a husband is observed surreptitiously giving vitamin pills to his children the week after his wife, for the first time, confesses her feeling that he has been right concerning his vituperative lectures about the worthlessness of vitamins in the face of American dietary habits.

b) FEEDBACK

Now what about the mechanisms that contribute to this self-regulatory process within the marriage or family? Here concepts drawn from cybernetics, particularly the notion of *servomechanisms,* are most appropriate (Wiener, 1962). Time and again, in discussions of the marital system, reference is made to thermostats, pressure gauges, gating mechanisms and the like. Central to each of these illustrations is the notion of the *feedback loop.* Instead of assuming that two events can only be related in a cause and effect fashion, two events can in certain circumstances be related in a circular fashion, characterized as either a positive or negative feedback loop.

In the positive feedback loop an increase in any component part of the loop will, in turn, increase the next event in the circular sequence. This is called a deviation-amplifying situation (Maruyama, 1963) and is primarily a self-destruction mechanism. Whether a deviation is in a positive or negative, higher or lower direction, the positive feedback loop sets up a runaway situation that eventually drives the system beyond the limits or range within which it can function.

The negative feedback loop, in contrast, establishes a balance between the deviations of different events within the loop. The classical physiological example is the pituitary-endocrine gland axis controlling hormonal levels in the body. As the hormone product of one component part of the axis increases, the hormonal product at the other end decreases and vice versa. In the marital system, a situation might exist in which an alcoholic husband and non-alcoholic wife engage in a repetitive sequence of behaviors that control actual level of alcohol consumed. Each time the husband decreases his alcohol intake, behavior on the wife's part, such as stocking the liquor cabinet or becoming increasingly argumentative, increases the likelihood of her husband's drinking. Conversely, an increase in the husband's drinking might be followed by his wife's suggestion that they return to a therapy group, or threats to leave him, or hiding money with which to buy alcohol.

The negative feedback loop has become a bread and butter concept for family systems theorists. It is now felt to be a critical component for normal stabilization of marriages. This aspect of cybernetic regulation is also felt to contribute heavily to the maintenance of chronic pathological patterns of behavior in marital systems.

3. *The concept of energy*

Any model that deals with living organisms must have in mind some concept of energy. Although this concept of energy may be peripheral to the issues to which the model is directed, at some point some formulation of what keeps the whole thing going is needed—where is the energy that drives the processes, that keeps the model functional? Systems models are not exempt from this requirement. However, it has not been easy to deal with this issue as regards living systems.

At a first level of explanation, the task is relatively simple. If energy is defined merely as the ability to do work, the traditional definition in physics, then the task is, of course, straightforward. Not only is it apparent that living systems require energy, but specific types of matter/energy, such as heat, light, essential nutrients and water, can be designated. Intimate knowledge of the biochemical pathways of intermediary metabolism even suggests the specific transformations that occur within living systems as matter is converted into energy and vice versa.

However, the systems model relies heavily on a second, more complex concept of energy, the concept of *entropy* (and its corollary, *negentropy*). Entropy is a principal concept in thermodynamics; it is the law of the degradation of energy. This law states that, over time, because heat energy cannot be converted into an equivalent amount of work, there will be a gradual degradational loss of energy in a particular system. As Miller (1965) tells us, "these changes, expressed statistically, constituted passing of the system from ordered arrangement into more chaotic or random distribution. The disorder, disorganization, lack of patterning, or randomness of organization of the system is known as its *'entropy'*" (p. 60).

But living systems may, over time, manifest exactly the opposite statistical trend. In other words, living systems show a tendency towards increased patterning, increased degree of organization, more and more complex structuring. The thermodynamic model was incapable of explaining such phenomena, and therefore relegated them to the realm of vitalism (a quasi-religious term). Systems theory returned the state of affairs to the realm of science by introducing the concept of *negentropy*. By distinguishing between open and closed systems, it can be seen that in living systems (all of which are open systems) energy can be freely transported into and out of the system, and a tendency toward increased patterning (organization), rather than increased randomness, can be supported—it has a potential source of energy.

But, the concept of negentropy is hardly a model of energy equivalent to, for example, caloric energy. Rather, it is a principle or rule that describes a tendency for the way energy and matter interact in living systems. Nevertheless, it is a critical concept, because it is the heart of the whole notion of the living system, the overriding principle that helps to explain what keeps the whole thing going. It is problematic in the sense that it is hardly an explanatory model, merely a descriptive one. It doesn't explain why growth and development occur, for example, but merely directs attention to a descriptive fact that growth and development lead to a state of greater patterning and a reduction of randomness within the organism.

Now another analogy, one which is most critical for systems concepts of marriage. This is the concept of *information*, which is defined as, in essence, the equivalent of negentropy. This means that information is a type of energy that leads to a reduction in the level of uncertainty within the system. Rapoport (1953) helps to bridge the gap between the original notions of thermodynamic energy and entropy, and this new notion of information or negentropy in the following way: Originally, he points out, "entropy was expressed in terms of the heat and temperature of the system." When energy is discussed in terms of kinetics, heat and temperature are connected with the movement of molecules in the system, and entropy becomes

> . . . a measure of the *probability* that the velocities of the molecules and other variables of the system are distributed in a certain way. The reason the entropy of a system is greatest when its temperature is constant throughout is because this distribution of temperatures is the *most probable*. Increase in entropy was thus interpreted as the passage of a system from less probable to more probable states (p. 158).

Once the notion of probability is introduced, then the concept of information falls readily into place, for information is directly related to the probability of occurrence of a particular event. The more probable the occurrence of the event, the less information connected with its occurrence.

Although information is still a descriptive concept, it has proven to be a phenomenally powerful one. Information, as a concept, helps in understanding how living systems can achieve the magnitude of complexity they have demonstrated. Whether dealing with human language or the genetic code incorporated in the DNA molecule, the magnitude of the multiplier effect that occurs when information is appropriately and efficiently packaged is striking. This concept has been powerful enough to convince some theorists that it is, in and of itself, sufficient to support a model of marriage and marital disorders.

The notion of communication, the process by which information is either changed from one state to another or moved from one point to another point in space is mentioned here only briefly and will be dealt with more fully when discussing the communications theorists.

In the discussion of the concepts of organization and control mechanisms, analogies between family systems and biological phenomena have been proposed. Communication, however, draws analogies from the information sciences, rather than the biological sciences. A system such as a marriage or family is viewed as an information-processing machine, and terminology that includes information bits, programs of behavior, and decoding failure is used to convey an image of marriage as a high-class computer (or perhaps a low-class computer).

4. *The dimensions of time and space*

Three major conceptual areas which are the building blocks of systems theory have been identified, and the critical concepts within each have been discussed to present a rounded picture of "pure" general systems theory. In order to complete the picture, two *dimensions* within which each of our theoretical concepts operate must be considered. These are the dimension of *space* and the dimension of *time*. Although each of these dimensions is so straightforward as to require little further explanation, it is most important to keep in mind the simultaneous existence of both dimensions. Although relatively easy to do in a theoretical discussion, it is far more difficult to deal simultaneously with both dimensions during clinical discussions.

Each of the conceptual areas—organization, control, and energy—takes on different qualities when discussed from the point of view of a spatial versus a temporal dimension. For example, organization or patterning observed along a spatial dimension is called *structure*. Patterning along a temporal dimension, on the other hand, is referred to as *process* or *function*. The pathologist, when viewing his slides at three different magnifications, had essentially frozen the time dimension, and was making his "systems judgments" based entirely on the spatial organization he observed. A psychoanalyst, on the other hand, pays very little attention to the physical space within which he and the patient operate, concentrating instead almost purely on the temporal arrangement of verbal production.

The therapist is obviously in the most advantageous position when observations can be made in a space/time continuum. But often, in the overwhelming mass of data with which he/she is presented, he/she finds him/herself inexorably drawn toward a choice of one or the other. For example, the therapist might be selectively attentive to the communicational patterning implicit in repetitive seating arrangements demonstrated by a family or the sequential order of speech during a conjoint interview, but might contend he/she could not process both simultaneously.

It will, nevertheless, be most important, when reviewing different systems theories of marriage, not only to keep in mind which dimensions the theorist uses, but also to ascertain what is given up by an emphasis on one dimension versus another. The next section will present three versions of systems theory conceptualizations of marital disorders and a brief review of relevant sociological theory. The particular versions chosen are meant to be representative of the most popular "systems" approaches currently being used by marital therapists. Although far from exhaustive, they present a clear picture of the diversity of ideas and emphases that all lay claim to being systems theoretical perspectives on marriage and marriage disorders.

SYSTEMS THEORY OF MARRIAGE: FOUR THEORIES

Scientific models serve a number of important functions. Included among these are the ability to stimulate theory building and the ability to focus attention on interesting questions (hypothesis generation). In clinical work they serve three additional functions of critical importance.

First, they organize the search for data. In the usual clinical situation the clinician is subjected to an information input of staggering proportions. These data must be given priority and reduced in a fashion that allows the clinician to generate meaningful clinical hypotheses. A good clinical model not only suggests such a priority, but also suggests a perceptual stance for the clinician to take in order to maximize the quality of data available to him.

Second, a theoretical model, in order to be useful in a clinical setting, must include a conceptualization of pathology. Although norms and normal variability are of relevance and importance, clinicians continue to live and die based on their ability to distinguish maladjustment from adjustment. It is therefore critical that they have available to them a set of suggested criteria against which selectively filtered data can be matched and adjudged acceptable or unacceptable.

And lastly, any clinical model worth its salt will also provide a blueprint for intervention. This blueprint usually includes at least two parts—a model suggesting why and how behavioral change occurs, and a suggested role for the clinician in the process of change.

Concepts of intervention based on the general systems model will be discussed in a companion chapter. This chapter will be concentrating primarily on what the general systems model suggests regarding how to organize data collection and to conceptualize pathology.

Version 1: Mental Research Institute and Communication Theory

Beginning with the seminal work examining communication patterns in families containing schizophrenic members, a multidisciplinary group at the Mental Research Institute (MRI) in Palo Alto has for the past 20 years been developing and refining theoretical concepts of marriage and family interaction based on communication theory. Because this work has played such a crucial part in the historical development of the family therapy movement, it is perhaps difficult at this point in time to place it in its proper perspective. A recent anthology (Sluzki and Ransom, 1976) and a major conference* have been organized around exactly such a critical review. By comparison, this discussion will obviously be only skimming the surface, highlighting the central organizing concepts and principles of this theoretical approach to families.

---

* "Beyond the Double Bind: Communication and Family Systems, Theories, and Techniques with Schizophrenics," a conference held on March 3-4, 1977 in New York City which included presentations by Gregory Bateson, Murray Bowen, Jay Haley, Albert Scheflen, John Weakland, Carl Whitaker and Lyman Wynne. Proceedings to be published by Brunner/Mazel, Inc., in 1978.

Major contributors to the MRI model have included the late Don Jackson, Gregory Bateson, Paul Watzlawick, James Weakland, Carlos Sluzki, and Jay Haley. As a group, they have been referred to as the "systems purists" in the family field (Beels and Ferber, 1969). This group, more than any other clinical group in the marital or family field, has adhered firmly to the tenet that the world is organized as a series of systems. Although the individual would certainly be acknowledged as a bona fide system in its own right, it is given no special priority over any other system. It makes just as much sense, this group would feel, to view a marriage or a family as the critical organizational unit as it does to concentrate efforts on the individual. The physical properties that obviously delimit the individual from the rest of the world, properties which are not paralleled by a marriage or a family, should not, they would argue, require treating the individual with any special reverence. In fact, in their more strident moments, these theorists might propose that the individual is a diversion, a biological entity to be sure, but a distraction if one's primary interest is an examination of behavior. This dramatic stance stems rather logically from this group's heavy reliance on cybernetics and communication theory.

To briefly recapitulate their argument: They start with an assumption which they call "the black box model" (Watzlawick, Beavin and Jackson, 1967). Fashioned after the problem faced by a demolitions expert having to defuse a bomb, or a cipher expert having to unravel the mysteries of a code transmitter, this model proposes that the workings of such a "black box" can be best described by delineating the rules that govern its functions. By paying strict attention to inputs and outputs, and the equations that describe the consistent relationships between these inputs and outputs, the black box expert can discover all he needs to know about how the box "works." Since he has no choice in such a situation (the bomb might explode or the cipher transmitter might be wired to self destruct if tampered with physically), it is reassuring to him that he can derive enough information from the above approach to make his critical decisions.

Now, how does such an argument apply to human behavior? To start with the individual for the moment, the extension of the black box model implies that the internal workings of the machine (in this case those thoughts and feelings that might be going on within the black box) are merely a distraction from the far more useful data regarding inputs and outputs (in this case communicational input and output). Speculations about fantasy life, motivation, or structural organization of the mind are interesting intellectual exercises, but merely confusing and perhaps down-right destructive if one's goal is to describe and understand the rules that govern human behavior.

"While it is true that these relations [intrapsychic factors] may permit inferences into what 'really' goes on inside the box, this knowledge is not essential for the study of the function of the device in the greater system of which it is a part" (Watzlawick et al., 1967, pp. 43-44). When one has such goals, trust is placed in communicational inputs and outputs, and those theories that can direct us toward a series of rules governing com-munication are used. Those theories, according to this group, include cybernetic theory, games theory, epistemology, and, of course, the more general principles of systems theory.

The same focus applies when considering marriage and marital dis-orders. Once again, the inner workings of the machine are ignored (in sharp contrast to the psychoanalytic view of the marital relationship as discussed in Chapter II), and instead all efforts are toward the study of communicational inputs and outputs. Thus marriage and the under-standing of marital disorders will be approached primarily from the perspective of communication theory. The model can be summarized as follows:

The first axiom is: "There is no such thing as non-behavior or, to put it even more simply: one cannot not *behave*" (Watzlawick et al., 1967, p. 48). If it is accepted that all behavior in an interactional situation has message value, is communication, it follows that no matter how one may try, one cannot not *communicate*.

Second, the communication which does occur can, for the purposes of study, be divided into the following categories: syntax, semantics and pragmatics.* Syntax centers on the ways in which information is trans-mitted. Such concepts as the encoding of information, channels of com-munication, the capacity, variability, noise, and redundancy inherent in the communicational transmitting system and the patterning of speech over time are concepts derived from information theory that are applied to this particular aspect of the study of communication. For marriages, in this area such qualities as who-to-whom speech, percentage of speak-ing time (dominance over the channels of communication), parsimony

---

* Watzlawick, Beavin and Jackson (1967) indicate their indebtedness to Charles W. Morris (1938) for this categorical approach to the study of communication, and to Ralph Carnap (1942) for his discussion of its applicability to semiotics. This earlier work provided the firm theoretical grounding for the application of the syntax-seman-tics-pragmatics distinctions to human communication.

of speech, and ratio of information to noise in marital communication are considered.

The second category is the area of *semantics* or the meaning of the communicational act. Here, the ability of the receiver to understand the communication transmitted is of particular interest. In marriages, the clarity of language, the existence of shared private communicational systems (such as code words of rich symbolic meaning or private gestures), and concordance versus confusion of communication are all of interest.

The third category is what has been called the *pragmatic* aspect of communication. Pragmatics refers to the behavioral effects of communication. For example, is a message acknowledged or disavowed? Does marital communication serve a mutually supportive function for both spouses, or is it a source of behavioral conflict? For the MRI group the terms communication and behavior are used synonymously, and therefore attention to the pragmatic aspect of communication within marriage can be used virtually *exclusively* to describe and define the rules of behavior that exist within a particular marriage.

In addition to these three aspects of communication (syntax, semantics, pragmatics), a distinction can also be made between the "report" aspect of a particular communicational act and its "command" aspect. The distinction here is between the conveying of information (the report aspect) versus those statements or aspects of statements that address the *relationship* between the communicants (the command aspect). Since obviously the study of marriage deals with an interactional communicational system, it must be recognized that the two partners in the marriage must not only send information back and forth, but must also, through communication, define the nature of their relationship to each other.

At a simple level, the command aspect of a particular communicational act might be that part of the communication which defines for the listener whether to label the information about to be received as critically important or relatively trivial. In an ongoing relationship, however, each communicational act might also contain a command function that introduces or reinforces a more complex series of statements defining the relationship between husband and wife. For example, consider the following sequence of interactions.

A husband and wife are seated at the dinner table. The wife is relating the events of her day, including the people she has talked to and places she has visited. Her husband reads the newspaper and emits occasional grunts. After 20 minutes of such "conversation" his wife says, "You haven't heard a thing I have said, have you?" He denies this accusation vigorously, and repeats, with some accuracy, the last item she has just mentioned to him. She then continues her recitation as his eyes return to his newspaper article.

Concentrating only on the command aspects of this communicational sequence, several conclusions could be drawn about the nature of this marital relationship. For starters, the wife in this instance gives her husband one command message, that she is engaged in an information exchange of rather trivial magnitude, while she is relating the events of the day, but then a second command message retrospectively 20 minutes later. Although this second command message indicates that the sequence which has just transpired is more important than originally met the eye because it is symbolic of his lack of attentiveness to her, she accepts a response from him that hardly addresses the issue at hand. His ability to have somehow managed to track her last statement at the same time he was engrossed in the newspaper is hardly evidence that his receiver was properly tuned to either the channel or volume she retrospectively indicated was appropriate. Her willingness to accept such a response from her husband might, in fact, reinforce his tendency to treat her verbal communication as trivial. One such exchange might pass by the boards without comment. But if a series of exchanges, very similar in form, were a nightly occurrence in this marriage, then it might be concluded that a pattern of communication existed within this marriage that had particular and describable dimensions.

Such a pattern of communication is felt to reflect a *rule* about the nature of the marital relationship. Jackson (1965), in particular, has emphasized the importance of such rules as a useful concept in defining the nature of the marital relationship. His view of the early phase of marriage, for example, is of a kind of a bargaining game in which two people work out the rules that will subsequently govern the nature of their relationship to each other. Whether the people involved are consciously aware of the fact that such a process is occurring is, in his view, irrelevant. What is important is that observation of behavior between people during courtship and early marriage demonstrates that such bargaining does go on and, furthermore, demonstrates that it occurs within the context of communication.

The term "marital quid pro quo" is Jackson's term for the initial bargain that is struck between husband and wife. It can be thought of as the basis upon which the marriage contract will be written. Such a contract, if written in broad and flexible strokes, might serve the couple well for many years to come. A narrowly or too rigidly defined quid pro quo, on the other hand, might place the couple at risk in the face of stresses or strains that require change in the communicational patterns. Although the notion of the marital quid pro quo is analogous to the behaviorist's notion of a marital "contract," quid pro quo often is applied to an abstracted condensation of interactional behavior rather than a direct analysis of concrete aspects of behavior.

A heavy reliance in this theoretical approach on notions drawn from cybernetics has already been noted. In the section on basic concepts of general systems theory, Jackson's contributions to the concepts of control and homeostasis were discussed. In the MRI model of marriage these concepts are developed within a communications framework. If feedback loops are assumed to be a central mechanism for achieving a homeostatic steady state within a marital system, then one assumes these feedback loops will be found in specific communicational patterns. For example, consider the following clinical situation described by Watzlawick et al. (1967):

> Suppose a couple have a marital problem to which he contributes passive withdrawal while her 50% is nagging criticism. In explaining their frustrations, the husband will state that withdrawal is his only *defense against* her nagging, while she will label this explanation gross and willful distortion of what "really" happens in their marriage: namely, that she is critical of him *because* of his passivity. Stripped of all ephemeral and fortuitous elements, their fights consist in a monotonous exchange of the messages, "I will withdraw because you nag" and "I nag because you withdraw" (p. 56).

They also provide a diagrammatic depiction of this sequence of communicational acts (see Figure 4), clearly a diagram of a steady state, homeostatic situation, based strictly on communication.

If the basic argument of the MRI model is accepted up to this point, then it follows naturally that pathological behavior, including marital psychopathology, can be described adequately and sufficiently in communicational terms. Pathological behavior is synonomous with pathological communication. What features make a particular communicational act "pathological"? It is beyond the scope of this chapter to present the argument in any exhaustive detail, but several critical concepts can be introduced as anchor points.

(1) First, the concept of *sequencing* or *patterning* of communication

FIGURE 4

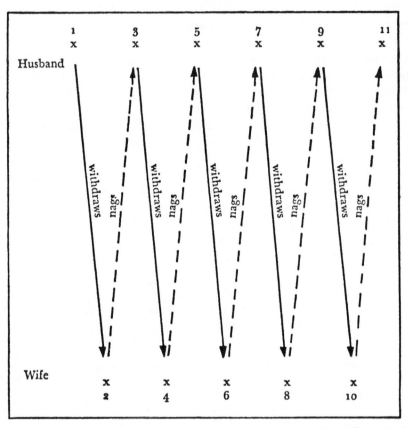

From: Watzlawick, P., Beavin, J. H., and Jackson, D. D., *Pragmatics of Human Communication.* Norton, New York, 1967.

must be considered. It is unlikely that a single act of communication, by itself, can be judged pathological or nonpathological. Instead, that judgment emerges from an examination of a series of communications and the nature of their stochastic or patterned qualities. At the risk of over-simplification, it can be said that there are two basic choices to make in the search for patterns.

The first is to concentrate on the syntactical and semantic qualities of the pattern of communication and determine the degree of clarity and confusion in the communicational sequence under examination. Such an approach suggests concentrating on the content of speech, an approach perhaps best exemplified by the landmark studies of Wynne and Singer (1963). These investigators compared families with schizophrenic, delinquent, and normal children and used as their discriminating variables such aspects of communication as the clarity of meaning in verbal exchanges. A second approach is to concentrate on the pragmatic aspects of the marital pattern of communication. Here the relationship between transmitter and receiver is of particular interest. Discriminating variables for defining communication as pathological then center around clarity not of content, but of the command aspect of communication. In a sequence of communicational acts, each message transmitted can meet one of three alternative fates at the hands of the receiver. It can be accepted, rejected, or, as a potentially more ominous option, disqualified. This last option is a style of communication in which a person invalidates either his own or the other person's communications. Self-contradictions, inconsistencies, subject switches, and systematic misunderstandings are suggested examples that lead to such a disqualification of communication.

(2) A second major concept related to pathological communication is the notion of paradox and paradoxical communication. A paradoxical communication is one which, simply put, moves in two opposite and internally inconsistent directions at the same time. It is surely a feature of everyday life, and in moderate doses is quite manageable. When, however, marital or family communication patterns take on paradoxical features at critical times in the life of the marriage or family, then trouble is just around the corner. If, for example, at times of crisis, or as a characteristic component of family problem-solving, or as a major model related to child rearing, the family resorts to paradoxical communication, then the situation, according to the MRI model, becomes rapidly pathological.

A type of paradoxical communication that has been specifically implicated as an etiological factor in schizophrenia is the *double bind*. The "double bind" refers to a communicational situation in which two logically inconsistent messages are simultaneously communicated, and there is also a third message, an injunction against commenting about this inconsistency.

A typical example given of a double bind communication might be a greeting ritual between a schizophrenic son and his mother who has come to visit him at a psychiatric hospital. As she comes toward him he moves to kiss her but she pulls away at the last moment. When he feels her pulling away from him and turning the side of her face toward him, he drops his arms, looking puzzled. At which point his mother says, accus-

ingly, "Aren't you happy to see me?" Mother has sent two logically inconsistent messages to her son, the physical message implying a desire not to
be embraced, and the verbal message chiding her son for his lack of
affection. In addition there is the implicit message that he is not to comment on this inconsistency, nor is he allowed to escape the field (his
emotional bonds to his mother prevent him from doing so).

Although there is currently some controversy about the role of this
type of communicational pattern in the etiology of schizophrenia, it
should be evident that it is a frequent pattern of communication in marriages and families. It is being underscored here, however, because of its
historical role in the development of the communication theory of marriage espoused by the Palo Alto Group (see Sluzki and Ransom, 1976,
for a complete discussion of the double bind theory).

(3) A third concept addresses symptom formation; it is an attempt to
conceptualize symptomatic behavior in communicational terms. In contrast to the psychoanalytic concept of symptom formation as an attempt
at conflict resolution (see Meissner, Chapter II), or the behaviorist notion
of symptoms as learned behavior (see Weiss, Chapter IV), systems-com-
municational theorists are prone to treat the symptom as a nonverbal
communicational message. Although the message may be confined to the
symptomatic individual alone (that is, a statement being made by that
individual via the symptom chosen), it is also proposed that the symptom
may be expressing a communicational message for the system as a whole.
Thus depression in one spouse may be expressing a message of marital
depression. Or schizophrenic behavior in one child of a family may be
reflective of a psychotic communication with the family system as a
whole (Bateson et al., 1956).

Version 2: Minuchin and Structural Family Theory

Minuchin's elegant theory of marriage and the family, as well as
the strikingly differentiated style of therapy that derives from this theory,
is based on a series of clearly defined premises, and equally clearly defined
conceptual priorities. What emerges is a model that is straightforward
and easy to comprehend, whether or not one agrees with its conclusions
(Minuchin, 1974).

The model is based on three major assumptions. The first assumption
states that man is not the master of his own fate. As Minuchin puts it,
the individual operates within a social context and it is the context
that defines the constraints within which individual behavior must exist.

An individual's psychic life, Minuchin contends, is "not entirely an internal process." Instead, there is a never-ending interaction between the individual and his context which mutually affect and influence each other over time. The second major assumption is that this social context can be seen as having a structure. The third major assumption is that some structures are good and some structures are bad. This is an assumption about the existence of structural pathology.

The structure of the marriage is evident if three dimensions are examined: (1) organizational characteristics (membership, systems versus subsystems, and boundaries); (2) the patterning of transactions over time as a measure of the internal development of the system; and (3) the system's response to stress.

What does Minuchin mean by each of these dimensions? Consider first the *organizational* dimension. Minuchin places heavy emphasis on what, within a systems theory, could be called the concept of level. For him, the marital dyad is best conceptualized as a subsystem within the family, a subsystem which in turn is composed of two individual subsystems (husband and wife). In like fashion, he would divide the family system into parental and childhood subsystems. But his point of departure from "pure" systems theory is his belief that the marital subsystem is not merely something that exists whenever two people decide to get married. It is, in effect, an *inherent* and necessary part of the family system. This is because the marital system is defined not only in terms of membership, but also in terms of function.

What about boundaries? Once again, Minuchin utilizes a concept from pure systems theory. The boundaries of a particular system are "the rules defining who participates, and how" (1974, p. 53). The function of boundaries is "to protect the differentiation of the system. Every family subsystem has specific functions and makes specific demands on its members; and the development of interpersonal skills achieved in these subsystems is predicated on the subsystem's freedom from interference by other subsystems" (1974, p. 53). A central notion to Minuchin's thinking is that marriages, in order to grow and prosper, must have clear boundaries. Clear boundaries insure that husband and wife are clearly enough defined as a separate system to be protected from interference by competing subsystems, such as in-laws or children. [Bob and Alice F., the hypothetical couple in the introductory section (see page 298), were asked by Minuchin to discuss their children, a logical part of his assessment interview used to determine the clarity of boundary between the parental and childhood subsystems within the family.] At the same time, boundaries must not be so rigid as to prevent interaction between the marital subsystem and the outside world, or between husband or wife as individuals within their separate subsystems, such as their work systems.

Clarity of boundaries therefore becomes a major parameter in evaluating the marriage's level of functioning. Minuchin identifies three general types of boundaries: disengaged, enmeshed, and clear boundaries, which he postulates exist on a continuum. Although he states that these terms do not refer to a qualitative difference between functional and dysfunctional types of boundaries, but rather to a transactional style or preference for a certain type of interaction, his theory implies that clarity of boundaries certainly makes it easier for a marriage to survive and thrive.

As already mentioned, the priority of boundaries is also important insofar as it subsidizes the functional capacity of the inherent or generic needs of any social system. For the marriage, the relative clarity or lack of clarity in boundaries might significantly influence the extent to which parents can exercise appropriate authority in dealing with their children, or the extent to which husband and wife can agree on a functional distribution of decision-making capacities within the marriage. The oft repeated story of the wife who attributes the stability of her marriage to the fact that her husband makes all important decisions (such as who should be elected President and what our stance should be in the SALT negotiations), while she handles the minor things (where they should live, where they should go on vacation, and what they should spend their money on) would be explained in structural theory utilizing the language of functional versus dysfunctional boundaries rather than a more traditional explanation utilizing the language of roles.

The second structural dimension Minuchin highlights is the *patterning of transactions*. Although this dimension is analogous in many respects to the notions of homeostasis and cybernetic control postulated by the MRI model of marriage, it is more diffuse in the data base it uses. Whereas the MRI model directs our attention to specific communicational acts, Minuchin's concept of patterned transactions uses a wider data base. Of particular importance is his sensitivity to the relationship between context and behavior. Transactions are not merely communicational acts between transmitters and receivers; they also include intricate interrelationships between environmental contexts and individual behavior.

Because patterned transactions are, in this model, conceptualized more in spatial than temporal terms, it is the relationship between different variables in space, rather than the sequential order of their occurrence, that becomes the critical variable on which Minuchin relies to make his judgments. This may be an overstatement of the case, since clearly Minuchin uses the back and forth sequence of husband and wife interactions to identify repetitive patterns. But these sequences are used to determine the juxtaposition of different functional roles within the transaction. These juxtapositions, first between context and behavior and second between husband and wife, allow one to make statements about the transactional structure within the marriage.

A marital combination might include a forceful, decision-making husband and a quiet, reticent wife. Although this conclusion might be based on observation of repetitive transactions, the implication is that husband, wife, and context are three parts of a jigsaw puzzle that interlock in a characteristic fashion. Such an image is quite different from the sequential diagrams associated with a communicational analysis of marriage. This emphasis on the fitting together of parts and on the constraints placed on behavior by the context in which the behavior occurs effectively removes the notion of motivation from transactions. It does not deny motivation—it merely indicates that it is no longer necessary to describe behavior in motivational terms. As a consequence of this stance, statements about behavior take on a distinctively non-judgmental flavor. It no longer becomes necessary to place blame on one spouse or the other for pathological transactional patterns; instead patterns occur because a particular fit has been established. Change the fit, and the pattern of behavior will also change. This willingness to disregard motivation as a determinant of behavior is clearly one of the aspects of systems approaches to marriage that most sharply differentiates it from the psychoanalytic approach.

Minuchin mentions two constraints on the form that transactional patterns will take. The first is the generic or inherent needs of the social system. The second is determined by the shared expectations of individual family members, in this case each spouse within the marriage. Once again, these notions about constraints on transaction are considerably broader in scope than the more finely honed notions about communicational acts in the MRI model.

The third dimension which defines the structure of a marriage is its *response to stress*. Although there are four potential sources of stress on the family (interaction between individuals and extra-familial forces, interaction between the family and extra-familial forces, developmental transition, and idiosyncratic sources), an underlying family structure can be identified in the common patterns of adaptation to stress that emerge. While one can roughly distinguish two forms of attempted adaptation— one of which leads to adjustment, the other one leading to increased rigidity—the emphasis is on parts that fit together in a particular organizational pattern.

Many of Minuchin's concepts have a certain vagueness to them that makes more precise definition difficult. Minuchin prefers to think of his model as a model of therapy, rather than a theoretical model. Nevertheless, the emphasis on structural concepts within the model has specific consequences that should be underscored. Most prominent among these is a difficulty in dealing with process variables over extended periods of time. Although he freely acknowledges the importance of developmental issues and concepts of adaptation, both the structural model and the style of therapy that emerges from it deal very much with the here and now. The emphasis is on maps, in which structural variables are represented in a spatial dimension only; past history, although interesting, does not necessarily have a logical or consistent role in conceptualization of normality and pathology in this model. The emphasis on stress and adaptation to stress is a logical extension of the conceptual reliance on structure. As shall be seen, it also plays a central role in sociological systems theory, a systems approach also emphasizing structure and organization.

Version 3: Murray Bowen and Family Systems Theory

The third version of systems theory of marriage and marital disorders is the body of concepts introduced by Murray Bowen during the period from 1955-75. Although it seems appropriate to include Bowen's work in this review, both because it represents a major theoretical contribution and because it clearly falls within the framework of holistic or organismic theories encompassed by general systems notion, Bowen himself might well voice surprise at this decision. Witness his following statement on the matter:

> It is grossly inaccurate to consider Family Systems Theory [Bowen's original name for his theoretical constructs] as synonymous with general systems, although it is accurate to think of Family Systems Theory as somehow fitting into the broad framework of general systems theory. There are those who believe Family Systems Theory was developed from general systems theory in spite of my explanation to the contrary. At the time my theory was developed, I knew nothing about general systems theory. Back in the 1940s I attended one lecture by Bertalanffy, which I did not understand, and another

by Norbert Wiener which was perhaps a little more understandable
. . . However it developed, Family Systems Theory as I have defined
it is a specific theory about human relationship functioning that has
now become confused with general systems theory and the popular,
non-specific use of the word *systems* (Bowen, 1976, pp. 62-63).

With that word of caution, therefore, Bowen's theory will be described.

As was the case with the MRI group, Bowen's interest in family relationships was stimulated by a series of studies of families containing schizophrenic members. These studies, which were carried out at NIMH during
the 1950s, were unique in that they included direct observation of families that were hospitalized *conjointly* on a research ward. Bowen's work
with these families impressed him with what he called the "emotional
stuck-togetherness" that characterized the flavor of their interactions. He
christened this quality the "undifferentiated family ego mass" (Bowen,
1960), a term that gained considerable popularity because of its ability
to capture and describe the emotional atmosphere in schizophrenic
families.

For the next ten years Bowen elaborated and refined a series of eight
separate concepts which he incorporated into a family theory initially
called Family Systems Theory (Bowen, 1966), but now referred to as the
Bowen theory (Bowen, 1976).

At the core of the model is Bowen's contention that a biological approach leads one to postulate the existence of two parallel processes, an
emotional process and an intellectual process, as the two fundamental
components of human behavior. In keeping with what he characterizes
as his roots in biology, he postulates that man's emotional process is the
behavioral manifestation of an "emotional system, an intimate part of
man's phylogenetic past which he shares with all lower forms of life, and
which is governed by the same laws that govern all living things" (Bowen,
1976, p. 60). The intellectual process, on the other hand, stems from an
intellectual system rooted in the cerebral cortex and "involves the ability
to think, reason, and reflect, and enables man to govern his life, in certain
areas, according to logic, intellect, and reason" (Bowen, 1976, p. 60).

Bowen is also quite clear-cut about which of these systems is the preferable one. The emotional system, a carryover from man's more primitive
origins, can only get him into hot water. By contrast, the intellectual
system represents man at the pinnacle of his powers. Bowen's position on
this matter is so strong that it leads him to define emotional illness as "a
disorder of the emotional system." The theory that develops from this
basic core is organized into eight separate concepts discussed below.

(1) *Differentiation of self.* Each individual can be placed on a continuum of functioning along an axis defined as the degree of fusion versus differentiation between emotional and intellectual functioning. Fusion implies that behavior is dominated by the emotional system and therefore impulsive, instinctual, and primitive. Differentiation implies behavior determined by the intellectual system. Bowen's implication is that an analogy can be made between growth and differentiation of cells, tissues, organs and their respective biological functions, and the growth and differentiation of behavior. The analogy is between the presumed higher level of differentiation in specialization as phylogenetic embryologic development proceeds, and the parallel differentiation of behavior. From an interactional point of view, the assumption is that the more fused the individual is on this continuum, the more difficult it will be for him to establish relationships that preserve his individuality and separateness.

(2) *Triangles.* This concept refers to a three-person emotional configuration which Bowen contends is the basic building block of any emotional system, including marriages and families. Although two-person systems may exhibit relative stability during periods of calm, at times of stress the two-person system is highly unstable, and the tendency of such a dyad is to attempt to involve or incorporate a third person, thereby establishing a triangle. If tension continues to increase even after a triangle has been established, then additional people are incorporated and a series of interlocking triangles is established. Bowen's version of the family is of such a series of interlocking triangles.

These triangles, depending upon their construction, can in turn be thought of as having relative degrees of stability or instability. Their relative stability, according to Bowen, will be directly related to the level of differentiation achieved by each of the members of the triangle. If, in a moment of stress, a two-person relationship is able to "triangle in" a third person and establish a fused triangle, then an emotional system will result and, according to Bowen, pathology will be perpetuated. If, on the other hand, the third person can maintain an outside position, that is, remain differentiated, then there will be increased pressure on the dyad to in turn become more differentiated themselves. Bowen's style of therapy, at least insofar as he defines the role of the therapist, is based primarily on this theoretical concept.

(3) *Nuclear family emotional system.* The two previous concepts addressed first a theoretical notion of individual functioning, and second a general rule regarding the nature and construction of human relation-

ships. This third concept "describes the patterns of emotional functioning in a family in a single generation" (Bowen, 1976, p. 78). Here Bowen contends that the same continuum that he used to describe individual functioning, the fusion-differentiation continuum, can also be used to classify or describe family functioning. Marriage, says Bowen, is a union of two people operating at similar levels of differentiation. This concept is critical to Bowen's notion of marital disorders. The more highly fused the marital system, the more at risk of marital pathology is the relationship. In fact, he states that the amount of undifferentiation that exists in a particular marriage will manifest itself specifically in three different directions: the area of marital conflict; the emergence of sickness or dysfunction in one's spouse; and a tendency to project marital problems onto children, leading to the impairment of one or more children.

(4-8) A fourth concept, the *family projection process,* deals with the mechanism by which the nuclear family emotional system potentially creates impairment in one child. A fifth concept, *emotional cut-off,* deals with the relationship between the individuals in a marriage and their families of origin. Again the issue is fusion versus differentiation, in this case the extent to which the marital dyad is differentiated from the preceding generation. A sixth concept, *multi-generational transmission process,* is Bowen's explanation of the emergence of severe psychopathology in one member of a particular generation. The last two concepts, *sibling position* and *societal regression,* are peripheral to this discussion, and are mentioned only for the sake of completeness.

Bowen's theory implies that current behavior is the result of a long process over many generations of patterned relationships that are both pre-determined and self-perpetuating. He contends this is so because like individuals marry (each spouse comes to the marriage with similar baseline levels of "differentiation"), and because families rarely change dramatically from generation to generation. His theories suggest a very different view of the concepts of organization and control from the two theoretical models previously discussed. Whereas the basic pattern of marital process may surely be expressed in brief communicational exchanges of the type most frequently analyzed by the MRI group, the same pattern is also expressed in broad strokes of family themes and myths as they develop over multiple generations. In fact, Bowen finds these historical data particularly important in helping individuals within a particular marriage to delineate the heritage they are either benefiting from or struggling against. Although Bowen shares with Minuchin an interest in context as it determines and structures behavior, context is very differently defined. Historical context, rather than structural context, is emphasized.

*Version 4: Contributions from Family Sociology
to the Systems Perspective*

Up to this point, the versions of systems models of marriage and marital disorders have been models specifically addressed to problems of clinical psychopathology. As such, they have been couched in terms familiar to the marital therapist. The links between the theoretical clinical model and potential suggestions for therapeutic intervention have been clear-cut. In this fourth section the emphasis will be on social science theory addressing basic processes in the social institutions of marriage and the family. These theories, by and large, were not intended to address clinical issues per se and their specific relevance to psychotherapeutic intervention may therefore be less clear-cut than the relevance of the models already discussed. Nevertheless, a rich and comprehensive body of theory about marriage and family has evolved from the intensive efforts of social scientists, especially sociologists, in this area.

An attempt to categorize the major conceptual approaches used by family sociologists led Hill and Hansen (1960) to identify five "frameworks" which they felt not only addressed the major dimensions of interest related to the study of the family, but which could also be clearly distinguished one from another. These frameworks were: the institutional-historical, the structural-functional, the symbolic-interactionist, the situational, and the developmental approaches. Of these five frameworks, the structural-functional and the developmental frameworks have drawn most heavily on general systems concepts and language in their formulation. Although systems theory has been applied with considerable success to other areas of sociological theory, as, for example, Buckley's (1967) discussion of social organization from a system's perspective, for the purposes of this chapter it will suffice to concentrate on a discussion of the structural-functional and the developmental theoretical approaches to marriage and the family.

The *structural-functional approach* in sociology is most thoroughly developed in the writings of Talcott Parsons and his colleagues at Harvard University (Parson and Bales, 1955). Using concepts and a language that are at this point in the chapter quite familiar, the structural-functional approach attempts to understand social facts by exploring their reciprocal relationships with one another. While, on the one hand, social facts are related to specific organizations (the structural component), on the other hand, they may also be reciprocally interrelated one with another in a relatively consistent fashion (the functional component). A model based on structural components that have functional relationships to one another defined by their reciprocal actions on each other is clearly an alternative phrasing of the general systems concept that circular causality is a preferable explanatory model to the more traditional reductionistic cause and effect model.

Parsons argues, furthermore, that *social systems* can best be understood if one examines the nature of their functional relationships with one another. According to this analysis, any social system is composed of subsystems, each of which addresses itself to one of four major functional problems: adaptation, goal attainment or gratification, integration, and pattern maintenance of the system. In order to meet these functional needs and/ or solve related problems, most societies, according to Parsons, develop four subsystems which he terms, respectively, the economy, the polity, the community, and the value system. Although for a particular society the actual structural components of a subsystem might vary from the structural components designated by a different society to deal with the same functional problem, Parsons' basic contention is that somehow these functional problems must be met, and so the functional analysis is a useful framework for comparing one society to another. For example, economic activity associated with a functional problem of adaptation might be handled in one society by such structural organizations as banks and government regulatory agencies, while in another society it might be handled primarily by the nuclear family unit via home industry.

When the structural-functional level of analysis is applied to the family, the same categorical system is used to identify four functional problems and to define a series of subsystems within the family responsible for dealing with each of these problems. So we have the familiar model of a larger system that is, in turn, broken down into smaller structural components. The emphasis, however, is not so much on the structural characteristics of these component parts as it is one the functional problems to which the subsystems are addressed. It is assumed that the necessity of performing functions via reciprocal interactions with other social forces will impose upon each of the subsystems a series of tasks. It is further assumed that in order to accomplish these tasks functional behavior will be shaped along relatively reproducible lines or dimensions, which are potentially discoverable if one carries out a systematic analysis of societal behavior.

How is such a level of analysis useful to the clinician in the conceptualization of marriage and marital disorders? First, it provides a categorical system that can be used to classify family functions, and presumably to distinguish pathological from non-pathological family functioning. Bell and Vogel (1960) have carried out such a functional analysis of family behavior and, in the process, sketched in sharply defined terms the relationship between the nuclear family and the functional components of the larger society.

Second, the structural-functional model implies a natural order to the way social systems, including the family, are organized. By stressing the common functional problems that families must address, it carries with it the clear-cut implication that partial or total compromising of any of these functions will create pathology within the family. Because the emphasis is on tasks that must be accomplished as part of the solution of functional problems, it draws attention to the stresses and strains placed on the family if the natural social organization of the nuclear family is for any reason disrupted. For example, the sheer volume of work that one spouse must assume on the death of his or her partner and the consequent stress placed on the nuclear family will be readily apparent to the clinician operating within the structural-functional framework.

Third, the structural-functional framework presents the family in its larger social context. For the clinician, whose perception is often easily distorted by the case method approach to diagnosis and intervention, a level of analysis that addresses the family as a social institution avoids the temptation to become overly immersed in detail and individual variation, and, in the process, lose sight of the forest for the trees.

An additional point should be mentioned briefly. Structural-functional theories are intended to form a comprehensive model not only of the relationship between the nuclear family and the overall social system, but also of the relationships between the family and personality development of individuals within the family. Parsons and Bales (1955) have addressed this issue at length in their discussion of how functional aspects of the family influence socialization and role behavior. Systems concepts of levels of organization, relationships between subsystems, boundaries delineating organizational structure, and the like are drawn upon freely to delineate these different structures and processes.

The *developmental approach* in sociology stems from the conceptual work of Reuben Hill and his colleagues at the University of Minnesota.

In contrast to the structural-functional approach which was developed initially as a theory of social systems and only later adapted to the study of the nuclear family, the developmental approach from its inception was meant to address the need for a theoretical framework for the family. It is, by and large, an integrative approach, drawing heavily on prior theoretical work in sociology, including structural-functionalism. As such, it borrows freely such concepts as role, norms, goal orientation and the conceptualization of the family as a social system. In addition to these earlier conceptual ideas, however, this new approach has attempted to systematically deal with the social time dimension. It has, therefore, added to the above earlier concepts a series of additional ideas dealing with those orderly sequences that give to the life history of the family a sense of structured regularity over time, the sine qua non of the developmental approach.

Hill (1971) has provided the following synopsis of the developmental approach in family sociology:

> The most frequently used concepts in the family developmental framework cluster around four distinct issues of conceptualization:
>
> (1) Concepts about the family collectivity as a system in its own right, in which the conceptual categories of its "systemness" are specified; namely, a system that is relatively closed, boundary maintaining, equilibrium seeking, purposive and adaptive.*
>
> (2) Concepts of structure such as position, role, norms, role clusters, and role complexes, which tell us what recurring, repetitive and reciprocal features may be seen when examining this framework internally and statically.
>
> (3) Concepts of goal orientation and direction and the corollary concepts of the allocation phenomena which illuminate the task performing and functioning features of the family.
>
> (4) Concepts dealing with orderly sequences, the sequential regularities observable in the family over its life history, such as role sequences, careers of family positions, intercontingencies of careers, and stages of development (p. 11).

---

* Note the description of the family by Hill as a "relatively closed" system. He is making this judgment based on a comparison of the family with other *social systems.* This judgment would therefore not be in conflict with the earlier characterization (p. 315) of the family as an open system insofar as it is a living, rather than a non-living, system. As regards the concept of energy exchange with extra-family social systems, Hill would agree that the family is an open system, although not as open as most social systems.

One can see in this summarization the heavy reliance on concepts already introduced by the structural-functional approach. It should, therefore, also be apparent that similar benefits accrue to the clinician who appreciates the work of Hill and his colleagues to those already mentioned in connection with the work of Parsons and Bales. The developmental approach, however, in contrast to earlier sociological views, treats the structural and functional components of families not as static entities, but as processes which follow reproducible sequential orders. The core concept is, of course, the notion of a life cycle, that is, a series of stages or "categories" which occur in a sequential order of approximately similar sequence from one family to another.

Several life cycle schema have been suggested. They differ primarily in their relative emphasis on staging as tied to childhood developmental sequences. Most versions of the family life cycle have also been designed for the traditional nuclear family and are not always easily adaptable to alternate life-styles. As an example, Duvall (1971) has suggested an eight-stage life cycle which unfolds as follows: (1) married couples (without children); (2) child bearing families (oldest child, birth-30 months); (3) families with preschool children (oldest child 30 months-6 years); (4) families with school children (oldest child 6-13 years); (5) families with teenagers (oldest child 13-20 years); (6) families as launching centers (first child gone to last child leaving home); (7) middle-aged parents (empty nest to retirement); (8) aging family members (retirement to death of both spouses). As can be seen in this scheme, not only are stages associated primarily with child development, but they are also keyed to the age of the oldest child. The implicit assumption is that the family will face and hopefully meet a succession of developmental tasks imposed upon it by the interactions of its oldest child, not only within the family but also in his/her dealings with the outside world.

Duvall's scheme has the advantage of parsimony in its willingness to limit itself to eight critical life stages for the family. Its drawback, on the other hand, is its inability to differentiate the more subtle family changes associated with the birth of additional children. Rodgers (1973) has introduced a 24-category family life cycle keyed not only to the development of the oldest child but also to the position of the "last of the line" child in the family. Perhaps with a growing appreciation of the developmental distinctions that occur in adulthood, as well as childhood, an even more complex family life cycle will soon be suggested that takes these additional distinctions into account.

Lastly, the concept of the family developmental task, defined by Duvall as those "basic family tasks particularized and specified for a given stage of development in the family life cycle" (p. 150), should be underscored. Once again, these stage-critical developmental tasks are most frequently discussed in relation to parent-child interaction, but could, with very little extrapolation, be applied to husband and wife over the life history of a particular marriage. Table 1 outlines these developmental tasks.

INTEGRATING THE FOUR SYSTEMS PERSPECTIVES

The preceding sections reviewed four different versions of marriage and marital disorders from a systems perspective. The task at this point is to suggest an approach which might help to integrate these different theoretical approaches. Since each of these versions is a proposed clinical model, three essential benefits (described previously) might accrue if a particular approach is successful: First, the model will lead to selectivity in data gathering procedures; second, the model will include a concept of family pathology; and third, the model will suggest a strategy for change.

At first glance, it might be difficult to accept that all four versions are in fact "systems models" of marriage. As noted, even some of the theorists might themselves challenge this contention. Nevertheless, each of the models presented is in fact a holistic theory of marriage in which primary attention is paid not to the individual husband and wife, but to the nature of the relationship between the spouses.

However, lest this discussion wind up in the same state of confusion experienced by the fictitious couple at the beginning of the chapter, it is essential to seek some rhyme or reason to what might appear, at first glance, to be a confusing theoretical field. An easy way out of the dilemma would be to conclude that a process of selective adaptation has occurred. Different clinical notions about marriage and family pathology merely reflect a differential concentration on selected aspects of general systems theory. For example, Minuchin places heavy emphasis on concepts of organization, with his stress on marriage as a subsystem of the larger family system, with a definition of pathology closely linked to his concepts of boundaries, and with his sensitivity to the relationship between behavior and context. The MRI group, on the other hand, places heavy emphasis on concepts of control, with particular attention to their version of homeostasis and feedback mechanisms.

However, it should also be clear that each of the versions of family systems reviewed takes into account *some* version of all three conceptual

TABLE 1

Stage-critical Family Developmental Tasks through
the Family Life Cycle

Stage of the family life cycle	Positions in the family	Stage-critical family developmental tasks
1. Married couple	Wife Husband	Establishing a mutually satisfying marriage Adjusting to pregnancy and the promise of parenthood Fitting into the kin network
2. Childbearing	Wife-mother Husband-father Infant daughter or son or both	Having, adjusting to, and encouraging the development of infants Establishing a satisfying home for both parents and infant(s)
3. Preschool-age	Wife-mother Husband-father Daughter-sister Son-brother	Adapting to the critical needs and interests of preschool children in stimulating, growth-promoting ways Coping with energy depletion and lack of privacy as parents
4. School-age	Wife-mother Husband-father Daughter-sister Son-brother	Fitting into the community of school-age families in constructive ways Encouraging children's educational achievement
5. Teenage	Wife-mother Husband-father Daughter-sister Son-brother	Balancing freedom with responsibility as teenagers mature and emancipate themselves Establishing postparental interests and careers as growing parents
6. Launching center	Wife-mother-grandmother Husband-father-grandfather Daughter-sister-aunt Son-brother-uncle	Releasing young adults into work, military service, college, marriage, etc., with appropriate rituals and assistance Maintaining a supportive home base
7. Middle-aged parents	Wife-mother-grandmother Husband-father-grandfather	Rebuilding the marriage relationship Maintaining kin ties with older and younger generations
8. Aging family members	Widow/widower Wife-mother-grandmother Husband-father-grandfather	Coping with bereavement and living alone Closing the family home or adapting it to aging Adjusting to retirement

From: Duvall, E. M., *Family Development*, Lippincott, New York, 1971.

areas identified as the essential building blocks of system theory: organization, control, and energy. The issue clearly is not one of lack of recognition of the importance of these three conceptual areas; rather, the issue appears to be one of selective emphasis. Each of the systems theorists, for example, would agree that such concepts as structural organization, or communication, or transgenerational patterns of behavior are relevant and meaningful for a systems theory of marriage. They might disagree strongly, however, about the relative power of each of these variables in predicting behavior, in distinguishing pathological from non-pathological behavior, and in offering guidance to the therapist about how to operate in a clinical situation. Rather than entering directly into this argument by detailing the merits and liabilities of each of the models presented, it would perhaps be more profitable to identify a few concepts which might be useful in discriminating between these different theoretical models.

This discussion of the different systems models of marriage will be organized around three important variables. The first variable is the differential position of each model regarding the two dimensions identified as critical for systems concepts—the dimensions of time and space. The second variable is the model's relative allegiance to principles of homeostasis versus principles of adaptation. The third variable is the relative level of abstraction of the basic building blocks used within the respective models.

1. Time Versus Space

Even in the best of all possible worlds, time and space cannot be artificially separated. Events, at least insofar as they are experienced, occur simultaneously in both these dimensions. As pointed out in the discussion of morphology versus physiology, it is possible in certain investigative situations to actually freeze time. A clear-cut example is a microscopic slide examined by the pathologist. But in this process of freezing time, the living system has been killed. Therefore, in work with living systems the dimension of time can be ignored, but cannot effectively be eliminated.

In terms of data relevant to marriages and marital pathology, the time dimension is treated in one of three systematic ways. First, it can be considered to be of critical importance, moved to center stage, and have its essential integrity preserved. In other words, data can be observed in a real-time dimension. Second, the importance of time can be acknowledged, but made more manageable by condensing it. This is the most frequent stance taken during a psychotherapy session, in which the interviewer might ask for a condensed narrative of life events from the patient or client. There is, of course, a limit to the extent to which time can be condensed if we are to do justice to the process or function being elicited. The condensation of a three generational history, for example, in the course of a 60-minute initial interview perhaps violates time to such an extent as to make it no longer meaningful as a systems dimension.

The final choice is to ignore time entirely. Of course this does not mean denying its existence; it merely means either taking it for granted or finding it not particularly helpful as a discriminating variable. When this final attitude is taken, behavior is viewed as ahistorical or as patterned primarily in terms of structure, rather than in terms of process.

When we compare the four different models on this time dimension, we see that the MRI group clearly presents the model that is most acutely sensitive to the importance of preserving a real-time dimension in the collection of data, in its notion of disorder, and in its strategy for change. Not only do these researchers concentrate on communication as the critical behavioral variable, but they are also exquisitely sensitive to communication as a process variable, that is, in preserving the sequential ordering of events over time. On the other hand, more than any other approach, the MRI model treats behavior as ahistorical. Attention is paid only to the here and now; events are only rarely placed in their developmental perspective.

At the other end of the spectrum, Bowen's model by and large ignores time as a critical variable. His time perspective is so broad, stretching over at least three generations of behavior, that the data actually collected cannot possibly retain an accurate sequential order. Nor does he seem to value process variables as they unfold during the therapy session itself.

The developmental model suggested by social scientists is, of course, dependent on a time dimension, inasmuch as developmental stages are thought to occur in a specific sequential order. Minuchin's model, on the other hand, although certainly sensitive to developmental issues, prefers to emphasize the ordering of events in space, rather than the ordering of events in time.

Although each systems version of marriage and the family takes a somewhat different stance in its use of a time dimension, it has already been noted that all of these models place heavy emphasis on patterned relationships and patterned events. The difference between patterning over time (process) and patterning in space (structure) has also been noted. An inverse relationship between emphasis on process and emphasis on structure might also be predicted in the different versions of the systems model.

Minuchin illustrates this inverse relationship nicely. When Minuchin, in the course of therapeutic work with a family, assigns a task, the goal is a restructuring of the organizational relationships between family members. It is often immaterial which sequential order the family chooses to carry out the task; instead, the critical issue is which family member assumes what role or which responsibility within the task. He might deem it important that a withdrawn and passive father assume responsibility for disciplining an anorectic daughter. As long as this disciplining occurs in some approximation to the girl's eating behavior, the more precise sequential ordering of behaviors would be judged of secondary importance.

The MRI group, on the other hand, shows far less sensitivity to the relationship between behavior and the psychosocial context within which it occurs. Chapter VII on systems therapy includes a series of specific directives to the potential therapist, directives drawn from the theoretical perspective of the MRI group. As can be seen, the directives usually apply across the board. Everyone is asked, for example, to speak only for him/herself, and such issues as the structural context of parents communicating with children versus intramarital communication are not addressed.

Both Bowen and the sociologists use both time and space as appropriate dimensions within which to seek patterns of family life. Their treatment of these dimensions, however, is at a macro-analytic level, rather than the micro-analytic analyses of behavior one associates with both the communication approach and structural family theory.

The major point being made is that by selecting a relative emphasis on time or space, in either macro- or micro-analytic frameworks, these different models preselect the types and quality of patterns they will define as important. Subsequent clinical decisions, especially as regards pathological versus non-pathological behavior, will flow quite naturally from these earlier distinctions.

2. *Control Versus Adaptation*

Although systems theorists would hardly challenge a statement that adaptation is a crucial mechanism ensuring the survival of living organisms, their predilection has been to emphasize instead those mechanisms of control that allow the living system to regulate its internal and external environment. Perhaps this merely represents a chauvinistic bias in favor of concepts one had a direct hand in developing. Adaptation, having achieved taken-for-granted status, tends to be pushed into the background, the focus instead shifting to the newer concepts of homeostasis and cybernetic regulation.

The implications for clinical work are unfortunately all too familiar. The clinician becomes extremely sensitive to each and every mechanism used by marital partners to regulate and control the pace of their relationship. Symptoms are defined exclusively in terms of "stabilization of the system." And marriage is viewed as an inherently rigid relationship, often destructive to individual growth. (Even the term "negative feedback" has an unintentional pejorative ring to it.)

To what extent have the systems theorists fallen prey to this tendency to emphasize control at the expense of adaptation? Perhaps the social scientists have managed to strike a healthy balance between these two important concepts. The clinicians, unfortunately, mention adaptation only in passing, if at all. Although the manner of control may differ from version to version (control via communication in one version, control via multi-generational tradition in a second, control through the establishment of structural context for behavior in a third), marriage in all three versions has an intricate and elaborate system of checks and balances, but seemingly little motivation or functional capacity for adaptation. Surely this is an unfortunate oversight—an error of omission rather than commission. Nevertheless, it adds a distinct flavor to the work of marital systems therapists and should therefore be altered in the future.

Haley (1973), in his discussion of the work of Milton Erickson, underscores a critical feature of Erickson's work—his belief that symptoms are, in fact, unsuccessful behavioral efforts at adaptation. Haley writes:

> We have progressed to an ever wider view of the function of symptoms and other human problems in the last 20 years. Symptoms were once seen as an expression of an individual independent of his social situation . . . Next came the idea that symptoms were an expression of a relationship between people and served some tactical purpose between intimates . . . Now there is a yet wider view . . . symptoms appear when there is a dislocation or interruption in the unfolding life cycle of a family or other natural group. This symptom is a signal that the family has a difficulty in getting past a stage in a life cycle (pp. 41-42).

3. Concrete Versus Abstract Concepts

The third variable concerns the relative level of abstraction used by the theorists in framing their key concepts. Although most theoretical concepts are by their very nature abstractions, they can be found in a language that permits the use of a wide variety of types of data for their verification. Take, for example, the concept of the family rule, and contrast it with Bowen's concept of the undifferentiated ego mass.

Family rules are statements about interactional behavior extrapolated directly from pragmatic aspects of communication. A particular family rule might be based on such data as speaking time for each interactant, behavioral posturing associated with communication, patterns of interruption associated with decision-making, or other observable events. These types of data are relatively concrete in nature. The undifferentiated ego mass, on the other hand, is a synthetic concept based on the abstract, subjective impressions of the clinical observer. In making such a judgment, the clinical observer uses a wide variety of observations and *reactions,* many of which are processed at a subconscious level, and uses such a product to form a judgment that is presumably unique to each family being observed.

The concepts introduced by the four "versions" can be placed on a continuum from relative concreteness to relative abstraction. Bowen and the social scientists, for example, clearly have a predilection for highly abstract concepts; Minuchin and the MRI group introduce concepts that are primarily concrete in nature.

Is the abstract-concrete distinction of any value when attempting to apply these theoretical models to clinical situations? Debate on this issue would probably be heated and inconclusive. I would argue, however, that difficulties with systems theory are more prone to arise when models jump willy-nilly from one level of abstraction to another—when mixed metaphors become the order of the day. Systems theory is particularly vulnerable in this regard because it is conceptualized as a unifying theory. In this sense it is presumed to be capable of absorbing and integrating concepts from otherwise widely disparate scientific disciplines. Its power to incorporate ideas, however, often seems greater than its power to reject silly or trivial notions. Several instances have been noted in which adaptation of biological constructs to family systems theory has been carried out with little regard for the inherent dangers in mixing concrete and abstract concepts. At the same time, nevertheless, adopting principles observed in biological and physical systems to behavioral and social systems (where appropriate) is clearly important.

Finally, there is the issue of validation. Systems theory, with its emphasis on holistic thinking and interrelationship of parts, cannot be subjected to traditional experimental investigation. Instead, the pattern of relationships between parts of the system must be assessed by other means. When dealing primarily with abstract concepts, clinical observations provide most of the data to validate such systems hypotheses. Concrete theoretical concepts, on the other hand, utilize quantitative as well as qualitative data, data which can be measured. Such data are better suited to the manipulations that must be carried out when attempting to validate the power of the systems hypotheses.

This discussion underscores the point made earlier that the various "systems models" of marriage proposed by clinicians and social scientists remain partial theories, still vying for adherents, not yet directing efforts at synthetic enterprises. The one exception to this generalization is the work of Reuben Hill and his colleagues, who have attempted to integrate systems thinking into their developmental model of the family (Hill, 1971).

Surely yet another version of the systems theory perspective of marriage seems the last thing one would want at this point. Yet that is exactly what the next section of the chapter proposes to present. It is being introduced at this point for two reasons: First, it is a model that has synthetic potential-capability for absorbing and organizing major tenets of the models already presented; second, it introduces a strong biological bias, a feature underrepresented in the discussion of marriage and marital disorders presented thus far.

A BIOLOGICALLY-ROOTED SYSTEMS MODEL OF MARRIAGE

General systems theory, as has been noted, was developed in part to deal with certain aspects of scientific exploration that traditional reductionistic-mechanistic science appeared unable to tackle. Traditional science, with its models based on linear causality and its systematic style of progressive hypothesis generation and hypothesis testing, has obviously served us well. But many complex issues, particularly in the life sciences, when reduced to simpler or more manageable concepts or hypotheses, seem to virtually disappear before one's eyes. By introducing such concepts as organization and relationships between parts, general systems theory aims at providing the means to tackle these more complex issues. How well has this new model done?

Although it may be much too early to render a final verdict, in the behavioral and social sciences, at least, the benefits are still more promised than accrued. The current dilemma is succinctly illustrated in an article by George Engel (1977) entitled "The Need for a New Medical Model:

A Challenge for Biomedicine." Dealing specifically with the relationship between psychiatry and medicine, Engel argues that a crisis of sorts now exists which he proposes to understand and potentially remedy by analyzing the nature of models currently used and their shortcomings. The core issue is a quite familiar one, namely, the extent to which a model of disease should be limited to somatic parameters or should include psychosocial parameters as well. The biomedical model, which Engel identifies as the dominant model of disease today, is described as follows:

> It assumes disease to be fully accounted for by deviations from the norm of measurable biological (somatic) variables. It leaves no room within its framework for the social, psychological, and behavioral dimensions of illness . . . It also demands that behavioral aberrations be explained on the basis of disorder (somatic, biochemical or neurophysiological) processes. Thus, the biomedical model embraces both reductionism, a philosophic view that complex phenomena are ultimately derived from a single primary principle, and mind-body dualism, the doctrine that separates the mental from the somatic (p. 130).

Engel argues that this model, despite its scientific elegance and the impressive discoveries that it has stimulated, remains in the last analysis perhaps merely a model of convenience. It is convenient in the sense that it allows the scientist to feel that disease has been explained utilizing both methods and findings he/she has high confidence in. However, Engel argues, such a stance yields a false sense of confidence. In actual fact, the expression of disease is clearly dependent on cultural, social and psychological considerations, as well as the biological variables which are most often considered. (The earlier example of pneumococcal pneumonia illustrated this point.) Engel proposes a biopsychosocial model which includes the patient as well as the illness as the preferable scientific model of disease.

Why is Engel's article being cited at such length? The first reason is to underscore the striking similarity between the problems faced by von Bertalanffy in the 1920s and the problems being addressed by Engel in the 1970s. In fact, Engel himself underscores this similarity:

> The struggle to reconcile the psychosocial and the biological in medicine has had its parallel in biology, also dominated by the reductionistic approach of molecular biology. Among biologists too have emerged advocates of the need to develop holistic as well as reductionistic explanations of life processes, to answer the "why?" and "what for?" as well as the "how?" (p. 134).

One can perhaps view this parallel as an example of the success of general systems theory. However, it is distressing to observe the continued need for a clarion call to holistic thinking. If such a characterization is accurate, it would appear that general systems theory, no matter how appealing its conceptual framework might initially appear to be, has not yet provided a consistent direction to follow that will be profitable in expanding understanding of biological and social systems. Although its potential power can be appreciated each time the deficits of traditional models are highlighted by their inability to account for multiple variables, it would appear that its initial promise as a *unifying* model has yet to be realized.

What about the examples of systems theory as applied to marriage and marital disorders? It must be concluded here as well that these are only a series of interesting conceptual starts. Once again, there is difficulty in developing a single, compelling holistic theory of marriage. Understanding of marital relationships and marital disorders has been helped immensely by knowledge of organization, control mechanisms, and concepts of energy expressed in terms of communication and information; but it has been extremely difficult to keep all of these notions simultaneously in mind. Instead, the various family theorists wind up emphasizing their own part of the pie.

In the present attempt to categorize the various systems approaches to marriage, it was indicated that family theorists were finding it particularly hard to simultaneously work with static versus process variables, and homeostatic versus developmental variables. Although each of the family theorists would almost certainly acknowledge the validity of simultaneously accounting for structure and process, and homeostasis and morphogenesis, the clinical situations within which data are collected and judgments are made appear to demand a narrowing down of focus because of their complexity. The theorists reviewed would probably argue that the dimensions they have chosen are the ones that, in their opinion, are most helpful in defining clinical pathology and developing strategies for change.

We probably have not yet discovered the right combination, as evidenced by our difficulties in embracing any single version of family systems theory to the exclusion of others, and by the difficulty experienced in successfully drawing analogies between marital and family systems and other living systems. (On this latter point, this lack of success is certainly not for want of trying. Witness the analogies to membrane boundaries, differentiation, and so forth.)

Although hardly a sophisticated explanation, those analogies that seem to work best are analogies that at their root are commonsensical. The communication theory analogy of marriage proposed by the MRI group makes sense because our physiological ability to transmit and receive complex communicational messages is definitely a fundamental property permitting us to engage in complex behavioral and social systems. We know what it means in complex social systems to gain control over the channels of communication. It is obviously not a coincidence that every revolutionary movement in our day and age includes capture of all available radio and telecommunications stations as a top priority, "day one" objective.

Analogies that work less well frequently seem to stretch similarities beyond their commonsensical limits. Bowen's use of the concept of "differentiation of self" is such an example. Note the following statement from Bowen's most recent description of his theory (1976):

> I . . . chose to use concepts that would be consistent with biology and the natural sciences . . . The concept of differentiation was chosen because it has specific meaning in the biological sciences. When we speak of the "differentiation of the self," we mean a process similar to the differentiation of cells from each other (p. 58).

Bowen's desire to root his theory in biology cannot be faulted. Where he has perhaps gone astray is in his notion that his concept, the differentiation of self, can be thought of as, in effect, a logical extension of biological phenomena associated with growth and development.

Nevertheless, one of systems theory's specific goals is an attempt to identify similar properties or isomorphies across different levels of organization (Rapoport, 1976). The notion is that by treating sets of related events as systems, such a goal will be achieved. In this way one can identify the fundamental laws and principles that operate commonly in all levels of organization, while at the same time pinpointing those aspects of relationships and functions that are unique to the particular system under study.

In again reviewing current notions of marriage and marital disorders, what conclusions can be drawn about the links formed between this theory and biology? In the area of control (homeostasis and feedback mechanisms), links to biology are quite impressive. In fact, as already noted, these terms as applied to marriages and families are direct extensions of similar concepts in human physiology (Cannon, 1939; Jackson, 1957). Concepts of marriage based on information and communication theory (one of the ways of defining energy concepts in systems terms) also have their direct analogy in biology. Genetic encoding and the biochemistry of protein metabolism have been found to be consistent with an information processing model. But perhaps even more compelling is knowledge about the structure of the human perceptual system. Both the visual and auditory systems are clearly organized as pattern recognizing structures which decode complex afferent stimuli at the periphery of the nervous system. This allows highly complex information to be passed on to central association areas.

Therefore, in at least two of the three major conceptual areas—the areas of control and of energy (as represented by information)—systems notions of marriage can be built on fairly clear-cut biological roots that make sense. There is, however, another concept of energy in living systems that needs to be addressed. This concept can be subsumed under the more general area of growth and development. The historical review of the development of systems theory pinpoints the phenomenon of *ordered growth* as one of the critical issues that could not be addressed using a reductionistic-mechanistic approach.

All complex biological organisms go through a predictable sequence of stages called a *life cycle.* Although these stages obviously run one into the other, and although there are surely processes that are common to all stages, it is useful to identify specific events or processes that seem more highly associated with one stage than another.

At the earliest part of the life cycle continuum, simple structural dimensions are used to label stages. Thus, in embryology, the one cell stage, the two cell stage, the four cell stage, and so on, are discussed. As things become more complex, more complex notions or structures are used upon which to base our staging (Erikson, 1963; Baer and Wright, 1975). For example, the concept of epigenesis is introduced in embryology to denote the progressive differentiation of tissue structures from previously undifferentiated cells. Biological growth and development, especially the phenomena associated with embryological cell differentiation, remain one of the great mysteries of biology. Nevertheless, even though the "how" of this process remains mysterious, there is clear consensus not only that it does occur, but also that it is a critical property of living systems.

What course of action should be taken in drawing parallels between the marital system *as a social system rooted in biology,* and the biological constraints within which the individual members of the marriage must operate? Bowen has urged starting with the concept of cell differentiation. But that process is the one understood least well. If it is a somewhat ethereal process in biology, surely it cannot translate into a less mystical concept when applied to marital interaction. There are, however, other phenomena related to growth and development that are better understood. One has already been mentioned—growth and development is staged, with each stage representing a kind of building block which is a necessary foundation for subsequent stages. In other words, biological growth and development unfolds according to a set sequential order. A second impressive fact is that growth and development does not necessarily proceed smoothly. When viewed along its time continuum, it appears to move in spurts and starts, with, for example, short periods of rapid growth interspersed between long periods of relative quiescence.

Utilizing these aspects of growth and development, what can be added to a systems model of marriage? There have been two major theoretical approaches that have been suggested. The first is to deal with the issue of growth and development along similar lines used to develop notions about control in living systems. Simply put, the argument is as follows: Just as it was proposed that living systems are steady states, with the notion of homeostasis or morphostasis describing the process by which systems maintain the steady state, so a concept must also be introduced to describe how living systems change, for surely living systems have distinct phases during which time they move to levels of higher complexity and organization. Such a concept can be called *morphogenesis*. To follow the argument through—if the negative feedback loop is proposed as a critical phenomenon associated with homeostasis, then a positive feedback process must also be proposed as a critical phenomenon associated with morphogenesis. This is the argument that has been advanced by Buckley (1967) in his general systems approach to social systems. Drawing primarily on Maruyama's (1963) categorization of cybernetic feedback mechanisms, he characterizes negative feedback as activated by error or deviation, but also counteracting deviation, while positive feedback, although also activated by deviation, results in amplification of deviation. Speer (1970), in his review of this work, characterizes the two processes as follows:

> The negative feedback process, or morphostatic function, is essentially . . . the traditional cybernetic type of feedback. The main point is that, after receiving mismatch information, deviation counteracting operations are triggered so as to bring the individual's or system's behavior or status back into congruence or convergence with the extant internal standards or the system's governing criterion values. . . . The positive feedback or deviation amplifying process

also begins with error or mismatch information resulting from a comparison of data about behavior with internal standards or criteria. The difference is that the subsequent effector operations do not act to reduce the discrepancy but rather act to increase the divergence between the system's or member's status and the original goal or standard values (p. 267).

Earlier views of these positive, deviation amplifying processes proposed that such processes are ultimately destructive to the system. Unchecked inflationary spirals are a frequently cited example in the sphere of economic systems. Buckley, in contrast to these earlier views, "believes that the positive feedback processes are the underlying vehicles by which social systems 'grow,' create, and innovate, and consequently views them as *morphogenetic* processes (literally, form or structure changing processes)" (Speer, 1970, p. 267).

Suppose these theoretical concepts were applied to clinical situations in marriage and families. Would such an analysis be satisfactory? For certain situations it appears to be highly relevant (Hoffman, 1971). However, although these positive and negative feedback processes can be identified in many clinical problems, this level of analysis seems by and large to miss the boat. For example, if presented with the familiar clinical situation of a family struggling with an acting out, promiscuous adolescent, the family's interactional behavior can be conceptualized in terms of negative and positive feedback, homeostasis and morphogenesis, but what is missing from such analysis is the *activating mechanism* that initiated the process in the first place. In cybernetic language, the behavior observed would be called an "error-activated" mechanism. But is this the best biological analogy if what in fact is being observed is a developmental stage called adolescence, a stage which characteristically includes, as one of its parameters, an attempt on the part of one individual to separate from the family system? (Perhaps a more accurate description of this "family life cycle" stage is a redefinition of the family system based on the biological imperative experienced by one member of the family system.)

Must the notion of psychobiological growth and development, firmly rooted in biology, be rejected and replaced with a cybernetic analogy, in order to employ systems thinking? Certainly not. However, the emphasis must be changed to incorporate the notions of staging and critical events introduced above. It may even be possible to include notions of timing and stages in the language of cybernetics and feedback loops. But first let us consider what can be done with the notion of the life cycle alone.

As already noted, the family life cycle is a core concept in the developmental approach to family theory (Duvall, 1971; Glick, 1955; Hill and Rodgers, 1964). Although the definitions of the starting and ending points for the "life" of the marriage are by necessity more forced than those of the conception and death of the individual, it is quite useful clinically to separate marriage into a series of life stages. On the other hand, because this theory comes from social scientists rather than biological scientists, the "critical events" associated with each stage are usually defined as tasks. This definition need not be accepted as comprehensive, however. It has emerged in this fashion primarily because a developmental model of marriage and the family has received so little attention from people with strong ties to both biological and behavioral sciences.

How might a model of marriage and notions of marital disorders look if a developmental perspective were incorporated into basic systems notions? In rough outline it would take shape in the following way. Marriage would be defined as a concrete system that had a clearly defined inception and a clearly defined ending (the marriage ceremony and the death of one's spouse or divorce). The life of the marriage would be divided into a series of stages delimited by transition periods. While a natural sequence of developmental stages for the marital system might be proposed, the environmental context within which the system operates must also be carefully considered. (Environmental context is defined here as the external psychosocial context within which the marital system is structured and functions.) Although this environmental context does not necessarily have a "life" of its own, it might manifest changes that have an impact on a marriage in a non-random fashion. These changes might be unanticipated (for example, major changes in climate or major changes in the political order), or anticipated (increased financial earning capacity or physical relocations). These changes clearly may be of a magnitude as to demand a response from the marital system. On the other hand, there are aspects of the environmental context that might have a biological life of their own. These elements might adhere to their own process, the timing and nature of which potentially place stresses and constraints on the marital system. An example here might be the growth and development of a child of this marriage. (Environmental context is defined here as the external psychosocial context within which the marital system is structured and functions.)

Two simultaneous processes might therefore be conceptualized, each of which contributes to the growth and development of a particular marriage—one set of processes is primarily related to the internal development of the marriage; the other set of processes is primarily related to changes in the environmental context.

As a picture of the marital system in a temporal/spatial dimension begins to develop (both time and space should be included in a systems model), two types of patterns emerge. The first pattern is an evolving structure associated with each stage in the life history of the marriage, a structure which includes both spatial organization (where people live, the identity and size of the social network, the nature of the marital subsystem within the larger family system, and so forth) and temporal organization or processes (including communication style, distribution of role function, and the like). During any particular stage, the marital system is governed, by and large, by principles of homeostasis. Although clearly a dynamic steady state, with a rich complex of inputs and outputs, the marriage, within a particular stage, manifests a characteristic style of organization and behavior, and has an established set of responses and rules for keeping organization and behavior within acceptable limits.

One would expect, therefore, that, at the midpoint of any particular stage, a marriage is in a relative state of quiescence, percolating along at a predictable and patterned style. Although this style may be more or less inventive, more or less adaptive, more or less "functional" in terms of the marriage's ability to maximize its resources and productivity, what would be found on close examination of such a marriage would be phenomena associated primarily with maintenance patterns. Distinctions between pathological and nonpathological systems at midstage would therefore center very much around the richness and flexibility of maintenance processes exhibited by the particular marriage. Although certainly influenced by individual value judgments, a generally agreed upon range of richness and flexibility might be definable.

The progression from one stage to another is marked by a period of transition. Transitional behavior may be necessitated by intra- or extra-system demands. But whatever the source, these demands place strains upon existing maintenance programs beyond the capacity of the marital system to continue to function within more static limits. At present it must be assumed that transitions brought about by biologically determined developmental changes have different qualities from transitions imposed on the marital system by external events. Unfortunately, however, there exists very little systematic knowledge in this area. Perhaps the work in sociology concerning families under stress can be viewed as an example of externally imposed transitions and this work can be compared with Haley's description of the family life cycle as biologically determined transitions. Suffice it to say that at this point in time different characteristic behaviors of families manifesting each type of transition probably can be described. It also seems clear that biological transitions, as currently defined, relate primarily to individual biological changes within the marriage and larger family. Most of the staging in the family life cycle, for example, is based on the growth and development of children at one end of the cycle, and the effects of aging at the other end of the cycle.

In any event, this model of marital systems would propose a series of transitions during which time both the organization and function of the system would change dramatically to meet the changing needs imposed upon it. During these time periods, adaptational behavior would presumably take precedence over homeostatic behavior. One model that might be invoked for these transition periods is a kind of military alert where resources are mobilized, communication is narrowed down and directed, and decision-making is streamlined. Another, very different model, sees these transition points as involving major jumps within the marriage from one level of organization to another and from one state of complexity to another. Transitions are then associated with bursts of energy, rapid changes in form and style, and major shifts in direction.

Such a model seems at this point to be perilously close to a psychoanalytic developmental model. Erikson's (1963) psychosocial developmental model, the "Eight Ages of Man," for example, has a strikingly similar flavor, with its emphasis on stages, on transition periods, and on critical tasks associated with each stage. (Duvall, 1971, has incorporated Erikson's approach in her developmental model of the family.) Far from being disturbed by this similarity, however, we should, in fact, be reassured by this sign that a biologically based systems model might have unifying capacities. It is most unlikely that a model that either relegates the individual to a markedly secondary position or attempts to eliminate him entirely as a focus of legitimate attention will ever be fully satisfying. No matter how sensitive a model might be to interactional and organizational principles of systems, too much is risked if the biological parameters of growth and development within the individual are ignored. The conceptual leap here is the systems notion that a *relationship* can have a very similar aging process, and that attention to the nature of the aging process will help immensely in the clinical setting.

To summarize the basic proposals up to this point: the concept of a family life cycle which includes a developmental sequence for marriage is emphasized. This life cycle is composed of a series of stages divided by transition periods. Stages characteristically manifest dynamic steady-state principles with an emphasis on homeostatic mechanisms. Transition periods characteristically involve major shifts of energy, with changes in the negentropy of the system as a whole manifested in recognizable changes of the structure and process within the marriage and family. Adaptational mechanisms are critical during transition periods.

If the marital and family life cycle is characterized in such a fashion, then clearly models must be developed that are useful both for stages and for transition periods. As long as it is clear that a particular family might manifest markedly different behavior, not only as regards staging versus transitional behavior, but also from one stage to another, and as long as those specific aspects of the family life cycle the model is attempting to describe are clearly defined, then the fact that the models developed are partial rather than complete models need not be of concern. Models often fall naturally into one of two groups: models that deal with the maintenance of existing behavior, and models that propose mechanisms for transitional behavior.

Two examples from the theoretical literature should help to illustrate these distinctions. First, the author's *systems model of alcoholism* (Steinglass, Weiner and Mendelson, 1971) is an example of a family model addressing maintenance behavior within a developmental stage. Second, Wolin, Bennett and Noonan's (unpublished) model of *family identity*, which incorporates concepts of ritual and myth, is an example of a family model addressing transitional behavior from one developmental stage to another. They are specifically interested in the transition from family of origin to family of procreation. This model, therefore, deals with the transition between the stage that Duvall would characterize as the "family as a launching center" and the formation of new satellite families, beginning their own marital systems.

The Systems Model of Alcoholism will be described first. The specific concern in this model is how to adequately describe the relationship between a chronic disease process and the family system. A controversy typically arises in the literature discussing family factors and chronic disease, centering around the debate about whether family factors consistently associated with a specific disease process contribute etiologically to the onset and maintenance of the disease itself or are the result of the common source of stress placed on families by the disease. Chronic alcoholism and allergic reactions such as asthma are two examples of conditions that have stimulated the above controversy.

The Systems Model of Alcoholism attempted to resolve this controversy in the following manner. First it attempted to distinguish between those families in which abusive drinking might serve the function of a signal or sign of stress within the family system and those families in which alcohol served a significant role in systems maintenance. Second, it proposed that, if a family system remained structurally and economically intact in the face of abusive drinking behavior, it had by definition reached a dynamic state, and it could be assumed a priori that drinking behavior and the family's interactional behavior were structurally and functionally interrelated. Third, it proposed that alcohol abuse, because of its profound behavioral, cultural, societal, and physical consequences, might assume such a central position in the life of some families as to become an *organizing principle* for interactional life within these families. In such families the term "alcoholic system" would be justified as a family label.

Since, according to this model, the "alcoholic system" was in a steady state, one would be justified in inferring that the alcoholic behavior was in effect *stabilizing* the family system. As already mentioned in the discussion of the concept of homeostasis, stability in the family system does not necessarily imply a healthy state of affairs; it merely implies that the family has incorporated mechanisms that act to restore the family's specific sense of balance whenever events occur that tend to disrupt this balance.

As the systems model of alcoholism was developed and substantiated by clinical and experimental data, the notion that drinking behavior was playing a specific role in homeostasis for the "alcoholic system" received considerable support (Steinglass, Davis and Berenson, 1977). In a study of marital couples one or both of whom were chronic alcoholics, who were conjointly hospitalized and observed during states of sobriety and intoxication, these marital couples were found to cycle between *two distinct interactional states*—a sober interactional state and an intoxicated interactional state. In addition, observations indicated, somewhat surprisingly, that the intoxicated interactional state was, if anything, even more non-random, and in this sense even more highly patterned, than behavior observed during states of sobriety. Furthermore, it appeared that the transition from sober to intoxicated behavior ap-

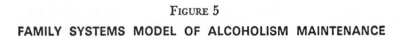

FIGURE 5

FAMILY SYSTEMS MODEL OF ALCOHOLISM MAINTENANCE

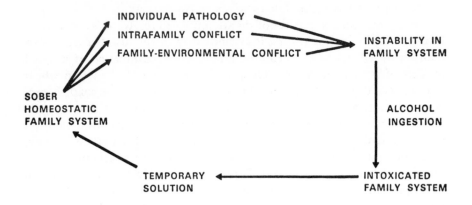

peared to serve a specific functional role for these marital couples, a role that was felt to be primarily problem-solving in nature. Although it was felt that three different types of problem-solving activities were associated with alcoholism (problem-solving associated with individual psychopathology, intrafamilial conflict, or conflict between the family and the external environment), in each case the emergence of the intoxicated interactional state appeared to temporarily restabilize the marital system.

Figure 5 is an illustration of this model. As can be readily seen, it is a circular model, relying heavily on concepts of homeostasis and feedback loops. Such a circular model implies that the overall pattern of behavior for the couple has reached a steady state. This model obviously does not attempt to explain the transition from the pre-alcoholic to the alcoholic state in the life history of the marital couple, nor does it propose a mechanism of transition that would move the family to a new stage of organization. It does not contend that such transitions are impossible, since clearly they have been observed clinically. Instead, it proposes to deal specifically with *maintenance behavior within one stage of the developmental cycle of a particular marriage.*

The Wolin-Bennett-Noonan model of *family identity,* in contrast, deals specifically with transition and growth. It is offered in part as an explanation of how a newlywed husband and wife develop an identity for their marriage which distinguishes it from the identities of the two families the husband and wife grew up in. Many family theorists have, of course, addressed this fundamental problem. Jackson's notion of family rules and the marital quid pro quo have already been discussed as one notion of how this process occurs. Wolin et al. rely primarily on the anthropological concepts of myth and ritual to develop their unique model.

This model unfolds in the following fashion: Wolin et al. contend that just as the individual-level construct of ego identity, as defined by Erikson and Goffman, has proven useful in understanding the psychological growth and development of the individual, a notion of a "family identity" might prove to be an equally useful family-level construct. Describing this concept as the family's "subjective sense of its own situation, continuity, and character," they contend that each family has a shared belief system or a set of implicit assumptions passively accepted by all family members, assumptions which serve to govern interactional behavior within the family. Although these shared assumptions might not be consciously recognized by individual family members, they gain expression in the form of family themes (Hess and Handel, 1959), family myths (Ferreira, 1966) and family constructs (Reiss, 1971).

Although family identity is a concept that can be useful in describing regulatory mechanisms a family might use in their day-to-day behavior, its particular usefulness is in describing the connections established between generations of the same family. In this sense it can be thought of as a framework within which the developmental sequence of the family occurs. Although it obviously does not itself provide the impetus for development, it helps to define constraints within which the particular flavor or coloring of the developmental process occurs. A newlywed couple, whatever their conscious protestations to the contrary, are not free to establish an identity for their marriage totally divorced from their prior individual experiences within their families of origin. Rather, they shape or form a fresh identity within general guidelines they bring with them. Wolin et al. propose two specific mechanisms that provide the vehicles for such a process: family rituals and family myths.

Family rituals are defined as those repetitive behaviors which take on a symbolic communicational function because the stereotypic form within which the behavior is repeated has some special meaning and satisfaction for its participants. Rituals of family life are by and large secular and occur around such family activities as dinner time, holidays and vacations, family ceremonies, and the entertainment of unusual guests. Rituals are "created" by the family, contend Wolin-Bennett-Noonan, not only to deal with problems of everyday life, but also to assist the family "as it tries to deal with life cycle transitions such as birth, adolescence, marriage, and death, and as it struggles to meet crises such as illness or financial loss." They also emphasize the similarity between such family rituals and those "culture wide rituals such as rites of passage which society uses to direct its members' transition from one stage of their life cycle to the next."

As a clinical example of how family rituals might serve to shape transitional behavior for the family, suppose the oldest child in the family is being sent off to first grade and for the first time will be staying in a school setting for the lunch-time meal. Two weeks after school starts the child, during a late afternoon conversation with her mother, relates in considerable detail all of the wonderful things she gets to do during lunch-time at school, including such seemingly trivial items as eating her dessert before her sandwich, talking while she is eating and discovering that she didn't choke, and sitting in a different seat around the table each day. Her mother listens with some amusement and conscious emotional detachment. Several days later, however, she casually remarks to her husband that dinners have recently felt quite chaotic with his coming home at a different time each evening, with the children running away from the table the minute the meal is over, and with a distinctly hurried atmosphere having replaced the earlier feeling of peacefulness they had come to associate with their dinner-time meals. Citing as her primary rationale her feeling that dinner-time is the one daily occasion for the entire family to be together, she and her husband agree to pay increased attention to the reestablishment of a family dinner-time hour.

Wolin et al. might argue that in such a hypothetical situation the family uses ritualistic behavior to express for the young child the critical symbolic components of the family's identity, thereby assuring that the transition, not only of the individual child but of the entire family, into this a new stage in their development will take place within guidelines consistent with the family's identity. Although the child may develop her own set of rituals associated with behavior in school, they will presumably be compatible with her family identity as well as distinguishable from her family rituals—"one set of behaviors is what I do when I am in school, another set of behaviors is what I do when I'm at home."

Family myths, the second mechanism associated with the establishment of the family identity, are defined as "an individual's recollection of his or her family history in the near and distant past. The family myth is a blend of fact and fantasy incorporating crucial events and notable personalities in the family's history." Insofar as family myths are narratives that often incorporate information about family rituals as they were performed in previous generations, Wolin et al. think of family myths as a "shorthand method" for educating one's children about the family's past, especially those aspects that one hopes to continue in the next generation as part of a transgenerational family identity.

The most difficult developmental transition to conceptualize is that which occurs when two individuals from separate families marry and give birth to a new family. Although this new family will ultimately shape its own unique identity, if it is to have any historical continuity with its ancestral past, it must have a mechanism for incorporating the central beliefs and traditions of its earlier generations. Although one might persuasively argue that during the earlier years of marriage a couple establishes an amalgam composed of a unique combination of selected ingredients from individual families of origin, Wolin et al. argue that the more frequent occurrence is a disproportionate influence of aspects of the family identity from either the husband's or wife's origin family. They have labeled the predominant origin family the "family of heritage" for the new nuclear unit. This family of heritage, they have proposed, provides a pool of family myths upon which the new nuclear family can draw in shaping their own ritualistic behavior. In addition, specific family rituals may be passed on (incorporated) in the behavior of this new family. Although the underlying process that gives rise to the transition and translation of family identity from one generation to the next may well involve expression of unconscious assumptions, specific contracting and negotiation, and personal experiences of the new couple (those processes that have been most frequently mentioned by family theorists in this regard), the concepts of family ritual and family myths provide a specific behavioral mechanism to effect the transition itself.

Although both the "systems model of alcoholism" and the "family identity model" view marriage and the family within the broad framework of systems theory (that is, they would accept the notion of a marriage as an interactional system with properties separate and apart from the additive effects of the individuals involved), the models have a distinctly different flavor consequent upon the questions to which they are addressed. One model addresses the mechanisms which maintain ongoing behavior; the other model addresses transitional mechanisms.

The proposed developmental model of marriage provides a logical and appropriate place for both. An unnecessary choice between these models is not forced upon us.

A SUMMARY STATEMENT

In developing basic concepts and reviewing different versions of the systems perspective of marriage and marital disorders, it has repeatedly been emphasized that a useful clinical model serves three distinct purposes: (1) It directs attention to relevant data; (2) it provides a conceptual basis for pathology; (3) and it suggests a strategy for therapeutic intervention. What might be said about the current state of the systems theory art?

It is clear from this review that a veritable theoretical buffet is offered from which to choose, and that a series of models is now available, making significant inroads into the three areas identified as critical to clinicians. However, these models also at times differ dramatically in the data they use and in their actual definitions of pathology; therefore, it would be predicted that they would suggest quite different styles of intervention. These differences can be best understood if each of these models is labeled a partial theory and categorized by underscoring its differential reliance on certain critical concepts associated with general systems theory. It is particularly around their differential treatment of the dimensions of time and space, and their relative reliance on concrete or abstract concepts and data, that the theories can be most meaningfully distinguished one from another.

As these theories were critically reviewed, their heavy emphasis on concepts of control and steady state mechanisms, versus their relative lack of sophistication regarding concepts of growth and development, adaptation, and increasing complexity of organization was noteworthy. A major advantage of systems theory (as stated by Miller, 1965) is its ability to forge links between behavioral sciences and the natural sciences, especially biology. In this spirit a systems model of marriage was offered in rudimentary form that relies most heavily on concepts of growth and development but also offers a framework within which the partial theories described above can be juxtaposed and found each to have their separate and distinctive value.

REFERENCES

Armstrong, R. H. Systems and psychodynamics: Paradigms in collision? Paper presented at Georgetown Family Symposium, October, 1970.

Baer, D. M. and Wright, J. C. Developmental psychology. *Annual Review of Psychology*, 1975, 25, 1-82.

Bateson, G. *Steps to an Ecology of Mind*. New York: Ballantine, 1972.

Bateson, G., Jackson, D. D., Haley, J. and Weakland, J. Toward a theory of schizophrenia. *Behavior Science*, 1956, 1, 251-264.

Beckett, J. A. General systems theory, psychiatry and psychotherapy. *International Journal of Group Psychotherapy*, 1973, 23, 292-305.

Beels, C. C. and Ferber, A. Family therapy: A view. *Family Process*, 1969, 8, 280-318.

Bell, N. W. and Vogel, E. F. *A Modern Introduction to the Family*. Glencoe: Free Press, 1960.

Bowen, M. Theory in the practice of psychotherapy. In: P. J. Guerin (Ed.), *Family Therapy: Theory and Practice*. New York: Gardner Press, 1976.

Bowen, M. The use of family theory in clinical practice. *Comprehensive Psychiatry*, 1966, 7, 345-374.

Bowen, M. A family concept of schizophrenia. In: D. D. Jackson (Ed.), *The Etiology of Schizophrenia*. New York: Basic Books, 1960.

Buckley, W. *Sociology and Modern Systems Theory*. Englewood Cliffs, New Jersey: Prentice-Hall, Inc., 1967.

Cannon, W. D. *The Wisdom of the Body*. New York: Norton, 1939.

Carnap, R. *Introduction to Semantics*. Cambridge: Harvard University Press, 1942.

Duvall, E. M. *Family Development*. New York: Lippincott, 1971.

Engel, G. L. The need for a new medical model: A challenge for biomedicine. *Science*, 1977, 196, 129-135.

Erikson, E. H. *Childhood and Society* (Second Edition). New York: Norton, 1963.

Ferreira, A. J. Family myths. In: I. M. Cohen (Ed.), *Psychiatric Research Reports 20*. Washington, D. C.: American Psychiatric Association, 1966.

Fisher, L. On the classification of families. *Archives of General Psychiatry*, 1977, 34, 424-433.

Glick, P. D. The life cycle of a family. *Marriage and Family Living*, 1955, 18, 3-9.

Glick, P. D. and Parke, R. New approaches in studying the life cycle of the family. *Demography*, 1965, 2, 187-202.

Gray, W., Duhl, F. J. and Rizzo, N. D. *General Systems Theory and Psychiatry*. Boston: Little, Brown, 1969.

Haley, J. *Uncommon Therapy: The Psychiatric Techniques of Milton H. Erickson, M.D.* New York: Norton, 1973.

Hess, R. D. and Handel, G. *Family Worlds*. Chicago: University of Chicago Press, 1969.

Hill, R. *Family Development in Three Generations*. Cambridge, Mass.: Schenkman, 1970.

Hill, R. Modern systems theory and the family: A confrontation. *Social Science Information*, 1971, 10, 7-26.

Hill, R. and Hansen, B. A. The identification of conceptual frameworks utilized in family study. *Marriage and Family Living*, 1960, 22, 299-311.

Hill, R. and Rodgers, R. H. The developmental approach. In: H. T. Christensen (Ed.), *Handbook of Marriage and the Family*. Chicago: Rand McNally, 1964.

Hoffman, L. Deviation-amplifying processes in natural groups. In: J. Haley (Ed.), *Changing Families*. New York: Grune & Stratton, 1971.

Jackson, D. D. The study of the family. *Family Process*, 1965, 4, 1-20.

Jackson, D. D. Family rules: The marital *quid pro quo*. *Archives of General Psychiatry*, 1965, 12, 589-594.

Jackson, D. D. The question of family homeostasis. *Psychiatric Quarterly Supplement*, 1957, 31, 79-90.

Jackson, D. D. The eternal triangle. In: J. Haley and L. Hoffman (Eds.), *Techniques of Family Therapy*. New York: Basic Books, 1967, 174-264.

Kafka, J. S. Ambiguity for individuation: A critique and reformulation of double-bind theory. *Archives of General Psychiatry*, 1971, 25, 232-239.

Kantor, D. and Lehr, W. *Inside the Family*. San Francisco: Jossey-Bass, 1975.

Lederer, W. J. and Jackson, D. D. *The Mirages of Marriage*. New York: W. W. Norton, 1968.

Maruyama, M. The second cybernetics: Deviation-amplifying mutual causal processes. *American Scientist*, 1963, 51, 164-179.

Miller, J. G. Living systems: Basic concepts. *Behavioral Science*, 1965, 10, 193-237.

Minuchin, S. *Families and Family Therapy*. Cambridge: Harvard, 1974.

Minuchin, S., Baker, L., Rosman, B., et al. A conceptual model of psychosomatic illness in children. *Archives of General Psychiatry*, 1975, 32, 1031-1038.

Morris, C. W. Foundations on the theory of signs. In: O. Neurath, R. Carnap and C. O. Morris (Eds.), *International Encyclopedia of United Science*, Volume 1. Chicago: University of Chicago Press, 1938, pp. 77-137.

Olson, D. H. Marital and family therapy: A critical overview. In: A. S. Gurman and D. G. Rice (Eds.), *Couples in Conflict*. New York: Aronson, 1975.

Parsons, T. and Bales, R. F. *Family, Socialization and Interaction Process*. Glencoe, Illinois: Free Press, 1955.

Pitts, J. L. The structural-functional approach. In: H. T. Christensen (Ed.), *Handbook of Marriage and the Family*. Chicago: Rand McNally, 1964, pp. 51-124.

Rapoport, A. General systems theory: A bridge between two cultures. Third Annual Ludwig Von Bertalanffy Memorial Lecture. *Behavioral Science*, 1976, 21, 228-239.

Rapoport, A. What is information? *Synthese*, 1953, 9, 157.

Reiss, D. Varieties of consensual experience. I. A theory for relating family interaction to individual thinking. *Family Process*, 1971, 10, 1-28.

Reiss, D. The multiple family group as a small society: Family regulation of interaction with nonmembers. *American Journal of Psychiatry*, 1977, 134, 21-24.

Ritterman, M. K. Paradigmatic classification of family therapy theories. *Family Process*, 1977, 16, 29-48.

Rodgers, R. H. *Family Interaction and Transaction: The Developmental Approach*. Englewood Cliffs, New Jersey: Prentice-Hall, 1973.

Ruesch, J. Analysis of various types of boundaries. In: R. R. Grinker (Ed.), *Toward a Unified Theory of Human Behavior*. New York: Basic Books, 1956.

Skynner, A. C. R. *Systems of Family and Marital Psychotherapy*. New York: Brunner/Mazel, 1976.

Sluzki, C. E. and Ransom, D. C. (Eds.). *Double Bind: The Foundation of the Communicational Approach to the Family*. New York: Grune & Stratton, 1976.

Solomon, M. A. A developmental, conceptual premise for family therapy. *Family Process*, 1973, 12, 179-196.

Speer, D. C. Family systems: Morphostasis and morphogenesis or "Is homeostasis enough?" *Family Process*, 1970, 9, 259-278.

Speigel, J. *Transactions: The Interplay Between Individual, Family, and Society*. New York: Science House, 1971.

Steinglass, P., Davis, D. I., and Berenson, D. Observations of conjointly hospitalized "alcoholic couples" during sobriety and intoxication: Implications for theory and therapy. *Family Process*, 1977, 16, 1.

Steinglass, P., Weiner, S. and Mendelson, J. H. A systems approach to alcoholism: A model and its clinical application. *Archives of General Psychiatry*, 1971, 24, 401-408.

von Bertalanffy, L. *General Systems Theory*. New York: George Braziller, 1968.

Waters, W. and Fried, F. General systems analysis of emotions. *Journal of Operational Psychiatry*, 1976, 7, 16-31.

Watzlawick, P., Beavin, J. H. and Jackson, D. D. *Pragmatics of Human Communication*. New York: Norton, 1967.

Watzlawick, P., Weakland, J. and Fisch, R. *Change: Principles of Problem Formation and Problem Resolution*. New York: W. W. Norton, 1974.

Wiener, N. *Cybernetics, or Control and Communication in the Animal and the Machine*. Cambridge, Mass.: MIT Press, 1962.

Wolin, S. J., Bennett, L. A. and Noonan, D. L. Ritual, myth and family identity (unpublished manuscript).

Wynne, L. and Singer, M. Thought disorder and family relations of schizophrenics: I. Research strategy. *Archives of General Psychiatry*, 1963, 9, 191-198.

VII

Marital Therapy from a Systems Theory Perspective

Carlos E. Sluzki, M.D.

The problems posed by any attempt at discussing the treatment of human systems are complex and exceedingly difficult to solve, for, viewed from any angle, therapy, like art, is unteachable. Only repertoires of forms can be transmitted, together with a certain intellectual grounding for them. This chapter is aimed at proposing some of those forms, as well as their conceptual roots.

Introduction

Marital and family therapy is not simply a treatment method. It is a whole new way of conceptualizing human problems, of understanding behavior, the development of symptoms, and their resolution. The qualitative shift in the conceptual framework that characterizes the interpersonal systems approach to the couple requires that one utilize the *transactions between individuals,* rather than the characteristics of each given individual, as primary data. Even when, for one reason or another, attention is zeroed in on one person, his/her behavior is analyzed in terms of its power to affect and shape the behavior of other members of the system and in terms of the variables of the eco-system that may have affected it. This approach is based on an original epistemology concerned, broadly speaking, with the notion of information and organization, with communication processes as they occur within systems.

When observing couples' interactions, a system-oriented therapist will take into consideration effects, rather than intentions. The effects of behaviors upon behaviors, the way interpersonal sequences are organized, will be carefully noted, while, on the contrary, no inference will be made about the motivations of the participants. Even further, issues about motivation or intention will be considered irrelevant to the understanding of interpersonal processes. This choice must not be taken as the blunt denial of the existence of motivation, intentions, or human volition in general. It only happens that those inferences do not add any relevant information for purposes of conceptualizing and/or treating marital disorders from a systems perspective. For those trained in the intrapsychic tradition, this strategic preference, this switch from intention to effect, must be zealously watched, as the old habits tend to sneak back and therapists may find they are once again engaged in 'exercises of reconstruction about what has been happening "inside the black box," as cyberneticians say, and worse, applying value judgments derived from those reconstructions.

As happens with the applications of any model, the utilization of a systems vantage point for the understanding and modification of the way couples interact necessarily requires focusing on certain behaviors and interpersonal processes *at the expense of others**—selectively observing events, filtering in those observables that are relevant to the model. This presentation will deal, therefore, with gross simplifications of highly complex interactional processes pertaining to social systems with an evolving history of their own and immersed in multiple, larger, constantly changing, overlapping social organizations. However, such simplification must not be considered a fallacy of the model, for the power of the model as a scientific device rests in its capacity to simplify and organize the subject matter (in addition to its capacity to explain and predict).

To teach therapists to "think systems" has been my main activity during recent years. In doing so, I followed a training format that went from theory to technique. That is, I started by speaking about general principles and progressively specified the concrete application of those

---

* This is true even within the systems model. From Jackson's revolutionary "The Question of Family Homeostasis" (1954) on, a number of authors have developed rich, internally consistent, intellectually attractive models of therapy for couples and for families coherent with a systems framework, while utilizing remarkably dissimilar conceptual tools and therapeutic strategies. Compare, for instance, Haley (1963, 1973), Bowen (1972), Minuchin (1974), and Kantor and Lehr (1975): All of them are sound examples of a systems vantage point; each of them is original and distinct.

principles. But that tack did not prove to be the best choice, for what I considered fascinating general principles seemed to be more relevant to the teacher than to the students. The latter, quite unmoved by general principles, were, however, consistently attracted by the pragmatics of the concrete applications. That observation stimulated me, quite recently, to make a 180° turn in my training strategy and start with the concrete and specific, deferring to later stages the gradual instillation of some theory.

This approach—from technique to theory—is followed in this chapter, which consists of a series of "naked" prescriptions about concrete, rather specific therapeutic interventions which can be carried out by the therapist whenever a member of a couple, or both members of it, display certain types of behaviors during the course of a session. Each prescription is separately formulated and conceptually grounded. The overall series, far from being an exhaustive list, constitutes an open-ended attempt to conceptualize treatment principles. However, if you, the reader, follow these prescriptions even loosely, they may lead your work with couples to rather unusual and quite fascinating places, through generating experience conducive to a systems exploration and systems intervention. Perhaps, they may even stimulate you to create a systems model of your own for the treatment of couples, which would be indeed the best possible way to learn. Let us, then, end this prologue and begin with the series.

PRESCRIPTIONS FOR THERAPEUTIC INTERVENTIONS

> #1. If A speaks in first person plural in reference
> to opinions, judgments or values, *then* tell A
> to use first person singular.

Example: A: ". . . whenever the subject of money arises, we get immediately all uptight."

Therapist: (to A) "I'd rather you would speak just for yourself right now. So, whenever the subject of money arises, you feel uptight."

A: "But it happens to both of us."

Therapist: (sticking to program) "I'm not questioning that possibility. But I'd rather use each of you as experts on yourselves, not on the other, so I'd rather you speak for yourself and let B speak for himself. Well, you were saying that whenever the subject of money arises. . . ."

From the very first steps of a treatment, it may be convenient to establish and maintain a set of communicational premises aimed at neutralizing, or at least making evident, certain fixed rules of the couple about spokesmanship and roles, as reflected in their linguistic style. One of them has to do with the use of the first person plural for referents other than facts or events. It constitutes a special case of what will later be discussed as "mind-reading." A special prescription about it is presented solely because this situation tends to appear early in the first interviews and, therefore, it becomes a testing ground for the couple's modality of negotiation with the therapist about premises of therapy, as well as for the couple's ability to make shifts and changes.

As happens with any relationship, from the very beginning of the therapy the participants are proposing rules about the definition of the therapeutic relationship. In fact, there are very few basic premises about which the participants tend to agree, such as who will be labeled as the expert (not *how*, not *for what*, not *for whom*, just *who*), who is going to be paid (not *who pays*), and where are they going to meet (not *when*). But even those premises are shaky. For instance, the expertise of the therapist is often questioned or challenged whenever the behavior of the expert does not match the a priori expectations of the couple; that is, the couple may strongly disagree in regard to how the expertise is going to come about or be implemented, and toward whom.

The case is particularly blatant in those couples in which one spouse is labeled as "the patient" and other as "the informer" or "helpful middle-person." The latter will frequently use the first person plural, and that usage states and explores the collective agreement on that role. To question it, to say "speak for yourself," challenges radically that role, and therefore a rule of the couple. This explains why this apparently minor communicational restructuring intervention may meet unusual resistance. Therefore, as with the rest of these therapeutic prescriptions, apply it gently but persistently.

> #2. If A speaks in impersonal terms about personal matters (such as value judgments and opinions), *then* tell A to make a personal statement.

Example: A· "People don't come home at three in the morning without letting you know they are going to be late."

> *Therapist:* (to A) "So it makes you feel bad when Joe comes home at three in the morning without previously warning you about the delay. To be more precise, what do you feel when that happens?"

This proposition establishes the basis for a cardinal premise that must be maintained and conveyed at all cost: Value judgments emanate from human beings, and not from objects or situations per se. That is, they are opinions, not immutable facts. The reification of values automatically externalizes them and transforms them into stone-carved truth. Demystifying value judgments is a necessary step toward changing them or, at least, toward introducing the possibility that alternative values or meanings can be equally legitimate, regardless of how compatible they may be with that of the holder or of the mainstream of the culture.

Putting the value judgment back into the speaker dramatically eliminates a strong ally of the speaker, the "generalized other," a powerful collective enemy against which the partner has to fight. Needless to say, it also clearly establishes that therapists do not organize the therapeutic field on the basis of rights and wrongs, or goods and bads.

The establishment of this premise may also represent for the couple a step toward reaching a first agreement—that they *disagree in terms of values or opinions*. This is a starting point for negotiations radically different from the conviction on the part of either than one is right and one is wrong, or, more frequently, that one is sane and the other crazy, or that one is good and the other evil.

#3. If A makes an unsubstantiated reference to B's subjective state ("mind-reading"), *then* ask A what it is that A perceives, differentiating perceptions from inferences.

Example: A: "And she doesn't like me to say those kinds of things about us."
Therapist: "Rather than checking it with you, B, let me ask you, A, how is it that you know that B doesn't like it?"

To mind-read is to assume that one can know what is in the mind of the other person—his/her thoughts, feelings, intentions, or motivations— without the need for information or verification by the other. Mind-

reading can be a powerful interactional tool with devastating consequences: If a spouse knows what his/her mate thinks or feels better than
he/she does, then no argument is going to convince the spouse of the
contrary.

Mind-reading is a frequent intervention of parents with children, and
of brainwashers about victims. The difference between one and the other
extreme of the situation—between a benign anticipation and a paralyz-
ing disqualification—can be sometimes assessed either by the context and
function of the mind-reading statement or by the response of the
recipient—sometimes just the baffled facial expression will do. There is
no way out of this bind within the system. It locks and perpetuates roles
and rules about who is sick or bad and who is healthy or good. It requires an outside intervention to be untangled.

The systematic questioning of mind-reading statements will, sometimes,
by itself attain dramatic changes in the couple's patterns of interactions.
More frequently, it will simply shatter assumptions previously taken for
granted by the couple, and contribute to the establishment of the general
rule that, in the session, each one will be considered an expert about
him/herself and not about the partner.*

> #4. If A speaks to you about B (rather than to B),
> *then*: (a) keep looking at A rather than at B
> while A speaks; and (b) tell A to speak to,
> not about B; or (c) ask A how he/she feels
> about it; or (d) address a comment about A
> to B.

It may be quite obvious, but nevertheless quite crucial, to point out
that, while the study of couple pathology requires an analysis of dyadic
systems, the study of the treatment of marital disorders implies the
analysis of triadic systems.

One unavoidable characteristic of human triads is their tendency to
establish coalitions, that is, alliances of two of the members established
for their mutual benefit or strength vis à vis the third member, implying

---

* An original approach to the detection and clinical handling of "mind-reading"
and other semantic ambiguities (including those dealt with in prescriptions #1 and
#2) can be found in Bandler and Grinder (1975).

relationships characterized by inclusion and by exclusion.* The process of coalition-seeking and coalition negotiation, which generally runs rampant in the beginning of any couple's treatment, requires careful monitoring and laborious calibration if the therapist wishes to establish instrumental ground rules, or metacommunicative principles, that will frame and guide an effective course of treatment. One of these rules is that "the therapist is going to establish only shifting, instrumental coalitions without binding himself/herself to stable, aprioristic ones or following the culturally established patterns of negotiation" (Sluzki, 1975, p. 71). The establishement of this rule results from a protracted accumulation of experiences in the course of the treatment, rather than from any one statement of principles about it.

This prescription consists of four parts, each of which will be discussed separately.

> (a) If A speaks to you *about* B (rather than *to* B),
> *then* keep looking at A rather than at B while
> A speaks.

The process of probing, proposing, bargaining and establishing rules about relationships—both relationships in families and in the context of therapy—happens occasionally through explicit verbal exchanges. The bulk of these transactions occurs, however, only implicitly, through the myriad exchanges of information that take place constantly by means of both linguistic and non-linguistic components of speech, and by nonverbal processes (postures, gestures, movement, distances and the like). Our body behavior can convey our own sets of premises as forcefully as words can. One cannot *not* communicate, as Bateson, and so many after him, said.

The statement conveyed by looking at the member of the couple who is speaking *about* the other can be perhaps clarified by its opposite. What would be implied if the therapist looked at B while A was speak-

---

* A considerable amount has been written about coalitions, from the first inquiries about the nature of interaction in groups of three published at the turn of the century by one of the founders of modern sociology, Georg Simmel (e.g., 1902), to Haley's (1963) insightful observations and prescriptions about coalitions in family therapy, to Caplow's (1968) elegant paper on inclusions and exclusions to the present author's article on coalitions (Sluzki, 1975). The reader is referred to that literature for any inquiry in depth on the subject.

ing about him/her? Perhaps the implied statement is "Now, what do you have to say in your defense?" or "So *that* is what he/she does!" That is, looking at B while A was speaking would be the equivalent of aligning with A and of taking A's statements as descriptions of reality—not as A's perceptions and opinions. It happens that when A is speaking about B, A is really speaking about A, and the therapist should be clear about this and act accordingly.

> (b) If A speaks to you about B (rather than to
> B), *then* tell A to speak *to*, not *about* B.*

Example: A: "She always sees the negative side of things."
    Therapist: (to A) "Would you mind saying that to her now?"
    A: "But I've told her the same thing a million times."
    Therapist: (sticking to instruction) "Well, then, once more won't hurt."
    A: "Frustrated. Frustrated and furious, doctor."

Example: A: "Jim is always late from work."
    Therapist: (to A) "Would you please tell that to Jim?"
    A: "All right. Jim, you never arrive at home on time. I've asked you that a hundred times, we've changed dinner hours another hundred, and nothing—you're still always late!"
    Therapist: (to A) "Could you tell Jim how you feel about it?"
    A: "Frustrated. Frustrated and furious, doctor."
    Therapist: (to A) "Tell him that."
    A: (to B) "It really infuriates me and frustrates me a lot when I find myself, once again, waiting for you, with everything ready for dinner and steaming up."

When the therapist is the recipient of the complaint, the implicit request of that statement is that he/she do something about it. On the other hand, when the members of the couple speak to one another, the weight of the responsibility for the change is transferred back onto them. At the same time, the therapist has further defined the nature of

---

* While this is a cherished axiom of those family therapists involved in the so-called "growth" approach, I should credit Alan and Eva Leveton (personal communication) for their having highlighted this point in unpublished didactic material prepared by them.

his/her relationship with the couple: The therapist is not going to be the middle-person, or take sides, or pass judgment. The nature of the observable is also defined—interpersonal processes rather than individual statements.

The "speak to, not about" instruction is a powerful tool to activate in the session in order to unveil the drama of the conflict, for it allows direct access to the couple's process under duress. It is important that the therapist remain consistent with this prescription, addressing the participants in second, rather than third, person whenever feasible. That is, he/she also has to speak to, not about the patients. That may require, surprisingly, a good deal of concentration and occasionally some linguistic juggling.

An exception to this reminder is the use of dialogue with a co-therapist *about* the couple, in the couple's presence, which is a tactic that can be utilized occasionally in order to muffle heavy interventions or establish the grounds for paradoxical prescriptions.

> (c) If A speaks to you about B (rather than to B), *then* ask A how he/she feels about it.

This intervention can be utilized as a less intense version of "Speak to, not about," as the latter may imply for the couple a far more radical departure from their expectation about the therapist's behaviors. Apparently, therapists are expected to ask about feelings, but not to redirect the flow of interaction.

In addition, this intervention proposes and models an effective style of communication, establishing the precedent that affects can be explicitly included as pieces of information rather than being taken for granted (thus allowing for countless mistaken "mind-readings").

In the last example, "How do you feel about it?" follows, and is followed by, a "Speak to, not about." Thus, the expression of feelings complements other maneuvers, and enriches the interaction. To pick up the dialogue of that example:

Therapist: (to A) "Could you tell Jim how you feel about it?"
A: "Frustrated. Frustrated and furious, doctor."
Therapist: (to A) "Tell *him* that."
A: (to B) "It really infuriates me and frustrates me a lot when I find myself, once again, waiting for you, with everything ready

for dinner and getting overcooked, or else ready to go out and
feeling bored."
Therapist: (to A) "And how, habitually, do you express, to Jim,
your fury and frustration?"
A: "I clam up. I don't speak to him for hours."
Therapist: "Well, that sounds to me more like a hurt response than
anger."
A: "Well, I *feel* hurt. . . ."

Here, "hurt" is a mild relabeling of "fury and frustration" aimed at
creating a more workable situation: The overall effect on both partners
of a transaction involving "hurt" in one member allows much more
leeway in terms of exchanges and negotiations than that generated by
"fury." Relabeling will be further discussed later in this chapter.

A final comment about the example. Although the therapist is aiming
at generating interactions between A and B, the whole excerpt is one in
which the speakers are A and the therapist. B seems to be, so to speak,
shielded by the therapist. In fact, that was precisely the intention of the
therapist: While favoring interactions between the members of the couple
through "Speak to, not about," he forcefully establishes and monitors
the conditions for that exchange, in order to increase the feasibility of a
positive experience. At the same time, by addressing A he is following
some of the previously mentioned prescriptions about coalitions. However, the therapist would have to balance this undue attention to A (or
this excessive protection of B) later in the session. Otherwise, he would
have created a risky imbalance in the relative "weight" of his relationship with each member of the couple.

(d) If A speaks to you about B (rather than to B),
then address a comment to B about A.

Example: A: "When he does that kind of thing it drives me crazy."
Therapist: (to B) "She sounds really angry, doesn't she? What
kind of feelings does her anger trigger in you?"

This type of intervention is especially useful when the communication
between members of the couple is becoming difficult due to their intense anger, a situation that requires some defusing before a more direct
interaction between them can be attempted. In those circumstances, it
constitutes a very powerful maneuver aimed at maintaining equidistance

in stormy waters. Through statements such as the one above, both A and B are being told that the therapist has not established a coalition with A or with B, and that therapy is focused on the reciprocal perspectives, without having either dismissed A for what A said or B for what has been said about B. It will take subsequent interventions consistent with this approach to further establish the rule of circumstantial coalition with, but basic equidistance from, both members of the couple.

> #5. If A is consistently defined as the "victimizer" (or as the "identified patient") by B, *then*:
> (a) reduce physical distance with A, and/or
> (b) mirror A's body position.

These prescriptions expand the repertoire of techniques that can be used in order to evade a coalition, in this case, with B. They signal that the therapist will not accept the couple's definition of the relationship with the therapist as one in which he/she will align with the "victims" or the "non-patients," as expected and prescribed by social norms.

The concepts of "victimizer" and of "victim" are utilized here in terms of a configuration of reciprocal roles, that is, as a rule in the relationship in which both members participate with equal responsibility. The same can be said of "identified patient" (IP), a role with complementary counter-roles which contribute as much as the IP to the maintenance of the system. The presence of these configurations allows the therapist to predict that the couple is going to propose a definition of the therapeutic relationship which will involve a coalition between the therapist and the "victim" versus the "victimizer" or between the therapist and the "healthy" spouse against the IP. If the therapist falls for that, he/she loses perspective as well as any chance of modifying the system.

Therefore, in order to signal lack of agreement with their proposition about the definition of the relationship, the therapist displays body signs indicating willingness to coalesce with the other one. The two behaviors contained in this instruction signal that intention.* Needless to say, this

---

* The reader who wants to explore further communicational function of the behaviors included in this prescription, as well as expand this repertoire with other equally expressive displays, should consult the work of Scheflen (1974, 1976), who has registered the most insightful observations on territoriality and the interpersonal patterns of body behavior, including the message values of body distance, body mirroring and leg crossing.

is *not* a stable alliance and the therapist remains in that bond only as long as it may take for the message to be received by the couple that he/she will not engage in the other configuration. Once that is clear, he/she will have to withdraw into the strategic oscillations that characterize the coalitionary process in couples therapy.

> #6. If A and B concur in defining A as victim and B as victimizer, *then* find a way of reversing the roles/labels and state the reversal forcefully.

The positions of "victim" and "victimizer" are the result of a punctuation in the sequence of events, that is, of an arbitrary decision on the part of one or both participants about who leads and who follows. The issue of "punctuations," as well as procedural matters dealing with this prescription, will be discussed in the context of #7, which is partly a concrete application of this prescription. In the case of victim-victimizer couples, as well as in symptomatic-nonsymptomatic dyads, it is difficult for members to change *from within* the rules that govern the system. They require an outside intervention to step out of recurrent patterns.*

The following constitutes an example of such an intervention in a dyad: The present author recently saw a couple who were locked in a relationship in which the wife's nagging, complaining negativism contrasted sharply with the husband's appeasing optimism. Each of them was expressing mounting dissatisfaction and resentment, and both concurred in defining her as the victimizer and him as the victim. I praised her for having decided to take the heavy load of the villain (cf., Prescriptions #6 and #8), though to help to make him look good while she remained the "mean one" must have had some kicks for her. But, I continued, there are no kicks like the kicks of being the "good guy," and he was selfishly keeping most of the assets to himself. They looked quite surprised, but went along with the reasoning and the metaphors. I prescribed that he should respond to any statement of hers by being as pessimistic as possible—regardless of how really pessimistic he might be at that moment, without leaking to her the true nature of his feelings. I prescribed her to remain as pessimistic as before, "in order not to make

---

* The protagonistic couple of Albee's "Who's Afraid of Virginia Woolf" provides a paradigm of impotence from within. (Cf. an outstanding interactional analysis of that play in Watzlawick et al., 1967.)

the task more difficult for him" (cf., Prescription #11). To analyze these prescriptions: (1) The prescription acknowledged that he *could* be genuinely pessimistic; (2) her habitual behavior was being relabeled as a gesture of good will; (3) if they followed instructions, they would quite quickly reach a deadlock that would force her to extricate the positive side of the matter; (4) nobody—but the therapist, perhaps—would be blamed for any escalation into pessimism between them, totally eliminating any label of victim and victimizer; and (5) they were being granted a humorous way out of confrontations, used by them thereafter on occasions. In fact, both expressed a remarkable reduction of the conflicts and a general improvement in the relationship from there on, while I, correspondingly, expressed concern about their unexplainable and too dramatic change (cf., Prescriptions #9 and #12).

A word of caution. If the couple's agreement on who is the victim or victimizer strikes the therapist as very farfetched, the agreement may represent a "folie à deux" or other strong family myth, in which case it should either be challenged very cautiously, or an alternative track, such as working toward changing the pattern while retaining the couple's definition of it, could be chosen (cf., Prescription #15).

> #7. If A and B describe a sequence of events that leads to conflict or to the emergence of symptoms, *then* search for the events or steps that precede what has been described as the first step in the sequence. If you cannot specify it, nonetheless state its existence. If it has been detected, and is accepted by A and B as possible, then repeat the cycle (i.e., search for a still previous step, or at least assert its existence).

Except perhaps in the very early stages of parent-child relationships, there is no totally passive, victim-like position in interpersonal situations within small systems. All members are contributing parties to the interactional sequences, the behavior of each member being induced by and in turn inducing the other. At the most, in certain circumstances one of the actors *appears* to be the victim. However, this constitutes an "optical illusion" derived from the fact that observers—and frequently also the participants—*punctuate the sequence arbitrarily*. That is, the chicken/egg puzzle is arbitrarily solved by designating one of the participants as the initiator and the other as the reactor. But, is it that he nags because she withdraws or that she withdraws because he nags?

The punctuation of the sequence of events is the result of the arbitrary and almost unavoidable introduction of context markers in the sequence of interactions (Bateson and Jackson, 1964). Even though some behaviors may be defined as *stimuli,* some as *responses,* and some as *reinforcement* (a calibration of the stimulus in the light of the response), each communicational act can be considered "simultaneously a stimulus, a response and a reinforcement, according to how we slide our identification . . . up and down the series" (Bateson, 1963, p. 176).

Leaving aside those couples who display a conflict format centered in punctuations—"you nag, no, you withdraw" type—most couples reach agreement about punctuation of events both in their history and in their present life, and any quest for alternative punctuations may meet with considerable resistance on their part. However, persistence may uncover many family myths and other covert agreements, and may provide leads toward dramatic restructuring of the rules of the relationship.

A couple was seen in conjoint therapy after one interview with the woman triggered a stormy depression, which was accompanied by bursts of unbearable anxiety and somatic symptoms such as daily vomiting, headaches and abdominal pain. The proposition of the therapist that there was some behavior in the nonsymptomatic partner that preceded and contributed to explain the IP's symptoms was met with total incredulity by both partners. In a subsequent crisis of the symptomatology that followed a period of quiescence, the therapist was able to detect and show to both members that when the husband started to experience anxiety due to mounting responsibilities in his complex job, the wife would respond to that cue with a flair of symptoms. Immediately, the husband would become involved in taking care of her and simultaneously his anxiety would vanish, freeing him for an effective performance at work (which became quite shaky due to his anxiety once when she was on vacation and a new requirement of his job took place). As a result of this observation, the therapist expressed his worries about what would happen to the husband if her symptoms subsided (Prescription #9), suggested to her that she produce symptoms out of phase (Prescription #10) and centered his attention on the husband's anxiety, acknowledging the wife's valuable contribution whenever she reported experiencing symptoms (Prescription #8). The whole symptomatic pattern broke within three months, after five years of plaguing the couple's life, as they replaced their hidden homeostatic agreement with one that was more mutual and did not require the presence of symptoms.

> #8. If A complains about a symptom, *then* find a way of complimenting A for what A is doing for B.

This prescription, still a spinoff of #6, is also the first of a series of prescriptions centered in positive connotation, symptoms prescriptions and paradoxical interventions.* It can be utilized to set in motion the notion that the therapist is going to apply a dialectic logic instead of the traditional causal one utilized up to that moment by the couple (and, in fact, by most people). There are several messages embedded in this prescription: A is defined as having control over the symptoms at a certain level; the connotation of the symptom is changed, from negative to positive, as the symptom is defined as having some positive value (it is accomplishing a useful function for the other member of the couple) —therefore, a certain shared responsibility of A and B over the symptom is implied; and the therapist will not confront the system by means of suppressing the symptom. Overall, a viewpoint characterized by the emphasis on interpersonal processes and shared responsibility is introduced.

In several examples throughout this chapter, the prescription to "compliment the symptom" appears as an introductory step for more complex paradoxical interventions, that is, for interventions which generate a bind that can only be solved by the patients' extinguishing the symptomatic behavior or breaking interactional stereotypes (cf., for instance, the case included in the comment to Prescription #6).

> #9. If symptomatic member A reports a decrease in in the intensity of symptoms in the last week(s), *then* express vague worries and recommend a slight relapse, even soliciting the aid of B to achieve that relapse, and/or express worry that B may develop some symptoms.

---

* The reader interested in pursuing this theme beyond the limits of these short comments should consult, in the first place, the innovative work of Haley (1963, 1977), as well as Watzlawick, Weakland and Fisch (1974) and Selvini Palazzoli et al. (1975).

Symptomatic patients and their mates may try to avoid change by attempting to define the symptom as something devoid of context. The interactional view allows the therapist to see otherwise: Symptoms accomplish functions for the system, and all members contribute somehow to their maintenance. But, how to proceed with this assumption without transforming the session into an arena for the confrontation of the two ideologies—the couple's and the therapist's? Beyond the sterility of a discussion about intentionality, the risk lies in appearing to be as explicitly aligned with the system's tendencies toward change. The habitual response of the members of this alignment is to hurry and stabilize the system following the patterns already familiar to them, and hence strengthen the status quo and the symptoms.

In fact, order (morphostatic properties) and change (morphogenesis) are complementary tendencies of interpersonal systems. They maintain a fine balance through complex homeostatic processes. When any living system deviates toward one of the poles, processes are activated that pull the system in the direction of the opposite tendency, thereby keeping the system within a clearly defined equilibrium between both. The triumph of the morphostatic tendencies are total rigidity and death of the system. The triumph of morphogenesis is total dissolution and, equally, death of the system. The balance between both tendencies is crucial both for stability and for change within the system.

Therefore, if the therapist wishes to favor change within a rigidified system, he/she should transit along that fine line. That can be done, in some cases, by maintaining a front defending stability while freeing the system from restrictive rules that prevent the members from working out changes. Symptoms, frequent barometers of these processes, can be useful tools in this type of paradoxical intervention, as has already been illustrated in the last example.

The prescription of symptoms—be it the very symptom that brought the couple to the consultation or any other one—is a powerful therapeutic tool that can be introduced—in general, with amazingly little resistance—through the tack followed by this prescription (and the next ones up to #13).

> #10. If A has a symptom that fluctuates within the day or the week, *then* instruct A to select times in which the symptom improves to tell B that it is worse.

It was mentioned above that couples with a symptomatic member tend to punctuate the sequence of events in such a manner that the symptom appears to be the (uncalled for, unintentional) *stimulus,* and that the partner's behavior is defined as the *response.* Ways to alter that punctuation were also proposed (Prescriptions #6-9). The present prescription is still another way of dealing with these issues.

Through prescribing a symptom to a symptomatic member in the presence of the mate, the therapist aims at shattering the very pattern that perpetuates the symptom. That effect occurs through two mechanisms: (a) When the patient is told "fake the symptom, and fake it well," the other member of the dyad is implicitly being told that the symptomatic behavior to which he/she may be exposed to *may* be false, therefore inhibiting "spontaneous" responses that in turn may reinforce and perpetuate the symptom; and (b) it subtly increases the consensus about the patient's control over the symptom, and decreases the chances of his/her claiming spontaneity. At the same time, it evokes its counterpart, that if the subject can *produce* a symptom through a prescription, he/she may also be able to *reduce* it. One of the key interactional attributes of symptoms, namely, the fact that they are considered spontaneous by the participants, is drastically questioned by a well-placed symptom description.

This prescription is illustrated in several examples in this chapter. To provide still another one: It corresponds to a first interview with a couple whose explicit problem was centered in her stubborn insomnia, recent loss of appetite, and fluctuating weakness and irritability which she related to her insomnia. She had four offspring from previous partners and had been living with this mate for some three years. He expressed worries about her symptoms and elegantly tolerated her condition, as well as his role as healthy partner of a sick lady. The exploration of the context or origin, as well as any function the symptom might have been serving in the system (i.e., the effects of the symptoms on his behavior, or on the behavior of any other member of the family), failed to produce any additional meaningful information.

In the course of that interview, the therapist stated that the symptoms the woman was presenting were correlates of depression without feelings of sadness. The man reacted immediately by stating, defensively, that she didn't have any reason to be sad. To defuse, the therapist proposed that maybe it had to do with old sadness (nothing to do with the present context) and prescribed that, in the course of the next week, she should behave as though she were very, very sad, especially on those days in which she was least sad, and asked him to help her in that task by letting her express her sadness without trying to counter-argue or shush her. The therapist added that they would probably find the task surprisingly difficult to comply with. She agreed that it was against the grain of her tendencies to show her sad side. The man stated, in turn, that he did not foresee any difficulty in his share, because, "After all, she may be just acting it."

In the next session, they reported that she cried as never before, and that he felt that he was helping her get rid of the pain by just being there, instead of feeling defensive about it. Two stormy sessions followed in which several current frustrations were discussed, and the crisis subsided with a drastic change in the couple's style of coping with conflict. The presenting symptoms were not even mentioned during that period, and when explored, they were reported as having vanished.

The symptom prescription seemed to accomplish the function of facilitating a break in an otherwise repetitive cycle that kept them locked, until then, in their respective roles of sick and sane.

> #11. Whenever a prescription of a behavior or of a symptom is made, the more basic the implied change, the more trivial it should be made to appear: involve both members in the prescription and admonish that, in spite of it sounding trivial, they will find it difficult to comply.

The maintenance and exacerbation of conflicts, problems or symptoms are frequently the result of the positive feedback loop created by those very behaviors of other members of the system aimed at resolving the difficulty; thus, the attempted solution becomes part of the problem (cf. Haley, 1963; Hoffman, 1971; Watzlawick et al., 1974; Wender, 1968).

The benevolent prescription by the therapist of those same behaviors which are considered symptomatic by the members of the system severely challenges the very rules that tend otherwise to perpetuate the symptoms. The illegitimate, spontaneous, parasitical behavior becomes legitimate, non-spontaneous and a useful part of the process. The complaint becomes the compliance and the disappearance of symptoms a non-compliance. The very behavior that was used previously as a marker of roles becomes now the result of a prescription by the therapist. The system is robbed of a basic rule.

The more challenging the change implied by the prescription, the less it should appear to be: Otherwise, the investment of the therapist in the specific change becomes itself a marker, and the members of the couple may tend to utilize the alternative outcomes of the prescription to reward or punish the therapist, or each other. For the same reason the expression of doubts is included: Whatever the outcome, the therapist will have made a correct prediction, which precludes any improvement or relapse made "in his behalf." Further, relapses may even be encouraged, a strategy that, as already discussed in regard to Prescription #10, conveys the notion that the symptomatic or problematic behavior is under the control of the actor, rather than an allegedly random process. Once this is established, the main interactional value of a symptom, its being there *in spite of* the participants, is lost, and, with it, the symptom itself.

The reason behind the recommendation of prescribing behaviors to both members must be quite clear by now—to further establish their joint responsibility for the problem and its solution, through further blurring the distinction between symptoms or problematic behaviors and their counterpart in each member.

A rather long example will illustrate several of these prescriptions.

It relates to the couple already introduced in the example for Prescription #7. Their conjoint treatment started with a façade of an individual therapy: a 30-year-old wife of a diplomat was brought to the office, completely crippled by a myriad of severe emotional and somatic symptoms—oppressive headaches, daily vomiting, intense anxiety and severe depression, all triggered by a move to San Francisco from their country due to his work. Her husband was engaged promptly in the treatment, and shortly afterwards therapy clearly was dealing fully with what Jackson (1965a) named the "marital *quid pro quo.*" In their case, the trade-off was that her symptoms allowed him to be free of anxiety—mainly around death and departures—which otherwise overwhelmed him occasionally, and his protective behavior allowed her to remain child-like while in control of most of the decisions in the relationship.

The sequence described here corresponds to a period in which they were dealing with the prospect of another move because of a change in his job responsibilities. During the session she complained of headaches and anxiety—one-tenth as intense as previously, but nonetheless there.

In the course of that session, I praised her for her sacrifices on behalf of the couple, praised him for allowing her to be so useful, and proceeded to prescribe for him, almost as a game, that in the next week he should try another tack: Instead of appeasing her whenever she complained of her symptoms, he should tell her immediately his own worries or problems, competing with her to see who suffered more, regardless of the "true" intensity of his problems or worries. In turn, I instructed her to be very sensitive about her body, and to communicate to him whenever she felt anything unpleasant.

In the following session, predictably, they reported that he was quite anxious and she didn't have any symptoms, even though she felt irritable. He commented, frustrated, that she hardly gave him any chance to express his worries, that she flooded him with her problems and symptoms. I told him to tell it to her (Prescription #4). He did. She answered that, in fact, she was fully aware of how worried he was about his future job and he replied that what really worried him was how to wrap up neatly his present responsibilities. She brushed him off: "But, dear, you don't have any problems whatsoever in the office right now; everything is under control." I commented that it seemed to me that her definition of helping, right then, was to appease, while his definition of being helped was to be listened to. He agreed. She stated, tears in her eyes, that the fact of the matter was that she also felt frustrated because he did not allow her to open up to him, a statement which startled him. He told her, astonished, that her statement went completely against his sense of how things were, and that he considered himself very sensitive in relation to her and allowed her to speak to him about anything whenever she felt anxious in order to facilitate her relief. She told him, quite tenderly, that that was true whenever she was loaded with symptoms, but it was not so for those things that truly worried her the most, that for those other things he was like a father, shushing her, minimizing her, treating her like a child.

I pointed out that what she described was also what she did with him when she minimized the issue of the office. I stressed the fact that the shushing technique probably had been useful for both of them, but both were saying it was no longer satisfying. They both agreed and concurred that they would try to defend their right to be anxious. I proposed a new twist: "When you detect anxiety in your mate, ask yourself, 'What is going on with me?' and whenever you feel yourself anxious, ask yourself, 'What is going on with my mate?'"

> #12. If the couple reports having complied with the task or prescription, *then* express surprise and predict amiably that it cannot last and that they will find it difficult or even fail next time.

The maneuver wraps up the three previous ones. Its rationale is the same as for the prediction of difficulties in the compliance of a seemingly trivial symptom prescription: to divest the symptom of any value as "reward" or "punishment" vis à vis the therapist.

This presentation can be enhanced further if the therapist also praises the couple for having achieved something that is difficult, namely, complying with a symptom prescription, a statement that further reframes the symptom as a non-spontaneous behavior while binding the couple in a positive experience of joint creation (in spite of the fact that what they have created is identical to what brought them to the consultation!)

> #13. If A (and/or B) expresses and/or attributes to the other feelings that have negative connotations in our culture—i.e., a connotation that to have those feelings is to be mad or bad or sick—*then* relabel or reframe that feeling into one of positive connotation.

To reframe or relabel consists of changing the frame of reference against which a given event is considered or judged, thus changing the meaning and value-judgment of the event (without any change in the event itself.)

When a patient, who seeks consultation due to vomiting that seems to be triggered by stressful events, is told, "Good, you should not stop vomiting until those things that bother you change. How wise of your body to devise such a clever way of forcing some changes in your unpleasant situation!" the complaint (vomiting), is not at all changed but the frame (from something that "just happens" to something that is purposeful) and its value, from negative (as an annoying symptom) to positive (as behavior leading to change), are both changed.

Reality depends on our beliefs. There is not one given interpretation of it that is more "correct" than the other. At the most, there are some that are more consensual than others. Therefore, different observers may in turn provide different meanings to the same given act. With the attribution of meaning comes a value judgment—the adjudication of a given value within different "scales" such as goodness-badness, sanity-madness, health-sickness. And those values, when firmly attached to members of a family system, pin them down to fixed roles, as they consolidate interactional roles within the family.

The simple act of relabeling someone's "anger" as hurt, or someone's "depression" as sadness, or someone's symptom as an act of kindness and good will, exerts a dramatic, exorcizing effect on the system (see, for instance, the example from Prescription #4c).

It is important to point out here that to *relabel* a problem or a symptom does not mean to *minimize* it (an issue discussed in depth by Haley, 1977). There are specific cases in which a symptom may be underplayed— through maneuvers such as that of "inflating" a minor symptom of the nonsymptomatic member in order to achieve a symmetrical stand with both members. But, overall, to simply minimize a symptom can be not only a futile wishful thinking but even a disqualification that may endanger the therapy.

#14. If A talks "crazy" in the midst of an interaction between you and B, *then* tell A not to interrupt or distract and follow your interaction with B.

In one of the training videotapes produced at the Philadelphia Child Guidance Clinic in recent years, entitled "Coming Home from the Hospital," there is a sequence that illustrates this point vividly—even though it takes place in a session with a larger family. The therapist, Gary Lande, M.D., is speaking with the parents of an adolescent daughter who has been just released from a mental hospital, when the identified patient introjects into the conversation a bizarre statement about clothes and their symbolic meaning. The therapist tells her benevolently, "We don't fall for that type of thing here," and goes on with the conversation with the parents. No further crazy talk takes place in the whole session, even though the identified patient participates actively.

This prescription on "crazy talk" is an illustration of the principle that, if the symptomatic behavior is deprived of its interactional power, of its value as a message, a substantial contribution to its elimination has occurred. Through dealing with "crazy" behavior as if it were mere "misbehavior," the therapist *de facto* relabels the symptom with a non-pathological tag. At the same time, he/she will provide the other, non-symptomatic members with a model of how the symptomatic behavior can be handled.

> #15. If you detect a family myth, *then* do not shatter it. Handle it with care. At the most, demystify slowly while supporting it with words. Even when members of the couple themselves suggest that the myth may not reflect the reality, appear doubtful.

As was discussed in detail by Jackson (1965a and b), a marital couple can be described as a rule-governed system, in which the relationship between members is structured by, or organized through, typical and repetitive patterns of interaction. The rules underlying those redundancies can be abstracted as a governing principle of family life.*

From a systems perspective, the notion of *rule*—which is a system attribute defining the members in terms of their relationship—replaces in good measure the notion of *role*, which has an individual connotation, as well as an a priori definition. The notion of family rule is a good example of the qualitative shift in the conceptual framework that characterizes the interpersonal systems approach: It requires that the *transactions between individuals* are used as primary data, rather than the characteristics of each given individual.

Family myths are a special case of stubborn family rules. Ferreira (1966, p. 86) has defined *family myths* as "well-systematized beliefs shared by all family members, about their mutual role in the family, and the nature of their relationship," even though those beliefs often defy existing evidence. Ferreria also pointed out that, once developed, the family myth tends to remain unshattered as an ordering force in the relationship, accomplishing at the couples' level much the same function as defenses serve for individuals. A direct questioning of the validity of a myth may seriously threaten the continuity of the treatment.

One of Ferreira's own examples well illustrates this concept: "In family

---

* It must remain clear that a rule is an inference, a simplifying metaphor created by the observer to define the regularity.

A, the husband has to drive the wife wherever she may need to go, oftentimes to the detriment of his business activity, since she does not know how to drive a car, nor does she care to learn. Although this pattern has been in operation since they were married some 16 years ago, she explains it in terms of not being 'mechanically inclined,' a statement which the husband immediately endorses and corroborates" (Ferreira, 1966, p. 86). As is quite obvious, the myth encompassed both members of the couple, establishing fixed rules and a mystified explanation for their reciprocal behavior.

Prescription #15 further stresses the notion, proposed in #11, that the therapist should work along the system's basic pattern rather than challenging frontally the rules that perpetuate it (this "working along" is what Minuchin named "joining operations"*). Throughout the interview the therapist probes different rules, and attempts gently to challenge them. This will prove to be feasible with those rules that are not crucial to the maintenance of the homeostatic, basic coping mechanisms of the couple, while the couple may react defensively when some organizing principles—and family myths frequently accomplish that function—are questioned. That doesn't mean that they should not be dealt with, but that those issues should be worked with without challenging them explicitly; the function that the myth accomplishes for the system should be discovered, and rendered unnecessary, leaving it to the couple to unveil the myth, if they choose to do so, or to let it fade away into oblivion, if they prefer. The goal is to help the couple to get beyond the stereotype, to "unstick" the partners rather than to convince them at any intellectual level that they were mistaken, or that the therapist was so bright (which is but another way of stating that therapy should be at the service of the couple, rather than at the service of the therapist's own narcissism).

> #16. If you find yourself not understanding what is going on with the couple, *then* cease paying attention to content, and observe verbal patterns, sequences, gestures and postures, and/ or observe your own emotions, attitudes or postures.

---

* The reader is interested in a detailed, skillful analysis of these strategies should consult Minuchin (1974).

This and the subsequent prescriptions are variations of the dictum, "If you don't like what you are getting, change *your* behavior." They aim specifically at dealing with the not infrequent situation of the therapist finding him/herself unable to understand what is going on in the session, and failing to detect meaningful regularities, to understand *quid pro quo*, to devise effective interventions, or other such problems. These difficulties are frequently the result of operating within the constrictions of the system, and therefore having lost perspective or distance.

Prescription #16 relates to the fact that one of the ways in which a therapist may lose distance and become entangled in a small group process is through being pulled by a fascination for content. In that case, a fresh start can be made by shifting the focus of attention to other equally rich sources of information which may provide more naked clues about interactional processes.

A practical question that has been posed is: "If you find yourself not understanding . . ."—for how long? As each therapist has a different degree of tolerance for ambiguity, that question cannot be met by a blanket answer. A rule of thumb is that when a therapist notices that he/she is engaged in an active internal dialogue in which he/she is telling him/herself "I don't understand," at that moment he/she is starting a move toward differentiating from the system, which in turn indicates that the therapist had been previously "sucked in." That constitutes a good opportunity to apply this prescription and/or the ones that follow.

> #17. If the actual observation of the couple's interactional process fails to give you a meaningful understanding, *then* switch to the exploration of the couple's history.

This paper has dealt with observables rather than with reconstructions. That choice rests in the conviction that if any process or event in the history of a couple has had any repercussion in their present relationship, what counts is not the original event but its current, isomorphic representation in present patterns, styles and rules. But, for reasons having to do with the couple or with the therapist, there are occasions when the therapist fails to develop a workable hypothesis on the basis of those observables. In such circumstances, the therapist may concentrate in the development of hypotheses that relate the present conflict with the couple's history and/or with the history of the members' lives prior to the establishment of the dyad. Prescription #17, reflecting that change of focus, rescues the historical process as an important source of information for the development of therapeutic strategies. Its value does not rest solely on providing clues toward the reconstruction of the couple's evolvement of norms, agreements and myths. The revisitation of anecdotes may also prove to be a useful way of working through lagging misunderstandings. In addition, the *process* of information-gathering can be, in itself, a rich terrain to observe interactional process and even specific styles evoked by the discussion of different periods in the history of the couple. Finally, the developmental perspective is crucial in order to study how the couple has dealt with previous family "passages" and to predict the mismanagement of future predictable crises.

In fact, the mere act of sharing with the couple the hypothesis that the development of the present marital conflict or symptom is part of a transition crisis in the family's life cycle often has a powerful positive effect, as they begin to view their situation less as an arbitrary, whimsical or idiosyncratic event, and more as an explainable problem. However, that relief is not equivalent to change. Awareness or understanding of problems and change are quite different things.

#18. If even then you find yourself unable to detect meaningful regularities and/or to produce change, *then* increase the number of participants in the session (introduce offspring or parents or co-therapists).

This last prescription derives from two observations. One is that on occasion the couple may not be the critical unit of analysis, as it may not include all the protagonists of the interpersonal drama. It is not an infrequent observation that, when treatment of a couple fails to show progress, a qualitative leap takes place when the couples' offspring—or her mother, or his sister, or any other relative—is included in a session. The effect is often the unveiling of issues that were up-to-then mystified, showing other sides of conflicts or triggering confrontations that appeared dormant until then. The second observation has to do with the fact that the same leaping effect may be achieved by the introduction of a co-therapist, who re-aligns drastically the coalitionary field and frees the first therapist from interpersonal traps.

CONCLUSIONS

To say that a therapy session is the result of a combination of these prescriptions or any other specific behaviors of the therapist is obviously and irritatingly unsatisfactory. It may be necessary to master most of the prescriptions of this repertoire in order to be an accomplished therapist. But that does not tell us anything about timing, combining interventions, the style used in delivering them and other *sui generis* variables that, however amenable to formalization they may be in the long run, constitute right now what can be described as *the art* of therapy.

Most of the interventions prescribed above have been not only defined but also conceptually grounded. It may be useful to formulate at this point an overall summary of the key theoretical notions that underlie and provide conceptual homogeneity to the prescriptions. They are the following:

—symptoms accomplish functions in systems; relabeling and prescribing symptoms can drastically undermine that function and render them unnecessary;

—semantic ambiguities contribute to define interactional rules about roles and about reality; when these ambiguities are clarified, roles are restructured and reality reshaped;

—throughout therapy, therapists and patients constantly negotiate and renegotiate the nature of their relationship; the process of coalition formation and restructuring reflects that process and becomes a meaningful arena for therapeutic interventions;

—roles, such as victim/victimizer, and patient/non-patient, are the result of family rules conjointly defined and agreed upon by all members; to challenge those rules challenges those roles;

—the way in which a sequence of events is punctuated and reality is organized results from (arbitrary) agreements by the participants; this principle has clear consequences in planning therapeutic interventions; a change in punctuation breaks stereotypes and may radically alter interactional rules and family myths.

Considering another, more general, level of abstraction, this chapter portrays a major epistemological shift in the behavioral sciences, a qualitative jump that results from the incorporation of the systems vantage point. It affects the unit of analysis, the process being observed, the type of goals and the type of means, and even the logic being utilized. This epistemological revolution is characterized by

a shift from individual to larger systems;
a shift from content to process;
a shift from interpretations to prescriptions;
a shift from intentions to effects;
a shift from origins to present, self-perpetuating loops;
a shift from roles to rules;
a shift from symptoms to functions;
a shift from linear causality to cybernetic circularity.

REFERENCES

Bandler, R. and Grinder, J. *The Structure of Magic*. Palo Alto: Science and Behavior, 1975.

Bateson, G. Exchange of information about patterns of human behavior. In: W. S. Field and W. Abbot (Eds.), *Information Storage and Neural Control*. Springfield, Ill.: Charles C Thomas, 1963.

Bateson, G. and Jackson, D. D. Some varieties of pathogenic organization. In: D. M. Rioch and E. A. Weinstein (Eds.), *Disorders of Communication*. Baltimore: Williams & Wilkins, 1968. Also in: D. D. Jackson (Ed.), *Communication, Family and Marriage*. Palo Alto: Science and Behavior, 1968.

Bowen, M. Family psychotherapy. *American Journal of Orthopsychiatry*, 1972, 31, 40-60.

Caplow, T. *Two Against One; Coalition in Triads*. Englewood Cliffs, N. J.: Prentice-Hall, 1968.

Ferreira, A. J. Family myths. *Psychiatric Research Report 20*, American Psychiatric Association, 1966. Also in: P. Watzlawick and J. H. Weakland (Eds.), *The Interactional View*. New York: Norton, 1977.

Haley, J. *Strategies of Psychotherapy*. New York: Grune & Stratton, 1963.

Haley, J. Toward a theory of pathological systems. In: G. Zuk and I. Boszormenyi-Nagy (Eds.), *Family Therapy and Disturbed Families*. Palo Alto: Science & Behavior, 1967.

Haley, J. *Uncommon Therapy: The Psychiatric Techniques of Milton H. Erickson, M.D.* New York: Norton, 1973.

Haley, J. *Problem Solving Therapy*. San Francisco: Jossey-Bass, 1977.

Hoffman, L. Deviation-amplifying processes in natural groups. In: J. Haley (Ed.), *Changing Families*. New York: Grune & Stratton, 1971.

Jackson, D. D. The question of family homeostasis. *Psychiatric Quarterly Supplement*, 1957, 31 (1), 79-90. Also in: D. D. Jackson (Ed.), *Communication, Family and Marriage*. Palo Alto: Science and Behavior, 1968.

Jackson, D. D. Family rules—Marital quid pro quo. *Arch. Gen. Psychiat.*, 1965 (a), 12, 589-594.

Jackson, D. D. The study of the family. *Family Process*, 1965 (b), 4, 1-20. Also in: P. Watzlawick and J. H. Weakland (Eds.), *The Interactional View*. New York: Norton, 1977.

Kantor, D. and Lehr, W. A. *Inside the Family*. San Francisco: Jossey-Bass, 1975.

Minuchin, S. *Families and Family Therapy*. Cambridge: Harvard University Press, 1974.

Scheflen, A. E. *How Behavior Means*. New York: Aronson, 1974.

Scheflen, A. E., with Ashcraft, N. *Human Territories: How We Behave in Space-Time*. Englewood Cliffs, N. J.: Prentice-Hall, 1976.

Selvini Palazzoli, M., Boscolo, L., Cecchin, G. and Prata, G. *Paradosso e Controparadosso*. Milano: Feltrinelli.

Simmel, G. The number of members as determining the sociological form of the group. *American Journal of Sociology*, 1902, 8 (1), 1-46 and 158-196.

Sluzki, C. E. The coalitionary process in initiating family therapy. *Family Process*, 1975, 14 (1), 67-77.

Sluzki, C. E. and Ransom, D. C. (Eds.). *Double Bind: The Foundation of the Communicational Approach to the Family*. New York: Grune & Stratton, 1976.

Watzlawick, P., Beavin, J. and Jackson, D. D. *Pragmatics of Human Communication*. New York: Norton, 1967.

Watzlawick, P., Weakland, J. H. and Fisch, R. *Change: Principles of Problem Formation and Problem Resolution*. New York: Norton, 1974.

Weitman, S. R. Intimacies: Note toward a theory of social inclusion and exclusion. In: A. Birenbaum and E. Sagarin (Eds.), *People in Places: The Sociology of the Familiar*. New York: Praeger, 1973.

Wender, P. H. Vicious and virtuous circles: The role of deviation-amplifying feedback in the origin and perpetuation of behavior. *Psychiatry*, 1968, 31, 317-324.

VIII

A Review of the Research on the Effectiveness of Marital Therapy

NEIL S. JACOBSON, PH.D.

Marital therapy, like individual psychotherapy, has developed largely in an empirical vacuum. The analogy between the two modalities is striking, although perhaps not surprising. The original clinical innovations of the psychoanalysts spawned a myriad of disciples and tributary movements; the advocates of each vigorously and zealously sang the praises of their particular approach, and the vigor of their advocacy far outstripped the rigor with which they critically examined the efficacy of their techniques. Only in the 1950s, after psychotherapists had been describing their clinical procedures for over 50 years, did Carl Rogers (1951) and his associates begin to insist upon empirical verification of their own client-centered intervention strategies. This movement toward the scientific study of behavior change in therapy continued into the 1960s with the advent of behavior therapy; outcome studies investigating behavior modification were the most sophisticated at that time, at least from a methodological standpoint. Now, in the 1970s, the promise of a scientifically based, empirically validated technology of behavior change looms on the horizon.

The development of marital therapy has paralleled the growth of individual psychotherapy from a collection of anecdotal clinical descriptions to a gradually emerging technology whose intervention strategies are being studied scientifically. Olson (1970) has documented the early phase of this development; more recently Gurman and Kniskern (in press) have spoken to the relative abundance of scientific investigations of marital therapy recently appearing in the literature. These published reports vary from anecdotal, subjective accounts of the effectiveness of a particular treatment to elegantly designed, well-controlled studies. It is very important to distinguish not only between the extremes on this continuum, but also among investigations which lie somewhere in between in terms of their methodological sophistication. The former extreme consists of reports which sanguinely suggest promise for alleviating marital distress. However, from a scientific standpoint such reports are of limited utility, since they neither objectively demonstrate the efficacy of their procedures nor further our understanding of the mechanisms by which such positive changes might come about. At the other extreme, controlled studies of therapeutic outcome do allow for certain probabilistic claims to be made regarding the advocated treatment package's efficacy; furthermore, given appropriate controls, they render it possible to ferret out the active ingredients of effective treatments for alleviating marital distress.

As this review will indicate, research has only begun to answer such questions, and, in fact, has at this stage raised more questions than it has answered. Thus, readers who hope to garner definitive information regarding which marital therapy strategies actually "work" will be significantly disappointed. However, this chapter will point to certain directions and identify certain converging trends in the outcome literature; as a result, some clinicians will be somewhat assured that they are on the right track, while others might begin to question some of their assumptions. Above all, this chapter will document the beginnings of experimental investigations of marital therapy, and will hopefully serve as a guide for investigators of marital therapy outcome in the future.

This chapter is organized into subsections, each of which reviews important experiments within a particular area of marital therapy outcome investigations. The first section on methodology essentially defines the characteristics of outcome research as the term is used in the chapter; the domain of published reports which are included in subsequent sections is delimited in this section by the specification of methodological prerequisites. Following this section are summaries of the two areas of marital therapy about which a substantial body of outcome literature has been accumulated: communication training, and behavioral marital therapy. Following these sections is an overview of studies investigating a variety of approaches and parameters relevant to the treatment of couples. Concluding the chapter is a summary of studies which applied marital therapy to two clinical problems: alcoholism and sexual dysfunctions.

The author's bias is admittedly a behavioral one, and this will certainly be apparent at various points in the chapter. However, rather than reflecting a commitment to a behavioral exchange model of marital distress, the bias primarily reflects a predilection for the rigorous methodological stance practiced both by behavioral clinicians and behavior therapy investigators. The real bias in this chapter is a strong belief in the importance of an experimental analysis of marital therapy procedures. As the title suggests, it is a review of *research* on marital therapy, rather than a review of marital therapy techniques. Interesting, provocative treatment approaches, even if widely practiced by marital therapists, are not discussed in this chapter unless they have been subjected to empirical evaluation. It is thus extremely regrettable that, despite the numerous treatment strategies acknowledged in the chapter, two out of the three perspectives described in this book (psychoanalytic and systems theory) are not represented. Few would deny the popularity of either the psychoanalytic (cf., chapters by Meissner and Nadelson, this volume) or the systems theory (cf., chapters by Sluzki and Steinglass, this volume) approaches to marital therapy. However, neither perspective can claim even a single outcome experiment investigating its effectiveness. The absence of studies investigating systems approaches is partially explained by the emphasis of these theorists on *family,* as opposed to *marital,* therapy. While there have been outcome studies looking at various systems approaches applied to child problems (cf., Gurman and Kniskern, in press), these studies are beyond the scope of this chapter, since its purpose is to evaluate the effectiveness of various clinical strategies on *marital relationships.*

Some additional discussion is warranted regarding the absence of outcome studies investigating the effectiveness of psychoanalytic or psychodynamic marital therapy. This paucity is consistent with the dynamicist's history of eschewing controlled investigation of therapy outcome with individual clients. Although it was at one time argued that psychoanalysis was too complex a phenomenon for careful, scientific study, a recent volume which included interviews with prominent pyschoanalytically oriented writers clearly suggests that most current writers of this persuasion accept the importance and the feasibility of subjecting their

techniques to controlled investigation (Bergin and Strupp, 1972). Therefore, it is even more puzzling that, despite current adherence to the view
that outcome research is important, it is seldom conducted. In a very
revealing paper published in the *Journal of the American Psychoanalytic
Association,* Engel (1968) analyzed the deterrents to the growth of psychoanalysis as a science. Since psychoanalysis has developed outside academic,
scientific institutions, and since its perpetuation has occurred in settings
only peripherally concerned with research, psychoanalytic clinicians tend
not to be interested or skilled in the principles of research. In this country, psychoanalysis has developed in isolation from the behavioral sciences
and has traditionally excluded those who would tend to be iconoclasts in
this regard, namely, nonmedical practitioners trained in research. In
light of this chapter's endorsement of scientific research as the optimal
path to increased knowledge as well as verification of therapeutic approaches to marital therapy, it is hoped that in the coming years psychoanalytic leaders will enter the mainstream of scientific inquiry so that
their methods of clinical practice can be scrutinized and evaluated in
the same arena as others discussed in this chapter.

METHODOLOGICAL CONSIDERATIONS

Psychotherapy outcome research has as its basic purpose the elicitation
of information regarding the effectiveness of a particular treatment
strategy. What separates outcome research from more qualitative, anecdotal discussions of treatment is its potential for allowing probabilistic
cause-effect conclusions to be drawn about the relationship between a
particular treatment and a particular outcome. A minimal requirement
of such research is that it be designed in such a way that objective, unbiased estimates of the effects of a given treatment are possible. Through
appropriate research design, these estimates should be uncontaminated
by alternative explanations for change; that is, given that an investigation of outcome provides evidence for the effectiveness of a treatment,
hypotheses which compete with the treatment as the basis for change
should be ruled out through the utilization of proper controls. This is
what is meant by an *internally valid* study. More ambitious, perhaps, but
still fundamental to the pursuit of knowledge regarding psychotherapy
procedures, are investigations which allow us to generalize from the
results of a given study to the use of similar treatments with other clients,
in other settings, when the treatment is conducted by other therapists.
Such considerations define the degree of *external validity* contained in
the study.

Some of the specific prerequisites of internally valid outcome research are enumerated below.

Outcome Criteria

In order to adequately assess the effectiveness of a treatment procedure, it is absolutely essential that objective ways of measuring therapeutic change are utilized. In correspondence with the necessity for objectivity, measures of change must be unbiased. Since both the principal investigator and the therapist participating in the study have an inevitable investment in the positive outcome of a treatment under investigation, their subjective estimates of the effectiveness of their treatment, while valuable and interesting, are unacceptable as the sole dependent measures in an outcome investigation.

Some data from perhaps the most well-designed outcome study in the history of psychotherapy research will help illustrate the dangers of relying on therapist reports. Sloane, Staples, Cristol, Yorkston, and Whipple (1975) compared psychoanalytic psychotherapy to behavior therapy in an outpatient psychiatric setting. Therapists, clients, and independent psychiatrists rated clients' degree of improvement after therapy. Therapists' ratings of improvement correlated with the ratings of assessors, clients, and informants .13, .21, and —.04, respectively. Thus, therapist estimates of their clients' change bore little relationship to change as estimated either by objective assessors or the clients themselves. The correlation between assessors' ratings and clients' ratings was much higher, $r = .65$.

Client self-reports measures are useful and informative indices of therapeutic change. However, client reports of increased marital satisfaction must be viewed with appropriate skepticism, since such reports of improvement may be determined by a variety of factors other than actual changes. The most familiar and obvious basis for distortion in client self-reports is the "hello-goodbye" effect; at the end of a treatment regime, clients may be motivated to report increments in satisfaction by a wish to please the therapist. Similarly, in order to justify either the financial investment or the output of time and effort undergone in therapy, couples might be predisposed to view therapy as successful and consequently report positive changes on a self-report instrument. An additional consideration in the utilization of self-report inventories is their degree of correspondence to *actual* marital satisfaction. A plethora of self-report inventories exist in the literature, and only a small portion of them have been empirically *validated;* without such validation, one must speculate hazardously about the extent to which positive changes on such an inventory correlate with actual changes in marital satisfaction.

One nonempirical form of validity which on the face of it seems sufficient for an inventory's use is *face validity;* an instrument contains face validity when it intuitively corresponds to the kinds of questions one would ask of a couple in attempting to gauge their degree of marital satisfaction. To the extent that a self-report measure approximates questions which directly ask a couple how satisfied they are with their marriage, face validity is obtained. However, the greater the face validity of an instrument, the more susceptible an instrument is to demand characteristics and social desirability variables.

An ideal self-report inventory is one in which the way to answer in the direction of marital satisfaction is disguised, so that the risk of demand characteristics determining couples' responses is somewhat minimized. However, it is essential that the validity of such instruments has been demonstrated. To further rule out the possibility of demand characteristics accounting for positive change, controls for such variables should be included in outcome investigations, usually through the inclusion of comparison control groups.

Even when client self-report instruments have been well validated, and appropriate controls have been instituted, their potential for bias and distortion requires that they not be used as the sole criterion for determining the effectiveness of a treatment intervention. Couples enter into marital therapy with presenting complaints, which often amount to specific behaviors on the part of the partner which each spouse desires to be changed. If these complaints are not modified by concrete changes in these target behaviors as a function of therapy, it is problematic to argue that treatment was successful. To the extent that the alleviation of such complaints can be objectively measured, they are ideal outcome measures. Unfortunately, since couples seldom correspond to one another in terms of their presenting complaints, between-group studies are extremely difficult to conduct using such measures. One way of maintaining the integrity of couples' idiosyncratic complaints and still investigate the effectiveness of a treatment procedure is by treating each couple as a separate outcome experiment, using a single-case experimental design (Hersen and Barlow, 1976). More will be said of such procedures below.

Observable measures of couples' behavior, taken either in the clinical setting or in the home, can constitute a highly objective and sensitive index of change. For example, couple interaction can be divided into discrete, operationalized behavioral categories, and coded reliably by trained raters who are blind to the experimental situation. Of course, just as in the case of self-report measures, the behavioral categories must correspond to couples' presenting complaints in order to be valid measures of therapeutic change for a particular couple. Moreover, in order for such a behavioral rating system to be clinically useful, change in its categories must be a valid indication of change in marital satisfaction. The validity of such instruments can only be determined empirically.

Design Considerations

Detailed descriptions of treatment procedures

Outcome investigations should contain concrete descriptions of each treatment intervention used in the study in order that the study could be easily replicated by another investigator. To simply say that couples were given "communication training," for example, is of little help when a reader is attempting to glean from a particular study exactly what the nature of the clinical intervention was.

Control groups

In order to isolate a particular treatment as an independent variable which has a positive effect on marital functioning, it is vitally important that these effects be compared to some baseline provided by a similar sample of couples who have received no treatment. The necessity for waiting-list control groups in therapy outcome research is universally recognized; it is therefore surprising that so many so-called outcome investigations fail to utilize such groups in the marital therapy literature. Although uncontrolled group data can be mildly suggestive of a given treatment's effectiveness, it is unacceptable to attribute such positive changes to the treatment being investigated. One hundred uncontrolled investigations of a given treatment, all suggesting improvement among treatment couples, constitute 100 uninterpretable studies; even when considered together, the cumulative total of these studies fails to establish causal relationships between a given treatment and positive changes. A related point concerns comparative outcome studies which compare two different types of marital therapy; such studies do not preclude the necessity for waiting-list control groups. Even when one treatment is significantly more effective than another, it could be that changes in a comparable waiting-list control would be equivalent, or even superior, to the favored treatment. At some point in the future, when the "spontaneous remission" rates of specific populations of couples are well known, it may be possible to dispense with such control groups. However, given the present state of ignorance, no-treatment control groups remain essential.

The inclusion of a no-treatment control group is only a minimum requirement in investigations of marital therapy outcome. If an investigator wishes to be able to attribute positive changes occurring in therapy to his hypothesized "active ingredients," other aspects of a treatment intervention must be ruled out as contributors to positive outcome. Treatment programs designed to alter the functioning of a distressed couple are usually complex and multifaceted, and include a myriad of factors other than those which the investigator deems responsible for change. These "nonspecific" aspects of the treatment setting must be controlled for, in order to isolate the experimenter's hypothesized "active ingredients" as essential for positive change. Nonspecific control groups allow for the parcelling out of such factors (Jacobson and Baucom, 1977). As the forthcoming review will indicate, such control groups are virtually absent from the marital therapy outcome literature.

Random assignment

The random assignment of subjects to various treatment conditions is another elementary principle of experimental design. Randomization maximizes the likelihood that the groups being compared will be equivalent, on the average, on all extraneous factors. The comparison of two or more groups of subjects, already intact on some other dimension, precludes the definitive interpretation of positive results.

Follow-up

A technique for treating couples is of little value if the gains occurring during treatment do not persist after the termination of active therapy. Follow-up data are the only way that one can be certain that treatment gains extended beyond the period of time when regular meetings with the therapist took place.

This has been a cursory, skeletal summary of some of the basic methodological requirements of outcome research in marital therapy. There are a great many other important considerations which will be discussed in the evaluation of specific studies. Some of the more common considerations include the careful specification of client population characteristics, use of multiple therapists, and the handling of couples who dropped out of treatment prior to the termination of the treatment program.

Qualitative Reports

Gurman and Kniskern (in press), in their comprehensive review of the marital therapy literature, list about two dozen reports of marital therapy outcome in which the primary criterion for measuring the procedure's effectiveness was the therapist's subjective estimate. Usually, these figures are summarized in terms of a percentage of couples improved as opposed to unimproved. According to the standards for outcome research enumerated above, these reports do not qualify as scientific investigations, and therefore will not be discussed at length. This does not imply that such reports are not useful, since many of them do generate hypotheses which can later be tested in controlled investigations; even in their present subjective state, they are often quite helpful to the practicing clinician, who seldom has the luxury of awaiting the results of controlled investigations.

These reports tend to support the efficacy of the procedures utilized; however, the types of intervention strategies used are at times left unspecified, while at other times the procedure in question is enumerated in some detail. Because it is impossible to rule out the possibility of therapist bias in such studies, the positive findings are very difficult to interpret. Moreover, the virtual absence of follow-ups in such studies, as well as the dearth of comparison control groups, further obfuscates the meaning of such reports. Gurman and Kniskern justify their inclusion by the close correspondence between the percentage of reported success in these studies and those of better controlled studies. However, the percentages of reported success across elegantly designed outcome studies are quite variable. In addition, the fact that therapists tend to report three-fifths to two-thirds of their couples improved as a function of therapy may be more a function of therapist-shared perceptions than of actual client improvement. Qualitative reports such as these may be of greater sociological interest than of interest as credible statements about the effects of marital therapy; in other words, perhaps couples therapists are predisposed to perceive a certain percentage of their clients as improved, regardless of actual change occurring in therapy. Clients might cooperate in this endeavor by creating the impression of better functioning at termination in order to justify, both to themselves and to their therapist, the costs of the therapeutic venture. The absence of long-term reports regarding the maintenance of improvement, reports which would shed light on the ubiquity of this demand effect, contributes to such suspicions. Of course, it could also be true that a large percentage of these subjective reports do accurately reflect the potency of the procedures described. Unfortunately, without the necessary rigor, the validity of these reported gains is impossible to determine.

COMMUNICATION TRAINING

One of the most widely investigated strategies for treating couples has been that rather heterogeneous group of procedures which focus on teaching couples how to communicate more effectively. The treatment programs tend to be highly structured with a didactic, educational format. Extensive use is made of role-playing techniques, and programmed texts of some kind are often used to supplement the instructions provided by the therapist during treatment sessions. Homework assignments are often utilized. Although such communication training modules are sometimes presented to couples individually, more often the treatment takes place in couples groups.

Communication Training Based on Carkhuff's Model

Pierce (1973) reported some data evaluating a communication approach based on a model put forth by Carkhuff. Carkhuff's system is an offshoot of the elements of communication advocated and popularized by Carl Rogers (1951). In Pierce's study couples were treated in groups, with the primary focus on teaching "empathy" skills. Through role-playing techniques, couples were taught to attend to one another's communication, and to listen more accurately. Therapists provided feedback, in addition to modeling effective communication.

Five couples met in a group for two hours once a week for a total of 25 hours. They were compared with two control groups who received insight-oriented therapy provided by different therapists. Couples in the control groups were selected from a different population; they consisted of the parents of emotionally disturbed children who sought therapy for their child's problems. The primary dependent variable used in the study involved 15-minute interviews conducted with each spouse before and after therapy; the interviews were rated by trained raters for skill in communication and degree of self-exploration. On both measures, couples in the experimental treatment group changed in the positive direction significantly more than did control group couples.

Methodological difficulties abound in this study, rendering the results uninterpretable. First, a randomized control group was not used; further, couples in the control group were not presenting with marital dysfunctions, and any differences between the two groups could be due to the lack of distress exhibited by such couples to begin with, or to any one of a number of differences which might have existed between the two populations. Second, no validity data were presented in regard to Pierce's designated change measure. The reader is forced to accept on faith the sensitivity of these measures to actual changes in marital satisfaction. Third, no follow-up data are presented.

Wells, Fiqurel, and McNamee (1975) investigated a similar communication training approach with distressed couples. Couples met for eight weekly two-hour sessions and were taught communication skills according to Carkhuff's model. Data were reported for two groups of three couples each. Couples were described as white and middle class. Change was measured using three self-report inventories—the Locke-Wallace Marital Adjustment Scale (MAS), and two subscales of the Barrett-Lennard Relationship Inventory. The MAS is a well validated index of marital adjustment, known to reliably differentiate between distressed and nondistressed couples. Mean scores for participating couples indicated significant changes on all measures in the direction of improved marital adjustment.

The strength of this study lies in its careful, detailed specification of treatment procedures, rendering it easily replicable by independent investigators. Unfortunately, the absence of a no-treatment control group precludes the attribution of positive changes to the treatment procedures. Moreover, couples' posttest mean score on the MAS (93.5), while 20 points higher than the pretest mean, still falls within the distressed range. One might therefore question the *clinical significance* of couples' changes. Finally, follow-up data were not presented.

Cotton (1976) compared the Carkhuff-defined treatment with a behavior-exchange treatment derived from Weiss, Hops, and Patterson (1973), and an attention-placebo control group. Twenty-four couples met in subgroups of from two to four couples for two hours twice a week for two weeks, with eight couples in each treatment condition. A series of self-report measures failed to uncover significant differences between groups.

In summary, the data are not as yet in on communication training of the Carkhuff variety. Studies reporting positive findings were uncontrolled, and the one study which included a placebo control group failed to demonstrate the effectiveness of the communication training procedure.

Conjugal Relationship Enhancement (CRE)

CRE is another type of structured communication training program, developed by Bernard Guerney (1977). Like the Carkhuff model, CRE attempts to teach couples skills in empathy, the ability to express feelings directly, and the ability to accurately clarify the partner's feelings. Differences between the two approaches are largely procedural rather than substantive or theoretical. CRE uses a group format where spouses alternate playing the roles of speaker and listener. While role-playing they practice the skills of expressing and clarifying feelings respectively. The therapist first models the skills, and then provides feedback during the practice sessions.

Rappaport (1976) evaluated this approach in a study where couples received marathon group sessions: two four-hour and two eight-hour sessions spread over a two-month period. Subjects served as their own controls in that they were tested twice prior to undergoing treatment, with a two-month waiting period in between.

Couples were solicited for this study through advertising to the Pennsylvania State University student body by mail, newspaper, and posters. Of 39 couples who were originally recruited for the study, 13 dropped out during the original two-month waiting period; this left 26 remaining, 21 of whom completed the training program. These couples averaged 28.2 years of age, and were married for an average of 5.5 years. Four couples were treated in each group. Inexperienced graduate students functioned as group leaders. Dependent measures included both behavioral and self-report measures. Both speaker and listener responses were rated according to scales developed by the investigators; adequate reliability was established for the scales. Self-report measures included the MAS and a number of others.

On most of the measures, couples did exhibit significant positive changes from pretest to posttest; no such changes were manifested during the waiting period. Although this combination of findings is mildly suggestive of a treatment effect, a causal relationship between treatment and outcome has not been established. In a within-subject design such as this, internal validity is not established simply by testing subjects at two points in time prior to introducing the experimental treatment. None of the alternative explanations for change which are present in uncontrolled studies are ruled out by this design, although they are rendered somewhat less likely by the waiting period. In order for within-subject designs to be internally valid, it must be demonstrated that the changes which occurred in the treatment group were due to the treatment itself;

this can only be accomplished through the use of reversal designs, multiple baselines, or another similar procedure (cf., Hersen and Barlow, 1976).

Another difficulty in Rappaport's study lies in the client population used. The method of recruitment suggests that these couples were less distressed than a clinical population; Rappaport provides no evidence to the contrary. Furthermore, one-third of the couples in the original sample dropped out of therapy during the waiting period. One might speculate that these were the most distressed members of the sample; again, no data were provided to suggest otherwise. The relative youth and short duration of the marriages suggest a mild degree of distress.

Rappaport is to be commended for his utilization of both behavioral and self-report measures as change criteria. However, no evidence is provided as to the validity of the behavioral measures. The measures included ratings of empathy, feeling expression and the like; it is unclear what relationship, if any, these variables have to marital satisfaction. The measures are derived from the investigator's theoretical notions regarding what kinds of communication are important in a successful marriage. In other words, the validity of the measures depends on the validity of the theory; however, the ability of the theory to describe the specific types of communication which are important in a well-functioning couple remains speculative.

Finally, as in the other investigations summarized thus far, follow-up data are not provided.

CRE has been evaluated in three controlled studies. Collins (1971) compared couples receiving CRE to an untreated control group. Couples were solicited in the same ways as were Rappaport's couples, and the population appears to fall somewhere in between the nondistressed and mildly distressed range. After five treatment couples dropped out, 24 couples remained in the experimental group and 25 in the untreated group. Couples were treated in groups of three couples each, led by graduate student therapists. Groups met for a six-month period. Change was measured by four self-report inventories. On two of the measures, CRE couples improved significantly more than did untreated couples, while on the other two the experimental group was also favored, but the trends were nonsignificant. Follow-up data are not reported.

In a well-designed experiment utilizing couples who were somewhat distressed, Ely, Guerney, and Stover (1973) compared couples who randomly either received a ten-week CRE program or remained on a waiting list. After a ten-week interval, control couples received treatment and then were reevaluated. In addition to evaluating change by a series of self-report measures (Ely Feeling Questionnaire, Primary Communication Inventory, Conjugal Life Questionnaire), behavioral observations were used. Couples role-played in 12 standardized situations, and trained observers reliably rated each spouse on feeling expression and feeling clarification.

On both observational measures and on two of the three self-report measures, significant differences were found favoring CRE couples. Furthermore, when control couples finally received the treatment, they improved to a degree commensurate with the changes achieved by treatment couples. Follow-up data on treatment couples were not reported.

Finally, Wieman (1973) compared CRE with a behavioral exchange (BE) treatment and a waiting-list control. This study is described in detail in the section on BE approaches. CRE couples did improve on a series of self-report measures relative to an untreated control, although there were no differences between it and the BE program.

Thus, three controlled studies attest to the efficacy of CRE, suggesting that it is a very promising clinical procedure. Optimism must remain tentative, however, since only one of these studies utilized even a mildly distressed couple population, and none has evaluated the approach with severely distressed couples. Furthermore, although the investigators of CRE are to be applauded for their use of multidimensional outcome criteria, their observational measures have not been sufficiently validated, a restriction which forces one to confine conclusions to the self-report data. Since such data are particularly vulnerable to alternative interpretations based on demand characteristics and placebo effects, it is unfortunate that control groups which would have ruled out such interpretations were not included. Finally, the absence of follow-up data renders an assessment of the maintenance of treatment effects impossible. Therefore, although the results of CRE investigations warrant optimism, a great deal of further experimentation is necessary if conclusions are to become more definitive.

Minnesota Couples' Communication Program (MCCP)

A well-designed and carefully reported study conducted by Miller, Nunnally, and Wackman (1976) evaluated the "Minnesota Couples' Communication Program" (MCCP). In MCCP, couples are taught both "awareness skills," designed to help them understand their relationship, and "communication skills," designed to help them make changes in their relationship when such changes were necessary. Couples were treated in groups, four or five couples per group. Each group met with one or two group leaders one or two nights per week for four consecutive weeks.

Thirty-two couples were randomly divided into a treatment group and a waiting-list group. These couples were recruited from a university community through an announcement; the sample consisted of well-educated, relatively nondistressed couples. Dependent measures were derived from the investigators' theoretical rationale for the treatment program; on the basis of couples' taped interaction before and after therapy, ratings were made of "recall accuracy" (how accurate each partner is at recalling an interaction pattern) and "work pattern communication" (the ability of couples to sustain open-style communication about their relationship). Each of these measures was operationally defined. On both measures, treatment couples changed in the desired direction; these changes were significantly greater than those in the untreated group. Fourteen of the 16 treatment couples improved on at least one of the two measures; the typical pattern was for couples to improve on only one of the two measures.

Despite the positive results of the Miller et al. study, two methodological limitations restrict the interpretation of the findings. First, the subject population is best described as an analog population in that the couples were nondistressed; the investigators themselves acknowledge that the treatment at this stage is not appropriate for distressed couples. Second, although the measures used accurately reflect the program's treatment goals, it is not clear whether the couples received what they wanted from the program, or the extent to which overall relationship satisfaction was enhanced by the treatment program. One wonders whether or not four weeks of such training can produce *permanent* or at least long-term changes in couples' communication patterns; the absence of follow-up data renders these questions unanswerable.

Campbell (1974) conducted a similar controlled investigation evaluating MCCP. Sixty couples were randomly assigned to experimental or control conditions. Testing occurred only at posttest time. Measures included two self-report questionnaires and observational ratings based on a five-minute audiotape recording of the couple discussing "things you do that irritate each other." Most measures yielded significant differences favoring the treatment group. However, Campbell found a significant *negative* correlation between a couple's perception of their communication effectiveness and evaluator rated effectiveness, which forces one to question either the validity of the assessment procedures or the efficacy of treatment.

Although these two controlled studies offer some preliminary indication of the effectiveness of MCCP, research needs to be conducted utilizing assessment procedures of demonstrable validity, nonspecific control groups, actual clinical populations, and follow-ups.

Miscellaneous Communication Training Procedures

Kind (1968) assessed the effects of a brief, "here and now" communication training approach. Couples underwent 14 hours of treatment, with nine couples assigned to the experimental treatment and nine to a minimal treatment control. Couples were treated in groups. A series of behavioral and self-report measures were used to evaluate the effects of treatment. No significant differences were found between the treatment and control groups.

Cardillo (1971) evaluated a communication training program in which couples were taught to express feelings more adequately and to listen to their spouses more empathically. Twenty couples who were referred from a local mental health center were randomly assigned to two treatment groups of ten couples each. Both groups of couples were taught communication skills, but only one group focused on specific problem areas in their relationship. Change was measured using two self-report inventories, the Interpersonal Perception Method and the Tennessee Self-Concept Scale. Although both groups reported changes, there were few significant differences between them. The absence of a no-treatment control group precludes attribution of these positive findings to the treatment procedures.

McIntosh (1975) compared three treatment approaches to training couples in communication skills: highly structured, partially structured, and non-structured groups. The structured group, like most of the studies already reported, was based on teaching skills in empathy, active listening and feeling expression. However, McIntosh added a behavioral exchange component to his technology; the specifics of this intervention strategy will be summarized in the section on behavioral approaches. A no-treatment control group was included in the design. None of the groups changed significantly from pretest to posttest on the criterion measures. None of the treatments showed changes which were significantly greater than those shown by the waiting-list control group.

Cassidy (1973) evaluated the effectiveness of a more eclectic approach to communication training than the ones discussed so far. A variety of communication skills were taught using feedback, modeling, and behavior rehearsal strategies. The measures used to evaluate change included a problem checklist and changes in target behaviors as reported by couples. Self-report measures were also used. A no-treatment control group was used in the study. Differences between the treatment and control groups were statistically significant on all measures; treatment couples improved relative to the changes manifested by the untreated condition. This study is to be commended not only for its use of a no-treatment control group, but also for its dependent measures, which were probably more sensitive to the presenting complaints brought in by couples than the measures used in the studies already reported. Unfortunately, demand characteristics cannot be ruled out as an explanation for the positive findings; moreover, whether or not communication training *per se* was responsible for the changes, rather than a host of nonspecific factors which were not controlled for, is open to question. The absence of follow-up data also makes it difficult to ascertain the long-term significance of couples' changes.

Pilder (1972) compared what he called laboratory training (LT) to a control group using therapist ratings and self-report ratings as change criteria. LT is an eclectic approach to teaching interpersonal skills to couples. Half of 60 couples underwent an LT workshop. Treatment couples improved more than control couples at posttest only on therapist ratings. However, at a nine-week follow-up, significant change was manifest on one of the two self-report measures.

Finally, Hines (1975) randomly assigned 12 couples to an eclectic communication training group, a traditional insight-oriented group, or a control group. Each treatment group met for two hours a day on five consecutive days. Prior to and following treatment each couple interviewed one another, alternating between roles of "helper" and "helpee." Trained observers rated each spouse for degree of helpfulness. The communication training group was significantly more effective than either of the other two groups.

To summarize these miscellaneous findings, three controlled studies support the effectiveness of various forms of communication training, while three others cast doubt on their effectiveness.

Summary of Communication Approaches

A number of studies have found significant differences favoring structured communications training approaches to marital discord when compared to untreated controls. Conjugal Relationship Enhancement appears to be the most well documented of the nonbehavioral communications approaches at present. The Minnesota Couples' Communication Program also has received some support from controlled investigations. Data are equivocal and somewhat contradictory in regard to both the Carkhuff model and other more eclectic communication training approaches. All of the studies are plagued by methodological problems enumerated above: Reliance on analog populations, unvalidated dependent variables, lack of follow-up findings, and the failure to utilize nonspecific control groups preclude definitive interpretations of current data. However, there seems to be some cause for cautious optimism that structured, systematic communication training, particularly communication training of the CRE variety, can be an effective treatment for mildly distressed couples.

BEHAVIORAL EXCHANGE APPROACHES

Although the application of behavior modification to the treatment of marital discord has been relatively new (the first reported study was published by Stuart in 1969), over the past seven years an extensive amount of research has been reported. This behavioral research will be extensively reviewed, both because of the methodological rigor in its research investigations, and because of the relatively large number of controlled studies which have emerged. Jacobson and Martin (1976) reviewed the literature through 1975; their review and others like it (e.g., Greer and D'Zurilla, 1975) emphasize the careful attention that has been devoted not only to the evaluation of treatment procedures, but also to the development of reliable, valid instruments for assessing marital satisfaction. Perhaps the greatest strength in the behavioral research to date lies in the multidimensional analysis of change during treatment procedures. Much of the credit for the development of sensitive assessment instruments is reserved for Weiss, Patterson, Hops, and their associates (Birchler, Weiss, and Vincent, 1975; Vincent, Weiss, and Birchler, 1975; Weiss, Hops, and Patterson, 1973; Wills, Weiss, and Patterson, 1974). Weiss et al. (1973) have developed a series of self-report measures of marital satisfaction (Areas of Change Questionnaire, Marital Status Inventory, Marital Activities Inventory), which have been carefully analyzed and validated. Similarly, a highly useful quasi-observational checklist (Spouse Observation Checklist) has been developed for use in the home by spouses; the checklist allows for the assessment of both frequencies of various spouse behaviors and phenomenological impressions of "pleases" and "displeases." This checklist has been found to be a good predictor of the day-to-day levels of marital satisfaction (Wills et al., 1974). Finally, and perhaps most importantly, the group has developed a behavioral rating system for coding spouse interaction according to various communication and problem-solving dimensions. Ratings on this system, the "Marital Interaction Coding System" (MICS) (Hops, Wills, Patterson, and Weiss, 1971), reliably differentiate between distressed and nondistressed couples (Birchler et al., 1975; Vincent et al., 1975) and correlate highly with other validated measures of marital satisfaction (Weiss et al., 1973). Recently a similar scale has been developed by Gottman and his associates (Gottman, Markman, Notarius, and Gonso, 1976).

The behavioral approach is based on a theory of marital discord which emphasizes faulty behavior change operations as important determinants of marital distress. It is assumed that distressed couples either lack or fail to emit the skills necessary to make desired changes in the marriage when conflicts arise. These deficits are usually conceptualized in operant terms. Thus, distressed couples are thought to utilize aversive control strategies rather than positive reinforcement strategies in attempting to bring about changes in their relationship.

Based on this model, behavioral intervention strategies are designed to teach couples how to bring about changes in their relationship more effectively. Essentially, couples are taught techniques for becoming efficient behavior modifiers in their own home. Usually two types of skills are taught. First, problem-solving and communication skills are emphasized in order that couples learn to talk more effectively with one another, particularly around conflict areas. Second, contingency management skills such as positive reinforcement, shaping, and pinpointing target behaviors are usually part of the treatment package. These two components are united through the implementation of change agreements whereby exchanges are made and often specified in the form of written contingency contracts (cf., Jacobson and Margolin, in press).

Uncontrolled Reports

Much like the outcome research in communication training, uncontrolled studies were the predominant mode of investigating treatment efficacy during the first few years that outcomes of this approach were reported. Although such reports can be suggestive of treatment efficacy, causal relationships between treatment and outcome cannot be derived.

Stuart (1969) evaluated a contingency contracting procedure with four couples who showed similar presenting complaints: Husbands complained of an insufficient frequency of sexual activity, while wives complained about their husband's unwillingness to engage them in conversation. Stuart had the couples, who were each treated separately, form written contracts where sexual activity was made contingent upon husband's increased conversation. A point system was used where a certain amount of conversation resulted in certain requisite sexual activities. All couples recorded both frequency of conversation and of sexual activity. Data indicated increases in both target problems to a degree which satisfied both spouses. Follow-ups at 24 and 48 weeks following treatment termination indicated that the changes were maintained. Treatment averaged seven hours per couple spread over a ten-week period.

Among the noteworthy aspects of Stuart's report is the inclusion of outcome measures which are extremely sensitive to the presenting complaints of the spouses. Rather than using standardized measures, Stuart had couples count frequencies of the very problems which brought them to therapy. There is little question as to the validity of such measures. The only difficulty with data collected by spouses is their questionable reliability. Many factors might influence such frequency counts other than actual amount or duration of the reported behavior, such as inaccurate recording or demand characteristics. Again, the main limitation of the study is that it is uncontrolled.

Weiss and Patterson (Patterson, Weiss, and Hops, 1975; Weiss et al., 1973) reported data on the outcome of ten couples who received a multifaceted treatment program, including various communication and problem-solving techniques, and training in contingency management skills. Couples were young, well-educated, and mildly distressed. Using the MICS, rates per minute for both "facilitative" and "disruptive" behaviors were derived, based on taped interactions of couples' problem-solving interaction before and after treatment. These behaviors were reliably coded by trained raters. Overall, couples exhibited significantly more facilitative behavior and significantly less disruptive behavior after therapy. Looking at the couples individually, eight of the ten improved on these observational measures. On the checklist described earlier, husbands reported significantly more "pleasing" wife behaviors and significantly fewer "displeasing" wife behaviors after therapy; wives reported significantly more "pleasing" husband behaviors after therapy; however, changes in "displeasing" husband behaviors were not significant. Again, looking at couples individually, complete data on eight couples indicated that six couples improved on this checklist. Self-report measures also showed significant changes from pretest to posttest.

Since much of the posttest data was collected three to six months after the end of treatment, some evidence as to the persistence of treatment gains is offered. Confidence in these results is further strengthened by the use of multiple outcome measures, including valid instruments measuring observable behavior. It should be recalled, however, that no control group was used, thereby failing to establish internal validity.

Azrin, Naster, and Jones (1973) investigated a four-week behavioral exchange procedure termed "reciprocity counseling." Couples received this procedure after undergoing three weeks of "catharsis" counseling. This latter condition was an attempt to control for nonspecific attention-placebo effects. Change was evaluated by a self-report measure completed by each spouse nightly. Eleven of 12 treated couples reported significantly more "happiness," as measured by this scale, than they had reported at the end of the placebo procedure. Ratings did improve from the time of pretesting until the end of the placebo procedures. Follow-ups of up to a year indicated that 11 of 12 couples remained significantly improved.

The design of this study is reminiscent of the Rappaport (1976) study reported earlier; it must be emphasized that simply by following one treatment with another, and then demonstrating that positive changes occurred only upon implementation of the second procedure, one does not establish a causal relationship between the second treatment and outcome. Moreover, the Azrin et al. study can be criticized for relying on one self-report measure as the sole criterion of outcome; indeed, the instrument used was constructed for the purposes of the study, and its reliability and validity had not been established.

Analog Studies

A great many of the outcome studies investigating behavioral marriage therapy are best conceptualized as analog studies. Such studies are best considered analog studies because they are characterized by one or both of the following factors: utilization of a nondistressed client population or a very brief, relatively discrete intervention procedure only vaguely similar to those used in actual clinical settings. Given that naturalistic outcome research is costly, time consuming, and difficult to conduct rigorously, analog studies can be extremely useful in demonstrating functional relationships between specific treatment variables and changes in marital behavior. However, it is often hazardous to generalize from the findings of these studies to naturalistic treatment settings. An exhaustive review of these studies is presented by Jacobson and Martin

(1976). Only a few well-controlled studies and ones that are recently completed will be presented here.

Roberts (1975) attempted to train normal, nondistressed couples in contracting skills. Thirty couples were randomly assigned to a contracting group, a nonspecific control, and an untreated control. Couples were treated by one of three therapists for three one-hour sessions. Two self-report measures found the contracting group to improve significantly more than the untreated control, with trends favoring the contracting group over the nonspecific control. It is very difficult to generalize these findings to an actual clinical situation, since treatment was so brief and the couples were nondistressed. One of the major difficulties in generalizing from work with analog studies is the possibility of a ceiling effect when measuring change; since they are scoring relatively high on most indices of marital satisfaction to begin with, there is not as much room for change, and consequently it is difficult to demonstrate significant treatment differences between groups.

Margolin (1976) had undergraduate therapists treat distressed couples in one of three conditions: a behavioral (B), a behavioral-cognitive (B-C), or a nondirective (N) condition. Interventions were brief (two meetings). All couples practiced communicating in regard to conflict-related topics, with feedback provided by the therapist. Nondirective couples focused on "spouse's reactions and feelings"; the therapist used techniques such as reflection, and modeled expressiveness and understanding. Behavioral couples were provided with a cuing system whereby spouses could press a button eliciting a pleasant tone upon emission of a "helpful" communication by the spouse. An aversive noise, which could be eliminated only by a helpful remark, sounded automatically if a helpful remark was not forthcoming within a specified time period. The B-C group differed procedurally from the behavioral group in that the pleasant tone sounded and the aversive tone was avoided only in the event that the spouses agreed on the presence of a helpful remark by one partner. In addition, B-C couples received comments from the therapist which attempted to restructure their cognitions regarding their relationship problems; couples were told to attribute their problems to faulty communications and negotiation skills, rather than to personality defects in the partner.

The results were mixed. On the MAS, B-C couples improved significantly more than couples in the other two groups; on MICS measures of undesirable negative behavior, as well as on negative behavior recorded by spouses in the home, the three groups all changed equivalently and significantly in the desired direction. On the self-report measures of positive behavior, the B and B-C groups improved more than the N group; on the positive behaviors rated in the laboratory, B-C couples changed the most.

The results suggest the potency of a relatively short-term intervention designed to help couples reinforce more positive communications. The differences between B-C and B couples are difficult to interpret, since they differed procedurally in a number of ways in addition to the re-attribution component of the B-C condition. The consistent reduction of negative behavior across treatment conditions might be a function of nonspecific variables common to all three conditions, but since a control group was not included, repeated testing or the passage of time cannot be ruled out.

These analog studies suggest that even a very brief behavioral intervention, whether focused on contingency contracting or communication, can be facilitative. Margolin's study is impressive since her couples were genuinely distressed; yet positive results were obtained in a two-session intervention.

Controlled Studies

Jacobson (1977a) investigated the effects of a multifaceted treatment package on distressed couples; although his couples were solicited from newspaper advertisements, pretest scores on the various measures indicated that these couples fell within the distressed range. Treatment involved training in communication and problem-solving skills, along with contingency contracting. Problem-solving training differed from nonbehavioral communication training in that the skills which couples were taught were oriented toward making them more effective behavior modifiers. Couples were taught how to use positive reinforcement in a problem-solving situation through modification of both their verbal and nonverbal behavior. Also, couples learned more efficient strategies for solving problems, such as defining problems and solutions specifically and in behavioral terms, shaping, and focusing on one problem at a time. Ten couples were randomly assigned to either a treatment or an untreated group. Treatment couples met for eight one-and-a-half-hour sessions individually with a therapist. Groups were compared on MICS measures of negative and positive behavior, as well as on the MAS. In addition, each treatment couple served as a separate single-subject experiment. Using data collected by couples in the home, multiple baseline analyses were conducted on target behaviors according to guidelines specified by Hersen and Barlow (1976).

On all between groups measures, treatment couples changed significantly more than did untreated couples. Within-subject measures corroborated these findings. The results were maintained at a one-year follow-up. The use of both within-subject and between subject controls, multiple, well-validated outcome measures, and a relatively long follow-up add to confidence in these findings. Since only one therapist was utilized (the principal investigator), the generalizability of the results is limited. Also, it is unclear what aspects of the treatment program are responsible for its effectiveness.

These deficiencies were corrected in a subsequent study (Jacobson, in press a) comparing two very similar behavioral treatments to a nonspecific control group, as well as to an untreated control group. Working with a similar client population, 32 couples were randomly assigned to one of the four treatment conditions and one of three therapists. The nonspecific treatment group was a very similar procedure to the behavioral treatments, differing only in that couples in this condition did not receive training in problem-solving and contracting skills. Manipulation checks confirmed that the nonspecific control group was perceived as credible and bona fide, both by clients and by naive undergraduates. On two behavioral measures (MICS "positive" and MICS "negative"), as well as one self-report measure (MAS), behavioral couples improved significantly more than couples in either of the two control groups. On a second self-report measure, all three treatment conditions (including the nonspecific control group) improved more than the untreated group. Six-month follow-up data on the MAS found that differences between the behavioral groups and the control groups were maintained.

Finally, Jacobson (1977b) conducted a series of single-subject experiments with a population of severely distressed couples. Using multiple baseline analyses on data collected in the home by couples, a treatment intervention emphasizing training in problem-solving skills was tested against a nonspecific procedure in which the therapists instructed couples to change their behavior in positive ways. After receiving three sessions of the nonspecific procedure, problem-solving training was introduced on one conflict area at a time. The results, confirmed by self-report and MICS measures, indicated that all six of the couples improved significantly; in five of the six cases, multiple baseline analyses confirmed that behavioral interventions were responsible for the improvement.

To summarize the results of Jacobson's research: In three separate studies, the effectiveness of behavioral marriage therapy was confirmed. Controls for nonspecific factors made it possible to isolate the specific behavioral training components as necessary for positive change. Positive results were found for both severely and moderately distressed populations. One study further isolated training in problem-solving skills as an effective ingredient in and of itself. Since the principal investigator served as at least one of the therapists in all three of the studies, the findings need to be replicated across a wider variety of therapists before one can be confident about generalizability. However, this body of research provides significant support for the effectiveness of this form of marital therapy.

Tsoi-Hoshmand (1976) compared a similar behavioral treatment program to a waiting-list control. She utilized three self-report measures as indicators of change. The measures were all well-validated, and shown to reliably differentiate distressed from nondistressed couples. Although unusually young and well-educated, the couples used in this study comprised a bona fide clinical population. All couples were treated by the principal investigator. Couples were seen at a number of different geographical locations, and random assignment to groups was not part of the design. Therapy sessions averaged 1-1½ hours in length, and the number of treatment sessions averaged 8.3. On all three change measures, statistically significant differences favored couples in the behavioral treatment group. Follow-up of one to four months indicated improvement in 70 percent of the couples treated.

Unfortunately, methodological difficulties preclude definite interpretation of the findings in this study. Since couples were not randomly assigned to groups, differences between the two groups could be a function of discrepancies of the two populations. Equally important, significance was found only when spouses were analyzed as individuals. This type of analyses violates one of the prerequisites for the use of analysis of variance—the independence of each observation in the sample. Nonparametric statistics should have been used. Therefore, despite the positive findings, this study does not add significantly to confidence in the effectiveness of a behavioral approach to marital therapy.

Harrell and Guerney (1976) tested a group behavioral treatment program involving communication training and contingency contracting. Each group included three couples and one therapist. Groups lasted for two months, in eight weekly two-hour sessions. Sixty couples recruited from a university community were randomly assigned to a treated and untreated control condition. In addition to self-report measures (including the MAS) and MICS categories, couples were rated on a conflict negotiation task. Experimental couples improved significantly more than untreated couples on the behavioral tasks. However, none of the self-report measures discriminated between the two.

These results stand in puzzling contrast to those of Jacobson. Although couples did change their behavior in desirable ways, various self-report indices of marital satisfaction suggested little change as a result of therapy. The most obvious difference between the procedures used by Harrell and Guerney and those used by Jacobson is that Harrell and Guerney treated couples in groups whereas Jacobson's couples were all seen individually. Perhaps group treatment is sufficient in that couples can learn the appropriate behaviors and utilize them while under the stimulus control of the therapy sessions. However, it may be that the inevitable decrease in individual attention afforded to couples in a group precludes the frequent monitoring and feedback necessary for the skills to generalize to the home situation. The lack of change on the self-report measures may indicate that the skills are not used at home, and that they have not resulted in increased satisfaction. It is also possible that self-report changes in other studies reflect demand characteristics, which were more powerful in an individual therapy situation than in a group therapy situation. However, Jacobson's (in press a) use of a nonspecific control group suggested that demand characteristics did not account for changes on the MAS. Harrell and Guerney's findings are unlikely, therefore, to simply reflect the absence of a demand effect.

Thus far, most of the discussed training programs utilized both some form of communication training and also some type of contingency contracting procedure. It is unclear at this stage which component of the package accounts for the largest percentage of reported effectiveness. Roberts (1975) found that contracting training alone was effective with nondistressed couples. Jacobson (1977b) found that communication and problem-solving training alone were sufficient to produce positive changes in severely distressed couples. His procedure included all elements of the behavioral exchange approach except the written specification of contingencies for compliance and noncompliance with change agreements. However, contingency management procedures such as shaping, pinpointing problem behaviors, and the like were included in the training procedures. Recently Turkewitz (1977) compared a communication training procedure (including both behavioral and non-behavioral components) without instructions in contingency management to a condition which included, in addition to communication training, training in behavior exchange skills. Neither group utilized written contingency contracts. All couples (ten per group) were treated individually by one of five therapists. Compared to an untreated control group, both treatment groups improved significantly on self-report measures. However, there were no differences between the two treatment groups. On behavioral measures, the three conditions did not differ from one another. There was an interesting interaction between age and treatment conditions: Younger couples found the addition of behavioral exchange training to be facilitative, while older couples improved more without behavioral exchange procedures (these findings are discussed in greater detail in O'Leary and Turkewitz, Chapter VI).

As for the importance of contingency contracting, there is little evidence as yet. Jacobson (in press a) found two forms of contracting equally effective, whereas Jacobson (1977b), and Turkewitz (1977) reported positive results without utilizing written contracts. Further comparisons between the various components of these treatment packages are an important priority of future research.

Comparative Outcome Studies

Of the five studies to be reviewed below, four were technically analog studies, since the treatment populations were constituted of nondistressed couples. They were included in this section despite their analog status, since they do compare a behavioral treatment program with programs derived from alternative theoretical perspectives.

Fisher (1973) compared group behavior therapy with an Adlerian group format and an untreated control; change in marital satisfaction was measured by perceptual congruence between members of a couple. (Perceptual congruence has been shown to correlate highly with marital satisfaction.) Forty-one couples were assigned to the three conditions on a random basis. Groups met for six treatment sessions. Three of four self-report measures, including a measure of perceptual congruence, indicated that behavioral couples improved significantly more than did Adlerian couples. There were no differences between the Adlerian condition and the control condition.

Fisher's use of a nondistressed sample limits the relevance of these findings. In addition, his treatment goal, increased perceptual congruence, is unique, and at this point it is unclear how it relates to the treatment goals specified by behavioral investigators in other outcome studies.

Wieman (1973) compared a type of behavioral marital therapy to a program based on conjugal relationship enhancement (CRE). Thirty-six couples responding to a newspaper advertisement were randomly assigned either to one of these conditions or to an untreated control condition. Couples met in groups of four for eight weekly sessions. Three therapist pairs were used. Couples in the behavioral condition were taught behavioral exchange skills, without additional communication training. On various measures of marital adjustment, there were no significant differences between the two treatment conditions, although both were significantly more effective than the control condition. Improvements were maintained at a ten-week follow-up. Unfortunately, no behavioral measures were taken; it would have been interesting to know if the same behavior versus self-report discrepancy that was found in the Harrell and Guerney (1976) study would have been found in this study. It should be noted that the behavioral exchange model used here was only part of the total package used by Fisher (1973), Jacobson (1977, in press a), Tsoi-Hoshmand (1976), and Turkewitz (1977).

Venema (1975) compared communication training *à la* Rappaport (1976) with a contingency contracting procedure. He also included a third condition which combined the two. The participating couples, who were relatively nondistressed, participated in a program which took the form of a seven-week workshop. The results on a series of self-report indices indicated that none of the groups made remarkable changes; the combination group tended to manifest the most positive changes followed by the behavioral group, and then the communication group. Like Wieman's study, Venema's findings are of limited value due to his exclusive reliance on self-report measures, and his use of a behavioral exchange treatment which included only a subset of the intervention strategies employed by other investigators. Specifically, his package excluded training in communication and problem-solving skills.

This same criticism can be leveled at Cotton's (1976) study, already described in the previous section. Cotton's BE condition did not contain a problem-solving or communication training module. Similarly, Cotton utilized only self-report measures. Therefore, his finding of no differences between communication training and BE is difficult to interpret.

Finally, in the only comparative outcome study utilizing genuinely distressed couples, Liberman, Levine, Wheeler, Sanders, and Wallace (1976) evaluated two types of groups: a behavioral group, and an "interaction-insight" group. The behavioral group followed a format which included training in communication and behavioral exchange skills, and contingency contracting procedures. The interaction-insight group was a less structured group designed to establish cohesiveness, model empathic communication, allow couples to express their feelings about the marriage without using mutual recriminations or blaming, give the couples concrete suggestions for making changes which would improve the marriage, and help couples gain insight and awareness into the impact their interpersonal behavior had on the relationship. The behavioral group included four couples; the interaction group included five couples. The same three therapists led both groups. As outcome measures, the investigators used self-reports (including the well-validated instruments developed by Weiss and his associates (Weiss et al., 1973) as well as the MAS), recordings of "pleasing" behavior in the home, and observed behavior before and after therapy, coded using the MICS. On all of the self-report measures, both groups improved significantly, but there were no differences between them. On five of the six behavioral categories derived from the MICS, couples in the behavioral group improved significantly more than couples in the interaction-insight group. One year follow-up data taken from two of the self-report measures suggested that changes on the part of both groups were maintained.

Summary of the Research on Behavioral Marriage Therapy

The available evidence tentatively suggests that behavioral exchange programs, when they include either communication, problem-solving training alone or communication training plus behavioral exchange, are an effective treatment for marital problems. In all of the controlled studies conducted thus far, with the exception of Turkewitz (1977), behavioral treatments have been found to be significantly more effective than the control groups on objective, behavioral measures. And with one exception (Harrell and Guerney, 1976), on self-report measures behavioral groups have been found to be significantly improved relative to their corresponding control groups. Jacobson's studies (in press a, 1977a, 1977b) have demonstrated that the hypothesized active ingredients of the treatment package—training in communication, problem-solving, and contingency management skills—are the factors responsible for change. There is some indirect evidence that couples treated alone improve more than couples treated in groups.

However, results have not been entirely consistent across studies. In investigations by Turkewitz (1977) and Harrell and Guerney (1976), results were inconsistent from one measure to another. Turkewitz (1977) found evidence for the effectiveness of behavior therapy on self-report measures but not on behavioral measures; Harrell and Guerney (1976) found exactly the opposite. At this point there is no way to reconcile these findings either with one another, or with those where the results were consistent across measures (Jacobson, 1977a, 1977b, in press a). Further research into the measures used to assess change may identify some of the sources for these discrepancies. One very speculative interpretation is suggested here. The observational measures commonly used by behavioral investigators may be limited in terms of their validity; recent research has suggested as much (Gottman et al., 1976). In the study by Turkewitz, where the MICS coding system was used as the basis for behavioral observations, and such observations were used as general measures of change, there were no differences between groups, although self-report measures did yield significant group differences. This discrepancy may be due to the lack of validity of the MICS. In other studies using the MICS coding system, treatment approaches were oriented specifically toward changing the behaviors measured by the categories of the MICS system. For these studies, the MICS contains face validity, and one would expect treatment effects in a successful program. Similarly, in Harrell and Guerney's (1976) study, where couples were relatively nondistressed, the changes on observational measures may again reflect the specific treatment focus of their groups on changing behaviors reflected by the MICS categories. However, self-report measures, validated on the basis of their ability to distinguish between distressed and nondistressed couples, may be subject to a ceiling effect when used with a sample of relatively nondistressed couples, like those in the Harrell and Guerney (1976) study. This ceiling effect may militate against demonstrating treatment effects.

Whether or not the behavioral approach to treating couples is more effective than other approaches is open to question. The results of comparative outcome studies are equivocal. In one case (Fisher, 1973), behavior therapy was clearly superior to an Adlerian group. In another study (Liberman et al., 1976), behavior therapy was superior to an interaction-insight group on behavioral, but not on self-report, measures. In three studies (Cotton, 1976; Venema, 1975; Wieman, 1973), behavior therapy was effective, but not more effective, than a nonbehavioral communication training group treatment. However, these studies provided only self-report measures of change. Also, the behavioral procedures used in these studies, were, in each case, only a part of the commonly used treatment package.

Questions regarding which aspects of a behavioral approach are most effective remain unanswered. However, from the available literature it appears that those aspects of the approach which emphasize communication training are necessary and possibly sufficient. Jacobson (in press a) found no difference between two kinds of contingency contracting, both of which were used in addition to training in problem-solving and communication training; one possible interpretation of these data is that the contracting procedure itself was extraneous. Jacobson (1977b) also found that a communication training approach was, by itself, sufficient to induce improvement in severely distressed couples. Turkewitz (1977) found that communication training plus behavioral exchange was no more effective than communication training alone. When communication training was not made part of a behavioral approach (Cotton, 1975; Venema, 1975; Wieman, 1973), the program was no more effective than another approach, which was, ironically, based on a different model of communication training. Anecdotally, many investigators have reported that couples respond more positively to the communication, problem-solving mode, than to the contracting mode (as in Jacobson, 1977b; Liberman et al., 1976). Those treatments which are found to be as effective as a behavioral approach also emphasize communication training (Venema, 1975; Wieman, 1973). It may be that the most effective element in the behavioral approach is the one which is the least unique to a behavioral approach.

MISCELLANEOUS OUTCOME INVESTIGATIONS

The communication training programs and the behavioral exchange programs are the only treatment paradigms which can claim a body of research literature at this time. This is unfortunate, because in practice couples are treated from a wide variety of theoretical perspectives, and in many ways a review of the outcome literature is incomplete without focusing on all of the major approaches used by clinicians in intervening with distressed marriages.

This section addresses a number of important research questions which have received some attention in outcome investigations. First, the question of time-limited versus long-term, open-ended treatment is examined. Second, the effectiveness of bibliotherapy and programmed instruction will be discussed in reference to a particular study. The relative effectiveness of conjoint, concurrent and group marital therapy will be discussed. Finally, a number of miscellaneous outcome studies will be summarized. None of these questions has been adequately resolved on the basis of current research, but the issues are sufficiently important to warrant mention of all studies which address them.

To a large extent, marriage counseling sprang forth from traditional social casework (cf. Olson, 1970). The systems perspective and the tendency to view behavioral disturbances as interactional are inherent in social casework. Traditionally, social casework with families has combined an insight-oriented, psychoanalytic perspective with intervention strategies that are more reality-oriented than traditional insight therapies. Clinical interventions tend to be aimed at solving current problems, and making changes in family systems. Despite this relatively practical framework, working with families and couples has been traditionally viewed as a process which requires extended, long-term therapy. The traditional model of family casework assumes that, if institutional constraints are absent, therapy should be continuous, long-term and in-depth. In a now classic study, Reid and Shyne (1967) compared the standard, traditional casework model with brief, time-limited (eight sessions) therapy with disturbed families and couples. The study was a large-scale endeavor spanning a number of casework agencies and eight social worker therapists. One hundred and twenty cases were randomly assigned to either continuous, time-unlimited casework or brief time-limited casework and to one of the therapists. The therapists were given no instructions as to how the interventions should be conducted, with the exception of the imposed time limit. Interestingly enough, copious process analyses of therapy excerpts in both conditions revealed few radical differences in the types of intervention strategies used. The primary difference seemed to be that the directive, advice-giving aspects of the casework occurred earlier in the brief condition.

A number of dependent measures were used to evaluate outcome, but the principal evaluative criteria were the ratings of independent clinicians, otherwise not participating in the study and blind to the experimental conditions. Clients were rated prior to, at the termination of, and six months following casework. To summarize the vast array of reported data, brief casework yielded a significantly higher improvement rate at termination (85 percent as opposed to 63 percent for extended casework), and a significantly lower deterioration rate (2 percent as opposed to 17 percent). These differences persisted at the follow-up evaluation, and were corroborated by client self-reports. In an unsuccessful attempt at replicating these findings, Wattie (1973) found no differences between the two types of treatment.

Of course, both sets of findings lead to the unmistakable preference for short-term casework, for reasons of clinical efficiency if not for greater effectiveness. Despite the absence of a control group in these studies and the lack of purely objective behavioral measures, the case for brief, time-limited therapy is compelling. At present one can only speculate as to the reasons for the apparent effectiveness of short-term treatment. Certainly, a clear-cut impending termination date which is known in advance both to therapist and client creates clear expectations about when progress is to be expected. Efforts are likely to be mobilized and maximized on both sides. Neither interactant can afford to become lazy and sacrifice certain sessions due to the knowledge that therapy can be prolonged indefinitely. Therapist and client must be more demanding of one another, treatment sessions are more tightly structured, and change simply occurs more rapidly. At any rate, it is becoming increasingly clear that therapeutic benefit does not require the year or more that was once felt to be sacred and necessary, either when it comes to treating couples or individuals.

Hickman and Baldwin (1971) investigated another important clinical issue in marital therapy, the potential value of programmed instruction devoid of actual therapist contact. The investigators evaluated a programmed text which taught various communication skills, and compared it to an unspecified "traditional" marriage counseling procedure. Thirty distressed couples were randomly assigned to either one of the two treatment procedures or to a waiting-list control group. All therapy sessions in the traditional marriage counseling were conducted by a counseling graduate student. A semantic differential self-report measure suggested the superiority of traditional marriage counseling over the untreated group. In the four-week treatment, no other comparisons attained statistical significance. Reconciliation rates were 30 percent for the control, 50 percent for the programmed text, and 90 percent for traditional counseling. This is one of the few studies to date which has evaluated a do-it-yourself instructional manual. The results paint a pessimistic picture for the ability of couples to improve without a therapist. Given the impressive results found in the other treatment condition, it is unfortunate that the procedures used were not specified. Considering the paucity of empirically-documented evidence for the effectiveness of marital therapy, it would be desirable to know the interventions that had such a marked impact on this distressed population of couples.

Another major area of controversy within marital therapy is the general question of which modality is most effective. Some have advocated treating couples concurrently, that is, seeing each spouse separately; others have advocated conjoint marital therapy, that is, treating the couple together; others have advocated treating couples in groups. Although the latter two modalities have been the most prevalent forms advocated by clinicians, there is really very little evidence to bring to bear on this issue. There is some indirect evidence, as has already been mentioned, that behavioral approaches are more effective when couples are seen conjointly but individually. However, what little data exist in the nonbehavioral literature are equivocal. Macon (1975) compared couples groups with conjoint therapy. The goals of treatment for both groups consisted of improved communication, increased ability to recognize and meet the needs of one another, improved role functioning and the resolution of role conflicts, the acquiring of problem-solving skills, ability to express positive feelings, increased self-esteem, as well as enhanced esteem for spouse.

No control group was used in the study. Couples comprised a distressed population, and 33 of these couples were randomly assigned to the two treatment conditions. Two self-report measures were used to assess outcome. Marked improvement was demonstrated in both groups, although differences between them were not significant. Given these results, the investigator quite appropriately recommended the use of couples groups on the basis of economy. Unfortunately, the absence of an untreated control makes it difficult to interpret the findings.

Graham (1968) compared a condition involving four hour-long conjoint sessions with one in which there were two individual sessions with each spouse plus a four-hour conjoint session. An untreated control group was included. Included in the treatment offering conjoint sessions only was a manipulation in which the therapist verbally reinforced positive responses directed toward the partner. Trends bordering on significance were found favoring the conjoint group ($p < .10$), with reconciliation rate used as the dependent measure. The investigator interprets these findings as supporting the efficacy of the therapist's reinforcing client positive responses. However, it is equally plausible to account for the difference by the fact that all therapy sessions were held conjointly in the superior condition.

Cookerly (1974) compared conjoint marriage counseling, concurrent marriage counseling, and group marriage counseling using the MMPI scales as measures of improvement. Sixty-three predominately middle-class couples were randomly assigned to one of three groups and one of three experienced counselors. Each form of counseling spanned a duration of 12 treatment hours, although couples in the concurrent group were allowed twice as much therapy time, since each spouse met for 12 hours with their counselor. On both the Depression and Psychasthenia scales, plus a combined overall pathology score, concurrent counseling was significantly more effective than conjoint counseling, with other group comparisons inconclusive. Again the absence of an untreated group precludes definitive interpretation, and the increased time afforded to concurrent couples may explain the differences. The MMPI scales, being measures of individual functioning, are questionable criterion measures for assessing relationship distress.

There is clearly an insufficient amount of evidence from which to conclude anything regarding the relative effectiveness of conjoint, concurrent and group marital therapy. It does seem clear, on the basis of studies reviewed by Gurman and Kniskern (in press), that conjoint therapy is generally a more effective way of treating couples than simply treating one spouse alone, assuming that the problem is a relationship problem. However, concurrent therapy involves both partners, and if the effectiveness of conjoint therapy is due primarily to such involvement, it may make little difference whether or not the couple is seen together. On the other hand, theorists of virtually every theoretical persuasion recommend conjoint or conjoint group therapy over concurrent. Since both of the former are more cost effective, perhaps, when we consider this collective clinical intuition, conjoint therapy is the treatment of choice pending further research. There is scant basis for deciding between conjoint therapy and conjoint group therapy, except for the greater efficiency of the latter. Evidence already mentioned regarding their relative effectiveness in behavior therapy is extremely indirect and speculative.

Griffin (1967) examined and compared experienced with inexperienced therapists in the treatment of marital problems. Only wives were participating in therapy. Change was measured by wives' perceptions of themselves and of their husbands in regard to level of regard, empathy, congruence, unconditionality of regard, and willingness to be known, using the Barrett-Leonard Relationship Inventory. Experienced counselors were social workers with a minimum of three years supervised experience; inexperienced therapists were graduates of social work schools who did not meet the "experience requirements." Sixty distressed couples were randomly assigned to an experienced therapist, an inexperienced therapist, or an untreated control. Therapy lasted for two months. Statistical tests failed to uncover differences between experienced and inexperienced therapists.

Matanovich (1970) examined an encounter group marital counseling program in its effects upon perceptual changes among treated spouses. This approach was compared to a "problem-centered" approach on the

Leary Interpersonal Checklist and on the number of reconciliations. Forty distressed couples were randomly assigned to one of four groups: a group using the Encounter tapes, which met for six sessions of three hours duration; a briefer form of the Encounter tapes group, which met for four sessions of one hour each; a problem-centered group, meeting for two individual hour-long sessions and one two-hour conjoint session, and an untreated control. In general, the results showed significant differences in reconciliation favoring encounter group couples over controls.

Christensen (1974) was generally unsuccessful in demonstrating the effectiveness of a marital treatment program designed to increase "interspouse supportiveness." Ziegler (1973) found no differences between an extended (one session of long duration) form of marriage counseling and continuous group treatment. Friedman (1975), in a study where the identified patients were "depressive neurotics," found an unspecified form of marriage counseling effective on the basis of a series of self-report measures of marital functioning, although it was not significantly superior to minimal contact in effecting changes on measures of individual depression on the part of the identified patient.

To summarize the studies presented in this section, a variety of different approaches to treating couples, most of them not carefully specified, were found to effect positive changes. The relative advantages of treating couples in groups versus conjointly versus concurrently remain unclear, although one study found concurrent therapy to be more effective than conjoint therapy. Some negative evidence was presented as to the value of programmed instruction, and one study suggested that inexperienced therapists can effect change equivalent to that produced by more experienced therapists. Most significantly, two studies suggest that brief, time-limited treatment is at least as effective as extended treatment.

It is premature to reach any definite conclusions regarding many of the important procedural parameters which potentially mediate the effectiveness of marriage counseling. Future research will hopefully shed light on the relative advantages and disadvantages of treating couples in groups, the pros and cons of using opposite-sexed co-therapists instead of one therapist, and the importance of therapist experience.

MARITAL THERAPY FOR ALCOHOLICS AND THEIR SPOUSES

Of all the individual behavior problems treated by various forms of psychotherapy, excessive alcohol consumption has most often been viewed as a problem relating to a dysfunctional family system. Many therapists have viewed marital distress as a likely mediator of alcoholism, and various theories describe the types of marital interaction patterns likely to be predictive of alcohol-related problems (Paolino and McCrady, 1977). One consequence of this literature has been a tendency to view marital therapy as an important adjunct, if not the treatment of choice, for married alcoholics. Although only a small amount of controlled research has examined these techniques, the prevalence of this point of view warrants a separate section on the use of marital therapy in treating alcoholism.

Gliedman (1957), in an exploratory investigation, collected data on nine chronic alcoholics and their spouses who participated in concurrent group therapy and then combined group therapy. Both drinking status and self-report measures of marital satisfaction were assessed before and after group treatment, as well as at various follow-up times.

For five months, the alcoholic patients met twice weekly with Gliedman acting as the therapist. A female psychologist served as group leader for the wives, who met once weekly. Only four of the couples later volunteered to involve themselves in three months of weekly combined group sessions, in which the two therapists acted as co-therapists. Unfortunately, the procedures characterizing the two sets of groups were not clearly specified. Of the nine couples who participated in concurrent group treatment, four of them reported significant drops in monthly expenditures for alcoholic beverages. Two of these were patients who went on to participate in the combined groups. These two couples continued to exhibit improvement, both at the termination of the combined group treatment and at follow-up; the other two patients continued to purchase alcohol at rates similar to those found initially. Sobriety was found to correlate highly with positive feelings about the marriage. From the data, it is not clear whether or not the groups were facilitative, either in terms of the patient's drinking status or in terms of improving the marriage.

Ewing, Long, and Wenzel (1961) reported a concurrent group treatment program for alcoholics and their wives. Both groups were described as psychodynamically oriented. Data were reported on the 32 alcoholics; in half of the cases, the wife agreed to participate in the groups. It was found not only that attendance of the wife greatly increased the likelihood of the husband's remaining in the groups for more than six months, but that the alcoholics were much more likely to remain either totally sober or very much improved for at least three years after the termination of treatment when the wives participated (30 percent for husbands attending alone, and 73 percent for husbands whose wives also attended). This is a correlational study, since couples were not randomly assigned to conditions where the wife either attended or did not attend. Therefore, the differences in reported sobriety might reflect differences already inherent in the two populations of couples. The couples in which the wives attended were probably more motivated; this might have accounted for the greater improvement exhibited by patients in this group. The authors do not report how they assessed sobriety; given the difficulties in ascertaining alcohol consumption in the real world, it is impossible to rule out the influence of demand characteristics on the reported findings. Smith (1969) similarly reported that abstinence rates as well as improvement rates were higher for male alcoholics whose wives participated in weekly group therapy sessions concurrent with their husbands' inpatient treatment.

Burton and Kaplan (1968) undertook a long-term follow-up study comparing alcoholics and their spouses who had experienced group marital counseling to couples where either or both spouses had received individual counseling. Assignment to condition occurred on a nonrandom basis, according to when patients approached the agency for assistance. Follow-ups varied in length for different patients, but since group counseling procedures had terminated more recently, these couples were reached sooner following therapy termination than couples where only individual counseling was used. Despite the fact that a significantly higher percentage of such clients reported benefit from counseling, the results are uninterpretable because of the systematic differences in follow-up length between conditions. Moreover, return rates of follow-up questionnaires were much higher for the group counseled couples, again possibly because the follow-up request followed therapy termination more closely in time.

Corder, Corder, and Laidlaw (1972) treated inpatient alcoholics and their wives, using a four-day intensive workshop, which followed normal inpatient services for a random proportion of the patients. After a four-week program, the wives joined for a series of group therapy sessions following a transactional analysis format. Also included in the workshop were a series of meetings and lectures, meetings with representatives of community agencies, and meetings of Alcoholics Anonymous and Al-Anon. Six-month follow-ups indicated that 85 percent of the control group patients had resumed drinking, compared to only 43 percent of those undergoing the workshop. Assuming the reliability of these reports, this is an impressive demonstration of facilitation by wives' participation in their husbands' treatment.

Cadogan (1973) studied an eclectic form of group therapy for alcoholics and their wives, emphasizing problem-solving, feeling expression, and learning the impact their behavior had on one another. Forty couples were randomly assigned to an experimental or a control group. Therapy was continuous, without a time limit; groups were led by a psychologist and an alcoholism counselor. Six months after discharge from the hospital, abstinence rates were 45 percent for the experimental group and only 10 percent for the control group; these differences were statistically significant. On the basis of marital inventories, there were no differences between the two groups in terms of marital satisfaction.

Hedberg and Campbell (1974) compared four behavior therapy approaches to the treatment of alcoholism, one of which was a marital therapy approach. The other treatment conditions included systematic desensitization, covert sensitization, and electrical aversive conditioning. Each treatment program was conducted on an outpatient basis, and each lasted for a year. Six months after treatment had ended, the marital therapy group showed the highest improvement rate for patients whose goal had been abstinence. Eighty percent of the couples aspiring toward abstinence attained their goal, compared to 60 percent of the desensitization subjects, 36 percent of the covert sensitization subjects, and none of the aversive conditioning subjects. If the goal had been controlled drinking rather than abstinence, attainment occurred for 60 percent of the marital therapy subjects, whereas the attainment rate for all treatments combined was 62 percent. Overall, 74 percent of the marital therapy patients attained their treatment goals, compared to 55 percent for all subjects combined. Whether or not these differences are significant is unclear, since statistical analyses were not provided.

In summary, there is some evidence that treating alcoholism as a marital problem can facilitate the diminution of alcohol consumption. Although all of the studies are plagued by methodological limitations, two controlled studies were able to significantly improve the abstinence rate by involving the wives of the alcoholics in the treatment. Given the lack of controls for nonspecific variables, and given the difficulties in assessing the level of alcohol consumption, these results must be regarded as tentative.

SEX THERAPY

Since the publication of *Human Sexual Inadequacy* by Masters and Johnson (1970), the treatment of sexual dysfunctions has become a mammoth industry, spawning numerous books (such as Hartman and Fithian, 1972; Kaplan, 1974), a new journal (*Journal of Sex and Marital Therapy*), and a panoply of clinics and training centers across the country. Most of these have reported impressively high success rates (for example, Masters and Johnson reported 97.8 percent cure for premature ejaculation, including in their report a five-year follow-up!)—results which are doubly impressive considering that sexual dysfunctions have been traditionally thought of as intractable clinical problems (as in Hastings, 1963).

A more sober appraisal of the efficacy of the sex therapies must begin at the level of analysis consistent with this chapter, that is, with an evaluation of the controlled research. An examination of the voluminous literature relating to sex therapy techniques over the past seven years reveals a startling paucity of controlled studies. As shall be seen, the controlled research that does exist requires tempering this optimism regarding the magical cures reported by sex therapists. But before reporting a few of the illustrative controlled studies, any analysis of the sex therapy literature must begin with the work of Masters and Johnson. It is from their research that the sex therapy bandwagon sprang forth, and the optimism regarding the reversibility of sexual dysfunctions is still primarily based on their data.

As Caird and Wincze (1977) have pointed out, the results reported by Masters and Johnson are based on an extremely unusual, selective sample of the dysfunctional population. In order to even be accepted into their treatment program, clients had to present a sexual dysfunction relatively unencumbered by additional marital or individual behavior problems. This selection criterion results in a sample of clients quite discrepant with the dysfunctional clients typically presented to the practicing clinician (Caird and Wincze, 1977). In addition, clients who appeared at Masters and Johnson's St. Louis office had to be sufficiently wealthy to afford a $2,500 fee for a two-week treatment program, not to mention a two-week vacation from work in order to reside in St. Louis for the duration of treatment.

Moreover, Masters and Johnson relied exclusively on client self-reports in assessing the degree of clinical benefit. To the normal cautions which must be entertained in evaluating data based on such self-reports, recent research by Wincze, Hoon, and Hoon (1977) must be added. These investigators found very low correlations between self-report and physiological measures of sexual functioning in dysfunctional women, such that despite positive self-reports of therapeutic benefit, none of the objective measures showed clinically significant changes. Considering the factors which might prompt clients to report positive benefits after undergoing the costly, intensive treatment program of Masters and Johnson, their findings must be interpreted with caution. Controls which might have ruled out such nonspecific factors as demand characteristics were not included.

Similar interpretive difficulties interfere with evaluation of the work of other sex therapists (for example, Kaplan, 1974). Turning to controlled research, Obler (1973) compared systematic desensitization procedures with a psychoanalytically oriented group treatment and an untreated control group in the treatment of sexual dysfunctions. Sixty-four subjects, including both males and females with mixed sexual dysfunctions, were matched on various relevant characteristics and assigned to one of the three conditions. Desensitization subjects were seen individually by the investigator for 15 weeks; sessions lasted for 45 minutes. A standard imaginal desensitization procedure was utilized, involving training in progressive muscle relaxation, hierarchy construction, and the graded pairing of the relaxation response with hierarchy items. Graphic aids, such as videotapes of actors engaging in various sexual activities, were used occasionally to facilitate imagery. Subjects were instructed to refrain from *in vivo* sexual activity until they had been desensitized to the corresponding imaginal items. Assertive training was added as an adjunct procedure to aid subjects in their social functioning with members of the opposite sex. Group therapy subjects met with two trained "neo-Freudian" therapists for one-and-a-half-hour weekly sessions. The focus of these groups was on open discussion of subjects' sexual and social problems, using analytic interpretations.

Improvement was measured in a number of ways. All subjects kept a diary of sexual experiences occurring during the course of therapy, including a designation of "success" or "failure" for each encounter. "Success" was operationally defined according to the nature of each particular subject's dysfunction. Physiological data (heart rate and galvanic skin response) were recorded while subjects were viewing films of actors exhibiting the subject's dysfunction. Finally, self-report measures of sexual and general anxiety were included. During the course of treatment, success rates among desensitization subjects were .42 for females and .61 for males. This compared favorably to group therapy (.03 for females and .03

for males) and untreated (.02 for females and .02 for males) ratings. Comparing the desensitization group to the other two groups combined, differences were statistically significant for females ($p < .0005$), males ($p < .05$), and for males and females combined ($p < .0001$). Physiological reductions in anxiety were also significantly greater for desensitization subjects. Self-report measures of sexual anxiety tended to corroborate these findings, although pre-post measures of general anxiety level did not discriminate between the groups. Informal success rates indicated that over 90 percent of the desensitization subjects were sexually functional at the conclusion of treatment, compared to only 0.025 percent in the other two groups. A one-and-a-half-year follow-up indicated maintenance of these results, although actual follow-up data were not reported.

Although Obler's findings are an impressive demonstration of the effectiveness of desensitization in improving sexual functioning, two major cautions must be mentioned. Desensitization subjects were explicitly instructed to avoid anxiety-inducing sexual encounters during treatment; although females did not seem to be substantially affected by these instructions, males in the desensitization group did attempt sexual activity much less frequently than group treatment subjects. These differential instructions might account for the superiority exhibited by desensitization subjects on the measure of percentage "success." The clinical significance of Obler's findings might also be questioned. Only 42 percent of the females' sexual encounters were successful during the course of treatment, despite the instructions to refrain from anxiety-inducing sexual encounters. Even though these results were significantly greater than the results for the other two conditions, it could be argued that 58 percent failure is still a dysfunctional rate!

Mathews, Bancroft, Whitehead, Hackman, Julier, Bancroft, Gath, and Shaw (1976) have recently reported a rather ambitious outcome study comparing three forms of treatment for sexual dysfunctions: systematic desensitization plus counseling, directed practice *à la* Masters and Johnson plus counseling (M&J), and directed practice with minimal therapist contact (MC). The population consisted of both female and male clients, and in each instance a partner was involved. Three male-female therapist teams split the duty, although half of the subjects were assigned to only a single therapist. Of the 18 dysfunctional males, 13 were impotent; 12 had some degree of premature ejaculation, and one exhibited ejaculatory failure. Thirteen of the 18 dysfunctional women were nonorgasmic, while 17 complained of a low degree of sexual arousal and interest. There was one case of vaginismus.

Dependent variables included ratings both of the overall relationship and of the sexual relationship, conducted by independent psychiatrists prior to treatment, one month following treatment, and at a four-month follow-up. Client self-reports were also utilized. There were no significant differences between the treatment conditions on any of the measures, despite the clear trends in favor of the Masters and Johnson approach on all the measures. The failure of these differences to achieve statistical significance appears to reflect considerable variability within treatments. At the one-month follow-up, only 50 percent of the desensitization subjects were rated as improved, compared to 75 percent of the Masters and Johnson subjects and 66 percent of the minimal contact subjects. However, none of the desensitization subjects deteriorated as a result of treatment, whereas two minimal contact subjects and one of the Masters and Johnson subjects exhibited deterioration. At the four-month follow-up, the desensitization improvement rate dropped to one-third, M&J to two-thirds, and MC to 7 out of 12. However, none of the desensitization subjects was rated as having deteriorated, compared to one M&J subject, and one-third of the MC subjects. There was an interaction between the factor of one versus two therapists and treatment: M&J subjects treated by two therapists improved more than any other combination of therapist and treatment. Just as in Obler's study, men seemed to benefit from treatment more than women; for example, on the basis of therapist ratings, only two of the 18 female subjects had become more orgasmic by the time of the last follow-up.

Any conclusions based on this study must be tentative, due to the absence of statistically significant differences between groups. The exclusion of an untreated control group further obfuscates the interpretation of these findings. But given the disappointing results in the imaginal desensitization condition in this study and in another controlled study (cf. Kockott, Dittmar, and Nusselt, 1975), there seems little reason to recommend it as a continuing treatment for sexual dysfunction. This study strengthens the suspicion that Obler's findings were both artifactual and clinically insignificant, and provides additional evidence that the directed practice approach created by Masters and Johnson is often an effective strategy for improving sexual functioning. However, neither of the two standard treatment approaches evaluated by either Obler (1973) or Mathews et al. (1976) seems to have been effective at helping women achieve an orgasmic response. It is the treatment of female sexual dysfunction which will now be examined.

Wincze and Caird (1976) compared standard desensitization with a procedure termed "video desensitization" in the treatment of essential orgasmic dysfunction in women. Even though three-fourths of the 21 subjects reported not experiencing orgasm during sexual activity, their primary complaint was anxiety in the sexual situation.

Video desensitization is identical to standard desensitization except that instead of imagining anxiety-provoking sexual scenes, subjects view them on videotaped sequences. Using a procedure similar to that already described by Obler (1973), Wincze and Caird produced a series of films corresponding to various potential hierarchy items, using actors.

Based on a variety of self-report measures of sexual anxiety, the investigators found that only the video procedure was consistently superior to an untreated control group either at posttesting or at a three-month follow-up. Only 25 percent of the nonorgasmic women reported that they were able to achieve orgasm following treatment. Thus, video desensitization seems to be an effective procedure for reducing sexual anxiety in dysfunctional women, but does not seem to be a particularly effective treatment for facilitating orgasmic responsiveness in nonorgasmic women. These findings also contribute to the suspicion that imaginal desensitization is a relatively ineffective procedure for treating sexual dysfunctions, particularly in lieu of intervention strategies utilizing some form of *in vivo* procedure.

LoPiccolo and Lobitz (1972) reported an apparently promising *in vivo* procedure for training women who had never achieved orgasm to become orgasmic. The treatment strategy begins with instructions in masturbation, and proceeds in a series of graded steps to progressive involvement of the partner. In a series of uncontrolled case studies, self-report data indicated that 100 percent of a sample of dysfunctional female clients became orgasmic through the use of this technique. In the only controlled study investigating the effectiveness of this directed masturbation strategy, Kohlenberg (1974) was able to demonstrate, for three female clients, a functional relationship between the technique and improvement in self-rated sexual arousal. Furthermore, all three of the women reported experiencing orgasm, both through masturbation and through sexual relations with a partner. Kohlenberg established internal validity through the use of the single-case design referred to as a multi-subject baseline design by Hersen and Barlow (1976). Kohlenberg had three clients collect data on each sexual encounter by having them rate their degree of sexual arousal on a ten-point scale and, also, note whether or not they had achieved orgasm. He then introduced his directed masturbation technique at different points in time for each client; after eight sessions for client #1, 12 sessions for client #2, and 24 sessions for client #3. For each client, self-reports of increased arousal remained relatively stable throughout baseline recording, and increased substantially upon the implementation of treatment. By staggering the time at which treatment was introduced, and establishing that positive changes occurred only upon the introduction of the treatment, Kohlenberg was able to demonstrate that this directed masturbation technique was responsible for these changes. Despite these positive findings, more recent research has indicated that even when directed masturbation is included in a behavioral treatment package, dysfunctional women are often unsuccessful in learning to attain orgasm during intercourse, although they do improve in other aspects of their sexual functioning (Munjack, Cristol, Goldstein, Phillips, Goldberg, Whipple, Staples, and Kanno, 1976; Schneidman and McGuire, 1976).

Measurement of sexual functioning remains a critical problem in the assessment of treatment effects. A study that was already mentioned by Wincze, Hoon, and Hoon (1977) evaluated a treatment program for women who reported little arousal or interest in sex. At the conclusion of therapy, they all reported that their sexual functioning was much improved, and that they had greatly benefited from therapy. However, on a variety of sexual arousal indices, including self-reports, behavioral measures, and physiological measures (vaginal capillary engorgement), there were virtually no changes as a function of treatment. The authors concluded that the clients were reporting improvement despite the *actual* lack of change. Their results call into question all of those studies which rely on such subjective assessments of change, as well as those reports which use the inferences of independent psychiatrists based upon the clients' subjective impressions of change. This includes most of the research discussed in this section, but is particularly damning of the work of Masters and Johnson (1970), since they relied almost exclusively on such measures.

In summary, when the effectiveness of sex therapy is examined, the evidence in favor is far less compelling than the proliferation of enthusiasts would imply. Standard systematic desensitization appears to lead to modest treatment effects, and is apparently inferior to *in vivo* treatments emphasizing directed practice. Desensitization using videotaped stimuli seems to be effective in reducing women's anxiety in the sexual situation, but appears to have little impact on their orgasmic capacity. Directed masturbation appears at this point to be the most promising technique for facilitating the orgasmic response in dysfunctional women.

Conclusions and Future Directions

The two approaches to marital therapy which emerge from the literature as the most promising are the behavioral and the conjugal relationship enhancement approaches. This is not to say that either receives an unequivocal endorsement on the basis of the current outcome literature, since the results are not totally consistent and are limited in terms of external validity. However, both approaches are supported by well-controlled studies. Other approaches have not been investigated with sufficient frequency to warrant any conclusions about their efficacy. Extrapolating from the social casework research, one might tentatively suggest that marital therapies which are brief, time-limited, and relatively structured are to be recommended on the basis of current research.

Structured communication training, whether behavioral or nonbehavioral, seems to be emerging as the *sine qua non* of effective marital therapy. The burden of proof is now on advocates of less structured, long-term approaches to demonstrate their effectiveness relative to these communication-oriented approaches. A research development which would be most welcome at this stage would be well-controlled, comparative outcome studies scrutinizing approaches which have hitherto gone uninvestigated. Until such research is conducted, structured communications training of some kind appears to be the treatment of choice for mild to moderate marital problems.

The important procedural parameters of marital therapy remain virtually uninvestigated, and must be viewed as important subjects for future research. *First,* component analyses of both conjugal and behavioral exchange approaches must be conducted in order to determine which aspects of these treatment packages are contributing most to their effectiveness. *Second,* group treatment versus individual conjoint treatment must be evaluated more thoroughly. *Third,* the merit of involving a co-therapist must be investigated.

Marital therapy has only begun to be studied with various populations of disturbed individuals. With the exception of one study on depressed neurotics which produced equivocal findings, most of the extant work has been conducted with alcoholics and sexually dysfunctional clients. The alcoholism literature is mildly suggestive of positive benefits to be derived from marital therapy, and the sex therapy literature is somewhat promising, particularly in terms of reversing male dysfunctions.

Marital therapy is slowly moving toward a firmer foundation in scientific inquiry. The research is still sufficiently ambiguous to allow one's extrapolations to be tempered by subjective biases, as is evidenced by the rather different conclusions deduced from the same literature by Gurman and Kniskern (in press). The goal of outcome research is to produce data from which the conclusions are unmistakable, where there is little room for individual interpretive biases. Although science, even at its best, is sufficiently subjective to render this goal largely unattainable, such aspirations are necessary in the desirable transformation of marital therapy from art to science.

REFERENCES

Azrin, N. H., Naster, B. J. and Jones, R. Reciprocity counseling: A rapid learning-based procedure for marital counseling. *Behaviour Research and Therapy*, 1973, 11, 365-382.

Bergin, A. E. and Strupp, H. H. *Changing Frontiers in the Science of Psychotherapy.* Chicago: Aldine, 1972.

Birchler, G. R., Weiss, R. L. and Vincent, J. P. A multidimensional analysis of social reinforcement exchange between maritally distressed and nondistressed spouse and stranger dyads. *Journal of Personality and Social Psychology*, 1975, 31, 349-360.

Burton, G. and Kaplan, H. M. Group counseling in conflicted marriages where alcoholism is present: Client's evaluation of effectiveness. *Journal of Marriage and the Family*, 1968, 30, 74-79.

Cadogan, D. A. Marital group therapy in the treatment of alcoholism. *Quarterly Journal of Studies on Alcohol*, 1973, 34, 1187-1194.

Caird, W. and Wincze, J. P. *Sex Therapy: A Behavioral Approach.* New York: Harper & Row, 1977.

Campbell, E. E. The effects of couple communication training on married couples in the child-rearing years: A field experiment. Unpublished doctoral dissertation, Arizona State University, 1974.

Cardillo, J. P. Effects of teaching communication roles on interpersonal perception and self-concept in disturbed marriages. *Proceedings, 79th Annual Convention of the American Psychological Association*, 1971, 440-442.

Cassidy, M. J. Communication training for marital pairs. Unpublished doctoral dissertation, UCLA, 1973.

Christensen, D. J. The effects of intramarriage self-esteem and decision-making on a structured marriage counseling program emphasizing inter-spouse supportiveness. *Dissertation Abstracts International*, 1974, 35, 3141A.

Collins, J. The effects of the conjugal relationship modification method on marital communication and adjustment. Unpublished doctoral dissertation, Pennsylvania State University, 1971.

Cookerly, J. R. The reduction of psychopathology as measured by the MMPI clinical scale in three forms of marriage counseling. *Journal of Marriage and the Family*, 1974, 36, 332-335.

Corder, B. F., Corder, R. F. and Laidlaw, N. D. An intensive program for alcoholics and their wives. *Quarterly Journal of Studies on Alcohol*, 1972, 33, 1144-1146.

Cotton, M. C. A systems approach to marital training evaluation. Unpublished doctoral dissertation, Texas Tech University, 1976.

Ely, A. L., Guerney, B. G. and Stover, L. Efficacy of the training phase of conjugal therapy. *Psychotherapy: Theory, Research and Practice*, 1973, 10, 201-207.

Engel, G. Some obstacles to the development of research in psychoanalysis. *Journal of the American Psychoanalytic Association*, 1968, 16, 195-204.

Ewing, J. A., Long, V. and Wenzel, G. G. Concurrent group psychotherapy of alcoholic patients and their wives. *International Journal of Group Psychotherapy*, 1961, 11, 329-338.

Fisher, R. E. The effect of two group counseling methods on perceptual congruence in married pairs. Unpublished doctoral dissertation, University of Hawaii, 1973.

Friedman, A. S. Interaction of drug therapy with marital therapy in depressive patients. *Archives of General Psychiatry*, 1975, 32, 619-637.

Gliedman, L. H. Concurrent and combined group treatment of chronic alcoholics and their wives. *International Journal of Psychotherapy*, 1957, 7, 414-424.

Gottman, J., Markman, H., Notarius, L. and Gonso, J. *A Couple's Guide to Communication*. Champaign: Research Press, 1976.

Graham, J. A. The effect of the use of counselor positive responses on positive perceptions of mate in marriage counseling. *Dissertation Abstracts International*, 1968, 28, 3504A.

Greer, S. E. and D'Zurilla, T. Behavioral approaches to marital discord and conflict. *Journal of Marriage and Family Counseling*, 1975, 1, 299-315.

Griffin, R. W. Change in perception of marital relationship as related to marriage counseling. *Dissertation Abstracts International*, 1967, 27, 3956A.

Guerney, B. G. *Relationship Enhancement*. San Francisco: Jossey-Bass, 1977.

Gurman, A. S. and Kniskern, D. P. Research on marital and family therapy: Progress, perspective and prospect. In: S. L. Garfield and A. E. Bergin (Eds.), *Handbook of Psychotherapy and Behavior Change: An Empirical Analysis*. New York: Wiley, in press.

Harrell, J. and Guerney, B. Training married couples in conflict negotiation skills. In: D. H. L. Olson (Ed.), *Treating Relationships*. Lake Mills, Iowa: Graphic Press, 1976.

Hartman, W. E. and Fithian, M. A. *Treatment of Sexual Dysfunction*. Long Beach: Center for Marital and Sexual Studies, 1972.

Hastings, D. W. *Impotence and Frigidity*. London: Churchill, 1963.

Hedberg, A. G. and Campbell, L. A comparison of four behavioral treatments of alcoholism. *Journal of Behavior Therapy and Experimental Psychiatry*, 1974, 5, 251-256.

Hersen, M. and Barlow, D. H. *Single Case Experimental Designs*. London: Pergamon, 1976.

Hickman, M. E. and Baldwin, B. A. Use of programmed instruction to improve communication in marriage. *Family Coordinator*, 1971, 20, 121-125.

Hines, G. A. Efficacy of communication skills training with married partners where no marital counseling has been sought. Unpublished doctoral dissertation, University of South Dakota, 1975.

Hops, H., Wills, T. A., Patterson, G. R., and Weiss, R. L. Marital interaction coding system. Unpublished manuscript, University of Oregon, 1971.

Jacobson, N. S. Problem solving and contingency contracting in the treatment of marital discord. *Journal of Consulting and Clinical Psychology*, 1977 (a), 45, 92-100.

Jacobson, N. S. The role of problem-solving in behavioral marital therapy. Paper presented at the annual meeting of the Association for the Advancement of Behavior Therapy, Atlanta, December, 1977 (b).

Jacobson, N. S. Specific and nonspecific factors in a behavioral approach to marital discord. *Journal of Consulting and Clinical Psychology*, in press (a).

Jacobson, N. S. A stimulus control model of change in behavioral marital therapy: Implications for contingency contracting. *Journal of Marriage and Family Counseling*, in press (b).

Jacobson, N. S. and Baucom, D. H. Design and assessment of nonspecific control groups in behavior modification research. *Behavior Therapy*, 1977, 8, 709-719.

Jacobson, N. S. and Margolin, G. *Marital Therapy: Strategies Based on Social Learning and Behavior Exchange Principles.* New York: Brunner/Mazel, in press.

Jacobson, N. S. and Martin, B. Behavioral marriage therapy: Current status. *Psychological Bulletin*, 1976, 83, 540-556.

Kaplan, H. S. *The New Sex Therapy.* New York: Brunner/Mazel, 1974.

Kind, J. The relationship of communication efficiency to marital happiness and an evaluation of short-term training in interpersonal communication with married couples. *Dissertation Abstracts International*, 1968, 29, 1173B.

Kockott, G., Dittmar, F., and Nusselt, L. Systematic desensitization of erectile impotence: A controlled study. *Archives of Sexual Behavior*, 1975, 4, 493-500.

Kohlenberg, R. Directed masturbation and the treatment of primary orgasmic dysfunction. *Archives of Sexual Behavior*, 1974, 3, 349-356.

Liberman, R. P., Levine, J., Wheeler, E., Sanders, N., and Wallace, C. Experimental evaluation of marital group therapy: Behavioral vs. interaction-insight formats. *Acta Psychiatrica Scandinavica*, 1976, Supplement.

LoPiccolo, J. and Lobitz, L. The role of masturbation in the treatment of orgasmic dysfunction. *Archives of Sexual Behavior*, 1972, 2, 163-171.

Macon, L. B. A comparative study of two approaches to the treatment of marital dysfunction. (Doctoral dissertation, University of Southern California, 1975.) *Dissertation Abstracts International*, 1975, 36, 4026-4027A.

Margolin, G. A comparison of marital interventions: Behavioral, behavioral-cognitive and non-directive. Paper presented at the meeting of the Western Psychological Association, Los Angeles, 1976.

Masters, W. H. and Johnson, V. E. *Human Sexual Inadequacy.* Boston: Little, Brown, 1970.

Matanovich, J. P. The effects of short-term group counseling upon positive perceptions of mate in marital counseling. *Dissertation Abstracts International*, 1970, 31, 2688A.

Mathews, A., Bancroft, J., Whitehead, A., Hackman, A., Julier, D., Bancroft, J., Gath, D. and Shaw, P. The behavioral treatment of sexual inadequacy: A comparative study. *Behaviour Research and Therapy*, 1976, 14, 427-436.

Miller, S., Nunnally, E. W. and Wackman, D. B. Minnesota Couples Communication Program (MCCP): Premarital and marital groups. In D. H. L. Olson (Ed.), *Treating Relationships.* Lake Mills: Graphic Press, 1976.

Munjack, D., Cristol, A., Goldstein, A., Phillips, D., Goldberg, A., Whipple, K., Staples, F., and Kanno, P. Behavioral treatment of orgasmic dysfunction: A controlled study. *British Journal of Psychiatry*, 1976, 129, 497-502.

McIntosh, D. M. A comparison of the effects of highly structured, partially structured, and non-structured human relations training for married couples on the dependent variables of communication, marital adjustment, and personal adjustment. *Dissertation Abstracts International*, 1975, 36, 2636-2637A.

Obler, M. Systematic desensitization in sexual disorders. *Journal of Behavior Therapy and Experimental Psychiatry*, 1973, 4, 93-101.

Olson, D. H. Marital and family therapy: Integrative review and critique. *Journal of Marriage and the Family*, 1970, 32, 501-538.

Paolino, T. J. & McCrady, B. S. *The Alcoholic Marriage: Alternative Perspectives.* New York: Grune & Stratton, 1977.

Patterson, G. R., Weiss, R. L. and Hops, H. Interpersonal skills training for couples in early stages of conflict. *Journal of Marriage and the Family*, 1975, 37, 295-303

Pierce, R. M. Training in interpersonal communication skills with the partners of deteriorated marriages. *Family Coordinator*, 1973, 22, 223-227.

Pilder, R. J. Some effects of laboratory training on married couples. Unpublished doctoral dissertation, United States International University, 1972.

Rappaport, A. F. Conjugal relationship enhancement program. In: D. H. L. Olson (Ed.), *Treating Relationships*. Lake Mills, Iowa: Graphic Press, 1976.

Reid, W. J. and Shyne, A. W. *Brief and Extended Casework*. New York: Columbia University Press, 1967.

Roberts, P. V. The effects on marital satisfaction of brief training in behavioral exchange negotiation mediated by differentially experienced trainers. *Dissertation Abstracts International*, 1975, 36, 457B.

Rogers, C. R. *Client-Centered Therapy*. Boston: Houghton-Mifflin, 1951.

Schneidman, B. and McGuire, L. Group therapy for nonorgasmic women: Two age levels. *Archives of Sexual Behavior*, 1976, 5, 239-247.

Sloane, R. B., Staples, F. R., Cristol, A. H., Yorkston, N. J. and Whipple, K. *Psychotherapy versus Behavior Therapy*. Cambridge: Harvard University Press, 1975.

Smith, C. G. Alcoholics: Their treatment and their wives. *British Journal of Psychiatry*, 1969, 115, 1039-1042.

Stuart, R. B. Operant-interpersonal treatment for marital discord. *Journal of Consulting and Clinical Psychology*, 1969, 33, 675-682.

Tsoi-Hoshmand, L. Marital therapy: An integrative behavioral-learning model. *Journal of Marriage and Family Counseling*, 1976, 2, 179-191.

Turkewitz, H. A comparative study of behavioral marital therapy and communication therapy. Unpublished doctoral dissertation, SUNY at Stony Brook, 1977.

Venema, H. B. Marriage enrichment: A comparison of the behavioral exchange negotiation and communication models. Unpublished doctoral dissertation, Fuller Theological Seminary, 1975.

Vincent, J. P., Weiss, R. L. and Birchler, G. R. A behavioral analysis of problem-solving in distressed and nondistressed married and stranger dyads. *Behavior Therapy*, 1975, 6, 475-487.

Wattie, B. Evaluating short-term casework in a family agency. *Social Casework*, 1973, 54, 609-616.

Weiss, R. L., Hops, H. and Patterson, G. R. A framework for conceptualizing marital conflict, a technology for altering it, some data for evaluating it. In: L. A. Hamerlynck, L. C. Handy and E. J. Mash (Eds.), *Behavior Change: Methodology, Concepts, and Practice*. Champaign: Research Press, 1973.

Wells, R. A., Fiqurel, J. A. and McNamee, P. Group facilitative training with conflicted marital couples. In: A. S. Gurman and D. Rice (Eds.), *Couples in Conflict: New Directions in Marital Therapy*. New York: Aronson, 1975.

Wieman, R. J. Conjugal relationship modification and reciprocal reinforcement: A comparison of treatments for marital discord. Unpublished doctoral dissertation, Pennsylvania State University, 1973.

Wills, T. A., Weiss, R. L. and Patterson, G. R. A behavioral analysis of the determinants of marital satisfaction. *Journal of Consulting and Clinical Psychology*, 1974, 42, 802-811.

Wincze, J. P. and Caird, W. K. The effects of systematic desensitization and video desensitization in the treatment of essential sexual dysfunction in women. *Behavior Therapy*, 1976, 7, 335-342.

Wincze, J., Hoon, P. and Hoon, E. Sexual arousal in women: A comparison of cognitive and physiological responses by continuous measurement. *Archives of Sexual Behavior*, 1977, 6, 230-245.

Ziegler, J. S. A comparison of the effect of two forms of group psychotherapy on the treatment of marital discord. *Dissertation Abstracts International*, 1973, 34, 143-144A.

IX

Contemporary Marital Therapies: A Critique and Comparative Analysis of Psychoanalytic, Behavioral and Systems Theory Approaches

ALAN S. GURMAN, PH.D.

INTRODUCTION

In the last decade, marital therapy has evolved into one of the most significant psychotherapeutic interventions in the mental health field. In addition to its obvious relevance to marital conflicts, marital therapy increasingly has been invoked as a potentially powerful general mode of intervention for a wide variety of clinical problems traditionally treated by individual psychotherapy. Affective disorders (Davenport, Ebert, Adland, and Goodwin, 1975; Feldman, 1976; Friedman, 1975; Greene, Lee, and Lustig, 1975), alcoholism (Burton and Kaplan, 1968; Cadogan, 1973; Gallant, Rich, Bey and Terranova, 1970; Smith, 1967, 1969; Steinglass, Davis and Berenson, 1975), sexual dysfunction (Kaplan, 1974; Kinder and Blakeney, 1976; Masters and Johnson, 1970; Mathews, Ban-

---

This chapter is dedicated to Jesse, who made a couple a family. Thanks are extended to Drs. Roger Knudson and David Rice for their helpful comments on an earlier draft of this chapter.

croft, Whitehead, Hackman, Julier, Bancroft, Gath and Shaw, 1976; Sager, 1974) and even obsessive (Stern, 1973) and compulsive rituals (Boyd and Bolen, 1970) have become the target for treatment in the social context of the marital dyad. Two-generational conflicts focused on childhood "behavior problems" have increasingly been examined in the context of parental conflict (Levitt, 1971; Oltmanns, Broderick and O'Leary, 1976; Patterson, 1975; Reisinger, Frangia and Hoffman, 1976; Shepherd, Oppenheim and Mitchell, 1966).

Such a prominent role in the delivery of mental health services has not always characterized the marital therapies. The conceptual history of marital therapy has, until recently, been quite weak and has been little more than a "technique in search of a theory" (Haley, 1969; Manus, 1966; Prochaska and Prochaska, Chapter I). Indeed, the substantive history of marital therapy has emerged primarily from the history of family therapy. Marital therapy adopted much of family theory long after the establishment of marital therapy as an area of independent clinical practice. In addition, three important historical forces have slowed the development of both the conceptual and the empirical base for couples therapy.

First, contemporary marital therapy did not begin with the advancement of a new theory or method of practice by a single founder, as did psychoanalysis; nor did it emerge from basic experimental research as did behavior therapy. Rather, it emerged rapidly in response to the felt needs of clients (Olson, 1970) and was often conducted under the rubric of marriage *counseling*, with rather different aims and strategies than those that characterize contemporary marital *therapy* (Gurman and Kniskern, 1977c).

Second, the autonomy and unconnectedness of the several independent professional disciplines committed to marital and family study, such as psychiatry, clinical psychology, social work, family sociology, and the ministry, while offering the potential for useful cross-fertilization, have actually yielded multidisciplinary antagonisms and adversarial jousts. The use of differing value structures regarding marital and family life and the treatment of dysfunctional systems and early clinical experience with vastly different clinical populations further fragmented the simultaneous developments in the field. Moreover, the absence, until relatively recently, of clinical psychology's involvement in the field in part delayed significantly the growth of the scientific study of marital process and change (Gurman, 1971).

Finally, a general devaluing of the very notion of treating marital systems directly, deriving from the psychoanalytic *Zeitgeist* of the first half of this century (and continuing even more recently, as in Giovacchini, 1965), and a related devaluing of psychological treatment by non-physicians hardly helped to facilitate interprofessional collaboration. Theory-specific concerns about the dilution of the transference relationship considered necessary to produce positive therapeutic change, and related concerns about the limited potential for dealing with "depth" material in a triadic treatment setting, while totally lacking empirical support, impeded advances in the field for several decades. Indeed, the "classical" model of marital therapy (Giovacchini, 1965) was, and still is, indistinguishable from psychoanalysis.

The last few years, however, offer reason for renewed optimism about the substantive conceptual and empirical future of the marital therapies. This is particularly evident in the rapid growth of research in the area. Whereas in 1972 there existed fewer than 30 published studies on the outcomes of couples therapy (Gurman, 1973a, 1973b), there now exist over 150 such studies, a great many of which are reasonably well designed and the majority of which meet at least minimal methodological requirements (Gurman and Kniskern, 1977c). On the conceptual front, marital therapy seems finally to have broken new ground and developed methods of clinical investigation and intervention which, while at times overlapping with theories of family process, have particular salience for the understanding and explanation of *marital* process and dysfunction.

SCOPE AND GOALS OF THE PRESENT CHAPTER

Not unlike individual therapists, marital therapists have recently either spawned or endorsed a flood of new schools or systems of "therapy" for couples in conflict, such as fair fight training, encounter weekends, transactional analysis and Gestalt therapy. None of these approaches offers empirical evidence of its efficacy and most offer but the weakest of theoretical substance. Indeed, the proliferation of faddish therapies for marital discord is a distinct danger, given both the youth of the field and the largely nonexistent legal regulation of its clinical practice (Gurman and Rice, 1975).

This chapter will focus intensively on a critical analysis of the three major approaches to couples therapy that to date provide the most substantive models for the understanding and treatment of couples in conflict: psychoanalytically oriented theory, systems theory, and social learning theory. The strengths and weaknesses of each approach will be examined in terms of the adequacy of each approach in dealing with the issues of marital attraction and choice and the nature of marital dysfunction, conflict and satisfaction/dissatisfaction. The remainder of each of the first three sections of this chapter will then discuss in some detail what appear to be the major controversial themes, assumptions and issues inherent in the conceptual perspective under consideration.

Each of these sections will conclude with a brief revisiting of some of the major practical problems and issues involved in the relatively *strict* application of each of these approaches to the treatment of marital disorders and will also note the major conceptual and technical strengths and advantages offered by each perspective. As will be seen later in this chapter, each of these approaches shares a good deal in common and appears to be becoming rather syncretistic and integrative, if not eclectic, in everyday application. Still, a consideration of each perspective in relatively pure culture, as it were, will allow a better understanding and appreciation of what each offers uniquely to the treatment of couples in conflict.

A systematic comparative analysis of the three approaches will then be presented and will emphasize, among other matters, the dimensions of treatment goals, the nature of the therapeutic relationship, and the therapeutic process. Throughout the remainder of this chapter, frequent reference will be made to the conceptual and applied models put forth in the preceding chapters by Drs. Meissner, Nadelson, Weiss, O'Leary and Turkewitz, Steinglass and Sluzki. In addition, the works of a number of other theoreticians, clinicians and researchers from each of these three perspectives will also be examined in an attempt to present a more comprehensive consideration of the three conceptual frameworks addressed in the present volume. It should be noted that this chapter does not critically consider "psychoanalytic theory," "systems theory" or "behaviorism," but focuses on each of these perspectives as specifically applied to the treatment of marital disorders. A fully comprehensive examination of *all* of the assumptions, premises and treatment techniques of these approaches obviously would require a volume unto itself.

The Psychoanalytic Perspective

There can be little doubt that psychoanalytic thought has had a greater impact on the conceptualization of the human condition than any other psychological paradigm. In the therapeutic context, psychoanalytically oriented therapists began to examine the nature of marriage and marital conflict long before applications to family life of systems theory or social learning theory even existed (Ackerman, 1958; Giovacchini, 1958; Mittelman, 1948; Oberndorf, 1938). Orthodox individual psychoanalytic treatment practices, however, precluded the inclusion of the spouse in the therapeutic transaction (Gurman, 1971) for decades. Perhaps as a result, there has been surprisingly little psychoanalytic theory development that has focused explicitly on the marital relationship. Meissner's contribution to this volume (Chapter II) adds significantly and impressively to this literature. Moreover, while a great many marital and family therapists appear to have been influenced by psychoanalytic thought (Group for the Advancement of Psychiatry, 1970), there exists but a paucity of marital treatment interventions derived directly from such an orientation, and most influential psychoanalytically oriented marital therapists, in fact, appear to be closet "technical eclectics" (for example, Ables and Brandsma, 1977; Martin, 1976; Nadelson, Chapter III; Nadelson, Bassuk, Hopps and Boutelle, 1975; Sager, 1976; Skynner, 1976). With the general recent increase of attention to the treatment of marital and family conflict in psychiatric and psychological circles, there appears to have been almost a rediscovery of the analytic perspective on marriage. For example, Dicks' (1967) articulate and brilliant text on the object-relations approach to marriage went out of print about 1972, to be reissued about four years later. Research on relatively pure forms of psychoanalytic treatment of marital disorders is nonexistent, however (see Gurman and Kniskern, 1977c; Jacobson, Chapter VIII). While a great many of the treatment experiences in the empirical literature on marital therapy have definitely had a psychodynamic flavor, it would certainly be inaccurate and misleading to characterize these interventions as anything other than pragmatically eclectic (Gurman, 1973b; Gurman and Kniskern, 1977c).

Marital Choice, Satisfaction and Conflict

Psychoanalytic attention to the choice of marital partners, and ensuing satisfaction and conflict, has been significant. This should come as no surprise since psychoanalytic theory is predominantly a developmental perspective (Meissner, Chapter II). Despite Kubie's (1956) assertion that the process of marital choice is not amenable to scientific study, since marital choice is considered to be largely unconscious, a good deal of speculation as well as a controversial body of empirical work has emerged within a broadly conceived psychoanalytic framework.

The most inclusive perspective on the unconscious factors operative in mate choice is that of *need complementarity*. At its core, this model

(Winch, 1952, 1955, 1958; Winch, Ktsanes and Ktsanes, 1954) posits that through homogamy of social characteristics there is established a "field of eligibles" (potential mates) and through a "heterogamy of motives" mate selection occurs. These motives are termed "need complementarity" or, more specifically, *unfulfilled* personality needs, which may be of two kinds: (1) those in which partners differ in degree, and (2) those in which partners differ in kind. These needs were selected from Murray's (1938) well-known list. In psychoanalytic terms, this proposed process represents a form of idealization in which, as Meissner (Chapter II) says, "the object becomes a substitute for some unattained ego ideal of the subject" (page 41).

While early results generally supported this position (Winch, 1952, 1955, 1958; Winch et al., 1954), several attempts to replicate these findings have failed (e.g., Heiss and Gordon, 1964; Murstein, 1961, 1967; Schellenberg and Bee, 1960). Several major methodological deficiencies in these researches also add to the theory's questionable empirical status (Tharp, 1963). Moreover, the *structure* of complementary need patterns presumed to influence mate choice is unspecified, for example, *how much* lack of fulfillment of a given need is to be compensated for by *how much* fulfillment of another need; if the needs of both spouses are met, but just barely, should a more lasting or satisfying relationship be predicted than when some needs are virtually completely fulfilled and others are entirely unsatisfied? Do discrepancies and/or congruencies of some needs exert a greater influence on mate selection than others? Moreover, as Meissner notes, "the hypothesis of complementarity of needs . . . seems to concern not only the type of need, but also the intensity and developmental immaturity of the need" (page 45). This more refined analysis has not yet been examined empirically. Such issues represent the essence of the difficulty inherent in such conceptual schemes in terms of predicting, evaluating, and, of most relevance here, treating conflicted relationships.

Moreover, the need complementarity hypothesis is vastly oversimplified. It assumes that need complementarity exists along the same dimensions for both individuals, as, for example, when it predicts a person who needs nurturance will be attracted to a person who needs to be nurturant. In fact, there is some evidence (Elizer and Klein, 1974) to the contrary, that dysfunctional couples are complementary or, more accurately, compensatory, with regard to *different* areas of individual conflict. Thus, spouse A manifests a form of compensation for spouse B by being nonproblematic in these domains laden with conflict for B, and vice versa.

This finding is reminiscent of Bowen's (1966) notion of "overfunctioning" and "dysfunctioning" in problem marriages.

Additionally, the need complementarity hypothesis fails to consider that similarity and/or complementarity (at both overt and covert levels) may exert their influence differently in functional and dysfunctional relationships. Thus, Murstein (1961) found similarity of needs to be more frequent than complementarity of needs among normal couples, and Tharp (1963) and Jacobson and Matheny (1962) have argued that similarity of traits as the basis of mate selection predominates along normal couples while complementarity of traits predominates among neurotic couples. The latter hypothesis is perhaps more in keeping with clinical evidence (e.g., Eidelberg, 1956) that normal couples select mates on the basis of anaclitic (dependent) object choice, while neurotic couples select mates on the basis of narcissistic (self-esteem) object choice, the two major paths to such choice delineated by Freud (1914). Still, it must be recognized that most intimate object choices involve both anaclitic and narcissistic dimensions and that the two are at best difficult to differentiate.

The problem with even this sort of more refined analysis (the complementary nature of "overfunctioning" and "dysfunctioning") is that it obscures the clinical observation that the interaction, in marriage, of overtly different personality types may function in such a way as to allow conflicted partners to avoid conscious confrontation of what are largely *similar* dynamic themes. This is reminiscent of Meissner's (Chapter II) assertion that clinical couples "tend to choose partners who have achieved an equivalent level of immaturity, but who have adopted opposite patterns of defensive organization" (page 43). For example, Barnett (1971) exquisitely detailed the nature of the unconscious interaction in the obsessional-hysteric marriage. He emphasized that while for the hysteric narcissism is largely in the service of dependency and for the obsessive dependency is in the service of narcissism, both such spouses are primarily conflicted around the issue of establishing and maintaining a manageable level of intimacy. Thus, overt stylistic differences and apparently different needs in ongoing marital interaction (as opposed to a somewhat more static marital choice) often reflect conflict over the same more fundamental dynamic theme. As Skynner (1976, p. 43) states it, "Couples are usually attracted by shared developmental failures." Giovacchini (1965) has adopted a similar position on the issue.

A rather simplified clinical application of the need complementarity hypothesis will divert the therapist's attention from the fact that overt behavioral styles may or may not be the outcomes of individual defensive operations, as, for example, the rational, articulate, and seemingly imperturbable husband whose overt style functions as a defense against both dependency and hostility. Thus, the clinician must proceed cautiously in inferring the need status of marital partners. Indeed, in terms of clinical assessment, this raises a very thorny issue: Is the relationship style of a given partner a characterological pattern of defense against antagonistic strivings or can it at times be taken at face value and understood without reference to unconscious forces?

To some extent, clarification, if not resolution, of the vexing problems noted above for the hypothesis of need complementarity in marital choice can be found in the writings of psychoanalytic clinicians. While these clinicians (for example, Aldous, 1973; Araoz, 1974; Dicks, 1967; Napier, 1971; Sager, 1976; Sager, Kaplan, Gundlach, Kremer, Lenz and Royce, 1971) are also wedded to a need complementarity framework, they are wedded to it in a critically different way. That is, in terms of ongoing marital dynamics, perhaps the major deficiency in the classical (Winch, 1952) model of need complementarity is that it is a relatively static construct because of its nearly exclusive focus on individual mate selection. Thus, the hypothesis purports to explain how person A chooses person B, and vice versa, but says little about how, or why, A and B choose each other as a *joint* venture. This unspoken process, variously referred to as "collusion" (Dicks, 1967), "family projection process" (Bowen, 1966), "pseudo-identification" (Eidelberg, 1948), "trading of dissociations" (Wynne, 1971) or "merging" (Boszormenyi-Nagy, 1967), involves the active, yet unconscious, collaboration of two partners, wherein each partner does not merely "choose" the other, but enters into an implicit agreement to both choose the other on the basis of one's own unfulfilled needs *and* to form an implicit "contract" (Sager, 1976; Sager et al., 1971) to meet the unfulfilled needs of the one chosen. Moreover, implicit in this contract is a "clause" that each partner will join with the other to protect each partner from those aspects of intra- and interpersonal experience that are laden with conflict (anxiety) (Dicks, 1967). Thus, the contract is one oriented toward the maintenance of each partner's consistent self-perception and, therefore, the unconscious agreement is to "see" the partner as the partner needs to "see" him/herself. Stated in this manner, the need complementarity hypothesis is one not merely of two co-occurring (sets of) events, but one of a shared exchange process in the definition of self. The function of this venture is, according to Dicks (1967), "to rediscover lost aspects of their primary object relations, which they had split off or repressed" (p. 69). Thus, *collusion, while geared toward anxiety reduction and avoidance of conflict, is seen as a potentially growthful collaboration, that is, as an adaptive attempt to resolve conflicts through specific relationships.* Stewart et al. (1975, p. 163) described the splitting (of psychic functions) and collusion involved in mate choice as "an attempt to establish ego boundaries and a sense of identity through difference."

Despite the growth-oriented purposiveness of marital choice, however, conflict is obviously all too common. In fact, the very same personal characteristics that initially attract one person to another rather routinely become the overt focus, if not the sources, of marital conflict. When "the honeymoon is over," that is, when spouses begin to sense the reality of who their mates really are, rather than seeing them through the distorted perceptions of their own needs, the potential for conflict exists. Undoubtedly a major force in the choice of a marital partner is that of idealization, that is, the ego's repression of ambivalent feelings toward the love object, and the concurrent conscious perception of only the good aspects of the mate. Thus, in the psychoanalytic perspective, conflict may ensue with the return of the repressed, such that the complementarity which initially appeared to be, and was felt as, non-ambivalent now becomes reattached to intrapsychic conflict surrounding an individual's felt needs and wishes. What is problematic is not necessarily that the partner cannot meet his/her partner's needs, but rather that the inherent contradictions within each partner's needs make them impossible to fulfill.

Conflict may also appear when each partner's unconscious expectations of the other are simply entirely unrealistic—what Meissner (Chapter II) refers to as "the inevitable frustration of inappropriate needs" (page 44). Or conflict may emerge when there is a change in one or both partners' needs or role demands, as for example, at critical developmental points such as the birth of the first child, the return to work of a non-working spouse, and so on. None of these events per se will stimulate marital conflict. Rather, conflict is likely in "the presence in one or both parties of rigid and relatively undifferentiated object relations schemata into whose Procrustean bed all must fit" (Rausch, Barry, Hertel and Swain, 1974, p. 47). A successful marriage and one capable of managing conflict requires "a flexible readiness *in each partner* to change their role behavior in response to the other's needs of the moment" (Dicks, 1967, p. 31, emphasis added). This emotional flexibility "betokens a secure sense of identity-adequate ego strength. It means that the self is sufficiently at ease in varied aspects of itself . . . a person with this degree of ego-strength can bear to see the partner as different, and the self as distinct from the partner, without feeling threatened . . . by contrast" (Dicks, 1967, p. 31).

The emerging theme in the above discussion is that the psychoanalytic perspective requires that for a "successful" marriage to obtain, each partner must be (relatively) free from neuroticism. This state, of course, in turn requires that each partner feels comfortably individuated from his/her family of origin (Framo, 1976; Meissner, Chapter II; Napier, 1971) so that intimacy is possible. If this is not the case, symptoms may develop either as a consequence of or as a defense against the state of fusion (Karpel, 1976), the feared unconscious meaning of intimacy for persons not individuated from their own parents (Overturf, 1976). The difficulty with this position is that it seems entirely possible and, indeed, not uncommon in the writer's experience, that *marital conflict can occur in the absence of significant individual psychopathology in either or both marital partners.* As Weiss (Chapter IV, page 235) states, "marriage and intimacy in general set up fairly common requirements which have to be met by the participants." Thus, for example, Helez (1973) distinguished among a "marital neurosis," in which a neurosis develops in one or both spouses in a way connected to the marriage, "interlocked neurotics," both of whom show some sort of personality disorder, and "neurosis perpetuated in the marriage."

Writing from an object-relations** framework, Dicks (1967) postulated three major levels or sub-systems that determine marital interaction: (a) the public sub-system of sociocultural values and norms; (b) the sub-

---

* But since all forms of marital conflict are not of the same type or level, a conflict between two people with no significant individual pathology may be identical in terms of overt behavior to a conflict between two "less healthy" individuals, but it would be an error to call the conflicts equivalent or to approach the two cases with the same therapeutic technique.

** Because object relations theory has exerted a significant influence on marital and family therapy and because it will be central to many issues discussed in this chapter, it is important to distinguish it from classical psychoanalytic theory. While object-relations theory had its roots in Freud and in the phenomena of transference and resistance in treatment, in general it has represented an evolutionary attempt within psychoanalytic thought to move beyond an outmoded natural science conception of human experience. Thus, Guntrip (1971, p. 12) writes that with object-relational thinking "we see the shift from (early Freudian) psychobiological instincts to the ego or self," and that "object-relational thinking (is) the gradual emergence to the forefront of what was always . . . the real heart of Freud's revolutionary approach to the mental illnesses . . . that is to say mental disturbances that are not specifically the result of physical causes, but profound disturbances of the normal courses of emotional development of human beings as persons" (p. 194).

system of personal norms, conscious judgments, which are "consciously held ego-attitudes in actual behavior" (p. 130); and (c) "the unconscious forces . . . (that are) the 'repressed' or 'split-off' internal ego-object relations" (p. 131). Dicks (1967, p. 133) noted that for a marital relationship to endure, "It would seem necessary for at least two of the three subsystems postulated to function with credit-balances of satisfaction over dissatisfaction to both partners." Thus, he argued, "Social affinity plus congruence of deep object-relations can withstand strong divergencies of personal norms and tastes," and "Strong agreements over personal norms and values plus deeper object-relations can override large cultural and social distance and incongruities."

Presumably, though unstated by Dicks, congruence of sociocultural factors and personal values and norms can also override existing unconscious conflict, at least for some couples. But more relevant here is the clinical observation that a notable, albeit undetermined, proportion of couples who seek conjoint therapy may be quite unconflicted at the unconscious level while experiencing profound distress due to conflict at either the "socio-cultural" or conscious attitudinal level. A not uncommon example of this type involves couples who share a mature mutual object relationship and similar interests and tastes, but who are jointly distressed by cultural and perhaps familial pressure deriving from different religious, racial and ethnic backgrounds. To argue in such cases that one or both partners are insufficiently differentiated from their families of origin or demonstrate low ego-strength would be to assume a position that is quite insensitive to the reality constraints on such a relationship. Perhaps an even more common example is the couple in which each member has grown over a period of time, usually several years or more, and simply no longer satisfies the newly developed, current needs of his/her mate. Here, conflict may result from positive, naturalistic change in each partner, such that the issue is not that there are levels of their "contract" (Sager, 1976) that are conflictual and unfulfilled, but that one or both partners now wish, for *healthy* reasons, not to renew the contract. A perhaps more unfortunate variation on this theme occurs when there has been clear differentiated growth on the part of one partner only. Of course, it is reasonable to argue that a structurally "healthy" marriage of two "healthy" individuals would be able to shift to accommodate such changing needs.

Thus, the danger for clinical practice is that the therapist may "see" levels of intrapsychic conflict occurring in the marital relationship when none, or little, exists, but where it is required by the therapist's conceptual scheme. Sager et al. (1971, p. 493) stated "contractual transactions *often* represent attempted solutions of intrapsychic difficulties" (emphasis added). The question unanswered by the psychoanalytic perspective is, *when do marital difficulties* not *reflect unconscious individual conflicts?* Of course, the systems and behavioral models also leave this question (and its opposite) unanswered. Moreover, in clinical practice it is quite difficult to know the extent of each partner's unconscious conflict early in treatment since few couples present themselves for therapy at this level of concern. "Underlying" conflicts, if they exist for a given couple, emerge only in the course of therapy.

Related to this issue is the implicit theme that complementarity is undesirable when it reflects an attempt to fulfill neurotic needs, but is desirable when this is not the case.* Whether or not this is true, this position poses a major stumbling block to rational assessment in couples therapy. A couple who has sought treatment for their relationship problem is, by virtue of their admission of conflict, quite likely to be *assumed* by the therapist to be engaged in neurotic complementarity struggles. How the therapist is to tell the difference between such very real struggles and other sources of conflict is quite unclear.

Perhaps the major deficiency in the psychoanalytic construction of marital conflict lies in its insufficient attention to the current and actual sources of interaction that maintain marital conflict beyond the distortions engendered in the "marital transference" (Araoz, 1974). Psychoanalytic approaches do, in fact, acknowledge that marital conflict cannot be entirely accounted for on the basis of perceptual distortions. As several writers (for example, Greenspan and Mannino, 1974; Lloyd and Paulson, 1972; Stewart et al., 1975) emphasize, the projected aspects of the self manage to find at least some reality basis. Stated otherwise, neurotic individuals seem to choose partners whose behavior will confirm their projections by acting upon them, thus protecting the projection from naturalistic modification by reality testing. What the psychoanalytic approach fails to emphasize, however, is that an indeterminate yet clinically significant portion of disturbed marital interaction is likely to have become functionally autonomous of its origins and, thus, is not reducible to such a motivational analysis. *Regardless of the extent to which marital conflict may have been initially determined by unconscious forces, current interaction not only reinforces shared collusions, but also offers fertile ground for secondary, but very real and salient difficulties that must be*

---

* Of course, one can also make the argument that "successful" fulfillment of neurotic needs is desirable, and perhaps inevitable.

treated independently of the historically underlying dynamic struggle. Wachtel (1976) has developed a similar argument in the context of individual conflict. While systems therapists and behaviorists probably have swung too far on the "here and now" versus "there and then" pendulum, as discussed later in this chapter, they remind us, in an important way, that present interpersonal behavior is often maintained without significant reference to symbolic processes, transference, or the unwitting intrusion of the past into current interaction. Whether intimate interpersonal behavior can be changed to assure durability and generalizability without reference to such factors is an, as yet, unaddressed empirical issue. Moreover, it is important to recall Yalom's (1975) point that "it is the reconstitution of the past, not simply the excavation of the past, that is crucial" (p. 28).

Finally, it needs to be noted that, not unlike most areas of psychoanalytic thought, there is little, if any, empirical evidence for any of the following notions central to the analytic perspective: (1) that neurotic versus non-neurotic complementarity can be reliably differentiated; (2) that the individuals in conflicted marriages are any more or less neurotic than those in non-conflicted relationships; (3) that such individuals utilize different or less effective collusive defensive operations (cf., Shumaker, 1976); (4) that there is any relationship between the developmental failure to individuate from one's family or origin and subsequent marital difficulties; (5) that distortions in the perception of one's spouse primarily reflect transferential reactions to one or both of an individual's parents or other early significant figures; or (6) that individual psychopathology manifest in the marital relationship can be validly differentiated from simple failure to enact culturally prescribed gender roles (cf., Barry, 1970; Hicks and Platt, 1970; Laws, 1971).

Moreover, no existing operational definitions have yet received empirical study for any of the following (among others) central psychoanalytic constructs: "collusion," "projective identification," "marital transference," "idealization," "fusion," "differentiation," "individuation." Witkin's (Witkin, 1965; Witkin and Goodenough, in press) research on field dependence-independence, which actually deals with differentiation in ways not unlike those of object-relations theorists, may be applicable here, but has not yet been tied to the marital relationship. While psychoanalytic theory may have thus far afforded a set of constructs rich in their conceptual potential for understanding the nature of marriage and marital conflict, only empirical study will allow us to determine whether such notions deserve any greater status than that of convenient explanatory fictions. It is important to remember, however, that explanatory fictions may still generate useful clinical interventions, as shall presently be seen.

The Process and Technique of Conjoint Treatment: Themes, Assumptions and Issues

The treatment of marital disorders in a conjoint treatment context raises several extremely important issues and problems for the psychodynamicist. It will be argued here that the *classical* psychoanalytic position (as in Giovacchini, 1965) does not offer a meaningful approach to the treatment of marital disharmony since its goals cannot be differentiated from and, in fact, are exactly the same as, those of the psychoanalysis of the individual. Adherents to the *classical* view and mode of practice are essentially unconcerned with the nature of the marital relationship per se in which the analysand experiences dissatisfaction. The focus here, at any rate, will be on the process and techniques of *conjoint* treatment conducted within a psychodynamic perspective. Some controversial issues involved in the so-called "individual treatment" of marital problems will also be addressed.

1. The goals of therapy: I. Individual personality change "versus" facilitation of marital interaction

Traditional analytic misgivings about the conjoint treatment of spouses center on matters of transference development and dyadic resistance to change. These issues will be considered in some detail shortly; they highlight the central theoretical and clinical issue in the treatment of marital difficulties: What are the goals of such intervention? Writers in the psychoanalytic perspective seem to have adopted two positions on this question. The more conservative view is represented by that of Hulse (1956), who has maintained that the focus of marital therapy should be on the psychopathology of the individual who has marital conflicts, not on the conflict itself. Therefore, he advocates the "cure or improvement of *underlying emotional illness*" (p. 247, emphasis added) rather than the modification of disturbed interaction patterns. This view is supported by Boas (1962), who argued that symptomatic improvement in marital disharmony constitutes an insufficient therapeutic outcome since movement is not based on "real structural changes" within the individual personality. Several other writers have adhered to this viewpoint (Jackson and Grotjahn, 1958, 1959; Leichter, 1962; Westman, Carek and McDermott, 1965) which is quite consistent with several psychoanalytic dicta against the conjoint treatment of family members.

Other writers (for example, Burton, 1962; Beukenkamp, 1959; Blinder and Kirschenbaum, 1967; Linden, Goodwin and Resnik, 1968) view conjoint therapy in terms of its potential for facilitating adaptive interpersonal behavior between marital partners as a result of increased self-understanding. Although the emphasis here is on marital interaction, proponents of this position do not argue against the development of insight but, in fact, foster it (for example, Perelman, 1960; Papanek, 1965; Gottlieb and Pattison, 1966; Leslie, 1964). Treatment goals are primarily the improvement of the quality of human interaction, with intrapsychic growth and awareness seen as the means to this end and not as ends in themselves. These writers see both insight and action (behavior) as necessary concomitants of positive therapeutic change. In contrast, those whose main concern is the remediation of individual pathology view the marital relationship and, therefore, marital disharmony as basically irrelevant to the therapeutic task, except insofar as they accentuate the pathology of individual marital partners. In this sense, such therapy is not marital therapy at all. The parallel between these competing psychodynamic viewpoints and those of classical Freudianism versus interpersonal psychodynamicism (such as Sullivan, Horney, Fromm, Erickson) is clear.

Clinicians who are psychoanalytically *oriented* prefer to see marital disharmony as the manifestation of a breakdown in the patterning of mutual gratification of the neurotic needs of both spouses, as discussed in the preceding section on marital conflict. Hence, the goals of therapy for most dynamically oriented marriage therapists involve not the restructuring of individual "psyches," but the restructuring of both spouses' internally based perceptions of, expectations of, and reactions to each other—that is, those aspects of personality functioning which are of specific import to the marital relationship.

Thus, *in contrast to the all too common caricatured critiques of psychoanalytically oriented marriage therapy, the truth is that most therapists operating in this framework do not set up a dichotomy between individual personality change and change of marital interaction. Quite the contrary, in an interpersonal dynamic framework, the one cannot occur without the other* (see, for example, Wachtel's superb (1976) discussion of this viewpoint in the individual therapy context). Unlike systems theory-based treatment and behavioral treatment, psychoanalytically oriented marital therapy aims toward both individual personality change and dyadic change and is concerned primarily with present characterological defenses and ways of interacting with one's spouse. *The psychoanalytic approach generally has attempted to transcend the false dichotomy between individual change and dyadic change.* Indeed, in psychodynamically oriented conjoint marital therapy, it is quite common for a good deal of individual work to occur. This practice is consistent with Meissner's (Chapter II) emphasis on the need of marital partners to develop a sense of self that is both more differentiated and internally integrated. Therapists of this persuasion will attempt to realize such bilateral yet interactive gains by interventions geared toward facilitating each spouse's encountering of his/her mate "as a safe, real person" (Dicks, 1967, p. 43). To accomplish this, treatment highlights conflict over the partners' differences and the failures of complementarity (Ackerman, 1965) by interrupting and labeling the collusive processes which simultaneously and paradoxically both generate *and* attempt to diminish anxiety in each partner. The therapist's intermediate goal, then, is to put each partner in touch with significant aspects of his/her mate's character which are omitted from awareness (Greenspan and Mannino, 1974). In so doing, the aim is to bring to light the relationship between each partner and the fended off and projected aspects of him/herself as it is experienced in the mate.

The main danger in such a construction of therapeutic goals can be seen to reside not in the goals per se but in the ambiguity usually surrounding their operationalization. For example, Ackerman (1965) has written that, "To a large extent, diagnosis rests on the therapist's special interest on what he is trying to do about marital condition . . . only as we become engaged in the adventure of therapy, do we achieve, step by step, a systematic diagnosis" (pp. 163-164). This position is quite consistent with the traditional individual psychoanalytic notion that, in effect, accurate diagnosis, in the sense of understanding the nature of the difficulties at hand, emerges only as a result of treatment. Where this stance is adhered to in the extreme, there is a real possibility of fostering an unfocused and even misdirected therapeutic experience. The main problem, then, as in all psychoanalytically oriented treatment, is that regardless of whether one focuses on individual or dyadic change, or both, the criteria for such changes often remain only implicit within the mind of the therapist. Psychoanalytically oriented therapists are primarily concerned, in marital as well as in individual treatment, with basic "structural" changes which, as Strupp and Hadley (1977) note, are inferential abstractions and can be judged only by experts, that is, psychoanalytically trained therapists. But such assessments of structural change cannot exist in pure culture, as it were; they must be based on the judge's knowledge of the patient's behavior and, in Strupp's (Strupp and Hadley, 1977) tripartite model, his sense of "well-being." This is not to argue that the psychotherapist possesses no special and unique vantage point for assessing the outcome of the therapy; in fact, there is a rather substantial literature that is persuasive of quite the opposite (Mintz, 1977).

2. The goals of therapy: II. Breadth and depth

A related matter of goals that is particularly relevant to psychoanalytically oriented marriage therapy centers on the breadth (how wide-ranging) and depth (how reconstructive of personality) of the changes that are sought. As Butcher and Koss (1978) note, "Many psychotherapeutic contacts, whether or not they initially were planned to be, turn out to be brief ones." In individual psychotherapy, high percentages of patients terminate in the first 6-8 sessions (Garfield, 1971). No doubt some of these terminations are premature ones reflecting poor patient motivation, mismatching of patient and therapist personality characteristics, and other such factors. But it is also true that many individuals seek psychological help with the expectation that the treatment will be a brief experience (Butcher and Koss, 1978) and this may be especially true of persons from lower socioeconomic or lower educational strata (Lorion, 1973, 1974). Recent reviews of marital therapy research (Gurman, 1973b; Gurman and Kniskern, 1977c) indicate that about two-thirds of such treatment lasts between 1 and 20 sessions. (This figure is not skewed by the inclusion of treatments explicitly time-limited either for clinical or research purposes, since few of the studies examined employed any time restriction). Since the overwhelming majority of marital therapies are short-term,* it appears necessary to consider what would generally be the appropriate breadth and depth of goals. This issue is especially salient for psychoanalytically oriented marriage therapists who, by virtue of their training and view of the nature of "good" psychotherapy, are likely to set goals "higher" than either behaviorally or systems oriented marital therapists. At the same time, though, the history of brief psychotherapy has been largely a history of brief psychodynamic psychotherapy (Butcher and Koss, 1977). It thus seems appropriate to examine the major parameters of brief (individual) analytically oriented psychotherapy to assess their relevance to and likely implications for psychoanalytically oriented

---

* Indeed, using the cut-off of 40 sessions considered by several influential writers to still qualify as brief psychotherapy (Balint, Ornstein & Balint, 1972; Malan, 1963, 1976; Sifneos, 1972), a reasonable estimate would be that no more than 20 percent of marital therapies continue beyond this criterion marker.

marriage therapy. Although intensive therapy of couples and families also occurs (such as Boszormenyi-Nagy and Framo, 1965), especially in private practice, relatively brief interventions are modal in the practice of marriage therapy, so that an emphasis upon this style of practice would seem to offer the framework with the broadest applicability and relevance to the greatest number of clinicians.

While several influential models of brief psychoanalytic therapy exist (Alexander and French, 1946; Balint et al., 1972; F. Deutsch, 1949; Ferenczi, 1920; Malan, 1963, 1976; Mann, 1973; Sifneos, 1972), there are a number of defining characteristics common to most such approaches. The overall goals of such therapies are one or more of the following: "the removal or amelioration of the most disabling symptoms as rapidly as possible; prompt re-establishment of the patient's previous emotional equilibrium; development of the patient's understanding of the current disturbance and increased coping ability in the future" (Butcher and Koss, 1977).

In brief psychotherapy, therefore, it is widely agreed that personality reconstruction is quite impossible. This is perhaps the most difficult characteristic of short-term therapy for many psychoanalytically oriented therapists to deal with. In order to work toward limited goals, the therapist must abandon his "therapeutic perfectionism" (Malan, 1963). In addition, he must not yield to his "prejudices of depth" (Wolberg, 1965). "Depth" work in psychotherapy involves dealing with conflict material that is far from consciousness, that is disturbing upon its expression, or which reflects early childhood experience. Dealing with such material in brief therapy involves, at the least, the establishment of a very trusting relationship with a therapist and, ideally, the emergence of a very positive transference. When one considers the fact that the great majority of marital therapies follow the initial appearance of one "identified patient" and that the "second spouse" is typically rather resistant to becoming involved in treatment except as the identified patient's "caretaker" (Aldous, 1973), one can see that a strong *working alliance* between the therapist and *each* member of the couple is often quite difficult to achieve, at least until several therapy sessions have been held. Stated otherwise, in marital therapy the therapeutic alliance "implies that the couple, as *individuals* and as a unit, have the ability to identify with the (analytical) approach of the marital therapist" (Smith and Grunebaum, 1976, p. 354, emphasis added). Part of this "approach" involves the assumption that there is not one "ill" partner, but that therapy is to be directed toward both the dyadic needs of the relationship *and* the conflicts of each individual in that relationship as they are manifest in the marital interaction. Thus, "motivational constellations" for entering therapy (Smith and Grunebaum, 1976) such as "looking for the exit," "looking for an ally," "looking for reentry," and "response to an ultimatum," common in the beginning of couples treatment, obviously work against the rapid establishment of a therapeutic alliance and would seem to preclude, at least initially and often longer, the ability of the therapist to deal with "depth" issues. In fact, quite often a substantial proportion of the entire course of couples therapy is directed toward establishing just such an alliance and, by definition, redefining the task of treatment from that of treating one "sick" spouse to that of helping each individual, as well as the relationship, to grow. Even in the minority of clinical couples who jointly seek therapy, in an apparent spirit of cooperativeness, resistance to change is usually significant and derives both from each partner's anxiety about change as well as from dyadically shared resistances (collusion) to change (Gurman and Knudson, 1978). These forces, in addition to a likely short-term course of treatment, render the probability of major structural (intrapsychic) changes in each partner low.

Still, in abandoning therapeutic perfectionism, there may be a parallel with the medical dictum, "do no harm." *One should be willing to work for limited change at the content level only so long as such intervention does not produce negative effects at the meta-level.* This argument is developed later in this chapter and elsewhere (Gurman and Knudson, 1978) with specific reference to the behavioral approach to marriage therapy, but it applies as well to brief psychoanalytically oriented couples therapy. The fact that most marital therapy is brief must not be taken as a rationale for the position that "since time is so short, we have to do *something.*" The next step in this logic usually takes the form of a definition of positive change limited to only one level. *While personality reconstruction may be quite unlikely in brief marriage therapy, nothing should be done by the therapist in brief therapy that would make such positive personality reconstruction less likely than when the couple began therapy. The therapist in brief therapy aims at limited goals, one of which is to keep alive in the patient the idea that more is possible.* This position suggests a subtle but important difference from a skills training model which tends to end when a person has acquired the necessary skills as defined by the therapeutic model and where a return to therapy would be indicated only if there were failure experiences in applying these skills.

A second defining characteristic of brief psychotherapy is equally salient in the treatment of couples—a focus on present life circumstances and a correspondingly limited attention to childhood experiences. Such focused interviewing and present-centeredness are also quite consonant with the nature of most precipitating events that lead a couple into conjoint treatment. Most couples enter therapy, whether by the "identified patient" or joint route, in response to a crisis in their relationship. Such a crisis may be as overt as the recent exposure of an "affair" of one of the partners or as subtle as the shifting but difficult to define expectations each spouse has of the other, as for example when one spouse has evidenced more individual growth over time and no longer lives up to the implicit and unconscious contract that initially fostered the couple's attraction (Sager, 1976; Sager et al., 1971). Under these conditions, many couples are so distressed that *their* initial goals, often in some measure of contrast to the goals of their therapist, are to reestablish rather immediate order in the face of emotional chaos. Thus, a crisis-intervention model (Butcher and Maudal, 1976; Caplan, 1964) is often the appropriate one in initial contacts with conflicted marriages. The "danger" here for psychoanalytically oriented therapists is that *the successful resolution of a marital crisis may preclude the couple's interest in further exploration or change in their relationship since anxiety, the major force operating to initiate a couple's entry into therapy, has been substantially reduced.*

An important shift from dominant psychoanalytic technique under these circumstances is that *the therapist's interpretations need to be more integrative than regressive. Thus, the therapist cannot assume the stance of waiting until significant repressed strivings emerge over time, but must interpret important marital dynamics at a point in time that, in the traditional analytic mode, would often appear premature.* Moreover, the therapist must make genetic links to current interpersonal suffering (the chronic and presently endured pain emphasized by Mann, 1973) that are far more tentative and tenuous than those that ideally reflect a state of awareness "just beyond" that of the patient in individual psychotherapy. While regressions of a sort are common to all marital and family therapy (Gurman and Kniskern, 1978b, 1978c), they usually are not of the magnitude encountered in exploratory, reconstructive psychoanalytically oriented individual therapy. This is particularly true because of the gross interferences in the development of the transference neurosis that are inherent in most conjoint treatment. The role of transference in couples therapy will be considered in greater detail below and is discussed by Meissner (Chapter II) and Nadelson (Chapter III).

Related to the above consideration is the oft-repeated (e.g., F. Deutsch,

1949; Malan, 1976; Mann, 1973) requirement that brief psychotherapy deal primarily with one "central issue" (Mann, 1973) that has three major parameters: (a) it is both genetically and adaptively important; (b) it is interpersonal in nature; and (c) it is manifest or potentially manifest in the transference relationship. The first of these requirements for focusing brief therapy with couples has already been addressed; the second parameter is obviously inherent in the nature and source of the problem at hand. The manifestation of the presenting problem in the transference relationship will be examined shortly. Mann (1973) argues that there are a finite number of "universal conflicts" around which such a focus can center, independence-dependence, activity-passivity, self-esteem, and unresolved or delayed grief. All these conflicts involve the management of object loss. Analogously, there are several universal conflicts inherent in intimate relationships that are reflective of both the individual and the marital life-cycles. These include, but are not limited to, developing autonomy from one's family of origin and establishing a marital commitment, resolving ambivalence over intimacy with one's partner, managing the inevitable conflict surrounding dependency in a marital relationship, establishing workable modes of conflict-resolution, decision-making and negotiation, clarifying role expectations, and developing functional channels for the expression of both positive and negative feelings.

The selection of (usually) one such central issue that taps into both the conflictual and the developmental aspects of the marital relationship precludes a treatment that "covers the waterfront" and requires not the "evenly hovering attention" of the psychoanalyst but the decisively focused intervention of a therapist whose energy is simultaneously directed toward both individuals in treatment and toward their joint personality as evidenced in the marital transaction.

Such a brief therapeutic context also requires a great deal more therapist activity than is common to most psychoanalytically oriented therapy. Wolberg (1965) has written that passivity is "anathema" in short-term individual psychotherapy. Marital therapy, regardless of its theoretical underpinnings, will flounder without an active and, at least at times, even directive therapist. Hidden agendas, unexpressed needs and feelings, and other factors often must be brought to the light of day by the therapist quite confrontively and forcefully if therapeutic progress is to be achieved in a limited time framework. Such directiveness on the therapist's part is, of course, quite antithetical to the more reflective style of the psychoanalytically oriented individual psychotherapist.

Directly related to this matter is the fact that most brief therapies, except perhaps those unswervingly aligned to the psychoanalytic model (such as Mann, 1973), require a great deal of technical flexibility on the part of the therapist. Such treatment is severely limited in its applicability unless a variety of intervention strategies are not only available in the therapist's repertoire but are also valued by the therapist. The truth of the matter is that *psychoanalytically oriented marriage therapy is largely "analytic" in the way it organizes the complex material at hand and conceptualizes the nature of marital discord, but is, of necessity, quite pragmatic, if not eclectic, in its selection of actual therapeutic interventions* (this assessment is reflected in Nadelson, Chapter III). This technical eclecticism is seen, for example, in a recent text by Ables and Brandsma (1977) who take the position that "theory is employed as a means of *understanding and appraising* individual dynamics manifest in present and interactional behaviors" (p. 2, emphasis added). Writing from an ego-psychological perspective, they add (p. 10) that "the therapist (has to be) cognizant of the limitations of any cognitive, problem solving approach and aware of the necessity for modifications and additional techniques in working with spouses." Similarly, Berman and Lief (1975), while emphasizing that "the interrelationships between intrapsychic and interpersonal factors are at the heart of marital therapy" (p. 584), and seeming to favor a classification scheme of marital problems based on personality style and psychiatric terminology, nonetheless endorse a "systems-behavioral approach (as) particularly helpful" (p. 584). Even Sager (1976) and Martin (1976), both decidedly psychoanalytically oriented by training and current preference, at times employ essentially the same sort of contracting strategies as used and developed by behavior therapists (such as O'Leary and Turkewitz, Chapter V; Weiss, 1975; Weiss, Birchler and Vincent, 1974; Weiss, Hops and Patterson, 1973), despite the fact that the "contracts" they see as most influential of marital discord are unconscious! And Nadelson (Nadelson et al., 1977) includes among her intervention strategies the "clarification of communication patterns," developing the "tools for effective problem-solving," and the negotiation around "concrete and specific concerns, i.e., budget, housework, etc."

Thus, a number of psychoanalytically oriented marriage therapists seem to have independently reached the same conclusion—that even while operating out of a dynamic conceptual framework, the conjoint treatment of marital couples requires a great deal of technical flexibility and pragmatism. As has been argued here, these modifications and even deviations from "standard" analytic technique are virtually inescapable in marriage therapy because of its generally short duration.

3. *Transference: Its role in conjoint therapy*

In Nadelson's (Chapter III, Nadelson et al., 1977) model of treatment, the use of a variety of strategic interventions in psychoanalytically oriented couples therapy tends to characterize the *initial* phase of treatment. Nadelson et al. (1977) note that during this phase of therapy, "While underlying dyanmic issues and transference feelings may be identified by the therapist they are not interpreted," and add that, "Many couple therapists consider treatment complete once the couple has developed workable problem-solving techniques . . . but if the couple is to work through conflict . . . more extensive transference work is indicated." This next phase of therapy focuses on the transference resistance and the development of a therapeutic alliance. Nadelson's position on this sequence of therapeutic developments is at odds with many other psychoanalytically oriented marriage therapists who from the beginning of treatment consider the establishment of the therapeutic alliance a prerequisite for more behavioral sorts of change (as in Smith and Grunebaum, 1976) and who emphasize resolution of transference issues as the *sine qua non* of therapy, as in individual psychoanalysis, rather than as the sort of elective, growth-oriented experience implicit in Nadelson's approach. Thus, for example, Dicks (1967) writes that

> The (therapist) fulfills the role of a transitional object whose task is not only to accept the (patients') projections and unreal expectations but also to respond to these communications . . . and increase the patient's insights . . . only a resolute sticking to the acceptance and interpretation of negative transference will help . . . (not) succumbing to the infantile accusations . . . that defeat *the aim of therapy: the working through of the past in the transference* (pp. 232-233, emphasis added).

Other influential clinicians also emphasize the primacy of the working through of the transference in conjoint therapy (as in Araoz, 1974; Sager, 1967). Indeed, the nature of transference development and its management is probably the most controversial conceptual and technical issue engendered in the conjoint psychoanalytic treatment of couples. Gurman (1971) has elaborated these issues in the context of couples' group therapy and the focus here will be on the conjoint format only. Three major issues will be considered: (a) the extent to which transference can be fostered in conjoint therapy; (b) the necessity of therapeutic regression for positive and lasting change; and (c) the use and role of transference analysis in the context of an active and generally brief therapeutic encounter.

The most extreme form of the transference relationship, and that prized by orthodox psychoanalysts as the major active mechanism of therapeutic change, is the *transference neurosis* which is said to exist

> when a patient is reenacting in the treatment relationship a pano-
> rama of neurotic conflicts, including many that are rooted in his
> childhood experience, and when his cumulative transference reac-
> tions have become so pervasive as to make therapy and the therapist
> the central concerns in his life (Weiner, 1975, p. 220).

Weiner (1975) notes that while there are no precise criteria by which to differentiate a transference *neurosis* from transference *reactions,* the former is often proposed as the essential characteristic distinguishing psychoanalysis from psychoanalytically oriented therapies. Several of the important factors that increase the probability of the development of a full-blown transference neurosis are:* (1) relatively longer therapeutic encounters—many psychoanalysts believe that the modal analysand re-quires at least one to one-and-a-half years of therapy four or five times per week for such transference development (Kepecs, 1977); (2) limited participation of the therapist as a real object, that is, a high degree of therapist anonymity and ambiguity and a corresponding lack of the therapist's direct expression of his own views; and (3) relative constancy of the therapist's behavior (Gill, 1954). Obviously, the lay (and, at times, professional) stereotyped image of the psychoanalyst as a "blank screen" or "mirror" probably has little in common with most current psycho-analytic practice but is reinforced by "demand characteristic" behavior of analysts at annual meetings and remains relatively impervious to modifi-cation because of most psychoanalysts' reticence to say, or allow to be seen, what they really do behind closed doors.**

---

* Here I am speaking in modal terms. Obviously, there is a good deal of variability in individuals' proneness to develop intense transference reactions and personality dif-ferences influence the rapidity of such reactions. For example, hysterical personalities who are almost always immediately expressive of their feelings are, in general, more likely to develop strong and rapid transference reactions than obsessive-compulsive personalities. Likewise, a small percentage of patients may develop full-blown trans-ference neuroses in the first few treatment hours.

** This only partially playful image was suggested to me by my psychoanalytic col-league and friend, Norman S. Greenfield, to whom I am grateful for teaching me most of what I understand about psychoanalytic canon and psychoanalytic reality.

Reviewing the above criteria for increasing the depth of the transference, it will be readily apparent to any experienced marriage therapist that conjoint marital therapy, except under infrequently occurring conditions, is quite unlikely to be able to safeguard the transference and, conversely, is almost guaranteed to "contaminate" it. The brevity of most marital therapy is one factor working against the development of a strong transference. Moreover, the therapist's constancy and anonymity are difficult if not impossible to achieve in large measure in couples therapy. For example, a marital therapist is continually "taking sides" (Zuk, 1968) for the purpose of undermining collusions and supporting the expression of emergent feelings, and, as hard as she/he may try not to, finds it difficult to suppress his/her own values about such "loaded" issues as sexuality, extramarital affairs, divorce, child-rearing, gender roles and the expression of anger. In fact, many marital therapists believe it is essential that, at times, the therapist explicitly reveal his values about and experiences with such issues when they touch on the suffering of his/her patient couples. Such behavior dilutes the transference but is not seen as either destructive of the therapeutic encounter in general or, more specifically, of the use of the patient-therapist relationship for therapeutic ends. This position will be elaborated shortly.

Thus, to summarize the degree to which the transference is generally able to be stimulated to a significant degree in conjoint, psychoanalytically oriented couples therapy, it is argued that the probability of the emergence of a transference *neurosis* is extremely low and the intensity of transference reactions, while not as severely limited as the transference neurosis, is typically a good deal less than in individual psychoanalytically oriented psychotherapy. In addition, a feature unique to the treatment of couples (and families, as distinct from the group therapy of non-related individuals) further weakens the intensity of each spouse's transference to the therapist: *The most powerful transference relationship in marriage therapy exists between the husband and wife* (Whitaker, 1975) and their families of origin (Boszormenyi-Nagy and Spark, 1973). Indeed, this thesis is consistent with Meissner's (Chapter II) analysis of the core of the marital transaction.

The second parameter of the transference issue in marital therapy raises the equally controversial issue of whether, in fact, significant patient regression in treatment is necessary in order to yield significant clinical change. Consistent with Wachtel's (1977) stance on this issue in the context of the individual psychotherapy, the position taken here is that *extensive regression is not necessary in order to yield meaningful* *and enduring change in the individual partners to a marital relationship or in that relationship itself.* Despite the significance of this statement, the viewpoint represented almost reflects a moot point since, as argued above, the regressive transference neurosis has little opportunity to flower under the prevailing atmospheric conditions of conjoint treatment. In an active and brief therapeutic encounter (here, marital therapy), in which a clear focus or series of foci *must* be maintained, "Patient and therapist are active collaborators . . . often explicitly discussing goals and how to achieve them. In such a context the therapist's role is largely demystified . . ." (Wachtel, 1977, p. 281). Moreover, when consideration is given to the fact that marital therapy frequently involves a *series* of marital therapy experiences (with the same therapist) focused around newly emergent themes in the family life-cycle,* it becomes even more clear that extensive regressive experiences are not required for genuine change and growth in intimate relationships. Marital therapy, then, not infrequently requires a series of therapeutic encounters analogous to Deutsch's (1949) "sector analyses." To disregard the significance of this phenomenon demands a view of psychotherapy that endorses treatment as a way of solving life's problems rather than as a catalyst to living life.**

How can transference be utilized, rather than sidestepped, in an active, focused and brief therapeutic encounter such as marital therapy? Wachtel's (1977) viewpoint is pertinent to the sort of conjoint marital therapy described here:

> transference is . . . not really a reaction stemming solely from the past and unrelated to what the therapist "really" does or what he is like. Transference must always be understood as the patient's idiosyncratic way of construing and reacting to what the therapist is

---

* I am indebted to my friend and colleague, David G. Rice, for helping me accept the notion that a couple's return to therapy is probably more a sign of the success than of the failure of earlier treatment.

** In the context set here, with its emphasis on the need for focused and active intervention by the marital therapist, it is not surprising that I endorse the role of the marital therapist as one of an "expert in human relations," in Harry Stack Sullivan's terms, rather than "that of an irrationally feared or revered parental figure" (Wachtel, 1977, p. 281). In this ego-oriented approach, it is fitting to again cite Wachtel's (1977) position that "the therapist's strategy . . . is one of continually trying to clarify and sort out the feelings (of the patient) generated as they develop, to accept and articulate the feelings of the present adult rather than trying to recreate the feelings of the long-ago child" (p. 281). Clearly, such an approach is quite consistent with the therapeutic styles and convictions of the majority of currently influential psychoanalytically oriented (or at least psychoanalytically influenced) marital therapists such as Martin (1976), Raush et al. (1974), Luthman (1974), Framo (1976) and, especially, Sager (1976; Sager et al., 1971).

doing—and the therapist is never doing "nothing," even when he is being silent or reflecting back a question instead of answering it (p. 112).

Thus, transference reactions occurring in a focused and active couples therapy will include important information on each partner's (and on the joint dyad's) feelings, perceptions, misperceptions, attributions of therapist intent, motivation and loyalties, and so forth, about specific therapist interventions. Only a very arid and narrowly conceived view of the sorts of "material" that are worthy of useful transference interpretation would exclude the above-generated reactions from its purview.

The position espoused here is, in fact, quite in keeping with current object-relations approaches to psychotherapy. For example, Stewart et al. (1975) consider the situation in which, in an early meeting with the patient, the therapist feels sarcastic toward him without any obvious contribution from the patient to induce this feeling. Rather than assuming that such a feeling represents a countertransference reaction (of course, it may, but it need not), they argue that "this valuable information may be stored to await further validation or, *if time is a factor,* the therapist may discreetly inquire whether the patient frequently finds himself the object of other people's irritation and sarcasm" (Stewart et al., 1975, p. 164, emphasis added). In the context of usefully employing psychoanalytic treatment principles in brief conjoint couples therapy, the reason for the added emphasis in the preceding quotation should be self-evident.

Finally, it must be acknowledged that the potential for countertransferential acting-out on the part of the marital therapist is heightened under such goal-oriented, active and relatively self-revealing therapeutic conditions which, as has been argued here, are inherent in effective conjoint treatment. As difficult as it is to avoid unconscious collusion in any individual psychotherapy, it is many times more trying to do so when working with marital couples, especially since the painful issues involved in "their" relationships are nearly impossible for most marital therapists not to encounter in their own, current intimate relationships. Personal therapy for the marital therapist may often be useful in this regard, but it is just as likely that, in treating marital relationships, untoward countertransference reactions may reflect conscious attitudes, beliefs and values as much as they may reflect unconscious conflict.* In sum, staid

---

* While referring to such conscious attitudes as countertransference may seem to some readers contradictory to the oft-cited *unconscious* nature of countertransference, it is, in fact, quite consistent with the views of several psychoanalytic writers, such as Heimann (1950, 1960) and Grossman (1965).

formulations of the nature of the transference in marital therapy, and rigid attempts to fit this treatment format to the requirements of traditional psychoanalytic (and even some contemporary psychoanalytically oriented) practice are doomed to failure. It should be clear, however, that modifications of the usually expected thrust of the transference relationship and modifications, albeit significant, of the *use* of the transference in marriage therapy are not only required by the active and brief nature of most couples treatment, but, in fact, when used judiciously, offer the marriage therapist an entrée into the marital transaction that is unique among the three approaches to marital therapy discussed in this book. Moreover, *the use and understanding of the transference in a form modified from classical individual treatment comprise what are probably the only features of psychoanalytically oriented couples therapy that are unique to this approach.*

4. *Present vs. past-centeredness*

The immediately preceding discussion of the use of the patient couple's reaction to the real and present aspects of the person and behavior of the marital therapist, in addition to the symbolically displaced aspects of that relationship, is analogously relevant to the husband-wife interaction itself. Perhaps the greatest potential weakness of any attempt to apply psychoanalytic thought to the treatment of couples in conflict is the tendency engendered by the adoption of such a framework to undervalue the significance of *current* interpersonal behavior for the maintenance and even the creation of dysfunctional relationships. Symbolic events, perceptual distortions and marital transference reactions are salient dimensions in the determination of marital satisfaction and growth and must be reckoned with in conjoint treatment. To the extent that factors such as these are largely ignored by behavioral and systems-oriented therapists, so, too, do psychoanalytically oriented therapists underestimate the power of real and present interpersonal behavior. It is not that psychoanalytically oriented therapists working with couples tend to restrict their awareness of the latter sources of influence to the ways in which each spouse perpetuates the other's characterological defenses. Rather, the problem is the *relative* denigration of therapist interventions designed to have direct and immediate influence on ongoing, observable marital transactions. Still, in fairness to most real, rather than caricatured, psychoanalytically oriented practice, it is important to recall Yalom's (1975, p. 75) argument that

> It makes better sense to say that the analyst makes excursions into historical research in order to understand something which is interfering with his *present* communication with the patient . . . than to say that he makes contact with the patient in order to gain access to biographical data (emphasis added).

Where such action-oriented techniques are used by psychoanalytically oriented therapists, they seem to be viewed as offering "mere" symptomatic relief. What such therapists seem to overlook is the fact that such symptomatic behavior is not always or necessarily motivated by unconscious conflict but that unconscious conflict can be *caused* by so-called symptomatic behavior. For example, consider a couple recently seen: Mr. and Mrs. B came to the first interview together and both agreed that their marriage had been "on the rocks" for several years due, they said, to an almost uninterrupted "lack of intimacy." Their non-intimate relationship was reflected by their rare sexual encounters, avoidance of self-disclosure about feelings generated both in their independent professional lives and in their actual marital interaction, and their unwillingness to confront each other about the accumulated mutual resentments of a disappointing life together. Both partners offered sufficient individual histories in the first three sessions to account for the tenuousness of their intimate relationships based on patterns of blame and avoidance in their families of origin. It was rather easy to see how each partner avoided making real contact with the other for fear that frustrated dependency needs would be painfully thwarted. It was also the case that their distancing behavior, motivated by this fear, *generated* their strong feelings of non-intimacy.

In the therapy that evolved, both the motivations for mutual avoidance *and* the current conflict-producing avoidance were addressed. Of course, neither partner was initially aware of his or her fear of experiencing dependency needs. What was equally significant was that in the perspective offered by this therapist, the unconscious inclinations of both partners could be substantially accounted for by their current pattern of living. Consistent with Wachtel's (1977) argument that motives can be usefully viewed as both cause *and* effect, it was felt that direct intervention could contribute to changing these unconscious yearnings and fears. The use of active, even behavioral, intervention was directed toward modifying the current sources of unconscious concerns and the tasks chosen for this purpose were directed by the therapist's understanding of the underlying psychodynamics of each partner. In this way, the model employed was parallel to that used by Feather and Rhoads (1972) in the psycho-analytic-behavioral treatment of phobias.

The possibilities for an integration of psychoanalytic and behavioral (as well as, perhaps, other action-oriented therapies) marital therapies are real and not illusory (see Wachtel, 1977). Their integrated use with couples has rarely been addressed, partially because of the artificial and unnecessary political separation of past and present in the therapeutic models of most marriage therapists.

5. *A cautionary note on the "individual" therapy of marital disorders*

It seems fitting that the conclusion of this analysis of several of the key issues in the use of a strictly psychoanalytic paradigm for the treatment of marital disorders returns to the controversial issue with which it began, the question of individual "versus" relationship change. As has been noted at many points in this section of the chapter, for decades there have been serious concerns expressed by therapists of a psycho-analytic persuasion about including relatives in individual psychotherapy. This section will briefly examine the possible consequences of *excluding* relatives (spouses) from psychotherapy. It should be made clear that the issue addressed here is not the effect of psychotherapy, generically speaking, on the spouse, but the effect on the partner in individual psycho-therapy for the treatment of *marital* problems. While the issues here are not unique to psychoanalytically oriented therapies, since at least some behavior therapists, for example, find it appropriate to treat half of the marital pair (e.g., Goldstein, 1971; Goldstein and Francis, 1969), they do have particular relevance to insight-oriented uncovering therapies.

Gurman and Kniskern (1978b) recently reviewed the existing empirical evidence on deterioration in marital and family therapy and determined that the rate of reported negative therapeutic effects as a result of indi-vidual therapy for marital discord was *twice* (11.6 percent *vs.* 5.6 percent) that of treatment formats in which both spouses were involved in one manner or another, through conjoint, conjoint group, concurrent or collaborative therapy. Moreover, the *success* rates of these one-spouse versus both-spouses-in-treatment formats were, conversely, strikingly in favor (65 percent versus 48 percent) of the latter approaches as an aggregate (Gurman and Kniskern, 1978c).

Hurvitz (1967) has described eight types of problems which frequently result from the treatment of one spouse (the wife) when marital problems exist: (1) the transference may complicate the basic relationship between the spouses; (2) the transference may create or complicate the specifically sexual problems between the spouses; (3) the problems that the spouses have in their marriage come to be regarded as less amenable to their own efforts to work them out; (4) the wife may regard the failure of therapy as her husband's fault; (5) the wife's therapy offers her a permissive setting within which she disparages her husband with impugnity and thereby reinforces her negative attitudes toward him; (6) the husband may be made to feel that he is a superfluous person in his wife's therapy and that she does not need him to overcome her problems; (7) the wife's gains in therapy tend to make her husband feel inadequate; (8) the husband may resist the wife's efforts to impose a new interaction pattern upon their relationship.

Kohl (1962) studied 39 marital partners of inpatients treated with individual psychotherapy, focusing on a patient's clinical improvement or recovery as the precipitant of a pathological reaction or psychiatric problem in his/her marital partner. Several types of reactions occurred: recurrence of alcoholism after a long period of abstinence, threats of divorce, resentment toward the therapist as well as toward the treatment, and depression mixed with acute anxiety.

> An ambitious 29-year-old woman, wife of a business executive who was admitted to the hospital for treatment of a manic excitement, described her marriage as "ideal" but at the same time expressed relief upon being able to assume an independent existence during her husband's confinement to the hospital. She also confessed that she was prepared and eager to assume directorship of his corporation if he failed to recover. In spite of his lack of cooperation and threats of divorce, she fully supported his treatment. *Only when the patient displayed encouraging signs of improvement and increasing confidence in his therapist did she react pathologically by depression, acute anxiety and indirect criticism of the therapist.* Through intensive treatment both partners were eventually able to make effective compromises and to establish a more mature adjustment (Kohl, 1962, p. 1038, emphasis added).

While deterioration does not occur only in individual treatment of marital disorders, this therapy format appears especially likely to produce such negative effects on a variety of criteria; those negative effects appear both on measures of the non-treated spouse's psychological functioning and on measures of the quality of the marital relationship per se (Gurman and Kniskern, 1978b). Gurman and Kniskern (1978b) found, in their review, a rate of deterioration (11.6 percent) in individual "marital" therapy that far exceeded the rate (5.6 percent) for other treatment formats. Clearly, the potential negative effects of treating one married partner in supposed isolation from his/her mate must be reckoned with by therapist who would endorse such practices.*

Some Additional Practical Considerations

The above sections have considered what appear to be the major conceptual issues, themes, and constraints inherent in a psychoanalytically oriented approach to the treatment of couples in conflict. Some common clinical issues have also been adumbrated in this context. This section will briefly present some additional very practical matters and problems that are likely to arise in the conduct of a predominantly psychoanalytically focused conjoint marital therapy.

(1) As has been stated in numerous ways above, primary reliance on interpretation of the *therapist-patient* transference relationship, with insufficient and unbalanced corresponding attention to the husband-wife transference, can divert the therapist from what is both the major source of resistance and the major potential source of an individual's growth in marriage. Moreover, the active and focused nature of conjoint couples therapy that is required within a brief treatment context further necessitates a significantly modified use of transference analysis.

(2) The therapist must be able to establish, on the one hand, a careful balance between an actively guiding yet confronting style of relating and, on the other hand, a manner of interpretation that is rather sensitively tuned to patients' capacities to withstand emotional stress. As Sager (Sager et al., 1971) notes

> A patient usually experiences relief when he attains insight into the reasons for his smoldering rage and irritability, which may have been puzzling and disturbing. On the other hand, confronting a spouse with the deep disappointments he has suffered in marriage can be destructive initially, and the therapist must be sensitive to the potentially disruptive effects of his interpretations upon the relationship (p. 493).

---

* The ethical implications of providing individual psychotherapy for marital problems are salient enough that when such a treatment possibility occurs in my practice, usually as the result of the steadfast refusal of one partner to enter conjoint therapy, I routinely insist that the second spouse come to at least part of one therapy session, at which time I inform both partners of the possibility of my seeing one of them alone on the condition that both understand the potential for secondary negative effects of an even apparently successful individual therapy. Thus informing both partners of this potential therapy-induced result not infrequently changes the resistant spouse's mind about entering conjoint therapy.

While a working alliance needs to be established rather quickly in brief therapy, it is often necessary to produce at least some rather tangible change in the marital relationship relatively early in order to begin to enlist the cooperation of a particularly resistive spouse (Nadelson's more active, step-wise approach described in Chapter III addresses this issue). The composite picture of a deterioration-inducing marital therapist described by Gurman and Kniskern (1978b) seems more likely to characterize a psychoanalytic treatment approach than either a behavioral or systems-oriented format.

> It is perhaps best described as one in which the therapist does relatively little structuring and guiding of early treatment sessions, uses frontal confrontations of highly affective material very early in therapy rather than reflections of feeling, labels unconscious motivation early in therapy rather than stimulating interaction, gathering data, or giving support, or does not actively intervene to moderate interpersonal feedback in families in which one member has very low ego-strength (p. 11).

(3) The therapist must guard carefully against the tendency of some couples to use self-revelation and dynamic formulations not as keys to understanding, but as weapons with which to passive-aggressively inflict wounds. There is also the related danger of marital partners' using such understanding as a defense against feeling or behavior change. This latter problem is hardly unique to psychoanalytically oriented marital therapy, but may be even more difficult to contravene here than in the analogous process in individual therapy, especially if a co-therapist is not involved in the treatment. Moreover, even the most articulate of insights is never an acceptable criterion of change, but must be used as a vehicle for change.

(4) A very basic strategic issue involves the sequencing of treatment goals. Should the therapist seek symptom reduction before attempting more fundamental structural intrapsychic change and directing greater attention to the transference relationship, as Nadelson (Chapter III; Nadelson et al., 1977) suggests, or should direct transference work, as opposed to the therapist's unspoken awareness of transference manifestations, be central to the treatment process from rather early in the encounter? Undoubtedly, both courses of action are called for under different circumstances, but the nature of these therapeutic decision-making criteria remains unresolved and, indeed, essentially unaddressed. Again, as noted earlier, the sequencing of goals should never be such

that achieving one set of goals would make it even more difficult later to achieve other or more ambitious goals.

(5) Because most psychoanalytically oriented training does not encourage a high degree of therapist activity, initiative-taking, and explicit, collaborative goal-setting, there is a potential danger in the use of predominantly psychoanalytically focused treatment of the therapist's avoidance of taking responsibility for some important aspects of the treatment process. This position is in no way intended to underestimate the very powerful effects of patient (couple) variables, such as motivation for change, psychological orientation and capacity to engage in an exploratory venture, and at least some evidence of commitment to the marital relationship. Still, acknowledging the couple's contribution to effective marital therapy does not absolve the therapist of the responsibility to be responsive to the felt needs and goals *of the couple,* in addition to his/her own targets for change. This is particularly the case with regard to symptom reduction, which is not meant here to be equivalent to symptomatic treatment.

(6) There is a good deal of disagreement among psychotherapists about what type of individual or couple is most likely to profit from differing treatment models. For example, while most psychoanalytically leaning therapists exercise a large amount of caution about whom they select for intensive treatment, at least some influential members of the analytic community believe that patients of a wide range of character types are suitable for brief psychoanalytically oriented therapy (Malan, 1976; Mann, 1973). More to the point in the marital context, psychoanalytically oriented therapists have not clearly addressed the central issue of whether motivation *for insight* is a necessary prerequisite for effective conjoint treatment. Indeed there is little evidence that it is a powerful prognostic sign in individual psychotherapy (Luborsky, Singer and Luborsky, 1975).

(7) Finally, it must be acknowledged that while psychoanalytic object-relations theory has added enormous depth to the understanding of the subtleties and vagaries of the marital relationship, it has thus far yielded few technical innovations of specific import to the treatment of dysfunctional intimate relationships. As has been noted earlier, this shortcoming has been reflected in the common adoption by psychoanalytically oriented marriage therapists of interventions generated not only outside the analytic framework, but conceived within orientations and perspectives usually thought to be irreconcilable with psychoanalytic theory and treatment. While further refinements of analytic technique developed

in the individual therapy context may be found to be useful for couples work, the continuing progress and advance of a psychoanalytic approach to conjoint therapy would seem to hinge in a most important way upon the emergence of dynamically constructed interventions designed specifically for the treatment of couples in conflict. The relative lack of such interventions is perhaps the weakest technical dimension of the psychoanalytic approach; as a result, most dynamicists have to become eclectics when treating couples.

Particular Advantages and Strengths of the
Psychoanalytic Approach

(1) The psychoanalytic (object relations) paradigm of marital choice, conflict and interaction offers a rich perspective with which to understand the interactive influences of individual psychological development on the vicissitudes of intimate relationships. In so doing, it offers a conceptual basis for appreciating the continuous nature of marriage as a logical outgrowth of prior interpersonal experience and, paradoxically, the adaptive potential of marital conflict.

(2) In like manner, the psychoanalytic perspective offers a model that substantially bridges the gap between private, inner experience and public, outer behavior. Of special relevance to the treatment of marital conflict, this perspective allows an understanding of both the function *and* meaning of marital behavior that otherwise appears quite puzzling, such as the hostile spouse who condemns his/her partner for the other's lack of attentiveness as a means of avoiding his/her own anxiety about showing tenderness.

(3) The psychoanalytic approach offers conflicted couples an opportunity for cognitive mastery of at least part of their suffering.

(4) Of particular clinical importance, the psychoanalytic approach, through its use of the transference, offers an opportunity for immediate affective interpersonal learning and for correcting misperceptions and distortions of interpersonal experiences that other approaches, such as the systems and behavioral, almost entirely eschew. Viewing the use of the patient-therapist relationship as an important vehicle for change offers the marital therapist many degrees of freedom toward flexible intervention which are more likely to be lost in more symptom-focused treatments.

THE BEHAVIORAL PERSPECTIVE

Behavior therapy, or more accurately, clinically applied social learning theory, offers the most recent important perspective on marital dysfunction and treatment. In the last decade, several influential workers in the area independently initiated the application of learning principles to disharmonious marital relationships (Azrin, Naster and Jones, 1973; Goldiamond, 1965; Lazarus, 1968; Liberman, 1970; Stuart, 1969a, 1969b, 1975). The most significant contributions have come from the Oregon Marital Studies Program (Birchler, Weiss and Vincent, 1975; Hops, Wills, Patterson and Weiss, 1971; Royce and Weiss, 1975; Vincent, Weiss and Birchler, 1975; Weiss, 1975, Chapter IV; Weiss et al., 1974), their followers (Jacobson, 1977a, 1977b) and Gottman's group (Gottman, 1975; Gottman, Notarius, Markman, Bank and Yoppi, 1976). A flood of clinical reports of both an anecdotal (Baird and Redfering, 1975; Fensterheim, 1972; Hickok and Komechak, 1974; Liberman, 1970) and experimental (Carter and Thomas, 1973; Eisler, Miller, Hersen and Alford, 1974; Goldstein, 1976; Wieman, Shoulders and Farr, 1974) nature have followed and enough substantive study of both the behavioral determinants of marital satisfaction and dissatisfaction and of the outcomes of behavioral marriage therapy has accumulated to prompt the appearance of a large number of reviews of behavioral assessment and treatment programs (Greer and D'Zurilla, 1975; Jacob, 1976; Jacobson, Chapter VIII; Jacobson and Martin, 1976; Olson, 1972; Patterson, Weiss and Hops, 1976; Weiss, Chapter IV; Weiss and Margolin, 1977).

Marital Choice, Satisfaction and Conflict

Behavior therapists have said little about the process of marital choice. This is not accidental since behavioral marriage therapists, like behavior therapists in general, have little concern with the past. Rarely does history-taking in behavioral couples therapy extend in time beyond the history of the marriage itself (D'Zurilla, 1976) and most workers in the area attempt no comprehensive or systematic assessment of the *development* of the relationship, placing an almost exclusive emphasis upon present behavior (cf., O'Leary and Turkewitz, Chapter V). Since behavioral marriage therapists view dyadic behavior only in its current contexts, the notion of *stages* of marital relationship and of the marital life-cycle (Berman and Lief, 1975) have generally been considered to be of little relevance to their clinical practice (Gurman, 1975b; Gurman and Knudson, 1978), although Weiss (Chapter IV) has begun to explicitly acknowledge their importance.

For the behavior therapist, presumably, those factors that influence current marital satisfaction involve the very same types of determinants and processes of initial interpersonal attraction and marital choice. Unfortunately, no behavioral marriage therapists have yet integrated or applied to their work the variety of cognitive-learning hypotheses (such as Byrne and Lamberth, 1971; Clore and Byrne, 1974; Huston, 1974; Lott and Lott, 1974; Murstein, 1971) that have been advanced to explain marital choice, although such attention might add the presently lacking developmental framework. This section will examine the social learning view of the ingredients of a successful marriage.

The most basic assumption in this regard is that successful and unsuccessful marriage can be reliably differentiated on the basis of the concurrent relative strength of reciprocity and coercion (Patterson and Hops, 1972; Reid, 1967) existing within the relationship. Several studies (Birchler and Webb, 1975; Birchler et al., 1972; Birchler et al., 1975; Vincent et al., 1975) have found that partners in distressed marriages behave quite differently (utilizing less positive and more aversive control strategies) when interacting (problem-solving) with their spouses than when interacting with strangers. It is on this basis that the argument is developed that what is functional or dysfunctional in the marital relationship is situation-specific (Franks and Wilson, 1976), that is, that marital behavior is based, if not entirely, then nearly so, on the immediate present behavior of the other spouse. Indeed, Stuart (1969a) advanced the "self-evident" premise that ". . . the impression which each spouse forms of the other is based on the behavior of the other. Accordingly, when one changes his behavior, there are corresponding changes in the other's impressions and perceptions of him" (p. 677). A similar position is taken by Weiss (Chapter IV): "As behaviors change we would expect that cognitions catch up with these changes . . ." (page 172). More elaborated extensions of this inference involve behavioral arguments against the interactional relevance of the personalities of the individuals concerned.

However, there exists an equally plausible alternative interpretation of these spouse-stranger differences, one more in keeping with psychoanalytic thinking: It is possible that these data point to the interactional difficulties that certain *individuals* have *in intimate relationships* and that the use of coercion and lack of reciprocity demonstrated in these studies is simply tapping into the *characterological* relationship deficits found among people in unsatisfactory marriages. This inference, of course, would be nearly impossible to study empirically, as it would require the interaction-testing of individuals in several intimate relationships and order-effects would be sizeable. Still, the clinical observation that many divorced individuals, left to their own devices, seem to repeat the errors of their first marriage in subsequent relationships would appear to argue in favor of the proposition that at least *some* important aspects of intimate relationships are determined by relatively enduring characteristics of individuals which transcend specific dyadic pairings.

That people do behave differently with their spouses than with strangers is not particularly surprising and is, in fact, commonsensical. To argue that data yielding such transactional differences weaken the position of trait or developmental theories is to entirely miss the very fundamental non-equivalence and, hence, non-comparability of intimate versus superficial relationships which are based only upon current interaction and which wholly lack their own developmental history, privately shared meaning systems (this concept is considered by some behaviorists, as in Stuart's [1975] "core symbols") and transactional rules. As Sager (1976) notes, "Each spouse stimulates defensive maneuvers in the other that may or may not be characteristic of that partner in another relationship" (p. 28). Or as Dicks (1967) argues, "The special feature of such apparent hate-relationships in marriage is that they occur within the framework of a compelling sense of belonging. The spouses are clear in their minds that they would not dream of treating anyone else but each other in this way" (p. 70).

Thus, for a behaviorist, a successful marriage is one that is reinforcing; a reinforcing marriage is one that is satisfying; and a satisfying marriage is one that is successful. As Glisson (1976) points out, an obvious tautology exists within this conceptualization, in addition to the potential circularity of the very notion of reinforcement itself (Hilgard and Marquis, 1961). Behavior therapists appear to be using the term "reinforcement" on a *post hoc* explanatory basis, perhaps even as a metaphor. That is, there has been little empirical demonstration that the reinforcements ("Pleases") offered by one spouse to another actually exert a controlling influence on the other's behavior. Relying upon a couple's verbal reports of what is "pleasing" and "displeasing," while economical of time, represents a practice hardly in keeping with operant behavior control procedures which, of course, require non-inferential and non-hedonistic measurement, under naturally occurring contingencies, of the response strength of behaviors to be controlled.

It is also important to note an important theoretical problem engendered in the behavior therapist's concurrent use of spouse-recorded behaviors, that is, Pleases (P's) and Displeases (D's), and observer-coded behaviors, such as the MICS. While multidimensional assessment is generally to be preferred in the psychotherapeutic context (Bergin, 1971;

Gurman and Kniskern, 1978c), it needs to be recognized that having spouses code their own behavior is more consistent with the tenets of exchange theory (Thibaut and Kelley, 1959) than is coding by external observers, since the payoff of a behavior is more a function of receiving (perceiving?) the behavior (Gottman, 1975), than of simply exhibiting the behavior (Gergen, 1969). As Gottman (1975) notes, "A smile may be a smirk to a spouse, or an interruption may display interest." Or, as Glick and Gross (1975, p. 510) have pointed out, "To view all communications as being of equivalent intensity or quality ignores a critical component of interaction style which determines the level of gratification received." Gathering data in these two ways (spouses' versus observers' coding of behavior) elicits information relevant, in effect, to two different but complementary theories, that is, exchange theory versus operant theory.

In fact, a more basic problem is involved in the notion of reciprocity of positive reinforcement. High base rates of "positive" behavior for spouses are not equivalent to reciprocity. While non-distressed couples may appear to reciprocate positive behaviors more often than distressed couples, this may in fact be an artifact of the higher (base-rate) probability of positive behavior in satisfied couples. Consistent with the above-mentioned apparent post hoc use of the notion of "reinforcement" is Gottman's (1975) argument that "what needs to be demonstrated is that significant reduction in uncertainty is gained about a particular consequent (behavior) by knowledge of a particular antecedent (behavior)." In sum, the behaviors in question must be distributed contingently. The temporal conditional probability (Gottman, 1975) of targeted marital behaviors, as distinct from the relative base rate probabilities of such behaviors, has rarely been demonstrated in behavioral research on couples' interaction. Thus, high base rates of "positive" behavior alone do not allow proper use of the notion "social reinforcement," which use must, of course, depend on the demonstrated effect (change in contingent probability) of the behaviors in question.

The potential explanatory weakness of the notion of reciprocity is perhaps best adumbrated with reference to the "Doll's House Marriage" (Pittman and Flomenhaft, 1970), as portrayed in Ibsen's classic play, in which the wife's extreme dependency and overt incompetence are balanced by an overly successful and "strong" husband. This is a not uncommon form of a relationship in which "reinforcement reciprocity" is hardly present on an observable level. Yet such relationships are often enduring and genuinely satisfying to their participants. Moreover, a number of marital relationship patterns have been described (Cuber and

Harroff, 1965) which are stable over time an dsatisfying but which seem quite lacking in *overt* mutual reciprocity.

The behavioral model seems to revere the symmetrical relationship, in which two people give and get qualitatively symmetrical behavior, thereby minimizing differences between the two partners.* In fact, of course, as implied above, there are numerous complementary relationships, often described as "traditional," which maximize (overt) differences, and in which each spouse "exchanges dissimilar but need-fulfilling behavior evoked by the other" (Berman and Leif, 1975). While the notion of reinforcement reciprocity may have appeal to the androgyny-oriented professional marital therapist, it is clear that many marriages in our culture are deeply satisfying to people despite an absence of *behavioral* reciprocity. Even Weiss (Weiss and Margolin, 1977) notes that "none of the (behavioral) approaches have reported on couples whose interest is predominantly a traditional role-oriented marriage. The considerable egalitarian emphasis of these (behavioral) approaches . . . might well run into difficulty with such clients" (page 585). Or, as Weiss (Chapter IV) notes in this volume, ". . . it would seem that behavioral approaches to marriage are best suited to relationships which already subscribe to more egalitarian than traditional ideological components" (italics omitted).

Implicit in the behavioral viewpoint is the assumption that marital disharmony derives from the same sources, insufficient reciprocity of positive reinforcement, at all stages of the individual and marital life cycle. Just as the same behaviors involved in challenging adult authority and seeking autonomy have very different developmental meanings for a two-year-old and a 32-year-old, and may be seen as more age-appropriate in the first case, so do the topographically similar conflicts of married couples take on different meanings at various life-stages. For example, the tenuous intimacy of couples in their early forties is not the same problem as the ambivalent intimacy of couples in their early twenties. In the former situation, complaints of "lack of affection" may point to the second spouse's concern about his/her perceived decreased sexual attractiveness, for example, while in the case of the younger couple, low rates of "affectional behavior" may suggest problems in developing autonomy from one's family of origin, assumption of the new roles of adulthood, and the like. A mere increase in the rate of affectional behaviors,

---

* While it is true that spouses may request, and exchange, *any* type of behaviors in the treatment process, the *ultimate* interactional goal of such exchanges is the qualitative symmetry of *overt* reinforcing events.

while constituting an apparently positive therapeutic change, obscures the developmental meaning of the previously low rate of such behavior and is likely, in and of itself, to leave untouched, and perhaps unexamined, the more basic issues of which a low behavioral output *may* be but the public expression. Although O'Leary and Turkewitz (Chapter V) do not discuss their findings of differential effectiveness of different behavioral techniques with younger and older couples in this context, their data point to the need for specifying different behavioral treatment procedures for different couples' problems. Still, it seems unlikely to the present writer that they would infer different underlying unconscious processes and defensive operations in these two patient groups.

It is assumed in the behavioral view that marital difficulties arise from faulty behavior change efforts (Patterson and Hops, 1972) and that marital conflict is equivalent to "an interchange in which one or both members of a dyad demand immediate change in the behavior of the other person and the other person does not comply" (Patterson et al., 1976, p. 244). Even a cursory examination of the conditions commonly precipitating a marital crisis, however, reveals numerous instances of severe marital conflict in which ineffective and misguided (i.e., the use of aversive consequation of the spouse's behavior, resulting in negative reinforcement, hence, "coercion") "behavior change operations" and demands for immediate behavior change that go unmet are hardly at issue, except perhaps via a very exaggerated stretching of the definition of "behavior change operations." A well-disguised and hidden extramarital affair, in which the spouse involved in an outside sexual relationship derives enormous satisfaction through the passive-aggressive expression of hostility, can serve as an all too common illustration of clear marital conflict in the absence of any demand for immediate change on the part of the other spouse.

Because behavior therapists ignore the simultaneous existence of multiple levels of the relationship, they are forced to assume a peculiar definition of conflict. Consider the definition of conflict in Raush et al. (1974, p. 30), ". . . any situation or process in which two or more social entities are linked by at least one form of *antagonistic psychological relation* or at least one form of *antagonistic interaction*" (emphasis supplied). Behavior therapy, by focusing only on content, limits itself to one part of this definition of conflict, the antagonistic interaction. It is curious to find psychotherapists who deny the necessity of taking into account psychological relations.

As Raush et al. (1974) point out, their definition takes into account covert conflict, "the possibility of conflict between two people even though they do not emerge in the usual signs of conflict such as shouting, arguing and fighting" (p. 30). As noted earlier, the behavioral definition of conflict permits behaviorists to assert as self-evident some things which contradict assumptions basic to most theories, as in the case of Stuart's (1969a, p. 677) premise that behavior change yields "corresponding changes in the other's impressions . . . of him." This premise is not "wrong." It is simply incomplete, even from a social learning point of view. An "impression" is based on the other's behavior *as interpreted* through the individual's perceptual system which has developed out of his experiences with previous significant others. If, however, behavior is, in fact, interpreted (perceived), then a change in husband's behavior *may or may not* change his wife's impressions and expectations. In most cases, the marital problem will be in a "hot" area, an area in which one or the other is emotionally vulnerable and, therefore, may be *less likely to be able to recognize, respond to, or learn from new experiences.* As Raush et al. (1974, p. 48) argue, "of all human relationships marriage has the greatest potential for reintegrating the schemata associated with anxieties of childhood," that is, tapping into a "hot" area so that an old (and inappropriate) battle is either fought or avoided. Clara Thompson's (1964) discussion of Sullivan (1953) is relevant here

> Interpersonal relations . . . refer to more than what actually goes on between two people. There may be "fantastic personifications" such as for instance the idealization of a love-object. . . . One may also endow people falsely with characteristics taken from significant people in one's past. An interpersonal relationship can be said to exist between a person and any one of these more or less fantastic people . . . as well as between a person or group evaluated without distortion (pp. 215-216).

Thus, the production of behavior change does not guarantee a parallel change in the way behavior is perceived. In this context, Weiss' (Chapter IV) comment that "If indeed cognitions are independent of the empirical (daily) events of the marital interaction, we would merely require a technology for changing attitudes independently of behavioral events" (page 171) seems unduly cavalier about the implicitly asserted ease ("merely" require) with which such interpersonal attitudes may be modified.

Even more striking is the difficulty encountered by the social learning perspective when faced with the common situation in which one spouse appears at a clinic with apparent "individual" symptoms which present no obvious dyadic basis, such as depression (Feldman, 1976; Friedman, 1975), but which from other points of view are replete with transactional meaning (Gurman and Knudson, 1978).

Behavior therapists also do not address the question of why some individuals are more prone to use aversive than positive control strategies in intimate relationships. What are the factors that increase the probability of, in a sense, a high operant level of such behaviors? Presumably, the response to this question would make reference, *ex post facto*, to the learning histories of the individuals, allude to probably vicarious learning via modeling of parental interaction, and so forth. Such an analysis, however, would not address, or at least consider immediately important for intervention, the likely faulty generalizations made from previous interpersonal experiences to present behavior patterns. As noted earlier in the commentary on the psychoanalytic approach to couples therapy, an active intervention style, even one focused largely on current behavior, does not preclude the use of a developmental framework for understanding present interpersonal behavior.

The Process and Technique of Conjoint
Treatment: Themes, Assumptions and Issues

Behavioral marriage therapists, more than any other group, have recently developed extremely systematic intervention procedures, with clearly differentiated treatment modules (see Gurman and Knudson, 1978; Weiss, 1975). Inherent in the behavioral approach to therapy is a strong emphasis upon empirical evaluation and validation of therapeutic outcomes. The conclusiveness of this research will be addressed briefly later in this chapter and is considered at length elsewhere (Gurman and Kniskern, 1978c; Jacobson, Chapter VIII). These empirical matters notwithstanding, several emergent themes and assumptions* that appear to characterize the behavioral approach raise some very basic issues about the nature of marriage and its change in the therapeutic encounter.

1. *Rationality in intimate relationships: Goal and potential*

The task-oriented, data-oriented and ahistorical approach of behavioral marriage therapy appears to revere the rationality of the observing ego. In caricatured form at least, couples are assumed to enter therapy (a) with both partners acknowledging the fact of a *relationship dysfunction,*

---

* Parts of this section, up to, "Some Additional Practical Considerations," are adapted from Gurman and Knudson (1978).

(b) to the maintenance of which each partner, by admission, contributes in some way. It is further implied (c) that these two "rational" adults, are, in large part, directly open to the therapist's suggestions and counsel on how to achieve behavior change and, therefore, in their own rational self-interest, (d) will not, in any substantial way, resist the therapist's interventions to achieve such change. It is also implicit in the behavioral model that (e) each partner has enough self-control and ego-strength and (f) enough commitment to the marital relationship that they will be able to deal with changing their relationship in a gradual, step-wise, and problem-by-problem fashion.

Clinical experience with couples not seen in the highly structured and formalized setting of the university-based clinical research laboratory persuades that one or more of these assumptions are misguided in the overwhelming majority of cases. It is, for example, a well-known clinical fact that only a very small percentage of couples actually treated present themselves as a dyad to a clinic or private practitioner. Much more commonly, one spouse, usually the wife, presents alone, with vague complaints of depression, existential *angst*, or other symptomatic behaviors. This "identified patient" is, in the reality of both a psychoanalytic and communications theory understanding of marital disharmony, the messenger of the couple, announcing to the audience of the therapist that previously satisfying or at least satisfactory modes of resolution of marital conflict and achievement of satisfaction in that relationship are no longer working effectively. In this context, the "second" spouse, if he appears at the therapist's office at all, does so, more often than not, in the role of the caretaker, whose only purpose in appearing is to "help my spouse with her problem." Such a second spouse typically will not acknowledge his active contribution to "her problem" and commonly will even deny that "her problem" in any way implies any dysfunction within the *relationship*, except perhaps as a secondary phenomenon.

Therefore, resistance to the therapist's interventions is virtually guaranteed and is explicitly expected by both psychoanalytically oriented and communications oriented therapists. Resistance to therapeutic influence also characterizes most couples who do not so blatantly use the therapy admission ticket of one "ill" partner. In fact, as General System Theory tells us, it is a property of any ongoing social system to resist change from within or from without. In the specific case of the marriage, much of this systemic resistance to change derives from the couple's agreements as to how the marital relationship is to be defined, that is, the marriage contract. One may wonder why behavior therapists have not discussed this source of potential resistance, particularly since their conceptualization includes "contracts" and marital *quid pro quo* as basic components.

Part of the explanation may lie in the fact that the use of the "contract" construct by behavior therapists differs from its use in most other conceptual systems. *As it is used outside behavioral discussions, the marriage contract is conceptualized as multi-leveled.* Sager's (Sager et al., 1971) classic paper and recent text (Sager, 1976) distinguish among conscious and verbalized, conscious but not verbalized, and unconscious levels of contractual agreement. In his formulation it is explicitly recognized that *contracts at one level of experience may directly contradict those at another level.* Communication models (such as Watzlawick et al., 1967) are most likely to emphasize the distinction between "content" and "relationship" level contracts. Jackson (1965, p. 12) exemplifies the latter view in his assertion that "the marital quid pro quo . . . is a *metaphorical* statement of the marital relationship *bargain;* that is, how the couple has agreed to *define themselves* within this relationship" (emphasis added). *In such a view, the key aspect of the contract negotiation process is not a mere reciprocal offering of behaviors; it is a bargain about definition of self.*

Such a conception appears broadly consistent with a wide variety of theoretical models including Laingian (1961), Rogerian (1961), Sullivanian (1953), and object-relations theory (Dicks, 1967; Raush et al., 1974), as well as those of symbolic interactionists such as Goffman (1959). As behavioral marriage therapy becomes somewhat more eclectic, such a broadening view of the function of quid pro quo is inevitable, as is evidenced by O'Leary and Turkewitz' (Chapter V) rather frequent, yet cautious, references to the contributions of Sager (1976; Sager et al., 1971). Perhaps there is initial evidence of this in Weiss' (Chapter IV) comment that, "Behaviors may have objective market value but more often relate to self-esteem or personal worth of the partners" (page 190). Is this an existential analysis of behavioral analysis?

To the extent to which the marriage contract is an agreement by each spouse to support the other's perception of self-in-relation-to-other, change would be predicted by analytic workers to be resisted in precisely the same way an individual defends against change in his/her own self-concept. Such resistance would be greater to the extent to which the marriage contract involves what Whitaker (1975) has aptly called a "pseudo-therapy" agreement—bargains which provide solutions to the spouse's intrapsychic difficulties.

The psychoanalytic notions of projective identification and collusion (Aldous, 1973; Dicks, 1967; Greenspan and Mannino, 1974; Lloyd and Paulson, 1972; Meissner, Chapter II; Stewart et al., 1975) help to clarify the self-definitional nature of *quid pro quo* and the potential roadblock put forth by rather straightaway attempts to engage couples in exchanges of desired overt behavior. Lloyd and Paulson (1972) point out that in a conflicted marital situation each partner "maintains an internal world that the other supports. By confirming each other's projections, they help each other to maintain a closed internal system, *protected from modification by reality*" (p. 410, emphasis added). It is when these intrapsychically agreed upon roles break down that the couple, or one member of the couple, becomes distressed or symptomatic. Thus, even among couples who initially appear to want to change, there is a tremendous internal pressure, generated by the desire to maintain one's own self-esteem and psychic boundaries, to continue to behave in modes that reinforce one's perception of one's spouse and, thereby, of one's self. Perhaps this explains, in part, why some couples withhold from each other reinforcements they are *capable* of providing. Therefore, there is almost always ambivalence about changing, hence there is almost always resistance to the therapist's influence. In this context, it is difficult to accept the proposition of Weiss and Margolin (1977) that resistance, or non-compliance with the therapist's change efforts, merely represents client skill deficits. Even among apparently "rational" marital partners, *the real and most salient exchange or quid pro quo is the reciprocal exchange of behaviors that confirm each partner's projections.* Thus, this analysis agrees with Weiss (Chapter IV) that in "well functioning relationships . . . each person has reinforcement value for the other" (page 187) but adds that such "reinforcement value" is also present in poorly functioning marriages, though perhaps at a different level of experience.

In this context, regardless of whether one speaks of unconscious contracts, relationship level contracts, or collusion, it is now quite understandable that many couples are often unable to rationally change their behavior in a step-by-step, contract-by-contract manner since such a focusing therapy, calling for relatively immediate behavior change, may directly challenge the collusive bonds of the couple. One aspect of this argument merits elaboration: Couples in conflict often cannot be rational in their "contract" change attempts. As Bancroft (1975) noted in a recent article on behavioral couples therapy:

> the behavior approach . . . requires both partners to behave like adults. One is explicitly asking them to do so when negotiating treat-

ment contracts with them. *Much of the success of treatment will depend on how successful the therapist is in persuading them to keep to such an an adult role, when all too often behaving like children has become well established in their coping behavior . . . therefore, the therapist is only prepared to work with the "adult," and this is one reason why such an approach is not suitable for all cases* (p. 152, emphasis added).

Furthermore, one may question whether it is a desirable therapeutic oucome for couples to become predominantly and more efficiently "adult" in their relationship. Perhaps an optimal therapeutic outcome within any system of marital therapy is that both partners become comfortable and even skilled at being both adult and childlike together and become able to flexibly interchange roles and combinations of roles as life-conditions require. To this end, couples treatment would appear to require exploration of the irrational, the non-linear and the unconscious.

2. *The primacy of overt behavior*

Olson (1972), in what was probably the first review of behavioral marriage therapy, asked in the title of his paper, "Are behavior counts all that count?" This issue of the presumed primacy of publicly observable (social) behaviors has been addressed many times, so the arguments for and against the position will not be belabored here. Rather, "behavior" needs to be put in some broader contexts relevant to couples' interactions and problem-solving.

The Stoic philosopher Epictetus in the first century A.D. said, "It is not the things themselves which trouble us, but the opinions that we have about these things." Thus, when one married partner complains, say, of his spouse's extreme criticalness, a behavior therapist would likely try to produce a decrease of "critical verbal behaviors" and an increase of incompatible positive behaviors on the part of the second spouse. This is an example of first-order change (Watzlawick et al., 1974). On the other hand, a systems-communication-oriented therapist might respond, "I think you should *thank* her constantly criticizing you because that shows just how much she cares about you." This "reframing," or changing "the conceptual and/or emotional setting or viewpoint in relation to which a situation is experienced" (Watzlawick et al., 1974, p. 95) and placing it "in another frame which fits the 'facts' of the same concrete situation equally well or even better" (p. 95), thereby changing its meaning, is an example of second-order change. Thus, it is not the case that "behavior is behavior is behavior," but rather that behavior *means.*

The practical implication of this viewpoint is that "solving the problem" can be accomplished on many levels, only one of which may be changing the frequency of a targeted behavior and only one of which requires acceptance of the stated or presented problem as the central issue. While behaviorists have generally eschewed therapist behaviors that smack of "interpretation," O'Leary and Turkewitz (Chapter V, page 275) come surprisingly close to this in clearly supporting what the communicationists call reframing or relabeling behavior, noting that "The therapist must help the spouses *reinterpret* each other's behaviors in a more positive and/or realistic way" (emphasis added). O'Leary and Turkewitz' (Chapter V) attempt to begin incorporation of cognitive interventions is also refreshing in this regard.

Yet another way of expressing this issue is that most behavioral marital therapists have largely ignored the power and salience of private events in marital behavior. A simplistic Skinnerian framework has been largely abandoned as the be all and end all of therapeutic change for most contemporary behavior therapists, as exemplified in the work of Bandura (1969), Mahoney (1974), Mahoney and Thoresen (1974). While it is true that, to a limited extent, behavior therapists do consider a patient's phenomenology in couples therapy, as in assessing "Pleases" and "Displeases," they have paid almost no attention to considering the private events in marital interaction as themselves the targets for change, but have seemingly viewed them as either epiphenomena of public behavior change or, at most, discriminative stimuli for such behavior. The reader conversant with social learning theory (for example, Bandura, 1969), recent work on self-control and private events (for example, Jacobs and Sachs, 1971; Kanfer and Karoly, 1972), and the role of cognition in human behavior (for example, Beck, 1976; Ellis, 1973; Mahoney, 1974; Meichenbaum, 1977), will readily recognize that such cognitive-conceptual private events, and systems-dynamic approaches to dealing with these events, as implied above, can be incorporated into a behavioral couples therapy strategy without comprising the unique advantages of methodological (versus metaphysical or radical) behaviorism (Mahoney, 1974).*

An interesting and important corollary of the "behavior is behavior is behavior" philosophy is the implicit assumption in most behavioral marriage therapy of the apparent ease with which causality can be established. Thus, a wife might complain of her husband's sarcastic "put

---

* While both of the behavioral chapters in this volume (Weiss, Chapter IV; O'Leary and Turkewitz, Chapter V) acknowledge the need for considering private events, neither offers a technology for change in this arena.

downs," yet ignore or, more likely, be unaware of the fact that her husband usually behaves this way only after the wife has refused sexual contact. Far more often there is involved, then, a circular causality, rather than a unidirectional linearity, in which there are chains of interaction such that a stimulus X_1 triggers a response Y_1 which, in turn, becomes the stimulus X_2 for another response Y_2, etc. (Olson, 1970). The point in the interactional sequence at which one intervenes or "punctuates" the interaction (Watzlawick et al., 1967) is totally arbitrary, that is, "the" cause or discriminative stimulus of another person's behavior does not exist unto itself, but is "chosen" by a patient, couple or therapist. Spouses typically choose causal explanations that put their partner in the villain role, while therapists choose those that suggest equal contribution to dysfunctional patterns. For example, a wife complaining of her uptightness about initiating sex with her husband and denying, with her husband's agreement, that she ever does anything but respond to "his" advances might be asked by the theraipst, "Tell me, how do you get your husband to initiate sex?" Thus, the point is that the therapist need not accept the client's definition of problematic reality, but may (and often must) himself define a new reality for the couple.

Hence, for most couples, *therapy will have to produce change in perceptual processes as well as in overt behavior, though direct alteration of the latter offers no assurance of the former also occurring.*

Because interventions in behavior therapy focus largely on content, their impact may be paradoxical at the relationship level. A striking example is provided by the behaviorist's distinction between "coercion" and "reciprocity." While behaviorists emphasize the desirability of replacing coercion with reciprocity, both of these can be seen as equivalent at the meta-level in the fundamental sense that *both are forms of control.* Consider, for example, the husband who stops threatening to beat his wife if she will not provide him with sex at least twice a week (aversive control) and contracts instead to wash the dishes once a week and pick up his dirty socks daily in exchange for sex (positive control). Wife is is still providing sex in response to a demand. At the meta-level, control is control is control. To deny the importance of this distinction is to say, in effect, that there is no difference between the husband-wife relationship and the client-prostitute relationship other than legal documents. Dicks (1967, p. 36) well expresses an alternative point of view: ". . . the foundations of a marriage (are) a mutual affirmation of the other's identity as a lovable person, not as a coitus machine for tension release."

The "good faith" contract (Weiss et al., 1974) seems to have been developed in response to a partial recognition of the problem inherent in control, even of a "positive" variety. By continuing to ignore the multiple-level nature of contracts, however, the "good faith" model is subject to the same difficulties as the model it purportedly improves upon. Assume, for example, that husband spends 10 minutes before dinner with the children. He does this not in exchange for a reciprocal change in wife's behavior, but simply for a bottle of beer presented by wife. What is the impact on wife? In the short run she may report increased satisfaction with husband's behavior. There is no apparent reason to believe that in the long run she will come to feel that husband sees either her or their children as more lovable (worth spending time with). There is, however, reason to speculate that she may eventually conclude that husband sees her as a mobile beer dispensing machine.*

Instead of "good faith," Bach (1971) suggests that what is called for is *unilateral commitment*: "I will do this for you because I want to please you" (because you are a lovable person). Perhaps many behavior therapists have been blinded to such a possibility because of their gallant attempts to retain "controlling environmental contingencies" as part of their formulation.

Of interest in this regard is Gottman's (1975; Gottman et al., 1976) behavioral model of a "good relationship" which emphasizes that *noncontingent* positive exchanges and *lack* of reciprocity characterize stable, mutually satisfying marriages. The basis for this sort of relationship must then be two individuals who have a clear sense of self as separate and whole, not dependent on the other for survival. This is the link to the literature which suggests, recognizing that there is a debate, that extrinsic reward may reduce intrinsic motivation (Levine and Fasnacht, 1974). Attributional theorists claim that our future behavior will be determined on the basis of how we attribute the causality of our behavior. As Levine and Fasnacht (1974) argue, there are dangers in using external rewards for behaviors that are of some intrinsic interest. Specifically, external rewards may lead to a decrease in interest because reinforcement may shift attention from the activity to the reinforcer.

Perhaps these laboratory observations reflect the oft-heard comment from one spouse to another in treatment, "I want you to (show interest

---

* While it could be argued (as in Jacobson, Chapter VIII) that existing research on behavioral marital therapy which shows significant positive changes in self-reported marital satisfaction following such interventions weakens this argument, elsewhere (Gurman and Kniskern, 1978c) it has been concluded that this evidence is not sufficiently convincing to invalidate the present view.

in me, be affectionate to me, etc., etc.) because *you* want to, not because we're in therapy (or because the therapist says you should)." As Weiss (Chapter IV) states, "Forced rewards, like solicited compliments, lose their value" (page 189).

Perceiving oneself to be the primary locus of causation for one's own behavior is critical. An individual who has a sense of worth as a person (unconditional positive self-regard) will not be (feel) dependent on another for survival and will see him/herself as the locus of his own behavior. Indeed, this is the essence of Bowen's position (1976a, 1976b, 1976c). Note that when a person makes a noncontingent expression of affection, a behavior therapist may actually work to change that. In Wills et al. (1974), an example is offered in which husband washes wife's car as, in husband's view, an expression of affection. (Weiss, Chapter IV, would argue that such behavior is "more properly" labeled "instrumental and personal services.") These therapists are critical of the husband's failure to understand the difference between an "instrumental" and an "affectional" behavior and aim to train the husband in the latter "skill." Again, it is as if only the form, the content, matters: Saying "I care" regardless of internal feelings is affection, while washing wife's car (with love) is not.

It may be, in fact, that learning *how* to negotiate in marriage is more important and will have longer range beneficial effects than the outcomes of specific negotiations. Weiss (Chapter IV) seems to acknowledge this in his comment that "much can be accomplished with the first three areas (of relationship accomplishment) so that relatively few problems require the full treatment of contracting and negotiation training" (page 203). Content is often subservient to process.

3. Marital conflict and the expression of feelings

Behavior therapists appear to denigrate the expression of feelings in intimate relationships and cast them aside as mere "catharsis." Actually, there is little evidence that merely catharting is a useful therapeutic venture (Marshall, 1972); in fact, unbridled expression of feelings, rather than relieving inner tension, may actually reinforce the tendency to express feelings in non-adaptive ways. But experientially and phenomenologically oriented therapists do not endorse feeling expression *per se* as being of value. Rather, such expression serves to define relationships. The contrast here between a behavioral and an experiential model of marital and therapeutic process can be illustrated by comparing some of what Luthman (1974) calls "lethal" processes in families with several "displeasing" (and, by implication, "negative") items from the Oregon group's Spouse Observation Checklist:

> *Lethal "rule" A*: Any comment family members make about another is viewed as an attack, whether the comment is a question, compliment, or an actual criticism (p. 119).
>
> "Displeasing Behavior": Spouse offered unsolicited advice.
>
> *Lethal "rule" B*: The fact that family members may be different from one another . . . is viewed as a threat (p. 120).
>
> "Displeasing Behavior": Spouse showed no interest in *my* hobby.
> Spouse did not respect *my* opinion.
>
> *Lethal "rule" C*: Everything must be reasonable, nice and polite (p. 121-122).
>
> "Displeasing Behavior": Spouse interrupted me.
> Spouse complained.
> Spouse criticized (my body, my smoking, etc.).

These examples are non-trivial and cannot be argued against by simply saying that these items are taken out of context or that they involve mere semantic differences. In fact, behavioral couples therapists argue that there is a fundamental link between assessment and therapy. The P/D list is an integral part of the Oregon treatment package. So, to list "Spouse did not respect my opinion" as a "D" is, in fact, to assert that such behavior should be eliminated from the marriage. But one cannot legislate or teach "respect." Furthermore, what kind of life results from the two people never arguing? Note, in this regard, Weiss' (Chapter IV) statement that he prefers to "deal with fighting strategically by removing the situational antecedents which lead to fighting." If successful, such strategies, by definition, eliminate fighting behavior, a desirable goal for behavior therapists, because fighting is implicitly destructive. O'Leary and Turkewitz (Chapter V) offer what appears to be a more moderate position in not encouraging "negative feelings regarding something a spouse cannot change. . . ." O'Leary and Turkewitz' discussion of the role of negative feeling expression in behavioral marriage therapy seems much more in keeping with a broader clinical framework than do previously published accounts of behavioral approaches.

This is the rub. What looks like "disrespect" at a content level may communicate great "respect" at the meta-level. Wife says to husband, "When it comes to politics, your head is really up your you-know-what." Behavior therapists called this a "D" (very destructive). However, the relationship message may be something like, "I have enough confidence in our relationship and enough respect for your strength that I can let go, lose my temper, and bounce a few insults off you—I know you aren't fundamentally wounded by this."

Just as feeling expression serves to define relationships at the meta-level of communication, so, too, do therapeutic paradigms serve to define implicit desired relationship themes. There exists the possibility that a therapeutic experience focused entirely on isolated behaviors, rather than on their emergent themes and functions as well, may be training efficient but fragmented people who respond to "pieces" of each other. Consider Jacobson's (1977b) position that "if the actions on the part of one person upset the other, these actions are justifiable targets for change regardless of their *intended* consequences" (original italics). The implication of this stance is that the reasons for such "actions," which may be quite beyond the scope of the marital transactional influence, are to be ignored as irrelevant to the therapeutic change process, while a "piece" of the possible internal conflict manifest in the "action" is to be addressed forthrightly.

Nor do behavioral admonitions concerning the need to avoid behavior changes that involve a spouse's repertoire skill deficit, e.g., sexual dysfunction, sufficiently address this problem. The danger of creating "as if" persons (Deutsch, 1942) is clear in Jacobson's (1977b) discussion of the development of a "collaborative set" between partners in treatment: "Couples must be persuaded to *act as if* they are facing a common problem, their dysfunctional relationship" (emphasis added), and in Stuart's (1975) intervention, reminiscent of the Oregon "love days," in which he asks the couple to "*act as if* their relationship were a success for three to five weeks" (p. 248, emphasis added). While role-playing *specific* affective responses, as in the case of a preorgasmic woman's rehearsal of certain components of sexual arousal and orgasm (Lobitz and LoPiccolo, 1972), may eventually yield the response without premeditation, it appears unlikely that most couples would be able to role-play very genuinely a "successful marriage" on the mere exhortation of the therapist.

Luthman (1974) asserts that "anger is very much attached to aliveness, sexuality, and creativity. To repress it is to deaden oneself in all these areas" (page 112). Yet this is one of the overall impacts of the P/D list: Do not complain, criticize, interrupt, disagree harshly, show disinterest, and the like. "Be docile, be quiet, be still," to borrow a phrase. There is such a push in behavioral marriage therapy to quickly move the couple away from "conflictual" interaction that it would seem that behavior therapists would strongly disagree with the statement by Sonne (1973) that often therapy must aim to "rekindle the conflicts in the marriage so they may be resolved and the marriage relibidinized" (p. 7). This position is quite contrasted to behaviorists' acceptance of behavior usually lacking social impropriety as indicative of marital dysfunction. Follingstad et al. (1976), for example, found that "functional" couples engaged in less criticism, interruption and disagreement than did "dysfunctional" couples, but also offered each other less eye contact. There is no reason to assume, on the basis of their report, that these couples were dissatisfied with their relationships. There is reason, however, to wonder whether "functional" couples, as described therein, were emotionally "dead." In this context, it is very important to heed O'Leary and Turkewitz' (Chapter V) observation that "changing these problematic areas by encouraging the distressed couple to behave more like a non-distressed couple will not necessarily create a happy marriage" (page 258).

Where, then, in the behavioral approach is the "hedonistic component" which Weiss (Chapter IV) agrees must be present in marriage? Is sexuality to be the source of all intimate hedonism? To complicate the matter further, at least in principle, Dicks' (1967) observation, in discussing the outcomes of marital therapy must be noted: "If we are told they quarrel much more than before it's difficult to assess if this is an advance or a deterioration. Nor, if they no longer fight, whether they have no bones of contention or whether they have ceased caring" (p. 308). Even the establishment of unambiguous target goals, directionally tailored to the needs of a given couple, does not circumvent the issue in this kind of situation, which is posited here to be one of a conflict between levels of analysis of the change addressed, in which even the achievement of behavioral change as aimed for does not, ipso facto, assure that the relationship meaning of such change exists in a one-to-one correspondence with the observed, overt change. More concretely, following Dicks' (1967) proposed scenario, a couple who initially complain of bitter arguments at high frequency may fight rarely as therapy terminates. Such a change *may* be unequivocally positive; it also may signal that the couple has learned to avoid conflict and to deny and repress negative feelings. A trained behavioral observer (as used, for example, in the MICS) could not detect such a subtle difference. Only the expert inferential judgment of a skilled psychotherapist could discriminate such nuances.

As Raush et al. (1974) note, "*Both* avoidance and engagement provide pathways to escalation or attenuation of conflict. Engagement does offer greater prospect for growth, but may . . . place greater burdens on both the individuals and the dyad" (p. 106).

Of course, there are couples whose process is so unproductively aggressive or destructive that they need to be pinned down and focused on a specific issue or behavior. But the behavior therapy literature seems to suggest that the therapist's task is only to shift the interaction pattern. This returns the issue to the earlier discussion, that there are levels of conflict and dealing with the interaction-conflict may be only a prelude to exploration of the covert conflict against which the behavioral pattern was erected as a defense.

4. The therapist as technician

Obviously, techniques are important in couples therapy. To argue otherwise would be quite out of touch with reality. Alexander and Parsons (1975) have stated the issue succinctly: "Do you take your game plan and expertise into therapy or does your technology and game plan take you?" It is curious that while marital therapists are, by definition, treating relationships, almost nothing is mentioned in the clinical behavioral literature on marriage therapy of the *patient-therapist* relationship which, after all, is the vehicle by means of which more specific treatment techniques can be applied.

Let us leave aside from this discussion the more complex issues of learning through modeling—for example, in therapy conducted by cotherapists (which practice, by the way, most behavioral couples therapists [O'Leary and Turkewitz, Chapter V, excluded] follow without empirical evidence for its necessity). The question of what are the personal qualities of the marital therapist which facilitate a couple's engagement in the process of therapy must be considered. Although this area has received scant empirical study, it is quite likely that most, if not all, the personal therapist attributes that influence the outcome of individual psychotherapy (Gurman and Razin, 1977) are also powerful in the context of therapies that directly treat relationships. In fact, evidence is now beginning to accumulate to show the powerful effect of therapist variables on treatment outcome in behavioral marital-family therapy (Alexander,

Barton, Schiavo and Parsons, 1976; Roberts, 1975; Thomlinson, 1974). It is unfortunate that, in a zealous effort to expand the technological and technical base and powers of couples therapy, behavior therapists generally have not emphasized the importance, in the therapist's behavior, of these very same interpersonal skills the therapist teaches to his clients (cf., Wilson and Evans, 1977). O'Leary and Turkewitz (Chapter V) have taken a major and refreshing step forward by beginning to emphasize the centrality of these personal dimensions of marital therapy in a social learning context. Perhaps the major weakness in their discussion of the therapist-client relationship, however, is that they construe those relationships in dyadic (therapist-husband, therapist-wife) terms only, and fail to comment on the different nature of engagement with a *system*.

In a different context, the present author's position on this issue has been stated quite directly:

> We had begun to be concerned about what we saw in many quarters of psychotherapy as increasing trends toward the "technologizing" of treatment. While we were not concerned with the *development* of effective new treatment techniques . . . we *were* concerned about what we saw as a growing tendency, springing from this development, to consider therapy as consisting *solely* of "the applition of the right technique" for "the right patient." While it is debatable whether such a purely technological approach to psychological dysfunction is desirable, if indeed it could be developed (and we doubt that this is possible on a broad scale), we do not now in fact have any systematic technology to apply. . . . It is our feeling, therefore, that it does not seem any wiser to proceed as though applying "the right technique" is all we need to do than it does to pretend that there *are* no techniques to apply, but only "a good relationship" to be offered. Both approaches, in our view, are gross oversimplifications of what psychotherapy . . . has to offer (Gurman and Razin, 1977, p. xi).

Sluzki (Chapter VII) has stated it more pointedly: ". . . therapy, like art, is unteachable. Only repertoires of forms can be transmitted, together with a certain intellectual grounding for them" (p. 366).

Some Additional Practical Considerations

In addition to the generic intervention strategies and their attendant conceptual matters described thus far, there are several commonly occurring practical questions and clinical situations that need to be addressed in the practice of behavioral couples therapy.

(1) Operant management procedures clearly emphasize the superiority

of attempting to increase positive (desired) behavior rather than to decrease negative behavior. This is reasonable on two related grounds: (a) the use of aversive consequences in behavior control is replete with practical problems affecting its efficacy (Azrin and Holz, 1966), and (b) the use of operant interventions to decrease target behavior would no doubt return couples to the use of coercive strategies that lay at the core of their difficulties in the first place. Still, it is quite uncertain whether attempts to decelerate undesired behavior should ever (and if so, when) accompany attempts to accelerate desired behavior. The lack of clarity on this issue is demonstrated in O'Leary and Turkewitz' (Chapter V) contrasting (to Weiss') view that, in some instances, working to decrease negative behaviors is necessary. Certainly, serious acting-out behavior, such as physical assault, must be dealt with forthrightly by the therapist and will not await gradual increments in incompatible, positive behavior. In some other cases, of course, partners may be willing and able to stop negative behavior, but may reject the goal of taking steps to increase positive marital interactions. Such changes, while being far from most therapists' ultimate treatment goals, need not be dismissed as trivial.

(2) It is unclear whether the use of communication training and negotiation training are additive in their effects or whether, on the other hand, one alone may at times be sufficient. Indeed, Weiss (Chapter IV) now acknowledges that negotiation training becomes superfluous for some couples in treatment. Turkewitz and O'Leary (1976), for example, found exchange procedures superior to communication training with younger couples and the reverse with older couples. Presumably, some younger couples have not escalated the breadth of their conflict to the extent that relatively simple exchanges are met with resistance. Other studies (Cotton, 1976; McIntosh, 1975; Wieman, 1973) have found no difference between these forms of intervention, although one analog study (Venema, 1975) did demonstrate an additive effect for the two approaches in combination.

(3) Still undetermined is the matter of whether good faith contracts (Weiss et al., 1974) are more advantageous than *quid pro quo* contracts. It has been argued (Jacobson and Martin, 1976; Weiss, 1975; Weiss et al., 1974) that in relationships severely lacking in trust, the *quid pro quo* approach forebodes failure in that the "who goes first" issue is quite salient. Jacobson (1977b) found both contracting formats superior to both a non-specific control treatment and a waiting list control, but not different from each other. The immediate clinical relevance of this study is questionable, however, in that all the behavioral change indices (MICS)

were based on couples' problem-solving behavior while dealing with *hypothetical* marital problems (from an inventory) and real but *minor* problems in their own relationship. The validity and generalizability of Jacobson's findings are weakened still further by Weiss' (Chapter IV) suggestion that contracting and negotiation are "best reserved for couples whose skill levels are very low."

(4) It remains to be determined whether some classes of behavior are more salient in effective problem-solving than are others. It is also likely that certain codes are more important in problem-solving with particular marital problems than are others.

(5) Narrowly conceived behavioral interventions may run aground when the skill needed to honor a behavioral exchange is absent from the spouse's repertoire. While behavior therapists clearly state the need in such a situation to teach the deficient spouse the skill in question, there are numerous clinical situations in which "skill training" may not meet the therapeutic task—for example, the characterologically "tight," obsessive husband whose fear of his own dependency needs (Barnett, 1971) will not allow him to be non-sexually affectionate with his wife; or the stereotypically passive, "weak" wife whose husband's requests for greater self-sufficiency on her part are painfully associated with childhood experiences of parental abandonment.

Moreover, excessive clinical attempts to increase the skill repertoire of a partner whose life theme is, say, to remain in a helpless, childlike position may run the risk of buying into the marital system's offering of an identified patient and predictably enlist the "healthy" spouse as deputy therapist, thereby possibly precluding that partner's eventual involvement in the treatment process in a meaningful manner in terms of transactional problems within the relationship.

Finally, of course, a spouse's assertion that a given requested behavior is not within his/her repertoire may at times represent not the "unavailability" of the behavior but rather a fear of losing power (based on the withholding of a reinforcing behavior, a "P") in the dyad by acknowledging the presence of the requisite skill. Such maneuvers, of course, require interpretive probing by the therapist.

(6) The behavioral model may also run into difficulty in the common situation in which one spouse's request for behavior change represents totally unrealistic expectations of either the partner or of marriage in general. Such expectations may yield to one or another variant of cognitive (Beck, 1976) or rational-emotive (Ellis, 1973) therapy, a treatment approach which clearly deals with factors not directly accessible to public

observation, but one increasingly employed by behavior therapists in the practice of individual psychotherapy (for example, Mahoney, 1974) and, at times, by broad spectrum behavioral marriage therapists, such as O'Leary and Turkewitz (Chapter V). At other times, however, a more psychoanalytic approach will be indicated in order to identify the unconscious determinants of the initial marital contract (Sager et al., 1971) so steadfastly defended by the spouse.

(7) People with rigid or brittle personality structures also pose potential problems for the behavioral marriage therapist. For example, the spouse who denies that his/her partner has anything reinforcing to offer raises the issue, phenomenologically, of that spouse's fear of dependency. For not a few people, acknowledging the reinforcement potential of the partner is perceived as a blow to one's self-esteem, as: "If I need his/her behavior, I'm weak." For others, any negatively valenced innuendo is felt as an outer and complete condemnation of the whole person. This may occur even when the therapist has assiduously attempted to teach couples how to pinpoint behavior, eschew character descriptions, and avoid motivational inferences. For such people, even the most benign request for positive behavior change is heard devastatingly. Clearly, a more subtle, supportive and gradual entrée into the marital transaction is called for on the part of the therapist; O'Leary and Turkewitz' (Chapter V) statement that "it is unlikely that there are no current satisfactions," while probably "true" in most cases, does not seem to resolve the dilemma as portrayed here.

(8) Perhaps the most difficult realm of common marital problems arises for the behavioral model when there is a questionable degree of commitment to the marital relationship (Tsoi-Hoshmand, 1975). "Cooperative problem-solving" is an ideal which can usually be hoped for as an outcome of treatment but not routinely expected or easily inculcated as an early step in treatment. Behavioral exchanges require that partners consider the partnership above absolute individual gain (Kimmel and Havens, 1966). Couples need to accept the "give to get" (Rappaport and Harrell, 1972, p. 203) philosophy as the basic ground rule of their relationship. Often, the adoption of such an attitude may itself be sufficient to produce remarkable changes in a conflicted marriage. Many married people can be expected to so severely question their partners' commitment to the relationship that *they* will be unwilling to negotiate for change: "You show me 'good faith' by making some changes on your own, *then* I'll expose myself."

Two special problems are subsumed under this issue. The first involves

the couple either leaning toward or in the process of divorce. Since negotiated behavior changes may well imply a permanent commitment to
the marital relationship, other approaches may be needed. A likely behavioral response to this problem, that the couple "try out" a relationship based on mutual positive reinforcement, would often be naive and
almost as a rule insensitive to the felt needs and consumer demands of
such a couple. Moreover, obviously severe limitations would be placed
on behavioral approaches during separations and other strategies may
be needed (for example, Toomin, 1972). In addition, no behavior therapist has yet addressed the issues of grief, loss and anger inherent in the
dissolution process.

Finally, adherence to a strict social learning modular approach would
seem to preclude the discovery of the routine "hidden agendas" with
which so many couples enter treatment, as, for example, one partner
seeking "expert" confirmation of the acceptability and appropriateness
of divorce. Obviously, couples do not always enter marital therapy because of their initially presented reasons. O'Leary and Turkewitz' contribution to this volume (Chapter V), unlike most other published behavioral accounts, seems to reflect awareness of this.

Particular Advantages and Strengths of the Behavioral Approach

(1) The behavioral approach offers a viable alternative to the circular
and non-productive "mind-reading" engaged in by many couples. In its
emphasis on explicit clarification of each partner's expectations of the
other partner and of the marriage, it works against useless personality
labeling and trait attribution. In this way, "objectification" (Weiss, Chapter IV), among other strategies, may serve as a useful means by which
the "rules" of which communicationists speak can be made explicit and
changed. In like fashion, such pinpointing may offer a concrete strategy
to aid in the differentiation of self (Bowen, 1976a, 1976b, 1976c). But
note that a partner's inference of his/her mate's feelings or motivations
is not necessarily of this order; when such inferences are in the service
of defensiveness or attack, they are best avoided, but such inferential
behavior may also offer the basis for genuine empathy.

(2) The highly focused nature of behavioral marriage therapy offers
two particular clinical advantages over both the systems and psychoanalytic approaches. First, it dramatically highlights the equal responsibility of marriage partners for the future and quality of their relationship, and, in this way, explicitly works against spouses' mutual blaming
tendencies. Of course, psychoanalytic and systems approaches similarly

highlight the mutuality of marital discord. Secondly, such a focused approach facilitates the identification of major thematic difficulties in the relationship so that dimensions of the marriage that are not problematic need not receive unnecessary attention. Psychodynamic and systems approaches are also concerned with thematic issues, but at a different level of experience. In this way, a behavioral style of initial assessment may have a great deal to offer in the elucidation of a central issue (Mann, 1973) or "sector" (Deutsch, 1949) of the relationship around which treatment interventions may be usefully planned. The potential for combining a behavioral approach to assessment (though not necessarily requiring the use of all the usual behavioral assessment methods and components) with a broadly conceived psychoanalytically oriented intervention format, especially in brief marital psychotherapy (see The Psychoanalytic Perspective, above), has yet to be explored in depth, but seems worthy of clinical experimentation.

(3) While behavior therapists have not described (and might be unwilling to acknowledge the appropriateness of) the use of their assessment procedures for this purpose, these procedures have tremendous practical utility in diagnosing sources and areas of resistance to change. Behavioral assessment, as described by O'Leary and Turkewitz (Chapter V) and Weiss (1975; Weiss, Chapter IV; Weiss et al., 1973; Weiss and Margolin, 1977), allows relatively immediate determination of marital partners' ability and willingness to acknowledge their mutual impact and of each partner's ability and willingness to admit (even in the face of hostility and disappointment) to the sources of pleasure and satisfaction supplied by the other. At a meta-level, much valuable information can be readily obtained simply by noting the responses of partners, both during therapy sessions and outside the sessions, to even the most rudimentary of homework assignments. For example, it is not uncommon in the present author's experience that the spouse who is most often labeled as resistant, either by referring mental health professionals or the mate, emerges as the partner most willing to engage in active change-related assignments.

(4) Behavioral approaches, because of their highly instructive, educational tone, are likely to be met with greater cooperation than, say, psychoanalytically oriented methods, from couples who are not psychologically sophisticated or insight-oriented. Thus, the possession of behavioral intervention skills greatly increases the range of potential patients with whom the marriage therapist can work productively.

(5) The behavioral approach, not unlike some systems-based ap-

proaches (as for example, Minuchin, 1974; Watzlawick et al., 1974), provides a reminder of the responsibility of the therapist to produce positive treatment outcomes. Such an implicit message need not underestimate the contribution of patients to the efficacy of marital therapy. While one may, as has been done in this chapter, raise certain issues about the choice of variables deemed most important by behavioral marriage therapists, it is absolutely clear that neither psychoanalytic nor systems advocates have even begun to approach the level of effort expended by behaviorists in assessing their therapeutic outcomes and attempting to validate empirically their central theoretical propositions (but compare: Gurman and Kniskern, 1978c; Jacobson, Chapter VIII). As in other areas of behavior therapy practice, *the behaviorists' metamessage of the importance of assessing what constitute useful versus irrelevant treatment components and of attempting to define and refine specific treatments for specific problems offers an attitudinal model for integrating practice and research that, with few exceptions (for example, Minuchin et al., 1975; Stanton and Todd, 1976) the systems and psychoanalytic approaches have largely ignored and to which they might well aspire.*

THE SYSTEMS THEORY PERSPECTIVE

The systems theory approach to marriage and the family chronologically represents a middle (between psychoanalytic and behavioral) model of human interaction, its vicissitudes and its treatment. While the broad conceptual groundwork of General System Theory has existed for decades in such fields as biology and engineering, and has been applied frequently in psychiatry and psychology (for example, Allport, 1961; Grinker, 1967; Menninger, Mayman and Pruyser, 1963), its influence on models of human behavior dysfunction is relatively recent. Moreover, while such notable figures as Bowen, Bateson, Jackson and Haley began to "think systems" in the 1950s in their research on schizophrenia, the systems framework for the treatment of marital and family relationships, as Guerin (1976) points out, was clearly a minority point of view as recently as 1970. Indeed, the death in 1971 of Nathan Ackerman, the major psychoanalytic proponent in the family therapy movement, may have hastened significantly the emergence of systems thinking. The rise of General System Theory (Bertalanffy, 1962, 1966, 1973; Berrien, 1968; Buckley, 1967; Miller, 1965a, 1965b) and its relevance to psychiatry and psychology in particular has been chronicled elsewhere (Bertalanffy, 1966; Gray and Rizzo, 1969). The present consideration of systems theory will be restricted to its application to the understanding of marital inter-action and the treatment of marital disorders.

Indeed, it is quite inaccurate to refer to "the" systems theory perspective as at the beginning of the last paragraph. First, such a label usually is meant to imply the application of *general* systems theory to marriage and the family. While it is undoubtedly true that some broad principles of general systems theory have been significantly incorporated into marital-family therapy, as a reading of Steinglass (Chapter VI) shows, it would be inaccurate and misleading to assert that "systems" therapies are based entirely or even nearly so on general systems theory, as shall be seen shortly. The reality of the situation is that there have evolved a number of *family* systems *theories*, with a wide range of adherence to and deviation from the language and logic of *general* systems theory. In point of fact, it is absolutely essential to distinguish between general systems theory and family systems theories since several influential family systems theories have emerged in the last few years, notably the strategic therapy of Haley (1963b, 1976) and Milton Erickson (Haley, 1973), the communications-oriented therapy of the Palo Alto group (Watzlawick, 1976a, 1976b; Watzlawick, Beavin and Jackson, 1967; Watzlawick, Weakland and Fisch, 1974; Weakland, 1976; Weakland, Fisch, Watzlawick and Bodin, 1974), the Structural Family Therapy of Minuchin (Camp, 1973; Liebman, Minuchin, Baker and Rosman, 1976; Minuchin, 1974; Minuchin, Baker, Rosman, Liebman, Milman and Todd, 1975), the eclectic communications therapy of Satir (Luthman, 1974; Satir, 1967, 1972; Satir, Stachowiak and Taschman, 1975), and the Family Systems Theory of Bowen (Bowen, 1961, 1966, 1976a, 1976c), now formally referred to as Bowen Theory (Bowen, 1976b).

Part of this terminological confusion is highlighted by Bowen (1976b):

> On a broad level, people believe that "system" is derived from general systems theory, which is a *system of thinking about existing knowledge* (p. 56, emphasis added). . . . Family systems theory has been confused with general systems theory, which has a much broader frame of reference and *no specific application to emotional functioning*. It is very difficult to apply general systems concepts to emotional functioning except in a broad, general way (p. 62, emphasis added).

As noted at the beginning of this chapter, marital therapy adopted much of family theory long after the establishment of marital therapy as an area of systems-oriented interventions. Indeed, while several important papers from the systems perspective have specifically dealt with the treatment of marital discord (for example, Haley, 1962a), the majority have focused on two- (or more) generational family systems. This is not surprising since so much of the early research on family systems centered on the pathogenesis of schizophrenia and since, in any systems view, the marital dyad is seen as a sub-system of the family, as Steinglass points out (Chapter VI). Indeed, systems perspectives on marriage and marital therapy are better thought of as perspectives on the marital dyad subsystem of the marital partners' families of origin. Perhaps for this reason, and in sharp contrast with both the psychoanalytic and behavioral approaches, it is impossible to identify (if, indeed, it is even possible to conceptualize) any major free-standing "school" of *marital* therapy that is in any way allegiant to general systems concepts.

The format of this section of this chapter will deviate somewhat from those of the previous discussions of the psychoanalytic and behavioral approaches to marriage and marital therapy. While all the major systems approaches noted earlier (Strategic Therapy, the Palo Alto model, Structural Family Therapy, Bowen Theory, and the work of Satir) obviously have commonalities in principle (see Steinglass' review, Chapter VI), in practice they are at times quite divergent, if not at odds with one another. So, while this chapter is oriented toward a comparative analysis of the psychoanalytic, systems and behavioral perspectives, it seems necessary here to move laterally and examine two of these major systems approaches. Satir's approach (Satir, 1967, 1972; Satir et al., 1975) will not be discussed because, in this writer's view, her work represents an eclectic mélange of communications principles, Gestalt therapy, bioenergetics, object-relations theory, rational-emotive and behavioral therapy, and client-centered therapy (Gurman, 1977). The influential and extremely significant contributions of Minuchin (1974) also will not be discussed here since the Philadelphia Guild Guidance Clinic group has not yet published reports of its work with couples, perhaps because its triadic and nearly exclusively two-generational clinical emphasis and the clinical populations with whom it has been most successfully used (anorexic and asthmatic children and adolescents— Liebman et al., 1976; Minuchin et al., 1975—and drug addicts—Stanton and Todd, 1976) have not yet been systematically applied to the treatment of the marital subsystem in isolation. For an excellent comparative paradigmatic study of Structural Family Therapy and the communications approach of the Palo Alto group, the reader is referred to the recent work of Ritterman (1977). In addition, Steinglass (Chapter VI) considers the Structural approach to the marital subsystem of the family.

Thus, this section will focus on Bowen theory and the communications perspective, including the contributions of Haley (1962a, 1963b, 1976). While the communications approach and the strategic approach are not identical or interchangeable, they share a great deal in practice and are certainly complementary.

Bowen Theory

This consideration of Bowen theory will not include Bowen's influential work with multiple family groups (1976a), but will focus only on the marital dyad. Such a focus is quite consistent with Bowen's (1976c) position that:

> Theoretically, a family system can be changed if any triangle in the family is changed, and if that triangle can stay in meaningful emotional contact with the others. Practically, *the two spouses are usually the only ones who are important enough to the rest of the family and who have the motivation and dedication for this kind of an effort* (p. 392, emphasis added).

Moreover, this discussion of Bowen theory will not be as extensive as the discussions of the other approaches to couples therapy examined in this chapter. Although Bowen's work has exerted a significant influence on family therapy, especially along the East coast, Bowen theory is not as frequently taught in training centers as are the other approaches discussed in this chapter and volume; in fact, it appears to have remained somewhat in the wings of the national and international therapeutic stage. Still, Bowen theory seems to be gaining adherents rapidly (Foley, 1974). It is important that this contribution be dealt with here both to illustrate the divergence of treatment models generally subsumed under systems theory and, in keeping with Steinglass' (Chapter VI) analysis, to demonstrate that in addition to the system-maintaining and stabilization possibilities of systems-derived therapies, such as the Palo Alto group, there have also been attempts to apply systems thinking to the mechanisms of marital and family growth and development.

Marital choice, satisfaction and conflict

The central construct of Bowen's theory is that of *differentiation of self* or its opposite, *fusion*. With this notion Bowen implicates the functioning and experience both of individuals and of relationships. In the individual domain, differentiation refers to the ability of a person to distinguish between the *feeling* process and the *intellectual* process (Bowen, 1976b), or between intuitive and rational processes. In the relationship domain, fusion or lack of differentiation is reflected in a family's *emotional stuck-togetherness* (Bowen, 1976a), or undifferentiated family-ego mass (Bowen, 1966). Bowen (1976b) argues that an individual's level of differentiation is largely determined by the time he/she leaves his/her family of origin. He notes, "two spouses begin a marriage with life-style patterns and levels of differentiation developed in their families of origin" (Bowen, 1976b, p. 79). Moreover, such pairings do not arise accidentally since each individual tends to repeat in all future relationships the style of relating learned in the parental family. Thus, poorly differentiated individuals "seek other equally dependent relationships in which they can borrow enough strength to function" (Bowen, 1976b, p. 70).

What often creates problems, however, in such a mate choice is that people tend to choose spouses who have the same levels of differentiation. This assumption is reminiscent of, if not identical to, Meissner's (Chapter II) comment that clinical couples, as well, perhaps, as others, "tend to choose partners who have achieved an equivalent level of immaturity, but who have adopted opposite patterns of defensive organization" (p. 43). It is also similar to Skynner's (1976, p. 13) observation noted earlier that "couples are usually attracted by shared developmental failures." Thus, for Bowenites, individuals (a) tend to seek out partners who repeat early familial experience and experience-of-self; (b) are attracted by potential mates who function at the same level of psychological development but manifest complementary overt behavior styles; and (c) expect their mates to make up for their own developmental failures. While Bowen asserts that he has largely deleted psychoanalytic thinking from his theory in going "from couch to coach" (Bowen, 1970), it appears that he has merely moved the couch from the horizontal to the vertical plane!

Conflict in marriage, then, arises when both individuals are poorly (internally) differentiated and the attendant fusion results in anxiety for one or both spouses: "People with most fusion have most of the human problems, and those with the most differentiation, the fewest" (Bowen, 1976b, p. 66). Conflict can also appear when one individual is sufficiently stressed and "tension" develops in that individual or in the marital dyad, resulting in symptoms or dysfunction. In addition, the complementarity of psychological-emotional functioning, described by Bowen (1966) as the "overfunctioning" and "underfunctioning" of the spouses, is implicit in his notion of one spouse being "dominant" and one "adaptive" (Bowen, 1976b, p. 79). Because of the partners' respective overt behavioral styles and the mechanisms each partner has learned in order to deal with interpersonal anxiety, the "dominant" spouse becomes what Aldous (1973) refers to as the "caretaker" of the "ill" partner. But since, as Bowen states, people pick spouses who have the same levels of differentiation, then it is clear that which spouse becomes symptomatic is relatively arbitrary and moot and that the emergence of marriage-related symptomatology in one spouse must be as the result of an implicit agreement between the spouses at an unconscious level.

A re-examination of the earlier discussion of these issues in the section of this chapter on the psychoanalytic perspective makes it clear that in Bowen theory the necessary and sufficient conditions for conflict in marriage and the process of symptomatic emergence in one spouse are indistinguishable from those postulated by object-relations writers (such as Dicks, 1967; Meissner, Chapter II; Skynner, 1976). Mouton Rothschild is Mouton Rothschild whether served in a cut crystal carafe or in a paper cup! It seems likely that Bowen's assertion (1976b, p. 54) that he has developed "a completely different (from psychoanalytic) theory about emotional illness" is exaggerated, since there is a great deal of overlap with other theories. Relabeling of existing constructs is not uncommon in the development of new "schools" of psychotherapy. Still, it would seem that alternative strategies for modifying and contemporizing psychoanalytic thought in clinical practice (such as Feather and Rhoads, 1972; Wachtel, 1977), some of which are considered in the section of this chapter on the psychoanalytic perspective, hold out greater promise.

The question arises, then, is Bowen theory a "systems" theory? Bowen writes (1976b, p. 62) that "At the time my theory was developed I knew nothing about general systems theory," yet the choice of the concept of differentiation was explicitly based (Bowen, 1976b, p. 58) on his attempt to use "biological concepts to describe human behavior" because it has "specific meaning in the biological sciences." Bowen may have "known" nothing of general systems theory, but, in contrast to his assertion that general systems theory has "no specific application to emotional functioning" (Bowen, 1976b, p. 62), he clearly writes in terms consistent with the most fundamental characteristic of general systems theory that there is a set of principles which can guide our thinking about *all* systems, whether living or mechanical. If, then, Bowen's ideas about the nature of marriage and marital conflict are, while not identical to, still consistent with both general systems theory (a positive conclusion that would be endorsed by Steinglass, Chapter VI), and, as has been argued, with psychoanalytic theory, then might there not be a potential rapprochement between general systems theory and psychoanalytic theory? Indeed, such a synthesis seems clinically viable (Gurman and Knudson, 1978). While Bowen theory is seen to be largely an ego-psychological one in which the central concept of fusion is offered as descriptive of individual functioning and in which the system is viewed as a collection of individuals (Klugman, 1975a, 1975b), this individualizing perspective hardly requires what often appears to be an arbitrary and artificial splitting of intrapsychic and interpersonal functioning, as discussed in the section on the psychoanalytic perspective.

The process and techniques of conjoint
treatment: Themes, assumptions and issues

It follows from the above that the goal of therapy for Bowen is to work toward each marital partner's increasing differentiation of self, both intra-individually and from one's family of origin. This process involves a "de-triangling" of the basic "molecule of any emotional system" (Bowen, 1976a, p. 233), the triangle, a three-person system. The concept of triangles "provides a way of reading the automatic emotional responsiveness so as to control one's own automatic emotional participation in the emotional process" (Bowen, 1976b, p. 53). The concept of triangulation is similar to Minuchin's (1974) focus on the interplay between the parental and sibling subsystems, as well as to the notion of collusion in the seminal work of Framo (1970). It involves the bringing into the emotional process of the marital dyad a third person who is scapegoated and thus serves as a buffer between the spouses and also functions as an available external object for the realignment of the fusion between husband and wife.

While this notion was developed by Bowen in his observations of the interaction patterns of families with a schizophrenic member, it applies as well to nonpsychotic families and to married couples who are childless. As Klugman (1975a) notes, "Each fused communication involves a triangulation, a bringing in of a third person or object who acts as mediator or deflector in the relationship" (p. 3, emphasis added). Thus, childless couples may invoke religious beliefs, science, or other supposed sacred cows or external standards ("A woman is not supposed to be assertive"; "It's not a man's job to diaper the kids"; "A spouse should never be critical of his/her mate") as the third point in the triangle and, thereby, avoid taking "I position stands" (Bowen, 1976c, p. 398), for to do so would begin to break up the couple's problematic fusion. In effect, achieving the "I position" is a direct antidote to collusion or mutual projective identification (Dicks, 1967; Lloyd and Paulson, 1972; Stewart et al., 1975), as discussed in the preceding section of this chapter. As Bowen (1976a, p. 251) states, "If any member can control his (collusive) emotional response, it interrupts the chain reaction" (parenthesis added). In object-relations terms, each member of the marital dyad will attempt to use the therapist as a transitional object upon whom to project his own conflicts and will try to draw the therapist into the (unconsciously) expected role of significant figures familiar to the patient, that is, she/he will work to elicit the "appropriate" countertransference reaction of the therapist.

To this end of increasing differentiation, four essential intervention strategies are used (Bowen, 1976c). The first is *defining and clarifying the relationship between the spouses,* corresponding roughly to the assessment stage of therapy. It is characterized by isolating and defining "the more prominent *stimulus-response* mechanisms (contingencies?) and to teach the spouses to be *observers"* (Bowen, 1976a, p. 262, parenthesis and emphasis added). Doing so gives the couple "some (stimulus?) control, the act of observing confers still more control" (Bowen, 1976a, p. 262). A second objective of the early part of therapy is for partners to talk directly to the therapist "in the calmest, low keyed, most objective possible way" so that each spouse is able "to listen and to 'really hear,' without reacting emotionally, for the first time in their lives together" (Bowen, 1976c, p. 394). *The similarity between this phase of Bowen therapy and the early treatment modules of "objectification" or pinpointing and the "support-understanding" relationship accomplishments of behavior therapists* (Weiss, Chapter IV; O'Leary and Turkewitz, Chapter V) *is astounding, given the almost orthogonal stated premises about marriage and marital conflict adhered to by these respective treatment approaches.* For example, Bowen's (1976c, p. 396) statement that "Often the careful definition of the (emotionally fusing) mechanism is enough to defuse it" (parenthesis added) seems to be touching on precisely the same observation made by Weiss (Chapter IV) that formal negotiation and contracting are often unnecessary and that a good deal can be accomplished in behavioral marriage therapy by progressing through the first three stages of treatment—objectification, support-understanding, and problem-solving. What behavior therapists at times tend to denigrate in terms of intuitive clinical artistry, however, does not seem to be of the same order of loss engendered in a Bowenite therapist's lack of empirically tested and specific assessment devices and protocols and his/her less direct and systematic training of basic communication skills.

The second therapist function, that of *keeping self de-triangled from the family emotional system* is, as noted, essential. The therapist's effort is to deflect any attempt by either spouse to triangulate him into their dysfunctional process by not being manipulated into taking sides with either partner. Bowen argues emphatically (1976a, p. 258, parentheses added):

> If the therapist can remain operationally outside the emotional system between the parents (*read*: spouses) while actively relating to each, the (parents) begin differentiating selfs from each other. . . . Conflict between two people will resolve automatically if both remain in emotional contact with a third person who can relate actively to both without taking sides with either.

The emphasis here on the therapist's active role is remarkably similar to the role described in the first section of this chapter as an essential element in all forms of brief, psychoanalytically oriented marital therapy. Moreover, the therapist's emotional nonparticipation also seems to be geared toward a de-emphasis of the patient-therapist transference and, as noted earlier, toward an intentional interruption of the couple's manifest collusive behavioral patterns. It will be recalled, however, that in the section on the psychoanalytic perspective, it was argued that the therapist's side-taking function is not necessarily destructive, but can, in fact, be quite facilitative of change.

Bowen's third strategic element involves *teaching about the functioning of emotional systems.* Unlike some other systems therapies (such as Minuchin, 1974; Watzlawick et al., 1974), wherein direct explication of the salient parameters of interpersonal relating and change is strategically viewed as inappropriate, Bowen is at times "quite didactic" (Bowen, 1976c, p. 398) and may communicate "important principles of systems theory" (Bowen, 1976a, p. 265). Bowen (1976c, p. 398) is quite explicit on this issue: "Some teaching or instruction is necessary with any kind of psychotherapy." In this way, Bowen deviates from orthodox psychoanalytic principles, but is philosophically in concert with the behaviorists.

The final core component of the therapist's function requires *taking "I position" stands,* which involves the therapist's clearly defining himself in relation to the marital partners. It is assumed that doing so forces the spouses to relate to each other in like fashion. Although it is not stated as such, it is reasonable to assume that when this outcome follows, a process of modeling, as well as one of identification with the therapist, constitutes an important part of the active mechanism. This treatment component, while undoubtedly significant in couples therapy, can, of course, be supported and understood from an existential, object-relations, client-centered, or behavioral viewpoint.

Some additional practical considerations

Bowen has always been associated in the family field with early research on the process of multigenerational transmission of psychopathology and his self-view as an empiricist is clear. He has written that he chooses "to use only concepts that would be consistent with recognized science" (Bowen, 1976a, p. 58), such as biology. This statement suggests that his therapeutic work is based on scientific evidence, which, by inference, suggests that the concepts and treatments are empirically validated. However, he has reported no empirical data relevant to these constructs. Bowen (1976b, p. 62) asserts that his systems theory "is a specific theory about the functional *facts* of emotional functioning" (emphasis added). Among such "facts" are: differentiation of self discriminates between psychologically dysfunctional and functional individuals and relationships; one must increase differentiation for therapy to be successful; there exists empirical evidence of therapy conducted according to Bowen theory; and various levels of differentiation of self can be accurately assessed and meaningfully measured. Indeed, there is no acceptable conclusive research evidence to support the first three of these "facts." Data relevant to the fourth "fact" follow.

Bowen (1976a) offers a detailed description of persons functioning at various levels of differentiation of self. The Differentiation of Self Scale is a semantic differential type, ranging from 0 ("ego fusion") to 100 ("differentiation of self") and it is "comparable to a scale of emotional maturity except that this theory does not use the concept of maturity or immaturity" (Bowen, 1976a, p. 235). Like maturity, however, differentiation of self cannot involve only a single dimension. Any significant and complex psychological process, state, or trait is inherently multidimensional. There exists no evidence to support Bowen's notion (1976b, p. 61) that "all human problems exist in a *single continuum*" (emphasis added). Moreover, Bowen (1976a) offers no supporting empirical evidence for his elaborate descriptions of the functioning of individuals at various levels of differentiation, nor any data in support of its reliability or validity. Indeed, Bowen notes (1976a, p. 235) that, "At the highest point on the scale is a postulated level of complete differentiation of perfect self, which man has not yet achieved," that is, levels of 75 to 100 are "more hypothetical than real" (Bowen, 1976b, p. 73). The noted American reinforcement theorist Robert Thorndike once said, "If something exists, it exists in some amount, and can be measured." But if a "level" of 75 to 100 does not exist, it obviously cannot be measured. Then why offer a "scale" to measure something that cannot be measured, since it does not exist? Such questions and issues have been clearly anticipated: A level of 75 to 100 "conveys an erroneous impression of the human phenomenon to concretistic thinkers who are searching for another instrument to measure human functioning" (Bowen, 1976b, p. 73). Moreover, "Once it is possible to see the phenomenon, there it is, operating in full view, right in front of our eyes. Once it is possible to see the phenomenon, it is then possible to apply the concept to hundreds of different human situations. To try to apply it without knowing it is an exercise in futility" (p. 73).* Reification of hypothetical constructs abounds in Bowen theory: ". . . the way *the* undifferentiation is distributed to children. *It* focuses first on one child. If the *amount* is too great . . . etc., etc." (Bowen, 1976b, p. 82, emphasis added). Bowen again implies a quantifiable dimension, but with no adequate definition or validation of his construct. While clearly all valuable knowledge is not empirical, it is inappropriate to propose an interval scale for an as yet non-quantifiable, vaguely defined concept and to encourage its use when it has yet to achieve even the status of an experimental evaluation tool. Psychoanalysts have for decades offered constructs lacking empirical validity and hypotheses which cannot be disconfirmed. Those are sufficient scientific deficiencies to warrant the plethora of criticisms levied against psychoanalytic theory and therapy. Bowen's theory is similar in presenting untestable hypotheses, and arguing that one cannot "apply it without knowing it" takes his theory out of the realm of scientific inquiry. Arguments about "concretistic thinkers" thus become superflous and misleading.

Exaggerated and empirically unsubstantiated claims of efficacy and of superiority to alternative treatments (e.g., "Results of this calm, intellectual, conceptual approach with families have been much more success-

---

* Perhaps I am one of the concretistic thinkers to whom Bowen refers, but I fail to comprehend the applied *or* conceptual usefulness of a "scale" that measures an implied substance ("it") which one is potentially able to "see." Bowen's argument is reminiscent of the not uncommon argument of psychoanalytic therapists that only *they* can truly evaluate outcome.

ful than emphasizing the 'therapeutic' expression of feeling" [Bowen, 1976c, p. 395]) are hopefully unimpressive to today's sophisticated psychotherapist.

Particular advantages and strengths of Bowen theory

As has been seen, one of the most influential systems theory approaches to the understanding and treatment of marital disorders merges perceptibly into object-relations theory. While an expected response to this position would argue that the above analysis is merely playing with words in the above consideration of Bowen theory and simply translating from one language to another, such a rebuttal would seem weak in the light of the striking similarities both of conceptualization and of clinical intervention documented. While a critical eye needs to be cast toward certain of Bowen's postulates and procedures, such as the Differentiation of Self Scale, Bowen also offers much that is of widespread usefulness on tactical clinical grounds. In addition to the parallels between Bowen thinking and treatment and that of psychoanalysts such as Meissner (Chapter II) and Nadelson (Chapter III), there is significant technical overlap with contemporary behavioral marriage therapy. While Bowen might take umbrage at the idea, *Bowen theory may be the only currently existing approach to marital therapy that has the potential, in some modified form, of simultaneously (a) operating out of a developmental framework, (b) paying explicit attention (though in different words) to the rules and meta-rules of intimate relationships, and (c) implementing therapeutic change strategies that are rather readily teachable, which center on current observable transactions, and which include a significant didactic-educational component.* Stated otherwise, *Bowen therapy seems to offer a treatment capable of using some of the best of what psychoanalytic, communications and behavioral therapies have to offer.* Finally, unlike the Palo Alto communications-oriented therapy and Haley's strategic therapy, to be discussed next, Bowen theory offers a treatment model that is explicitly evolutionary and oriented toward growth and development in intimate relationships.

Communication Theories

This section will consider communications theories, a systems model of marital interaction and therapy more directly tied to and derived from general systems theory. As Broderick (1971, p. 12) has pointed out, communication theory is not equivalent to general systems theory, but "articulates with general system theory, borrowing many concepts and constructs from it." Steinglass (Chapter VI) seems to echo this view. It should be noted that there is certainly no one communication model of human behavior. But of the various models put forth (such as Grinder and Bandler, 1976; Ruesch, 1969; Scheflen, 1969), the paradigms emerging from the Mental Research Institute of Palo Alto (e.g., Haley, 1963a, 1963b, 1976; Jackson, 1965, 1967; Sluzki, 1975; Sluzki, Chapter VII; Watzlawick, 1976b; Watzlawick et al., 1967, 1974; Weakland, 1976; Weakland, et al., 1974) have undoubtedly had the greatest impact on mental health professionals' conceptualization of psychopathology and psychotherapy. Indeed, the communication training emphasis in behavioral marriage therapy (Weiss, Chapter IV; O'Leary and Turkewitz, Chapter V) and in other approaches (such as Nadelson, Chapter III), as well as the rapidly proliferating use of communication training for purposes of marital enrichment (Gurman and Kniskern, 1977), traces a significant part of its lineage directly to these models. While there are detectable differences between the intervention strategies of Haley, on the one hand, and Jackson, Weakland, Watzlawick et al., on the other, they are considered together here because of their common heritage and essential parallels and similarities.

Specific constructs emanating from general systems theory or communication theories will not be considered in detail here. To do so would require an analogous analysis of key concepts in psychoanalytic thinking (such as repression, denial, the structure and economics of the unconscious, introjection, and others) and behavioral thinking (for example, reinforcement, functional analysis of behavior, stimulus generalization, and so on) that is well beyond the scope of this chapter and which is dealt with rather comprehensively in other chapters in this volume, as well as elsewhere. Rather, concepts used in general systems theory (such as circular causality, equifinality, entropy, homeo- and heterostasis, positive and negative feedback, and the like) and those deriving from family systems theory (for example, rules and myths, coalitions and alliances, double-bind, paradoxical communication, first- and second-order change) will be used and referred to with the assumption of the reader's familiarity with them.

Marital choice, satisfaction and conflict

In contrast to other systems views of marriage, such as that of Bowen discussed earlier, family communication theorists have been mute on the issue of marital choice. Presumably, individuals chose partners whose styles of interaction are familiar to them on the basis of past interpersonal experience, in such a way as to maintain felt phenomenological equilibrium and a view of self-in-relation-to-others that is consistent across time and relationships. Conversely, relationship stimuli which threaten to disrupt the individual's "steady" state view of self as experienced in interaction presumably will be counteracted through negative feedback processes, as yet unspecified in the evaluation of choosing a marital partner.

Since communicationists have yet to be heard on the question of marital choice, it is difficult and perhaps even inappropriate here to speculate on this issue beyond the admittedly broad stroke just painted. In any case, it is quite clear that communication purists would certainly disavow the possible relevance of unconscious need fulfillment, repetition of childhood experience, and the like. Some of the postulates offered by cognitive behaviorists, on the other hand, might be more easily accommodated by the communicationists, such as reciprocity of reinforcement, social bargaining and exchange, and so forth, although these notions would probably be dealt with metaphorically rather than concretistically.

Also consistent with a social learning view would be the communicationist's agreement that marital conflict does not follow from existing psychopathology in people who marry one another, but that such conflict is produced as a *result* of their interactions. The exclusionary (of intrapsychic determinants) position that interaction is the cause of marital conflict is central to communications models. *For communicationists, like behaviorists, the genesis of a system or of a conflict is simply not as important as the current organization of the interaction.* For Haley, the central issue is that of working out overt shared agreements about previously covert and undiscussed matters (Haley, 1963a). But such agreements are often not arrived at overtly and rationally, as in the behavioral treatment approach. Indeed such "rules" (Ford and Herrick, 1974; Haley, 1963a), while including the issue of which rules to follow, are not centered primarily on behaviors to be exchanged or changed, but on the matter of who is to make the rules.

Marriage, as a process of defining relationships, is seen as largely a process of the struggle for power and control, and conflict reflects these same dimensions. Conflict is not inherent in the attempt to define a relationship, but is made likely by the fact that conflicted couples communicate at multiple levels simultaneously (Haley, 1963a), on what are called the report and command levels (Watzlawick, et al., 1967). When such paradoxical communication occurs, spouses often cannot resolve their conflicts on their own because change always requires progress to the next higher level of Logical Types (Watzlawick et al., 1974) and interpersonal systems typically do not have rules that allow the changing of their own rules. To do so would require one or both spouses to meta-communicate, thereby stepping outside the communicational constraints of their ongoing interactional process (system); doing so is militated against by built-in homeostatic or deviation-counteracting mutual cause processes.

This view of the nature of communicational conflict is certainly a reasonable one which may be complemented by other theoretical positions, though perhaps not in ways that would be acceptable to communication purists. Klugman (1975a), in a brilliant unpublished paper, argues that there are important similarities between the Bowenian and communicationist views of conflicted interaction. His central argument is that fused people, in Bowen's terms, equal paradoxical communicators: "Symptomatic behavior may be viewed as a system of communications, one designed to support the delusion of fusion" (p. 4). Amplifying this analysis, Klugman (1975a, p. 5) writes that:

> Contradictions between different levels of communication, that is, paradox, allow for a feeling of closeness through talking, without the danger of really defining an "I position," and without fear of the contradiction being pointed out, since its communication on separate levels also carries the message that this discrepancy may not be discussed. Paradoxical communication has, as its goal, avoidance of open expression of ambivalence. To point to a defense mechanism is to point, implicitly, to what it is defending. Thus, paradox carries the prohibition against its own discovery.

Klugman's analysis clearly goes a most useful step beyond conventional discussions of communicational conflict in that it points to the *purposiveness* of such styles of relating. This purpose is revealed to be one of protecting (defending) the individual from the anxiety attendant upon differentiation of self. Klugman argues further that the "communication style of a person . . . reflects his level of fusion . . . fusion implies avoiding 'I positions' which implies unclear, paradoxical or contradictory communication and vice-versa" (1975a, p. 6). Writing from an object relations framework, Dicks (1967, p. 121) goes a step further in explicating the implication of Klugman's view: "What object-relations theory would call unconscious collusion is described by Haley in phenomenological and behavioral terms." Dicks (1967) adds that "the sources of the paradoxical, confusing messages and signals (are) in the splits between the conflicting but shared ego system" (p. 122).

Raush (Raush et al., 1974) elaborates how object relations schemata, that is, a structure for organizing experience and giving meaning to events, can bridge communication and conflict theories. Raush argues that the images one holds of one's self and of others, together with the needs and affects characterizing the relationships between the images, set constraints upon the ways in which interpersonal messages will be received (perceived). Thus, a poorly differentiated (in Bowen's sense) individual with, by definition, rigid and narrow perceptual capacities, is restricted in the variety of available decoding channels for processing information. This restriction *within an individual* has an important implication for communication theory in that "the restriction in variety of any part of the system limits the system as a whole . . . a reduction in the variety (of the system or its subsystems) . . . will limit the ability of the system to adapt to new circumstances" (Raush et al., 1974, p. 25). Rigid object relations schemata make it likely that such individuals will see their spouses in terms of past relationships instead of as "real contemporary people" (Raush et al., 1974, p. 46).

In considering the analyses of Dicks (1967) and Raush (Raush et al., 1974), it may be posited, in agreement with Klugman (1975a), that *the mechanism of collusion requires paradoxical communication for its maintenance and, at the same time, produces paradoxical communication.* As Raush et al. (1974) note, "A collusive joint pattern of avoidance seems particularly likely to foreclose the possibility of shift to a metacommunicative level" (p. 80). Thus, communication theory, Bowen theory, and object relations theory address the same underlying phenomenon in different ways. The present author is in agreement with Klugman's assertion that this same phenomenon is translated through different levels, that is, communicationists conceptualize interaction on the dyadic level, while Bowenites operate on the monadic level, to which obviously can be added that object relations theorists also focus on the monadic level. Just as was argued in the section of this chapter on the psychoanalytic perspective that puristic psychoanalytic stances at times allow therapists to create an unnecessary split between past and present and between internal and interactional views of human behavior, so, too, it is seen here and in the previous examination of the behavioral approach, that in Weiss' (Chapter IV) terms, "individualizing" and interactional approaches are only very arbitrarily orthogonal or antagonistic. Friedman (1965) has presented a similar argument regarding Haley's strategic approach. Raush et al. (1974, p. 50) state the matter well, that an object relations perspective "helps avoid the twin dangers of a mona-distinct view of personality and a purely role-playing or stimulus-control view" because "(object relations schemata) are personality structures . . . but they need others to become operative" (p. 49). Adding an object relations dimension to the pragmatics of communication thus seems to begin to deal with the conceptually (if not, in the view of communica-tionists, clinically) important question of why some individuals are more inclined than others to meta-communicate and engage in counterpro-ductive power struggles.

While Haley's (1963a, 1963b) central focus in marital conflict is on the power struggle between spouses, the major problematic dimension of communication for Watzlawick et al. (1974) is cognitive. That is, con-flict often ensues when people (here, spouses) fail to differentiate be-tween a "difficulty" and a "problem" or when "the solution becomes the problem" (Watzlawick et al., 1974, p. 31) through the mishandling of difficulties. There are three ways in which such a mishandling occurs: (a) "A solution is attempted by denying that a problem is a problem, action is necessary, but it is not taken"; (b) "change is attempted regard-ing a difficulty which for all practical purposes is either unchangeable or nonexistent; action is taken when it should not be"; or (c) "an error in logical typing is committed . . . either by attempting a first-order change in a situation which can be changed only from the next higher logical level . . . action is taken at the wrong level" (p. 39).

What is problematic "is the meaning attributed to the situation, and therefore its consequences, but not its concrete facts" (Watzlawick et al., 1976, p. 95). For the contemporary Palo Alto group, conflict between spouses is the result of attributional deficiency, or cognitive misconcep-tions. These "utopia syndromes" (Watzlawick et al., 1974, p. 47) are all based on "the premises (of the syndrome which) are considered to be more real than reality. . . . This distinction between facts and premises about the facts is crucial for an understanding . . . of change" (p. 54). The similarity between this perspective and that elaborated recently by behavior therapists and cognitive therapists (such as Beck, 1976; Ellis, 1973; Mahoney, 1974; Meichenbaum, 1977; Seligman, 1975) is overwhelm-ingly clear. Indeed, the "premises" of which Watzlawick et al. (1974) speak are identical, for example, with the "irrational assumptions" and categorical imperatives ("should," "ought," and "must") that form the core of the rational-emotive model of the production and maintenance of psychopathology (Ellis, 1973), and with the "implicit assumptions," "arbitrary inferences," and so forth, of Beck's (1976) cognitive approach. As was seen, however, the therapeutic interventions that follow from these models are tremendously different from those of the Palo Alto group. What is most striking, however, in all of this is that despite the near identity of these models, nowhere in the Palo Alto group's writings are Ellis or Beck referred to, and nowhere in the writings of Ellis or Beck are the contributions of the Palo Alto group acknowledged. O'Leary and Turkewitz' (Chapter V) comment that "The cognitive trend, however, has not had significant inroads in the practice of behavioral marital therapy" (p. 105) is equally applicable to communications-oriented approaches. Apparently, it is much farther from the San Francisco Bay area to Philadelphia and New York than cartographers would have us believe.

The process and technique of conjoint treatment: Themes, assumptions and issues

One of the great, or perhaps meaningless, controversies among family systems therapists is the matter of who shall be treated in therapy. Some, such as Whitaker (1975) and Minuchin (1974), believe that the therapist is greatly hampered by the absence of any family member and thus insist that the whole family be present, at least initially. Others, such as Bowen (1976b, 1976c), prefer to work with what they see to be the central subsystem of the family, and still others argue that all psychotherapy "is" family therapy because change in any one component (person) of the family system produces change in the total system. Even traditional individual child psychotherapy can be viewed and defended from a family systems point of view (Montalvo and Haley, 1973). Just as general systems theory is a way of conceptualizing existing knowledge, *it at times appears that a family systems therapy model is an attempt to redefine and subsume all existing psychotherapies.* In the marital context, whether the treatment of one spouse "is" marital therapy is a definitional matter. Indeed, to say this is quite in keeping with the communicationist's view that reality is how you define it. But whether individual therapy "is" or "is not" marital therapy is a question that must be separated from the matter of the *effects* of carrying out treatment in these two formats. This is an empirical matter. As discussed in detail elsewhere (Gurman, 1975a; Gurman and Kniskern, 1978b, 1978c) and briefly in the first part of the present chapter, the existing research evidence points in the direction of a significantly lower rate of improvement and a significantly higher rate of deterioration in the individual treatment of marital difficulties than in the treatment of marital problems with both spouses involved. This comparative difference is particularly marked in the case of conjoint (including conjoint group) therapy. Thus, while some systems therapists may argue that individual treatment is a conceptually acceptable intervention into family or marital systems, the data contradict the wisdom of such a position. Thus, for reasons other than the mere symmetry of chapter subsections, this section will focus on conjoint treatment within the communications models.

(1) *Symptoms always have interpersonal meaning in current relationships.* A most basic assumption for communicationists is that individual symptoms are ways of attempting to define and control relationships. Two questions are: (1) Do all psychiatric symptoms have functional interpersonal intent? and (2) When symptoms are interpersonally relevant, do they necessarily invoke current relationships?

First, the assumption that symptomatic behavior is functional for relationship reasons has been raised in the preceding discussion of an object relations view of communicational paradoxes, in which it was argued that contradictory levels of communication not only serve relationship functions but also serve individual psychic defensive functions, such as avoiding anxiety. In addition, it can be postulated from a phenomenological-humanistic perspective that the functional value of successfully controlling an intimate relationship lies in its potential for maintaining a consistent self-view and, thereby, self-esteem. Thus, *attempts to define intimate relationships represent more fundamental attempts to define one's self.* Thus, symptomatology serves both relationship and individual ends.

But is it necessary to argue that the so-called identified patient *always* serves an important function for the marital relationship? The central notion of homeostasis has developed as an almost sacred doctrine in family systems circles the corollary that if a patient improves, someone else in the family (here, perhaps, the spouse) will *automatically* get worse unless the other members of the family are also treated.* As Wahlroos (1976, p. 9) comments:

> This often happens, but by no means does it *always* happen. In many cases, a patient (in individual therapy) has improved and his family members have responded *favorably* to his improvement by

---

* Lest this point be misconstrued as contradicting the earlier discussion of deterioration following the individual treatment of one partner to marital conflict, it should be emphasized that that earlier discussion concerned the possibility, not the automaticity, of such negative therapeutic effects.

improving themselves. . . . There are also families in which the improvement—or the worsening—of a family member seems to make no difference at all! *We just do not know under what conditions the theoretical postulates of family homeostasis apply and under which conditions they do not apply* (first italics added).

It may be asserted, then, that the belief of the *necessary* interpersonal meaning of an individual's symptomatology is based on a confounding of consequences and functions. While it is reasonable to argue that, if not all, then nearly all, individual symptomatology produces *consequences* for one's marital partner and, therefore, for the marriage relationship, this is not equivalent to the argument that such dysfunctional behavior is, functionally speaking, intended to control such a relationship *or* that the second spouse necessarily is a primary contributing force in the dysfunctional partner's misery. Indeed, the depression of a husband fired unexpectedly from his job may have disastrous marital consequences deserving of professional therapeutic attention, but his depression does not originate in the marital interaction (though it may be maintained thereby), nor does it necessarily have an implicit "command" component to his wife of "take care of me." Indeed, more parsimonious and empirically substantiated conceptual models for this depressive episode exists (Beck, 1976; Seligman, 1975).

The point here is that not infrequently the "identified" patient (who happens to be married) *is* the patient and the relationship is not, although the relationship may require therapeutic intervention as a set of phenomena secondary to the suffering of an individual. *Individual dysfunctioning does not necessarily reflect relationship conflict; in fact, individual functioning at times may* precipitate *relationship conflict.* Moreover, while individual symptomatology undoubtedly is often equilibrating for a relationship, the fact, well known to clinicians, should not be overlooked that such symptomatology also serves organismic functions, that is, has intra-individual, autoregulating consequences and purposes. In statistical language, communications theory, like general system theory, seems to emphasize "between effects" and to largely ignore "within effects." Steinglass' (Chapter VI) contribution to this volume offers an important model within which the individual need not be "lost" as she/he often is in discussions of general systems theory as applied to the family.

With regard to the second issue of the presumed relevance of individual dysfunction to *current* interpersonal relationships, it is difficult to imagine how most systems therapists deal with a person who does not have a family. Perhaps a more reasonable model is suggested by Wahlroos (1976, p. 9), who sees:

> symptoms as falling on a *continuum* from those which are relatively *unrelated* to current interpersonal transactions, to those symptoms which are almost *entirely* an integral function of current family relationships, with most symptoms falling somewhere in between these extremes (italics in original).

(2) *Defining (redefining) the couple's problem is best achieved through paradox.* In truth, the communicationist's view that people get "stuck" by their definition of a problem is hardly unique to this model and, in fact, is characteristic of all psychotherapeutic approaches (Raimy, 1975). The differences among competing models reside in the alternative ways of construing experience which they offer to their clientele. Since reality is how you define it, there is nothing in the communicationist's perception of a couple's problematic reality that is inherently truer or better than alternative definitions. Clinically, the important question is whether one set of alternative perceptions is more effective than another set in producing therapeutic change. Thus far there is little convincing evidence in either individual (Luborsky, Singer and Luborsky, 1975) or marital-family therapy (Gurman and Kniskern, 1978c) that any one set of definitions of reality is superior to others.

This discussion, therefore, will consider whether the use of paradox, though paradoxical tasks, relabeling, or "reframing" (Watzlawick et al., 1974; Weakland et al., 1974), and the like, has particular advantages over alternative clinical methods for changing a person's outlook on his/her/their difficulties.

The use of paradox (therapeutic double-binds) is based on the notion that "rules," all second-order realities, are relative. In addition, it is argued that when the therapist permits and encourages usual (symptomatic) behavior, the patient tends to discontinue it (Haley, 1963a). Thus, communicational paradox is used for either (or both) of two reasons: It presents an alternative cognitive definition that is just as fitting of the "facts" of the clinical situation as that offered by the couple, and/or it places control of the clinical problem in the therapist's hands. Whichever of these motivations applies for the therapist in a given situation, the result is the same—the patient (couple) perceives the therapist's command as "illogical" and "unreasonable" because of the shift of premises. Having been forced to step outside their first-order belief, the couple presumably cannot continue to be dysfunctional, at least eventually.

Whether such interventions are effective (produce the desired change) is a matter for empirical verification, not assumption. To date, there is absolutely no evidence of the efficacy or superiority of this means of redefining a couple's reality. The only existing outcome data on this approach (Weakland et al., 1974) are quite unconvincing: Experimental controls were entirely absent; outcome was reported only from the therapist's vantage point; and even if the outcomes could be trusted as validly assessed, they certainly could not be attributed to the use of paradoxical injunctions and reframing alone, since a host of therapeutic strategies were used in the treatments reported.

On the other hand, therapeutic interventions based on almost exactly the same premises as those of the communicationists and aimed also at changing the assumptive set of patients have been developed by other clinicians (for example, Ellis, 1973; Beck, 1976) and have received a noteworthy degree of empirical support for their efficacy (Mahoney and Arnkoff, 1978). Rather than offering couples apparently "irrational" premises, these approaches, rational-emotive and cognitive therapy, work toward teaching patients more rational ways of thinking and of construing experience. Data on important clinical questions are often lacking, but when they exist it is probably wise that they be heeded. Watzlawick recently commented at a national conference that, "Statistics are like bikinis: what they reveal is suggestive, what they conceal is vital."* This witticism notwithstanding, Haley and the Palo Alto group have yet to even begin to disrobe!

Moreover, *while marital interaction may be better accounted for from the viewpoint of circular causality, this would not require that the therapist avoid the use of linear solutions.* For example, the use of assertive training, so common in behavioral marriage therapy, would seem to offer a viable "rational" intervention for paradoxically communicating couples. The cure of a problem says nothing about its etiology.

(3) *Symptom change facilitates system change, or content is inferior to process.* One of the major empirically untested assumptions in most family systems theories is that there is nearly a one-to-one correspondence between behavior change and other dimensions of change. Minuchin (1974) comments that, "By changing the relationship between a person and the familiar context in which he functions, one changes subjective experience" (p. 13). And Haley (1976) agrees, ". . . the main goal of therapy is to get people to behave differently and so to have different

---

* K. Strelnick, personal communication, March, 1977.

subjective experiences" (p. 49). These stances are remarkably similar to the approaches of those behavior therapists who regarded feelings and other internal (private) experience as epiphenomena of overt behavior change. But contemporary behavioral practitioners generally and specifically in the context of marital therapy no longer assume such a correspondence (see Weiss, Chapter IV and O'Leary and Turkewitz, Chapter V). Indeed, there is a vast amount of research evidence (Strupp and Hadley, 1977) that feelings of well-being and even reliably counted behavioral changes do not show any consistently high positive correlation. Perhaps nowhere is this independence demonstrated more strikingly that in recent research on the treatment of phobias where it is commonly found that a subject can, after treatment, touch a snake, ride elevators, or give public speeches at a frequency implying improvement, yet remain subjectively "anxious" and/or physiologically aroused. Couples do not bring their complaints to a therapist because of dysfunctional communication patterns, unmet unconscious needs, or insufficient positive reinforcement reciprocity, but because they (or one spouse) hurt experientially. Whatever the causes or maintaining variables of such suffering, *an effective marital therapy must offer evidence that it has relieved symptomatology where and in the terms in which it hurts.*

The basic assumption of communicationists in this regard is that when change has been achieved in one domain of experience, it radiates to all other domains, described above, from the behavioral-interactional to the subjective. This assumption also appears in analogous form in the standard contention by systems-oriented therapists that a therapeutic focus on process is superior to a focus on content. This assumption is explained by reference to the general systems notion of equifinality, that is, that no matter where one begins the conclusion will be the same:

> For example, if one takes a system view of an ongoing interrelationship such as a marriage, it is not necessary nor even useful to spend a long time getting a history of the couple. Whether the subject is money, sex, children, or in-laws, the pattern will be the same . . . the clinician need only get some idea of the couple's interaction in a given area to understand how they relate (Foley, 1974, pp. 42-43).

"All roads lead to Rome"—except those that lead elsewhere! And in marital therapy there are numerous one-way streets, some streets with "No U-turn" signs, as well as some dead ends. The equifinality construct (premise) allows the logical conclusion that content is irrelevant, since if the couple adequately resolves problem A (say, the presenting complaint), the process by which they did so will generalize to problems B, C, D, ad infinitum. However, if psychotherapy research of the last 20 years has taught us anything, it is that different problems require different solutions and that the same solution (therapeutic method, technique, or strategy) does not solve all problems. Indeed, belief in the converse of this position has probably done more to hinder the progress of psychoanalytic therapy than any other single factor. Moreover, there are countless instances in the experience of every psychotherapist in which problem A is remediated without any effect whatsoever on problems B, C, and so on. This is both a clinical and an empirical fact. What, then, could be the rebuttal of the strategic therapist or communications therapist but to take the indefensible position that problem A had not "really" changed, despite even concrete, measurable, countable evidence to the contrary? There is no adequate rebuttal that would support the equifinality principle in psychotherapy.

Finally, symptom-focused marital therapies also assume that symptom change is equivalent to and/or at least facilitative of system change and that such changes as may occur will be self-maintained:

> The family system has self-perpetuating properties. Therefore, the processes that the therapist initiates within the family will be maintained in his absence by the family's self-regulatory mechanisms (Minuchin, 1974, p. 14).

As Weiss and Margolin (1977) note in this regard, it is assumed that the satisfaction with the behavioral outcome is derived from the execution of the behaviors themselves. Also, since communication-oriented therapies include little or no explicit skill learning, it is further assumed that therapeutic intervention will allow the desired behaviors to occur *de novo*. Stated otherwise, these approaches assume that natural reinforcement will take over once the problematic interaction pattern has been changed. Such a stance seems unduly optimistic. The oft-heard litany of the behaviorist should suffice to make the point here and deliver the message to many systems-oriented therapists that generalization should be planned, rather than lamented (Baer, Wolfe and Risley, 1968).

Some additional practical considerations

Several other issues of everyday practical relevance need to be considered briefly. While some of these matters may not be unique to a communications-oriented marital therapy, they do seem to be particularly relevant in this instance.

(1) In many important ways, the individual is lost in communication-oriented therapies of the Palo Alto type. In part, this is due, as discussed above, to an unnecessary conceptual splitting of the individual and the interpersonal. This split has also ensued because of purist communicationists' near-total denunciation of the clinical significance of unconscious factors. Indeed, this position is quite similar to that which probably all behaviorists have stood by for years, and which most still do, despite the fact that some leading behavioral clinical researchers are now at least acknowledging that the study of the unconscious *may* be relevant to the practice of cognitive behavior therapy (Mahoney, 1977).

Communicationists have thrown the baby out with the proverbial bath water by resisting the temptation to acknowledge that the unconscious is an important sub-subsystem of influential forces within the subsystem of the individual. For example, while it is convenient to attempt to explain or describe all resistance phenomena in the language of "the system," it is painfully clear that there are situations in marriage therapy in which it is simply far more reasonable to believe that one spouse is, as an individual, a great deal more resistance to therapeutic input than the other. While resistance in couples therapy often is a joint resistance, whether viewed from a psychodynamic or a systems-oriented viewpoint, there are a not insignificant proportion of times when the impasse reached by the therapist is better accounted for on the basis of *one* partner's anxieties about change. Communicationists might even agree with this observation, but would proceed to deal with the resistance in what, at times, may be a most unfortunate manner. Various paradoxical methods have been suggested (for example, Haley, 1963a; Watzlawick et al., 1974) for this purpose. While it is an empirical question whether such paradoxical strategies "work" in the case of resistance, it is also important to consider that such a momentary success may be but a Pyrrhic victory, in that the therapist may have lost an opportunity for immediate and salient interpersonal learning by leaving his own person out of the transaction and, instead, shifting an interpersonal conflict between patient and therapist to the level of technology.

Moreover, when are non-individualizing interventions simply out of place? If the patient's phenomenological experience of such interventions as the communicationist may offer is not at all positive, what then? Is a referral made to a colleague with a different orientation? Stated otherwise, when are the communicationists' treatment strategies *not* indicated? Indeed, this is a question worth addressing to all the approaches to marital therapy discussed in this volume. But this writer's reading of the status of these competing models is that the communication purists are the most vocal in their unwillingness to incorporate therapeutic interventions that do not neatly fit into this world view. For example, Haley's (1976) assertion that for him, and presumably the Palo Alto group, "The emphasis is not on a method but on approaching each problem with special techniques for the specific situation" (p. 1) seems to be belied routinely. Are not the bulbar squeeze, assertive training, thought-stopping, in vivo desensitization, interpretation of transference reactions, and the like "special techniques" relevant to marital therapy that have served clinicians well? Are such interventions used by communicationists?

(2) Because communicationists' interventions are often right-brained rather than rational, a tremendous amount of variance in the efficacy of their interventions must rest on the intuitive wisdom of the therapist. While this may be no different in principle from what occurs in other therapeutic approaches, there seems to be a particular danger in the communication treatment model of using rather wild interventions. Admittedly, this is not required by the treatment model, but may ensue from its (mis-)use, especially among relatively inexperienced marriage therapists. It has been the present author's experience on numerous occasions in supervising novice marital therapists to see them offer their couples what they thought were useful "irrational" suggestions without paying any attention to the timing of such interventions, or to the meaning of such suggestions for the patient-therapist relationship. Perhaps such ill-timed maneuvers reflected the sentiment of some of the most influential communications-oriented therapists: "This is not a therapy in which the therapist's personality factors . . . enter; it is a therapy based on his skills, and on his learning operational procedures and carrying them out" (Haley, in Levant, 1977).

The broader implication of such a statement seems to be that technique matters above all else, a position commonly held as well by behavior therapists, but quite unsupported by hundreds of empirical studies (Gurman and Razin, 1977). Moreover, what many communicationists offer as techniques are certainly not of the same order as techniques used by marriage therapists of other theoretical persuasions and because of the lack of systematic research on the uses and limitations of their techniques, many a therapist has acted as though the use of "irrational" strategies gave him/her license to do whatever seemed fitting at the moment. While influential communications therapists did not supervise these therapies and certainly are not liable for their effects, they are responsible for making clear, especially to young marital therapists, the limitations of their techniques and the conditions under which they are better not used. To date, they do not appear to have done so (see, for example, Sluzki, Chapter VII).

(3) Finally, as noted earlier, communicationists find it unnecessary to teach their couples the principles of behavior change, quite unlike behavioral, psychoanalytically oriented, or Bowenite clinicians. In addition to the assumptions of natural reinforcement, and the like, noted above in regard to therapeutically induced changes, some other matters arise in this context. What type of client is likely to carry out paradoxically tasks that are offered within little or no explanatory cognitive framework? It is tempting to speculate that such responsive clients must be either quite naive or dependent and compliant. But more central to this issue is the matter of what the couple takes away from therapy in addition to symptom reduction. Behavior therapists have been showing in an impressive way the last few years that clients' abilities to cope with numerous problems in their lives have been vastly underestimated in the past. Many people are able to learn and apply with success systematic behavior change principles in their natural environment. Beyond the assumption of homeostatic regulation of therapy-induced change, what do the communications therapies offer couples such that they can become, and continue to be, their own problem-solving therapists when the wizardry of the therapist is not available? This is quite unclear.*

Particular advantages and strengths of the communications approach

(1) The communications-systems approach usefully challenges assumptions about the site of psychopathology and provides an important reminder that human behavior, whether functional or dysfunctional, usually occurs in an interpersonal context. It helps to challenge reifying tendencies so that, for example, what social psychology has taught for years is recognized—that a psychiatric diagnosis is not a verbal label for an entity within one individual, but the result of a complex labeling process in which the diagnostician must be viewed as part of the interactional field in which particular patient behaviors and verbal reports occur. This system model requires that therapists be, metaphorically speaking, good

---

* There is a maxim that says, "If you are hungry and I give you a fish, you may live for one day; but if, instead, I teach you *how* to fish, you may live for many, many years."

statisticians and recognize that "between effects" often (though not always, as argued) account for a good deal of the variance in intimate relationships.

(2) The communications approaches also provide a reminder of the importance of attempting to develop and apply problem-specific treatment interventions, much as the behavior therapists do. Whether the outcome goals aimed for in some communications-based marital therapy are the most appropriate goals is a matter of taste, speculation and personal preference. But the *achievement* of a chosen goal must be demonstrated in a convincing manner, regardless of its nature, if the marital therapies are to offer service of enduring value.

(3) While some may take issue, as done above, with the clinical wisdom of some communications treatment strategies, it seems likely that a therapist's mastery of some of the basic strategic skills proposed by the communicationists (as, for example, in Sluzki, Chapter VII) may offer invaluable aid in working with certain couples, especially those with limited interest in or motivation for working beyond symptom resolution, those whose treatments, for whatever reason, must be very brief and would thereby preclude more casual exploration of multiple dimensions of the marital relationship, and the like.

(4) Communications approaches present a challenge to try to change that which can be changed and to accept that which cannot be changed. Like all psychotherapies, they as yet offer little wisdom to be able to know the difference between the two. But, in their normal fallibility, *communication-systems approaches may be the most influential of the major contemporary marital therapies in helping therapists to overcome their own "Utopian syndromes," which at times derive from conceptual models of ideal therapeutic practice as well as from the narcissistic strivings of individual therapists.*

A COMPARATIVE ANALYSIS OF PSYCHOANALYTIC, BEHAVIORAL AND SYSTEMS APPROACHES

Having critically examined the three major contemporary approaches to marital disorders and marital therapy, this last section will take a more systematic, multidimensional comparative look at the three models. What is presented here is derived both from the first three sections of this chapter, as well as from examination of the chapters in this volume by Meissner and Nadelson and Paolino (psychoanalytic), Weiss and O'Leary and Turkewitz (behavioral) and Steinglass and Sluzki (systems). Some of the observations presented here do not derive explicitly from the earlier sections of this chapter, but flow naturally from them and from a careful reading of other material in this volume. Consistent with the format and limitations of the preceding discussions, this section will not present a comparative examination of behavioral therapy, psychoanalysis, or systems theory, but will focus instead on the similarities and differences among these approaches as they apply specifically in the marital context. Comparative analyses of the broader schools of thought represented in this volume are presented elsewhere (as in Barrett-Lennard, 1965; Birk, 1972; Eysenck, 1959; Marks and Gelder, 1966; Murray, 1963; Ritterman, 1977).

The analysis here will parallel the format of presentation of the preceding sections of this chapter: first, a comparison of the three approaches (actually, four since Bowen therapy and communications-oriented therapy are considered separately) under consideration in terms of their models of marital choice; next, in examination of the competing views of the nature and causes of marital conflict; and, finally, a focus on several dimensions of the actual process of conjoint treatment. The chapter will conclude with a few comments on the status of research in marital therapy and will offer some thoughts toward the future of the marital psychotherapies.

Marital Choice

What is most striking with regard to marital choice is the nearly bimodal distribution of interest in the process evidenced in the four theories. The psychoanalytic and Bowen models place great emphasis on the process, while communicationists and behaviorists appear quite disinterested in how couples become couples in the first place. This is not surprising since the psychoanalytic and Bowen models are evolutionary, developmental perspectives on human behavior, while the communications and behavioral perspectives are nearly entirely present-focused. While neither the communicationists nor the behaviorists would disavow that there probably are relatively predictable and systematic components to the selection of an intimate partner, they would relegate its study to that of a perhaps interesting intellectual exercise that simply is not a requisite element in the successful treatment of couples in conflict. The central rationale for these groups' lack of concern with the selection process would be that, in effect, however we got here, we only stay where we are because of what we do now. The past maintains behavior only as it is manifest in the present, and therefore no special attention to the past *qua* past is needed (sic). In Sluzki's (Chapter VII) words, "if any process in the history of an individual has had any repercussions in the present life, that process will have an isomorphic representation in current processes" (p. 391).

In contrast, analytic workers and Bowenites have been quite explicit about what they see as the major determining forces in the selection of marriage partners. While psychoanalytically oriented theorists speak of unconscious need complementarity, projective identification, and the like and Bowenites speak of differentiation of self, fusion, triangles, and the like, these two conceptual models appear not only to be referring to the same underlying phenomena, but, in fact, to be merely using different words for precisely the same central dimensions. For example, the psychoanalytically oriented therapist's emphasis on the marital object choice as a transferential object from one's family of origin is indistinguishable from Bowen's observation that people tend to pick partners who repeat the family interactions with which they are familiar in their own early development; and the psychoanalytically oriented argue that people tend to choose mates with the same level of maturity and who share the same developmental failures, while Bowen speaks of the way in which people select mates with the same level of internal differentiation from one's parental family. They also agree that marital choice represents an attempt at finding intimate interpersonal conditions for individual growth.

Marital Satisfaction and Conflict

Consistent with their views of the nature of marital choice, the psychoanalytically oriented and Bowenites see as a necessary component of marital satisfaction the individual's development of autonomy or differentiation from one's family of origin. Inherent in this, of course, is that each spouse must have established a flexible manner of viewing and relating to other people (objects), so that one is able to view, without anxiety, one's marital partner as a person unto him/herself, with relatively little intrusion of past significant figures into one's perception. In learning terms, response generalization or the success or failure of discrimination would be used to explain these phenomena, although behavior therapists do not place any importance on the impact of the similarity of an individual's behavior with his/her spouse and his/her perceptions of and feelings toward parental figures. Clearly, communicationists and behaviorists view unconscious factors as either non-existent or at least irrelevant to the treatment of marital disorders. While an argument could be developed that the notion of meta-communication suggests at least a "subconscious" process, most systems-oriented marriage therapists would reject, or at least object to, such a view.

While behaviorists view the immediate causes of marital strife as resulting from faulty behavior-change efforts of one spouse toward the other, or both, and implicate the absence of rather specific relationship skills in the process, the other approaches assume that what the behaviorists would call skills reflect the response potentials already possessed by individuals, but which are blocked from use and expression because of conflict at either an unconscious or a communicational level.

On one very central matter in the area of marital conflict, there seems to be agreement among the four models, namely, that conflict is always the result of attempts to define the relationship between husband and wife. It is clear, however, that these perspectives offer very different explanations of the forces operating in such an attempted definition. Analysts speak of shared collusions and multi-level contracts; communicationists speak of the implicit rules of the relationship; Bowenites speak of fusion and the mutual fear of individuation; and behaviorists speak of inequitable exchange of reinforcing behaviors. In all cases and despite language differences among the theories, the argument would be that the individual's felt needs were not being met in the relationship as it existed.

For the psychoanalytically oriented, a partial explanation of the lack of need fulfillment would point to internally paradoxical, conflicting needs that seem to require contradictory behavior from one's spouse for their fulfillment. As argued earlier, these *internal* paradoxes may be the final common pathway of the paradoxical communications, at an observable level, to which the communicationists point. And Bowenites would say that, in effect, fused individuals have unrealistic expectations of the extent to which their partners are capable of fixing their developmental deficits. The paradox, or irony, in this view, however, is that while the partners will function differently overtly, one appearing to function well and one poorly, fundamentally both partners are equally undifferentiated and cannot possibly offer each other the "therapeutic" benefits each expects from the relationship. Behaviorists would point not to paradoxes but to discrepancies between what each partner wants from the other and what each is receiving, but would place relatively little emphasis on whether such desires are reasonable, in marked contrast to the psychoanalytically oriented. While behaviorists would say that each partner's desires were going unmet because the spouses lacked effective ways of directly expressing their needs in positive terms (with which position, by itself, none of the other approaches would disagree), the other approaches would routinely question the possibility of such needs being met according to the terms in which they were being sought.

The "reasons," as it were, why people seek to define their intimate relationships would also vary among our four theories. Psychoanalysts place great emphasis upon unconscious needs to avoid the anxiety attendant upon confronting the split-off parts of one's self in one's partner —hence, the need to control the partner's behavior and to continue to see the partner in ways conforming to one's own internal object-relations schemata. Bowenites use a different language in this regard, but seem to be addressing the same phenomenon. Haleyan communicationists see the reason for attempted definition of the marital relationship as residing in each partner's desire to establish control in what is basically the power struggle inherent in all relationships, but appear uninterested in *why* people try (need?) to control the definition of relationship and, thereby, relationships themselves. Both an existential and a cognitive-behavioral response to this issue, as well perhaps as a psychoanalytic response, would invoke the notions of perceived mastery or coping ability as the precursor to phenomenologically experienced self-esteem and a sense of internal control of one's destiny. While behaviorists would agree that a heightened sense of self-esteem might *follow* from such obtained influence over social reinforcement, they would strongly object to the idea that people work to obtain reinforcement because of a basic need to experience a positive self-image.

The Process of Conjoint Therapy

Here, some of the issues examined in the first three sections of this chapter will be considered, as well as some dimensions of the actual treatment process not previously considered. While numerous dimensions of the therapeutic process could be examined, this discussion will focus selectively on the following parameters that need to be addressed both conceptually and technically in any type of marriage therapy: (a) the role of the past and of the unconscious; (b) the meaning of presenting problems and the role of assessment; (c) the goals to be achieved, or the nature of the change sought; (d) the role of the therapist-patient relationship in achieving these goals.

The role of the past and of the unconscious

Table I presents a summary comparative view of the role of the past and of the unconscious in the treatment of dysfunctional marriages. Consistent with observations at various earlier points in this chapter, this analysis reveals a strikingly similar assumptive set on the part of communicationists and behaviorists regarding the importance (or lack thereof) of historical and unconscious factors in the actual treatment process. The message of these two approaches is that current problems are maintained by current forces, not by the past. While analytic and Bowenite therapists would agree that the past is relevant as it is manifest in the present, and that conflicts deriving from past experience require appropriate current objects (people) to become operative, they differ markedly from the communicational and behavioral views of the amount of attention to these factors required for couples therapy to be effective. An important technical difference between psychoanalytic and Bowenite usage of this arena exists, however, in that while psychoanalytically oriented treatment couples are encouraged to explore the impact of the past during therapy sessions, Bowenites are more likely to encourage each marital partner to work toward differentiation from their families of origin through active out-of-therapy encounters with their parents. On the other side, communicationists and most behaviorists might agree that descriptive elaboration of the history of each individual partner's prior experience and of its impact on current transactional patterns would be of interesting speculative value, but they would relegate it to the status of a useless intellectual exercise for immediate treatment purposes. O'Leary and Turkewitz (Chapter V) seem to take a more moderate stance on at least part of this issue in that they do regard the gathering of historical information about the marital relationships as rather important.

The nature and meaning of presenting problems and the role of assessment

Assessment is an area in all psychotherapeutic practice that raises some salient, and at times divisive, issues. To a large extent, of course, assessment reflects the theoretical biases of the therapist, in terms of what she/he thinks is most important to examine. In turn, where one looks and what one looks for significantly affect what one sees. An analogous situation is reflected in the time-honored, if not well-worn, observation that psychotherapy patients come to think and talk like their therapists, so that a person in behavioral treatment will think in terms of the antecedents and consequences of a specific behavior, a psychoanalytic patient will talk of denial, the symbolic meaning of dreams, and so forth.

TABLE 1

The Role of the Past and of the Unconscious in
Marital Therapy from Three Perspectives

Psychoanalytic	*Bowenite*	*Systems* *Communications*	*Behavioral*
1. Couple's understanding of conscious and unconscious aspects of *marital choice* process central to treatment	Couple's understanding marital choice process useful in treatment; therapist's understanding important		Couple's and therapist's understanding of unconscious aspects of marital choice process irrelevant to treatment; conscious aspects of some importance
2. *History of marital relationship* very important for treatment	History of marital relationship useful in treatment		History of marital relationship of limited usefulness in treatment
3. Attention to *individual unconscious dynamics* required for effective treatment	Individual unconscious dynamics said to be unimportant, but appear useful.		Individual unconscious dynamics totally irrelevant to treatment
4. Past conflict and experience, especially in family of origin, importance as manifest in current marital relationship	Past conflict and experience central to changing current relationship	Past conflicts and experience of only "academic" interest	Past conflicts and experience of very limited importance

Table 2 summarizes the three perspectives' views of selected assessment issues. All of the four treatment models emphasize the importance of careful early assessment, but vary tremendously in the degree to which standardized evaluation instruments and approaches are used, with behavior therapists clearly investing the most energy in this first phase of treatment. Assessment practices also vary widely in terms of the breadth of the procedures used, with the communications approach emerging as the only one that largely sticks to the initial presenting problem and does not routinely conduct a far-ranging evaluation of multiple aspects of the marital relationship, in a sort of "marital status exam" comparable to the mental status examination common in psychiatric settings. While communicationists focus rather more narrowly, at first, in their assessments, they seem to join forces rather soon with Bowenites and behaviorists in focusing on specific stimulus-response contingencies, while dynamicists are likely to emphasize interactional *themes*.

Of course, the issue here is somewhat muddled, in that Bowenites, communicationists and behaviorists alike view specific target problems as metaphors for, as representative of, broader classes of transactional patterns. Moreover, while presenting problems are taken at relatively face value by systemists and behaviorists, dynamically-oriented marriage therapists appear to acknowledge their importance, but view them as reflecting more basic, disguised, underlying conflicts, so that the *meaning* attributed to presenting problems is quite different from, say, the communicationists' view of symptoms as communicational messages, and the behaviorists' view of symptoms as learned behavior. Of course, from any perspective, the behavior of individuals or of dyads is learned. At least thus far, researchers have not pointed to endocrinological, neurophysiological or metabolic substrates of the choice of defense mechanisms or the use of paradoxical communications in intimate relationships!

Finally, all the perspectives agree, in one fashion or another, that the couple, or the marital relationship, is "the patient." Once again, communicationists are the deviant group in their almost wholesale lack of attention to individual variables. While behaviorists often campaign against what Weiss (Chapter IV) calls "individualizing" approaches, behaviorists are really quite concerned about such matters, as is evidenced in their efforts to teach marital partners, as individuals but in a dyadic context, communication skills, negotiation and bargaining skills, and the like. Clearly, the individualization that occurs in behavioral marital therapy is of a different order than that which occurs in psychoanalytically oriented therapy, but is in many ways more akin to the Bowenite emphasis on active, directive teaching of new ways in which individual spouses can begin to differentiate themselves from their parental families.

One other commonality among the perspectives is that each offers little guidance on the question of when therapeutic approaches other than their own are indicated for a given couple, when their own is the treatment of choice, or, indeed, when no treatment is the appropriate course of action!

The comparative importance of mediating and ultimate goals in marital therapy

While there is a range of opinion on the matter, marital and family therapists as a group are noted, if not notorious, for scorning the central

TABLE 2

The Nature and Meaning of Presenting Problems and the
Role of Assessment in Marital Therapy from
the Three Perspectives

Psychoanalytic	Bowenite	Systems Communications	Behavioral
1. Assessment is very important	Assessment is very important	Assessment is critical first phase of therapy	Assessment is critical first phase of therapy
2. Assessment largely reflects *idiosyncratic interests* of given therapist*	Assessment is *not standardized,* and relies entirely on therapist's clinical judgment, but centers on core themes/dimensions for all couples.		Assessment is flexible but *standardized* and uses carefully *tested and researched instruments* and interaction tasks
3. Assessment emphasizes interactional *themes,* but includes target complaints	Assessment emphasizes *rather specific stimulus-response contingencies*	Assessment centers on highly *specific problem behaviors* but views these as *metaphors* for broader classes of interaction patterns	Assessment focuses on themes somewhat, but emphasizes *specific stimulus-response contingencies*
4. Presenting problems acknowledged as important, but not taken at face value	Presenting problems taken at face value, but understood in terms of fusion	Presenting problems largely taken at face value, though clarification for specificity is required	
5. Presenting problems seen as reflecting *unconscious individual* as well as dyadic conflict resolution	Presenting problems seen as result of *tension in undifferentiated partners*	Presenting problems seen as *communicational messages* about power in marriage; or seen as the result of *faulty problem definition* or faulty previous change efforts	Presenting problems seen as *learned behaviors*
6. The relationship *and* the individual partners are all seen as "the patients"		The *relationship* is "the patient"	The *relationship* is "the patient," but individuals' *skill deficits* are central

* A distinction must be made between the painstaking anamnesis that occurs in (individual) psychoanalysis and the relative lack of agreement on what constitute necessary assessment dimensions in psychodynamic *marriage* therapy.

importance of manifest changes in the individual—changes that are basic to all individual psychotherapies. Parloff (1976) states that the matter at hand is one of a failure to differentiate between *mediating* and *ultimate* goals:

> Mediating goals are those which reflect the clinician's assumptions regarding the necessary steps and stages through which a patient must progress if the treatment is to be effective. These goals represent the postulated enabling or intermediate conditions which will permit the attainment of the ultimate goals. The ultimate goals of psychotherapy must, however, go beyond such hypothesized mediating variables as inferences regarding the resolution of neurotic conflicts, growth . . . enhancing the communicational systems, etc. (p. 317).

Mediating Goals

Table 3 presents a comparison of the relative importance attached to a number of mediating goals in marital therapy from the three perspectives. Obviously, such an analysis reflects both the factors deemed relevant by the present writer and his own assessments of the importance attached to these variables by the competing therapeutic paradigms. Others might have focused on different goal dimensions and/or rated their importance differently in different instances. What is offered here, then, represents one person's view of these selected parameters and certainly cannot be an effective substitute for carefully conducted research on the goal preferences of marriage therapists of differing persuasions (as, for example, Group for the Advancement of Psychiatry, 1970).

What is striking is that, according to the present analysis, there are quite a number of mediating or process goals that appear to be of major importance in all the theoretical perspectives under consideration: (1) the specification of problems; (2) the clarification of each spouse's individual desires and needs in the marital relationship; (3) redefining the nature of the couple's difficulties; (4) encouraging of each partner's recognition of his/her mutual contribution to the marital discord; (5) the recognition and modification of communication patterns, "rules," and interactional patterns; (6) increasing reciprocity; and (7) decreasing the use of coercion and blaming.

In addition, some other mediating goals are of at least moderate importance in all the treatment approaches: (1) increasing cooperative problem-solving; (2) the establishment of a positive working relationship between the couple and the therapist; (3) the modification of felt

TABLE 3

Comparative Importance of Mediating Goals in Marital
Therapy from the Three Perspectives

| | *Psycho-analytic* | Systems | | *Behavioral* |
		Bowenite	*Communi-cations*	
MEDIATING GOALS				
1. Specification of problem(s)	High	High	High	High
2. Clarification of attempted solutions	Moderate	Low	High	Moderate
3. Assessment of multiple aspects of marital relationship	High	Moderate	Low	High
4. Redefinition of problems	High	High	High	High
5. Recognition of mutual contribution to problem(s)	High	High	High	High
6. Establishment of working alliance	High	Moderate	Moderate	Moderate
7. Inclusion of children in therapy	Low	Low	High-Low	Low
8. Inclusion of partners' parents in therapy	Low	Low	High-Low	Low
9. Clarification of marital boundaries	High	Moderate	Low	Moderate
10. Clarification/specification of individual desires, needs, etc. in relationship	High	High	High	High
11. Modification of individual needs, etc.	High	High	High-Low	Low
12. Increased expressive and listening skills	High	High	Moderate-Low	Low
13. Increased reciprocity	High	High	High	High
14. Decreased coercion, blame, etc.	High	High	High	High
15. Cooperative problem-solving & increased conflict resolution skills	High-Low*	High	Moderate	High
16. Recognition and modification of communication patterns, "rules," etc.	High	High	High	High
17. Insight regarding historical factors	High	Moderate	Low	Low
18. Insight regarding current transactions ("interaction insight")	High	Moderate	Low	High
19. Increased differentiation	High	High	Low	Moderate
20. Resolution of marital transference	High	High-Moderate	Low	Low
21. Resolution of patient-therapist transference	High	Low	Low	Low

* Psychoanalytically oriented marital therapists clearly vary widely in this regard, with Nadelson (Chapter III) being rather unusually high on this dimension, in the present writer's view.

individual needs in the marriage; and (4) increasing each partner's ability to express their feelings clearly and directly and to "hear" his/her mate accurately.

The psychoanalytic model, however, seems to stand alone in its emphasis on achieving insight of both a historical and current sort, and on working to clarify and resolve transference reactions.

Ultimate Goals

While the analysis of ultimate goals (Table 4) reveals a commonality of therapeutic goals in certain areas, such as (1) increased role flexibility/adaptability; (2) resolution of presenting problems and decreased symptomatology; (3) a more equitable balance of power; (4) open and clear communication; and (5) increased self-esteem, there is a good deal of variability in the importance attached to a number of other possible ultimate treatment goals. What is most striking is the apparent concordance between psychoanalytic and Bowenite goals, on the one hand, the concordance between communicationists' and behaviorists' goals on the other, and the split between these two pairings. For example, behaviorists and communicationists evidence little concern for the resolution of putative individual neurotic conflicts or improvements of each partner's relationship with his/her own parents, while this is not true for the psychoanalytically oriented and Bowenites. The latter two groups are quite concerned with increasing the balance between the emotions and the intellect, while communicationists and behaviorists would be concerned with these areas only when they reflect major initial presenting difficulties.

The major parameters on which the four approaches appear to go their separate ways not surprisingly involve those that reflect the importance, or lack thereof, attributed to the impact of conjoint treatment on (1) each spouse's *and* the dyad's relationships outside their two-person subsystem; (2) the impact of treatment on characterological traits, conflicts and mechanisms for handling *intra*personal conflict, and vice versa; and (3) the establishment of a functional and adaptive balance between affect and cognition, or feelings and rational thinking.

What is most interesting in this writer's point of view is the contrast between the amount of overlap and agreement among the three perspectives on matters involving mediating treatment goals, on the one hand, and, on the other, the relative disagreement about ultimate goals. Perhaps this is not surprising at all when one considers that the divergence of opinion about the importance of many ultimate goals centers

TABLE 4

Comparative Importance of Ultimate Goals in Marital
Therapy from the Three Perspectives

	Psycho-analytic	Systems Bowenite	Systems Communications	Behavioral
1. Increased intimacy	High	Moderate	Low	Moderate
2. Role flexibility/adaptability	High	High	High	High
3. Toleration of differentness	High	High	Low	High
4. Improved sexual relationships and gender identity	High	Moderate	Low	Low-Moderate
5. Resolution of presenting problems	High	High	High	High
6. Balance of power	High	High	High	High
7. Inclusion of children in ther-intellect	High	High	Low	Moderate
8. Increased self-esteem	High	High	Moderate	Moderate
9. Clear communication	High	High	High	High
10. Resolution of neurotic conflict	High	High	Low	Low
11. Improved relationship with children	Moderate	High	High-Low	Low
12. Improved relationship with own parents	Moderate	High	High-Low	Low

on the degree to which the dimensions of change involved reflect currently measurable variables versus the degree to which the goals examined require a good deal of inference and speculation to establish whether they have been achieved. In Strupp and Hadley's (1977) terms, the issue is one of the importance attached to behavioral changes, changes reflecting a general sense of well-being, and structural changes.

The comparative importance of various therapist roles and functions in marital therapy

Before turning to a brief consideration of some empirical issues of a comparative nature, this section will attend to a dimension of the therapeutic process that is, to understate the matter, quite controversial in all psychotherapies. The issue is, to put it simply, the nature of the therapist's impact in the treatment process. What does a therapist do that makes a difference, and in what ways are the process and outcome of therapy affected by who the therapist is as a person? These issues have been considered in exhaustive detail in individual therapy (Gurman and Razin, 1977), but have received relatively little empirical study in marital and family therapy (Gurman and Kniskern, 1978c).

In a sense, the issue at hand is whether the therapist views his/her therapeutic influence as deriving primarily from technical skills or from an intense personal relationship with those whom he treats. In Alexander et al.'s (1976) terms, the distinction is one between "structuring skills" and "relationship skills." Table 5 shows the comparative importance attributed by the competing perspectives to selected therapist roles and functions.

All of the approaches attach major importance to four therapist activities: (1) directing and structuring the flow of therapy sessions and guiding the sequencing of treatment goals; (2) challenging the assumptions, beliefs, and attitudes of couples about the nature of marriage in general and of their difficulties in particular, and providing alternative world views; (3) clarifying communication; and (4) assigning out-of-therapy "homework" of various sorts. In addition, all the approaches except for the communications-oriented systems therapists believe it is important that the therapist provide an explicit rationale for the couple's difficulties and for the treatment that is proposed.

Thus, all the approaches seem to be in basic agreement about certain structuring activities in both the early and later phases of treatment. What is most striking in this analysis, however, is the manner in which these approaches to the treatment of marital disorders divide on other structuring (technical) and relationship dimensions. Teaching concrete interpersonal skills and imparting "expert" knowledge, and modeling new, more adaptive interpersonal behavior are activities given priority by all but the communicationists who, as noted in the section on the systems perspective, seem to make certain questionable assumptions about the existence of behaviors in individuals' repertoires and the mechanisms by which therapy-induced change is maintained.

The most decisive parting of the ways, however, revolves around the four therapies' views of the patient (couple)-therapist relationship and how it is used to achieve desired treatment goals. While Bowenites explicitly avoid getting intensely involved with couples, communicationists see the "relationship" largely as a power struggle to be won by the thera-

TABLE 5

Comparative Importance of Various Therapist Roles and
Functions in Marital Therapy from
the Three Perspectives

	Psycho-analytic	Systems Bowenite	Systems Communications	Behavioral
1. Teaches skills, imparts knowledge	Moderate	Moderate	Low	High
2. Models new modes of interpersonal behavior	Moderate	Moderate	Low	High
3. Directs, structures, sessions; sequences goals	Moderate	High	High	High
4. Clarifies communication	High	High	High	High
5. Gives practical advice, support	Moderate	Moderate	Low	High
6. Provides rationale for couples' difficulties and for treatment offered	High	High	Low	High
7. Encourages and supports expression of feelings	High	Moderate	Low	Moderate
8. Manipulates environment	Low	Moderate	High	Low
9. Assigns "homework"	High-Low*	High	High	High
10. Challenges couple's assumptions, beliefs	High	High	High	Moderate
11. Interprets patients' feelings and behavior, facilitates insight	High	Low	Low	Low
12. Facilitates and interprets transference	High	Low	Low	Low
13. Shares own values, uses self, including countertransference feelings and behavior	High	Low	Low	Low

* Assessment of the importance of such assigned out-of-therapy tasks is particularly difficult, in modal terms, within the psychoanalytic perspective because of the tremendous range of emphasis on this issue in actual practice; compare, for example, Dicks (1967) and Nadelson (Chapter III).

pist (albeit in the best interests of the couple), and behaviorists view the therapeutic relationship as simply the interpersonal backdrop which may facilitate the application of highly specific technical interventions. Indeed, "technique" (what you do) is far more important in these approaches than "style" (how you do it) or than the person you are who does it. For the psychoanalytically oriented, of course, the major vehicle of change in marital therapy derives from the unique relationship that evolves between the couple and their therapist(s), its subtle nuances and meanings, vicissitudes, and ultimate resolution.

While all the votes certainly are not yet in (if they ever will be), it seems quite likely that, except for a rather small number of highly focal marital difficulties, effective treatment will require the application of expert technical knowledge and skills in the context of a deeply personal, emotionally intense relationship between a marriage therapist and those married couples who come to him/her in distress.

Current Status of Marital Therapy Research

Only five years ago, research on the outcomes of marital therapy was virtually non-existent (Gurman, 1973a, 1973b), and only about 50 empirical reports of effectiveness could be found. There now exist well over 200 studies of marital and family therapy outcome (Gurman and Kniskern, 1978b, 1978c), as well as some 35 studies on marital enrichment programs (Gurman and Kniskern, 1978d). As Jacobson (Chapter VIII) notes in his review of research on the effectiveness of marital therapy, he has reached "rather different conclusions" about this literature than the present author (Gurman and Kniskern, 1978c). Since both examined the same research literature, yet reached different conclusions, it is likely that these differences are based on different evaluative assumptions. This section will briefly examine a few of the more important of these assumptions and some selected methodological issues relevant to the future conduct of research in this area. While a scientifically based, empirically validated technology of behavior change may be desirable, it seems quite unrealistic to expect "technology" to fully account for therapeutically-induced behavior change. The implicit philosophy of the therapist as technician, discussed in the section of this chapter on the behavioral approach, seems unsupportable on both clinical and empirical grounds (Alexander et al., 1976; Alexander and Parsons, 1975; Gurman and Kniskern, 1978c; Gurman and Razin, 1977; Roberts, 1975; Thomlinson, 1974).

The not uncommon argument that uncontrolled studies are virtually useless needs to be re-examined. The usual source of this viewpoint is dissatisfaction with subjective assessment of change, in that such measures are said to be "biased" and *therefore* useless. While on pristine methodological grounds this position is, of course, correct, one must wonder about the meaning, if not the extent, of such bias in considering the fact that numerous marriage therapists, in presenting the outcomes of their own therapy, have reported a believable proportion of the cases as having worsened (Gurman and Kniskern, 1978b, 1978c)! Therapists may be biased, but a large number also seem to be honest.

On the basis of the bias issue, researchers are often encouraged to disregard therapists' evaluations of change. What this stance fails to appreciate is that *the marital therapist, like any psychotherapist, offers a unique perspective on clinical change.* Fiske (1975) has argued persuasively that since a source of data is not a measuring instrument, attempts to eliminate disagreement among rating sources and reduce what is often thought of as error variance are futile. Fiske (1975, p. 20) argues:

> A source of data yields observations from a distinctive role providing distinctive experience. When an observer representing a source makes judgments about the complex variables of interest to current psychotherapeutic theory, he is actually processing his own experience. . . . Nearly exact agreement can be obtained only from inanimate measuring instruments or from observers functioning like instruments.

Fiske also notes (p. 23) that, "Instead of seeking to minimize (differences in perceptions), researchers should seek to identify the unique components of the perceptions and judgments from each source." Gurman and Kniskern (1978c), reviewing the results of behavioral marital and family therapy, noted that it was rare to find a behavioral treatment study in which the therapist's view of change was considered, and concluded that, "It is as if the implicit message were that despite the therapist's assumed expertise as a change-agent, he/she offers no uniquely valuable perspective in assessing clinical change!" Ah, paradox!

Researchers who routinely adopt the "therapist bias" position often also dismiss the empirical usefulness of client reports of change on the basis that such change is not "real" change since "real" change can only be based on objective therapeutic indicators. But just what is "real" change? Following Fiske's (1975) argument, such objective changes are no more real than those based on participants' evaluations and reports. They are, of course, different, but they certainly do not deserve the label of superiority often assigned to them. Indeed, objective indices *are* the "best" sources of assessment from certain theoretical perspectives, such as the behavioral perspective, and are, as the present author has emphasized elsewhere (Gurman and Kniskern, 1978c), requisite dimensions in any study of marital therapy outcome. But they are *not* inherently better than indices based on patients' and therapists' subjective assessments. Any measure that is valid, reliable and theoretically meaningful is useful in assessing the outcomes of marital therapy. It is ironic, of course, that those researchers who reject client reports of change in marital therapy often do accept clients' initial complaints and statements of suffering for both clinical and research purposes (compare: Jacobson, Chapter VIII, 1977a, 1977b). Arguments that behavioral measures are the most objective scientifically should not be equated with a belief that such measures are the most scientifically useful.

Finally, in contrast to Jacobson's (Chapter VIII) conclusions about the relative efficacy of different approaches to marital therapy, there follows a summary of the conclusions reached by the present author in his review of the literature on the outcomes of marital therapy (Gurman and Kniskern, 1978c): (1) Non-behavioral marital therapies produce beneficial effects in about 61 percent of cases; (2) when both spouses are involved in therapy, there is a much higher rate (65 percent) of improvement than when only one spouse is treated (48 percent); (3) the rate of deterioration in treatment involving both spouses is about half (5.6 percent vs. 11.6 percent) that occurring when only one partner is treated; (4) among non-behavioral therapy studies, treatment has emerged as superior to control conditions in 10 to 15 comparisons; (5) summing across both analog and naturalistic studies of behavioral marriage therapy, behavioral interventions have been superior to control conditions in 7 of 11 studies and superior to alternative treatments in 8 of 16 comparisons; (6) evidence of the efficacy of behavioral marriage therapy is no more persuasive than is the research on non-behavioral treatment because of its limitations in terms of too frequent use of non-clinical analog demonstrations with minimally distressed couples, the essential lack of replication of the influential Oregon group's work except for the studies of Jacobson (1977a, 1977b), and infrequent follow-up; (7) deterioration is as frequent in behavioral marriage therapy as in non-behavioral treatments; (8) there is no demonstrated superiority of relatively longer versus shorter-term marital interventions; (9) there is little consistent evidence that would support the use of videotape feedback or other apparatus-based interventions; (10) therapist relationship skills have major impact on the outcome of marital therapy regardless of the "school" orientation of the clinician.

It is clear that precious little is known empirically about the marital therapies, including those represented by the three major perspectives presented in the present volume. Such divergent conclusions about the current status of research on marital therapy as represented by Jacobson (Chapter VIII) and Gurman and Kniskern (1978c) themselves may offer usefully different vantage points for the generation of productive research and scholarly thought in the field of marital therapy.

SOME THOUGHTS TOWARD THE FUTURE OF THE MARITAL THERAPIES

In this volume, several substantive contemporary models of marriage and marital therapy have been presented and critically evaluated. Each comes from a different intellectual lineage and each offers different ways of construing the nature of what goes right and what goes wrong in the most significant voluntary relationship of our lives. These divergent views, when adopted by marital therapists, necessarily lead them to see the same proverbial elephant in different ways, though, as argued here, the therapeutic actions taken often are more similar than might at first be expected. Is the existence of multiple theories of marriage and marital therapy a boon or a bane? At this point, the field is fortunate to have differences of opinion; it is absolutely necessary that therapists, theoreticians and researchers alike continue to challenge, modify, and refine existing models, lest premature calcification becomes irreversible. Indeed, the sole purpose of theories is to be disproved. Thus, therapists, as well as their patients, will fare better in the long run if they adopt an attitude of cautious optimism about the wisdom offered by current psychoanalytic, systems and behavioral perspectives on marital disorders and their treatment, and accept none of them as a finished product.

Indeed, psychotherapeutic practices, like science, improve over time through small increments, not with cataclysmic revelation. The dominant marital therapies three decades from now will probably be as similar to contemporary marital therapies as a child is to his/her parents. They will have a definite heritage, will inherit some characteristics that are permanent and fixed, and will be dependent on their parentage for certain basic sustaining qualities and attributes, but ultimately define their own course in how they negotiate with the world. Undoubtedly, like children, they will reject certain assumptions, beliefs and values that they may have been wiser to have retained, but they will also grow by doing so. They will be similar to their parents, but not the same.

Indeed, the marital therapies of the future may well be the offspring of apparent miscegenation. The evolving hybrid will hopefully reflect and refine those generic factors that are common to all effective marital therapy and psychotherapy. Contemporary marital therapies are in an adolescent period. They owe their existence, in large part, to family theory, but are struggling to establish their own boundaries. Like adolescents, they are understandably very caught up in their own identities, in attempts to establish themselves as unique entities. Also like adolescents, competitiveness and self-image are at times paramount. Fortunately, the major contemporary marital therapies considered in this volume have matured rather well of late. Probably no psychoanalytic therapists would now endorse the position that psychoanalysis is always the intervention of choice, and behavior therapists, having established that they have a legitimate place in the therapeutic sun, have, in general, toned down their earlier claims of superior efficacy, and, indeed, have recently even begun to incorporate methods that would have been considered heretic. if not blasphemous, a decade ago.

Opposing schools of marital therapy, while still retaining a basic belief in their own substantiveness, have become more moderate in their claims and more sober in their assessments. Indeed, the available empirical evidence on the comparative efficacy of different treatment approaches strongly supports just such a cautious, but optimistic, trend (Gurman and Kniskern, 1978c), as discussed above. It has become apparent to marital therapists, as it has to other psychotherapists, that no single approach has won all the prizes in the Alice in Wonderland race for superiority. Indeed, the most useful general direction for the future development of the marital therapies is one that does not emphasize an adversarial "we're better than you" philosophy, but rather seeks to concretize the reality of the fact that, just as there are "different strokes for different folks," a taxonomy of marital therapy needs to be developed that, as much as possible, allows the specification of different therapies for different couples, with different problems, at different points in the family life-cycle, and so on. This oft-repeated litany of therapy researchers by now has become hackneyed, but is still fundamental. Successful marital therapies must be fitted to individuals and individual couples; the force-fitting of couples to favorite conceptual models will only create the sort of dissonance that can only be reduced, as it has in the past, by useless rationalizations invoking the untreatability of the couple, their lack of motivation, or other such fancy and fanciful myths of our own creation. Whether the newer marital therapies represent "delusions or deliverances" (Mahoney,

Kazdin and Lesswing, 1974, p. 11) or "fads or breakthroughs" (Shapiro, 1976, p. 154) will be determined by careful empirical study, not by politicized debate. The late Don Jackson seems to have had something like this in mind when, a decade ago, he wrote that "we cannot view diverse theories in an 'either-or' fashion, but must live with the idea that many discontinuous approaches should be investigated and given credence" (Jackson, 1967, p. 395).

Whether the theoretical perspectives examined in this book will be found to be harmonious in principle or whether such discontinuities as Jackson referred to will predominate should not obscure the fact that very, very little is known about what marital therapists of different persuasions actually do with couples. As behavior therapists have made clear, there is often a lack of correspondence between patient self-reports of behavior and others' observations of their behavior. Should the self-reports of marriage therapists be trusted any more than the self-reports of patients? Probably not. In the end, even the most impressive collegial discussions of why we do what we do in therapy, and of what we say we do in therapy, have no direct influence on the outcomes of our work. Obviously, what we do as therapists should have something in concert with what we believe as therapists to be important, but it is what we do that produces change or fails to produce it. Empirical study of our actions will be of greater use to our patients than unending musings in professional dialogues.

Of course, how we assess the outcomes of our clinical efforts with couples will reflect our differing value structures about the nature of the good life in marriage. Thus, we will measure our efficacy according to different criteria and, to some extent, are likely to continue to find ourselves comparing not only apples and oranges, which are at least of the same class, in that they are both fruit, but even comparing fruits with vegetables, vegetables with meats, and all of these with cookware! Our own narcissism, pride or self-respect will dictate that we do so; hopefully, we might at least agree to use some common indices to assess change even if, or especially if, they do not tap our favorite variables. Would it not be provocative and exciting to find, for example, that behavioral negotiation-training and contracting procedures produce significant increases in differentiation of self, or that the working through of the transference in marital therapy yields significant positive changes in a couple's ability to problem-solve constructively?

Indeed, the very existence of this book is testimony to the fact that we are all very concerned, in both a professional and in a personal way, with the future of marriage. Without doubt, marriage is the major test of one's life, having the potential to foster profound individual growth. While we may continue to disagree about what dimensions of marriage are most significant, we can agree in principle with Sigmund Freud's (1904, p. 259) assertion that, "there are many ways and means of practicing psychotherapy. All that lead to recovery are good."

REFERENCES

Ables, B. and Brandsma, J. *Therapy for Couples.* San Francisco: Jossey-Bass, 1977.

Ackerman, N. *The Psychodynamics of Family Life.* New York: Basic Books, 1958.

Ackerman, N. The family approach to marital disorders. In: B. L. Greene (Ed.), *The Psychotherapies of Marital Disharmony.* New York: The Free Press, 1965.

Aldous, N. R. Mechanisms of stalemate in conjoint marital therapy. *Canadian Psychiatric Association Journal,* 1973, 18, 191-197.

Alexander, F. and French, T. M. *Psychoanalytic Therapy: Principles and Applications.* New York: Ronald Press, 1946.

Alexander, J., Barton, C., Schiavo, R. and Parsons, B. Systems-behavioral intervention with families of delinquents: Therapist characteristics, family behavior and outcome. *Journal of Consulting and Clinical Psychology,* 1976, 44, 656-664.

Alexander, J. F. and Parsons, B. V. Cognitive and relationship components of short-term behavioral therapy with families. Paper presented at the Association for the Advancement of Behavior Therapy Meeting, San Francisco, December 1975.

Allport, G. *Pattern and Growth in Personality.* New York: Holt, Rinehart & Winston, 1961.

Araoz, D. L. Marital transference. *Journal of Family Counseling,* 1974, 2, 55-63.

Azrin, N. and Holz, W. Punishment. In: W. Konig (Ed.), *Operant Behavior.* New York: Appleton-Century-Crofts, 1966.

Azrin, N., Naster, B. and Jones, R. Reciprocity counseling: A rapid learning-based procedure for marital counseling. *Behaviour Research and Therapy,* 1973, 11, 365-382.

Bach, G. R. *Aggression Lab: The Fair Fight Training Manual.* Dubuque, Iowa: Kendall/Hunt Publishing Co., 1971.

Baer, D. M., Wolfe, M. M. & Risley, T. Some current dimensions of applied behavioral analysis. *Journal of Applied Behavior Analysis,* 1968, 1, 91-97.

Baird, E. and Redfering, D. L. Behavior modification in marriage counseling. *Journal of Family Counseling,* 1975, 3, 59-64.

Balint, M., Ornstein, P. and Balint, E. *Focal Psychotherapy.* London: Tavistock, 1972.

Bancroft, J. The behavioural approach to marital problems. *British Journal of Medical Psychology,* 1975, 48, 147-152.

Bandura, A. *Principles of Behavior Modification.* New York: Holt, Rinehart & Winston, 1969.

Barnett, J. Narcissism and dependency in the obsessional-hysteric marriage. *Family Process,* 1971, 10, 75-83.

Barrett-Lennard, G. T. Professional psychology and the control of human behavior. *Australian Journal of Psychology,* 1965, 17, 24-34.

Barry, W. A. Marriage research and conflict: An integrative review. *Psychological Bulletin,* 1970, 73, 41-54.

Beck, A. T. *Cognitive Therapy and the Emotional Disorders.* New York: International Universities Press, 1976.

Beck, D. F. Research findings on the outcomes of marital counseling. *Social Casework,* 1975, 56, 153-181.

Bergin, A. E. The evaluation of therapeutic outcomes. In: A. E. Bergin and S. L. Garfield (Eds.), *Handbook of Psychotherapy and Behavior Change.* New York: Wiley, 1971.

Berman, E. M. and Lief, H. I. Marital therapy from a psychiatric perspective: An overview. *American Journal of Psychiatry,* 1975, 132, 583-592.

Berrien, F. K. *General and Social Systems.* New Brunswick, N. J.: Rutgers University Press, 1968.

Bertalanffy, L. von. General system theory and psychiatry. In: S. Arieti (Ed.), *American Handbook of Psychiatry,* Vol. III. New York: Basic Books, 1966.

Bertalanffy, L. von. General system theory—a critical review. *General Systems,* 1962, 7, 1-20.

Bertalanffy, L. von. *General System Theory.* New York: George Braziller, 1973.

Beukenkamp, C. The noncommunication between husbands and wives as revealed in group psychotherapy. *International Journal of Group Psychotherapy,* 1959, 9, 308-313.

Birchler, G. R. and Webb, L. A social learning formulation of discriminating inter-action behaviors in happy and unhappy marriages. Paper presented at the South-west Psychological Association Meeting, Houston, April, 1975.

Birchler, G. R., Weiss, R. L. and Vincent, J. P. A multidimensional analysis of social reinforcement exchange between maritally distressed and nondistressed spouse and stranger dyads. *Journal of Personality and Social Psychology,* 1975, 31, 349-360.

Birchler, G. R., Weiss, R. L. and Wampler, L. D. Differential patterns of social rein-forcement as a function of degree of marital stress and level of intimacy. Paper presented at the Western Psychological Association Meeting, Portland, April 1972.

Birk, L. Psychoanalytic omniscience and behavioral omnipotence: Current trends in psychotherapy. *Seminars in Psychiatry,* 1972, 4, 113-120.

Blinder, M. G. and Kirschenbaum, M. The technique of married couple group ther-apy. *Archives of General Psychiatry,* 1967, 17, 44-52.

Boas, C. V. E. Intensive group psychotherapy with married couples. *International Journal of Group Psychotherapy,* 1962, 12, 142-153.

Boszormenyi-Nagy, I. and Framo, J. *Intensive Family Therapy.* New York: Harper and Row, 1965.

Boszormenyi-Nagy, I. Relational modes and meanings. In: G. Zuk and I. Boszormenyi-Nagy (Eds.), *Family Therapy and Disturbed Families.* Palo Alto, Calif.: Science and Behavior Books, 1967.

Boszormenyi-Nagy, I. and Spark, G. *Invisible Loyalties.* New York: Harper & Row, 1973.

Bowen, M. Family psychotherapy. *American Journal of Orthopsychiatry,* 1961, 30, 40-60.

Bowen, M. The use of family theory in clinical practice. *Comprehesnive Psychiatry,* 1966, 7, 345-374.

Bowen, M. From Couch to Coach. Address presented at the Georgetown University Symposium on Family Psychotherapy, Washington, D. C., October 1970.

Bowen, M. Toward the differentiation of the self in one's family of origin. In: F. Andres and J. Lorio (Eds.), *Georgetown Family Symposium Papers.* Washington, D. C.: Georgetown University Press, 1974.

Bowen, M. Family therapy and family group therapy. In: D. H. L. Olson (Ed.), *Treating Relationships.* Lake Mills, Iowa: Graphic Press, 1976 (a).

Bowen, M. Theory in the practice of psychotherapy. In: P. Guerin (Ed.), *Family Therapy.* New York: Gardner, 1976 (b).

Bowen, M. Principles and techniques of multiple family therapy. In: P. Guerin (Ed.), *Family Therapy*. New York: Gardner, 1976 (c).

Boyd, W. H. and Bolen, D. W. The compulsive gambler and spouse in group psychotherapy. *International Journal of Group Psychotherapy*, 1970, 20, 77-90.

Broderick, C. B. Beyond the five conceptual frameworks: A decade of development in family theory. In: C. B. Broderick (Ed.), *A Decade of Family Research and Action*. Minneapolis: National Council on Family Relations, 1971.

Buckley, W. *Sociology and Modern Systems Theory*. Englewood Cliffs, N. J.: Prentice-Hall, 1967.

Burton, G. Group counseling with alcoholic husbands and their nonalcoholic wives. *Marriage and Family Living*, 1962, 24, 56-61.

Burton, G. and Kaplan, H. M. Group counseling in conflicted marriages where alcoholism is present: Clients' evaluation of effectiveness. *Journal of Marriage and the Family*, 1968, 30, 74-79.

Butcher, J. N. and Koss, M. P. Research on brief and crisis-oriented therapies. In: S. L. Garfield and A. E. Bergin (Eds.), *Handbook of Psychotherapy and Behavior Change* (Revised edition). New York: Wiley, 1978.

Butcher, J. N. and Maudal, G. R. Crisis intervention. In: I. B. Weiner (Ed.), *Clinical Methods in Psychology*. New York: Wiley, 1976.

Byrne, D. and Lamberth, J. Cognitive and reinforcement theories as complementary approaches to the study of attraction. In: B. I. Murstein (Ed.), *Theories of Attraction and Love*. New York: Springer, 1971.

Cadogan, D. A. Marital group therapy in the treatment of alcoholism. *Quarterly Journal of Studies on Alcohol*, 1973, 34, 1187-1194.

Camp, H. Structural family therapy: An outsider's perspective. *Family Process*, 1973, 12, 269-278.

Caplan, G. *Principles of Preventive Psychiatry*. New York: Basic Books, 1964.

Carter, R. D. and Thomas, E. J. Modification of problematic marital communication using corrective feedback and instruction. *Behavior Therapy*, 1973, 4, 100-109.

Clore, G. L. and Byrne, D. A reinforcement-affect model of attraction. In: T. L. Huston (Ed.), *Foundations of Interpersonal Attraction*. New York: Academic Press, 1974.

Cuber, J. and Harroff, P. *The Significant Americans: A Study of Sexual Behavior Among the Affluent*. New York: Appleton-Century, 1965.

Davenport, Y. B., Ebert, M. H., Adland, M. L. and Goodwin, F. W. Lithium prophylaxis: The married couples group. Paper presented at the American Psychiatric Association Meeting, Anaheim, California, 1975.

Deutsch, F. *Applied Psychoanalysis: Selected Lectures on Psychotherapy*. New York: Grune & Stratton, 1949.

Deutsch, H. Some forms of emotional disturbance and their relationship to schizophrenia. *Psychoanalytic Quarterly*, 1942, 11.

Dicks, H. V. *Marital Tensions*. New York: Basic Books, 1967.

D'Zurilla, T. J. Marital problem solving: A cognitive-behavioral-relationship approach to marital therapy. Paper presented at the Association for the Advancement of Behavior Therapy, New York, December, 1976.

Eidelberg, L. *Studies in Psychoanalysis*. New York: International Universities Press, 1948.

Eidelberg, L. Neurotic choice of mate. In: V. Eisenstein (Ed.), *Neurotic Interaction in Marriage*. New York: Basic Books, 1956.

Eisler, R. M., Miller, P. M., Hersen, M. and Alford, H. Effects of assertive training on marital interaction. *Archives of General Psychiatry*, 1974, 30, 643-649.

Elizer, A. and Klein, M. M. Similarity, complementarity and difference of marital couples in problem and non-problem areas. *Israel Annals of Psychiatry and Related Disciplines*, 1974, 12, 145-155.

Ellis, A. *Humanistic Psychotherapy: The Rational-Emotive Approach.* New York: The Julian Press, 1973.

Eysenck, H. J. Learning theory and behavior therapy. *Journal of Mental Science,* 1959, 105, 61-75.

Feather, B. W. and Rhoads, J. M. Psychodynamic behavior therapy: II. Clinical aspects. *Archives of General Psychiatry,* 1972, 26, 503-511.

Feldman, L. Depression and marital interaction. *Family Process,* 1976, 15, 389-395.

Fensterheim, H. Assertive methods and marital problems. In: R. Rubin, H. Fensterheim, J. Henderson and L. Ullmann (Eds.), *Advances in Behavior Therapy.* New York: Academic Press, 1972.

Ferenczi, S. *Further Contribution to the Theory and Technique of Psychoanalysis* (1920). London: Hogarth, 1950.

Ferreira, A. J. Family myths and homeostasis. *Archives of General Psychiatry,* 1963, 9, 457-463.

Ferreira, A. J. Family myths: The covert rules of the relationship. *Comprehensive Psychiatry,* 1965, 8, 15-20.

Fiske, D. A source of data is not a measuring instrument. *Journal of Abnormal Psychology,* 1975, 84, 20-23.

Foley, V. D. *An Introduction to Family Therapy.* New York: Harper & Row, 1974.

Follingstad, D. R., Sullivan, J., Ierace, C., Ferrara, J. and Haynes, S. N. Behavioral assessment of marital interaction. Paper presented at the Association for the Advancement of Behavior Therapy, New York, December, 1976.

Ford, F. R. and Herrick, J. Family rules: Family life styles. *American Journal of Orthopsychiatry,* 1974, 44, 61-69.

Fox, R. The effect of psychotherapy on the spouse. *Family Process,* 1968, 1, 7-16.

Framo, J. Symptoms from a transactional viewpoint. In: N. Ackerman (Ed.), *Family Therapy in Transition.* Boston: Little, Brown, 1970.

Framo, J. Family origin as a therapeutic resource for adults in marital and family therapy: You can and should go home again. *Family Process,* 1976, 15, 193-210.

Franks, C. M. and Wilson, G. T. *Annual Review of Behavior Theory and Practice: 1976.* New York: Brunner/Mazel, 1976.

Freud, S. (1904). On psychotherapy. In J. Strachey et al. (Eds.), *The Standard Edition of the Complete Psychological Works of Sigmund Freud,* Vol. 7. London: Hogarth, 1953.

Freud, S. (1914). On narcissism. In: J. Strachey et al. (Eds.), *The Standard Edition of the Complete Psychological Works of Sigmund Freud,* Vol. 14. London: Hogarth, 1957.

Friedman, A. S. Interaction of drug therapy with marital therapy in depressive patients. *Archives of General Psychiatry,* 1975, 32, 619-637.

Friedman, L. An examination of Jay Haley's strategies of psychotherapy. *Psychotherapy,* 1965, 2, 181-188.

Gallant, P. M., Rich, A., Bey, E. and Terranova, L. Group psychotherapy with married couples: A successful technique in New Orleans Alcoholism Clinic patients. *Journal of the Louisiana State Medical Society,* 1970, 122, 41-44.

Garfield, S. L. Research on client variables in psychotherapy. In: A. E. Bergin and S. L. Garfield (Eds.), *Handbook of Psychotherapy and Behavior Change.* New York: Wiley, 1971.

Gergen, K. *The Psychology of Behavior Exchange.* Reading, Mass.: Addison-Wesley, 1969.

Gill, M. M. Psychoanalysis and exploratory psychotherapy. *Journal of the American Psychoanalytic Association,* 1954, 2, 771-797.

Giovacchini, P. Mutual adaptation in various object relationships. *International Journal of Psychoanalysis,* 1958, 34, 1-12.

Giovacchini, P. Treatment of marital disharmonies: The classical approach. In: B. L. Greene (Ed.), *The Psychotherapies of Marital Disharmony*. New York: The Free Press, 1965.

Glick, B. R. and Gross, S. J. Marital interaction and marital conflict: A critical evaluation of current research strategies. *Journal of Marriage and the Family*, 1975, 37, 505-512.

Glisson, D. H. A review of behavioral marital counseling: Has practice tuned out theory? *Psychological Record*, 1976, 26, 95-104.

Goffman, E. *The Presentation of Self in Everyday Life*. New York: Doubleday, 1959.

Goldiamond, I. Self-control procedures in personal behavior problems. *Psychological Reports*, 1965, 17, 851-868.

Goldstein, M. K. Behavior rate change in marriage: Training wives to modify husband's behavior (Doctoral dissertation, Cornell University, 1971). *Dissertation Abstracts International*, 1971, 32, 559B.

Goldstein, M. K. Increasing positive behaviors in married couples. In: J. D. Krumboltz and C. E. Thoresen (Eds.), *Counseling Methods*. New York: Holt, Rinehart & Winston, 1976.

Goldstein, M. K. and Francis, B. Behavior Modification of Husbands by Wives. Paper presented at the National Council on Family Relations Meeting, Washington, D. C., October 1969.

Gottlieb, A. and Pattison, E. M. Married couples group psychotherapy. *Archives of General Psychiatry*, 1966, 14, 143-152.

Gottman, J. The topography of marital conflict. Unpublished manuscript, Indiana University, 1975.

Gottman, J., Notarius, C., Markman, H., Bank, S. and Yoppi, B. Behavior exchange theory and marital decision-making. *Journal of Personality and Social Psychology*, in press.

Gray, W. and Rizzo, N. D. History and development of general systems theory. In: W. Gray, F. Duhl and N. Rizzo (Eds.), *General Systems Theory and Psychiatry*. Boston: Little, Brown, 1969.

Greene, B. L., Lee, R. R. and Lustig, N. Treatment of marital disharmony where one spouse has a primary affective disorder (manic depressive illness): I. General overview—100 couples. *Journal of Marriage and Family Counseling*, 1975, 1, 39-50.

Greenspan, S. I. and Mannino, F. V. A model for brief intervention with couples based on projective identification. *American Journal of Psychiatry*, 1974, 131, 1103-1106.

Greer, S. E. and D'Zurilla, T. J. Behavioral approaches to marital discord and conflict. *Journal of Marriage and Family Counseling*, 1975, 1, 299-315.

Grinder, J. and Bandler, R. *The Structure of Magic II*. Palo Alto: Science and Behavior Books, 1976.

Grinker, R. R., Jr. *Toward a Unified Theory of Human Behavior*. Second edition. New York: Basic Books, 1967.

Grossman, C. M. Transference, countertransference and being in love. *Psychoanalytic Quarterly*, 1965, 34, 249-256.

Group for the Advancement of Psychiatry. *Treatment of Families in Conflict*. New York: Science House, 1970.

Grunebaum, H., Christ, J. and Neiberg, N. Diagnosis and treatment planning for couples. *International Journal of Group Psychotherapy*, 1969, 19, 185-202.

Guerin, P. J. Family therapy: The first twenty-five years. In: P. J. Guerin (Ed.), *Family Therapy*. New York: Gardner, 1976.

Guerney, B. *Relationship Enhancement*. San Francisco: Jossey-Bass, 1977.

Guntrip, H. *Psychoanalytic Theory, Therapy and the Self*. New York: Basic Books, 1971

Gurman, A. S. Group marital therapy: Clinical and empirical implications for outcome research. *International Journal of Group Psychotherapy*, 1971, 21, 174-189.

Gurman, A. S. Marital therapy: Emerging trends in research and practice. *Family Process*, 1973 (a), 12, 45-54.

Gurman, A. S. The effects and effectiveness of marital therapy: A review of outcome research. *Family Process*, 1973 (b), 12, 145-170.

Gurman, A. S. Some therapeutic implications of marital therapy research. In: A. S. Gurman and D. G. Rice (Eds.), *Couples in Conflict: New Directions in Marital Therapy*. New York: Jason Aronson, 1975 (a).

Gurman, A. S. Misapplications and misuses of behavioral exchange programs in marital therapy. Paper presented at the Association for the Advancement of Behavior Therapy, San Francisco, December, 1975 (b).

Gurman, A. S. Much vigor, little rigor. *Contemporary Psychology*, 1977, 22, 67-68.

Gurman, A. S. and Kniskern, D. P. Behavioral marriage therapy. II: Empirical perspective. *Family Process*, 1978, in press (a).

Gurman, A. S. and Kniskern, D. P. Deterioration in marital and family therapy: Empirical, clinical and conceptual issues. *Family Process*, 1978, 17, 3-20.

Gurman, A. S. and Kniskern, D. P. Research in marital and family therapy: Progress, perspective and prospect. In: S. L. Garfield and A. E. Bergin (Eds.), *Handbook of Psychotherapy and Behavior Change* (Revised edition). New York: Wiley, 1978 (c).

Gurman, A. S. and Kniskern, D. P. Enriching research on marital enrichment programs. *Journal of Marriage and Family Counseling*, 1977, 3, 3-11.

Gurman, A. S. and Knudson, R. Behavioral marriage therapy: I. A psychodynamic-systems analysis and critique. *Family Process*, 1978, in press.

Gurman, A. S. and Razin, A. M. *Effective Psychotherapy: A Handbook of Research*. New York: Pergamon, 1977.

Gurman, A. S. and Rice, D. G. *Couples in Conflict: New Directions in Marital Therapy*. New York: Jason Aronson, 1975.

Haley, J. Marriage therapy. *Archives of General Psychiatry*, 1963 (a), 8, 213-234.

Haley, J. *Strategies of Psychotherapy*. New York: Grune & Stratton, 1963 (b).

Haley, J. An editor's farewell. *Family Process*, 1969, 8, 149-158.

Haley, J. *Uncommon Therapy: The Psychiatric Techniques of Milton H. Erickson, M.D.* New York: Norton, 1973.

Haley, J. *Problem Solving Therapy*. San Francisco: Jossey-Bass, 1976.

Hefez, A. Neurosis and marriage—a phenomenological analysis of disturbed married couple. *Israel Annals of Psychiatry and Related Disciplines*, 1973, 11, 81-90.

Heimann, P. On countertransference. *International Journal of Psychoanalysis*, 1950, 31, 81-84.

Heimann, P. Countertransference. *British Journal of Medical Psychology*, 1960, 33, 9-15.

Heiss, J. and Gordon, M. Need patterns and the mutual satisfaction of dating and engaged couples. *Journal of Marriage and the Family*, 1964, 26, 337.

Hickok, J. E. and Komechak, M. G. Behavior modification in marital conflict: A case report. *Family Process*, 1974, 13, 111-119.

Hicks, M. W. and Platt, M. Marital happiness and stability: A review of the research in the sixties. *Journal of Marriage and the Family*, 1970, 32, 553-574.

Hilgard, E. R. and Marquis, D. G. *Conditioning and Learning*. New York: Appleton-Century-Crofts, 1961.

Hops, H., Wills, T. A., Patterson, G. R. and Weiss, R. L. Marital interaction coding system. Unpublished manuscript, University of Oregon, 1971.

Hulse, W. C. Group psychotherapy. In: V. Eisenstein (Ed.), *Neurotic Interaction in Marriage*. New York: Basic Books, 1956.

Hurvitz, N. Marital problems following psychotherapy with one spouse. *Journal of Consulting and Clinical Psychology*, 1967, 31, 38-47.

Huston, T. L. A perspective on interpersonal attraction. In: T. L. Huston (Ed.), *Foundations of Interpersonal Attraction*. New York: Academic Press, 1974.

Jackson, D. D. The study of the family. *Family Process*, 1965, 4, 1-20.

Jackson, D. D. The individual and the larger contexts. *Family Process*, 1967, 6, 139-147.

Jackson, J. and Grotjahn, M. The re-enactment of the marriage neurosis in group psychotherapy. *Journal of Nervous and Mental Disease*, 1958, 127, 503-510.

Jackson, J. and Grotjahn, M. The efficacy of group therapy in a case of marriage neurosis. *International Journal of Group Psychotherapy*, 1959, 9, 420-428.

Jacob, T. Assessment of marital dysfunction. In: M. Hersen and A. Bellack (Eds.), *Behavioral Assessment: A Practical Handbook*. New York: Pergamon, 1976.

Jacobs, A. and Sachs, L. B. (Eds.). *The Psychology of Private Events*. New York: Academic Press, 1971.

Jacobson, D. and Matheny, A. Mate selection in open marriage systems. *International Journal of Comparative Sociology*, 1962, 3, 98-123.

Jacobson, N. S. Problem-solving and contingency contracting in the treatment of marital discord. *Journal of Consulting and Clinical Psychology*, 1977, 45, 92-100.

Jacobson, N. S. Specific and non-specific factors in the effectiveness of a behavioral approach to marital discord. *Journal of Consulting and Clinical Psychology*, 1978, 46, 442-452.

Jacobson, N. S. and Martin, B. Behavioral marriage therapy: Current status. *Psychological Bulletin*, 1976, 83, 540-556.

Kanfer, F. H. and Karoly, P. Self-control: A behavioristic excursion into the lion's den. *Behavior Therapy*, 1972, 3, 398-416.

Kaplan, H. S. *The New Sex Therapy*. New York: Brunner/Mazel, 1974.

Karpel, M. Individuation: From fusion to dialogue. *Family Process*, 1976, 15, 65-82.

Kepecs, J. Personal communication, April 1977.

Kimmel, P. R. and Havens, J. W. Game theory versus mutual identification: Two criteria for assessing marital relationships. *Journal of Marriage and the Family*, 1966, 28, 460-465.

Kinder, B. N. and Blakeney, P. Treatment of sexual dysfunction: A review of outcome studies. Unpublished manuscript, University of Texas Medical Branch, 1976.

Klugman, J. Towards a unified theory of family therapy. Unpublished manuscript, Yale University, 1975 (a).

Klugman, J. Towards a unified technique of family therapy: A meta-strategy of psychotherapy. Unpublished manuscript, Yale University, 1975 (b).

Kohl, R. N. Pathologic reactions of marital partners to improvement in patients. *American Journal of Psychiatry*, 1962, 118, 1036-1041.

Kubie, L. Psychoanalysis and marriage: Practical and theoretical issues. In: V. Eisenstein (Ed.), *Neurotic Interaction in Marriage*. New York: Basic Books, 1956.

Laing, R. D. *Self and Others*. London: Tavistock, 1961.

Laing, R. D., Phillipson, H. and Lee, A. R. *Interpersonal Perception*. New York: Springer, 1966.

Laws, J. L. A feminist review of marital adjustment literature: The rape of the locke. *Journal of Marriage and the Family*, 1971, 33, 483-516.

Lazarus, A. A. Behavior therapy and marriage counseling. *Journal of the American Society of Psychosomatic Dentistry and Medicine*, 1968, 15, 49-56.

Leichter, E. Group psychotherapy of married couples' groups: Some characteristic treatment dynamics. *International Journal of Group Psychotherapy*, 1962, 12, 154-163.

Leslie, G. R. The field of marriage counseling. In: H. T. Christensen (Ed.), *Handbook of Marriage and the Family*. Chicago: Rand McNally, 1964.

Levant, R. F. Client-centered approaches to working with the family: A review of new therapeutic, educational, and preventive models. *Paper presented at the California State Psychological Association, Los Angeles, March, 1977.*

Levitt, E. Research on psychotherapy with children. In: A. E. Bergin and S. L. Garfield (Eds.), *Handbook of Psychotherapy and Behavior Change.* New York: Wiley, 1971.

Levine, F. M. and Fasnacht, G. Token rewards may lead to token learning. *American Psychologist,* 1974, 29, 816-820.

Liberman, R. P. Behavioral approaches to family and couple therapy. *American Journal of Orthopsychiatry,* 1970, 40, 106-118.

Liberman, R. P., Levine, J., Wheeler, E., Sanders, N. and Wallace, C. Experimental evaluation of marital group therapy: Behavioral vs. interaction-insight formats. *Acta Psychiatrica Scandinavica,* 1976.

Liebman, R., Minuchin, S., Baker, L. and Rosman, B. L. The role of the family in the treatment of chronic asthma. In: P. Guerin (Ed.), *Family Therapy.* New York: Gardner, 1976.

Linden, M. E., Goodwin, H. M. and Resnik, H. Group psychotherapy of couples in marriage counseling. *International Journal of Group Psychotherapy,* 1968, 18, 313-324.

Lloyd, R. A. and Paulson, I. Projective identification in the marital relationship as a resistance in psychotherapy. *Archives of General Psychiatry,* 1972, 27, 410-413.

Lobitz, W. C. and LoPiccolo, J. New methods in the behavioral treatment of sexual dysfunction. *Journal of Behavior Therapy and Experimental Psychology,* 1972, 3, 265-271.

Lorion, R. P. Socioeconomic status and traditional treatment approaches reconsidered. *Psychological Bulletin,* 1973, 79, 263-270.

Lorion, R. P. Patient and therapist variables in the treatment of low income patients. *Psychological Bulletin,* 1974, 81, 344-354.

Lott, A. J. and Lott, B. E. The role of reward in the formation of positive interpersonal attitudes. In: T. L. Huston (Ed.), *Foundations of Interpersonal Attraction.* New York: Academic Press, 1974.

Luborsky, L., Singer, B. and Luborsky, L. Comparative studies of psychotherapies: Is it true that "Everyone has won and all must have prizes"? *Archives of General Psychiatry,* 1975, 32, 995-1008.

Luthman, S. *The Dynamic Family.* Palo Alto, Calif.: Science and Behavior Books, 1974.

Mahoney, M. *Cognition and Behavior Modification.* Cambridge, Mass.: Ballinger, 1974.

Mahoney, M. Cognitive therapy and research: A question of questions. *Cognitive Therapy and Research,* 1977, 1, 5-16.

Mahoney, M. and Arnkoff, D. Cognitive and self-control therapies. In: S. L. Garfield and A. E. Bergin (Eds.), *Handbook of Psychotherapy and Behavior Change.* Second edition. New York: Wiley, 1978.

Mahoney, M. and Thoresen, C. *Self-Control: Power to the Person.* Monterey, Calif.: Brooks/Cole, 1974.

Mann, J. *Time-Limited Psychotherapy.* Cambridge, Mass.: Harvard University Press, 1973.

Malan, D. H. *A Study of Brief Psychotherapy.* London: Tavistock, 1963.

Malan, D. H. *The Frontier of Brief Psychotherapy.* New York: Plenum, 1976.

Manus, G. I. Marriage counseling: A technique in search of a theory. *Journal of Marriage and the Family,* 1966, 28, 449-453.

Marks, I. M. and Gelder, M. G. Common ground between behavior therapy and psychodynamic methods. *British Journal of Medical Psychology,* 1966, 39, 11-23.

Marshall, J. R. The expression of feelings. *Archives of General Psychiatry,* 1972, 27, 786-790.

Martin, P. *A Marital Therapy Manual.* New York: Brunner/Mazel, 1976.

Masters, W. H. and Johnson, V. E. *Human Sexual Inadequacy.* Boston: Little, Brown, 1970.

Mathews, A., Bancroft, J., Whitehead, A., Hackman, A., Julier, D., Bancroft, J., Gath, D. and Shaw, P. The behavioral treatment of sexual inadequacy: A comparative study. *Behaviour Research and Therapy,* 1976, 14, 427-436.

Meichenbaum, D. *Cognitive Behavior Modification.* New York: Plenum, 1977.

Menninger, K., Mayman, M. and Pruyser, P. *The Vital Balance.* New York: Viking, 1963.

Miller, J. G. Living systems: Basic concepts. *Behavioral Science,* 1965 (a), 10, 193-237.

Miller, J. G. Living systems: Structure and Process. *Behavioral Science* 1965 (b), 10, 337-379.

Mintz, J. The role of the therapist in assessing psychotherapy outcome. In: A. S. Gurman and A. M. Razin (Eds.), *Effective Psychotherapy: A Handbook of Research.* New York: Pergamon, 1977.

Minuchin, S. *Families and Family Therapy.* Cambridge, Ma.: Harvard University Press, 1974.

Minuchin, S., Baker, L., Rosman, B., Liebman, R., Milman, L. and Todd, T. A conceptual model of psychosomatic illness in children. *Archives of General Psychiatry,* 1975, 32, 1031-1038.

Mittelman, B. Concurrent analysis of marital couples. *Psychoanalytic Quarterly,* 1948, 17, 182-197.

Montalvo, B. and Haley, J. In defense of child therapy. *Family Process,* 1973, 12, 227-244.

Murray, E. Learning theory and psychotherapy: Biotropic versus sociotropic approaches. *Journal of Counseling Psychology,* 1963, 10, 250-255.

Murray, H. *Explorations in Personality.* New York: Oxford University Press, 1938.

Murstein, B. I. The complementarity need hypothesis in newlyweds and middle-aged married couples. *Journal of Abnormal and Social Psychology,* 1961, 63, 194-197.

Murstein, B. I. Empirical tests of role complementarity needs, and homogany theories of marital choice. *Journal of Marriage and the Family,* 1967, 29, 689.

Murstein, B. I. A theory of marital choice and its applicability to marital adjustment. In: B. L. Murstein (Ed.), *Theories of Attraction and Love.* New York: Academic Press, 1971.

Murstein, B. I. and Beck, G. D. Person perception, marriage adjustment and social desirability. *Journal of Consulting and Clinical Psychology,* 1972, 39, 396-403.

Nadelson, C., Bassuk, E., Hopps, C. and Boutelle, W. Conjoint marital psychotherapy: Evaluative procedures. *Social Casework,* 1975, 56, 91-96.

Nadelson, C., Bassuk, E., Hopps, C. and Boutelle, W. Conjoint marital psychotherapy: Treatment techniques. *Psychiatric Quarterly,* 1977, 38, 11, 898-907.

Napier, A. Y. The marriage of families: Cross-generational complementarity. *Family Process,* 1971, 10, 373-395.

Oberndorf, C. P. Psychoanalysis of married couples. *Psychoanalytic Review,* 1938, 25, 453-475.

Olson, D. H. Marital and family therapy: Integrative review and critique. *Journal of Marriage and the Family,* 1970, 32, 501-538.

Olson, D. H. Behavior modification research with couples and families: A systems analysis, review and critique. Are behavior counts all that count? Paper presented at the Association for the Advancement of Behavior Therapy Meeting, New York, October, 1972.

Oltmanns, T., Broderick, J. and O'Leary, K. D. Marital adjustment and the efficacy of behavior therapy with children. Paper presented at the Association for the Advancement of Behavior Therapy, New York, December 1976.

Overturf, J. Marital therapy: Toleration of differentness. *Journal of Marriage and Family Counseling,* 1976, 3, 235-241.

Papanek, H. Group psychotherapy with married couples. In: H. Masserman (Ed.), *Current Psychiatric Therapies,* Volume 5. New York: Grune & Stratton, 1965.

Parloff, M. B. The narcissism of small differences—and some big ones. *International Journal of Group Psychotherapy,* 1976, 26, 311-319.

Patterson, G. R. The aggressive child: Victim and architect of a coercive system. In: E. Mash, L. Hamerlynck and L. Handy (Eds.), *Behavior Modification and Families.* New York: Brunner/Mazel, 1975.

Patterson, G. R. and Hops, H. Coercion: A game for two. Intervention techniques for marital conflict. In: R. Ulrich and P. Mountjoy (Eds.), *The Experimental Analysis of Social Behavior.* New York: Appleton-Century-Crofts, 1972.

Patterson, G. R., Weiss, R. L. and Hops, H. Training of marital skills. In: H. Leitenberg (Ed.), *Handbook of Behavior Modification and Behavior Therapy.* New York: Prentice-Hall, 1976.

Perelman, J. S. Problems encountered in group psychotherapy of married couples. *International Journal of Group Psychotherapy,* 1960, 10, 136-142.

Pittman, F. and Flomenhaft, K. Treating the Doll's House Marriage. *Family Process,* 1970, 9, 143-155.

Raimy, Y. V. *Misconceptions of the Self.* San Francisco: Jossey-Bass, 1975.

Rappaport, A. F. and Harrell, J. A behavioral exchange model for marital counseling. *The Family Coordinator,* 1972, 22, 203-212.

Rausch, H. L. Paradox, levels and junctures in person-situation systems. In: D. Magnusson and N. S. Endler (Eds.), *Personality at the Crossroads.* New York: Wiley, 1976.

Rausch, H. L., Barry, W. A., Hertel, R. K. and Swain, M. A. *Communication, Conflict and Marriage.* San Francisco: Jossey-Bass, 1974.

Reid, J. Reciprocity and family interaction. Unpublished doctoral dissertation, University of Oregon, 1967.

Reisinger, J. J., Frangia, G. W. and Hoffman, E. H. Toddler management training: Generalization and marital status. *Journal of Behavior Therapy and Experimental Psychiatry,* 1976, 7, 335-340.

Ritterman, M. K. Paradigmatic classification of family therapy techniques. *Family Process,* 1977, 16, 29-46.

Rogers, C. R. *On Becoming a Person.* Boston: Houghton-Mifflin, 1961.

Royce, W. S. and Weiss, R. L. Behavioral cues in the judgment of marital satisfaction: A linear regression analysis. *Journal of Consulting and Clinical Psychology,* 1975, 43, 816-824.

Ruesch, J. A general systems theory based on human communications. In: W. Gray, F. Duhl and N. Rizzo (Eds.), *General Systems Theory and Psychiatry.* Boston: Little, Brown, 1969.

Sager, C. J. Transference in the conjoint therapy of married couples. *Archives of General Psychiatry,* 1967, 16, 185-193.

Sager, C. J. Sexual dysfunctions and marital discord. In: H. Kaplan, *The New Sex Therapy.* New York: Brunner/Mazel, 1974.

Sager, C. J. *Marriage Contracts and Couple Therapy.* New York: Brunner/Mazel, 1976.

Sager, C. J., Kaplan, H. S., Gundlach, R. H., Kremer, M., Lenz, R. and Royce, J. R. The marriage contract. *Family Process,* 1971, 10, 311-326

Satir, V. *Conjoint Family Therapy.* Palo Alto, Calif.: Science and Behavior Books, 1967.

Satir, V. *Peoplemaking.* Palo Alto, Calif.: Science and Behavior Books, 1972.

Satir, V., Stachowiak, J. and Taschman, H. *Helping Families to Change.* New York: Aronson, 1975

Scheflen, A. E. Behavioral programs in human communication. In: W. Gray, F. Duhl and N. Rizzo (Eds.), *General Systems Theory and Psychiatry*. Boston: Little, Brown, 1969.

Schellenberg, J. and Bee, L. A re-examination of the theory of complementary needs in mate selection. *Marriage and Family Living*, 1960, 22, 227.

Seligman, M. P. *Helplessness*. San Francisco: W. H. Freeman, 1975.

Shapiro, A. K. The behavior therapies: Therapeutic breakthrough or latest fad? *American Journal of Psychiatry*, 1976, 133, 154-159.

Shepherd, M., Oppenheim, A. and Mitchell, S. Childhood behavior disorders and the child guidance clinic: An epidemiological study. *Journal of Child Psychology and Psychiatry*, 1966, 7, 39-52.

Shumaker, D. G. Object relations theory of dependency and its effect upon marital comparability. *Dissertation Abstracts International*, 1976, 37, 3097-3098B.

Sifneos, R. E. *Short-Term Psychotherapy and Emotional Crisis*. Cambridge, Mass.: Harvard University Press, 1972.

Skynner, A. C. R. *Systems of Family and Marital Psychotherapy*. New York: Brunner/Mazel, 1976.

Sluzki, C. E. The coalitionary process in initiating family therapy. *Family Process*, 1975, 14, 67-77.

Smith, C. G. Marital influence on treatment outcome in alcoholism. *Journal of the Irish Medical Association*, 1967, 60, 433-434.

Smith, C. G. Alcoholics: Their treatment and their wives. *British Journal of Psychiatry*, 1969, 115, 1039-1042.

Smith, J. W. and Grunebaum, H. The therapeutic alliance in marital therapy. In: H. Grunebaum and J. Christ (Eds.), *Contemporary Marriage: Structure, Dynamics and Therapy*. Boston: Little, Brown, 1976.

Sonne, J. C. *A Primer for Family Therapists*. Philadelphia: Thursday Press, 1973.

Stanton, M. D. and Todd, T. Structural family therapy with heroin addicts: Some outcome data. Paper presented at the Society for Psychotherapy Research Meeting, San Diego, June 1976.

Steinglass, P., Davis, D. I. and Berenson, D. In-hospital treatment of alcoholic couples. Paper presented at the American Psychiatric Association Meeting, Anaheim, California, 1975.

Stern, R. Contract therapy in obsessive-compulsive neurosis with marital discord. *British Journal of Psychiatry*, 1973, 123, 681-684.

Stewart, R. H., Peters, T. C., Marsh, S. and Peters, M. J. An object-relations approach to psychotherapy with marital couples, families and children. *Family Process*, 1975, 14, 161-178.

Strupp, H. H. and Hadley, S. W. A tripartite model of mental health and therapeutic outcomes: With special reference to negative effects in psychotherapy. *American Psychologist*, 1977, 32, 187-196.

Stuart, R. B. Operant-interpersonal treatment for marital discord. *Journal of Consulting and Clinical Psychology*, 1969 (a), 33, 675-682.

Stuart, R. B. Token reinforcement in marital treatment. In: R. D. Rubin and C. M. Franks (Eds.), *Advances in Behavior Therapy*. New York: Academic Press, 1969 (b).

Stuart, R. B. Behavioral remedies for marital ills: A guide to the use of operant-interpersonal techniques. In: A. S. Gurman and D. G. Rice (Eds.), *Couples in Conflict: New Directions in Marital Therapy*. New York: Aronson, 1975.

Sullivan, H. S. *The Interpersonal Theory of Psychiatry*. New York: W. W. Norton, 1953.

Tharp, R. B. Psychological patterning in marriage. *Psychological Bulletin*, 1963, 60, 97-117.

Thibaut, J. W. and Kelley, H. H. *The Social Psychology of Groups*. New York: Wiley, 1959.

Thomlinson, R. J. A behavioral model for social work intervention with the marital dyad (doctoral dissertation, University of Toronto, 1972). *Dissertation Abstracts International*, 1974, 35, 1227A.

Thompson, C. M. *Interpersonal psychoanalysis*. New York: Basic Books, 1964.

Titchener, J. The problem of interpretation in marital therapy. *Comprehensive Psychiatry*, 1966, 7, 321-327.

Toomim, M. K. Structured separation with counseling: A therapeutic approach for couples in conflict. *Family Process*, 1972, 11, 299-310.

Tsoi-Hoshmand, L. The limits of *quid pro quo* in couple therapy. *The Family Coordinator*, 1975, 24, 51-54.

Tsoi-Hoshmand, L. Marital therapy: An integrative behavioral-learning model. *Journal of Marriage and Family Counseling*, 1976, 2, 179-191.

Turkewitz, H. Communication training and behavioral exchange in the treatment of marital problems. Unpublished doctoral dissertation, SUNY at Stony Brook, 1977.

Turkewitz, H. and O'Leary, K. D. Communication and behavioral marital therapy: An outcome study. Paper presented at the Association for the Advancement of Behavior Therapy Meeting, New York, December 1976.

Vincent, J. P., Weiss, R. L. and Birchler, G. R. A behavioral analysis of problem-solving in distressed and nondistressed married and stranger dyads. *Behavior Therapy*, 1975, 6, 475-487.

Wachtel, P. L. *Psychoanalysis and Behavior Therapy: Toward an Integration*. New York: Basic Books, 1978.

Wahlroos, S. Some limitations of family therapy. *Journal of Family Counseling*, 1976, 4, 8-11.

Watzlawick, P. *How Real Is Real? Confusion, Disinformation, Communication*. New York: Random House, 1976 (a).

Watzlawick, P. The psychotherapeutic technique of "reframing." In: J. L. Claghorn (Ed.), *Successful Psychotherapy*. New York: Brunner/Mazel, 1976 (b).

Watzlawick, P., Beavin, J. H. and Jackson, D. D. *Pragmatics of Human Communication*. New York: W. W. Norton, 1967.

Watzlawick, P., Weakland, J. and Fisch, R. *Change: Principles of Problem Formation and Problem Resolution*. New York: W. W. Norton, 1974.

Weakland, J. Communication theory and clinical change. In: P. Guerin (Ed.), *Family Therapy*. New York: Gardner, 1976.

Weakland, J. H., Fisch, R., Watzlawick, P. and Bodin, A. M. Brief therapy: Focused problem resolution. *Family Process*, 1974, 13, 141-168.

Weiner, I. B. *Principles of Psychotherapy*. New York: Wiley, 1975.

Weiss, R. L. Contracts, cognition and change: A behavioral approach to marital therapy. *The Counseling Psychologist*, 1975, 5, 15-26.

Weiss, R. L., Hops, H. and Patterson, G. R. A framework for conceptualizing marital conflict, a technology for altering it, some data for evaluating it. In: L. A. Hamerlynck, L. C. Handy and E. J. Mash (Eds.), *Behavior Change: Methodology, Concepts and Practice*. Champaign, Ill.: Research Press, 1973.

Weiss, R. L. and Margolin, G. Marital conflict and accord. In: A. R. Ciminero, K. D. Calhoun and H. E. Adams (Eds.), *Handbook for Behavioral Assessment*. New York: Wiley, 1977.

Weiss, R. L., Birchler, G. R. and Vincent, J. Contractual models for negotiation training in marital dyads. *Journal of Marriage and the Family*, 1974, 36, 321-330.

Westman, J. C., Carek, D. J. and McDermott, J. F. A comparison of married couples in the same and separate therapy groups. *International Journal of Group Psychotherapy*, 1965, 15, 374-381.

Whitaker, C. A. A family therapist looks at marital therapy. In: A. S. Gurman and

D. G. Rice (Eds.), *Couples in Conflict: New Directions in Marital Therapy*. New York: Jason Aronson, 1975.

Wieman, R. J., Shoulders, D. I. and Farr, J. H. Reciprocal reinforcement in marital therapy. *Journal of Behavior Therapy and Experimental Psychiatry*, 1973, 5, 291-295.

Wills, T. A., Weiss, R. L. and Patterson, G. R. A behavioral analysis of the determinants of marital satisfaction. *Journal of Consulting and Clinical Psychology*, 1974, 42, 802-811.

Wilson, G. T. and Evans, I. M. The therapist-client relationship in behavior therapy. In: A. S. Gurman and A. M. Razin (Eds.), *Effective Psychotherapy: A Handbook of Research*. New York: Pergamon, 1977.

Winch, R. F. *The Modern Family*. New York: Holt, 1952.

Winch, R. F. The theory of complementary needs in mate selection: Final results on the test of general hypothesis. *American Sociological Review*, 1955, 20, 552-555.

Winch, R. F. *Mate-Selection: A Study of Complementary Needs*. New York: Harper, 1958.

Winch, R. F., Ktsanes, T. and Ktsanes, V. The theory of complementary needs in mate selection: An analytic and descriptive study. *American Sociological Review*, 1954, 19, 241-249.

Witkin, H. A. Psychological differentiation and forms of pathology. *Journal of Abnormal Psychology*, 1965, 70, 317-336.

Witkin, H. A. and Goodenough, H. Field dependence and interpersonal behavior. *Psychological Bulletin*, 1977, 84, 4, 661-689.

Wolberg, L. R. (Ed.). *Short-Term Psychotherapy*. New York: Grune & Stratton, 1965.

Wynne, L. C. Some guidelines for exploratory conjoint family therapy. In: J. Haley (Ed.), *Changing Families*. New York: Grune & Stratton, 1971.

Yalom, I. *Theory and Practice of Group Psychotherapy* (Second Edition). New York: Basic Books, 1975.

Yates, A. J. *Behavior Therapy*. New York: Wiley, 1971.

Zuk, G. The side-taking function in family therapy. *American Journal of Orthopsychiatry*, 1968, 38, 553-559.

Subject Index

Acrophobia, treatment of, 244
Acting out:
  and communication, marital, 140
  and denial, 99
  and therapy, 501
Adaptation, and family system, 343ff.
Adultery, 263
Affective disorders, treatment of, 445
Aggressor-introject, 37-39, 75. *See also* Introjection
Al-Anon, 432
Alcoholics Anonymous, 240, 241, 432
Alcoholism:
  and desensitization, 248
  family implications, 169
  and feedback, 313-14
  systems mode of, 356-59, 361
  treatment of, 243, 261, 397, 430-33, 445, 475
Alliances, therapeutic, 126-27
American Association of Marriage and Family Counselors, 4
American Association of Marriage Counselors, 12
American Institute of Family Relations, 12
American Psychiatric Association, 91, 302
American Psychological Association (APA), 1
Analog studies, 415-17
Anorexia, 508
Anxiety:
  defined, 243-44
  and sexuality, 433ff., 439-40
  social, 244

and therapy, 384-85, 475
Areas of Change Questionnaire, 220, 412
"As-if" personality, 33
Assertiveness training, 18, 185, 227, 248
Assortive theory, of mating, 169
Asthma, 508
Attribution theory, 182-83
Autism, treatment of, 290
Aversive consequences, 177, 178. *See also* Reinforcement
Aversive stimulus, 187, 232, 233. *See also* Reinforcement

Behavioral Exchange-Change model, 196-200, 408
Behaviorism. *See also* Behaviorism, and marital therapy; Reinforcement; Stimuli
  behavioral analysis, 174ff.
  behavioral system approach, 189ff.
    behavioral exchange model, 197
    integrative model, 205
    interaction categories, 199
  behavioral therapy, 90, 94. 243
    assessment, 538-40
    compared, 99, 533ff., 539ff., 549ff.
    goals of, 540-45
    and self-reports, 412ff., 423-24
    studies on, 395
    therapists, 545-48
  conceptions of, 168ff.
  evaluation of, 207ff.
  perspective on, 231ff.
  theory of, 457

567

Behaviorism, and marital therapy, 240ff., 479ff. *See also* Behaviorism
approach, 242ff.
cognitive movement in, 19
conjoint treatment, 487ff.
development of, 17-19, 248ff.
effectiveness of, 21, 22
future directions, 289-93
marital choice, 480ff.
outcomes of, 285-89
overt behavior, 491ff.
strengths of, 504-506
therapist in, 499ff.
treatment process, 256ff.
courtship stage, 256ff.
disengagement stage, 256, 283-85
engagement stage, 256, 265-67
marriage stage, 267ff.
Beth Israel Hospital, Department of Psychiatry, 102, 130, 154-59
"Beyond the Double Bind," conference, 318n.
Biomedical model, of disease, 347
Black box, model, 319-20, 367
Borderline personality, clinical case of, 134-35
Boundaries:
and marital functioning, 328
in systems theory, 306-308

Cambodia, invasion of, 6
Carcinoma, uterine, 305
Catharsis, and therapy, 415, 495
Cell structure, 304
Classical conditioning, 243-45. *See also* Behaviorism
Client-centered therapy, 395, 508
"Clockwork Orange," 165
Coalition negotiation, in therapy, 372, 372n.
Coercion process, 187
Cognitive approach, to therapy, 167, 172, 242, 245-47, 527
Cohabitation, 6, 8, 11
Colitis, ulcerative, pattern in, 61
Collaborative therapy, 13, 474
Collusion, and marriage, 452, 453, 457, 490, 520, 521
Combined marital therapy, 13, 120
"Coming Home from the Hospital," videotapes, 387
Communal marriage, 6, 8, 10, 11
Communications:
and biology, 316

categorical approach to, 320n.
charting of, 323-24
clarity in, 270-73
command aspect of, 325
and disengagement, 284-85
feeling expression in, 274-76
and marriage, 268ff., 285ff.
and MRI theory, 319
paradigm of, 242n.
skills in, 241, 404ff., 425, 427
theory of, 318ff.
verbal interactions, 273-74
Companionship marriage, 9-11, 191
Comparative outcome studies, 421-23
Compulsion. *See* Obsessive-compulsion
Concurrent marital therapy, 12-15, 117-18, 124-25
compared, 430
effectiveness of, 474
group, 14
Conditioning, aversive, electric, 433. *See also* Behaviorism; Reinforcement
Conjoint therapy, 13-14, 118-20, 478, 537
advantages of, 248-49, 254
and concurrent therapy, 430
couple comparison by, 428-30
effectiveness of, 474
goals of, 458ff.
group, 14, 249, 474
prescriptions in, 366ff.
symptoms in, 379
transference in, 467ff.
Conjugal Life Questionnaire, 408
Conjugal Relationship Enhancement (CRE), 406-408, 411
Conjugal Relationship Modification, 223
Conjugal therapy, 14
Consecutive therapy, 117
Context markers, of interaction, 379
Contingency management techniques, 18, 19, 178-79. *See also* Behaviorism, and marital therapy
Contraception, 155
Contracts:
and behavioral therapy, 489
behavior specification in, 277-78
consequences, positive, 280-83
construction of, 278-80
and contingency, 268, 421, 425
implicit, 452
levels of, 455-56
and marital therapy, 241, 276n., 277ff., 285, 289
and marriage, 113, 139-40

negotiation of, 490-91
psychoanalysis of, 140, 141, 503
and reciprocity, 228
training in, 46, 227
types of, 251-53
Control groups, in research, 401-402, 405, 417-21
Core symbols, 482
Co-therapy, 120-21, 253-55
"Counseling Readiness Questionnaire," 221
Counterconditioning techniques, 18, 19. *See also* Desensitization
Countertransference, 49, 52, 81, 124, 125. *See also* Psychoanalysis; Transference
and contracts, 140, 141
in marriage, 16
and therapy, 17, 117, 118, 121, 123-27, 148, 149, 152, 471
unconscious in, 471n.
Couples' Evaluation Questionnaire, 154-59
Couple's Guide to Communication, A (Gottman et al.), 276
Courtship:
and problem solution, 53
and therapy, 256ff.
Cybernetics, 367
and adaptation, 344
and analogy, 351, 352
circularity in, 393
and data, 328
and MRI theory, 319
and regulation, 314

Death of the Family, The (Cooper), 6
Decision-making, teaching of, 246
Delinquents, treatment of, 243
Denial, 518
and distancing, 149
and therapy, 116
Depersonalization, and marriage, 48
Depression:
bipolar, 55, 61, 135
case study of, 136, 240ff.
and communication, 326
and family systems, 525
and helplessness, 198
and identity, 34
and marriage, 109, 169
and neurosis, 430
and sadness, 382
scale on, 428
spectrum disorder, 169

and systems theory, 306
and therapy, 261, 379, 475
Desensitization, 181, 185, 244-45, 248, 264, 433, 435-39
Developmental framework, of sociology, 334, 336ff., 342, 346, 362
Differentiation. *See* Individuation-differentiation
Differentiation of Self Scale, 515-17
Discriminative stimulus, 177
Disengagement stage, of therapy, 256, 283-85
Displacement:
pathology in, 39
and transference, 82
Dissociations, trading of, 452
Divorce, trends in, 2ff.
case study of, 147
counseling on, 263
and cultural change, 4
law, 7
and male dominance, 4-6
monogamy, 4-5
rates, 2-3
remarriage, 292
and self-realization, 103
socio-economic change, 7
termination, 353
DNA, information in, 316
Dora case, 28, 100
Double bind:
and communications, 109, 325-26
and therapy, 526
Dream analysis, and therapy, 143-44, 149
Drugs, problems with, 55, 61, 508
Dyadic systems, and pathology, 371
Dysfunctioning, and marriage, 451

Eco-system, variables of, 366
Egalitarianism, and behavior, 184, 192
Ego, 470n.
boundaries of, 109, 453
and change, 115
and communication, 521
as concept, 92
control by, 106
development of, 101, 108
and differentiation, 345
in family, 331, 510
functions of, 37, 129, 136
gratification of, 32
and id, 94
ideal of, 41, 43, 105, 450
identity of, 68, 69

and love, 41, 43
pathology in, 144
and repression, 109-10
strength in, 102, 115, 139, 455, 488
syntonic, problems, 122
Ego and the Id, The (Freud), 94
Ego psychology, sociological dimension, 30
"Eight Ages of Man," 355
Embryology, stages in, 350
Emotional cut-off, 333
Emotional process/demand, 68
Empathy:
  and communication, 422-23
  development of, 119
  and ego, 136
  paternal basis of, 57
  of therapist, 287
  in therapy, 264, 275
  training in, 271-73, 404, 406
Encounter groups, 447
Engagement, and marriage, 43-44, 53
Engagement stage, of therapy, 256, 265-67
Entropy, 314, 518
Enuresis, treatment of, 290
Epigenesis, in embryology, 350
Equifinality, principle of, 518, 529
"Error-activated" mechanism, 352
Extinction. *See also* Behaviorism
  and marital relations, 248
  and reinforcement, 178, 179, 182
  term use, 265
  in therapy, 246-47
  in vivo, 245

Face validity, 400
Fair fight training, 447
Family Contract Game, 226
Family cycle, and development, 336ff., 340
Family Development (Duvall), 340n.
Family identity model, 356, 358-59, 361
"Family Neurosis and the Neurotic Family" (Spitz), 29
Family projection process, 452. *See also* Projection
Family systems theory, 70, 183, 299, 330-34. *See also* Systems theory
Fatty acids, production of, and stress, 312
Feedback, 349, 354
  loop, negative, 313ff., 344, 351, 352
  loop, positive, 313ff., 352, 383
  and systems theory, 20, 313ff.
Feelings Questionnaire, 286, 408

"Feelings Toward Spouse," questionnaire, 260
Feminism, and roles, 170
Fixation, and psychosis, 69
Follow-up, in research, 402
Free association, 126, 148. *See also* Psychoanalysis
Fusion, 457, 535

Galvanic skin response, and sexuality, 435
Gay marriage, 6
General systems theory. *See* Systems theory
General Systems Theory and Psychiatry (Gray et al.), 302
Gestalt therapy, 447
Good faith contract, 251-52
Grandiose self, 38
Greening of America, The (Reich), 6
Group for the Advancement of Psychiatry, 542
Group marriage, 6, 8, 10, 11
Group therapy, 13-14, 122, 254, 255
"Growth approach," to therapy, 373n.

Harvard University, 334
Headache, and therapy, 384-85
Heart rate, and sexuality, 435
Height, attitudes on, 9
Hepatoma, 304-305
Heterostasis, 518
Hierarchies, in systems theory, 309-11, 311n.
Holistic theory, 330
Homeostasis, 349
  and adaptation, 341, 344
  in agreement, 379
  biological, 311-12
  and data, 328
  and family systems, 524
  and feedback, 351, 352, 354
  maintenance of, 389
  and marriage, 120
  in systems theory, 20, 311ff.
  in therapy, 381, 532
Homosexuality, 61, 120
Human Sexual Inadequacy (Masters and Johnson), 245, 434
Hyperactivity:
  and reinforcement, 177
  treatment of, 290

Id:
  concept of, 92
  and ego, 94

Idealization:
  definition problem, 457
  in marriage, 110-11, 450, 486
  primitive, in love, 41-43
Identification, 490, 512. *See also* Identity
  of child, 56
  and generations, 57
  and introjection, 51n.
  and love, 41, 42
  and marriage, 16, 45, 47, 105
  and parental models, 73
  and therapist, 151
  and therapy, 142, 144
Identified patient (IP), role in therapy, 376
Identity. *See also* Identification
  and child development, 77-78
  development of, 36, 37
  diffusion in, 39
  of family, 76-77
  and marriage, 45, 47, 48
  maturity in, 35
  and object loss, 109
  personal, disorder in, 32-34
Impotency:
  case study of, 137
  treatment of, 436-37
Individual therapy:
  caution on, 474-76
  and conjoint therapy, 248-49
  described, 115-18
Individuation-differentiation, 46-48, 57
  and behaviorism, 181-83
  and blame, 49
  in cells, 350-51
  definition problem, 457
  establishment of, 34
  failure in, 33-34, 37-39
  in family, 510-13
  and fusion, continuum, 333
  and love, 42, 43, 47, 48
  in marriage, 105-107
  and neurosis, 50
  and parenting, 75, 76, 81
  and pseudomutuality, 71
  and self, 332, 349, 535
  and separation, 32, 33
  and therapy, 515, 540
Insight, and conjoint therapy, 478
Institutional-historical framework, 334
Insurance, and marriage therapy, 168
Integration, of self, 36
Interaction theory, of psychopathology, 169

Internalization, xiii
  and child development, 60, 73
  failure in, 33
  and introjection, 52
  and love, 42, 43
  and marriage, 26, 27
  and maternal rejection, 63
  and parenting, 57, 74
  patterns of, 51, 52
  role in, 37
  and transference, 82
International Congress of Psychoanalysis, 29
Interpersonal Checklist, 430
Interpersonal perception, 410
Interpretation of Dreams (Freud), 94
Introductory Lectures (Freud), 94
Introjection, xiii, 518
  and analysis, 85
  development of, 36-37
  and family system, 70-72
  and grandparents, 57
  and identification, 512
  and internalization, 52
  and love, 41, 42
  and marriage, 16, 17, 26, 27, 105
  and maternal rejection, 63
  organization in, 37-38, 39
  and paranoia, 53
  and parenting, 74-76
  pathogenic, 46-47
  patterns of, 50-51, 58
  and projection, 40, 170
  and transference, 81-84
Inventory of Marital Conflicts, 286

Journal of Sex and Marital Therapy, 434
Journal of the American Psychoanalytic Association, 398

Laboratory training (LT), effect of, 411
Latency, and child development, 77
Learning, and behavior, 232
Libidinal drives:
  and development, 92
  and love, 40
  and regression, 108
Life cycle, 193
  and family theory, 353ff.
  future of, 552
  labeling criteria, 350ff.
  literature on, 208-209
  and marriage, 204
  regression in, 470

and symptoms, 344
transition crisis, 391
Love, development of, 40-43

Marathon groups, 406
Marital Activities Inventory, 412
Marital Adjustment Scale (MAS), Locke-
    Wallace, 171, 228, 229, 259, 285,
    405, 406, 416-18, 420, 423
Marital Happiness Scale, 198, 213, 214,
    222, 223, 227, 228
Marital Interaction Coding System
    (MICS), 215, 218, 219, 221, 224-
    26, 228, 413, 414, 416-18, 429, 423,
    424, 483, 499, 501
Marital Status Inventory, 412
Marital therapy, 1ff., 199, 214. *See also*
    Behaviorism, and marital therapy;
    Marriage; Psychoanalysis, and mar-
    ital therapy; Systems theory, and
    marital therapy
  for alcoholics, 430-33
  communication training, 404ff.
  effectiveness of, 395ff.
  future directions in, 440-41
  and homeostasis, 10
  methodology, 398-402
  non-directive, 230
  and objectification, 207-208
  and problem solving, 224
  programs in, 1-2
  qualitative reports on, 403-404
  sex therapy, 433ff.
  studies of, 446
  trends in, 12ff.
Marital transference, definition problem,
    457. *See also* Transference
Marriage. *See also* Marital therapy
  contracts in, 113, 139-40
  evaluation of, 207ff.
  happiness in, 212
  and intrapsychic process, 106-108
  and mate selection, 104-106, 534-35
  problems in, 44ff., 108ff.
  satisfaction in, 535-37
  significance of, 44
  success in, criteria, 11-12
  types of, 6, 8, 10, 11
Marriage Consultation Center, 12
Marriage Contracts and Couple Therapy
    (Sager), 277
Marriage Council of Philadelphia, 12
Marriage stage, of therapy, 256, 267ff.
MAS. *See* Marital Adjustment Scale

Masochism. *See also* Sadism-masochism
  case study of, 142
  in marriage, 15, 193
Masturbation, instructed, 438-39
Maternal overprotection, and schizo-
    phrenia, 62ff., 75
Mechanistic world view, 302
"Me decade," 6
Menstrual history, questionnaire, 155
Mental Research Institute (MRI), 318ff.,
    328, 329, 331, 333, 339, 342, 343,
    345, 349
Merging, in marriage, 452
MICS. *See* Marital Interaction Coding
    System
Minimal therapist contact (MC), 436
Minnesota Couples' Communication Pro-
    gram (MCCP), 408-10, 412
Minnesota Multi-Phasic Personality In-
    ventory (MMPI), 428, 429
Mirages of Marriage (Lederer and Jack-
    son), 2, 276
Modeling:
  and learning, 499
  and therapy, 142
Monogamy, and divorce, 4-5. *See also*
    Serial monogamy
Morphastatic qualities, and therapy, 381
Morphogenesis:
  described, 351, 352
  and therapy, 381
Moses and Monotheism (Freud), 94
MRI. *See* Marital Research Institute
Multi-generational transmission process,
    333
Multiple regression analysis, 208, 210
Myths/rituals, family, 359-61, 388, 389,
    391, 392

Narcissism:
  and disorder, 39
  and internalization, 37
  and introjection, 37
  and love, 41, 43
  and marriage, 16, 451
  meaning of, 92
  and object choice, 105
  parental, 74, 78
  and personality structure, 42
  primary, 38
  in therapy, 116, 389
National Institute of Mental Health
    (NIMH), 2, 331

"Need for a New Medical Model" (Engel), 346
Negentropy, and systems theory, 314, 315
Negotiation. *See* Contracts
Neo-Freudian therapy, 435
Neuroendocrine system, 311-12
Neurosis:
    and anxiety, 94
    and conflicts, 542, 544
    incidence of, 457
    in marriage, 43, 451, 454-56
    in mothers, 61-62
    and needs, 13, 49-50
    in offspring, 62
    and parenting, 74
    pathogenic configuration, 52
    in therapy, 90, 99-101
Non-directive marital therapy, 230
Nuclear family, identity of, 361

Objectification, 228-30, 232
    and evaluation, 207ff.
    and relatedness, 201
    and therapy, 504, 513
Object relations, xiii, 25-27
    aim-inhibited, 42
    internalized, 41-42
    and introjection, 70
    and marriage, 44-46, 105-106, 449, 452-55, 454n., 537
    mother-infant, 107ff.
    and projection, 52
    theory on, 36, 457, 508, 517, 520, 521
Obligatory relationship, 190
Obsessional-hysteric marriage, 451
Obsessive-compulsion:
    clinical case of, 134-35
    treatment of, 243, 261, 446
Oedipal conflict, 28, 59-60. *See also* Psychoanalysis
    case study of, 145
    and child development, 77, 78
    and marriage, 74, 109
    and therapy, 117
Open marriage, 6, 8, 10, 11
Operant conditioning, 18, 177, 243-44. *See also* Behaviorism; Reinforcement
    and exchange theory, 483
    and interpersonal treatment, 186
    model of, 232
    term use, 265
Oregon Marital Studies Program, 217, 480, 496, 550
Organismic theory, 300ff., 330

Overdetermination, and pathology, 80
Overfunctioning, in marriage, 451
Overvaluation, in love, 41

Palo Alto Mental Research Institute, 507, 517, 518, 522, 523, 530, 531
Paranoid process, 36, 39, 40, 50, 53, 116, 120
Passivity and aggression, 112
Paternal rejection, 58
Path analysis, multiple regression, 208
Pavlovian model, 18. *See also* Behaviorism
Penis envy, 64
Pennsylvania State University, 406
Permeability, in systems boundaries, 307-308, 308n.
Philadelphia Child Guidance Clinic, 387, 508
Phobias:
    and anxiety, 528
    of school, 55, 60, 61
    treatment of, 244, 474
Placebo effect, 21, 405, 408
Pleasure sine wave, 199-200, 204
Pneumococcus, 304, 347
Pneumonia, 304, 347
"Positive Statement Procedure," 253
Pragmatics, and communication, 321
Pragmatics of Human Communication (Watzlawick et al.), 324
Premature ejaculation, treatment of, 436-37
Primary Communication Inventory, 261, 286, 288, 408
Primary-process thinking, and psychosis, 69
Problem-solving:
    and alcoholism, 433
    and behavior, 491
    and contracts, 253, 254
    cooperative, 503
    and interactions, 256, 481
    in marriage, 224ff., 232
    and psychoanalysis, 466
    and psychopathology, 358
    skill improvement, 268ff.
    teaching of, 246, 413
    term use, 268n.
    and treatment, 257, 417, 418, 428, 513
    and writing, 267
Project for a Scientific Psychology (Freud), 94
Projection, xiii, 26
    and analysis, 85

into child, 59
and countertransference, 81
and family process, 71, 72, 333
and fantasy, 28
and grandparents, 57
and introjection, 40, 170
and marriage, 16, 17, 106, 109, 110, 105, 150
and love, 42, 43
and maternal rejection, 63
and paranoia, 53
and parenting, 74-76, 80
pathology in, 39
patterns of, 50-52, 58
reciprocal exchange of, 490
and schizophrenia, 66-67
into spouse, 124
and therapy, 116
and transference, 82, 83
Projective identification, 51n., 109, 111, 457, 535
Protein metabolism, genetics of, 350
Pseudo-identification, 47, 452
Pseudomutuality, 71
Psychasthenia scale, 428
Psychoanalysis. *See also* Psychoanalysis, and marital therapy
advantages, 479
association, serial, 97-98
compared, 533ff., 539ff., 549ff.
conjoint, 467ff., 476, 478
on contracts, 277, 503
development of, 19, 27-31
diagnosis in, 460, 505
and family dynamics, 31ff.
goals in, 458ff.
individual, 474-76
influence of, 395, 397, 447
and life stages, 193
limitations of, 21-22, 474-76
and marriage, 15-17, 25ff., 113ff., 449ff.
mother-schizophrenic child dyad, 65ff.
and needs, complementary, 13
and neurosis, xii, 99-101
parents-child triad, 76ff.
present/past centeredness, 472-74
and psychotherapy, 399
and research, 398
and sexual dysfunction, 235
and structural theory, 329
and systems theory, 511-12
technique of, 92, 93, 126
term meaning, 91, 92
transference model, 80-84

unconscious in, 92-93
Psychoanalysis, and marital therapy, 89ff.
See also Psychoanalysis
case studies of, 130ff.
and contracts, 113
evaluative process, 127ff.
formats of, 113ff.
and homeostasis, 104
influence of, 12-13
and life cycle, 104
organization in, 101-102
stages of, 139ff.
contract, 139-41
initiation, 141-42
middle stage, 143ff.
termination, 149-52
and values, 103
Psychoanalytic Study of the Family, The (Flügel), 29
Psychotherapy, psychoanalytic. *See* Psychoanalysis; Psychoanalysis, and marital therapy
Psychotherapy by Reciprocal Inhibition (Wolpe), 244, 245

Questionnaires, 259ff., 409
on communication, 261-62
on contracts, 284
feelings toward spouse, 260
marital happiness, 259
self-description, 157, 260
on sexuality, 159-61
on therapy, 286
"Question of Family Homeostasis, The" (Jackson), 367n.
Quid pro quo, marital, 251, 252, 322-23, 359, 384, 390, 489, 490, 501

Random assignment, in research, 402
Rational emotive therapy (RET), 247, 508, 527
Reciprocity:
behavioral, 484
and coercion, 493-94
and control, 188
counseling, 255, 415
criteria for, 226
defined, 188
and inhibition, 244
and marriage, 195-96
models of, 242n.
overt, 483-84
and reinforcement, 223, 229, 243, 493-94, 519

training in, 223, 227
"Reciprocity Awareness Procedure," 266
Reductionistic/mechanistic science, 301, 304
Regression:
    case study of, 131-32
    in family, 333
    in marriage, 110, 111
    and object ties, 108
    parental, 74
    in schizophrenia, 67
    and symbiosis, 57
    and therapy, 133, 145
    and transference, 100, 125
Reinforcement. *See also* Behaviorism
    and alternative responses, 245
    behavior as, 379, 382
    circularity in, 482
    contingencies of, 182, 232
    and control, 200-201, 205, 206, 228, 234
    covert, 246
    and exchanges, 180-81
    generalized, 198
    identification of, 230
    and marriage, 189, 195-96
    natural, 532
    and nonoccurrences, 250, 269
    positive/negative, 177, 178, 187, 223, 232, 413, 483-84, 504
    primary, 178
    reciprocity in, 223, 229, 243, 484, 493-94, 519
    schedules of, 179, 182
    social, 241, 483
    spouse-controlled, 252, 253, 289
    stress on, 290
    and target behavior, 185
    term use, 265
    and therapy, 502
    tokens for, 250-51
    verbal, 281-82, 287
Relabeling, of problems, 386-87
Relationship Inventory, Barrett-Lennard, 405
Repression, 518
    and acting out, 99
    and consciousness, 96
    and love, 42
    in marriage, 105, 110, 111, 452-53
    meaning of, 92
    and object relations, 455
Resistance:
    theories of, 92

and therapy, 17, 105, 125-26, 140, 454n., 488
    and transference, 146
Roles, 522
    and affective response, 497
    and communication, 404
    and expectations, 465
    and life stages, 193
    and marriage, 170-71
    reversals in, 220
    segregated instrumental, 210
    and spokesmanship, 368ff.
    training in, 406
    transition in, 208

Sado-masochism. *See also* Masochism
    and love, 42
    and marriage, 105
    and object loss, 111
Scapegoating:
    and displacement, 72
    and marriage, 512
Scenes From A Marriage (Bergman), 8, 22n.
Schizophrenia:
    behavioral treatment of, 18
    child and mother, 61, 65ff.
    conference on, 318n.
    and double bind, 325-26
    in families, 60, 331, 512
    and narcissism, 42
    and separation, 34
    and siblings, 78, 79
    and symbiosis, 47
    systems theory on, 506
Science, 292
Science and Human Behavior (Skinner), 242
Sector analyses, 470
Self-actualization, 7, 8
Self-report measures, 157, 400, 417ff., 427
Semantics, and communications, 320
Semiotics, 320n.
Sensitization, covert, 433, 435. *See also* Desensitization
Serial associations, 97-98
Serial monogamy, as alternative, 4, 8, 10, 11
Servomechanisms, 313
Sexuality:
    case study of, 132, 136, 137
    conditioning of, 244-45
    contracts on, 279, 281-83
    and conversation, 203

and hedonism, 498
and identity, 65, 77-78
and initiation, 493
and love, 40-41
in marriage, 44-45, 137, 191
and parenting, 58-60
promiscuity in, 42
and psychoanalysis, 114
and psychosis, 68-69
questionnaire on, 159-61
satisfaction in, 247
stereotypical, 183
and therapy, 134-35, 167, 245, 265, 285, 397, 433ff., 445-46
Shaping, as learning, 180
Sibling position, in family system, 333
Situational framework, 334
Social learning theory, 186, 292
Social mobility, and education, 7
Somatic compliance, 30
Spearman-Brown formula, 259
Splitting, and love, 42
Spontaneous remission rates, 401-402
Spouse Observation Checklist, 412, 496
Stereotypic therapy, 118
Stimuli. *See also* Behaviorism
    aversive, 178, 198
    and behavior, 379, 382
    and control, 179-80, 193-96, 205, 206, 234, 522
    and desensitization, 244
    discriminative, 200, 271
    and marital relations, 248, 513
    model of, 301
    objectification of, 228
Stony Brook, therapy center, 240, 254, 256, 258, 277, 280, 281, 286n., 289, 292
Structural family therapy, 326-30, 507,, 508
Structural-functional framework, of sociology, 334-36, 337
Studies on Hysteria (Breuer and Freud). 95
Superego:
    concept of, 92
    defects in, 29
    demands of, 94
    function of, 37
Swinging, 6, 8, 264
Symbiosis:
    and infantilization, 61
    and mother-infant, 32, 36-37, 57
    and psychosis, 65-66, 68ff., 75, 79
    and regression, 57

Symbolic-interactionist framework, 334
Symptoms:
    interactional attributes of, 382
    and reinforcement, 386
    substitution of, 94
Syntax, and communication, 320
Systems of Family and Marital Psychotherapy (Skynner), 311n.
Systems theory, 170, 172, 298ff. *See also* Systems theory, and marital therapy
    and alcoholism, 356-59, 361
    advantages of, 362
    and behaviorism, 183-84, 491-92
    biologically-rooted model, 346ff.
    influence of, 397
    and life stages, 193
    and marriage, 19-22
    and sociology, 334ff.
    and time, 457
    theory integration, 339ff.
    weaknesses in, 345-46
Systems theory, and marital therapy, 90, 366ff., 506ff. *See also* Systems theory
    advantages of, 517
    Bowen theory, 509, 517
    communication theories, 517-23, 529ff.
    compared, 533ff., 538ff., 549ff.
    conjoint treatment, 523ff.
    marital satisfaction, 509ff.

Tennessee Self-Concept Scale, 410
Thermodynamics, and systems theory, 314-15
Tokens, for reinforcement, 250-51
Total Woman, The (Morgan), 10
Totem and Taboo (Freud), 29, 94
Traditional marriage, 191, 192
Transactional analysis, 328, 329, 432, 447, 482
Transference, xii, xiii, 124-25, 454n. *See also* Psychoanalysis; Psychoanalysis, and marital therapy; Transference neurosis
    and child-parent relations, 30
    complexity of, 27
    in conjoint therapy, 467ff.
    and couple interaction, 142
    and family, 40
    and internalization, 82
    and marital disorder, 114-15
    model of, 26, 80-85
    and needs, 49
    and projection, 52, 117
    and sexuality, 92

and systems theory, 514
and therapy, 12, 16, 17, 90, 100, 121,
    123-27, 129, 143ff., 148, 149, 152
and transitional mode, 52
Transference neurosis, xii, 81, 100-101,
    146, 464, 468n., 468ff. *See also*
    Transference
Transitional mode, of experience, 52-53
Triadic systems, and pathology, 371-72

Unconscious. *See also* Psychoanalysis
    association, serial, 97-98
    and conjoint therapy, 537-39
    making conscious, 92, 95-97
    meaning of, 92
    and symptoms, 93-95
University of Minnesota, 336
University of Oregon, Marital Studies
    Program, 201

University of Rhode Island, 5
Vaginismus, 437
Validity, in research, 398-400, 405, 407,
    415
Victim-introject, 37-40, 75. *See also* In-
    trojection
Victim-victimizer couples, 377
Videotapes, for therapy, 102, 148-49, 387,
    438, 550
Vietnamese war, and family instability, 7
Vomiting, reinforcement of, 386-87

Wait-list, control group, 285
Washington University, School of Medi-
    cine, 245
Watergate, 6
Wholeness, in systems theory, 306
"Who's Afraid of Virginia Woolf?" 377n.
Wolf-Man case, 28

Name Index

Abelin, E. L., 56, 86n.
Ables, B., 449, 466, 554n.
Ackerman, N. W., 28, 30, 50, 54, 56, 62, 76, 86n., 110, 114, 161n., 449, 460, 461, 506, 554n.
Adland, M. L., 445, 556n.
Adler, A., 421, 424
Agras, S., 60, 86n.
Ainslie, G., 99, 161n.
Albee, E., 377n.
Aldous, N. R., 452, 462, 490, 511, 554n.
Alexander, F., 97, 100, 101, 141, 161n., 546, 548, 554n.
Alexander, J. F., 462, 499, 554n.
Alford, H., 480, 556n.
Alger, I., 148, 161n., 163n.
Allport, G., 506, 554n.
Araoz, D. L., 452, 456, 467, 554n.
Armel, S., 246, 296n.
Arnkoff, D., 527, 561n.
Aved, B. M., 169, 239n.
Azrin, N. H., 186, 188, 198, 217, 223, 226, 227, 235n., 243, 251, 253, 255, 265, 266, 293n., 415, 441n., 480, 501, 554n.

Bach, G. R., 494, 554n.
Baer, D. M., 359, 363n., 529, 554n.
Baird, E., 480, 554n.
Baker, L., 507, 561n., 562n.
Baldwin, B. A., 254, 294n., 427, 442n.
Bales, R. F., 334, 336, 338, 364n.
Balint, E., 461n., 554n.
Balint, M., 461n., 462, 554n.
Bancroft, J., 436, 443n., 445, 446, 490, 554n., 562n.

Bandler, R., 371n., 393n., 518, 558n.
Bandura, A., 180, 235n., 247, 291, 293n., 492, 554n.
Bank, S., 186, 236n., 258, 294n., 480, 558n.
Barlow, D. H., 400, 407, 418, 438, 442n.
Barnett, J., 405, 429, 451, 502n., 554n.
Barrett-Lennard, G. T., 534, 554n.
Barron, S. H., 61, 88n.
Barry, W. A., 453, 457, 554n., 563n.
Barton, C., 500, 554n.
Basamania, B., 55, 86n.
Bassuk, E., 127, 164n., 449, 562n.
Bateson, G., 19, 20, 22n., 302, 318n., 319, 326, 363n., 372, 379, 393n., 506
Baucom, D. H., 402, 443n.
Beavin, J. H., 19, 24n., 183, 239n., 319, 320n., 324n., 365n., 507, 565n.
Beck, A. T., 246n., 289, 293, 293n., 492, 502, 522, 523, 525, 527, 554n.
Beck, G. D., 259, 295n.
Bee, L., 450, 564n.
Beels, C. C., 319, 363n.
Bell, N. W., 336, 363n.
Benedek, T., 57, 77, 86n., 141, 161n.
Bennett, L. A., 356, 358, 365n.
Benschoter, R. A., 149, 161n.
Berenson, D., 357, 364n., 445, 564n.
Bergin, A. E., 398, 441n., 482, 555n.
Bergman, A., 32, 87
Bergman, I., 8
Berman, E. M., 104, 161n., 466, 480, 484, 555n.
Bernard, J., 5, 7, 22n.
Berrien, F. K., 506, 555n.
Beukenkamp, C., 459, 555n.

Bey, E., 445, 557n.
Bienvenu, M. J., 258, 273, 274, 293n.
Birchler, G. R., 166, 188, 212, 215, 218, 220, 225, 228, 235n., 239n., 250, 252, 273, 277, 293n., 297n., 412, 413, 441n., 444n., 466, 480, 481, 555n., 565n.
Bird, B., 100, 161n.
Bird, H. W., 29, 87n., 118, 161n.
Bird, W., 13, 23n.
Birk, L., 534, 555n.
Blakeney, P., 445, 560n.
Blanck, G., 44, 76, 86n., 104, 106, 161n.
Blanck, R., 44, 76, 86n., 104, 106 161n.
Blechman, E. A., 226, 235n.
Blinder, M. G., 459, 555n.
Boas, C., 14, 22n., 458, 555n.
Bodin, A. M., 507, 565n.
Bolen, D. W., 446, 556n.
Boszormenyi-Nagy, I., 70, 86n., 452, 462, 469, 555n.
Boutelle, W., 127, 164n., 449, 562n.
Bowen, M., 20, 43, 54, 55, 61, 66-68, 77-80, 86n., 299, 305, 318n., 330-33, 342, 343, 345, 349, 363n., 367n., 393n., 451, 452, 495, 504, 506-17, 516n., 520, 521, 523, 532, 534-36, 538-40, 544, 546, 555n., 556n.
Bowlby, J., 107, 161n.
Boyd, W. H., 446, 556n.
Bradburn, N. M., 208, 235n.
Brandsma, J., 449, 466, 554n.
Breuer, J., 95, 161n.
Broderick, C. B., 517, 556n.
Broderick, J. E., 172, 237n., 258, 296n., 446, 562n.
Brody, S., 13, 22n.
Brown, 259
Buckley, W., 334, 351, 352, 363n., 506, 556n.
Budd, L. G., 209, 238n.
Burgess, E., 9, 22n.
Burlingham, D. T., 29, 86n.
Burton, G., 432, 441n., 445, 459, 556n.
Butcher, J. N., 461, 462, 464, 556n.
Butler, R. N., 104, 161n.
Byrne, D., 481, 556n.

Cadogan, D. A., 433, 441n., 445, 556n.
Caird, W. K., 434, 438, 441n., 444n.
Cambor, C., 13, 22n.
Camp, H., 507, 556n.
Campbell, E. E., 409, 441n.
Campbell, L., 433, 442n.
Cannon, K. L., 193, 208, 238n.
Cannon, W. D., 311, 349, 363n.

Caplan, G., 464, 556n.
Caplow, T., 372n., 393n.
Cardillo, J. P., 410, 441n.
Carek, D. J., 458, 565n.
Carkhuff, 404-406, 412
Carnap, R., 320n., 363n.
Carrol, E., 13, 22n.
Carter, H., 190, 235n.
Carter, R. D., 226, 227, 235n., 480, 556n.
Cassidy, M. J., 410, 441n.
Cautela, J. R., 246, 293n.
Cheek, F. E., 66, 86n.
Christ, J., 119, 122, 163n.
Christensen, D. J., 430, 441n.
Clark, L., 258, 293n.
Clore, G. L., 481, 556n.
Cobb, J. A., 186, 238n.
Cohen, M., 61, 87n., 274, 294n., 295n.
Cohen, R. A., 61, 87n.
Cole, C. L., 193, 238n., 291, 296n.
Cole, S., 292, 293n.
Coleman, R. E., 169, 236n.
Collins, J., 407, 441n.
Cookerly, J. R., 13, 14, 22n., 116, 161n., 428, 441n.
Cooper, D., 6, 22n.
Corder, B. F., 432, 441n.
Corder, R. F., 432, 441n.
Cornelison, A. R., 55, 87n.
Cotton, M. C., 405, 422, 424, 425, 442n.
Cozby, P. C., 274, 293n.
Crago, M., 169, 236n.
Craighead, W. E., 247, 293n.
Cristol, A. H., 289, 296n., 399, 439, 443n., 444n.
Cuber, J., 12, 22n., 483, 556n.
Cunningham, M. R., 209, 238n.

Daniels, R., 144, 162n.
Darrow, C. M., 103, 163n.
Datan, N., 104, 164n.
Davenport, Y. B., 441, 556n.
Davis, D. I., 357, 364n., 445, 564n.
Davis, J. D., 264, 293n.
Day, J., 71, 88n.
Dember, W. N., 291, 293n.
Deutsch, F., 462, 464, 470, 505, 556n.
Deutsch, H., 33, 86n., 497, 556n.
Deutsche, M., 108, 162n.
Dibastia, B., 259, 293n.
Dicks, H. V., 105, 108-11, 162n., 449, 452-55, 460, 461, 467, 482, 489, 490, 493, 498, 511, 513, 520, 521, 547n., 556n.
Dittmar, F., 437, 443n.
Duhl, F. J., 302, 363n.

Duvall, E. M., 338, 340n., 353, 355, 356, 363n.
Dysinger, R. H., 55, 86n.
D'Zurilla, T. J., 248, 268n., 293n., 294n., 412, 442n., 480, 556n., 558n.

Eaton, M. T., 149, 161n.
Ebert, M. H., 445, 556n.
Edelheit, H., 75, 86n.
Edmonds, V., 259, 293n.
Eidelberg, L., 451, 452, 556n.
Eisenberg, J. M., 247, 259, 293n.
Eisenberg, L., 60, 86n.
Eisler, R. M., 480, 556n.
Elizer, A., 450, 556n.
Ellenberger, H., 93, 162n.
Ellis, A., 246, 247, 293n., 492, 502, 522, 523, 527, 557n.
Ely, A. L., 14, 22n., 254, 271, 293n., 407, 408, 442n.
Engel, G., 346, 347, 363n., 398, 442n.
Engel, K., 219, 236n.
Erickson, M., 507
Erikson, E., 30, 39, 86n., 95, 103, 106, 162n., 193, 236n., 350, 355, 359, 363n.
Erikson, M., 344
Etzel, B. C., 256, 297n.
Etzioni, A., 292, 294n.
Evans, I. M., 262, 264, 297n., 500, 566n.
Ewing, J. A., 431, 442n.
Ewing, T. N., 264, 294n.
Eysenck, H. J., 534, 557n.
Ezriel, H., 122, 162n.

Fairbairn, W. R. D., 106, 107, 162n.
Farace, R. V., 195, 238n.
Farr, J. H., 480, 566n.
Fasnacht, G., 494, 561n.
Feather, B. W., 99, 162n., 474, 511, 557n.
Feldman, L., 445, 487, 557n.
Fensterheim, H., 185, 236n., 480, 557n.
Ferber, A., 319, 363n.
Ferenczi, S., 462, 557n.
Ferrara, J., 214, 236n.
Ferreira, A. J., 359, 363n., 388, 389, 393n.
Fiqurel, J. A., 405, 444n.
Fisch, R., 380n., 394n., 507, 565n.
Fisher, R. E., 421, 422, 424, 442n.
Fiske, D., 549, 557n.
Fithian, M. A., 434, 442n.
Fleck, S., 55, 56, 61, 86n., 87n.
Flomenhaft, K., 483, 563n.
Flügel, J. D., 29, 86n.
Foley, V. D., 509, 528, 557n.

Follingstad, D. R., 214, 222, 223, 228, 236n., 498, 557n.
Ford, F. R., 519, 557n.
Framo, J., 454, 462, 470n., 512, 555n., 557n.
Francis, B., 185, 236n., 248, 294n., 474, 558n.
Frangia, G. W., 446, 563n.
Frank, J. D., 90, 162n.
Franks, C. M., 481, 557n.
Frederiksen, 226, 238n.
French, T. M., 462, 554n.
Freud, A., 62, 86n., 87n.
Freud, S., x, 25, 28-30, 36, 40-42, 87n., 89, 90, 92-95, 97-100, 105, 110, 146, 162n., 451, 454n., 554, 557n.
Friedman, A. S., 430, 442n., 445, 487, 521, 557n.
Friedman, P. H., 249, 294n.
Fromm, E., 459
Fromm-Reichmann, F., 91, 92, 163n.

Gallant, P. M., 445, 557n.
Garfield, S. L., 461, 557n.
Gath, D., 436, 443n., 446, 562n.
Gebhard, P. H., 258, 294n.
Gelder, M. G., 534, 561n.
Gergen, K., 186, 236n., 483, 557n.
Gibson, R. W., 61, 87n.
Giffin, M. E., 29, 87n.
Gilbert, W. M., 264, 294n.
Gill, M., 93, 97, 139, 163n., 164n., 468, 557n.
Giovacchini, P., 117, 163n., 447, 449, 451, 458, 557n., 558n.
Glick, B. R., 483, 558n.
Glick, P. D., 3, 7, 22n., 190, 235n., 353, 363n.
Gliedman, L. H., 431, 442n.
Glisson, D. H., 482, 558n.
Goffman, E., 359, 489, 558n.
Goldberg, A., 439, 442n.
Goldfried, A. P., 246, 294n.
Goldfried, M. R., 246, 268n., 293n., 294n.
Goldiamond, I., 185, 236n., 248, 294n., 480, 558n.
Goldman, G., 262, 294n.
Goldstein, A., 262, 294n., 439, 443n.
Goldstein, M. K., 185, 223, 236n., 239n., 248, 294n., 474, 480, 558n.
Goldston, J., 274, 294n., 295
Gonso, J., 276, 294n., 413, 442n
Goodenough, H., 457, 566n.
Goodman, J., 246, 295n.
Goodwin, F W., 445, 556n

Goodwin, H. M., 459, 561n.
Gordon, M., 450, 559n.
Gottlieb, A., 459, 558n.
Gottlieb, S., 14, 22n.
Gottman, J., 186, 188, 189, 202, 217, 219, 220, 222, 224, 226, 236n., 258, 270, 276, 294n., 413, 424, 442n., 480, 483, 494, 558n.
Gould, R. L., 104, 163n.
Graham, J. A., 428, 442n.
Gray, W., 302, 363n., 506, 558n.
Greene, B., 12, 21, 22n., 120, 124, 125, 141, 163n., 164n., 445, 558n.
Greenfield, N. S., 468n.
Greenson, R., 126, 163n.
Greenspan, S. I., 51, 51n., 87n., 456, 460, 490, 558n.
Greer, S. E., 248, 294n., 412, 442n., 480, 558n.
Griffin, R. W., 429, 442n.
Grinder, J., 371n., 393n., 518, 558n.
Grinker, R. R., Jr., 506, 558n.
Gross, S. J., 483, 558n.
Grossman, C. M., 471n., 558n.
Grotjahn, M., 458, 560n.
Grunebaum, H., 119, 122, 127, 130, 163n., 164n., 462, 463, 467, 564n.
Guerin, P. J., 506, 558n.
Guerney, B. G., Jr., 216, 223, 226, 229, 236n., 254, 293n., 406, 407, 419, 420, 422-24, 442n.
Gundlach, R., 116, 164n., 452, 563n.
Guntrip, H., 454n., 558n.
Gurman, A. S., xii, xiii, 21, 101, 188, 217, 221, 236n., 249, 254, 255, 264, 289, 294n., 396, 397, 403, 429, 441, 442n., 445ff., 446-49, 461, 463, 464, 467, 474, 475, 477, 480, 484, 487, 487n., 494n., 499, 500, 506, 508, 512, 518, 523, 526, 531n., 546, 548-52, 559n.

Hackman, A., 436, 443n., 446, 562n.
Hadley, S. W., 460, 461, 528, 545, 564n.
Haley, J., 13, 19, 20, 22n., 23n., 114, 163n., 184, 193, 194, 236n., 318n., 319, 344, 363n., 367n., 372n., 380n., 383, 387, 393n., 446, 506-509, 517-23, 526, 527, 530, 531, 537, 559n., 562n.
Handel, G., 359, 363n.
Hansen, B. A., 334, 363n.
Haroff, P., 484, 556n.
Harper, R., 247, 293n.
Harrell, J., 216, 217, 226, 229, 236n., 238n., 249, 251, 296n., 419, 420, 422-24, 442n., 503, 563n.

Hartman, W. E., 434, 442n.
Hartmann, H., 29, 87n.
Hastings, D. W., 434, 442n.
Havens, J. W., 503, 560n.
Haynes, S., 214, 222n, 236n.
Hedberg, A., 433, 442n.
Heimann, P., 471n., 559n.
Heiss, J., 450, 559n.
Helez, 454
Henry, B. W., 169, 237n.
Herrick, J., 519, 557n.
Hersen, M., 400, 407, 418, 438, 442n., 480, 556n.
Hertel, R. K., 453, 563n.
Hess, R. D., 359, 363n.
Hickman, M. E., 254, 294n., 427, 442n.
Hickok, J. E., 250, 251, 294n., 480, 559n.
Hicks, M. W., 171, 208, 236n., 457, 559n.
Hilgard, E. R., 482, 559n.
Hill, R., 20, 305, 334, 336-38, 337n., 346, 353, 363n.
Hines, G. A., 411, 442n.
Hirsch, S. I., 71, 88n.
Hoffman, E. H., 446, 563n.
Hoffman, L., 352, 363n., 383, 393n.
Hogan, P., 13, 23n., 148, 161n., 163n.
Hollender, M. H., 120, 163n.
Holz, W., 501, 554n.
Homans, G. C., 187, 236n.
Hoon, E., 434, 439, 444n.
Hopps, C., 127, 164n., 449, 562n.
Hops, H., 166, 185, 215, 238n., 239n., 243, 248, 251, 253, 256, 289, 296n., 297n., 405, 412-14, 442n., 443n., 444n., 466, 480, 481, 485, 559n., 563n., 565n.
Horney, K., 459
Hulse, W. C., 458, 559n.
Hurvitz, N., 474, 560n.
Huston, T. L., 481, 560n.

Ibsen, 483
Ierace, C., 314, 336n.
Isaac, J., 171, 211, 213, 239n.

Jackson, D. D., 2, 3, 19, 20, 22n., 23n., 24n., 183, 186, 187, 194, 237n., 239n., 251, 276, 295n., 299, 305, 312, 319, 320n., 322, 323, 324n., 349, 363n., 364n., 365n., 367n., 379, 384, 388, 393n., 489, 506, 507, 518, 553, 560n., 565n.
Jackson, J., 458, 560n.
Jacob, T., 480, 560n.
Jacobs, A., 492, 560n.
Jacobson, D., 451, 560n.
Jacobson, N. S., xiii, 21, 185, 188, 217, 226,

228, 236n., 248, 252, 253, 256, 281, 294n., 395ff., 402, 412, 413, 415, 417, 418, 420-25, 442n., 443n., 449, 480, 487, 494n., 497, 501, 506, 548, 550, 560n.
Jesselyn, I. M., 61, 88n.
Johnson, A. M., 29, 87n.
Johnson, D. W., 256, 294n.
Johnson, S., 183, 237n.
Johnson, V. E., 245, 295n., 415, 434-37, 439, 443n., 562n.
Jones, E. E., 182, 237n.
Jones, R., 186, 235n., 243, 253, 265, 293n., 415, 441n., 480, 554n.
Julier, D., 436, 446, 562n.
Jung, C., 93

Kahn, M., 270, 273, 291, 294n.
Kanfer, F. H., 492, 560n.
Kanno, P., 439, 443n.
Kanouse, D. E., 182, 237n.
Kantor, D., 367n., 393n.
Kaplan, H. M., 432, 441n., 445, 556n.
Kaplan, H. S., 4, 23n., 114, 163n., 434, 435, 443n., 445, 452, 560n., 563n.
Karasu, T. B., 90, 91, 163n.
Karoly, P., 492, 560n.
Karpel, M., 454, 560n.
Katz, I., 274, 294n., 295n.
Katz, M., 270, 295n.
Kazdin, A. E., 244, 247, 293n., 295n., 553
Kelley, H. H., 18, 24n., 182, 186, 187, 237n., 239n., 483, 564n.
Kelly, G., 181
Kent, R. N., 260, 263n., 295n.
Kepecs, J., 468, 560n.
Kernberg, O., 36, 38, 41, 42, 87n.
Kimmel, C., 259, 295n.
Kimmel, P. R., 503, 560n.
Kind, J., 410, 443n.
Kinder, B. N., 445, 560n.
Kirschenbaum, M., 459, 555n.
Klein, E. B., 103, 163n.
Klein, M., 51n., 93
Klein, M. M., 450, 556n.
Kniskern, D. P., 188, 217, 221, 236n., 249, 254, 255, 264, 289, 294n., 396, 397, 403, 429, 441, 442n., 446, 447, 449, 461, 464, 474, 475, 477, 483, 487, 494n., 506, 518, 523, 526, 546, 548-52, 559n.
Knox, D., 252, 284, 295n.
Knudson, R., 445n., 463, 480, 487, 487n., 512, 559n.
Koch, J., 264, 295n.
Koch, L., 264, 295n.
Kockott, G., 437, 443n.

Kohl, R. N., 111, 163n., 475, 560n.
Kohlenberg, R., 438, 439, 443n.
Kohut, H., 38, 39, 87n.
Komechak, M. G., 250, 251, 294n., 480, 559n.
Koss, M. P., 461, 462, 556n.
Kremer, M., 116, 164n., 452, 563n.
Krupinski, J., 15, 23n.
Ktones, T., 15, 24n., 43, 88n., 450, 566n.
Ktones, V., 24n., 43, 88n., 450, 566n.
Kubie, L., 449, 560n.

Laidlaw, N. D., 432, 441n.
Laing, R. D., 489
Lamberth, J., 481, 556n.
Lande, G., 387
Langer, E. J., 182, 237n.
Langs, R., 95, 99, 163n.
Laszlo, C. A., 183, 237n.
Laws, J. L., 170, 171, 173, 193, 237n., 457, 560n.
Lazarus, A. A., 185, 237n., 244, 248, 295n., 480, 560n.
Lederer, W., 2, 3, 23n., 186, 187, 194, 237n., 251, 276, 295n.
Lee, R. R., 445, 558n.
Lehr, W. A., 367n., 393n.
Lehrman, N., 13, 23n.
Leichter, E., 458, 560n.
Leichter, G., 14, 23n.
Lennard, 405, 429
Lenz, R., 116, 164n., 452, 563n.
Leslie, G. R., 459, 560n.
Lespoll, J., 13, 22n.
Lesswing, 553
Levant, R. F., 531, 561n.
Leveton, A., 373n.
Leveton, E. E., 373n.
Levine, F. M., 494, 561n.
Levine, J., 253, 295n., 422, 443n.
Levine, M. D., 183, 237n.
Levinger, G., 165, 237n.
Levinson, D. J., 103, 163n.
Levinson, M., 103-104, 163n.
Levitt, E., 446, 561n.
Levy, D. M., 62, 87n.
Lewis, R. A., 193, 238n., 291, 296n.
Liberman, R. P., 249, 253, 254, 268, 295n., 422, 424, 425, 443n., 480, 561n.
Lidz, T., 29, 30, 47, 55, 56, 60, 65, **73**, 74, 78, 87n., 104, 163n.
Liebman, R., 507, 508, 561n., 562n.
Lief, H. I., 104, 161n., 466, 480, 484, 555n.
Linden, M. E., 459, 561n.
Lindsley, O. R., 243, 295n.

Litin, E. M., 29, 87n.
Lloyd, R. A., 456, 490, 513, 561n.
Lobitz, G. K., 183, 237n.
Lobitz, L., 438, 443n.
Lobitz, W. C., 245, 295n., 497, 561n.
Locke, H., 9, 22n.
Locke, H. J., 171, 212, 220, 222, 223, 228, 229, 237n., 247, 259, 295n., 405
Long, V., 431, 442n.
LoPiccolo, J., 245, 295n., 438, 443n., 497, 561n.
Lorion, R. P., 461, 561n.
Lott, A. J., 481, 561n.
Lott, B. E., 481, 561n.
Lovibond, S. H., 264, 295n.
Luborsky, L., 478, 526, 561n.
Luborsky, L., 478, 526, 561n.
Lustig, N., 445, 558n.
Luthman, S., 470n., 496, 497, 507, 561n.

Mace, D., 4, 7, 8-10, 12, 15, 23n.
Mace, V., 4, 7-10, 23n.
Macon, L. B., 428, 443n.
Mahler, M. S., 32, 87
Mahoney, M. J., 167, 246, 247, 293n., 295n., 492, 503, 522, 527, 530, 552, 561n.
Main, T. F., 105, 124, 163n.
Malan, D. H., 461n., 462n., 465, 478, 561n.
Mann, J., 462, 464-66, 478, 505, 561n.
Mannino, F. V., 51, 51n., 87n., 456, 460, 490, 558n.
Manus, G., 15, 23n., 446, 561n.
Margolin, G., 171, 173, 183, 185, 201, 202, 207, 210, 218, 220-22, 237n., 239n., 257, 297n., 413, 416, 417, 443n., 480, 484, 490, 505, 529, 565n.
Markman, H., 186, 219, 236n., 258, 276, 294n., 413, 442n., 480, 558n.
Marks, I. M., 167, 237n., 245, 251, 295n., 296n., 534, 561n.
Marmor, J., 113, 163n.
Marquis, D. G., 482, 559n.
Marshall, E., 15, 23n.
Marshall, J. R., 495, 561n.
Martin, B., 185, 188, 217, 237n., 248, 252, 294n., 412, 415, 443n., 480, 501, 560n.
Martin, P., 13, 23n., 29, 87n., 112, 113, 115, 118, 119, 161n., 163n., 449, 466, 470n., 562n.
Maruyama, M., 313, 351, 364n.
Mason, P., 61, 87n.
Masters, W. H., 245, 295n., 434-37, 439, 443n., 445, 562n.
Matanovich, J. P., 429, 443n.
Matheny, A., 451, 560n.

Mathews, A., 436, 437, 443n., 445, 562n.
Matross, R., 256, 294n.
Maudal, G. R., 464, 556n.
Mayman, M., 506, 562n.
McCrady, B. S., ix-xiii, 169, 238n., 431, 443n.
McDermott, J. F., 458, 565n.
McGuire, L., 439, 444n.
McIntosh, D. M., 410, 443n., 501
McKee, B., 104, 163n.
McNamee, P., 405, 444n.
Mead, 225
Meichenbaum, D., 246, 295n., 492, 522, 562n.
Meissner, W., xiii, 16, 25ff., 33, 36, 39, 42, 51n., 53, 55, 61, 75, 79, 87n., 88n., 101, 106, 107, 109, 123, 170, 181, 196n., 205, 326, 397, 448-51, 453, 454, 460, 464, 469, 490, 510, 511, 517, 533
Mendelson, J. H., 356, 364n.
Menninger, K., 506, 562n.
Metzger, N. J., 194, 238n.
Miller, A. G., 169, 236n.
Miller, B. C., 208, 209, 237n.
Miller, J. G., 306, 314, 362, 364n., 506, 562n.
Miller, M., 13, 22n.
Miller, P. M., 480, 556n.
Miller, S., 408, 409, 443n.
Milman, L., 507, 562n.
Milsum, J. H., 183, 237n.
Mintz, J., 461, 562n.
Minuchin, S., 20, 299, 305, 312, 326-30, 333, 339, 342, 343, 345, 364n., 367n., 389, 393n., 506-508, 512, 514, 523, 527, 529, 561n., 562n.
Mischel, W., 167, 170, 181, 237n.
Mitchell, S., 446, 564n.
Mittelmann, B., 12, 13, 15, 17, 23n., 29, 88n., 112, 117, 163n., 449, 562n.
Modell, A. H., 39, 88n.
Mohr, G. J., 61, 88n.
Montalvo, B., 523, 562n.
Morgan, M., 10, 23n.
Morris, C. W., 320n., 364n.
Mudd, E., 12
Munjack, D., 439, 443n.
Munroe, R. L., 163n.
Murray, H., 450, 534, 562n.
Murstein, B. I., 259, 295n., 450, 451, 481, 562n.

Nadelson, C., xiii, 17, 89, 90, 101ff., 127, 149, 163n., 164n., 181, 397, 448, 449, 464,

466, 467, 477, 517, 518, 533, 543n., 547n., 562n.
Napier, A. Y., 452, 454, 562n.
Naster, B. J., 186, 235n., 243, 253, 265, 293n., 415, 441n., 480, 554n.
Navran, L., 258, 261, 295n.
Neiberg, N., 119, 122, 163n., 164n.
Neugarten, B. L., 104, 164n.
Newton, I., 302
Nietzsche, 6
Nisbett, R. E., 182, 237n.
Noll, C. E., 208, 235n.
Noonan, D. L., 356, 358, 365n.
Nortan, A. J., 292, 295n.
Notarius, C., 186, 217, 219, 236n., 258, 276, 294n., 480, 558n.
Notarius, L., 413, 442n.
Nunberg, H., 94, 164n.
Nunnally, E. W., 408, 443n.
Nusselt, L., 437, 443n.

Oberndorf, C. P., 12, 15, 23n., 29, 43, 88n., 111, 117, 164n., 449, 562n.
Obler, M., 435-38, 443n.
O'Flaherty, K., 227, 239n.
O'Leary, K. D., xiii, 19, 166, 167, 172, 237n., 240ff., 243, 244, 246, 258, 260, 262, 264, 265, 289, 290, 295n., 296n., 297n., 421, 446, 448, 466, 480, 485, 489, 492, 492n., 496, 498, 499, 501, 503-505, 513, 518, 523, 528, 538, 562n.
Olson, D. H., 2, 13, 15, 19, 23n., 226, 235n., 258, 261, 286, 296n., 300, 364n., 396, 426, 443n., 446, 480, 491, 493, 562n.
Oltmanns, T. F., 172, 237n., 258, 296n., 446, 562n.
Oppenheim, A., 446, 564n.
Ornstein, P., 461n., 554n.
Orr, D. W., 100, 164n.
Overall, J. E., 169, 237n.
Overturf, J., 454, 563n.

Paolino, T. J., ix-xiii, 89ff., 169, 238n., 431, 443n., 464, 533
Papanek, H., 459, 563n.
Parloff, M., 2, 23n., 542, 563n.
Parsons, B. V., 499, 500, 548, 554n.
Parsons, T., 20, 334-36, 338, 364n.
Patterson, G. R., 166, 183, 185-87, 210, 215, 217, 218, 224, 226, 237n., 238n., 239n., 243, 248, 251, 253, 256, 258, 289, 296n., 297n., 405, 412-14, 442n., 443n., 444n., 446, 466, 480, 481, 485, 559n., 563n., 565n.
Pattison, E. M., 459, 558n.

Paul, G. L., 264, 296n.
Paulson, I., 456, 490, 513, 561n.
Pelham, W. E., 260, 296n.
Perelman, J. S., 459, 563n.
Phillips, D., 439, 443n.
Phillips, G. M., 194, 238n.
Pierce, R. M., 254, 271, 296n., 404, 405, 444n.
Pilder, R. J., 411, 444n.
Pine, F., 32, 87n.
Pittman, F., 483, 563n.
Platt, M., 171, 208, 236n., 457, 559n.
Popenoe, P., 12
Price, G. H., 260, 296n.
Price, M. G., 212-14, 222, 223, 238n.
Prochaska, J., xiii, 1ff., 9, 24n., 191, 446
Prochaska, J., xiii., 1ff., 191, 446
Pruyser, P., 506, 562n.

Raimy, Y. V., 526, 563n.
Ransom, D. C., 318, 326, 364n.
Rapaport, D., 93, 164n.
Rapoport, A., 315, 349, 364n.
Rappaport, A. F., 216, 217, 223, 224, 238n., 249, 251, 296n., 406, 407, 415, 422, 444n., 503, 563n.
Rausch, H. L., 453, 470n., 485, 486, 489, 499, 521, 522, 563n.
Razin, A. M., 499, 500, 531n., 546, 548, 559n.
Redfering, D. L., 480, 554n.
Reich, C. A., 6, 23n.
Reid, J. B., 186, 187, 194, 238n., 481, 563n.
Reid, W. J., 426, 444n.
Reis, W., 13, 22n.
Reisinger, J. J., 446, 563n.
Reiss, D., 312, 359, 364n.
Resnik, H., 459, 561n.
Rexford, E. N., 61, 88n.
Rhoads, J. M., 99, 162n., 474, 511, 557n.
Rice, D., 445n.
Rice, D. G., 447, 470n., 559n.
Rich, A., 445, 557n.
Ricks, D., 55, 88n.
Rioch, J., 123, 164n.
Risley, T., 529, 554n.
Ritterman, M. K., 302, 364n., 508, 534, 563n.
Rizzo, N. D., 302, 363n., 506, 558n.
Roberts, P., 416, 420, 444n., 500, 548
Robin, A. L., 246, 268n., 296n.
Robinson, E. A., 212-14, 222, 223, 238n.
Rodgers, R. H., 338, 353, 364n.
Rogers, C., 395, 404, 444n., 489
Rogers, L. E., 195, 238n.

Rollins, B. S., 193, 208, 238n.
Rosenbaum, A., 260, 296n.
Rosenblatt, P. C., 209, 210, 213, 238n.
Rosman, B. L., 507, 561n., 562n.
Rothschild, M., 511
Royce, J., 13, 23n., 116, 164n., 452, 563n.
Royce, W. S., 218, 225, 238n., 480, 563n.
Rubin, M. E., 186, 258, 294n.
Ruesch, J., 518, 563n.
Ryckoff, I. M., 71, 88n.
Ryder, R. G., 258, 286, 296n.

Sachs, L. B., 492, 560n.
Sager, C. J., 14, 17, 23n., 112, 113, 116, 120, 124-26, 130, 145, 164n., 247, 277, 296n., 446, 449, 452, 455, 456, 464, 466, 467, 470n., 476, 482, 489, 503, 563n.
Sanders, N., 253, 254, 295n., 422, 443n.
Satir, V., 13, 23n., 183, 238n., 507, 508, 563n.
Scanzoni, J., 3, 7, 10, 23n.
Scheflen, A. E., 318., 376n., 393n., 518, 564n.
Schellenberg, J., 450, 564n.
Schiavo, R., 500, 554n.
Schneidman, B., 439, 444n.
Sears, R. R., 259, 296n.
Seligman, M. P., 198, 238n., 522, 525, 564n.
Selvini Palazzoli, M., 380n., 393n.
Shapiro, A. K., 553, 564n.
Shapiro, R., 51n., 75, 88n.
Shaw, P., 436, 443n., 446, 562n.
Sheehy, G., 193, 238n.
Shepherd, M., 446, 564n.
Shoulders, D. I., 480, 566n.
Shumaker, D. G., 457, 564n.
Shyne, A. W., 426, 444n.
Sifneos, R. E., 461n., 462, 564n.
Simmel, G., 372n., 394n.
Singer, B., 478, 526, 561n.
Singer, L., 4
Singer, M., 325, 365n.
Skinner, A. E. G., 264, 293n.
Skinner, B. F., 18, 242, 243, 295n., 296n., 492
Skynner, A. C. R., 307, 311n., 364n., 449, 451, 510, 511, 564n.
Slipp, S., 68, 69, 72, 73, 88n.
Sloane, R. B., 289, 296n., 399, 444n.
Sluzki, C., x, xiii, 20, 176n., 183, 318, 319, 326, 364n., 366ff., 372, 372n., 394n., 397, 448, 500, 518, 532-34, 564n.
Smith, C. G., 432, 444n., 445, 564n.
Smith, J. W., 127, 130, 164n., 462, 463, 467, 564n.

Smith, P., 149, 161n.
Solomon, A., 13, 22n., 120, 124, 125, 141, 163n., 164n.
Solomon, H. C., 243, 295n.
Sonne, J. C., 498, 564n.
Spanier, G. B., 193, 238n., 291, 296n.
Spark, G., 469, 555n.
Spearman, 259
Speer, D. C., 351, 352, 364n.
Spitz, R., 29, 88n.
Spurlock, J., 61, 88n.
Stachowiak, J., 507, 563n.
Stanton, M. D., 506, 508, 564n.
Staples, F. R., 289, 296n., 399, 439, 443n., 444n.
Stein, M., 105, 164n.
Steinglass, P., x., xiii, 19, 20, 167, 183, 191n., 196n., 204, 205, 298ff., 356, 357, 364n., 397, 445, 448, 507, 508, 512, 518, 525, 533, 564n.
Stern, R. S., 251, 296n., 446, 564n.
Stewart, R. H., 453, 456, 464n., 471, 490, 513
Stone, A., 12
Stone, H., 12
Stover, L., 254, 293n., 407, 442n.
Strelnick, K., 527n.
Strupp, H. H., 398, 441n., 460, 461, 528, 545, 564n.
Stuart, R. B., 18, 19, 23n., 184, 186, 187, 196, 217, 223, 227, 239n., 243, 243n., 250, 251, 253, 255, 263n., 296n., 412, 413, 444n., 480-82, 486, 497, 564n.
Stucker, S., 274, 294n., 295n.
Sullivan, H. S., 92, 459, 470n., 486, 489, 564n.
Sullivan, J., 214, 222, 236n.
Swain, M. A., 453, 563n.
Szasz, T. S., 100, 164n.
Szurek, S. A., 29, 87n.

Taffel, S. J., 265, 296n.
Taschman, H., 507, 563n.
Terman, 259
Terranova, L., 445, 557n.
Tharp, R. B., 450, 451, 564n.
Tharp, R. G., 170, 236n.
Thibaut, J., 18, 24n., 186, 187, 239n., 483, 564n.
Thomas, E. J., 226, 227, 235n., 239n., 480, 556n.
Thomlinson, R. J., 500, 548, 565n.
Thompson, C., 486, 565n.
Thoresen, C., 492, 561
Thorndike, R., 516

Titchener, J., 126, 144, 147, 164n.
Titus, S. L., 209, 238n.
Todd, T., 506-508, 562n., 564n.
Toomin, M. K., 504, 565n.
Tsoi-Hoshmand, L., 419, 422, 444n., 503, 565n.
Turkewitz, H., xiii, 19, 166, 167, 240ff., 243, 258, 262, 265, 289, 290, 296n., 297n., 420-25, 444n., 448, 466, 480, 485, 489, 492, 492n., 496, 498-500, 503-505, 518, 523, 528, 538
Turner, A. J., 254, 297n.

Valins, S., 182, 237n.
Van Amerongen, S. T., 61, 88n.
Van der Veen, F., 259, 295n.
Venema, H. B., 422, 424, 425, 444n., 501
Vincent, J. P., 188, 215, 225, 228, 235n., 239n., 250, 252, 273, 277, 293n., 297n., 412, 413, 441n., 444n., 466, 480, 481, 555n., 565n.
Vogel, E. F., 336, 363n.
Von Bertalanffy, L., 300-302, 330, 347, 364n., 506, 555n.

Wachtel, P. L., 457, 459, 469, 470, 470n., 472, 474, 511, 565n.
Wackman, D. B., 408, 443n.,
Wahlroos, S., 524, 526, 565n.
Wallace, C. J., 253, 295n., 422, 443n.
Wallace, K. M., 171, 212, 220, 222, 237n.
Wallace, M., 228, 229, 247, 259, 295n., 405
Walter, C. L., 227, 239n.
Waring, M., 55, 88n.
Watson, A. S., 13, 24n., 118, 146, 164n.
Wattie, B., 426, 444n.
Watzlawick, P., 19, 20, 24n., 183, 186, 194, 239n., 319, 320, 320n., 323, 324n., 365n., 377n., 380n., 383, 394n., 489, 491, 493, 506, 507, 514, 518, 520, 522, 526, 527, 530, 565n.
Weakland, J., 19, 22n., 318n., 319, 380, 394n., 507, 518, 526, 527, 565n.
Webb, L., 481, 555n.
Weiner, B., 182, 237n.
Weiner, I. B., 468, 565n.
Weiner, S., 356, 364n.
Weiss, R., xii, xiii, 18, 19, 103, 164n., 165ff., 166, 169, 171, 173, 185, 186, 188, 201, 202, 207, 210, 211, 213, 215, 217-19, 221, 223, 225, 226, 228, 235n., 236n., 238n., 239n., 242n., 243, 246n., 248-53, 255-58, 270, 271, 273, 276, 276n., 277, 289, 290, 293n., 296n., 297n., 326, 405,

412-14, 423, 441n., 442n., 443n., 444n., 448, 454, 466, 480, 481, 484, 486, 487, 489, 490, 492n., 493, 495, 496, 501, 502, 504, 505, 513, 518, 521, 528, 529, 540, 555n., 559n., 563n., 565n.
Welch, J. J., 223, 239n.
Wells, R. A., 405, 444n.
Wender, P. H., 383, 394n.
Wenzel, G. G., 431, 442n.
Westman, J. C., 458, 565n.
Wheeler, E., 253, 254, 295n., 422, 443n.
Whipple, K., 289, 296n., 399, 439, 443n., 444n.
Whitaker, C. A., 14, 26n., 172, 239n., 318n., 469, 489, 523, 565n., 566n.
Whitehead, A., 436, 443n., 446, 562n.
Wieman, R. J., 223, 224, 229, 239n., 408, 421, 422, 424, 425, 444n., 480, 501, 566n.
Wiener, N., 313, 365n.
Wilcoxon, L. A., 244, 295n.
Williams, A. M., 212, 239n.
Wills, T. A., 210, 213, 239n., 412, 413, 442n., 444n., 480, 495, 559n., 566n.
Wilson, G. T., 244, 262, 264, 265, 291, 296n., 297n., 391, 481, 500, 557n., 566n.
Winch, R. F., 15, 24n., 43, 88n., 450, 452
Wincze, J., 434, 438, 439, 441n., 444n.
Winnicott, D. W., 52, 53, 88n., 107, 164n.
Withers, G., 259, 293n.
Witkin, H. A., 457, 566n.
Wolberg, L. R., 462, 465, 566n.
Wolf, S., 256, 280n., 297n.
Wolfe, M. M., 529, 554n.
Wolfe, T., 6, 24n.
Wolin, S. J., 356, 358-61, 365n.
Wolpe, J., 18, 24n., 243-46, 297n.
Woodward, A., 169, 237n.
Woolfolk, A. E., 265, 297n.
Wright, J. C., 350, 363n.
Wynne, L., 71, 88n., 318n., 325, 365n., 452, 566n.

Yale, E., 15, 23n.
Yalom, I., 457, 472, 566n.
Yankelovich, D., 7, 24n.
Yoppi, B., 186, 236n., 258, 294n., 480, 558n.
Yorkston, N. J., 289, 296n., 399, 444n.

Zetzel, E., 126, 164n.
Ziegler, J. S., 430, 444n.
Zimmerman, C., 6, 24n.
Zingle, H. W., 247, 259, 293n.
Zinner, J., 51n., 75, 88n.
Zuk, G., 469, 566n.